how to organize *just about* every-thing

Also in this series

How To Do (Just About) Everything
by Courtney Rosen

How To Fix (Just About) Everything
by Bill Marken

How To Buy & Sell (Just About) Everything
by Jeff Wuorio

how to organize *just about* every-thing

Peter Walsh

*More Than 500 Step-by-Step Instructions for Everything
from Organizing Your Closets to Planning a Wedding
to Creating a Flawless Filing System*

FREE PRESS

New York • London • Toronto • Sydney

FREE PRESS
A Division of Simon & Schuster, Inc.
1230 Avenue of the Americas
New York, NY 10020

For information about special discounts for bulk purchases, please contact Simon & Schuster
Special Sales: 1-800-456-6798 or business@simonandschuster.com

●com|press

Designed and produced by .com press
.com press is a division of Weldon Owen Inc.,
814 Montgomery Street, San Francisco, CA 94133

Printed in the United States by Phoenix Color
10 9 8 7 6 5 4 3 2 1

Library of Congress Cataloging-in-Publication Data
is available.

ISBN 0 7432 5494 5

CEO: John Owen
President and COO: Terry Newell
VP, International Sales: Stuart Laurence
VP, Publisher: Roger Shaw
Creative Director: Gaye Allen
Business Manager: Richard Van Oosterhout
Production Manager: Chris Hemesath
Co-Edition and Reprint Coordinator: Todd Rechner

Series Editor: Brynn Breuner
Managing Editor: Jennifer Block Martin
Consulting Editor: Bill Marken
Production and Layout: Joan Olson, Jody Ginsberg,
Phoebe Bixler
Illustrator: William Laird
Copy Editors: Jacqueline Aaron, Rick Clogher,
Gail Nelson-Bonebrake
Contributing Editors: Julie Thompson, Ginny McLean,
Sharon Payne, Jodi Greenberg, Spencer Weisbroth,
Françoise Hembert
Editorial Assistance: Renée Meyers
Proofreaders: Desne Ahlers, Gail Nelson-Bonebreak
Indexer: Ken DellaPenta

CONTENTS

YARD & GARDEN

STORAGE SOLUTIONS

EDUCATION & CAREER

BUSINESS & WORK

FINANCIAL PLANS

FAMILY AFFAIRS

TRAVEL & ADVENTURE

THE UNEXPECTED

INDEX

CONTRIBUTOR CREDITS

IN YOUR DREAMS

A NOTE TO READERS

When attempting to follow any of the advice in this book, please note the following:

Risky activities: Certain activities described in this book are inherently dangerous or risky. Before attempting any new activity, know your own limitations and consider all applicable risks (whether listed or not).

Professional advice: While we strive to provide complete and accurate information, this is not intended as a substitute for professional advice. You should always consult a professional whenever appropriate or if you have any questions or concerns regarding medical, legal or financial advice.

Physical or health-related activities: Be sure to consult a physician before attempting any health- or diet-related activity or any activity involving physical exertion, particularly if you have any condition that could impair or limit your ability to engage in such an activity.

Adult supervision: The activities described in this book are intended for adults only, and they should not be performed by children without responsible adult supervision.

Violations of law: The information provided in this book should not be used to violate any applicable law or regulation.

Sources and prices: Prices and sources for products and services listed in this edition were accurate at press time. Since the nature of any market is changeable, however, we cannot guarantee that any source listed in these pages will continue to carry items mentioned or even remain in business. Similarly, all prices mentioned in this book are approximate only and are subject to change.

Foreword

Is your household a fine-tuned model of efficiency? Or do you simply close the door when the piles and heaps get out of control? If your home, your calendar and your inbox are bursting at the seams, rest assured that you're not alone: We're all guilty of acquiring more and more stuff and have fewer places to put it. Schedules are overrun with commitments, checkbooks stagger under ever-increasing debt loads, and closets long for breathing room. Where does it end?

Being organized is the key to a simpler life, in which the things we own reflect who we are and everything has its place. *How to Organize (Just About) Everything* covers the typical organizing dilemmas—closets, garage, desk—but goes beyond mere cosmetic fixes to the root of the problem. You'll find tried-and-true strategies that will help everyone from the hopelessly scattered to the chronically late—bringing relief to the most hard core pack rat.

This definitive guide will help you organize your life from cradle to grave whether you're planning your family (249) or planning your estate (247). Tackle affairs of the heart and meet Mr. or Ms. Right (33), arrange a wedding (323) and orchestrate the perfect conception (251). Stay on top of your kids' schedules (277), homework (275) and birthday parties (344). When you need to get away from it all, investigate a trove of travel tips to help plan your honeymoon (339), a fishing trip to Alaska (448) or the perfect day at Disneyland (463). Discover a surprising range of topics in chapters devoted entirely to improving your community, planning celebrations and events and dealing with life's unexpected situations.

Your first tip: Start with chapter one (Get Organized) and get a handle on the basics. You'll learn how to Write an Effective To-Do List (3), Overcome Chronic Disorganization (8), Get Rid of What You Don't Want (12) and Set Goals (16). Check the difficulty level for each topic—the more paper clips, the more challenging the task—and the Tips, Who Knew? and Warning sidebars for additional insight. You'll be primed to declutter your home, streamline your workday, plot your career, master your finances and much, much more.

Thanks to all of our authors and professional organizers for expertly distilling organizing principles into concise topics (read more about them on the Contributors page). A tip of the hat to Julie Thompson and Ginny McLean for diving into the breach with flair and to managing editor Jennifer Block Martin for nailing it time and time again with style and grace. Special thanks to Brynn Breuner for deftly steering the project and without whom this book would never have seen the light of day, and to Ken, for making me brave.

So, conquer that clutter (37), find your keys (35) and welcome deadlines (6) with open arms. With *How to Organize (Just About) Everything,* you'll be ready for anything life throws at you.

Peter Walsh

GANIZE YOUR CONTACTS • GET RID OF WHAT YOU DON'T WANT • SAY NO WITHOUT FEELING GUILTY • BALANCE HOME AND WORK • LI
AIN • SCHEDULE TELEVISION WATCHING • DESIGN A HEALTHY LIFESTYLE • PLAN TO AVOID JUNK FOOD • CHOOSE A WEIGHT LOSS PLA
EET AN ONLINE DATE • PLAN THE PERFECT DATE • MASTERMIND A BREAKUP • PLAN YOUR SOCIAL CALENDAR • MEET MR. OR MS. RIGH
RT YOUR SOCK DRAWER • RETURN RENTALS ON TIME • TAKE CONTROL OF YOUR JUNK DRAWER • ORGANIZE THE MEDICINE CABINET
R CLEAN AND ORDERLY • DEAL WITH A PACK RAT • SELL STUFF ONLINE • ORGANIZE YOUR BOOKSHELVES • CATEGORIZE NEWSPAPER
E BETTER THROUGH LABELING • ORGANIZE JEWELRY • PLAN YOUR DREAM KITCHEN • CONQUER YOUR CLOSETS • ORGANIZE THE LIN
GANIZE SPRING CLEANING • KEEP THE FAMILY ROOM ORGANIZED • SET UP A BATHROOM SCHEDULE • ORGANIZE BATHROOMS • ORGA
GANIZE KIDS' ROOMS • ORGANIZE SPORTS EQUIPMENT • ORGANIZE KIDS' PLAY SPACES • SAFEGUARD YOUR HOME AGAINST ALLERGI
USE • USE HOME DESIGN AND PLANNING SOFTWARE • ESTABLISH YOUR HOME'S SPACE PLAN • INCORPORATE UNIVERSAL DESIGN PR
E BASEMENT • ORGANIZE THE GARAGE • ORGANIZE A TOOLBOX • SET UP A WOODSHOP • ORGANIZE YOUR WINE COLLECTION • PLAN
UDIO OR SMALL APARTMENT • MANAGE WARRANTY DOCUMENTS • MANAGE HOME-IMPROVEMENT PAPERWORK • MERGE TWO HOUSE
RGANIC VEGETABLE GARDEN • PLANT A KITCHEN HERB GARDEN • PLAN A BUTTERFLY GARDEN • DESIGN A BIRD GARDEN • DESIGN A C
ORGANIZE GARDENING TOOLS • ADD A POTTING BENCH TO A YARD • SCHEDULE FRUIT TREE MAINTENANCE • LAY OUT A SPRINKLER SY
SIGN A GARDEN PATH • SET UP A COMPOST SYSTEM • WINTERIZE PLANTS • SCHEDULE YARD WORK • STORE ANYTHING • STORE BUL
D HOBBY MATERIALS • ORGANIZE ART SUPPLIES • ORGANIZE GIFT WRAP AND SEASONAL DECORATIONS • ORGANIZE KIDS' SCHOOLWO
UR WEDDING DRESS AND OTHER TEXTILES • STORE A FUR COAT • STORE BICYCLES AND GEAR • STORE SKI GEAR • ORGANIZE CAMPI
HICH COLLEGE IS RIGHT FOR YOU • GET INTO A TOP COLLEGE OR UNIVERSITY • ACE THE COLLEGE ADMISSIONS TESTS • ORGANIZE YO
W SCHOOL • PREPARE FOR THE BAR EXAM • GET A DEGREE WHILE YOU'RE WORKING • WORK AT HOME WITH KIDS • GO BACK TO WO
RGANIZE YOUR JOB SEARCH • PREPARE FOR A CAREER CHANGE • OPEN A RESTAURANT • BECOME A PHYSICIST • BECOME A CONCER
EALITY-SHOW CONCEPT • BECOME A TALK-SHOW HOST • BECOME A PHOTOJOURNALIST • BECOME A MOVIE DIRECTOR • BECOME A M
ING SYSTEM • ORGANIZE YOUR BRIEFCASE • ORGANIZE YOUR DESK • ORGANIZE YOUR WORKDAY • GET A HANDLE ON E-MAIL • ORG
LARY REVIEW • CLIMB THE CORPORATE LADDER EFFECTIVELY • ADD A WORKSPACE TO ANY ROOM • ORGANIZE A HOME OFFICE • ORG
AVEL • WRITE A BUSINESS PLAN • SET UP A NEW BUSINESS • CREATE A MARKETING PLAN • AMASS A REAL-ESTATE EMPIRE • POLISH
MPLOYEE • FIRE AN EMPLOYEE • PASS ON A FAMILY BUSINESS • STAY ON TOP OF YOUR SALES GAME • RESTRUCTURE A COMPANY TO
EFEND AGAINST A HOSTILE TAKEOVER • ORGANIZE YOUR OFFICE FOR A MOVE • PREPARE YOUR BUSINESS FOR THE UNTHINKABLE • R
REPARE YOUR TAXES • ORGANIZE A LOAN APPLICATION • ORGANIZE IMPORTANT DOCUMENTS • SAVE FOR PRIVATE SCHOOLING • ORGA
LUB • TRACK YOUR INVESTMENTS • SURVIVE BANKRUPTCY • PLAN FOR RETIREMENT • PREPARE A PRENUPTIAL AGREEMENT • CREATE
ONEY • PLAN YOUR FAMILY • BUDGET FOR A NEW BABY • ORCHESTRATE THE PERFECT CONCEPTION • PLAN FOR ARTIFICIAL INSEMINA
AVE • ORDER BABY ANNOUNCEMENTS • ORGANIZE AN INTERNATIONAL ADOPTION • FOSTER A CHILD • ORGANIZE YOUR LIFE AS A NE
OORDINATE A FAMILY CALENDAR • PLAN FAMILY MEETINGS • ORGANIZE HOME SYSTEMS FOR ADD • PREPARE FOR A NEW CAT OR DOG
ACK-TO-SCHOOL • WIN THE HOMEWORK WARS • PLAN A FIELD TRIP • PLAN YOUR CHILD'S ACTIVITIES • PLAN YOUR CHILDREN'S SUMM
NLINE • ORGANIZE A GENEALOGICAL SEARCH • PREPARE FOR YOUR CHILD'S DEPARTURE FOR COLLEGE • ORGANIZE YOUR EMPTY NE
DERLY PARENTS' CARE • PREPARE FOR THE DEATH OF A SPOUSE • HELP YOUR ELDERLY PARENTS MOVE • ORGANIZE A HOME MEDICA
ORE TRIPS • SET UP ONLINE GROCERY SHOPPING • ORGANIZE RECIPES AND COOKBOOKS • PLAN THEME MENUS • CREATE EFFECTIV
EFRIGERATOR AND FREEZER • ORGANIZE CUTLERY AND KITCHEN TOOLS • ORGANIZE CUPBOARDS AND DRAWERS • ORGANIZE THE PA
UNCHES FOR KIDS • PLAN PARTY FOODS AHEAD • THROW A DINNER PARTY • FINISH DINNER ON TIME • PULL OFF A LAST-MINUTE PART
LTIMATE WEDDING CHECKLIST • BUDGET FOR A WEDDING • FIND THE PERFECT WEDDING RING • PLAN AN ELOPEMENT • SET UP A BAR
ONOR • EXECUTE BEST MAN DUTIES • HIRE A BAND • HIRE A BARTENDER • PLAN A SHOWER • ORGANIZE THE REHEARSAL DINNER • P
UCCESSFUL SLUMBER PARTY • PLAN A BAR OR BAT MITZVAH • PLAN A QUINCEAÑERA • PLAN A RETIREMENT PARTY • PLAN A FUNERA
ANUKKAH PARTY • ORGANIZE A HOLIDAY CRAFT PARTY • PLAN TO SPEND CHRISTMAS SOLO • PLAN THE PERFECT HOLIDAY GIFT EXCH
HE HOLIDAYS • STICK TO YOUR NEW YEAR'S RESOLUTIONS • PLAN THE PERFECT NEW YEAR'S EVE • PLAN A SEDER • PLAN A SPECIAL
OOD TREE • ORGANIZE A BICYCLE SCAVENGER HUNT • RUN A SPORTS TOURNAMENT • PUBLICIZE AN EVENT • PLAN AN ORGANIZATION
LAN A CONCERT IN THE PARK • ORGANIZE AN INTERNATIONAL CONCERT TOUR • ORGANIZE A FILM FESTIVAL • PLAN A FUND-RAISING
BUILD A COMMUNITY PLAY STRUCTURE • THROW A BLOCK PARTY • SET UP A NEIGHBORHOOD WATCH • CREATE AN EVACUATION PLA
RGANIZE A PROTEST OR MARCH • FIGHT CITY HALL • ORGANIZE A BOYCOTT • ORGANIZE A CLASS ACTION LAWSUIT • MANAGE GROW
CHOOL IN A THIRD WORLD COUNTRY • PLAN A TRIP • PLAN A TRIP WITH CHILDREN • TRAVEL WITH TEENS • BOOK AIRLINE TICKETS • F
OTORCYCLE TRIP • PLAN A TRAIN TRIP IN THE UNITED STATES • RIDE THE RAILS ABROAD • PREPARE A VACATION COUNTDOWN CHEC
UGGAGE • LOAD A BACKPACK PROPERLY • PLAN AN ELDERHOSTEL TRIP • ORGANIZE AN RV VACATION • PLAN A TRIP WITH AGING PAR
DELY DIFFERENT PEOPLE • PLAN SPRING BREAK • PLAN AN OVERNIGHT GETAWAY WITH YOUR SPOUSE • PLAN A VACATION SEPARATE
OLITICALLY UNSTABLE REGION • GET TRAVEL INSURANCE • GET IMMUNIZATIONS FOR TRAVELING • BOOK AN ADVENTURE VACATION •
LAN A FISHING TRIP TO ALASKA • PACK FOR A CAMPING TRIP • LEAD A BACKPACK TRIP • HIKE A FAMOUS TRAIL • PLAN A TOUR OF TH
NGLISH CANAL TRIP • PLAN A CROSS-COUNTRY AIRPLANE VOYAGE • PLAN THE PERFECT DAY ABROAD • PLAN A VISIT TO THE LOUVRE
LAN • PREPARE FOR AN ACT OF GOD • ASSEMBLE EMERGENCY KITS • PREPARE FOR SURGERY • PLAN YOUR RECOVERY • SURVIVE A
EING LOST • CONDUCT A SEARCH AND RESCUE OPERATION • PLAN AN INVASION • SURVIVE A POLITICAL COUP • PLAN FOR A TERROR

Get Organized

ESS • SET GOALS • STREAMLINE YOUR MORNING ROUTINE • ORGANIZE A CHORE SCHEDULE FOR KIDS • ORGANIZE YOUR CHORES • N
N YOUR WORKOUT SCHEDULE • SCHEDULE DOCTOR VISITS • PREPARE FOR COLD AND FLU SEASON • GET A DRASTIC MAKEOVER • ARI
Y UP • FIND YOUR KEYS • TIDY UP IN MINUTES • CONQUER CLUTTER • ACTUALLY SEE THE BOTTOM OF YOUR PURSE • ORGANIZE YOUR
LE CAR MAINTENANCE • ORGANIZE PET SUPPLIES • MANAGE GARBAGE AND RECYCLABLES • PREPARE GRAB 'N' GO ACTIVITY BAGS • ╴
AZINE CLIPPINGS • ORGANIZE YOUR PHOTOS • ARRANGE PHOTOS AND PICTURES • ARRANGE AN ART COLLECTION • END COLLECTION
T • ORGANIZE YOUR LAUNDRY CENTER • CREATE A SEWING CENTER • GET READY FOR THE HOUSECLEANER • ORGANIZE CLEANING SU
RYWAYS AND MUDROOMS • ORGANIZE A DORM ROOM • ORGANIZE YOUR SCHOOL LOCKER • MAKE YOUR HOME SAFE FOR SMALL CHI
PARE FOR SKYROCKETING ENERGY COSTS • USE FENG SHUI TO ORGANIZE YOUR HOME • DESIGN A NEW HOME WITH FENG SHUI • DES
PLAN A REMODEL • PLAN A MULTIMEDIA CENTER • TURN A BASEMENT INTO A MEDIA ROOM OR PLAYROOM • ORGANIZE THE ATTIC • C
SFUL ESTATE SALE • PLAN A YARD OR GARAGE SALE • PREPARE YOUR HOME FOR SALE • PLAN A MOVE • DOWNSIZE YOUR HOUSE • O
ECORATE FOR THE SEASONS • PREPARE A VACATION HOME FOR THE OFF-SEASON • PREPARE YOUR HOME FOR NATURE'S WORST • PR
GARDEN • PLANT A CUT-FLOWER GARDEN • DESIGN A SHADE GARDEN • DESIGN A DRY GARDEN • PLAN FOR A LONG-SEASON CONTAI
AN AND PLANT A LAWN • DESIGN A NEW LANDSCAPE • PLAN AN OUTDOOR KITCHEN • DESIGN A DECK OR PATIO • DESIGN A WATER FE
ES • STORAGE SOLUTIONS FOR ANY ROOM • ⋯ THE CAPACITY OF A SMALL ROOM • ORGAN
RTWORK • ORGANIZE MOVIES, MUSIC AND ⋯ IRLOOMS • STORE OUT-OF-SEASON CLOTHES
ENT • STORE PAINT AND OTHER HAZARDOU⋯ STORE A BOAT FOR THE WINTER • STORE A C
GE APPLICATIONS • PLAN YOUR COURSE OF ⋯ H PAPER • GET INTO GRAD SCHOOL • GET INT
LONG ABSENCE • SET UP AN INTERNSHIP • ⋯ N THE PEACE CORPS • PRODUCE A NEWSLETTI
• BECOME A COWBOY • BECOME A BRAIN S⋯ ATHOLIC NUN • ORGANIZE AN EXHIBITION • DE
OME A STUNT PERSON • BECOME A TOUR ⋯ • CONQUER YOUR PAPER PILES • CREATE A ╴
PUTER FILES • SCHEDULE APPOINTMENTS E⋯ NCE CALL • PREPARE FOR A MEETING • PREPA
ME NETWORK • CHOOSE THE BEST PHONE ⋯ TEM • MAKE A NETWORKING PLAN • PLAN YOU
ENTATION SKILLS • PREPARE A SPEECH • PR⋯ AN AN IPO • DELEGATE RESPONSIBILITIES • HIF
ROFITS • FORM A BOARD OF DIRECTORS • ⋯ AN A COMPANY PICNIC • PLAN A COMPANY RE
A FAILING BUSINESS • DISMANTLE A BUSINE⋯ • DESIGN A SAVINGS PLAN • SIMPLIFY BILL PA
FINANCIAL-AID PACKAGE • PLAN FOR COLLE⋯ E A HEALTH INSURANCE PLAN • START AN INV
UST • MAKE A WILL • EXECUTE A POWER O⋯ ESTATE • PLAN YOUR ESTATE • TEACH YOUR
PARE FOR AN IN VITRO FERTILIZATION • PRE⋯ ATERNITY WARDROBE • SET UP MATERNITY OF
PREPARE FOR CHILDBIRTH • STOCK A DIAPE⋯ LEND FAMILIES • CREATE A HOUSEHOLD ORGA
OOL YOUR CHILD • SET UP A CARPOOL • S⋯ HE BEST ELEMENTARY SCHOOL • ORGANIZE KI
FOR SUMMER CAMP • CHOOSE A SUMMER S⋯ R FAMILY COMPUTER USE • PLAN TO KEEP YO
R BOOMERANG KIDS • PLAN AN AMICABLE ⋯ EMENTS • ORGANIZE MEDICAL RECORDS • PLA
E • ARRANGE HOSPICE CARE • MAKE YOUR⋯ RECORDS • PLAN A WEEK OF MENUS • ORGANI
LISTS • COOK AHEAD • DETERMINE THE SH⋯ M WAREHOUSE STORES • EFFICIENTLY USE THI
IENTLY USE SPACE UNDER THE SINK • STO⋯ UR COUNTER SPACE • COOK FOR ONE • PLAN
DINNER PARTY FOR YOUR BOSS • PLAN DI⋯ PARTY • IMPRESS A DATE • PLAN A WEDDING •
VENT PLANNER • HIRE A PHOTOGRAPHER • ⋯ ACHELORETTE PARTY • PREPARE TO BE THE M.
NEYMOON • PLAN A BAPTISM • PLAN A BRI⋯ THROW A PARTY • PREPARE FOR HOUSE GUESTS • PLAN A CHILD'S BIRTHDAY PARTY •
A TO CUSTOM • PLAN AHEAD FOR A LOW-STRESS HOLIDAY • STAY WITHIN A BUDGET THIS CHRISTMAS • PREPARE A HOLIDAY FEAST •
NIZE GIFT GIVING IN ADVANCE • STICK TO YOUR GIFT DURING THE HOLIDAYS • PLAN A HOLIDAY OPEN HOUSE • REORGANIZE YOUR L
• ORGANIZE A HIGH-SCHOOL CLASS REUNION • PLAN A FAMILY REUNION • START A KNITTING CIRCLE • ORGANIZE A BOOK CLUB • S
• SHARPEN THE FOCUS OF AN ORGANIZATION • IMPROVE YOUR CHILD'S SCHOOL • PLAN A PROM • ORGANIZE A COMMUNITY THEATE
NIZE A PANCAKE BREAKFAST • PLAN A TOY DRIVE • HOLD A BARN RAISING • ORGANIZE A CHARITY WALK OR RUN • BUILD LOW-INCO
OTER-REGISTRATION DRIVE • RUN FOR LOCAL OFFICE • ORGANIZE A PETITION • ORGANIZE A RECALL • GET AN INITIATIVE ON THE BALL
OMMUNITY • PRESERVE OPEN SPACE • SAVE HISTORIC PROPERTIES AND LANDMARKS • SET UP A NONGOVERNMENTAL ORGANIZATIO
THE UNITED STATES • RENT A CAR ABROAD • MAKE HOTEL RESERVATIONS • ARRANGE EXECUTIVE ACCOMMODATIONS • PLAN A CRU
RE AN ITINERARY • PACK FOR A TRIP • PACK FOR A BUSINESS TRIP • PACK FOR A WEEK IN ONE CARRY-ON • PACK A DAY BAG • PREVE
NIZE A SAILING TEAM • PLAN A SAILBOAT CRUISE • PLAN A BICYCLE TRIP WITH A TOUR COMPANY • TRAVEL ABROAD • PLAN A VACATIO
SPOUSE • PLAN A TRIP TO A DIFFERENT CULTURE • FORAGE ABROAD • MAIL PACKAGES BACK TO THE UNITED STATES • PLAN A TRIP T
LK ROAD • PLAN A CLIMB OF MOUNT KILIMANJARO • PACK FOR A SAFARI • ORGANIZE A HUNTING TRIP • PACK FOR A FISHING OR HU
RKS • ORGANIZE A BACKCOUNTRY SKI TRIP • ORGANIZE A CAR RALLY • PLAN A WHALE-WATCHING TRIP • PACK FOR A VOYAGE AT SE
SYDNEY HARBOUR BRIDGE • PLAN A TRIP TO NEW ORLEANS FOR MARDI GRAS • PLAN A DAY AT DISNEYLAND • FORMULATE A FAMILY
IF YOU'RE ALONE • SURVIVE IF YOUR CAR BREAKS DOWN • DEAL WITH AMNESIA • FIGHT AN EBOLA OUTBREAK • FIGHT A FOREST FI
ESCUE A HOSTAGE • OUTSMART PIRATES • DELIVER A BABY • MAKE AN EMERGENCY LANDING • MAKE A JAIL BREAK • BECOME A MO

1 | Get Organized

How many times have you torn up the house looking for that one important item, or been paralyzed by the avalanche in your inbox, or spent far too many mornings in a dead sprint to get out of the house on time? Things that are left undone can be your own undoing—adding stress and wasting precious time. Organizing is the act of giving yourself more time and peace of mind.

Steps

Getting started

1 Try to understand the role in your life played by all those accumulated belongings. Many people hang on to belongings for comfort and security, and to remind them of who they've been and who they want to become. Paring down, however, doesn't have to be a painful process. Organizing takes whatever works best for you and makes it the norm rather than the exception.

2 Read 16 Set Goals. Then take an inventory of everything that's not working in your life, big or small. Is it pawing through your closet each morning for something to wear, or dreading planning dinner every night? Do you wish you had more time to work out, travel or write a book (see 496 Write the Great American Novel)? Now list everything that would make you feel better: Having bills paid on time (see 229 Simplify Bill Paying). Spending more time with your family. Being able to actually park your car in the garage. This inventory will reveal where your energy and time are needed and clarify your values.

The urge to purge

1 Choose an area from your inventory that needs help. Whether it's your overflowing office, your crammed closet or your bureau, roll up your sleeves.

2 Start small to avoid getting overwhelmed. If you don't have a entire day or weekend to devote to the project, carve out 20-minute chunks. Tackle the junk drawer during halftime. Take on the medicine chest while you're supervising baths (see 43 Organize the Medicine Cabinet). Setting a realistic time frame is key to getting stuff done.

3 Pull out everything from your target area and sort it into four piles: items to keep, items to sell or give away, items to fix and items to toss. Use boxes or large garbage bags to manage your piles, and keep one box to fill with items that belong elsewhere.

4 Put the misplaced items where they belong or in a temporary place. Take your discards to the garbage can and recycling bin.

Tips

Break the big jobs down into manageable tasks and tackle one room or area at a time to minimize disruption.

Be ruthless when you purge. For each item, ask: "Do I love this? Do I really need it? Can someone else use it?" If you haven't worn it, used it or needed it in a year, get rid of it. If you can replace something easily, trash it. If you have many similar items, keep one and pitch the rest.

Are you one of those people who keeps empty boxes for a possible future move or mailing? There's no shortage of cardboard boxes if you should ever need them. Break them down and set them out for recycling.

Who Knew?

Having trouble parting with certain stuff? Gather items into categories such as those in step 3. When you look at them all together, you'll wonder why you kept them to begin with.

Tape cassettes, laser disc players, old computers and cell phones are just taking up space.

Put your sell or donate box in the car (see 12 Get Rid of What You Don't Want). Now look through what you're keeping. Set aside anything that needs repairs, with a deadline of three months or so until they are too are sold or donated.

5 Make purging a routine. Of all the organizing principles, it's the most difficult, yet it yields the most visible results. If you have trouble letting something go, box it up for a year. If you still haven't needed it, you'll be more ready to toss it.

Keeping it together

1 Start creating new organizing systems by analyzing how you use and store your stuff (see 128 Store Anything). Some organizers call it being "motion minded." Hang a bucket filled with sponges, rags, soap and wax in the garage. Keep the coffeemaker next to the sink for water, and store coffee, filters and cups nearby. Pay attention to how often you use things as well. Place frequently needed items at eye level and at the front of shelves; put less frequently used items at the back, or on high or low shelves.

2 Ask yourself how a particular task or area could be made more efficient, and continue to refine your systems until you're happy with the result. Whatever you try, make it simple. Anything else sets you up for failure.

3 Purchase containers that fit the task. Clear, stackable, sturdy, air- and watertight containers offer security, access and visibility.

4 Label containers, folders, boxes and files clearly so everyone in the family knows where things go, and you can quickly identify contents. Unlabeled CDs, videotapes, folders or boxes are a guaranteed time waster. See 57 Live Better Through Labeling.

5 Be conscious about acquiring new stuff. Before you purchase something, make sure you have a place for it. Better yet, purchase something new only if you get rid of something old. Buy only what you'll really use—even if it's a good deal or on sale. Say no to castoffs from friends and family. When in doubt, live without. See 15 Live With Less.

6 Recognize that you can't do it alone all the time—that's part of being organized. Get help from relatives, friends or professionals if you can't keep up with routine chores; you aren't good at doing what needs to be done; you don't know how to do something and have no time to learn; or you recently went through a major life event such as a family death, divorce, job loss or change or a move. If you're too overwhelmed to even start, call in the cavalry (see 5 Hire a Professional Organizer).

Warning

Before you head out to buy new containers to stash your stuff, measure what's going in them first to make sure everything fits.

2 Set Priorities

If you had only a year to live, what would you do? How you choose to spend your time reflects what's truly important in your life. If you're constantly longing to have more time for the things and people you love, perhaps you need to shake up your priorities.

Steps

1 See 16 Set Goals. When your values are clearly defined, you can look at the things that are most important to you and compare them with how you actually spend your time and money.

2 Examine how you handle the conflicting demands of home, family, relationships and work (see 14 Balance Home and Work).

3 Pay attention to resentments—they often reveal needs that aren't being met. If you're growling at your children or spouse, you may be running on a deficit of time to yourself—to work out, read or simply be. If you resent the tasks that fill your workday, examine how they stack up to your career expectations (see 167 Prepare for a Career Change). Re-establish balance in your life by delving into the true source of your anger.

4 Say no to additional commitments. Sure, it feels great to be in demand, but consider what it will cost you to take on yet another thing you don't have time for. See 13 Say No Without Feeling Guilty.

5 Prioritize your spending. Write down what you'd like to have and be brutally honest about how much it will improve your quality of life. Then assess what it will really cost you to get the item— bearing in mind upfront costs, maintenance and potential credit card debt. When you spend your money on what you really need (like a reliable car), it makes it less painful do without things you merely want (like another pair of shoes). See 15 Live With Less and 228 Design a Savings Plan.

6 Keep the 80/20 rule in mind: 80 percent of the time is spent doing 20 percent of the work. Be aware of your peak energy periods and schedule your most critical tasks at those times. Bring the best of yourself to bear on the problems at hand and complete them more quickly and effectively. See 188 Organize Your Workday and 191 Schedule Appointments Efficiently.

7 Resist wasting time and energy surfing the Internet or constantly checking e-mail. Schedule those tasks after critical work is completed or in short power bursts. See 189 Get a Handle on E-mail.

8 Prepare for tomorrow. At the end of each day, make a to-do list for the next one. You'll keep track of your tasks and save valuable time. Prioritize critical or urgent items. See 3 Write an Effective To-Do List.

9 Reward yourself for priorities well set—and achieved. See 405 Plan a Trip.

Tips

If you can put off a task without penalty, do it.

Tackle fewer but higher priority tasks—you'll meet your goals faster.

Who Knew?

Schedule time in your calendar to play, rest, exercise, visit friends, have a date with your significant other or kids, or just be alone. Actually seeing your priorities in writing can make it easier to set aside time for them.

Warning

Don't be seduced by how easy a task appears—your time will be eaten up regardless of how important the job is, so spend that time wisely.

3 | Write an Effective To-Do List

How many times have you've gotten somewhere only to forget what you needed in the first place? Note to self: Writing to-do lists saves time, energy, stress and even gas. A good list lets you forget—once you have a written reminder, your mind is free to concentrate on other things. A to-do list even helps you meet your goals. Whether you're a legal pad, personal digital assistant (PDA) or back-of-the-phone-bill type, pick a system that works—and write it down!

Steps

1 Pull those scraps out of your pockets, purse and glove compartment, and gather them in one place. Where you choose to collect your thoughts depends on your personal style: If you like to cross things off, use a datebook, calendar or spiral-bound notebook that travels with you. If you prefer a more fluid system, write items on individual sticky notes and put them on a wall calendar. You can rearrange them as priorities change. Or stick the notes in your datebook and hit the road. See 11 Organize Your Contacts and 265 Create a Household Organizer.

2 Investigate the many electronic options for list makers. Your PDA is a great repository for all of your lists, including movies to rent, gifts to buy and business contacts who expect a call that day.

3 Categorize your to-dos, keeping like items together such as calls to make, things to buy and errands to run. Other categories might include gifts, projects, contacts, thoughts and goals. Order errand-related to-dos by shop and destination. See 4 Run Errands Efficiently.

4 Prioritize the items on your list to stay focused on what's critical (see 2 Set Priorities). Revisit your to-do list regularly to re-assess and reprioritize as situations change, and to check off completed items. Keep a "This Week" or "This Month" section for items that aren't immediate.

5 Buy a weekly calendar and use it for your to-do list. You can easily transfer leftover items to the next page, and you'll have a record of your entire year at the end.

6 Post a to-do list with projects that take 5 minutes or less to complete. Have family members choose and complete a task every evening—changing a burned out lightbulb, pumping up bike tires, putting the library books in the car or rearranging the towel closet. You'll free your weekends of small tasks and have time to tackle the big ones. See 36 Tidy Up in 15 Minutes.

Tips

Remember those crazy dreams—and save them. See 16 Set Goals and review a lifetime to-do list every six months or so. Jump start your list with 491 Learn to Fly, 490 Run a Marathon and 501 Be Happy.

Give kids their own to-do lists. They're an important and valued part of the family team, and your household routines will go much smoother. Even preschoolers will enjoy checking items off a list with pictures next to the words.

See ToDoListMagazine.com for more tips on handling life's details.

Put reading 9 Organize Your Thoughts on your list.

Create checklists on your computer so that you can update and print them easily.

Who Knew?

Stash your to-do lists strategically. For example, keep a workout list in your gym bag and you'll never leave your swim goggles home again.

4   Run Errands Efficiently

You look forward to the weekend for so many reasons—to relax, reflect and play. But if your downtime gets eaten up by trips to the supermarket, the library, the cleaners and every other spot on the map except your couch, then you need to retune your systems. Whether you live alone or have a large family, you can reclaim your free time by following these simple steps.

Steps

1   Read 10 Set Up a Reminder System and 2 Set Priorities. Make a list of your errands in order of priority, then group them by location so that you can get the most done in the shortest amount of time. Stick to your list.

2   Create an errand center in your house by setting up one of the following systems and encourage your entire household to use it (see 265 Create a Household Organizer).

- Post a blank laminated calendar and write in the month and the days of the week using an erasable marker. Then, on sticky notes, write down the errands to be completed and put the notes on the day the errands need to be done. Include any helpful phone numbers and directions.

- Pull out your spiral-bound to-do list (see 3 Write an Effective To-Do List) and create sections for to buy, to do and to fix. Use sticky notes to jot down any necessary phone numbers, contacts, addresses, measurements, serial numbers and other product-specific information that needs to come with you.

- Stash items near the door that need to go in the car. See 41 Return Rentals on Time.

3   Plan your most efficient route with errands grouped geographically. Save even more time by switching to a dry cleaner that's near the supermarket that's near your office. Plan your route so the grocery run comes last to prevent perishables from spoiling in the car. Or put a cooler in the trunk to hold those items until you get home. See 298 Organize Grocery Store Trips.

4   Stock up on frequently used nonperishable items only once a month to cut down on the number of shopping trips. See 302 Create Effective Shopping Lists.

Tip

Make sure your cellular phone is fully charged before you hit the road. You can call some of the people on your to-do list while running errands. Just don't talk and drive at the same time.

Who Knew?

If you use sticky notes, arrange them in the sequence of the stops you'll have to make.

Write down your list of errands on an envelope and insert any coupons, addresses or other notes.

5 | Hire a Professional Organizer

Suppose you have no talent at all for creating order out of chaos—much less for envisioning and implementing systems customized to your home and your way of life. It's time to call in a pro. Choose the type of professional services you need, then pick up the phone and get the show on the road.

Steps

1 Ask neighbors and friends for recommendations. Inquire about the nature of the work they had done, how long it took, if the professional organizer provided hands-on assistance and which methods were used. Also ask if they continued to be organized after the professional left.

2 Contact the National Association of Professional Organizers (napo.net) for information on the field as well as referrals. NAPO members are bound by a code of ethics that includes serving customers with competency, integrity and strict confidentiality.

3 Ask the same questions you would ask any consultant: What is your background and training? How long have you been in the business? What is your particular area of expertise? Are you member of a professional association? Can I call your references?

4 Find out how much the organizer charges. Fees vary widely based on geographic location, experience and the type of services provided. Most residential organizers charge an hourly fee that may range from $25 to more than $200; some work on a fixed-fee basis; and some use a combination of hourly and fixed fees. For large projects, professional organizers may contract their services for a defined period of time on a retainer basis.

5 Clarify who will do what. Depending on the nature and the scope of the work, organizers adapt their services to the needs of the customer. He or she may set up the new systems and let you do the work, plow through the job with you, or take care of it alone.

Tips

Professional organizers will often request an on-site consultation visit to better understand the nature of the problem and the extent of the services to be provided. Some charge for this visit, while others offer it for free.

Ask what supplies you'll need to have on hand, such as bins and trash bags for sorting.

Who Knew?

Many organizers specialize in working with children, students, seniors or people with ADD. See 268 Organize Home Systems for ADD.

Some professional organizers will run errands for you.

Residential	Workplace	Events
Purge, declutter and organize all rooms, attic, basement and garage.	• Devise effective filing systems.	Prepare for the sale of a house.
Design a well-organized kitchen and bathroom.	• Improve paper and work flow.	Organize the packing and unpacking for a move.
Organize closets.	• Define and implement information and records management (for legal, medical and other offices).	Supervise an estate sale.
Organize collections, memorabilia and photographs.	• Implement time-management and goal-setting strategies.	Plan and coordinate business and family events.
Organize garage sales.	• Organize finances for bookkeeping.	Give seminars, workshops and training on professional organizing strategies.
Organize a home office.		Plan meetings.
Devise effective filing systems.		

6 | Meet Deadlines

You were the type who always pulled all-nighters to cram for exams. Now you're still doing the same thing as deadlines loom, whether it's for filing taxes, mailing holiday cards or completing work assignments. Use these tips to break down large projects into bite-size chunks and break the cycle. Soon you'll be making those deadlines—with time to spare.

Steps

1 Read 16 Set Goals and 2 Set Priorities.

2 Identify when your project must be completed, then calculate how much time you have to do it. Depending on the project, this could be days, weeks or months.

3 Take into consideration what may sidetrack you. The more time-critical the task, the more important it is that you're realistic about what else is on your plate.

4 Break large projects into smaller subtasks. For example, you can divide wedding planning into getting a dress, finding a reception location, hiring a caterer and so on (see 324 Create the Ultimate Wedding Checklist). To come up with an accurate schedule for the project, estimate how long you'll need to complete each subtask, making sure to build in time for unforeseen circumstances or delays.

5 Define each subtask, and set start and end dates for each. Make sure you continually evaluate how realistic your time frame is. If you're running out of time, and there's nothing you can do about it—such as the meeting starts in 48 hours—then get creative and start trimming tasks.

6 Create a check list and schedule for each subtask (see 3 Write an Effective To-Do List). Use whatever system works for you to stay on track: a daily check-in with your schedule, a tickler file on the dining-room table or an alarm on your personal digital assistant (PDA).

7 Enlist help from reliable colleagues or friends—you'll not only save time but also empower others on your team when they contribute to the overall project. Delegate all tasks except those that only you can get done. Schedule regular meetings with your team to make sure subtasks remain on schedule and within budget.

8 Cut corners where you can without affecting the overall quality. Re-evaluate your deadline and keep consolidating tasks and cutting extras until you can get the job done.

9 Take care to assess the situation with a calm head as you go along. Big projects can quickly snowball.

Tip

Use scheduling software such as Microsoft Project to help set up your tasks and automatically adjust critical dates when delays crop up. Make use of the Sheets feature to organize and keep a record of all relevant information.

10 Identify certain tasks that may be holding up the works or are simply not going to get done in time. If possible, hire someone to help you.

11 Gather your team after the deadline has been met. Discuss the project and determine if goals were met, how the process could have been improved and how team members performed. Ask for honest feedback from everyone with the understanding that your ultimate desire is improved performance on the next deadline.

7   Deal With a Flood of Mail

Save on long-distance rates! Don't miss this sale! Pay this bill! While the U.S. Postal Service prides itself on delivering the mail come rain, sleet or snow, you could use some shelter from the storm. Reclaim your kitchen counter—and your life—by adopting one or all of these strategies.

Steps

1 Keep your filing system simple and weed on a regular basis. See 185 Create a Flawless Filing System and 184 Conquer Your Paper Piles.

2 Establish a mail station in your home or office using, for example, two baskets and a trash can. Sort mail immediately and try to touch each piece only once: act on it, file it or throw it out.

3 Recycle junk mail without opening it.

4 Keep a basket at hand where you can toss the magazines and catalogs. Once the basket is full, recycle the contents after tearing out (and filing) any articles you want to keep. See 52 Categorize Newspaper and Magazine Clippings.

5 File only those papers you need to retain, such as taxes and personal documents. Ask your accountant to clarify how long you should keep different documents. In general, keep bills from the previous month, then shred and toss them once they're reconciled. (You'll need to hang on to bills longer if you're self-employed—see 232 Organize Important Documents.) When in doubt, ask yourself if you can obtain a legitimate copy of a document if you had to.

6 Protect yourself against identity theft. Shred any documents that contain account numbers, Social Security numbers or other personal, sensitive information.

Tips

See 229 Simplify Bill Paying.

Opt for electronic subscriptions of magazines and newspapers, if available, and print out only what you want to read.

Who Knew?

Cut down on the amount of junk mail you receive. Remove your name from junk-mail lists by contacting the Direct Marketing Association (www.dmaconsumers.org/offmailinglist.html).

Warning

If you don't have a shredder, tear up and separate pieces of sensitive documents.

8 | Overcome Chronic Disorganization

You've battled a chaotic house, office and desk all your adult life. Bills go unpaid because you've misplaced them, trash piles up and you're wearing your last pair of clean socks. Regardless of your best efforts and unflagging desire to overcome the clutter, nothing seems to work. Take heart. The following strategies may get you on the way to overcoming chronic disorganization.

Steps

General tips

1 Identify the reasons why you are terminally disorganized. Do you have ADD or ADHD? If so, this is a clinical disorder that can be treated. See also 268 Organize Home Systems for ADD.

2 Take it one step at a time. Before you can mop or vacuum the floor, you need to pick up the toys, clothes and shoes. Reward yourself for each tiny task, and you'll be inspired to keep going.

3 Learn to let go of unrealistic expectations. Your home or office may not win any cleanliness awards, but having a system that works for you will make the difference.

Pair up

1 Hire a pro if even thinking about the task ahead overwhelms you. See 5 Hire a Professional Organizer.

2 Hire a weekly cleaning service to help you keep your home clean. See 64 Get Ready for the Housecleaner.

3 Ask a friend or relative to be your "organizing buddy." It will greatly increase your chances for success. Pick someone you trust and who can be totally honest, because he or she will be a hands-on partner every step of the way. Your buddy will help you overcome your reluctance to part with objects, haul your discard pile to the curb and help you figure out what to do with the remainder. Together, read 1 Get Organized for details on downsizing.

Clothes and objects

1 Clear a table or an area of the floor to use as a sorting stage. Define sections for the following categories: keep, give away or sell, fix, and discard.

2 Stand at a distance from your stuff and have your buddy be the one to pick up each item for you. This will make it easier for you to determine what to do with it.

3 Instruct your buddy to put each item in the appropriate pile.

4 Go through the keep pile and distill it further. Make sure everything that stays has a home in your house.

Tips

Tackle one room at a time. Each effort you make is a step in the right direction.

Contact the National Study Group on Chronic Disorganization (nsgcd.org) for tips and referrals to professional organizers.

Clutterless Recovery Groups (clutterless.org) has a bulletin board for people seeking clutter buddies.

Who Knew?

Read 184 Conquer Your Paper Piles and 185 Create a Flawless Filing System. When filing papers, pick up each document and mutter (yes, mutter!) the first sentence that comes to mind. Have your buddy write that sentence on the folder and place the document inside. Examples are "Things I've Been Putting Off," "Stuff I Can Never Find," "The Good Old Days," and "When I Win the Lottery."

Or, organize your folders around emotionally oriented subject areas. For example, keep folders containing packing and travel checklists, travel insurance, and passport together in a drawer labeled "Stuff for Traveling."

5 Donate designated items to charity, and set up a yard sale or eBay.com account to sell the rest (see 12 Get Rid of What You Don't Want). Ask your buddy to put the discard items in the trash if you can't bear to do it.

Pare down

1 Define an in/out ratio that will help you keep your clutter under control. For example, if you bring an item into your environment, get rid of two items. Your clutter will decrease dramatically.

2 Keep the lid on clutter by scheduling regular maintenance sessions with your organizing buddy.

9 Organize Your Thoughts

Lightbulb! A brilliant idea suddenly strikes. But how do you maximize that creative thought before it disappears? Try mind mapping, a technique of organizing ideas visually created by Tony Buzan in *The Mind Map Book: How to Use Radiant Thinking to Maximize Your Brain's Untapped Potential.* Mind mapping helps you sift through complex thoughts and work out practical solutions. Use it to take notes, develop concepts or sketch out an overview. Give it a try during your next brainstorm.

Steps

1 Get a pencil with an eraser and a big piece of unlined paper. Write the project title, a short phrase or a symbol of your main idea in the center of the page. Then draw a circle around it.

2 Add other important concepts around the outside of the circle. Write quickly without pausing, judging or editing yourself. Use strong words instead of long explanations.

3 Think about the relationship of the outer items to the center one. Relocate relevant items closer to each other for more accurate or realistic representation of their interconnections.

4 Draw lines radiating out from the center circle and label them with the major subheadings.

5 Incorporate new ideas into the map appropriately. As you look for meaningful relationships between the ideas, you are mapping knowledge in a manner that will help you understand and recall new information.

6 Get creative: Combine concepts to expand your map, add more detail and explore tangents. For many people, symbols and pictures that represent ideas are easier to identify and remember than words.

Tip

People with dyslexia may find mind mapping particularly helpful since it relies on images and colors, and not words.

Who Knew?

Look for software at MindGenius.com and ConceptDraw.com, among others, if you would like to produce high-quality maps that you can easily edit and redraft. A computer mind map will also allow you to write sentences of explanation for yourself or others while keeping extra information hidden until it is needed.

10 | Set Up a Reminder System

What if there existed a magic system—one that always told you what bills needed paying or birthday cards sending (and when), where to find directions to the company retreat and when the cutoff was for buying season tickets? Relax. It exists—and in a format that works the way you do. Train yourself to use a reminder system and you'll never forget to take care of a critical item again.

Steps

1 Buy a wire step rack or accordion envelope and folders marked with the months of the year. Number a set of plain folders for the current month, one for each day (you'll reuse these every month). Slip all folders into the rack or envelope.

2 Pull all time-sensitive notes, stickies, papers, bills and invoices from their scattered locations. File each in the folder that corresponds to the date on which you need to deal with that item. Slip bills into folders 15 and 30 for payment on those days (see 229 Simplify Bill Paying). Stash your smog certificate in the folder for the week before it's due. Follow suit with all other paperwork.

3 Jump to the monthly folders for those items that require action next month or later in the year. Put year-end bank statements and 1099s in the March or April folder, your cruise tickets in the June one and a list of back-to-school supplies in September. When you get to the end of the current month, pull out the next month's file and stick all those items in the appropriate daily folders.

4 Make efficient use of your calendar if you're in the habit of checking it regularly. Sit down once a week and pencil in all the dates and deadlines you need to remember in the week (or month) to come. Or write action items on colored sticky notes for easy transfer to another day if plans change. Each day, move stickies onto your to-do list and take critical information with you.

Tips

Tie your reminder system to your planning calendar and to-do list so that you coordinate all three systems at the same time every day. See 3 Write an Effective To-Do List and 266 Coordinate a Family Calendar.

Get in the habit of taking a quick look at today's folder every morning.

Include names, addresses, phone numbers and directions when you're penciling in items to remember.

Who Knew?

Let your computer be your personal assistant. Set up automatic reminders with scheduling and calendar software. Synchronize your software with your PDA and take your reminder system with you.

11 | Organize Your Contacts

You have lots of great options when you finally upgrade that address book you've had since college. Paper-based planners, contact management software, personal digital assistants (PDAs) and smart mobile phones can all help you get your contact information in order.

Steps

1 Decide if you're an ink-and-paper person or if you like to deal in digital.

2 Use only one address book. Don't keep separate books for home, work and other activities; instead, keep all the information in a single address book that's broken out into categories.

Tip

PDAs and mobile phones equipped with Bluetooth can synchronize with Bluetooth-enabled computers if they're within a few feet of each other—and you don't have any cables or cradles to worry about.

3 Collect all your addresses before entering them. Don't forget club rosters, alumni address books, community resources, doctors and professional associations, in addition to your personal address book. Check that addresses are current and correct, and update those that aren't.

4 Keep track of birthday and holiday cards—whom you sent them to, and who sent them to you—in your book, and file reminders in your tickler system (see 10 Set Up a Reminder System).

Warning

Protect your information against loss. If you have a paper organizer, photocopy it regularly. If your system is electronic, synchronize and back up often, and don't let the batteries run down.

EQUIPMENT	FEATURES
Paper Organizers	• Classic printed organizers, such as Filofax and Franklin Covey, are fast and flexible, but they can be bulky and heavy. • Write names in ink, but addresses and telephone numbers in pencil. • Make sure your organizer can accommodate new pages when the address book gets full. You may need to buy them from the organizer's manufacturer.
Contact Management Software	• This software is aimed at salespeople, but it can be helpful for busy households, too. • Choose a product that can share addresses with your computer's e-mail program. Microsoft Outlook and Plaxo.com are some examples. • Look for software that will synchronize with your mobile phone or PDA. • Use the program's mail merge feature to personalize a form letter. You can even send personalized bulk e-mail. (Won't your friends love that?)
Personal Digital Assistants (PDAs)	• Small, lightweight and powerful, even an inexpensive PDA will beat a paper organizer in terms of features—but some find learning to write on a PDA a difficult obstacle. • Enter your information on your computer and then synchronize, rather than scratching all the information on the PDA's tiny screen. There's no sense in making this task more tedious than it has to be. • Tap into the other features that come with your PDA. For example, you can add a birthday to a person's address record, and then have that birthday appear on your electronic calendar (with a reminder a week beforehand). • Use the security feature on your PDA so that a password is required to access important addresses and phone numbers.
Mobile Phones	• Break out that user manual. Many newer phones have full address-book capabilities—not just numbers, but addresses and even birthday reminders. • Look into wireless data services, such as AOL MyMobile (mymobile.aol.com), MSN Mobile (mobile.msn.com) and Yahoo Mobile (mobile.yahoo.com), that you can access via your mobile phone. They include address-book functions. Find out if your phone service can support these.

12 Get Rid of What You Don't Want

You did it. You sorted your stuff—so now what do you do with those toss and give-away piles? There still may be use and life left in your discards, and with a little effort, you may even convert some castoffs into cold, hard cash as well as deductions on your next tax return. Use this chart to get started. Also see 95 Plan a Yard or Garage Sale and 50 Sell Stuff Online.

ITEMS	WHAT TO DO
Clothing	• Sell at a garage or yard sale or online.
	• Consign never-worn or designer-brand items less than 2 years old.
	• Sell vintage clothing (made more than 20 years ago) to retro stores.
	• Donate to charities and shelters. Worn out sneakers can go to Nike at nikereuseashoe.com.
Wire Hangers	• Give to dry cleaners or to charity stores (must be clean and in good shape).
Eyeglasses	• Donate to the Lion's Club Recycle for Sight program (lionsclubs.org). Drop-off locations include Goodwill, LensCrafters stores and community offices.
Towels, Blankets and Linens	• Drop off at a humane society.
	• Give items in decent, usable condition to shelters for homeless people and for battered women.
Magazines	• Donate to hospitals, nursing homes, veterans services and doctors' offices.
	• Donate magazine subscriptions to public libraries and schools.
	• Recycle.
Books	• Sell to book resale stores or online.
	• Donate to charities, schools and shelters.
Computers, Monitors, Printers, Scanners, Copiers and Fax Machines	• If only a year or two old, sell online or through the classifieds. Always use scrubbing software to remove all data from the hard drive.
	• Donate to ShareTechnology.org and other organizations if still working.
	• If equipment is not working or is outdated, contact your county waste-disposal department, computer or office equipment recycler or salvager for disposal guidelines. Often there is a nominal fee for disposal, typically calculated by weight, to pay for removing toxic components. See RecycleAPC.com. Remember, you can't throw these items in the trash.
Televisions, VCRs, Camcorders, Telephones, Stereos and Radios	• Sell or donate if in good working order (cell phones can go to programs such as DonateAPhone.com).
	• If not working, contact your county waste-disposal department for options. Often you pay a nominal fee or no fee at all for disposal.
Records, Cassette Tapes, CDs and Video Games	• If in excellent condition or of unusual interest, contact a reseller.
	• Sell at a garage or yard sale or online.
	• Donate all but records to shelters and schools.

ITEMS	WHAT TO DO
Batteries	• Check out BatteryRecycling.com for information on recycling used dry cells from cell phones, laptop computers, flashlights, cameras, watches, hearing aids, toys, two-way radios, electric tools, clocks and electronic devices.
Musical Instruments	• Sell to a resell store such as Music Go Round (musicgoround.com). • Donate to a school's music program.
Sports Equipment	• Sell equipment in excellent condition on eBay or to a resell store such as Play It Again Sports (www.playitagainsports.com), or donate to organizations like Second Swing (2ndswing.com). • Donate to youth sports programs or schools.
Plastic or Foam Packing Peanuts	• Drop off at a packing and shipping store for recycling (must be bagged, clean and dry).
Appliances	• If in working order, sell through the classifieds or a garage or yard sale. • Contact your county waste-disposal department or Sears.com to find a licensed appliance recycler. Expect to pay a fee for disposal.
Vehicles	• Donate to auto-maintenance technical schools or charities such as the Cystic Fibrosis Foundation (cff.org/cardonate), where the cars are sold at auction and the proceeds benefit programming. Contact the National Vehicle Donation Program (www.auto-donation.com) for more information. • Sell through the classifieds, CraigsList.org or other online services. • Sell to auto-salvage or scrap-metal dealers (usually they'll take only models less than seven years old).
Tires	• Contact local service stations, tire retailers or your county waste-disposal department (usually they charge a nominal fee for disposal).
Vehicle Batteries (car, boat, motorcycle, golf cart, snowmobile)	• Turn in the old battery when you buy a new one, since it can be illegal to put vehicle batteries in the trash. Otherwise the retailer will charge a $5 fee (refundable if you bring in the old battery with a receipt within 30 days). Drop off batteries at a Triple A location (aaa.com) during its annual Earth Day battery roundup. • Wear gloves when handling batteries, and keep all items upright in a sturdy box or container to prevent spills, shifting or tipping during transit.
TIPS	Charities can accept donations only of items in good to excellent condition with no need for repair. That means no rips, holes, stains or scratches. Donating items that fall outside the guidelines places a financial burden on the charity for additional dumpster costs. If your discards are too much for weekly garbage pickups, rent a dumpster. Your neighbors might split the cost to be able to clear our their garage, too. Look in the yellow pages under "Garbage and Rubbish Collection" or call (800) GOT-JUNK to arrange for pickup. If something isn't in good enough condition to sell or donate, put it out on the curb with a "Free" sign. If it doesn't disappear in a few days, toss it.

13 | Say No Without Feeling Guilty

Are you chronically overcommitted? Rushing from one task to another, with no time for yourself? The key is to have a strong vision of what you want to say yes to. Then you'll feel far more confident saying no.

Steps

1 Decide which activities you truly love. If you stay focused on those things, then the next time you are asked to volunteer or get involved in a time-consuming activity, just check in. If the request takes you too far from what you are already dedicating yourself to, it's easier to say no (see 16 Set Goals).

2 Get over the need to be nice. Stop being afraid to disappoint people, and let go of the sense of importance you get from being indispensable.

3 Be clear when you say no. Ambiguities like "Maybe after the first of the year" or "Let me get back to you" leave the other person thinking you're actually interested, when you're not.

4 Practice saying no in nonthreatening situations, when you have little at stake and success is almost assured. Then you'll work up to resigning from the board of directors and stop signing up for committee work. Learn that carving out time for yourself and your family requires no reason and no apology.

5 Say no to requests for money in simple language and give no explanation. Contribute to the causes that excite you and complement your values. Then you'll feel confident saying, "My contributions have already been allocated this year."

Tips

Keep it simple. The most effective nos are the least complicated. The more details you supply, the more likely the other person will challenge you or try to change your mind.

Make a compromise while you're learning to say no. If you're asked to bring cookies to an event, opt for store-bought sweets instead of slaving away in the kitchen.

Re-evaluate your current commitments. You may have agreed to a long-term commitment months ago, but now see that it's not working for you. Talk with the people involved and come up with an arrangement that works for everyone.

14 | Balance Home and Work

Missed another dinner party or recital because you were stuck at the office? Do you spend weekends catching up on work rather than being with your family or friends? The trick to creating a healthy balance is to be conscious of what you're doing and when you're doing it.

Steps

1 Read 16 Set Goals and ask yourself what really matters. To create the life you want, first define what's most important to you, then develop a plan that helps you prioritize and balance those things.

2 Assess your financial needs (see 228 Design a Savings Plan) to see if you or your spouse can cut back on work hours.

Tip

Take advantage of maternity and paternity leaves, sabbaticals, and other company-sponsored programs when available. See 162 Plan a Sabbatical and 256 Set Up Maternity or Paternity Leave.

3 Find out if your employer will allow telecommuting, job sharing or a part-time schedule. Look into child care assistance (for emergencies, during spring break and the holiday season, see 263 Arrange Quality Child Care); employee assistance on topics such as stress and time management; educational and training opportunities; and fitness membership assistance.

4 Put a cap on time spent on work whether you are in an office or at home. Let your family and co-workers know what those limits are. With clear parameters you'll work more effectively, and your family may be more supportive. When the time is up, stop working and focus on your family. Make vacations strictly off-limits for work.

5 Learn how to switch gears. Turn off your computer at 5:30 p.m. Stop multitasking at dinnertime so you can focus fully on your kids or spouse. Make 6 p.m. to 8 p.m. a no-phone zone.

6 Keep the clutter at bay. Prepare a house maintenance schedule and stick to it. If you can afford it, have your house cleaned on a weekly or biweekly basis. A well-maintained house requires less work to keep clean, which results in more time for family and fun. See 1 Get Organized, 37 Conquer Clutter and 36 Tidy Up in 15 Minutes.

7 Resist the urge to fill your family's time with scheduled activities. Practice, lessons and clubs will keep everyone's calendars full and stress levels high. Allow for completely unscheduled free time—even if it feels odd at first. See 266 Coordinate a Family Calendar.

8 Ask your family to use whatever message system you've set up (see 265 Create a Household Organizer).

9 Use the weekend for a real change of pace. If you work at a computer all day, crank up the volume on the weekend with a bike ride, gardening or a trip to a nearby park (see 452 Plan a Tour of the National Parks). If, however, you're racing nonstop all week long, then bask in quiet indolence come Saturday.

10 Build in time that's just for you. Make trades with your spouse to get time off from the house, the chores and the kids. Stay connected to friends. Make it a priority to work out and find a way to make it fun (see 25 Design Your Workout Schedule).

11 Do a status check every six months. Review your goals and your priorities. Continue to pare down belongings, commitments and responsibilities until you find a mix that works for you.

Warning

If the stress is overwhelming, talk to a professional therapist. Your work's human resources department may be able to confidentially refer you to counseling that's covered by your insurance.

15 Live With Less

It's been said that this is the first generation living in a total credit-card economy, one in which getting ahead has become more important than staying out of debt. As people become overwhelmed by working ever harder to pay for more stuff, frugal living is a hot topic again. Proponents of voluntary simplicity or living below your means (LBYM) make conscious spending decisions to live a full and rich life.

Steps

1 Read 226 Set Up a Budget and audit your own spending habits. Compare your expenses (including debt) with your income. If you're consistently spending more than you earn, it'll be no surprise that you're carrying a larger and larger debt load.

2 Make a list of short-, medium- and long-term financial goals (see 16 Set Goals). List in detail what you'll have to give up in order to meet each. Give yourself a reasonable period of time to practice your new spending habits in order to see progress.

3 Go through your belongings and get rid of as much as you can. See 1 Get Organized and 12 Get Rid of What You Don't Want.

4 Favor quality over quantity and buy the best quality you can afford. You'll save money in the long run since high-quality items last longer and require less maintenance. This applies to adult clothing, furniture, electronics and cars. On the other hand, buy used quality kids' clothing and toys every chance you get.

Tips

Charges made using your debit card are automatically deducted from your checking account—and therefore are interest-free.

Barter everything—babysitting to sewing to carpentry and plumbing—with family and friends. Type "barter groups" into a search engine for a wide range of bartering sites, groups and links.

Buy pre-owned quality items.

Cruise secondhand and thrift stores for quality and designer clothes at a fraction of their original price.

See 227 Get Out of Debt and 228 Design a Savings Plan.

AREA	ACTION
Spending	• Set up a budget against which you can track your expenses.
	• Pay cash rather than using a credit card. Cash lends transparency to your spending.
	• Refinance your mortgage at lower interest rates. Pay off high-interest loans first.
Debit and Credit Cards	• Use debit cards for your personal and household purchases so the money is automatically deducted from your checking account and no interest is charged.
	• Get rid of high-interest credit cards. Consolidate credit-card debt in a low-interest equity line of credit or low-interest credit card. Reduce the number of credit cards to one or at most two cards.
Saving	• With every paycheck, put some money aside in a savings account immediately.
	• Drop your spare change into a dedicated jar. At the end of each month, put the money into a savings account.
Entertainment	• Buy used books, music, videos and DVDs, or borrow them from the library.
	• Cancel subscriptions to magazines you don't read. Limit your newspaper subscription to the Sunday edition and read the online version during the week.
	• Cancel cable TV subscriptions and pick up a book instead.

16 | Set Goals

Goals and dreams aren't trivial. They reveal where hidden gifts, passion and vitality lie. Whether it's to skate in the Olympics, sing in a choir, remodel your bathroom or do stand-up comedy, when your goals are clearly stated, they are much more likely to be achieved.

Steps

1 Dream a little: What do you want to do, see, accomplish and experience? Look at a wide range of areas while you're mulling over your life and your values, including your career, the arts, physical achievements, finances, education and public service.

2 Ponder more personal goals: How do you want to feel? Do you want to have a family? Create a stronger one? How would you want those who love you most to describe you and the life you live? Would you like to change your mind-set or how you relate to people? Improve a core relationship? Be as truthful possible.

3 Review and reprioritize your goals until they reflect the life you want to live.

4 Set your lifetime goals. Then establish goals for 10 years from now, five years, one year—and then one month. Now prioritize them (review 2 Set Priorities).

5 Break each goal into subtasks that need to be completed. For example, if a financial goal is to be debt-free in two years (see 227 Get Out of Debt), you might decide to set up a budget (228 Design a Savings Plan), spend less than you make (15 Live With Less) and refinance your mortgage to lower your monthly payment. Set a time frame and priority for each subtask.

6 Use your daily to-do list (see 3 Write an Effective To-Do List) as a means to reach even your lifetime goals. Now that you've divided your goals into achievable tasks, incorporate those tasks into your list and pick them off, one at a time.

7 Review and reprioritize your goals regularly and when you suffer inevitable setbacks. You may find that they change over time, or that certain objectives get put on hold while you work on others.

8 Bear in mind that your goals may affect your loved ones. You might do this work together. If you have kids, bring them into the loop and fully consider their opinions. If an objective is to spend more time together as a family, and one solution is for you to work only part-time, ask family members what material goods they'd be willing to give up to get more time with you. You might be surprised. (See 14 Balance Home and Work.)

9 Commit to carrying out your plan of action. You've already gone further than most. Stay focused on the process and reward yourself—or at least notice—when something you've always wanted is actually attained.

Tips

In addition to not setting goals unrealistically high, be careful not to set goals too low. Aim for attainable goals that are just out of reach. When you accomplish one goal, you'll have the momentum to move on to the next.

Use rewards not only as a prize for achievement but also as an encouragement to continue on the road to your ultimate goal.

When you write down your goals, pay attention to your language. Replace "I should" and "I'll try" with "I will."

If you find you are having trouble meeting a particular goal, look deeper into the causes for this. Learn from the experience and either reprioritize the goal or move on to something else.

Warning

Beware of setting goals for yourself that are actually a veil for someone else's desires for you—your parents, your boss or your significant other.

ESS • SET GOALS • STREAMLINE YOUR MORNING ROUTINE • ORGANIZE A CHORE SCHEDULE FOR KIDS • ORGANIZE YOUR CHORES • NE
J YOUR WORKOUT SCHEDULE • SCHEDULE DOCTOR VISITS • PREPARE FOR COLD AND FLU SEASON • GET A DRASTIC MAKEOVER • ARF
UP • FIND YOUR KEYS • TIDY UP IN MINUTES • CONQUER CLUTTER • ACTUALLY SEE THE BOTTOM OF YOUR PURSE • ORGANIZE YOUR
E CAR MAINTENANCE • ORGANIZE PET SUPPLIES • MANAGE GARBAGE AND RECYCLABLES • PREPARE GRAB 'N' GO ACTIVITY BAGS • K
ZINE CLIPPINGS • ORGANIZE YOUR PHOTOS • ARRANGE PHOTOS AND PICTURES • ARRANGE AN ART COLLECTION • END COLLECTION
• ORGANIZE YOUR LAUNDRY CENTER • CREATE A SEWING CENTER • GET READY FOR THE HOUSECLEANER • ORGANIZE CLEANING SU
YWAYS AND MUDROOMS • ORGANIZE A DORM ROOM • ORGANIZE YOUR SCHOOL LOCKER • MAKE YOUR HOME SAFE FOR SMALL CHIL
ARE FOR SKYROCKETING ENERGY COSTS • USE FENG SHUI TO ORGANIZE YOUR HOME • DESIGN A NEW HOME WITH FENG SHUI • DES
PLAN A REMODEL • PLAN A MULTIMEDIA CENTER • TURN A BASEMENT INTO A MEDIA ROOM OR PLAYROOM • ORGANIZE THE ATTIC • O
SFUL ESTATE SALE • PLAN A YARD OR GARAGE SALE • PREPARE YOUR HOME FOR SALE • PLAN A MOVE • DOWNSIZE YOUR HOUSE • OI
ECORATE FOR THE SEASONS • PREPARE A VACATION HOME FOR THE OFF-SEASON • PREPARE YOUR HOME FOR NATURE'S WORST • PI
GARDEN • PLANT A CUT-FLOWER GARDEN • DESIGN A SHADE GARDEN • DESIGN A DRY GARDEN • PLAN FOR A LONG-SEASON CONTAIN
AN AND PLANT A LAWN • DESIGN A NEW LANDSCAPE • PLAN AN OUTDOOR KITCHEN • DESIGN A DECK OR PATIO • DESIGN A WATER FE,
ES • STORAGE SOLUTIONS FOR ANY ROOM   D THE CAPACITY OF A SMALL ROOM • ORGANI,
TWORK • ORGANIZE MOVIES, MUSIC AND O   IRLOOMS • STORE OUT-OF-SEASON CLOTHES
NT • STORE PAINT AND OTHER HAZARDOUS   STORE A BOAT FOR THE WINTER • STORE A C
E APPLICATIONS • PLAN YOUR COURSE OF   H PAPER • GET INTO GRAD SCHOOL • GET INT
LONG ABSENCE • SET UP AN INTERNSHIP •   N THE PEACE CORPS • PRODUCE A NEWSLETTE
BECOME A COWBOY • BECOME A BRAIN S   ATHOLIC NUN • ORGANIZE AN EXHIBITION • DE
OME A STUNT PERSON • BECOME A TOUR G   S • CONQUER YOUR PAPER PILES • CREATE A F
UTER FILES • SCHEDULE APPOINTMENTS EF   NCE CALL • PREPARE FOR A MEETING • PREPAI
ME NETWORK • CHOOSE THE BEST PHONE   TEM • MAKE A NETWORKING PLAN • PLAN YOU
NTATION SKILLS • PREPARE A SPEECH • PR   AN AN IPO • DELEGATE RESPONSIBILITIES • HIR
ROFITS • FORM A BOARD OF DIRECTORS • C   AN A COMPANY PICNIC • PLAN A COMPANY RET
FAILING BUSINESS • DISMANTLE A BUSINE   • DESIGN A SAVINGS PLAN • SIMPLIFY BILL PA'
FINANCIAL-AID PACKAGE • PLAN FOR COLLE   E A HEALTH INSURANCE PLAN • START AN INVE
UST • MAKE A WILL • EXECUTE A POWER OF   S' ESTATE • PLAN YOUR ESTATE • TEACH YOUR
ARE FOR AN IN VITRO FERTILIZATION • PREI   ATERNITY WARDROBE • SET UP MATERNITY OF
REPARE FOR CHILDBIRTH • STOCK A DIAPE   LEND FAMILIES • CREATE A HOUSEHOLD ORGA
OOL YOUR CHILD • SET UP A CARPOOL • ST   HE BEST ELEMENTARY SCHOOL • ORGANIZE KID
OR SUMMER CAMP • CHOOSE A SUMMER S   R FAMILY COMPUTER USE • PLAN TO KEEP YOU
R BOOMERANG KIDS • PLAN AN AMICABLE   EMENTS • ORGANIZE MEDICAL RECORDS • PLA,
• ARRANGE HOSPICE CARE • MAKE YOUR   ECORDS • PLAN A WEEK OF MENUS • ORGANIZ
LISTS • COOK AHEAD • DETERMINE THE SH   M WAREHOUSE STORES • EFFICIENTLY USE THE
ENTLY USE SPACE UNDER THE SINK • STO   UR COUNTER SPACE • COOK FOR ONE • PLAN
DINNER PARTY FOR YOUR BOSS • PLAN DII   PARTY • IMPRESS A DATE • PLAN A WEDDING •
ENT PLANNER • HIRE A PHOTOGRAPHER •   ACHELORETTE PARTY • PREPARE TO BE THE M,

Life's Nitty Gritty

NEYMOON • PLAN A BAPTISM • PLAN A BRI   THROW A PARTY • PREPARE FOR HOUSE GUESTS • PLAN A CHILD'S BIRTHDAY PARTY •
TO CUSTOM • PLAN AHEAD FOR A LOW-STRESS HOLIDAY • STAY WITHIN A BUDGET THIS CHRISTMAS • PREPARE A HOLIDAY FEAST •
NIZE GIFT-GIVING IN ADVANCE • STICK TO YOUR DIET DURING THE HOLIDAYS • PLAN A HOLIDAY OPEN HOUSE • REORGANIZE YOUR LI
• ORGANIZE A HIGH-SCHOOL CLASS REUNION • PLAN A FAMILY REUNION • START A KNITTING CIRCLE • ORGANIZE A BOOK CLUB • SI
SHARPEN THE FOCUS OF AN ORGANIZATION • IMPROVE YOUR CHILD'S SCHOOL • PLAN A PROM • ORGANIZE A COMMUNITY THEATE
NIZE A PANCAKE BREAKFAST • PLAN A TOY DRIVE • HOLD A BARN RAISING • ORGANIZE A CHARITY WALK OR RUN • BUILD LOW-INCON
TER-REGISTRATION DRIVE • RUN FOR LOCAL OFFICE • ORGANIZE A PETITION • ORGANIZE A RECALL • GET AN INITIATIVE ON THE BALL
OMMUNITY • PRESERVE OPEN SPACE • SAVE HISTORIC PROPERTIES AND LANDMARKS • SET UP A NONGOVERNMENTAL ORGANIZATIO
THE UNITED STATES • RENT A CAR ABROAD • MAKE HOTEL RESERVATIONS • ARRANGE EXECUTIVE ACCOMMODATIONS • PLAN A CRUI
E AN ITINERARY • PACK FOR A TRIP • PACK FOR A BUSINESS TRIP • PACK FOR A WEEK IN ONE CARRY-ON • PACK A DAY BAG • PREVEI
ZE A SAILING TEAM • PLAN A SAILBOAT CRUISE • PLAN A BICYCLE TRIP WITH A TOUR COMPANY • TRAVEL ABROAD • PLAN A VACATIC
POUSE • PLAN A TRIP TO A DIFFERENT CULTURE • FORAGE ABROAD • MAIL PACKAGES BACK TO THE UNITED STATES • PLAN A TRIP T
K ROAD • PLAN A CLIMB OF MOUNT KILIMANJARO • PACK FOR A SAFARI • ORGANIZE A HUNTING TRIP • PACK FOR A FISHING OR HU
RKS • ORGANIZE A BACKCOUNTRY SKI TRIP • ORGANIZE A CAR RALLY • PLAN A WHALE-WATCHING TRIP • PACK FOR A VOYAGE AT SE
YDNEY HARBOUR BRIDGE • PLAN A TRIP TO NEW ORLEANS FOR MARDI GRAS • PLAN A DAY AT DISNEYLAND • FORMULATE A FAMILY
IF YOU'RE ALONE • SURVIVE IF YOUR CAR BREAKS DOWN • DEAL WITH AMNESIA • FIGHT AN EBOLA OUTBREAK • FIGHT A FOREST FIF
ESCUE A HOSTAGE • OUTSMART PIRATES • DELIVER A BABY • MAKE AN EMERGENCY LANDING • MAKE A JAIL BREAK • BECOME A MC

17 | Streamline Your Morning Routine

Leaving the house in a mad dash is more the norm than the exception for many. Whether you live by yourself or with others, making a few minor changes to your morning routine will have you heading out the door on top of the world. The trick is nothing fancier than taking care of as much as possible the night before.

Steps

The night before

1 Check your calendar and to-do list to make sure you have everything you need for appointments the next day and to cue your memory for any other necessary items. See 3 Write an Effective To-Do List.

2 Program your coffeemaker to start brewing that black magic before you roll out of bed. Purchase an electric hot pot for tea, hot chocolate and instant oatmeal. Pull out the blender, bananas and other dry ingredients for smoothie production.

3 Set the thermostat to kick on 30 minutes before your alarm clock goes off so the house is toasty when you're climbing in the shower.

4 Move frozen food to the refrigerator to thaw for the next day's dinner. See 297 Plan a Week of Menus.

5 Choose your entire outfit for the next day and do the same for your young kids. Don't forget underwear, socks, shoes and accessories. You'll never have to stare blankly into the closet every morning— plus you'll have time to iron, shine, hem or sew.

6 Ask older children and teens to lay out their clothes, too. Load up a hanger with a complete outfit, or spread out clothes on the floor snowman-style. If you sign off on clothes the night before, that's a power struggle you don't have to deal with in the morning.

7 Prepare lunch fixings. Divide cheese, cut veggies and fruit into small plastic bags that can be grabbed in the morning. Assemble sandwiches or dish up a large pot of soup or chili into individual serving containers. See 314 Plan Healthy Lunches for Kids.

8 Double-check supplies. Make sure there's enough milk, cereal, bread and fruit. If not, send an able body to the store after dinner. Have him or her put gas in the car too, if you're running on empty.

9 Sort vitamins or medications into labeled pillboxes and put them on the breakfast table. Pour the cereal, too, if that helps speed things along.

Tips

Warm up kids' clothes in the dryer for a few minutes to ease them out of their pajamas and into clothes for a painless transition on frigid mornings.

Keep your morning free of bicker and balking by listing one or two breakfast options that your kids can choose from on a white board the night before.

Iron a whole week's worth of clothing over the weekend.

A kitchen timer helps keep preschoolers focused and on task in the morning.

See 68 Set Up a Bathroom Schedule.

10 Make sure your children's backpacks contain everything they need for the day, including uniforms, signed paperwork, book reports and projects (set up a checklist for older kids). Get your own bag and files ready as well (see 186 Organize Your Briefcase).

11 Determine whose turn it is to walk and feed the dog. You don't want to forget about Rover while everyone is rushing out the door. See 18 Organize a Chore Schedule for Kids.

12 Hang a shelf at the door with hooks for keys, and use a shelf, a basket or an entryway table to stash sunglasses, purses, lunches, backpacks, hats, mittens, and leashes and plastic bags (see 70 Organize Entryways and Mudrooms). Keep a jar of change for bus, train, parking and toll money. If you have out-of-the-ordinary items to remember, put a sticky note on your keys: "Bring snacks for soccer practice." Do a sweep to make sure important items are ready to go by the door.

In the morning

1 Set your clock a half an hour to an hour early to get some time to yourself. Work out, run a load of laundry, meditate, plan or prepare—in peace and quiet.

2 Get yourself ready first. If you're showered and dressed, you'll be better able to handle whatever comes up.

3 Use music to rock your routine. Choose one song to wake up to, another for someone's bathroom time and a third for someone else's dressing time. You can have a breakfast song, a getting-dressed song and a brushing-your-teeth song—whatever works. Burn a CD of everyone's favorites and make your morning an off-off Broadway hit.

4 Post morning to-do lists for each family member. Give prereaders one too, with pictures to cue their tasks.

5 Turn on the news only if you can resist watching for one more segment. Get the weather, the top news and the traffic report— and get out. Same goes for the newspaper.

6 Give your spouse, kids and yourself a treat. Whether it's waking up 15 minutes early for some snuggle time or occasional fresh blueberry pancakes instead of frozen waffles, spiking the routine with rewards makes it smoother and more enjoyable for everyone.

Who Knew?

Keep a stash of emergency supplies in the car: changes of clothes, hair brush, clips, pencils, snack bars and juice boxes. Keep a supply of portable yogurt, milk boxes (that don't need refrigeration) and small plastic bags packed with cereal for those mornings that are a complete disaster.

If you have young kids, use morning TV time strategically or not at all. Save "Sesame Street" as a reward for when clothes are on, breakfast is eaten and everything is ready to go.

18 Organize a Chore Schedule for Kids

To keep the house running smoothly and efficiently, every member of the family should be on the chore team. Picking up after themselves, keeping rooms picked up and beds made are not chores—they're just part of life. Assign chores based on kids' age and competence.

Steps

1 Make a list of all chores to be divvied up.

2 Separate tasks into three age categories: beginner (pre-schoolers), intermediate (grade schoolers) and advanced (high schoolers and adults).

3 Assign or allow kids to take turns choosing age-appropriate chores. Beginner tasks include helping set the table and sorting socks; intermediate chores include dishwasher duty and pet care; advanced tasks include cleaning the bathroom, vacuuming and helping with meal preparation.

4 Give adults the leftovers if there are not enough able little bodies in your home.

5 Add more and bigger jobs as kids demonstrate aptitude and competence.

6 Rotate chores so that everyone shares the more odious tasks.

Tips

To determine how many chores you should give a child, halve her age as a good rule of thumb. A 10-year-old would get five chores; a 16-year-old would have eight.

If a child whines about a chore or does it poorly, he gets an extra one the next week.

See 248 Teach Your Kids About Money for tips on allowances.

19 Organize Your Chores

Taking the time to develop a chore plan ensures that all of the rooms and their contents get cleaned on a regular basis, and that nothing is overlooked. Create a plan that accommodates your lifestyle so that you're not pulling out your cleaning supplies every day.

Steps

1 Amend the chart (right) to fit your home and schedule. Use a calendar or spreadsheet program to record your chores plan.

2 Keep the daily chores balanced over the course of the week so that one day doesn't have more chores than the others, and you're doing a little bit each day. See 36 Tidy Up in 15 minutes.

3 Gather sponges, cleaners, vacuums, brooms, mops and buckets into one centralized location. Or put everything you need for one room in a basket or bucket and keep it in that room. See 65 Organize Cleaning Supplies.

4 Save the dirtiest, grimiest surfaces for last. In each room, work from low-contamination areas to high. For example, when you

Tip

Read 66 Organize Spring Cleaning and 266 Coordinate a Family Calendar.

clean the bathroom, do the toilet last. This way you're not re-introducing germs to surfaces you've already cleaned.

5 Get some help. Read 18 Organize a Chore Schedule for Kids and recruit the rest of the household, or hire someone to clean.

FREQUENCY	CHORES
Daily	• Load and unload the dishwasher or wash dishes. • Nuke the sponge for 30 seconds to kill germs. • Wipe down and disinfect countertops and stovetop. • Move newspapers and magazines to recycling area. • Put toys and games away. • Return clothes to closets and throw dirty clothes in the laundry baskets. • Make the beds. • Clean cat litter box (if you're not pregnant—see 254 Prepare for a New Baby). • Sort the mail.
Weekly	• Pay bills and file paperwork (see 229 Simplify Bill Paying). • Drop off/pick up clothes from the dry cleaner. • Vacuum rugs and mop floors (more often if you have a pet). • Clean all kitchen surfaces and appliances. • Empty wastebaskets. • Clean bathrooms. • Wash bed linens (see 77 Safeguard Your Home Against Allergens). • Dust. • Take out trash and recycling. • Buy groceries (see 298 Organize Grocery Store Trips). • Sanitize cat litter boxes. • Wash and sort laundry.
Monthly	• Dust blinds. • Clean windows (one or two each month). • Clean mirrors. • Disinfect trash containers. • Clean the refrigerator inside and out (see 306 Efficiently Use the Refrigerator and Freezer).
Quarterly	• Dust the blades of ceiling fans. • Replace air filters in central air unit. • Replace water filters on tap and in coffeemakers. • Declutter cabinets and closets. • Drop off items to charity (see 12 Get Rid of What You Don't Want).

20 | Never Be Late Again

Are you punctually challenged? Always running behind? Are your friends tired of your tardiness? You've tried setting your clocks ahead and getting up earlier, but you're still late. When it comes right down to it, punctuality is actually a habit that you can develop. Start now.

Steps

1 Read 16 Set Goals. Then glean strategic tips from 17 Streamline Your Morning Routine.

2 Consider the costs of being chronically late: You risk censure at work, you negatively impact the lives of friends and colleagues and you jeopardize your child's record at school. Not to mention you crank up your own stress level. Voluntarily.

3 Make a commitment to arrive 5 minutes early—not just on time by the skin of your teeth, or on time only if traffic is easy and there's a meter right in front. Punctuality is a planning decision, not a sign of good character.

4 Assess your own timeliness. Compare how long you *think* it takes to get somewhere with the reality—if you're late all the time, this is easy. Are you perpetually 5 to 10 minutes late for appointments? Do you get to the movies when the opening credits are already rolling?

5 Scope out your destination in advance and find out how long it takes to get there. Always build in additional travel time, especially if the route is unfamiliar or if it's a long trip. Instead of being caught by surprise, take into account traffic, public transportation delays and potential parking difficulties. Write down directions and take the time to print out a map. Get a copy of public transportation schedules and routes.

6 Resist the urge to squeeze in "one more thing" on the way. When you're scheduling your day, write down when you'll have to leave in order to get to an appointment on time, and leave then. Don't delude yourself into thinking you now have extra time to do something else en route—even when you could.

7 Set a kitchen timer for 30 minutes before you have to leave if you tend to fritter extra time away and still end up rushing or late. When the timer rings, stop procrastinating and get a move on.

8 Start and end meetings on time. When time is running out, continue the discussion offline or schedule a follow-up meeting. See 191 Schedule Appointments Efficiently.

9 Make a date with your checkbook. Mark on your calendar two regular times every month (more if you need it) to take care of your bills rather than using those late notices as your call to action. See 229 Simplify Bill Paying.

Tips

Call immediately when you realize that you will be late.

Go to bed earlier, set the alarm earlier and get up earlier.

If you just can't seem to get to work by 9 a.m. because of traffic or kids' school schedules, for example, see if you can work from 10 a.m. to 6 p.m.

Who Knew?

If you are constantly late for work but are on time for appointments in your personal life, maybe it's because you hate your job. Do some soul-searching and think about getting a new job. See 167 Prepare for a Career Change and 166 Organize Your Job Search.

Have you ever been watching television and realized that three hours mysteriously went by? Sure, channel surfing is a guilty habit for some, but you can use your viewing time more wisely with a little fore-thought. And if you want to control your kids' television time, work with them to figure out optimal schedules.

Steps

1 Limit your television intake. Don't use the tube as background noise. Turn it off while you eat dinner, clean or go about other activities. Try turning on the radio instead. When the television is on, be sure there's a reason for it.

2 Talk to your kids about television. While you of course want to limit the hours they watch and control what they see, you'll also want to talk to them about the messages different shows and commercials are sending.

3 Consult the weekly guide and decide what to watch before flip-ping endlessly through each channel. This extra step will help you and your family think critically about how you spend your time in front of the tube.

4 Key in the selected shows' six-digit PlusCode number (using the keys of your remote control) if your video recorder supports VCRPlus (vcrplus.com) instant programming. These numbers are published in standard television listings in the United States, Canada and many other countries in the world. For instant pro-gramming to work, you must have completed the one-time process to map the VCRPlus assignment number with the dial channel number for each station received in your home.

5 Buy a digital video recorder. Any DVR owner is likely to say it's the greatest invention since sliced bread. TiVo, Ultimate TV, Replay TV and other brands of DVRs allow you to pause and rewind live television, and record a season's worth of shows with a click of a button. You always have a menu of programs that you've prerecorded. And you can fast-forward through commer-cials, limiting your child's (and your own) exposure to products. This way you can get through a 1-hour program in about 44 minutes.

6 Tape or buy several movies so you have them ready to pop in if you're in a "500 channels and nothing's on" funk.

Tips

Record your favorite shows to DVD to take with you on the plane if you're a frequent traveler. Play them on your laptop or portable DVD player.

There's a big difference between watching television for entertainment and watch-ing out of boredom. Choose your programs wisely.

See 137 Organize Movies, Music and Other Media.

Who Knew?

Set a weekly time limit. Have your kids identify their favorite shows, and together prioritize which shows make the schedule. Use the exer-cise to evaluate your own viewing habits and start making choices on how you want to spend your time.

If you get greedy and hack into your DVR to extend the hours, don't go crying back to the manufacturer if it stops working. Tampering with the box will void the warranty.

22 | Design a Healthy Lifestyle

Everyone knows that eating nutritious foods, exercising regularly and coping with stress are beneficial to the body and mind. But how do you balance work and family, friendships and hobbies without spreading yourself too thin? The solution is to incorporate these elements into a healthy lifestyle plan. Investing in professional assistance is a huge motivator and a small price to pay for a healthier, happier you.

Steps

1 Consult your doctor as you begin to map out your new lifestyle. He or she will help ensure a safe and beneficial regimen based on your age and physical condition.

2 Hire a personal weight loss and nutritional adviser to get you started. His or her guidance and expertise will help you formulate a plan that's right for you and, more important, help you stay on track when you stray. See 24 Choose a Weight Loss Plan.

3 Seek out a professional trainer that you can relate to and develop a fitness program that you'll enjoy and maintain for the long haul. Moderate exercise can improve your quality of life by firming muscles, controlling weight, strengthening the heart and lungs, improving circulation and digestion, burning calories, and building strength, endurance and flexibility. See 25 Design Your Workout Schedule.

4 Reduce your stress level by finding a mental or physical outlet that works for you. Exercise, yoga and meditation are proven to reduce stress and increase a feeling of well-being. Walking regularly has huge health benefits for people of all ages and fitness levels—and it's free.

5 Get enough sleep. Lack of rest weakens your immune system and makes you susceptible to illness and disease. Also, drink plenty of water. It eliminates toxins, increases energy, aids in weight loss, and promotes better brain function.

6 Plan your meals in advance to avoid unhealthy choices such as fast or prepackaged foods. A weekly menu will help you stick to a more balanced diet and choose healthier options at the grocery store. See 298 Organize Grocery Store Trips and 297 Plan a Week of Menus.

7 Make time for your family, your friends and yourself. Cultivating new relationships, enjoying a hobby and sharing time with your family will allow you to stay focused on what's truly important in life. See 14 Balance Home and Work and 15 Live With Less.

Tips

Go outside more often to enjoy the sunshine and fresh air. Sunshine helps the hypothalamus and pituitary glands regulate appetite, sleep, body temperature, sexual functions, water balance and hormones.

Visit your doctor regularly to maintain a healthful lifestyle and detect early signs of illness.

Read 27 Prepare for Cold and Flu Season.

Warning

Dieting can be extremely harmful to your body if it's not closely monitored. Make eating healthy part of your lifestyle, and you can eliminate crash dieting altogether.

Unless you move to a macrobiotic commune in Oregon, kicking the junk-food habit can be tough. Junk food is convenient, marketed aggressively, cheap to buy and hard to resist. Most Americans fail to lose weight because they're programmed to consume far too much and to choose foods that are saturated with fat and salt ("Supersize those fries?"). See 24 Choose a Weight Loss Plan and take steps to reform that junk-food junkie within you.

Steps

1 Eliminate temptation at home. Clear out all the junk from your cupboards, and get the whole family on board for the effort.

2 Lay a healthful foundation by stocking up on ingredients for nutritious meals, desserts and snacks. If you eat healthy food at home, you won't feel so bad when you splurge on an infrequent fast-food meal or candy bar.

3 Set realistic expectations for yourself by remembering to practice moderation. Total deprivation will only make your cravings more intense, so allow yourself a weekly treat for cutting back.

4 Identify those times of the day when you're most vulnerable to a junk-food attack. Is it that relentless 3 p.m. cookie craving? The phone call from your client-from-hell that spurs a run to McDonald's? Prepare ahead of time by having healthy, flavorful alternatives on hand—and if you still need to indulge, just have a bite or two and toss the rest. Better yet, schedule alternate activities for those times when you're most likely to face temptation.

5 Choose grilled or broiled versions of foods that are typically fried. Grilled chicken sandwiches, grilled chicken and rice bowls, sandwiches with no cheese and a small amount of mayonnaise, fat-free or baked chips, water, and salads with light dressing are available at most fast-food restaurants.

6 Focus on eating healthy foods. Be sure the snack foods you keep in plain sight and hidden away are all good choices. Keep a fruit basket on your kitchen counter, table or desk. If you stock the refrigerator with exclusively healthy foods, you'll eventually overcome the urge for fat and sugar-laden treats.

7 Avoid situations that may encourage a junk attack, like sitting in front of the television all evening. Resist those evil vending machines at work by bringing your own healthful snacks and leaving your pocket change at home.

8 Cook large quantities and put extra meals in the freezer. That way you won't be tempted to make a junk-food run on your way home from work. See 297 Plan a Week of Menus.

Tips

Listen to your appetite and adjust portions and ingredients—rather than deny yourself—to moderate your diet.

Give alternative, healthy fast food a try. The vegetarian fast-food industry is quickly expanding.

Get in the habit of reading food labels: If the first two ingredients are fat and sugar, it's junk food.

Warning

Don't take labels at face value. Many "low-carb," "low-fat" or "no-fat" products are still very high in calories and dangerous trans fats.

24 | Choose a Weight Loss Plan

News flash: There's no magic pill to make the pounds disappear. But there isn't a magic plan either. If you're really ready to fight the Battle of The Bulge, your arsenal needs to include plenty of determination and common sense as well as regular exercise and a healthy eating plan that will work for the long haul.

Steps

1 Decide how much weight you want to lose. Most dieters hope to shed about 30 pounds, but this goal could prove unrealistic and discouraging to many people.

2 Learn how to monitor not only your body weight, but your Body Mass Index (BMI), a number that shows weight adjusted for height. Find your BMI rating on the Centers for Disease Control and Prevention site (www.cdc.gov).

3 Discuss how much weight you really need to lose with your doctor or a registered dietitian. Map out a total plan and timeline to achieve your weight loss goals (see 16 Set Goals).

4 Glean tips from the popular diet plans. Weight Watchers advocates portion control, balanced nutrition and limited intake of starches and sugars. Members attend weekly meetings for support and tips. In the South Beach Diet's three-phased approach, you start out with major sugar and carbohydrate restrictions and gradually work complex carbs back in. Both South Beach and Atkins encourage a hefty intake of proteins and vegetables in order to trigger a slower release of sugars into the bloodstream and keep insulin levels steady. Figuring out a nutritional ratio for every meal, such as the Zone's mix of 40 percent carbohydrates, 30 percent protein and 30 percent fat may not hold up in the long run, but it will train you to make educated choices.

5 Get moving. Regular exercise not only burns calories and increases your general fitness level but also speeds up your metabolism, which then burns more calories. (See 25 Design Your Workout Schedule.)

6 Make calorie-burning choices. Take the stairs instead of the elevator and skip the golf cart rental. Every little bit counts.

7 Put a positive support team in place. Studies show that having a coach, mentor or support group (such as those at Weight Watchers and Jenny Craig) is a huge help when making lifestyle changes. Or, find a friend who shares your goals. It's much easier to stay motivated when someone else is slugging it out with you.

8 Work losing weight into your budget. Some plans cost money to join, others sell ready-made meals and books. And, fresh ingredients often cost more than fast food. You also may spend money joining a gym. You'll find the benefits far exceed any monetary drawbacks.

Tips

Remember that the key to any successful weight loss plan is to consume fewer calories than you burn, control the size of your portions, and eat a nutritionally balanced diet.

Drink lots of water and take a daily multivitamin.

See 499 Live to Be 100 Years Old.

Skepticism is a healthy thing when you're considering a hot new dieting plan.

Who Knew?

Studies show that the people who stuck with the four popular diet plans—Dean Ornish, Weight Watchers, Atkins and the Zone—for a year lost only about 5 percent of their body weight.

Warnings

Fast, drastic weight loss can cause serious damage to your health.

Fad diets are just that—fads. They don't stick around, because people come to the realization that they are not going to lose weight and keep it off just because they ate only meat, subsisted on grapefruit juice for 6 months or slurped cabbage soup. See FadDiet.com for a compendium of plans.

Whether you want to build muscle, increase aerobic capacity or just get into those jeans again, the only way to achieve success is to set up a workout schedule that fits your needs. The rewards of a steady workout schedule are priceless: lower stress, stronger heart and lungs, increased strength and flexibility, a shrinking waistline, better sleep and improved self-confidence. Keep at it long enough and eventually you'll crave a good workout.

Steps

1 Be realistic about your current fitness level and choose goals, classes and activities that are appropriate. If you can't remember the last time you put on those running shoes, start slowly to build both your strength and stamina without injuring yourself or burning out.

2 Invest in one or two sessions with a personal trainer. He or she can help you establish reasonable goals and present options that you may not have considered. See 16 Set Goals.

3 Start gradually. Do up to 30 minutes of cardiovascular work mixed with strength training three times per week or more. Also incorporate flexibility exercises into your workouts. Continually evaluate your progress and set new goals: As your general fitness improves, increase the length, frequency and intensity of your workouts.

4 Develop—with a qualified trainer's help—a weight-lifting program that meets your specific performance goals. Strength training is critical to athletic performance and osteoporosis prevention. Lifting is most effective done every other day so that fatigued muscles have time to rest and rebuild.

5 Be sure to work the entire body consistently and balance opposing muscle groups. For example, if you work your quadriceps, hit the less visible but equally important hamstrings, too. You'll gain overall strength and avoid injury.

6 Rotate your cardio work on the days you rest from weight lifting. Cross-train with a variety of activities instead of just one. You'll challenge different muscles, prevent injuries due to overuse and avoid burnout.

7 Aim for a heart rate within your training zone. Subtract your age from 220 and multiply it by 0.6 and 0.8 to determine the lower and upper limits of your training heart-rate zone (some formulas calculate slightly higher heart-rate limits for women). You will not achieve cardiovascular benefits unless your heart rate reaches that zone. Maintain this rate for a minimum 30 minutes at least three times a week.

8 Schedule time in your calendar to work out. If you've got it written down, you'll be more apt to keep the appointment.

Tips

Rule of thumb: Working out three times a week will maintain your fitness level; more will increase it.

Work out with a friend or join a group or club to stay motivated.

For a list of exercises, including how many calories they burn per hour, check out NutriStrategy.com.

Unless you have access to a gym at work, choose a facility that is near your office.

See 361 Stick to Your New Year's Resolutions.

Who Knew?

Always make warming up, cooling down and stretching part of your exercise routine.

Choose a diversified program you'll enjoy for the long haul. If you find yourself getting bored with your routine, change it up. Instead of running 5 miles, do 3 miles alternating sprinting with jogging or walking. Opt for the open road instead of a spinning class. Join a master's swim class.

Warning

When lifting weights or using any fitness machine, be aware of your form. If you're unsure that you are performing an exercise correctly, consult a trainer to avoid injury.

26 | Schedule Doctor Visits

Have you had a physical in the past decade? When was the last time you got your cholesterol checked? It's easy to miss these important tests, especially if you rely on your overworked doctor to remember to order them for you. Before you make an appointment, call your insurance company: Some offer free or low-cost mammograms, cholesterol tests and eye exams.

EXAM TYPE	WHO	HOW OFTEN
Physical	Men and women	Yearly.
Dental	Men and women	Twice a year after age 3.
Eye	Men and women	Every three to five years if you have no symptoms. Comprehensive exam every two years for ages 40 and up; after age 65, every year. Contact lens wearers and people with diabetes should get an annual exam at any age. Ophthalmologists and optometrists check for glaucoma, tumors of the brain or optic nerve, cataracts and retinal degeneration. If you're extremely nearsighted, you're at increased risk for all eye diseases and should be checked annually.
Breast	Women	Starting at age 20, clinical breast exam each year and monthly self-exams. Get first baseline mammogram between 35 and 40. Between 40 and 50, get a mammogram every other year; after 50, get one yearly. If your mother or sister had breast cancer before menopause and you are over age 25, get a baseline mammogram 10 years before the age your relative was diagnosed. If you're under 40 and find a lump, get a sonogram.
Prostate	Men	Get an annual prostate-specific antigen (PSA) blood-test screenings after age 50, or annually after 40 if you have risk factors like family history or being African-American.
Colorectal Cancer	Men and women	If you're over 50, get screened for colon cancer annually. If you have a history of inflammatory bowel disease, get tested more often. If you have a parent or sibling who had colorectal cancer or polyps before age 60, get tested 10 years before the age they were diagnosed. If you have had polyps at any age, start getting screened in your 40s. If you are at high risk, consider getting a colonoscopy first.

EXAM TYPE	WHO	HOW OFTEN
Gynecological	Women	Starting at age 18, get a yearly pelvic exam with Pap smear (test for cervical cancer); start younger if you are sexually active. If you have a history of abnormal Pap smears, ask for the new Hybrid II DNA test for chlamydia, a sometimes asymptomatic sexually transmitted disease that can lead to pelvic inflammatory disease and infertility. At menopause, get an endometrial biopsy if recommended by your doctor.
Bone Mineral Density	Women	Get a baseline bone scan at age 65; your doctor will then determine how often you should be tested. Get a bone scan after menopause if you have any risk factors: smoking, a history of nontraumatic fractures as an adult, low calcium intake, a history of steroid use or a weight of less than 127 pounds (57 kg). Ask for the entire bone-density printout (pictures of the scan in addition to the written report) for later comparisons.
Cholesterol	Men and women	Starting at age 20, have a fasting lipoprotein analysis every five years, which checks your total cholesterol: low-density lipoprotein ("bad" or LDL), high-density lipoprotein ("good" or HDL) and triglycerides.
Skin Cancer	Men and women	Between ages 20 and 39, have a complete body exam every three years. Get an annual exam with a digital imaging screening if you have a family history of skin cancer; if you have many moles, fair skin, red or blond hair, or freckles; and/or have had excessive sun exposure as a child or teenager, or if you are over 40. Do monthly self-exams to check for freckles, moles and suspicious lesions.
TIPS		Follow your pediatrician's guidelines for your child's vaccinations and checkups. Be prepared to supply up-to-date insurance information. Add a photocopy of the health care cards of all family members to your personal calendar so that you have the required reference information on hand when making appointments. See 289 Organize Medical Records. Bring a list of questions for the doctor. Once in the examining room, it's easy to forget them. Then write down the answers to your questions.
WARNING		This chart is only a guide. Talk to your doctor about your choices.

27 Prepare for Cold and Flu Season

Studies show that the average person contracts about three colds per year, and those who are in contact with young children get even more. While there's no cure for the common cold or the flu, you can take measures to protect yourself.

Steps

1 Know the difference between a cold and the flu (see chart, right). A cold can last two or three weeks; most people are better within seven to ten days. On the other hand, without proper care or attention, a flu virus can lead to bronchitis or pneumonia, each of which can cause permanent health damage. Each year, more than 100,000 people in the United States are hospitalized and about 36,000 die due to the flu and its complications.

2 Wash your hands. Frequent washing with warm water and ordinary soap for 10 seconds is one of the simplest and most effective ways to avoid catching a cold or the flu. Use antibacterial alcohol-based foams and gels when you don't have access to soap and water.

3 Disinfect your home regularly. Spray the surfaces in your bathroom and kitchen with a mild solution of 2 to 5 percent bleach in water to kill viruses and bacteria.

4 Get a flu vaccination if you're in a high-risk population:

• People living in long-term care facilities and group homes.

• Adults over the age of 65.

• Adults and children with chronic diseases such as diabetes, asthma, emphysema and kidney disease.

• Pregnant women who will be in the second or third trimester of their pregnancy during the flu season.

• People with weakened immune systems, such as HIV-positive individuals or cancer patients who are undergoing chemotherapy.

• Health care workers.

The vaccine is made with a killed virus that cannot give you the flu. Vaccines are not 100 percent effective, so you may still get a less severe case of the flu after receiving the vaccine. The vaccine takes about two weeks to become fully effective in your body, so prepare yourself before the season hits.

5 Discuss FluMist with your doctor if you are healthy and between 5 and 49 years. Approved in 2003 by the Food and Drug Administration, this flu vaccine is delivered through a nasal spray.

Tip

See 497 Cure the Common Cold.

Who Knew?

Ask your doctor about Tamiflu (oseltamivir phosphate) and Relenza (zanamivir), which both help lessen and prevent flu symptoms and duration. For these drugs to be effective, they must be taken when you are first exposed to others suffering from the flu. If someone in your home gets the flu, other family members can possibly avoid getting it by taking these drugs for at least seven days. A person exposed to the flu because of an outbreak in the community can take the drug for up to six weeks.

If you've got a cold, don't ask your doctor to prescribe antibiotics. They do not kill cold viruses and can lead to resistant strains of bacteria. Prevention is the best approach to combat the cold virus.

6 Eat a well-balanced diet. It's essential to building a healthy immune system, and it provides sources of energy and nutrition for optimal growth and development. Taking a daily multi-vitamin—especially when you're fatigued or stressed—also helps ensure that you will receive an adequate dose of minerals and vitamins.

7 Get plenty of rest. On average, humans require seven to eight hours of sleep every night. Lack of sleep can lower the immune system's ability to react when needed. Without sufficient sleep, the immune system is hard-pressed to keep up with its nightly repair work, and creates an opening for opportunistic diseases.

8 Stock your medicine cabinet with a supply of single-symptom drugs such as cough suppressants, pain relievers and antihista-mines. Cold symptoms tend to appear in sequence, not all at once, so multisymptom formulas often give you too much or not enough medicine for any given symptom. Avoid time-release capsules for the same reason. See 43 Organize the Medicine Cabinet.

Warning

The American Academy of Pediatrics recommends that aspirin and combination products containing aspirin not be given to children under 19 years of age during episodes of fever-causing illnesses, due to the risk of contracting Reye's Syndrome. Children's Tylenol and Children's Motrin are safe when administered according to directions.

SYMPTOMS	COLD	FLU
Fever	Rare in adults and older children, but can be as high as 102 degrees F (39 C) in infants and small children.	Typically around 102 degrees F (39 C), but can go up to 104 degrees F (40 C). Usually lasts three to four days.
Headache	Rare	Sudden onset, can be severe
Muscle Aches	Mild	Usual, often severe
Tiredness and Weakness	Mild	Can last two or more weeks
Extreme Exhaustion	Never	Sudden onset, can be severe
Runny Nose	Often	Sometimes
Sneezing	Often	Sometimes
Sore Throat	Often	Sometimes
Cough	Mild, hacking cough, can worsen	Usual, can become severe

28 Get a Drastic Makeover

Everyone has a least-favorite physical feature. According to the American Society for Aesthetic Plastic Surgery, more than 7 million cosmetic surgery procedures are performed in the United States each year. Some could use some nonsurgical help as well. So whether you're a straight guy in need of a queer eye or someone with a serious cosmetic issue to correct, you'll need a game plan.

Steps

General tips

1 Decide just how dramatically different you want your new-and-improved self to be. Making a list of what you'd like to change (hair, makeup, wardrobe, job, friends) will help you prioritize your goals. See 16 Set Goals.

2 Consider the costs. Include wardrobe additions, hair and makeup styling, fitness and nutrition consultants, new furniture and remodeling fees (see 85 Plan a Remodel), as well as potential surgery and several weeks or more to recover. A drastic new look doesn't come cheap. Establishing a budget will help you set your makeover limits and keep things in perspective. See 228 Design a Savings Plan.

Looks

1 Hire an image consultant to evaluate your current style, make wardrobe and beauty recommendations and tailor a makeover just for you. He or she will also connect you with the best stylists for your particular look. A full day's consultation usually runs about $1,200. To begin your search, check the yellow pages under "Consultants" and "Image Consultants."

2 Test new looks on Web sites such as the Makeover-o-Matic at Substance.com, VirtualMakeover.com and MyPersonalStyle.com. Scan your own photo and then test various hair and makeup schemes onscreen before you commit. Print your top picks on a color printer and bring the images for your stylist to work from. Style magazines are also a good source of ideas.

3 Take photos (front, sides and back) of your new style, cut and color. Then bring these photos when you return to the salon to make sure they get it right every time.

4 Get in shape and shed those extra pounds (see 24 Choose a Weight Loss Plan and 25 Design Your Workout Schedule).

Surgery

1 Decide what type of surgery you're interested in. Popular cosmetic surgical procedures include breast augmentation, eye lifts, face lifts, upper arm lifts, dental work, nose jobs and liposuction.

Tips

lenhance.com, an online directory, helps those seeking cosmetic plastic surgery find a specialist in their area and provides detailed information on the various cosmetic procedures available.

The Advanced Aesthetics Institute (advanced aestheticsinstitute.com) specializes in full-service makeovers. Clients are assigned a beauty consultant "concierge" who recommends both the services and the players—hairstylist, plastic surgeon and cosmetic dentist.

Who Knew?

Before a doctor will consider you a candidate for plastic surgery you'll have to lose as much weight on your own as possible.

Ask to see living examples of the surgeon's work, not just photos in a book. Ask to have a frank talk with former patients.

Confirm exactly what the quoted prices cover, since some plastic surgeons' offices quote the surgeon's fee separately. Factor in other costly items like the consultation, anesthesia, supplies, medication, facility fees, hospitalization, compression garments and blood testing.

Prices range from $3,000 to $12,000 depending on the surgeon, your geographic region and how much surgery you're having performed.

2 Interview several surgeons and ask how many procedures similar to yours each has performed, which is particularly important with new treatments. Identify a top-notch plastic surgeon via referrals from your physician and satisfied friends.

3 Make sure a prospective surgeon is certified by the American Board of Plastic Surgery and is a member of the American Society of Plastic Surgeons (plasticsurgery.org). The ABPS requires a five-year surgical residency plus two years of specialized training. Ask if doctors have surgical privileges at a hospital; if not, it's possible their credentials fell short, so tread carefully.

4 Make the most of every cosmetic surgery consultation, which will cost you around $50 to $100 each. Ask questions about the surgeon's education, specialties and experience. You'll want to know everything about what will be done to you. Make sure that you understand all the possible risks and complications involved with the procedure. See 467 Prepare for Surgery.

5 Plan conservatively on a two-week minimum rest period in order to facilitate recovery and tissue repair. If you break the recovery discipline by doing too much too soon, you might tear your sutures and cause long-term damage and put yourself right back in the hospital. See 468 Plan Your Recovery.

Lifestyle

1 Read 1 Get Organized and 37 Conquer Clutter, then clear out your home.

2 Throw out or give away pieces of furniture that have seen better days. See 12 Get Rid of What You Don't Want.

3 Experiment with bold colors and put a fresh coat of paint on your house—inside and out.

4 Create a budget (see 226 Set Up a Budget), make a list of what you need to buy (clothing, furniture, decor) and prioritize your list to keep costs in line. Shop to increase functionality and style at the same time—take a friend whose opinion (and taste) you trust, or hire an interior designer. Call your favorite department store and ask if they have a personal shopping service available.

5 Step out of your comfort zone and take a class in something you've always been interested in—wine tasting, art history and so on. Meet new people, make new friends. See 32 Plan Your Social Calendar.

6 Enjoy the new you!

Warnings

Make sure that any doctor you choose is a member of the American Society for Aesthetic Plastic Surgery. Check with your state's licensing boards or the Web site of the American Board of Medical Specialties (abms.org) to verify board certification.

Consider a rushed consultation a red flag. If a surgeon doesn't thoroughly advise you on possible side effects, potential problems and how much discomfort or disability to expect, you aren't getting what you need to give informed consent to surgery, which is your right.

29 | Arrange to Meet an Online Date

Does anyone meet without using the Internet these days? It's getting to the point when soon people will mistrust relationships that don't start at a keyboard. But there's always that first meeting. You need to be mindful of your safety in any dating situation but even more so with someone you've only met online.

Steps

1 Get a picture or two immediately. As shallow as it sounds, there's no sense in going forward if he or she is not your type.

2 Be restrained in deciding when to reveal your real e-mail address, and hold off giving out your phone number until you have established a solid, legitimate connection.

3 Meet as soon as possible, ideally after only four to six e-mail messages and a phone call. Late-night marathon sessions of pouring your heart out online can make strangers feel like soul mates—but you're not. Conduct the "getting to know you" phase in person or at least on the phone.

4 Be honest—you won't have to clean up things later. You can probably get away with little fibs ("'Survivor'? Never seen it. I was reading Proust last night."), but truth always works better. Likewise, be on the lookout for dishonesty from your new friend. Small lies can be a sign of deeper problems.

5 Share details of your life judiciously. Obviously, you want to get to know this person, but don't blurt. For both your physical and emotional safety, let the relationship progress slowly.

6 Arrange to meet in a neutral location that's well-lit and full of people. Don't give out your address, and don't drive together. No matter how close you may feel, you do *not* know this person.

7 Meet for coffee on the first date, rather than dinner. If you know in one minute that this person is completely wrong for you—and you will—a quick and painless exit is worth its weight in gold.

8 Enlist someone to help. Have a friend stay close by, out of sight, when you meet your date. Or you might even consider introducing the friend to your Internet correspondent. If your date doesn't like it, too bad.

9 Shut up and listen. Pay attention to things that don't feel right. If your date claims to really like kids but has never spent any time with them and hates mess and lack of control, that's valuable information.

10 Assess your overall compatibility with your date, not just your suitor's physical appearance. Do you like the person? Is his emotional baggage a carry-on or a steamer trunk? Does she listen to you or just wait until it's her turn to talk again? Keep your mind focused on exploring whether you two would be a good match and you'll do just fine.

Tips

Share what you know about this person with your friends and family, and listen to their feedback. They're concerned for your safety, and their opinions are worth having.

Pay attention to what your suitor says about previous relationships and why they ended. You might be the one to disprove the adage that history repeats itself, but probably not.

Warnings

Beware of conversational subjects that are off-limits. If your date refuses to discuss past relationships or family, you've probably got trouble.

Listen for conversational references to mental illness, medications and strange family histories.

Don't rush into physical intimacy; it's wiser and safer to wait until you know more about the other person. Why risk emotional regrets or worse, sexually transmitted disease?

You thought getting the date was the hard part? No, it's way too early to congratulate yourself—you're still just beginning. Now you have to come up with an exciting, memorable and fun series of events that will make you look like a romantic hero.

Steps

First date

1 Have a general idea about what you might do before you even ask about a date. If you suggest "Maybe we can get together sometime," and you get a favorable response, follow immediately with "Great, how about next Saturday?" The idea is to move the conversation directly to the specifics, rather than stand there stammering like a simpleton.

2 Plan first dates to be able to talk and get to know each other for a brief time in a nonthreatening environment. A rock concert is exciting, but too loud; dinner at an overly romantic restaurant can be too intense. Coffee? Good idea. Pick something that lets either of you easily slip away from an awkward first date.

3 Get tickets to a theater opening, a concert or a ball game. Make sure it's something your date will enjoy. Then, call well in advance of your planned meeting, and say that you might be able to get tickets for a big event. Ask your date if he or she would be interested. If the response is anything less than whole-hearted enthusiasm, sell the tickets to your brother-in-law.

4 Be decisive. If your first idea bombs, think of something else and remember that sitting and talking in a great environment is the whole idea. Acting beleaguered will get you nowhere fast. Your attitude is far more important than the activity.

Further along

1 Plan a picnic. It shows your organizational skills, as well as your appreciation of romance. Pack wine, a luscious feast and dessert. Remember that you'll need to bring everything, including a blanket, bottle opener, cutlery, plates, cups and napkins (see 321 Plan an Outdoor Party and 322 Impress a Date).

2 Stick to mainstream activities while you get to know each other. Until you know your date shares your tastes, keep the nude yoga classes and extreme rock climbing on the back burner. Granted, unusual activities can be a good way of filtering out those who have nothing in common with you, but they may also scare away qualified prospects.

3 Have a mental list of romantic spots. If things are going well, suggest a visit to one of them. It needn't be elaborate and shouldn't be forced. A bar with a great view of the city always works, or even a visit to a swing set in a park.

Tips

Keep your plan flexible. Chuck it altogether and improvise if something's not going well, or if it's going so well that you don't want to break the spell. Don't worry about sticking to a predetermined schedule that has you rushing from one event to another.

If your plans wash out, don't get discouraged—learn from your mistakes. And remember, bad dates can be a source of great stories (see 208 Prepare a Speech and 334 Execute Best Man Duties).

Warning

Arrange a meeting or pickup time and don't be late. Leave yourself plenty of time so that you arrive relaxed. See 20 Never Be Late Again.

31 | Mastermind a Breakup

"Who is this emotionally stunted crybaby and why are we having dinner together?" Does this sound like your last evening on the town? You know what you have to do. It's time to put on your breakup shoes and head out the door. Be firm, be gentle, but most of all—be gone.

Steps

1 Pick a time in the very near future. If you don't, a time will pick you—and it's guaranteed to be bad. You don't want to have a huge argument and break up during a six-hour car trip. Miles and miles of angry silence. Not relaxing.

2 Verify, as best as you can, that the time is considerate to your future ex. There's nothing to be gained by destroying someone on their birthday or while they're in the middle of critical business.

3 Do the deed in person. If the relationship is advanced enough to require this level of planning, have the courage and consideration to do the dumping face to face.

4 Pick a comfortable, private spot. You don't want to be in an airport terminal. You don't know what's going to happen. You could spend a lot of time sitting around crying. Bring a box of tissues.

5 Lie. There's no reason to be completely honest if it will cause needless pain. Why say "Five more seconds of your inane commentary about J.Lo and I'll slap you on the forehead" when it's just as easy to say "We just aren't compatible." On the other hand, most people can spot a lie a mile away, so strike a balance between brutal honesty and emotional truth.

6 Have an escape. Schedule the breakup for one hour before an appointment that you have to keep. That way you can escape gracefully without causing undo trauma.

7 If you are engaged, you'll have to do the following post-breakup:

• If invitations have already been sent, write a note to guests stating that the engagement has been broken. Do not include personal details, and keep it short.

• If wedding invitations have not been sent out, you may notify people via word of mouth.

• Return all engagement gifts.

• Unless the engagement ring has been in the bride's family for generations, it should always go back to the man. Others say that if the man breaks it off, the woman can keep it, but if she breaks it off then she has to give it back.

Tips

Don't backtrack. Once you've broken it off, don't relent. You'll regret it.

Retrieve any important belongings from your future ex before the breakup. You don't want your favorite leather jacket in hysterical enemy hands.

Burn a CD with a selection of classic breakup songs to play in that rare moment of weakness when you think you might just give your ex a call: "Achy Breaky Heart" (Billy Ray Cyrus), "Bed of Lies" (Matchbox 20), "Ex Factor" (Lauryn Hill), "Home Ain't Where His Heart Is Anymore" (Shania Twain), "Go Your Own Way" (Fleetwood Mac), "Take Another Little Piece of My Heart" (Janis Joplin) among others.

32 | Plan Your Social Calendar

A burden to some, raison d'etre to others, maintaining a workable schedule can be very challenging. Whether you're already a social Olympian or you just want to maximize your hobnobbing time, use the following steps to improve and streamline your social life.

Steps

1 Define the goal of your social life. If your only thought is to have fun, consider yourself among the lucky ones. Other reasons might include staying abreast of your enemies, networking, finding a mate or branching out from your circle of friends. Tailor your activities to meet your goals. See 33 Meet Mr. or Ms. Right, 34 Marry Up and 201 Make a Networking Plan.

2 Take out your personal organizer. Note birthdays, anniversaries, weddings, graduations, debutante balls, opening night for the opera and symphony, and other big occasions that you don't want to miss.

3 Work in events and meetings from the organizations you belong to, school functions and whatnot. Don't forget going to the gym—you need to stay fit in order to maintain your level of socializing. See 25 Design Your Workout Schedule.

4 Make time for good friends and simple get-togethers. A brunch or coffee date is a great time to reconnect with a good friend and share stories. Don't be so focused on attending big events and meeting new people that you ignore those closest to you.

5 Consider getting a personal digital assistant (PDA). These mini-computers may soon replace your bulging address book and calendar. They're small and convenient, and you can update your schedule on the fly. Prices start at about $250. See 11 Organize Your Contacts.

6 Know your party-stamina quotient—you don't want to burn out from too much activity. It's far better to be slightly underbooked than definitely overbooked, and much more pleasurable to leave yourself wanting more than to be overwhelmed. The occasional night at home to recharge is essential.

7 Know your limits and trust your personal preferences. Don't go to a restaurant with 20 people if you're not comfortable in large groups. There's nothing wrong with being reserved on occasion. Don't let friends and colleagues pressure you into events that aren't appealing. Read 13 Say No Without Feeling Guilty.

Tip

Always arrive with a small, tasteful gift for your host or hostess, such as flowers or wine. See 322 Impress a Date.

Warning

Watch costs. You won't have fun if you overextend your budget. Don't try to impress people with lavish spending if it exceeds your comfort zone. See 226 Set Up a Budget.

33 | Meet Mr. or Ms. Right

Can this really be planned? Hardly. The last thing you want is to become one of those desperate creatures who obsesses about the need to be married. Gear your planning toward enjoying yourself and at the same time increasing your exposure to potential mates.

Steps

1 Trust your instincts when it comes to knowing what you want. The older you get, the more discriminating your taste in potential mates becomes. This is a good thing.

2 Cultivate a wide circle of friends. Use e-mail, phone calls and birthday cards to keep in touch with as large a group as you can. If possible, be a social hub, the kind of person who brings different groups together. Instead of waiting for things to happen, get on the phone and initiate activities. Join a softball team or enroll in tennis lessons. See 201 Make a Networking Plan.

3 Control your anxiety about not having a mate. Your life is not on hold just because you haven't found someone. Take the time to enjoy yourself today. Read 501 Be Happy.

4 Move slowly and keep assessing compatibility. Don't try to convince yourself someone is Mr. Perfect when he might really only be Mr. Available.

5 Dump Mr. or Ms. Not Right immediately. You'll be much more successful in meeting someone appropriate if you're not carrying around the anchor of a failing relationship. See 31 Mastermind a Breakup.

6 Exploit gender concentrations. Gals, there are numerous guy-dominated activities where you will stand out. If you can ride a motorcycle, pilot a boat or argue about baseball with any skill at all, you'll be virtually worshiped by groups of men. Guys, at some point in her life every woman in the world has looked in vain for a skilled dancing partner. Sign up for dance classes.

7 Join a gym. In addition to helping you get fit, you get to see lots of active people in skimpy outfits. Gyms are basically like nightclubs but without all the pointless standing around. See 25 Design Your Workout Schedule.

Tips

If your friends don't like your mate, it's probably not a good match. They may be reluctant to be completely honest with you, but look for clues that there's a problem.

See 29 Arrange to Meet an Online Date and 30 Plan the Perfect Date.

Despite your slovenly wardrobe, uncouth demeanor and lack of charm, you feel that you're upper-class material. OK, fine. But how do you make the leap from reading the funnies to actually appearing on the social page? It will take hard work, conniving, patience and a lot of luck, but you might pull it off.

Steps

1 Be charming and fun. This is basic advice for anyone looking for a mate. Without these qualities you're really going to have a hard time of it.

2 Study the society page in your newspaper. It's essential that you're familiar with prominent families and local big shots. After a few weeks of investigations, you'll have a feel for the major players in the best circles. Focus on available prospects.

3 Upgrade your appearance. No matter how fabulous you already are (inside and out, of course) there's always room for improvement. Join a gym and lose the spare tire, get a new haircut and overhaul your wardrobe. See 28 Get a Drastic Makeover.

4 Enroll in finishing school to gain ease and familiarity with the finer points of social etiquette. Learn how to carry on witty and lively conversations, and if you lean toward bluntness, school yourself in the gentle art of diplomacy in all areas of your life.

5 Volunteer for a high-profile charity that attracts philanthropists. Any city is likely to have a publicly supported hospital, opera or symphony, or school. A fund-raising position will put you into direct contact with the well-heeled. If a conflict of interest arises, deal with it after that ring is on your finger.

6 Use your volunteer position to stay informed about major fund-raisers, opening night at the opera or ballet, polo matches and museum dedications. Your work will give you credibility and help secure invitations to all the hot events. Find dates from among your fund-raising contacts by subtly dropping the hint that it's their duty to accompany you to an upcoming event. Avoid over-playing the guilt card or you'll have an unwilling escort.

7 Join a prestigious club. You have many choices depending on your interests. A country club is an obvious choice. Many yacht clubs have associate or social memberships for people who don't actually have a boat or lots of cash. See 428 Organize a Sailing Team.

Tips

Marrying up will be successful in the long run only if you actually love your mate. Marrying just for money is likely to prove a disaster. See 287 Plan an Amicable Divorce.

You don't want to pick a mate just by reading the society page but you might as well see who's available. If nothing else, it will make the process interesting.

See 32 Plan Your Social Calendar.

Warning

When in doubt, keep your mouth shut.

GANIZE YOUR CONTACTS • GET RID OF WHAT YOU DON'T WANT • SAY NO WITHOUT FEELING GUILTY • BALANCE HOME AND WORK • LIV
AIN • SCHEDULE TELEVISION WATCHING • DESIGN A HEALTHY LIFESTYLE • PLAN TO AVOID JUNK FOOD • CHOOSE A WEIGHT LOSS PLAN
ET AN ONLINE DATE • PLAN THE PERFECT DATE • MASTERMIND A BREAKUP • PLAN YOUR SOCIAL CALENDAR • MEET MR. OR MS. RIGHT
RT YOUR SOCK DRAWER • RETURN RENTALS ON TIME • TAKE CONTROL OF YOUR JUNK DRAWER • ORGANIZE THE MEDICINE CABINET •
R CLEAN AND ORDERLY • DEAL WITH A PACK RAT • SELL STUFF ONLINE • ORGANIZE YOUR BOOKSHELVES • CATEGORIZE NEWSPAPER A
E BETTER THROUGH LABELING • ORGANIZE JEWELRY • PLAN YOUR DREAM KITCHEN • CONQUER YOUR CLOSETS • ORGANIZE THE LINE
GANIZE SPRING CLEANING • KEEP THE FAMILY ROOM ORGANIZED • SET UP A BATHROOM SCHEDULE • ORGANIZE BATHROOMS • ORGA
GANIZE KIDS' ROOMS • ORGANIZE SPORTS EQUIPMENT • ORGANIZE KIDS' PLAY SPACES • SAFEGUARD YOUR HOME AGAINST ALLERGE
USE • USE HOME DESIGN AND PLANNING SOFTWARE • ESTABLISH YOUR HOME'S SPACE PLAN • INCORPORATE UNIVERSAL DESIGN PR
E BASEMENT • ORGANIZE THE GARAGE • ORGANIZE A TOOLBOX • SET UP A WOODSHOP • ORGANIZE YOUR WINE COLLECTION • PLAN
JDIO OR SMALL APARTMENT • MANAGE WARRANTY DOCUMENTS • MANAGE HOME-IMPROVEMENT PAPERWORK • MERGE TWO HOUSE
GANIC VEGETABLE GARDEN • PLANT A KITCHEN HERB GARDEN • PLAN A BUTTERFLY GARDEN • DESIGN A BIRD GARDEN • DESIGN A C
RGANIZE GARDENING TOOLS • ADD A POTTING BENCH TO A YARD • SCHEDULE FRUIT TREE MAINTENANCE • LAY OUT A SPRINKLER SY
SIGN A GARDEN PATH • SET UP A COMPOST SYSTEM • WINTERIZE PLANTS • SCHEDULE YARD WORK • STORE ANYTHING • STORE BULH
D HOBBY MATERIALS • ORGANIZE ART SUPPLIES • ORGANIZE GIFT WRAP AND SEASONAL DECORATIONS • ORGANIZE KIDS' SCHOOLWC
UR WEDDING DRESS AND OTHER TEXTILES • STORE A FUR COAT • STORE BICYCLES AND GEAR • STORE SKI GEAR • ORGANIZE CAMPI
IICH COLLEGE IS RIGHT FOR YOU • GET INTO A TOP COLLEGE OR UNIVERSITY • ACE THE COLLEGE ADMISSIONS TESTS • ORGANIZE YC
W SCHOOL • PREPARE FOR THE BAR EXAM • GET A DEGREE WHILE YOU'RE WORKING • WORK AT HOME WITH KIDS • GO BACK TO WOF
GANIZE YOUR JOB SEARCH • PREPARE FOR A CAREER CHANGE • OPEN A RESTAURANT • BECOME A PHYSICIST • BECOME A CONCER
ALITY-SHOW CONCEPT • BECOME A TALK-SHOW HOST • BECOME A PHOTOJOURNALIST • BECOME A MOVIE DIRECTOR • BECOME A M
ING SYSTEM • ORGANIZE YOUR BRIEFCASE • ORGANIZE YOUR DESK • ORGANIZE YOUR WORKDAY • GET A HANDLE ON E-MAIL • ORGA
LARY REVIEW • CLIMB THE CORPORATE LADDER EFFECTIVELY • ADD A WORKSPACE TO ANY ROOM • ORGANIZE A HOME OFFICE • ORG
AVEL • WRITE A BUSINESS PLAN • SET UP A NEW BUSINESS • CREATE A MARKETING PLAN • AMASS A REAL-ESTATE EMPIRE • POLISH
IPLOYEE • FIRE AN EMPLOYEE • PASS ON A FAMILY BUSINESS • STAY ON TOP OF YOUR SALES GAME • RESTRUCTURE A COMPANY TO
FEND AGAINST A HOSTILE TAKEOVER • ORGANIZE YOUR OFFICE FOR A MOVE • PREPARE YOUR BUSINESS FOR THE UNTHINKABLE • R
EPARE YOUR TAXES • ORGANIZE A LOAN APPLICATION • ORGANIZE IMPORTANT DOCUMENTS • SAVE FOR PRIVATE SCHOOLING • ORGA
UB • TRACK YOUR INVESTMENTS • SURVIVE BANKRUPTCY • PLAN FOR RETIREMENT • PREPARE A PRENUPTIAL AGREEMENT • CREATE
DNEY • PLAN YOUR FAMILY • BUDGET FOR A NEW BABY • ORCHESTRATE THE PERFECT CONCEPTION • PLAN FOR ARTIFICIAL INSEMINA
AVE • ORDER BABY ANNOUNCEMENTS • ORGANIZE AN INTERNATIONAL ADOPTION • FOSTER A CHILD • ORGANIZE YOUR LIFE AS A NE\
ORDINATE A FAMILY CALENDAR • PLAN FAMILY MEETINGS • ORGANIZE HOME SYSTEMS FOR ADD • PREPARE FOR A NEW CAT OR DOG
CK-TO-SCHOOL • WIN THE HOMEWORK WARS • PLAN A FIELD TRIP • PLAN YOUR CHILD'S ACTIVITIES • PLAN YOUR CHILDREN'S SUMM
LINE • ORGANIZE A GENEALOGICAL SEARCH • PREPARE FOR YOUR CHILD'S DEPARTURE FOR COLLEGE • ORGANIZE YOUR EMPTY NE
DERLY PARENTS' CARE • PREPARE FOR THE DEATH OF A SPOUSE • HELP YOUR ELDERLY PARENTS MOVE • ORGANIZE A HOME MEDICA
ORE TRIPS • SET UP ONLINE GROCERY SHOPPING • ORGANIZE RECIPES AND COOKBOOKS • PLAN THEME MENUS • CREATE EFFECTIV
FRIGERATOR AND FREEZER • ORGANIZE CUTLERY AND KITCHEN TOOLS • ORGANIZE CUPBOARDS AND DRAWERS • ORGANIZE THE PA
NCHES FOR KIDS • PLAN PARTY FOODS AHEAD • THROW A DINNER PARTY • FINISH DINNER ON TIME • PULL OFF A LAST-MINUTE PART
TIMATE WEDDING CHECKLIST • BUDGET FOR A WEDDING • FIND THE PERFECT WEDDING RING • PLAN AN ELOPEMENT • SET UP A BAF
DNOR • EXECUTE BEST MAN DUTIES • HIRE A BAND • HIRE A BARTENDER • PLAN A SHOWER • ORGANIZE THE REHEARSAL DINNER • P
ICCESSFUL SLUMBER PARTY • PLAN A BAR OR BAT MITZVAH • PLAN A QUINCEAÑERA • PLAN A RETIREMENT PARTY • PLAN A FUNERA
NUKKAH PARTY • ORGANIZE A HOLIDAY CRAFT PARTY • PLAN TO SPEND CHRISTMAS SOLO • PLAN THE PERFECT HOLIDAY GIFT EXCH
E HOLIDAYS • STICK TO YOUR NEW YEAR'S RESOLUTIONS • PLAN THE PERFECT NEW YEAR'S EVE • PLAN A SEDER • PLAN A SPECIAL
OD TREE • ORGANIZE A BICYCLE SCAVENGER HUNT • RUN A SPORTS TOURNAMENT • PUBLICIZE AN EVENT • PLAN AN ORGANIZATIO
AN A CONCERT IN THE PARK • ORGANIZE AN INTERNATIONAL CONCERT TOUR • ORGANIZE A FILM FESTIVAL • PLAN A FUND-RAISING
3UILD A COMMUNITY PLAY STRUCTURE • THROW A BLOCK PARTY • SET UP A NEIGHBORHOOD WATCH • CREATE AN EVACUATION PLA
RGANIZE A PROTEST OR MARCH • FIGHT CITY HALL • ORGANIZE A BOYCOTT • ORGANIZE A CLASS ACTION LAWSUIT • MANAGE GROW
HOOL IN A THIRD WORLD COUNTRY • PLAN A TRIP • PLAN A TRIP WITH CHILDREN • TRAVEL WITH TEENS • BOOK AIRLINE TICKETS •
OTORCYCLE TRIP • PLAN A TRAIN TRIP IN THE UNITED STATES • RIDE THE RAILS ABROAD • PREPARE A VACATION COUNTDOWN CHEC
IGGAGE • LOAD A BACKPACK PROPERLY • PLAN AN ELDERHOSTEL TRIP • ORGANIZE AN RV VACATION • PLAN A TRIP WITH AGING PAF
DELY DIFFERENT PEOPLE • PLAN SPRING BREAK • PLAN AN OVERNIGHT GETAWAY WITH YOUR SPOUSE • PLAN A VACATION SEPARAT
DLITICALLY UNSTABLE REGION • GET TRAVEL INSURANCE • GET IMMUNIZATIONS FOR TRAVELING • BOOK AN ADVENTURE VACATION •
AN A FISHING TRIP TO ALASKA • PACK FOR A CAMPING TRIP • LEAD A BACKPACK TRIP • HIKE A FAMOUS TRAIL • PLAN A TOUR OF TH
IGLISH CANAL TRIP • PLAN A CROSS-COUNTRY AIRPLANE VOYAGE • PLAN THE PERFECT DAY ABROAD • PLAN A VISIT TO THE LOUVRE
AN • PREPARE FOR AN ACT OF GOD • ASSEMBLE EMERGENCY KITS • PREPARE FOR SURGERY • PLAN YOUR RECOVERY • SURVIVE A
ING LOST • CONDUCT A SEARCH AND RESCUE OPERATION • PLAN AN INVASION • SURVIVE A POLITICAL COUP • PLAN FOR A TERROR

SS • SET GOALS • STREAMLINE YOUR MORNING ROUTINE • ORGANIZE A CHORE SCHEDULE FOR KIDS • ORGANIZE YOUR CHORES • NE
YOUR WORKOUT SCHEDULE • SCHEDULE DOCTOR VISITS • PREPARE FOR COLD AND FLU SEASON • GET A DRASTIC MAKEOVER • ARR
JP • FIND YOUR KEYS • TIDY UP IN MINUTES • CONQUER CLUTTER • ACTUALLY SEE THE BOTTOM OF YOUR PURSE • ORGANIZE YOUR S
E CAR MAINTENANCE • ORGANIZE PET SUPPLIES • MANAGE GARBAGE AND RECYCLABLES • PREPARE GRAB 'N' GO ACTIVITY BAGS • KE
INE CLIPPINGS • ORGANIZE YOUR PHOTOS • ARRANGE PHOTOS AND PICTURES • ARRANGE AN ART COLLECTION • END COLLECTION C
• ORGANIZE YOUR LAUNDRY CENTER • CREATE A SEWING CENTER • GET READY FOR THE HOUSECLEANER • ORGANIZE CLEANING SUP
WAYS AND MUDROOMS • ORGANIZE A DORM ROOM • ORGANIZE YOUR SCHOOL LOCKER • MAKE YOUR HOME SAFE FOR SMALL CHILD
RE FOR SKYROCKETING ENERGY COSTS • USE FENG SHUI TO ORGANIZE YOUR HOME • DESIGN A NEW HOME WITH FENG SHUI • DESIG
PLAN A REMODEL • PLAN A MULTIMEDIA CENTER • TURN A BASEMENT INTO A MEDIA ROOM OR PLAYROOM • ORGANIZE THE ATTIC • OF
FUL ESTATE SALE • PLAN A YARD OR GARAGE SALE • PREPARE YOUR HOME FOR SALE • PLAN A MOVE • DOWNSIZE YOUR HOUSE • OR
CORATE FOR THE SEASONS • PREPARE A VACATION HOME FOR THE OFF-SEASON • PREPARE YOUR HOME FOR NATURE'S WORST • PRE
ARDEN • PLANT A CUT-FLOWER GARDEN • DESIGN A SHADE GARDEN • DESIGN A DRY GARDEN • PLAN FOR A LONG-SEASON CONTAIN
N AND PLANT A LAWN • DESIGN A NEW LANDSCAPE • PLAN AN OUTDOOR KITCHEN • DESIGN A DECK OR PATIO • DESIGN A WATER FEA
S • STORAGE SOLUTIONS FOR ANY ROOM • ... THE CAPACITY OF A SMALL ROOM • ORGANIZ
TWORK • ORGANIZE MOVIES, MUSIC AND O... RLOOMS • STORE OUT-OF-SEASON CLOTHES •
NT • STORE PAINT AND OTHER HAZARDOUS ... STORE A BOAT FOR THE WINTER • STORE A CA
E APPLICATIONS • PLAN YOUR COURSE OF ... H PAPER • GET INTO GRAD SCHOOL • GET INTC
ONG ABSENCE • SET UP AN INTERNSHIP • ... N THE PEACE CORPS • PRODUCE A NEWSLETTE
BECOME A COWBOY • BECOME A BRAIN S... ATHOLIC NUN • ORGANIZE AN EXHIBITION • DEV
ME A STUNT PERSON • BECOME A TOUR G... G • CONQUER YOUR PAPER PILES • CREATE A FL
TER FILES • SCHEDULE APPOINTMENTS EF... NCE CALL • PREPARE FOR A MEETING • PREPAR
E NETWORK • CHOOSE THE BEST PHONE ... TEM • MAKE A NETWORKING PLAN • PLAN YOUF
TATION SKILLS • PREPARE A SPEECH • PR... AN AN IPO • DELEGATE RESPONSIBILITIES • HIRE
OFITS • FORM A BOARD OF DIRECTORS • ... AN A COMPANY PICNIC • PLAN A COMPANY RET
FAILING BUSINESS • DISMANTLE A BUSINE... • DESIGN A SAVINGS PLAN • SIMPLIFY BILL PAY
NANCIAL-AID PACKAGE • PLAN FOR COLLE... E A HEALTH INSURANCE PLAN • START AN INVES
ST • MAKE A WILL • EXECUTE A POWER OF ... S ESTATE • PLAN YOUR ESTATE • TEACH YOUR H
RE FOR AN IN VITRO FERTILIZATION • PRE... ATERNITY WARDROBE • SET UP MATERNITY OR
EPARE FOR CHILDBIRTH • STOCK A DIAPE... LEND FAMILIES • CREATE A HOUSEHOLD ORGA
OL YOUR CHILD • SET UP A CARPOOL • S... HE BEST ELEMENTARY SCHOOL • ORGANIZE KID
R SUMMER CAMP • CHOOSE A SUMMER S... R FAMILY COMPUTER USE • PLAN TO KEEP YOU
BOOMERANG KIDS • PLAN AN AMICABLE ... EMENTS • ORGANIZE MEDICAL RECORDS • PLAN
ARRANGE HOSPICE CARE • MAKE YOUR ... ECORDS • PLAN A WEEK OF MENUS • ORGANIZ

**Daily
Debris**

STS • COOK AHEAD • DETERMINE THE SH... M WAREHOUSE STORES • EFFICIENTLY USE THE
NTLY USE SPACE UNDER THE SINK • STO... UR COUNTER SPACE • COOK FOR ONE • PLAN H
INNER PARTY FOR YOUR BOSS • PLAN DI... PARTY • IMPRESS A DATE • PLAN A WEDDING • C
NT PLANNER • HIRE A PHOTOGRAPHER • ... ACHELORETTE PARTY • PREPARE TO BE THE MA
EYMOON • PLAN A BAPTISM • PLAN A BR... GUESTS • PLAN A CHILD'S BIRTHDAY PARTY • P
O CUSTOM • PLAN AHEAD FOR A LOW-STRESS HOLIDAY • STAY WITHIN A BUDGET THIS CHRISTMAS • PREPARE A HOLIDAY FEAST • T
ZE GIFT-GIVING IN ADVANCE • STICK TO YOUR DIET DURING THE HOLIDAYS • PLAN A HOLIDAY OPEN HOUSE • REORGANIZE YOUR LIF
ORGANIZE A HIGH-SCHOOL CLASS REUNION • PLAN A FAMILY REUNION • START A KNITTING CIRCLE • ORGANIZE A BOOK CLUB • SE
SHARPEN THE FOCUS OF AN ORGANIZATION • IMPROVE YOUR CHILD'S SCHOOL • PLAN A PROM • ORGANIZE A COMMUNITY THEATEF
ZE A PANCAKE BREAKFAST • PLAN A TOY DRIVE • HOLD A BARN RAISING • ORGANIZE A CHARITY WALK OR RUN • BUILD LOW-INCOM
ER-REGISTRATION DRIVE • RUN FOR LOCAL OFFICE • ORGANIZE A PETITION • ORGANIZE A RECALL • GET AN INITIATIVE ON THE BALL
MMUNITY • PRESERVE OPEN SPACE • SAVE HISTORIC PROPERTIES AND LANDMARKS • SET UP A NONGOVERNMENTAL ORGANIZATION
HE UNITED STATES • RENT A CAR ABROAD • MAKE HOTEL RESERVATIONS • ARRANGE EXECUTIVE ACCOMMODATIONS • PLAN A CRUIS
AN ITINERARY • PACK FOR A TRIP • PACK FOR A BUSINESS TRIP • PACK FOR A WEEK IN ONE CARRY-ON • PACK A DAY BAG • PREVEN
E A SAILING TEAM • PLAN A SAILBOAT CRUISE • PLAN A BICYCLE TRIP WITH A TOUR COMPANY • TRAVEL ABROAD • PLAN A VACATIO
OUSE • PLAN A TRIP TO A DIFFERENT CULTURE • FORAGE ABROAD • MAIL PACKAGES BACK TO THE UNITED STATES • PLAN A TRIP TC
ROAD • PLAN A CLIMB OF MOUNT KILIMANJARO • PACK FOR A SAFARI • ORGANIZE A HUNTING TRIP • PACK FOR A FISHING OR HUN
KS • ORGANIZE A BACKCOUNTRY SKI TRIP • ORGANIZE A CAR RALLY • PLAN A WHALE-WATCHING TRIP • PACK FOR A VOYAGE AT SE
DNEY HARBOUR BRIDGE • PLAN A TRIP TO NEW ORLEANS FOR MARDI GRAS • PLAN A DAY AT DISNEYLAND • FORMULATE A FAMILY E
YOU'RE ALONE • SURVIVE IF YOUR CAR BREAKS DOWN • DEAL WITH AMNESIA • FIGHT AN EBOLA OUTBREAK • FIGHT A FOREST FIR
SCUE A HOSTAGE • OUTSMART PIRATES • DELIVER A BABY • MAKE AN EMERGENCY LANDING • MAKE A JAIL BREAK • BECOME A MOV

35 | Find Your Keys

Sometimes it's the things you use every day that can be the hardest to find. Creating consistent habits and permanent homes for keys, handbags, briefcases and other important items saves time and stress every time you leave the house.

Steps

1 Pick one location near the door to hold your key ring while you're at home. Practice putting keys in a basket, bowl or hook by the entry area as soon as you walk through the door so they're easy to find. If you are having a hard time getting into the habit of using your new holding spot, write a reminder on a sticky note and keep it on the outside entry door until the habit becomes routine.

2 Slim down massive key rings. Keep only frequently used keys for entry locks, security doors and vehicles on your everyday key ring to keep it light.

3 Sort through all other keys, testing to see that they actually open something. Toss those that you can't identify or that unlock things you no longer own.

4 Install a hook rack for keys in a handy location to hold the remaining keys, such as those for the mailbox, storage shed, bike lock, boat or neighbor's home. Identify each key with a colored key jacket or key tag. If security is an issue, use a wall-mounted key safe. See 57 Live Better Through Labeling.

5 Give an extra house key to a trusted neighbor for unexpected lockouts. If you have both upper and lower locks, identify which key opens which lock—or better yet, have both locks rekeyed to the same key.

6 Avoid stashing your keys in a coat pocket, as they're easy to forget when temperatures warm up and the coat stays in the closet.

7 To avoid losing a safe deposit box key, tape it to the inside of a frequently used cabinet or drawer. Note the location within a contents file for the box, kept in your home filing system. See 185 Create a Flawless Filing System.

8 Keep an extra car key in your wallet as a backup in case of accidental lockouts.

Tip

Keep the ignition or valet key to your car on a detachable clip in the glovebox for quick handoff to attendants at parking garages. If you frequently need to detach individual keys, invest in a valet-type ring, such as ones at KeyChains4You.com.

Who Knew?

Find a landing pad for purses, briefcases and backpacks somewhere near the entry so you can spot them quickly when you leave the house. A hanging accessory bag or shelving unit in the closet or a slim table in the hallway manages these items well. See 70 Organize Entryways and Mudrooms.

36 | Tidy Up in 15 Minutes

There's nothing more discouraging than spending an entire Saturday cleaning and organizing, only to find your home in a shambles again by Wednesday. Set aside 15 minutes each day to maintain your living space, and you'll minimize clutter buildup as the week marches on. Use the chart below as a guide for keeping your house together throughout the week.

Steps

1 Get the whole family to participate in daily home maintenance by assigning one small, quick job to each family member. Good tasks for kids include setting the table or vacuuming the main entry area. Post a reminder list with daily check-off boxes in the kitchen. See 18 Organize a Chore Schedule for Kids.

2 Avoid going from one floor of your home to another without returning something to where it belongs. Keep a basket next to the stairs. Make putting things away a routine.

3 Use superabsorbent microfiber cloths to trap dust and dirt. Feather dusters and rags often just blow dust and dirt around.

Tip

Keep a small caddy in each bathroom, filled with cleaners and paper towels, for quick cleanup when unexpected company drops by.

Who Knew?

A little dusting goes a long way. If you let dust build up, it becomes grime, which requires heavy-duty cleaning measures.

WHEN	TASK	
Monday	• Put away videos, games, CDs and tapes.	• Sweep, mop or vacuum the kitchen floor.
Tuesday	• Take newspapers, magazines and catalogs to the recycle bins.	• Check the supply of toilet paper, paper towels, and tissues.
Wednesday	• Pick up stray clutter and put it back to where it belongs.	• Dust all flat surfaces in living areas. • Clean all mirrors and glass tops.
Thursday	• Clear the clutter from dresser tops and put away items to be kept.	• Put away videos, games, CDs and tapes. • Vacuum all carpeted areas of the house.
Friday	• Pick up stray clutter and put it back to where it belongs.	• Sweep, mop or vacuum the kitchen floor.
Saturday and Sunday	• Return shoes from the entry area to the bedroom closets. • Return stray clothes to bedrooms or laundry.	• Clean the bathroom sinks and toilets. • Vacuum the main entry areas and halls.

37 Conquer Clutter

Over time, it creeps into the corners and cabinets, stairways and entryways, closets and cupboards of your home—clutter! Suddenly you're overrun with piles of unrelated stuff, some useful and some far from it. Junk-proof your life and keep only what you use and love.

Steps

1 Pick one area to focus your decluttering efforts on. Start small— just a drawer, shelf or closet floor. Sticking to a single small area will ensure that you get something accomplished. See 1 Get Organized.

2 Dress down. You're about to get dirty and sweaty, so wear clothes you don't mind messing up.

3 Decide how long each decluttering session will last. Set a timer or other prompt to let you know when to stop. Keep in mind that you will be most effective if you limit your sessions to a few hours at most. A whole day of decluttering can be overwhelming.

4 Bring bags and boxes to your decluttering location for collecting the items you no longer need or use.

5 Ask yourself these questions as you pick up each item to decide whether it stays or goes:

- Have I used this in the last two years?

- Is it a duplicate? Can I replace it easily if it's not?

- Does it need repair, and if so, is it worth repairing?

- Will I use it in the next year?

- Am I keeping it only for sentimental reasons?

- Is an unused item taking up space where I could store some- thing more valuable or useful?

- Does it belong elsewhere or to someone else?

- Do I love it?

6 Add that item to one of your boxes: Repairs, store returns, items to put elsewhere, items to return to others, items to sell, dona- tions, mementos, garbage, maybes and definite keepers.

7 Take action on each pile after you've handled every item:

- Put repair items in the car. Drop them off on your next errand run.

- Collect store returns along with their purchase receipts and put them all in one designated place. Return them when conven- ient—and before the store's money-back return period is up.

- Cart the box with your "belongs elsewhere" pile around the house, and replace everything. Find a permanent home for items; if possible, instead of another temporary spot you'll have to clean again.

Tips

If you are working in a room that is covered in clutter and you feel overwhelmed, box up a small quantity of stuff to take to your clear area to sort.

Walk around the living spaces of your home— kitchen, family room, entry areas—each evening with a box and gather all stray items. Redistribute or toss the box's contents before going to bed to keep the level of clutter manageable. See 36 Tidy Up in 15 Minutes.

Keep a donations box in or close to the laundry room for outgrown or unwanted clothes. Remember, though, that you should donate only items in good to excellent condition—clean, no rips, holes or stains. See 62 Organize Your Laundry Center.

Mix small decluttering jobs with other activities. Sort through the kitchen junk drawer while talking on the phone, or cull magazines while watching TV. See 42 Take Control of Your Junk Drawer and 52 Categorize Newspaper and Magazine Clippings.

To boost your efforts, pre- tend that you have to move and will be paying someone by the hour to pack and transport all your stuff. Marginal things lose their value quickly when you adopt this strategy.

- Box up mementos and items you aren't quite ready to let go of. List contents on the outside of the containers and place them in a storage area of your house. Look at these items again in six months to decide whether you want to keep them or let them go. See 296 Archive Family Records.

- Place items for donation in boxes or bags and move them to a holding area, ideally in the garage or storage space. Make arrangements for pickup or plan a time in your schedule for drop-off. See 12 Get Rid of What You Don't Want.

8 Clean your freshly decluttered area, and put the keepers in their permanent home.

9 Reward yourself with a tangible prize to reinforce and celebrate your success.

10 Find you next victim—a room, a shelf—and repeat the process until your home is clutter-free.

11 Select a permanent home for every new thing that comes into your life to prevent the clutter from building up again.

For every new item that comes into your home, get rid of something else (the in-and-out rule).

Warning

Be realistic about how long it will take you to get a handle on your clutter. It didn't get that way in a week, so you won't fix it in a week.

38 Actually See the Bottom of Your Purse

If your purse has become a dumping ground for every small item you encounter, it's time to banish the stale peppermints, four shades of lipstick and old receipts. Purging and reorganizing will help you find your keys, a pen or the bridge toll in record time. Follow the tips below and carry your clutch with confidence.

Tips

Buy a bag with a light-colored lining. It will make the contents much easier to see.

Photocopy all your cards and keep the copies in a safe location for quick retrieval in case your purse or wallet is lost or stolen.

Never carry your Social Security card in your wallet. You will need to produce the actual card only when securing employment.

Steps

1 Dump out contents onto a working surface and toss the trash. Pare down to the essentials. For example, carry one all-purpose lipstick versus several, and so forth.

2 Pull out notes, reminders and receipts, and transfer critical information to your to do list, calendar or tickler system. See 10 Set Up a Reminder System, 266 Coordinate a Family Calendar and 3 Write an Effective To-Do List.

3 Assess the bag's ability to hold what is left. Is it the right size? Could you go smaller or larger? If so, it's time to raid your closet or go shopping for a new purse.

4 Make the most of zipper pockets and open slots by assigning a specific item to each location. For example, use one pocket for your phone and another for sunglasses. Get in the habit of always returning items to their special spot.

5 Purge your purse weekly to keep it functioning at its best.

39 | Organize Your Shoes

Do you dread another morning of digging through a jumbled mess of loafers, slippers, boots and running shoes piled in your closet? Even if you do spot the pair of shoes you want, you may not be ready to shuffle off to Buffalo. Be well heeled and ready to meet each day with shoes that are are well organized.

Steps

1 Gather all your shoes from around the house into one place. Discard those that are beyond repair. Screen out pairs worth repairing and make plans to take them to a shoe repair shop.

2 Sort the shoes into groups. First sort by frequency of wear—daily or special occasion—then by color within each grouping. Further separate the groups by seasons.

3 Eliminate duplicates, footwear past its prime and shoes that no longer (or never did) fit. Keep only the pairs you love and wear.

4 Count how many pairs remain and shop for shoe organizers. Hanging cubby bags or shoe racks capitalize on extra vertical closet space or the back of a closet door. Horizontal shoe shelves maximize space between the bottom of hanging clothes and the floor.

5 Use these organizers to arrange your shoes. Place the current season's daily favorites front and center. Store out-of-season and special-occasion pairs on higher closet shelves in their shoe boxes—take a picture of each pair and tape to the outside of the box for instant identification. Put shoe trees in boots and store on the floor or from hanging shoe trees.

6 Repeat the process next season.

Tips

If you need additional shoe storage, place an over-the-door shoe rack or bag on the back of a bedroom door.

When traveling, always take a spare pair of shoelaces. See 60 Conquer Your Closets.

To minimize shoe clutter at a home's entry point, keep a large basket to hold shoes until they can be returned to each owner's closet. See 70 Organize Entryways and Mudrooms.

40 | Sort Your Sock Drawer

Argyles mixing with stockings? Bobby socks colluding with trouser socks? It's just not right. Take control of the situation and sort things out with a simple system. You'll save time each morning by skipping the missing-sock tango.

Steps

1 Pull all socks out of the drawer and onto a bed or table. Match up pairs of loose socks. Set aside those that need mending. Remove socks that are beyond repair, along with single socks, and reuse these for another purpose (see Tips) or toss.

2 Insert a drawer organizer. Use narrow shoe boxes or commercial sock boxes. Make use of as much space as possible, placing the boxes lengthwise in the drawer.

Tips

Give a second life to your worn cotton socks by using them as polishing cloths for shoes, silver, mirrors and more. They slip nicely over a hand and allow fingers to work into small areas.

3 Designate a small area as a holding place for lone socks. Toss them after a month.

4 Return the pairs to the drawer, grouping them in the boxes by color and type (pantyhose, sport, dress). Use a trifold method for storing the socks versus the cuff-over strategy. It's quicker and minimizes stretching of the cuff elastic.

5 Match up pairs as you sort each batch of clean laundry and place them in the appropriate box.

To avoid choosing the wrong color from your dark socks, label the end of each sock organizer with a color. Use labeled zipper-lock plastic bags to separate dark-colored pantyhose.

41 Return Rentals on Time

What treasures lie under that coffee-table chaos? Could it be the video you rented two weeks ago? Perhaps it's the library book due last month. If late fees and overdue items are sapping your cash— and putting a strain on friendships—it's time for a new system.

Tips

Some libraries may have additional drop-offs at post offices, grocery stores and city hall.

For added convenience, try using online library resources for your reading material. Check out NetLibrary.com or ClassicBookshelf.com for electronic books (aka e-books).

Steps

1 Choose a spot near the front door (a closet, a bookshelf, a cub-byhole) and place a container there to gather rental-store returns, borrowed items and library books. See 128 Store Anything.

2 Train yourself (and your family) to note the return dates of each rental item on the master calendar. Put a sticky note on the item itself or a reminder. See 266 Coordinate a Family Calendar.

3 Have family members develop the habit of checking the master calendar to see what needs to happen and note upcoming deadlines for returns.

4 Schedule the return errand in your daily to-do list, or assign someone to make the returns. See 4 Run Errands Efficiently and 3 Write an Effective To-Do List.

5 Cross off the note when the item is returned.

6 Renew the item by phone or online if you know you're going to be late. Many libraries offer this service.

7 Try services such as Netflix.com or Gameznflix.com. For a fixed monthly membership charge, you get three rentals at a time from your submitted favorites list, which you can keep as long as you like. These services send new movies or games only when you return the previous ones, so you don't pay any late fees. See 20 Never Be Late Again.

42 | Take Control of Your Junk Drawer

Everybody's got one—the inevitable junk drawer. What would you do without this catchall container of matches, batteries, nails, stamps, safety pins, birthday candles, useless keys and whatever else the cat dragged in? You don't have to live without it—just get these odds and ends better organized.

Steps

1 Remove the drawer's contents and place them on a table or countertop. Protect the work surface by putting down an old towel first.

2 Throw out the true junk—unidentified keys, expired coupons, dead pens, dried-up glue and broken clothespins. Keep only what you really intend to use.

3 Group the remaining items into piles, such as office supplies, household helpers and mailing items.

4 Relocate those things that belong somewhere else. Decks of cards go back with other games, assorted hardware to the toolkit and tees to the golf bag.

5 Organize the drawer with containers large enough to hold each pile. Recycle check or cigar boxes, or purchase drawer trays to create sections. Stick with square or rectangular shapes to maximize drawer efficiency.

6 Replace orderly piles in the drawer compartments. Sign up for occasional purging sessions to keep your junk drawer from getting too gunked up again.

Tips

Restrict yourself to just one junk drawer in the house.

Snack-size zipper-lock plastic bags are great containers for small items such as loose hardware (a set of screws or other parts). Put a piece of masking tape on the outside and label with a permanent label marker if you know what they belong to. See 57 Live Better Through Labeling.

43 | Organize the Medicine Cabinet

You look into it every day, but do you really see what has taken up residence in your medicine cabinet? Expired medications, dusty dental-floss dispensers and abandoned skin-care regimens are all signs that your cabinet is in need of some first aid. Follow this prescription for organization and you'll keep your cabinet in good health.

Steps

1 Purge any items you no longer use or that are too old. Likely candidates for disposal are old toothbrushes (replace every three months), out-of-date sunscreens (good for only one year after purchase), gunky nail polish, expired over-the-counter remedies (pills, creams and lotions), and expired prescriptions or medications that you no longer use.

2 Clean the cabinet's mirror, shelves and interior thoroughly with a disinfectant.

Tips

See 293 Organize a Home Medication Regime.

Date all over-the-counter medications when you purchase them if they don't have a printed expiration date. Discard them after one year.

3 Sort all the keepers and place them into categorized piles: vitamins, first aid, bath and body care, hair care, pain relief, cold and flu, makeup and nail care, dental care, eye care, feminine products and so on.

4 Buy small plastic trays or narrow baskets to put your piles into. Put those items you use most frequently on the bottom shelves.

5 Put remaining items (by pile) in labeled see-through containers. Select a cool, dark and dry storage area for prescription and over-the-counter medications to protect product efficacy.

6 Repeat this process with the cabinet and additional storage spaces twice a year to keep clutter from building up again.

Warning

Dispose of prescription and over-the-counter medications with care. Flush them down the toilet or place them in a tightly covered outdoor trash container so kids and pets can't get them. Also, for privacy's sake, remove the prescription information from the bottle before recycling it.

44 | Schedule Car Maintenance

It's not that it's hard to remember to stay on top of car-care chores; it's just that it's so easy to forget. Take your vehicle in for servicing at scheduled intervals and you'll avoid inconvenient breakdowns and costly repairs.

Steps

1 Find a reputable mechanic (if you don't already have one) to service your car. Survey friends and relatives for referrals, always checking on any service provider with your local Better Business Bureau (bbb.org).

2 Photocopy the recommended maintenance schedule for oil changes, tire rotations, fluid checks and tune-ups. You'll find this information in your car's manual. Enter key dates into your planner (see 266 Coordinate a Family Calendar).

3 Place a reminder in your calendar for the next service date, including a list of the maintenance to be done. When the reminder comes up, schedule an appointment.

4 Develop the habit of checking the oil each time you fill the car with gas. Use the first of each month as a reminder date for checking washer fluid levels, tire pressure and wear patterns. Put the reminder in your calendar until it becomes a habit.

5 Before road trips, do the following:

• Bring the oil level up to but not over the dipstick's "full" mark.

• Check the wear patterns and pressure of all four tires.

• Top off the automatic transmission fluid, power-steering fluid, brake fluid and coolant level as needed.

• Replace belts that are frayed or have glazed-looking undersides. Check coolant hoses for leaks and cracks.

Tips

See 48 Keep Your Car Clean and Orderly.

Regular application of a glass finish product such as Rain-X will keep windows clean longer and improve visibility in rainy conditions.

Keep yourself on time by filling up with gas on your way home instead of on the way out. See 4 Run Errands Efficiently for more ideas.

45 | Organize Pet Supplies

Pets come with almost as much stuff as people do. From cans and bags of food and treats, crates, leashes, toys, medications and kitty litter, there's plenty to keep track of when the animal kingdom takes up residence in your home.

Steps

1 Pour dry food into an air-tight aluminum, glass or heavy-duty plastic container with a close-fitting lid. Choose a size large enough to hold the contents of a food bag you typically buy. Keep the container close to food dishes. Save time with the automatic feeders (for animals who actually have portion control).

2 Stack cans of food on a lazy Susan or shelf. You'll be able to spin and find Fluffy's favorite flavor.

3 Place leashes and extra collars on hooks located near the most-used door or on the inside wall of an entry-area closet. Keep travel gear—Frisbees, collapsible water bowls and old towels—here as well. Keep a plastic bag tied around the leash so you'll never forget one when you go on walks. See 47 Prepare Grab 'n' Go Activity Bags.

4 Stow pet-care products, such as grooming supplies, medications and ointments in a bucket. Hang from the same hook you've got the leash on.

5 Corral toys and bones in a basket near the pet's bed or crate.

Tips

See 269 Prepare for a New Cat or Dog.

If you have to search for the packet of heartworm pills each time a dose is due, keep them in a pet file. Put the dosage dates in your calendar.

Who Knew?

Dry pet food will say fresh for six to nine months when stored in a cool, dry place. Soft, moist food will stay fresh for three to six months if kept in its original package with the top rolled tightly closed. Cover opened cans and refrigerate.

46 | Manage Garbage and Recyclables

Most homes weren't designed with an eye toward managing the growing issue of garbage and recyclable materials. And without a system, trash, bottles, cans and papers quickly take over even the most organized kitchen. Set up a system for keeping tabs on daily discards and enjoy the sweet smell of success.

Steps

1 Log on to your city's Web site and find out exactly what is recyclable or compostable. Some take cans and glass but not plastic; others take certain kinds of plastic and glass. Also find out if you have to separate glass and plastic or mixed paper and newspapers. Post a list of what you can and can't recycle on the inside of a cabinet door for easy reference.

Tips

Keep extra liner bags in the bottom of the garbage can so a new one is ready and waiting when you take out the trash.

Clean and disinfect trash and recycling containers once a month.

See 498 Save the Earth.

2 Select an out-of-the-way spot to put the recycling. Check out easy-to-open, stackable recycling bins at many home supply stores or HoldEverything.com. For many households, a garbage can under the sink with another can to its side for recyclables will do. If you're designing a new home or remodeling your kitchen, build in a space for recyclables into cabinet drawers. See 59 Plan Your Dream Kitchen.

3 Cut down on the amount of garbage you generate. Purchase products that use little or no packaging, and opt for individually wrapped packages only when there is no alternative. Buy reusable products, such as rechargeable batteries that you don't have to recycle after one use. Buy one general housecleaning product rather than a variety of products for different purposes.

4 Think before you toss. The items shown in the chart (below) are dangerous or toxic—you can't just throw them away with the regular garbage. Take used motor oil, fluids and antifreeze, for example, to the local gas station for recycling. Manufacturers can't reuse cans of motor oil or pesticide containers because they contain harmful residues. Take old tires to the gas station or an auto wrecker. Your city has information on proper disposal. See 12 Get Rid of What You Don't Want and 145 Store Paint and Other Hazardous Materials.

Place newspapers and other recyclable paper upright in a paper grocery bag near the area where you open and sort mail. As the bag fills, move it to the recycling bin for pickup and replace it with a new bag. See 7 Deal With a Flood of Mail.

SOURCE	HAZARDOUS HOUSEHOLD WASTE
Garage	Antifreeze, chrome polish, automotive cleaner, diesel fuel, auto-body filler, engine degreaser, automatic transmission fluid, gasoline, brake fluid, kerosene or lamp oil, carburetor cleaner, lubricating oil, car batteries, motor oil, car wax.
Garden Supplies	Fungicides, soil fumigants, herbicides, snail and slug poison, insecticides, rodent and gopher poison, weed killer.
Cleaning Supplies	Dry-cleaning fluid, mothballs and moth flakes, furniture and floor polish, rug cleaners, household cleaners, spot removers, metal polish.
Household Supplies	Aerosol cans, lighter fluid, batteries, mercury from a broken thermometer, butane lighters, pet shampoo, chemotherapy drugs, lice shampoo, flea powder, shoe dye and polish, fluorescent lamp tubes.

Tired of running around the house trying to put together everything you need at the last minute for a day trip or activity? Stow essential items in a designated tote bag in advance to save time and frustration when you want to get out the door quickly and enjoy your day.

TYPE OF BAG	CONTENTS		
Day-Trip	• Mini first aid kit • Wet naps • Bug repellent • Sunblock • Poncho or garbage bag for emergency raincoat	• Books or toys for kids • Change of underwear, socks and shoes for little ones • Bottled water, juice boxes • Snacks	• Small spray bottle of water for quick cooldowns and cleanups
Activity and Sports	• Shoes, cleats, skates, guards • Racket, stick, ball, puck and other equipment • Helmet, padding, gloves, cup and other protective gear	• Mat, strap and block (yoga and Pilates) • Athletic tape • Towel • Energy bars or healthy snack food	• Water bottle • Small first aid kit with bandages, gauze, antiseptic pads, ibuprofen • Instant ice pack • Ankle or knee brace
Beach	• Swimsuit • Swim diapers • Change of clothes • Sunhat • Sunglasses • Plastic bags for wet clothes	• Flip-flops, sandals • Sunblock, lip protector • Umbrella • Beach chairs • Towels • Cooler with snacks, drinks	• Surfboard, boogie boards, snorkel, fins, surf wax, wet suit, rash guard • Beach ball, Frisbee, paddleball • Sand toys
Dog Park	• Leash and collar • Plastic bags	• Water, collapsible dish • Treats for good dogs	• Frisbee or ball • Ratty towel
TIPS	In summer, fill water bottles halfway with water and then freeze them on their sides. Just before heading out, fill the rest of the bottle with water. The ice keeps the water cold longer as it melts. Restock each bag when returning home. Give children individual bags and put them in charge of restocking their own stuff. Designate shelves in an entry closet or attached garage for holding sport and activity bags in one spot so they're easy to grab when leaving the house. See 75 Organize Sports Equipment.		

While you might think of your vehicle as simply a means to get from point A to point B, in reality it's a portable household with everything you need and want while you're on the go. Setting up regular routines to maintain your abode on wheels will keep you humming happily down the road.

Steps

1 Empty everything out of the vehicle and trunk, discard the obvious garbage, and return coffee cups to the kitchen.

2 Sort the remaining items into piles, such as maintenance supplies, kids' stuff, music and videos, manuals and maps.

3 Clean all interior surfaces. Vacuum the floors and seats, wipe down the dash and doors, clean windows and shake out the floor mats.

4 Keep a trash bin on the floor of the back seat, or hang a trash bag from the dashboard.

5 Stash kids' toys, small books and travel games in a behind-the-seat organizer (a hanging shoe bag works, too), within reach of backseat passengers. Periodically rotate items in and out to keep kids interested.

6 Stow tapes and CDs in visor organizers. Separate kids' tunes from adult music.

7 Store the following in the glove compartment: owner's manual, maps, vehicle registration information (if required), auto club information, accident report form, notepad, pen, disposable camera, flashlight, list of emergency contact names and numbers, tire gauge, paper napkins and any other frequently needed or essential items.

8 Purchase or make an emergency kit for your vehicle and store it in the trunk or rear of the car. Include booster cables, a tire gauge, flares, reflective tape, a help sign, a screwdriver, pliers, a first aid kit, work gloves, a blanket, an old towel or rags, a jug of water and motor oil. See 466 Assemble Emergency Kits.

9 Put together a survival kit, especially if you live in a cold-weather climate. Include candles, waterproof matches, energy bars or candy bars, large plastic garbage bags and rubber bands. Keep larger items, such as cat litter (for slippery roads), a collapsible shovel, an extra blanket and heavy socks, hats and mittens (enough for several passengers), in a duffel bag or tub in the trunk or rear of the car. See 470 Survive If Your Car Breaks Down.

10 Tackle the car again every season. Restock all your kits; check your maintenance schedule to see when servicing is needed (see 44 Schedule Car Maintenance).

Tips

See 406 Plan a Trip with Children.

Keep a small cooler in the rear or trunk to carry refrigerated and frozen groceries so you can run more errands after shopping. See 4 Run Errands Efficiently.

Keep a small travel bag with a change of clothes in the trunk, just in case.

Protect maps from travel spills by storing them in zipper-lock plastic bags.

Keep a heavy-duty rubber band on the driver's side visor to hold parking tickets, directions, mileage logs and any other papers relevant to the day's travels.

Who Knew?

Keep your car smelling sweet by placing fabric-softener sheets under the seats or filling the ashtray with baking soda.

An old shower curtain stored in the trunk comes in handy as a cover for a summer picnic table, a drop cloth for changing a tire, or a protective tarp.

Warning

Remove trash that held milk products (latte cups, portable yogurt containers) before they start to reek.

"I might need it someday" is just one of the many excuses a pack rat pulls out to defend his or her right to stay knee-deep in clutter. And while you can't change your clutter bug overnight (or ever), there are ways to make the situation more manageable.

Steps

1 Set aside a time when you can have a frank conversation with your dear pack rat rather than deliver an endless attack of small jabs. Discuss the problems his or her clutter is creating in the household. Are there rooms you can't use because they are crammed with too much stuff? Is there a financial cost from paying for rental units to store everything? Could he or she actually find a specific item if needed?

2 Write down what these problems are. Ask clarifying questions. Agree on a limit to the space, time and money you'll devote to managing pack-rat clutter. This limit should be less than what is currently allocated.

3 Agree to a 30-day moratorium on getting anything new, even if it's free. That means no trips to the flea market, garage or yard sales, auctions, estate sales, souvenir shops or gift shops.

4 Begin working together in one small area. Piece by piece, sort through the stuff, decluttering as you go. When the process is underway and an organizing system well established, peel out and let the pack rat handle the job alone. If that's too overwhelming, call in a pro. (See 1 Get Organized, 5 Hire a Professional Organizer and 37 Conquer Clutter.)

5 Be patient and not judgmental with your pack rat as you make joint decisions about what to keep and what to eliminate. Pose questions that help him or her be more realistic about what to get rid of. See 8 Overcome Chronic Disorganization.

6 Act immediately on discarded items, removing them in bags or boxes and taking them to donation or disposal sites (see 12 Get Rid of What You Don't Want).

7 Repeat these sort-and-purge sessions until your pack rat has gone through everything. Extend the moratorium on acquiring new items if needed in order to finish the initial purge.

8 Talk about and agree on where the best place is for storing the pack rat's scaled-back possessions. If possible, set aside a separate room. Reach an agreement that the collections will stay

Tips

Create a visual reminder of the pack rat's space limitations by placing tape on the floor as a boundary line.

If there are duplicates of a particular item, ask the pack rat to pick a favorite to keep and donate the rest.

Warning

Hold the line: If the pack rat doesn't abide by the new agreement, box up the stuff and take to the dump. Then see 287 Plan an Amicable Divorce.

within the boundaries of that space. (See 56 End Collection Chaos.) Add shelving units if it makes the area more manageable. Put up a folding screen divider if the space borders on other living areas.

9 Set a good example for the pack rat and regularly get rid of your own unused possessions.

50 Sell Stuff Online

If you'd like to make some cash and you don't have the time, space or patience for a garage sale, set up your own cybershop. There are literally millions of people online looking for items to buy, and it couldn't be easier to connect with them. Use existing venues or set up your own Internet store.

Steps

1 Go to sites like Amazon.com or Half.com to sell used books, CDs and other items at a fixed price. You can list items in exchange for a percentage of the sale. Avoid sites that charge a fee for posting an ad.

2 List items that are hard to ship (garden furniture, a pool table, a futon) on sites such as CraigsList.org or in regional online classifieds, so that the buyer can pick them up in person.

3 Use auction sites to sell valuable collectibles, antiques and out-of-print books to the highest bidder.

4 Set up an online store. Check out Amazon.com, eBay.com and Yahoo Shopping (shopping.yahoo.com) for turnkey solutions to building an online store for a monthly fee. The bonus is that you tap into the heavy traffic of these popular sites and take advantage of their search engines.

5 Contact a company like Bidadoo.com, which can sell your stuff on eBay for you in exchange for a percentage of the selling price. These businesses edit and upload your photos and come up with the right bidding price after researching what similar items go for.

Tips

Image is everything when you sell online. Post copy that is free of errors. Include high-quality, well-cropped photos of your product as well as all dimensions.

See 95 Plan a Yard or Garage Sale.

Who Knew?

Consider paying a small fee to learn the ins and outs of online selling through community education classes or eBay University (pages.ebay.com/university).

In this age of changing media where you can download audio books, print out electronic books and find reference materials on virtually anything online, what is the purpose of owning a book? Truth is, books are still valuable, no matter how fast the digital world moves—or perhaps because of it. Pare down the literary mountain in your home and keep only those books you want.

Steps

1 Mull over the role books play in your life. Do piles of books make you feel cozy and literate? Are your shelves rich with volumes of literature, drama and history that you *know* would make you a better person if you read them—but that you also know you never will? To some people, books are sacred and not to be thrown away: Are your old college textbooks collecting dust? Do you still have a shelf of Encyclopedia Britannica volumes? Once you understand why you have the books you do, you can begin to figure out what to do with them.

2 Set aside a day, pick up several cardboard boxes and start the purge. Take your time (because you will leaf through old favorites) and sort your books into piles: those you're ready to give up; keepers; maybes; and those you probably won't ever read but think you should. Now get tough with yourself and go back through the maybes and probablys. Remind yourself that selling *Finnegan's Wake* does not mean you're not an intelligent person. Box up the discards for resale or donation. See 1 Get Organized and 12 Get Rid of What You Don't Want.

3 Decide what else you want to put on the shelves besides books, such as photo albums, magazines, videos, DVDs, cassettes and CDs. See 137 Organize Movies, Music and Other Media.

4 Stack the books and other items you would like to store and take a linear measurement of the piles, then compare that number to your available shelf space. If you're short on shelves, cull your "keep" pile or put up more shelves.

5 Separate books into categories according to your tastes: fiction, new literature, everything golf, the Civil War, cheap mysteries and cookbooks, for example. Sort movies into kids' and adult films (comedy, drama, action), CDs and tapes into genres.

6 Start putting everything back on the shelves. Reserve the most easily reached shelves for books, movies and music you enjoy frequently. Keep different categories of books on separate shelves or even in other rooms (unless you're lucky enough to have a library): atlas and reference books in the study, kids' books and videos in an easily accessed shelf in their room, new fiction on your bedside table and so on. Alphabetize extensive collections and sort by genre.

Tips

Avoid wasting your shelves on just a few very tall coffee-table books—instead, lay them flat in a stack of three or four on a shorter shelf. Place an objet d'art on the stack as a design accent. See 56 End Collection Chaos.

Label your shelves if you have a large collection and need to constantly refer to various volumes. See 57 Live Better Through Labeling.

See 300 Organize Recipes and Cookbooks.

Who Knew?

Store cassettes, CDs, videos and DVDs away from any heat sources that may be close to the bookshelf.

Don't fill every available inch of shelf space. Allow for growth, especially if you're a bookstore addict. Wean yourself, if you're turning over a new leaf (see 227 Get Out of Debt and 228 Design a Savings Plan) with frequent visits to the library. Or, wait to buy books until they come out in paperback. See 15 Live With Less.

7 Shelve magazines and periodicals in stand-up files labeled by publication and time period, for example, "Gourmet 2004." See 52 Categorize Newspaper and Magazine Clippings.

8 Set up a log on the computer if you have an extensive collection. Arrange titles alphabetically for each category and note the shelf or room the book is kept, and any that are on loan to a friend. Place a copy of the log in a binder on the bookshelf and keep the master log in your filing system. See 3 Write an Effective To-Do List.

Warning

If you're in an earthquake-prone area, secure free-standing bookshelves to the wall. See 105 Prepare Your Home for Nature's Worst and 73 Make Your House Safe for Small Children.

---

52 | Categorize Newspaper and Magazine Clippings

Has your stack of unread newspapers turned from a nuisance into a firetrap? Have you vowed to never again dig through a jumble of clippings just to find that certain article, recipe, exercising tip or decorating idea? Put an end to the endless pileup of information by creating a permanent home for all those loose but intriguing and useful articles.

Steps

1 Set aside a few hours to cull your piles. Go through the newspapers and magazines and cut out or photocopy the pages you want to keep. Don't read them. Recycle the rest.

2 Sort the clippings into general categories, such as finance, inspiration, health, gardening, recipes and project ideas. File by subject groupings into hanging files or an expanding accordion file.

3 Label your finished files with category names that help you recognize the contents. Name each file according to how you plan to use it; that will make it easier to find what you want later. For example, use the label "Travel Destination Ideas" instead of "Sunday Travel Section Articles." See 185 Create a Flawless Filing System.

4 Clip any new articles you want to keep and place them right away into the appropriate folder or binder section. Photocopy large papers down to 8½-by-11–inch size to fit in folders easily.

5 Pick up your clipping file when you're looking for something to read. You'll be familiar with what's available, and more likely to remember you have it when the need arises.

6 Keep magazines in handsome boxes and create a unified look on your bookshelves (see 51 Organize Your Bookshelves). Shop at stores such as Levenger.com, Hold Everything (holdeverything.com) and the Container Store (thecontainerstore.com).

Tips

If you are a do-it-yourselfer and you often clip information describing processes, set up a how-to binder, with tabbed categories such as repairs, home care, decorating, and yard and garden. Make an article index at the front of each category for quick retrieval.

Date recipes when you file them, and commit to either try or toss them within two years. See 300 Organize Recipes and Cookbooks.

53 | Organize Your Photos

You love snapping those pictures and then flipping through the newly developed packet of captured memories or scrolling through your digital images. But you may not love the next step—*doing* something with all those photographs. Start today to create a picture-perfect system for containing and protecting your photos.

Steps

Prints

1 Gather photos from every corner and closet of your home. You'll end up with a pile of stray photos and lots of packets.

2 Flip through the packets, note the event and date on the outside top edge, and put them in a shoe box. If it will be a while before you do anything with the photos, remove them from their paper envelopes and put them into labeled acid-free and PVC-free envelopes (such as those at RetrospectBySmead.com).

3 Buy several plastic recipe boxes with tabs. Create a list of categories such as "Summer 2002, Trip to France" or "Family Reunion." File all your loose photos into one of these categories or simply label the tabs (or boxes) by year for speedy sorting.

4 Choose a system to store and display your photos. Shop online at Exposures.com, Organize-Everything.com and other stores for acid-free albums and archival systems. Select a wooden photo box, insert a favorite photo into the glass lid, and slip hundreds of 5-by-7 photos inside—without hassling with plastic sleeves.

5 Cut yourself some slack if you think you should be making scrapbooks for photos but don't have the time just now. Protect the photos first, and reserve the option to create scrapbooks later.

6 Develop the habit of labeling and storing photos in albums as you process each roll of film. You'll always be able to pull out photos for projects and duplication as you need them.

Digital photos

1 Decide what you want to do with your photos. Do you just e-mail them to friends and family? Do you ever print out or blow up favorites? If you never print any, save your images to the 72-dpi size and free up massive amounts of room on your hard drive. If there's even a chance you'll want to print them, burn larger-resolution images to a CD and keep thumbnails (tiny screen representations that you can easily scroll through) on your computer.

2 Back up your files frequently. After you download the photos and trash the duds, burn the files onto a CD or DVD. Label the discs and store them on a spindle or in jewel cases or a CD book.

3 Store photos in a folder on your computer, or plug in an external hard drive and store them there to free up space on your system.

Tips

See 137 Organize Movies, Music and Other Media.

Buy the type and color of album that you like in quantity. A cluster of identical albums is much more visually appealing on a bookshelf than odd sizes and varied colors.

Create some albums around themes such as vacations or holiday celebrations.

Toss out prints and delete digital images that are blurry or badly exposed. Don't clog up your system with photos you don't want to see or share.

Investigate a variety of software programs such as iView Media Pro that let you create top-quality digital slide shows.

For fast and safe transfers, buy a digital-card reader that fits your particular type of camera and media card.

Who Knew?

Transfer negatives to labeled sleeve protectors (available at photo-supply stores or CenturyPhoto.com). Keep the protectors in an archival, acid-free binder or an expanding multipocket organizer. Include index prints, which show a thumbnail of each shot on a roll. APS-processed film comes with index prints; for 35 mm negatives, you can have an index print made for about $2.

Or buy an iPod and an adapter, and transfer digital photos on the fly from your camera to the iPod for 20 or 40 gigabytes of instant storage.

4 Transfer the digital photos from your camera to your computer and devise a consistent naming system. Create a folder structure, organizing the pictures first by year, then by event. For large events, such as weddings, you may need subfolders.

5 Take advantage of digital asset management software to make fast work of organizing and cataloging all of your digital photos. Macintosh users will love the incredibly easy-to-use and powerful iPhoto. Other programs such as Picasa (free from Google .com), Cumulus (canto.com), Portfolio (extensis.com), Adobe PhotoShop Album (adobe.com) and Paint Shop Photo Album (JASC.com) also have a dizzying array of features. Check platform requirements and consider what your needs are when weighing the costs of any asset management system. Alternatively, sign up for free (or cheap) services such as Shutterfly .com and Ofoto.com. Upload photos, create albums and share pictures with unlimited online storage as a bonus.

Warnings

Always make sure a CD is readable before deleting images off your hard drive.

Never use a ballpoint pen to label photos or CDs.

Heat, cold, humidity and direct sunlight will degrade photos, negatives and CDs. Store photo boxes, albums and other archives in areas where temperatures stay between 40 and 70 degrees F (4 and 21 C) and relative humidity stays below 60 percent. Avoid storing photos in basements and attics, or near vents.

54 | Arrange Photos and Pictures

An open wall or bare tabletop is a canvas just waiting for your photos and pictures to light it up. But before you start randomly pounding in nails and hooks, take some time to plan out the best approach for displaying your treasures.

Steps

1 Group similar photographs, framed prints and other artwork. Create a relationship among a variety of pieces. For instance, put black-and-white portraits together in one grouping, modern art pieces in another, and landscapes in yet another. Arranging pictures and photos around a theme brings purpose to an open space. Use an odd number of items on walls or tabletop groupings to create balance (unless you have just two pieces).

2 Choose frames that complement each other. A multitude of frame styles is distracting and detracts from the arrangement.

3 Cut out templates in brown kraft paper for each piece in a group (if you're hanging pictures on the wall) and label them to identify the item they represent.

4 Arrange a group's templates on an open wall, securing them with masking tape. Start with the largest piece in the center and then, working out to the sides, add smaller pieces. As a guide for spacing, allow no more than a hand's width between pieces in

Tips

Display artwork on an artist's easel for added dimension.

Arranging pictures and photos vertically makes a room seem higher. Likewise, horizontal arrangements make a room seem wider.

When hanging items on a papered wall, cut a small **V** through the wallpaper using a utility blade. Lift the **V** and drive the nail in underneath. If you move the picture or photo later, glue the wallpaper flap down again and no one will be the wiser.

Frame black and white pictures in all black or all white frames for a striking, classic arrangement.

Continued on next page

a group. Expand above and below as the space and number of items allow.

5 Continue adding and moving template pieces until you find the desired balance. Avoid hanging all items in a straight line. Varying heights add interest to the sight lines.

6 Line up the horizontal center of each group or of an individual piece so that it is at eye level on the wall. Average eye level falls between 5 feet 8 inches and 5 feet 10 inches. For homes with people of greatly varying heights, find the midpoint between the eye level of the tallest and shortest persons. You can also drop the centerline 1 to 2 feet in areas where the admirers will mostly be seated, as in a living room.

7 Choose hanging hardware strong enough to support the weight of each item (look on the hook's package for weight limitations) and suitable for the type of wall you have. Use two hooks when hanging heavy or wide items. Use specialty hangers designed for brick walls instead of drilling directly into brick or mortar. If you live in an earthquake-prone zone, take special care in hanging large and/or heavy items. Consult a professional for choosing appropriate hardware and techniques.

Leave nail holes worries behind: Try 3M Command Hooks (mmm.com), which can be removed from a wall without causing damage. They are especially helpful in rental units or college dorms where hooks and nails aren't allowed.

Warning

Plaster walls may chip or crack when you use picture-hanging hardware. Make sure to minimize damage by placing an **X** of tape centered at the desired location before hammering in the nail.

---

55 | Arrange an Art Collection

You've plunked down your hard-earned cash on another acquisition for your home museum. Now take the time to organize and protect your new treasure so that its value will only appreciate.

Steps

1 Read 56 End Collection Chaos. Take an inventory of all items in the collection. Include the title of the piece, artist's name, date of issue, current condition, when and where you purchased it, purchase price and current value.

2 Look into software to help you organize, catalog and manage collections. One example, Art and Antiques Organizer Deluxe (primasoft.com), is geared toward private and corporate collectors, small galleries, artists and dealers.

3 Protect artwork from heat sources such as chimneys and vents as well as direct sunlight when choosing display locations. Also beware of humidity and dampness or any area with fluctuating temperatures, such as a doorway or outside wall.

4 Find proper storage for pieces that are not currently on display or that you'll be rotating in and out of display areas. Avoid basements, attics and garages, which have moisture and temperature issues. An interior closet on the main floor is a good choice. Otherwise, contact a local art dealer regarding professional storage.

Tips

Store framed pieces in labeled shipping boxes, or place them upright with cloth protection between and under items. The cloth must not come into contact with the surface of an oil painting.

Gather in one location books, pamphlets, articles and any other information about each artist and work.

Warnings

Cigar and cigarette smoke damages artwork over time.

Never spray cleaner directly on the glass. Spray a cloth first, then wipe the glass, avoiding its outer edges.

You call yourself a collector; your friends think you're a pack rat. Yes, there can be too much of a good thing. Pare down your gaggle of Hummels and rare enamelware, then display the best of the lot.

Steps

1 Focus, focus, focus. You can't collect everything, so devote your space, time and money to a few favorites—or just one specialty. Try not to let unintentional collections distract you from the ones you love or have a great interest in.

2 Know when the time comes to either quit adding to your collection or sell it off. This will be determined by the space available for display and storage, your budget and how much time you have to manage and care for your collections.

3 Know what you own. Inventory and catalog all pieces in a database. Include the manufacturer, issue date, purchase price, series name and number, and any other pertinent information. It can also be helpful to photograph or videotape collections. Keep the photos or video in a safe location, along with a copy of the inventory. Place the original inventory near the collections for ready reference, or in a file drawer.

4 Get appraisals if individual pieces or the collection as a whole is valuable. Ask your insurance agent if your homeowner's or renter's policy is adequate for the full replacement cost of valuable collections.

5 Properly pack and protect surplus items that aren't on display, selecting containers based on the items' value and fragility. Log the contents of each container; keep the original log with other collection documents and a copy with the stored items.

6 Build or buy pieces to display and protect your collection (see chart below). Shop for these in craft, hobby or gift stores, and online.

Tips

Create a revolving display area for flat items such as photos, autographs, stamps and postcards by having a glass top cut to fit a coffee or end table.

Browse collector's magazines for resources for storage and organizing tools as well as for pricing information.

See 49 Deal With a Pack Rat.

Add and delete from the inventory catalog and storage logs as you acquire new items and rotate or eliminate existing ones.

Who Knew?

Displaying a unified collection has more impact from a design perspective than scattering pieces around a room.

Always include an organizing tool with any collection gift to a child. It gets him or her started in the right direction.

Racks and Shelves	Binders	Display Cases	Bowls
Matchbooks	• Trading cards	Figurines	• Wine corks
Golf balls	• Stamps	Dolls	• Beach glass
Teacups	• Coins	Ceramic villages	• Shells
Collector plates	• Greeting cards	Seashells	• Coins
Bells	• Postcards	Historical memorabilia	• Marbles
Model trains, cars	• Golf score cards	Jewelry	
Porcelain, enamelware	• Vintage produce labels	Crystal	
Silver serving dishes			

Live Better Through Labeling

Now that everything is in its place, how will you remember which bin holds what? Whether you use a handheld battery-operated labeler, color-coded stickers or even just a grease pencil, knowing what's where in a glance will help you stay organized.

Steps

1 Choose your labeler. File stickers or a battery-operated labeler are options. For slick surfaces such as plastic bags and tubs, use a grease pencil or write on masking tape. For fabrics, opt for a laundry marker or sew-in labels.

2 Color your world. Get different-hued key jackets to use the right key on the first try. Use colored tubs for each holiday, and plastic hangers to designate work, casual and dressy clothing.

3 Label containers of children's toys with pictures from packaging or catalogs and place them next to written labels.

Tip

Children are more likely to return playthings to the correct labeled container and at the same time will develop reading skills.

Warning

Always label any product you've taken out of its original packaging. Also transfer expiration dates.

LOCATION	WHAT TO LABEL
Kitchen	• Snack bins. • Storage containers for flour, sugar, rice, pasta and baking supplies. • Pantry shelves by category (soups, canned fruit or vegetables, condiments). • Refrigerated and frozen leftovers and cuts of meat (with date of storage).
Family and Living Room	• Shelves in bookcases or cabinets that store games and puzzles. • Containers or drawers that hold CDs, videotapes and DVDs. • Containers of kids' and adults' craft and art supplies. • Bins of toys—action figures, building blocks, dolls.
Bathroom	• Containers for various supplies—including first aid, cold and cough, body care, hair care and dental care.
Bedrooms and Closets	• Kids' dresser drawers, sorted by contents. • Storage boxes for out-of-season clothes. • Shoe boxes for seasonal or specialty footwear.
Basement, Attic and Storage Closets	• Paint cans labeled with a brush swipe of the color and the room. • Sets of china and glassware in protective cases.
Garage	• Bins for auto and garden supplies, tools, camping and sports equipment.
Home Office	• Magazine files holding catalogs or periodicals. • Grouped supplies contained in closets. • Wires and cords for computer and office equipment.

If it were true that all that glitters is gold, your jam-packed jewelry box might be worth a mint. But even if you don't own the crown jewels, keep your jewelry tidy—that way you'll always be able to pull out what you want without searching for the missing earring or untangling a chain.

Steps

1 Scan your jewelry with a critical eye. Eliminate out-of-style, worn-out, mismatched, never-worn and broken pieces. See 12 Get Rid of What You Don't Want.

2 Clean and fix any keepers that are tarnished or in disrepair.

3 Clean silver with silver polish or a jewelers cloth. Or rub the piece with toothpaste, using an old toothbrush to get into cracks. Rinse.

4 Clean gold, platinum and diamonds by dropping two Alka-Seltzer tablets in a glass of water and immersing the jewelry for about two minutes. Or soak for several minutes in a bowl of warm water with dishwashing liquid. Rinse and polish with a smooth, lint-free cloth or chamois.

5 Store like items together. Keep specialty items in their original boxes if you like, labeling the box's exterior. Storing silver pieces in felt jewelry pouches prevents tarnishing and keeps items ready to wear. (See 138 Store China and Family Heirlooms.)

6 Choose the best location and storage for your jewelry. A traditional jewelry box on a dresser can adequately accommodate smaller collections. Shallow dresser drawers outfitted with trays and organizers manage larger collections in style.

7 Protect valuable pieces of jewelry and items with great sentimental worth in an at-home safe or in a bank's safe-deposit box. Make sure you properly value and insure these items in case of loss (see 56 End Collection Chaos).

Tips

To prevent kinks from forming in link necklaces, run the chain through a straw and fasten the clasp. Lay it flat in a drawer or tray.

Create an attractive storage piece for pierced earrings by placing a cut-to-fit window screen or a piece of cross-stitch fabric in an easel frame. Secure earrings through the material.

See 326 Find the Perfect Wedding Ring.

Warning

Keep jewelry away from chlorine and harsh chemicals, which can erode the finish and polish of gems.

RGANIZE YOUR CONTACTS • GET RID OF WHAT YOU DON'T WANT • SAY NO WITHOUT FEELING GUILTY • BALANCE HOME AND WORK • LI
3AIN • SCHEDULE TELEVISION WATCHING • DESIGN A HEALTHY LIFESTYLE • PLAN TO AVOID JUNK FOOD • CHOOSE A WEIGHT LOSS PLA
EET AN ONLINE DATE • PLAN THE PERFECT DATE • MASTERMIND A BREAKUP • PLAN YOUR SOCIAL CALENDAR • MEET MR. OR MS. RIGH
ORT YOUR SOCK DRAWER • RETURN RENTALS ON TIME • TAKE CONTROL OF YOUR JUNK DRAWER • ORGANIZE THE MEDICINE CABINET
AR CLEAN AND ORDERLY • DEAL WITH A PACK RAT • SELL STUFF ONLINE • ORGANIZE YOUR BOOKSHELVES • CATEGORIZE NEWSPAPER
VE BETTER THROUGH LABELING • ORGANIZE JEWELRY • PLAN YOUR DREAM KITCHEN • CONQUER YOUR CLOSETS • ORGANIZE THE LIN
RGANIZE SPRING CLEANING • KEEP THE FAMILY ROOM ORGANIZED • SET UP A BATHROOM SCHEDULE • ORGANIZE BATHROOMS • ORG
RGANIZE KIDS' ROOMS • ORGANIZE SPORTS EQUIPMENT • ORGANIZE KIDS' PLAY SPACES • SAFEGUARD YOUR HOME AGAINST ALLERG
OUSE • USE HOME DESIGN AND PLANNING SOFTWARE • ESTABLISH YOUR HOME'S SPACE PLAN • INCORPORATE UNIVERSAL DESIGN PI
HE BASEMENT • ORGANIZE THE GARAGE • ORGANIZE A TOOLBOX • SET UP A WOODSHOP • ORGANIZE YOUR WINE COLLECTION • PLAN
TUDIO OR SMALL APARTMENT • MANAGE WARRANTY DOCUMENTS • MANAGE HOME-IMPROVEMENT PAPERWORK • MERGE TWO HOUSE
RGANIC VEGETABLE GARDEN • PLANT A KITCHEN HERB GARDEN • PLAN A BUTTERFLY GARDEN • DESIGN A BIRD GARDEN • DESIGN A C
ORGANIZE GARDENING TOOLS • ADD A POTTING BENCH TO A YARD • SCHEDULE FRUIT TREE MAINTENANCE • LAY OUT A SPRINKLER S
ESIGN A GARDEN PATH • SET UP A COMPOST SYSTEM • WINTERIZE PLANTS • SCHEDULE YARD WORK • STORE ANYTHING • STORE BUL
ND HOBBY MATERIALS • ORGANIZE ART SUPPLIES • ORGANIZE GIFT WRAP AND SEASONAL DECORATIONS • ORGANIZE KIDS' SCHOOLW
OUR WEDDING DRESS AND OTHER TEXTILES • STORE A FUR COAT • STORE BICYCLES AND GEAR • STORE SKI GEAR • ORGANIZE CAMP
HICH COLLEGE IS RIGHT FOR YOU • GET INTO A TOP COLLEGE OR UNIVERSITY • ACE THE COLLEGE ADMISSIONS TESTS • ORGANIZE Y
AW SCHOOL • PREPARE FOR THE BAR EXAM • GET A DEGREE WHILE YOU'RE WORKING • WORK AT HOME WITH KIDS • GO BACK TO WO
RGANIZE YOUR JOB SEARCH • PREPARE FOR A CAREER CHANGE • OPEN A RESTAURANT • BECOME A PHYSICIST • BECOME A CONCEI
EALITY-SHOW CONCEPT • BECOME A TALK-SHOW HOST • BECOME A PHOTOJOURNALIST • BECOME A MOVIE DIRECTOR • BECOME A N
LING SYSTEM • ORGANIZE YOUR BRIEFCASE • ORGANIZE YOUR DESK • ORGANIZE YOUR WORKDAY • GET A HANDLE ON E-MAIL • ORG
ALARY REVIEW • CLIMB THE CORPORATE LADDER EFFECTIVELY • ADD A WORKSPACE TO ANY ROOM • ORGANIZE A HOME OFFICE • OR
RAVEL • WRITE A BUSINESS PLAN • SET UP A NEW BUSINESS • CREATE A MARKETING PLAN • AMASS A REAL-ESTATE EMPIRE • POLISH
MPLOYEE • FIRE AN EMPLOYEE • PASS ON A FAMILY BUSINESS • STAY ON TOP OF YOUR SALES GAME • RESTRUCTURE A COMPANY TO
EFEND AGAINST A HOSTILE TAKEOVER • ORGANIZE YOUR OFFICE FOR A MOVE • PREPARE YOUR BUSINESS FOR THE UNTHINKABLE • F
REPARE YOUR TAXES • ORGANIZE A LOAN APPLICATION • ORGANIZE IMPORTANT DOCUMENTS • SAVE FOR PRIVATE SCHOOLING • ORG
LUB • TRACK YOUR INVESTMENTS • SURVIVE BANKRUPTCY • PLAN FOR RETIREMENT • PREPARE A PRENUPTIAL AGREEMENT • CREATI
ONEY • PLAN YOUR FAMILY • BUDGET FOR A NEW BABY • ORCHESTRATE THE PERFECT CONCEPTION • PLAN FOR ARTIFICIAL INSEMIN
EAVE • ORDER BABY ANNOUNCEMENTS • ORGANIZE AN INTERNATIONAL ADOPTION • FOSTER A CHILD • ORGANIZE YOUR LIFE AS A NE
OORDINATE A FAMILY CALENDAR • PLAN FAMILY MEETINGS • ORGANIZE HOME SYSTEMS FOR ADD • PREPARE FOR A NEW CAT OR DOC
ACK-TO-SCHOOL • WIN THE HOMEWORK WARS • PLAN A FIELD TRIP • PLAN YOUR CHILD'S ACTIVITIES • PLAN YOUR CHILDREN'S SUM
NLINE • ORGANIZE A GENEALOGICAL SEARCH • PREPARE FOR YOUR CHILD'S DEPARTURE FOR COLLEGE • ORGANIZE YOUR EMPTY NI
LDERLY PARENTS' CARE • PREPARE FOR THE DEATH OF A SPOUSE • HELP YOUR ELDERLY PARENTS MOVE • ORGANIZE A HOME MEDIC
TORE TRIPS • SET UP ONLINE GROCERY SHOPPING • ORGANIZE RECIPES AND COOKBOOKS • PLAN THEME MENUS • CREATE EFFECTI
EFRIGERATOR AND FREEZER • ORGANIZE CUTLERY AND KITCHEN TOOLS • ORGANIZE CUPBOARDS AND DRAWERS • ORGANIZE THE P
UNCHES FOR KIDS • PLAN PARTY FOODS AHEAD • THROW A DINNER PARTY • FINISH DINNER ON TIME • PULL OFF A LAST-MINUTE PAR
LTIMATE WEDDING CHECKLIST • BUDGET FOR A WEDDING • FIND THE PERFECT WEDDING RING • PLAN AN ELOPEMENT • SET UP A BA
ONOR • EXECUTE BEST MAN DUTIES • HIRE A BAND • HIRE A BARTENDER • PLAN A SHOWER • ORGANIZE THE REHEARSAL DINNER • F
UCCESSFUL SLUMBER PARTY • PLAN A BAR OR BAT MITZVAH • PLAN A QUINCEAÑERA • PLAN A RETIREMENT PARTY • PLAN A FUNER
ANUKKAH PARTY • ORGANIZE A HOLIDAY CRAFT PARTY • PLAN TO SPEND CHRISTMAS SOLO • PLAN THE PERFECT HOLIDAY GIFT EXC
HE HOLIDAYS • STICK TO YOUR NEW YEAR'S RESOLUTIONS • PLAN THE PERFECT NEW YEAR'S EVE • PLAN A SEDER • PLAN A SPECIA
OOD TREE • ORGANIZE A BICYCLE SCAVENGER HUNT • RUN A SPORTS TOURNAMENT • PUBLICIZE AN EVENT • PLAN AN ORGANIZATIO
LAN A CONCERT IN THE PARK • ORGANIZE AN INTERNATIONAL CONCERT TOUR • ORGANIZE A FILM FESTIVAL • PLAN A FUND-RAISING
BUILD A COMMUNITY PLAY STRUCTURE • THROW A BLOCK PARTY • SET UP A NEIGHBORHOOD WATCH • CREATE AN EVACUATION PL
RGANIZE A PROTEST OR MARCH • FIGHT CITY HALL • ORGANIZE A BOYCOTT • ORGANIZE A CLASS ACTION LAWSUIT • MANAGE GROV
CHOOL IN A THIRD WORLD COUNTRY • PLAN A TRIP • PLAN A TRIP WITH CHILDREN • TRAVEL WITH TEENS • BOOK AIRLINE TICKETS •
OTORCYCLE TRIP • PLAN A TRAIN TRIP IN THE UNITED STATES • RIDE THE RAILS ABROAD • PREPARE A VACATION COUNTDOWN CHEC
UGGAGE • LOAD A BACKPACK PROPERLY • PLAN AN ELDERHOSTEL TRIP • ORGANIZE AN RV VACATION • PLAN A TRIP WITH AGING PA
IDELY DIFFERENT PEOPLE • PLAN SPRING BREAK • PLAN AN OVERNIGHT GETAWAY WITH YOUR SPOUSE • PLAN A VACATION SEPARAT
OLITICALLY UNSTABLE REGION • GET TRAVEL INSURANCE • GET IMMUNIZATIONS FOR TRAVELING • BOOK AN ADVENTURE VACATION •
LAN A FISHING TRIP TO ALASKA • PACK FOR A CAMPING TRIP • LEAD A BACKPACK TRIP • HIKE A FAMOUS TRAIL • PLAN A TOUR OF T
NGLISH CANAL TRIP • PLAN A CROSS-COUNTRY AIRPLANE VOYAGE • PLAN THE PERFECT DAY ABROAD • PLAN A VISIT TO THE LOUVR
LAN • PREPARE FOR AN ACT OF GOD • ASSEMBLE EMERGENCY KITS • PREPARE FOR SURGERY • PLAN YOUR RECOVERY • SURVIVE A
EING LOST • CONDUCT A SEARCH AND RESCUE OPERATION • PLAN AN INVASION • SURVIVE A POLITICAL COUP • PLAN FOR A TERRO

SS • SET GOALS • STREAMLINE YOUR MORNING ROUTINE • ORGANIZE A CHORE SCHEDULE FOR KIDS • ORGANIZE YOUR CHORES • NE
YOUR WORKOUT SCHEDULE • SCHEDULE DOCTOR VISITS • PREPARE FOR COLD AND FLU SEASON • GET A DRASTIC MAKEOVER • ARR
UP • FIND YOUR KEYS • TIDY UP IN MINUTES • CONQUER CLUTTER • ACTUALLY SEE THE BOTTOM OF YOUR PURSE • ORGANIZE YOUR S
E CAR MAINTENANCE • ORGANIZE PET SUPPLIES • MANAGE GARBAGE AND RECYCLABLES • PREPARE GRAB 'N' GO ACTIVITY BAGS • KE
ZINE CLIPPINGS • ORGANIZE YOUR PHOTOS • ARRANGE PHOTOS AND PICTURES • ARRANGE AN ART COLLECTION • END COLLECTION C
• ORGANIZE YOUR LAUNDRY CENTER • CREATE A SEWING CENTER • GET READY FOR THE HOUSECLEANER • ORGANIZE CLEANING SU
YWAYS AND MUDROOMS • ORGANIZE A DORM ROOM • ORGANIZE YOUR SCHOOL LOCKER • MAKE YOUR HOME SAFE FOR SMALL CHILI
RE FOR SKYROCKETING ENERGY COSTS • USE FENG SHUI TO ORGANIZE YOUR HOME • DESIGN A NEW HOME WITH FENG SHUI • DESI
PLAN A REMODEL • PLAN A MULTIMEDIA CENTER • TURN A BASEMENT INTO A MEDIA ROOM OR PLAYROOM • ORGANIZE THE ATTIC • OF
FUL ESTATE SALE • PLAN A YARD OR GARAGE SALE • PREPARE YOUR HOME FOR SALE • PLAN A MOVE • DOWNSIZE YOUR HOUSE • OR
CORATE FOR THE SEASONS • PREPARE A VACATION HOME FOR THE OFF-SEASON • PREPARE YOUR HOME FOR NATURE'S WORST • PR
GARDEN • PLANT A CUT-FLOWER GARDEN • DESIGN A SHADE GARDEN • DESIGN A DRY GARDEN • PLAN FOR A LONG-SEASON CONTAIN
N AND PLANT A LAWN • DESIGN A NEW LANDSCAPE • PLAN AN OUTDOOR KITCHEN • DESIGN A DECK OR PATIO • DESIGN A WATER FEA
S • STORAGE SOLUTIONS FOR ANY ROOM •   THE CAPACITY OF A SMALL ROOM • ORGANIZ
TWORK • ORGANIZE MOVIES, MUSIC AND O   IRLOOMS • STORE OUT-OF-SEASON CLOTHES •
NT • STORE PAINT AND OTHER HAZARDOUS   STORE A BOAT FOR THE WINTER • STORE A CA
E APPLICATIONS • PLAN YOUR COURSE OF   H PAPER • GET INTO GRAD SCHOOL • GET INTO
ONG ABSENCE • SET UP AN INTERNSHIP •   N THE PEACE CORPS • PRODUCE A NEWSLETTE
BECOME A COWBOY • BECOME A BRAIN S   ATHOLIC NUN • ORGANIZE AN EXHIBITION • DEV
OME A STUNT PERSON • BECOME A TOUR G   • CONQUER YOUR PAPER PILES • CREATE A FI
UTER FILES • SCHEDULE APPOINTMENTS EF   NCE CALL • PREPARE FOR A MEETING • PREPAR
ME NETWORK • CHOOSE THE BEST PHONE   TEM • MAKE A NETWORKING PLAN • PLAN YOUI
NTATION SKILLS • PREPARE A SPEECH • PR   AN AN IPO • DELEGATE RESPONSIBILITIES • HIRI
OFITS • FORM A BOARD OF DIRECTORS •   AN A COMPANY PICNIC • PLAN A COMPANY RET
FAILING BUSINESS • DISMANTLE A BUSINE   • DESIGN A SAVINGS PLAN • SIMPLIFY BILL PAY
NANCIAL-AID PACKAGE • PLAN FOR COLLE   E A HEALTH INSURANCE PLAN • START AN INVE
ST • MAKE A WILL • EXECUTE A POWER OF   S' ESTATE • PLAN YOUR ESTATE • TEACH YOUR '
RE FOR AN IN VITRO FERTILIZATION • PREF   ATERNITY WARDROBE • SET UP MATERNITY OR
REPARE FOR CHILDBIRTH • STOCK A DIAPE   LEND FAMILIES • CREATE A HOUSEHOLD ORGA
OL YOUR CHILD • SET UP A CARPOOL • S   HE BEST ELEMENTARY SCHOOL • ORGANIZE KID
R SUMMER CAMP • CHOOSE A SUMMER S   R FAMILY COMPUTER USE • PLAN TO KEEP YOU
BOOMERANG KIDS • PLAN AN AMICABLE   EMENTS • ORGANIZE MEDICAL RECORDS • PLAN
ARRANGE HOSPICE CARE • MAKE YOUR   ECORDS • PLAN A WEEK OF MENUS • ORGANIZ

**Heart
& Home**

STS • COOK AHEAD • DETERMINE THE SH   M WAREHOUSE STORES • EFFICIENTLY USE THE
NTLY USE SPACE UNDER THE SINK • STOV   UR COUNTER SPACE • COOK FOR ONE • PLAN I
DINNER PARTY FOR YOUR BOSS • PLAN DI   PARTY • IMPRESS A DATE • PLAN A WEDDING •
NT PLANNER • HIRE A PHOTOGRAPHER •   ACHELORETTE PARTY • PREPARE TO BE THE MA
EYMOON • PLAN A BAPTISM • PLAN A BRI   THROW A PARTY • PREPARE FOR HOUSE GUESTS • PLAN A CHILD'S BIRTHDAY PARTY •
TO CUSTOM • PLAN AHEAD FOR A LOW-STRESS HOLIDAY • STAY WITHIN A BUDGET THIS CHRISTMAS • PREPARE A HOLIDAY FEAST • T
IZE GIFT GIVING IN ADVANCE • STICK TO YOUR DIET DURING THE HOLIDAYS • PLAN A HOLIDAY OPEN HOUSE • REORGANIZE YOUR LII
ORGANIZE A HIGH-SCHOOL CLASS REUNION • PLAN A FAMILY REUNION • START A KNITTING CIRCLE • ORGANIZE A BOOK CLUB • SE
SHARPEN THE FOCUS OF AN ORGANIZATION • IMPROVE YOUR CHILD'S SCHOOL • PLAN A PROM • ORGANIZE A COMMUNITY THEATEI
IZE A PANCAKE BREAKFAST • PLAN A TOY DRIVE • HOLD A BARN RAISING • ORGANIZE A CHARITY WALK OR RUN • BUILD LOW-INCOM
ER-REGISTRATION DRIVE • RUN FOR LOCAL OFFICE • ORGANIZE A PETITION • ORGANIZE A RECALL • GET AN INITIATIVE ON THE BALL
MMUNITY • PRESERVE OPEN SPACE • SAVE HISTORIC PROPERTIES AND LANDMARKS • SET UP A NONGOVERNMENTAL ORGANIZATION
HE UNITED STATES • RENT A CAR ABROAD • MAKE HOTEL RESERVATIONS • ARRANGE EXECUTIVE ACCOMMODATIONS • PLAN A CRUIS
E AN ITINERARY • PACK FOR A TRIP • PACK FOR A BUSINESS TRIP • PACK FOR A WEEK IN ONE CARRY-ON • PACK A DAY BAG • PREVE
ZE A SAILING TEAM • PLAN A SAILBOAT CRUISE • PLAN A BICYCLE TRIP WITH A TOUR COMPANY • TRAVEL ABROAD • PLAN A VACATIO
OUSE • PLAN A TRIP TO A DIFFERENT CULTURE • FORAGE ABROAD • MAIL PACKAGES BACK TO THE UNITED STATES • PLAN A TRIP T
K ROAD • PLAN A CLIMB OF MOUNT KILIMANJARO • PACK FOR A SAFARI • ORGANIZE A HUNTING TRIP • PACK FOR A FISHING OR HUN
KS • ORGANIZE A BACKCOUNTRY SKI TRIP • ORGANIZE A CAR RALLY • PLAN A WHALE-WATCHING TRIP • PACK FOR A VOYAGE AT SE
DNEY HARBOUR BRIDGE • PLAN A TRIP TO NEW ORLEANS FOR MARDI GRAS • PLAN A DAY AT DISNEYLAND • FORMULATE A FAMILY I
F YOU'RE ALONE • SURVIVE IF YOUR CAR BREAKS DOWN • DEAL WITH AMNESIA • FIGHT AN EBOLA OUTBREAK • FIGHT A FOREST FIR
SCUE A HOSTAGE • OUTSMART PIRATES • DELIVER A BABY • MAKE AN EMERGENCY LANDING • MAKE A JAIL BREAK • BECOME A MO

59 | Plan Your Dream Kitchen

Today's kitchens are the heart of entertaining and family life. Many house televisions and computers, in addition to numerous must-have cooking gadgets. Planning your own kitchen just the way you'd like it—pure heaven. Read on for tips to make your dream come true.

Steps

1 Read 85 Plan a Remodel. All of the information there applies to designing and remodeling a kitchen as well as an entire home.

2 Visit kitchen showrooms, open houses and home design stores, and take photos of what you like. Flip through magazines, and watch remodeling and cooking shows on television. Create two lists: a functional wish list (appliances, cabinet arrangements, islands and the like) and a list of style preferences (surfaces, colors, finishes and such).

3 Assess your storage needs. Count and measure pots and pans, plates and silverware, appliances, tools, linens, foods and ingredients, wines, special display items (vases, platters, artwork) and electronics (computers, televisions, radios). Use this information to determine how much cabinetry you need. Cabinets can tally up to half the cost of your new kitchen, depending on quality and material and whether they are stock units or custom-made.

4 Have all plumbing work done before the cabinets go in, when the walls are open.

5 Plan lighting and the placement of electrical outlets at this time, too. Three types of lighting are typically used in dream kitchens: ambient (for the room), task (for specific workstations, such as stoves or sinks), and spot (for display of food or decor). An electrician should also run television cable, telephone wire and computer network wire when the walls are open.

6 Choose surfaces carefully. Kitchens are hot, wet, messy places, so look for surfaces that balance cleanliness, durability and attractiveness. Ask about features of various surfaces—does will that gorgeous granite you covet, for example, become discolored under a hot pot?

7 Price out and prioritize all the elements of your dream kitchen, and reality-check this information against how much you're willing to spend. A kitchen remodel should not cost more than 15 percent of the total value of your house; if it does, you're overimproving. A new kitchen will return, at best, 80 percent of its cost in increased home value.

8 Make some strategic cuts to your plan, with an eye toward staying in budget without sabotaging your overall goals. Sensible cuts include keeping your current appliances (upgrade them later) and choosing semicustom cabinets rather than custom.

Tips

Don't skimp when buying cabinets. Get plywood panels (not particleboard) and insist on dovetailed or doweled drawer boxes. The quality of semicustom cabinets can be remarkably good.

Multiple sinks are common in high-end kitchens because they can separate food preparation from cleanup.

Who Knew?

Remember, you need to eat while your kitchen remodel is under way. If you can remodel in the summer, you can barbecue outside and eat salads and other simple meals. You may still end up washing your dishes in the bathtub. Some kitchen contractors will create a temporary kitchen in a laundry room or garage.

Certified Kitchen Designers have at least seven years of experience and training, have completed 60 hours of specialized training, and have passed a kitchen designers' exam.

9 Factor in the cost of a professional design. A kitchen designer typically charges 6 percent of the finished cost of the project, but may also work by the hour (at a rate of $50 to $150 per hour).

10 Understand how space and proportion work in your kitchen. The classic kitchen work triangle—the total distance between sink, stove and refrigerator—should be 12 to 26 feet (3.7 to 7.9 m). Working aisles should be at least 42 inches (107 cm) for one cook, 48 inches (122 cm) for two. Base cabinets plus counter-tops should be 36 inches (91 cm) high, but can be 42 inches (107 cm) high if they incorporate a seating area with stools. The bottoms of wall- or ceiling-mounted cabinets should be at least 18 inches (46 cm) above countertops and higher over stoves. Check local building codes.

60 | Conquer Your Closets

It's said that clothing, like other areas in life, follows the 80:20 rule—we wear 20 percent of our wardrobe 80 percent of the time. Cull your clothes and organize your closets, and you'll wear more of what you own more often—and have a closet even your mother would love.

Steps

Pare down

1 Set aside time to clear out your bedroom closet and sort through everything in it. This could easily take a full day. Read 1 Get Organized for the full drill.

2 Remove everything from the closet. While doing this, put any-thing that belongs somewhere else in a box; when you're done sorting, return things to their proper home.

3 Try on each item of clothing in a full-length mirror and ask your-self these questions: Does it fit? Is it in style? Is it in season? Does it need mending? How long has it been since I've worn it? Is it a duplicate? Is it comfortable? Does it look good on me? Do I love it?

4 Sort everything into one of four piles as you take them off: keep, repair, throw out (beyond repair), and sell or donate. See 12 Get Rid of What You Don't Want.

5 Get rid of near-duplicate items. Keep just two blazers instead of six, for example.

6 Pull out seasonal clothing from your "keep" pile and store it in a separate area. See 139 Store Out-of-Season Clothes.

Tips

If you've kept a lot of clothes for several years because you think they may fit again, choose just one favorite piece (as an incentive) and get rid of the rest. When you shed those pounds, reward yourself with a new wardrobe.

Use plastic or wooden hangers, not wire. Wire hangers don't support clothing well and make for a messy-looking closet.

Who Knew?

Some city housing codes require fluorescent lights in closets to save electricity.

Continued on next page

Organize what's left

1 See if your closet fits your newly pared-down wardrobe. Is there an area for long garments as well as short ones? Is the shoe storage adequate? Is there room for hats, ties, belts, purses and other accessories? If the closet is largely OK, skip to step 4.

2 Call in a professional if your needs are great and time is short. Look in the yellow pages under "Closets and Closet Accessories" for a company near you. Many custom closet design companies offer free in-home consultations.

3 Go to a specialty shop if your closet needs help, but you think you can do it yourself. Many organizing stores, such as the Container Store and Organized Living, offer free closet- and space-planning services. Bring your closet measurements and the amount of different spaces you need. (Planning and purchasing a system may involve several trips.)

4 Head for a department store, a home-improvement center or online retailers such as HoldEverything.com and TheContainer Store.com if your closet just needs a minor tweaking. Look for second rods, additional shelves, hanging shelves (with and without drawers) and zippered bags for sweaters.

5 Group your clothes in your new closet system. Options include organizing by type (all pants, shirts, skirts and blouses together), by use (work clothes, casual clothes, formalwear), by tone (light to dark) or by color. Choose a system that makes sense to you and that will be easy to maintain.

6 Take a picture of your finished closet and hang it inside the door for future reference and inspiration. (Send a copy to your mom.)

For long dresses, allow for 69 inches of hanging space; robes, 52 inches; dresses, 45 inches; pants, 44 inches; men's suits, 38 inches; women's suits, 29 inches; skirts, 35 inches; blouses, shirts, 28 inches; and pants (double hung), 20 inches.

Add a valet hook outside of your closet for hanging dry cleaning or just-ironed clothes, or for planning outfits.

61 | Organize the Linen Closet

In the ideal linen closet, you can see everything at a glance and find exactly what you need at a moment's notice. Putting your linen closet in order is as easy as sort, fold and stack.

Tips

Also read 140 Store Your Wedding Dress and Other Textiles.

Take a photo of your organized linen closet and post it inside the door for future reference. Or, label the shelves so you can remember what goes where.

Steps

1 Pull everything out of the closet and sort into categories: pillows, blankets, towels, sheets, table linens, dinner napkins and table runners. Anything else should be stored elsewhere.

2 Limit yourself to three sets of sheets per bed and three sets of bath towels, hand towels and washcloths per person. Either donate or make rags of old, worn or unused linens.

3 Sponge clean the shelves, then adjust them up and down to accommodate items. Add extra shelves if necessary. Aim for a height of 10 inches for sheets and table linens, 12 to 16 inches for towels, and 18 inches or more from the top shelf to the ceiling for bulky items, such as blankets.

4 Think small stacks, not leaning towers. Even if your shelves are at the standard 12 to 15 inches apart, take care not to cram them too tightly, or the whole stack will come tumbling down when you pull something out. You also want good airflow to keep linens smelling fresh.

5 Line shelves with acid-free tissue paper (available at art stores and LightImpressionsDirect.com).

6 Put bulky, lightweight, infrequently used items—such as pillows, comforters and quilts—on the highest or lowest shelf. Store them in their original zippered bedding bag to protect them from dust, allergens and humidity.

7 Sort towels by size or type. Fold towels in thirds lengthwise, then fold in half (matching the ends to each other), then fold in half again; this way they'll stack perfectly and fit most shelves. Or fold towels in half and roll them up for a spa look. Since towels are used the most, keep them within easy reach. Stash beach towels on a separate shelf with other seasonal items, or behind your bath towels.

8 Sort sheets into sets for each bed. Keep folded sets together by storing them inside the pillowcase. Place seasonal sheets, such as winter flannels or summer cottons, with other seasonal linens, or stack them behind your everyday sheets.

9 Fold tablecloths lengthwise and hang them on a wooden hanger covered with acid-free paper. Hang this on a hook or rod inside the closet door.

10 Put antique linens on the top shelf if they're not used often. Since they aren't easily cleaned, never put them on the floor of the closet, where they run the risk of water damage.

11 Keep relative humidity at 50 percent and temperatures at 60 to 65 degrees F (16 to 18C). Avoid extreme fluctuations of humidity and temperature levels. Inspect textiles regularly for mildew and mold, which can stain fibers and cause deterioration.

Place an open box of baking soda, activated charcoal or calcium carbonate in the closet to keep items smelling fresh.

Put the closet door to use: Add a hook to hang robes or shallow baskets for soaps. Mount a full-length mirror on the inside.

Who Knew?

If your linen closet is small, store linens in the rooms where they're used: table linens in a dining-room sideboard, cloth napkins in a kitchen drawer, guest towels and sheets in the spare bedroom.

Warning

Cardboard boxes, paper bags and plastic bags can damage fabrics. So can cedar chests, which neither kill moths nor deter carpet beetles. Instead opt for paradichlorobenzene moth crystals to aid in controlling insects.

62 | Organize Your Laundry Center

When did laundry get so complicated? The simplicity of pure cotton and clotheslines has morphed into complex science with a myriad of synthetic fabrics and care labels. And where you do the wash—in a tiny closet, a small corner of the garage or a full-blown dedicated laundry room—makes a difference. Streamline your laundry systems and train your family—and this constant chore will be less of one.

Steps

Train your team

1 Place laundry baskets or hampers in each bathroom and bedroom. Dedicate one for clothes needing repairs, stain treatment or hand-washing, and another one for dry cleaning.

2 Teach older kids how to do their own laundry. Even youngsters can match up socks and sort their dirty clothes into piles of colors and whites. Show your kids how to hang up clothes, and explain the difference between "dirty" and "worn, but still wearable" to cut down on the weekly load. Remind older kids to empty their pockets—any money found in the washer goes to the finder. See 74 Organize Kids' Rooms.

3 Clip clothespins to the side of each laundry hamper in the house. Teach family members to use them to mark stains on dirty clothes.

4 Make each family member responsible for returning folded clothes to his or her drawers.

Set up the ideal space

1 Create as much counter space for folding as your room allows.

2 Supplement natural light with bright, full-spectrum light to make spot checking easier.

3 Store cleaning products and supplies in cabinets or on overhead shelves away from small hands. Big cubbies at floor level will keep laundry baskets out of the way.

4 Install a retractable clothesline (like those in hotel showers) or a freestanding drying rack that you can pull out when needed. Keep the ironing board nearby—if space is tight, put it on an over-the-door rack along with the iron.

The dirty lowdown

1 Sort clothes by color and also by how dirty they are and what temperature they need. Wash lint distributors (towels and sweatshirts) separately from lint magnets (fleece garments and tights).

2 Zip zippers, hook hooks and button buttons on all garments before washing to minimize wear and tear.

Tips

Follow the instructions on care labels to prolong the life of your clothes.

Clean the dryer's lint trap after every load; it helps prevent fire hazards, and clothes will dry more quickly.

Treat spills on the spot: Blot stains and rinse with water immediately to keep them from becoming permanent.

Use multi-colored plastic laundry hampers to your advantage. Choose a different color for each family member, or use distinct colors to sort wash (whites in a white hamper, darks in a dark hamper).

Who Knew?

If you really like sticking to a schedule, earmark specific loads for specific days: Mondays are for whites, Tuesdays for darks, Wednesdays for towels, and so on.

Some communities frown on or actually prohibit clotheslines. So much for the sweet smell of sun-dried sheets!

Warnings

Sanitize your washer after a nasty load of greasy clothes, baby diapers or the dog bed. Fill the machine with hot water to the maximum level, add 1 cup of bleach, and run it for a full cycle (without any laundry). A rinse cycle will wash out the bleach.

3 Add appropriate products (detergent, bleach, fabric softener and so on) to each load according to the manufacturer's instructions.

4 Fill the washing machine, but don't cram clothes in. Corral small or delicate items into a mesh bag.

5 Dry loads of similar weights so you don't roast a favorite shirt while the towels are still tumbling.

After dry cleaning, remove the plastic coverings and let your clothes air out before you put them in your closet.

Never mix bleach and ammonia. Together, they form toxic gases.

---

63 Create a Sewing Center

You love to sew, but your supplies are squirreled away in random drawers and cubbies all over the house. What to do? Transform an extra bedroom, a large closet or even a quiet corner into a comfortable, productive sewing center where you can sew in peace.

Steps

1 See 196 Add a Workspace to Any Room.

2 Store hand tools, such as scissors, a rotary cutter and a magnifying glass, in stackable plastic drawers. Mount Peg-Board on the wall and hang up your frequently used tools, or slip them into a shoe organizer hung on a door.

3 Put good task lighting in your work area. A full-spectrum light source—direct sunlight through a window or a bright lamp—is important for seeing true colors.

4 Use a rolling suitcase to stow your sewing machine and a plastic box of supplies if you have to operate in a small space. The box holds zipper-lock plastic bags of all sizes with like items grouped together (threads, needles, trims, Velcro). If you're taking the machine on the road, toss in an iron and a mini pressing board.

5 Move the machine to the project rather than vice versa when working on large projects (sails, curtains, comforter covers). Re-hem drapes right at the source, without even taking them down.

6 Keep a list of measurements for projects you are considering tucked away in your wallet or purse and take advantage of buying opportunities as they arise. Keep a couple of fabric swatches from your couch, linens and so on to match colors on the fly.

7 Store extra fabric in gallon-size zipper-lock plastic storage bags. Organize these bags by color in a filing cabinet, filing boxes or clear plastic bins. Place your sewing patterns in plastic bags, too (picture facing outward), rather than forcing them back into their envelopes. Or, just fold and press patterns with a warm iron—they compress right down to slide back in their packets.

Tips

You can also store patterns by rolling them around gift-wrap tubes to keep them smooth and flat.

Keep a separate sewing kit with tiny thread spools and needles in a convenient location for quick mending. Save the hassle of getting into your big sewing kit just to sew on a button.

Pick up pins and needles with a magnet.

Many of these ideas also apply to craft rooms.

Who Knew?

Fabric glue is your best friend. When working with materials such as decorative trims, glue is much more efficient than sewing. (Duct tape, however, has been proven to last through only a couple of washings.)

64 Get Ready for the Housecleaner

Oh, the irony! You've hired a housecleaner, but every two weeks you run around the night before he or she comes, cleaning the house. If you're using the housecleaner as a nudge to pay the bills and put away the laundry, you've got bigger fish to fry. Follow these tips and you'll be able to enjoy the peace of a newly scrubbed house with far less of a prewash.

Steps

1 Discuss your wants and needs with your cleaning person so that you both understand the expectations. Most services will dust, vacuum, mop, take out the trash and clean bathrooms and kitchens. Typically, you'll have to negotiate chores like windows, dishes and laundry. Discuss these things at your house so you can make expectations very clear, room by room.

2 Write up a list that details what you covered in your meeting. Add special instructions, like "Never put my pants in the dryer" or "Don't use ant spray inside the house." List extras such as cleaning the fridge or washing baseboards in a separate section. Put your list out every time the housecleaner comes, especially if your needs or priorities change week to week. See 3 Write an Effective To-Do List.

3 Brush up on your housecleaner's native language if he or she is a non-English speaker. Or ask a friend who's fluent to translate your list. When you first meet with your housecleaner, and from time to time afterward, refer to the list to point out anything that may have changed.

4 Inform the housecleaner of any pets, keys, alarms or other specifics about your household.

5 Develop organizing systems to reduce the clutter you have to deal with so it doesn't build up before cleaning day (see 1 Get Organized). Pick up shoes, clothes, toys and laundry before the cleaner arrives, so that floors, beds, tables and counters can be cleaned properly.

6 Mark your cleaning day on the calendar so you remember to get cash ahead of time if you need to. See 265 Create a Household Organizer.

7 Set out clean sheets for the beds and towels for the bathrooms.

8 Put away valuables, important papers and other things you want to keep private or wouldn't want to be accidentally thrown away. See 184 Conquer Your Paper Piles and 7 Deal With a Flood of Mail.

9 Separate clothes you don't want machine-washed and dried rather than leave them in the dirty clothes. If it's a concern, sort laundry into piles (see 62 Organize Your Laundry Center).

65 | Organize Cleaning Supplies

You've got products that disinfect, clean, whiten, brighten, scrub and shine, but the trick is to find the one you want when you need it. Keep things simple, buy in bulk, and borrow some tips from the pros.

Steps

1 Set up a cleaning caddy in a plastic carrier or bucket. Include an all-purpose cleaning spray, glass cleaner, an old toothbrush, paper towels, scrapers, sponges, soft cloths and rubber gloves. Carry it from room to room when you clean, or keep one on each floor if you have a multistory house.

2 Hang brooms and mops from a closet wall. Make sure their "business" ends don't get damaged by resting on the floor. Replace brooms when edges are bent, broken or splayed, and sponge mops when they lose their shape.

3 Avoid buying specialized cleaners for every different job. An all-purpose cleaner can tackle the majority of your needs and saves money. In fact, you can make your own green cleaner recipes from lemon juice, Borax, baking soda and white vinegar. (Be sure to label this mixture so that no one mistakes it for a beverage.)

4 Stow your vacuum cleaner in an easily accessible place. Hang the hose from a hook to free up floor space. Keep a lightweight vacuum cleaner and a small step stool upstairs if you have a multistory house. That way, you don't have to haul heavy tools upstairs and down when you clean.

5 Store a set of cleaning supplies under each bathroom sink. See 69 Organize Bathrooms.

6 Toss that feather duster—it just moves dust around. Opt instead for an electrostatic cloth, or just a rag.

7 Store extra trash bags in the bottom of a wastebasket. When you empty the trash, you have a new bag waiting to line the can.

Tip

Fashion a wearable cleaning kit—a sturdy canvas apron with basic cleaning supplies in its pockets—that you can wear while you clean.

Warnings

Bleach and ammonia form the toxic gases chloramine and ammonium chloride if they're mixed. Always keep these two cleaning products away from each other, even in storage.

Keep products in their original containers so that safety information and directions remain with the product.

Always store toxic cleaning supplies out of reach of young children, and install childproof locks on your supply cabinet.

Springtime is the traditional time to remove the winter blues from your home and make it ready for the long days of summer fun. It's also a good exercise in taking stock of your home and its contents. Just make sure that you share the work—and the credit for a job well done.

WHAT	HOW
Air Conditioner and Heater	• Don't wait until the first really hot day of summer to check it out—schedule a service in early spring and fall.
	• Change the filters in the furnace.
Windows	• Do first before the day gets hot. Speed through the job with a squeegee and a water and ammonia mix rather than glass cleaner and newspapers.
	• Touch up paint on sills inside and out.
Clutter Busting	• Read 1 Get Organized and 37 Conquer Clutter. Have each family member take on a room and blast through it. Divvy up common living spaces and take on the shelves, surfaces and other clutter magnets. Create keep, sell or give away, and toss piles. (See 12 Get Rid of What You Don't Want.)
	• Clean cabinets and closets inside and out.
	• Empty kitchen cabinets and closets, and discard any unused items.
De-Griming	• Wash down the walls and doors with a mixture of trisodium phosphate (TSP) and water. Pay particular attention to the kitchen and bathrooms.
	• Spray your bathroom ceiling with a 50-50 solution of water and hydrogen peroxide. Don't wipe it off. This formula will help keep mildew from forming.
	• Hit the showers. Soak cotton balls in bleach and place them in mildewy corners of the shower or bath when you start cleaning. Remove when you leave; the mildew should be gone. Use rubbing alcohol to clean caulking.
	• Disinfect and whiten toilets with chlorine bleach. Let sit for 10 minutes to kill off the germs. Wear gloves.
	• Remove mildew from floors and walls by spraying on a mixture of ½ cup (4 fl oz/125 ml) chlorine bleach, ⅓ cup (3 fl oz/80 ml) powdered laundry detergent and 1 gallon (4 l) hot water, working from the base of the wall up. Wear gloves.
Fridge and Freezer	• With a trash can and a large cooler on hand, take everything out of the refrigerator and freezer. Throw away or put in the cooler. Scrub down all interior surfaces, including rubber gaskets around the doors.
	• Remove the grill along the bottom of your refrigerator. Locate the drip pan, using a flashlight if necessary. The pan will be sitting on the black condenser coils. Remove the pan and wash it with a mixture of warm, soapy water and bleach to kill any mold. Let dry and replace.
	• Locate the coils. They look like thin, black radiators and may be underneath the fridge or attached to the back. If the coils are in back, pull the fridge away from the wall. Use the vacuum attachments to get between the coils. Take care not to damage them.

WHAT	HOW
Floors	• Sweep or vacuum, then wet mop with appropriate cleaning products.
	• If you have discolored waxy buildup on your floors, purchase a wax stripper that's right for your floors. Rent an electric floor scrubber and a wet-dry vacuum. The scrubber scrubs away wax, and the wet-dry vacuum sucks up all the residue.
	• Wax the floor and seal when dry to provide a protective coat.
	• Power clean carpets and area rugs.
Odds and Ends	• Test and clean all smoke alarms and carbon monoxide detectors. Change the batteries in them twice a year.
	• Open and close your main water valve and the valves on all toilets and sinks. Look for leaks around your water heater.
	• Test and reset all ground fault circuit interrupters (GFCIs).
Exterior	• Recharge fire extinguishers.
	• Flush out your sump pump and make sure all fittings are secure.
	• Touch up interior paint. (Make sure you have adequate ventilation when painting entire rooms.)
	• Check your roof and gutters for leaves, snow and ice. Use a rake or broom to break up ice dams.
	• Patch cracks in the driveway, patio, paths and sidewalk.
	• Power-wash any wooden decks and check them for deterioration.
	• Patch and paint exterior walls and siding. Inspect and repair the roof.
	• Lubricate the doors and windows.
	• Get your chimney and furnace inspected and serviced.
	• Caulk windows and doors. Insulate any exposed pipes and bring garden hoses inside.
	• Trim tree branches that may become a hazard in winter.
TIPS	Use the weakest cleaner first, then graduate to stronger solutions when needed. This way you're least likely to harm surfaces with harsh, inappropriate cleaners.
	Pop moist sponges in the microwave oven for 20 seconds to kill germs.
	Spring cleaning is also a great time to change out your wardrobe. Wash and pack away winter clothes, and break out the short sleeves and beach towels. See 60 Conquer Your Closets.
	Stock up on trash bags, boxes, cleaning supplies and rags.

67 | Keep the Family Room Organized

Everyone wants their family room to be all things to all people. This is where friends and family gather to play games, do yoga, watch television, relax, read, do arts and crafts and more. With so many activities in one room, you need a strategy for keeping them contained.

Steps

1 Look for easy-care furniture when shopping for your family room. Fabrics should be stain resistant, and surfaces should wipe clean easily.

2 Choose multipurpose furniture, such as ottomans that serve as coffee tables with hinged lids for hidden storage; couches with built-in recliners; and bookshelves with drawers and cabinets for small items.

3 Design storage solutions when your budget allows it. Build hinged benches along a wall to hold toys, games, photo albums and media collections. Put cushions on top so the benches do double-duty for sleepovers.

4 Create seating clusters for different activities. Tuck the TV in a corner facing a large couch; arrange a pod of chairs near a good light for reading or crafts.

5 Dedicate several baskets, tote bags or bins for newspapers and magazines. Clip articles, rotate the stock and purge the containers regularly and ruthlessly. See 52 Categorize Newspaper and Magazine Clippings.

6 Store art and craft supplies in stackable containers that fit on your bookshelves or in a portable chest or rolling bin that can be tucked out of the way.

7 Set up a basket or box for pet toys. Train your pet so he or she knows where to find those toys—and, if you're smart, to put them away!

Tips

Slip a folding card table under the couch, and pull it out for puzzles, games and short-term art and craft projects.

Place a large basket or bin in a corner for things that find their way to the family room but belong elsewhere. Return the contents of this basket to their proper places regularly.

68 | Set Up a Bathroom Schedule

Tired of playing drill sergeant every morning, trying to hustle the kids in and out of the bathroom and off to school? Does the bathroom look like a war zone after everyone's finished? With some color coding and a schedule, daily bathroom battles can have to a peaceful resolution.

Steps

1 Set up staggered bathroom schedules if people outnumber plumbing. Set up the schedule based on who leaves the house first and who takes the longest to get ready. (Have the slow ones go last, so they don't push everyone else off schedule.) If several

Tips

See 17 Streamline Your Morning Routine.

Put a clock or kitchen timer in the bathroom to keep time.

people leave at the same time, and if a hairstyle can handle it, shower the night before. Post the schedule on the door.

2 Free up the shower by taking makeup and hair supplies out of the bathroom and into the bedrooms, where all that's needed is a mirror and a plug.

3 Assign each family member a different color towel and wash-cloth. Give everyone their own hook as well.

4 Keep a basket with makeup, clips, hair products, comb, brush and blow-drier outside the bathroom. As long as there's a plug and a mirror, serious primpers can continue their work without causing a bathroom bottleneck.

69 Organize Bathrooms

The bathroom may not be the biggest room in your house, but it's one of the most important. In addition to handling bathing and grooming chores, the bathroom is sometimes the only room where you can escape for a moment's peace. Get yours spiffed up and organized so it's a haven of tranquility.

Steps

1 Empty out all the shelves, drawers and cabinets, and put back only what you currently use or need. Dispose of expired products properly (see 43 Organize the Medicine Cabinet).

2 Eliminate countertop clutter. Choose a cosmetics organizer that's suitable for your makeup needs—a cabinet, drawers or storage unit. If you're a heavy-user, get a trunk-style case (similar to what makeup artists use) with foldout trays and dividers.

3 Separate your drawer space. Insert drawer organizers or sec-tioned trays to organize your makeup and grooming supplies. Don't be afraid to use other things such as kitchen utensil hold-ers to keep your beauty products in line.

4 Store shaving supplies in a cool, dry place. Keep cans of shaving cream away from extreme heat. Razors and scissors should be dried before storing and kept in sheaths for safety.

5 Make hard-to-corral items accessible. Use an attractive soap dish to store smaller items such as hair clips or ties.

6 Place a bathroom étagère or shelves over the toilet for extra storage space.

Who Knew?

Give everyone a plastic caddy for storing personal supplies, such as brushes, combs, shampoo and other hair products; toothbrushes, toothpaste and dental floss; makeup and other toiletries. If space is tight, these bins can stay in bedrooms when not in use.

Tips

Opened cosmetics have a shorter shelf life than most products: mascara, three months; liquid eyeliners and eye shadows, three to six months; compact powder, eight months. If there's a change in color, smell or consistency, get rid of the product.

Accept the fact that the bathroom is a good place to catch up on reading, and position a magazine rack near the toilet.

Warning

Store cosmetics away from light, humidity and extreme temperatures. Scent com-pounds in perfumes and colognes deteriorate in heat and sunlight.

70 Organize Entryways and Mudrooms

"Bring the outdoors inside," say the window manufacturers and houseplant growers. Those of us who clean floors would, frankly, prefer the outdoors to stay there. A functional mudroom or entryway—the natural home for boots and coats—keeps the whole house cleaner.

Steps

1 Start with an entryway that has a waterproof, resilient floor, such as concrete, tile, vinyl, laminate or stone. Carpeting will just get filthy.

2 Cover the entryway floor with high-quality doormats and washable area rugs. These are going to be real workhorses, so choose utility over appearance.

3 Clear out the clutter. Store in your entryway only those things that you need to have available when you walk out the door. Put seasonal or nonessential items elsewhere.

4 Pair a row of coat hooks or pegs to hold hats and scarves with a storage bench below where people can sit to remove their shoes.

5 Build or buy some cubbies for the entryway. These are great for keys, cell phones, gloves, hats, garden tools and other items.

6 Have a space heater or fan in the mudroom so wet things dry more quickly. If you're building a new house, designate a heating vent for this area, or install radiant heating in the floor.

Tips

If your house doesn't have a mudroom or entryway, consider installing a large waterproof awning over your back door. Have people take off their shoes and muddy garments there.

A canvas floor cloth, sealed with polyurethane, is another great option for foyer floors. You can paint it to match your décor—and wipe it clean when it gets filthy.

If you have a dog, move his dishes to the mudroom. Many dogs like to eat in privacy, and the mudroom's floor will resist spills and stains. See 45 Organize Pet Supplies.

71 Organize a Dorm Room

Question: How do you fit your books, clothes, linens, computer and other necessities into a space no bigger than a prison cell? Answer: With furniture that's vertical, functional and dual-purpose.

Steps

1 Find out what furniture is included with your room. Many dorms have suggested floor plans to maximize space; some schools won't let you bring your own furniture.

2 Use a footlocker-style trunk and stackable, interlocking plastic crates to transport your things to school. The crates can serve as storage units, and the trunk can double as a coffee table or an end table. Suitcases can store clothing and extra linens.

3 Bring only the clothes you'll wear for the next few months if you plan to go home on breaks. Fill in gaps and adjust for the seasons in spurts.

4 Use the chart (right) to maximize your dorm room.

Tip

See 284 Prepare for Your Child's Departure for College.

AREA	IDEAS
Storage	• A tall bookcase and a rolling file box, if permitted, are both useful and inexpensive space-expanding furniture pieces. • File cabinets or carts and expandable files keep papers organized. • Subdue your CD collection with a multimedia rack or CD storage boxes.
Studying	• Put up bulletin/magnetic boards to keep track of deadlines, and to express your personality. • Add a hutch on top of the dorm-issue desk for handy access to your ever-increasing collection of textbooks.
Layout	• Investigate ways to maximize the closet space. Buy multi-tiered racks and hangers, stacking open crates, and so on. • Set up a loft bed, which creates underbed space for a desk and storage. If your dorm doesn't permit lofts, increase available floor space by stacking the beds into bunks, or raise your bed on cinder blocks to slide in shallow underbed boxes or drawers.

72 Organize Your School Locker

If you're one of the lucky students whose school has not outlawed lockers (and who doesn't have to carry around a day's worth of books in an overstuffed backpack), then check out these tips for making your locker your home away from homeroom.

Steps

1 Install a shelf in your locker to double the horizontal storage space. You can find a variety of locker shelves and accessories online at stores such as Lockermate.com, StacksAndStacks.com and PotteryBarnTeen.com.

2 Stand your books upright (not stacked) with their spines out to see the titles and grab the book you need quickly.

3 Use a notebook or binder (or section) for each class. Color-code these binders with notebooks and book covers so that everything related to a particular class is the same color.

4 Save space and keep everything accessible by adding mirrors, pencil cups, clocks and picture frames. Many have magnetic attachments.

5 Carry your valuables—cash, laptop computers, digital cameras or MP3 players—with you; don't put them in your school locker. Better yet, leave them at home.

Tip

Before you shop for a school backpack, measure the width of your locker. It's extra handy to get a backpack or rolling bag that fits right into your locker—even when crammed with books.

Warning

Empty your trash and recycling, and remove unneeded items, at least once a week. Make sure you're not creating science experiments out of banana peels and sweaty gym clothes in the locker's nether regions.

73 | Make Your Home Safe for Small Children

You probably consider your home a safe place, but you might be unaware of certain conditions and products that can harm children, especially the youngest ones. Common sense coupled with some easy-to-use products and tools can make any home safer for everyone. Look for child-proofing products online and at drugstores as well as children's, hardware and department stores.

ROOM	TASK
General	• Place childproof covers on electrical outlets. • Keep hallways and exits well lit and clear of obstructions. • Shorten cords on window blinds, or use cord windup devices to prevent strangulation hazards. • Keep windows and doors locked to keep kids from climbing out or jamming their fingers. Make sure doors that are in frequent use cannot be locked. Use foam devices that cling to the door's edge and prevent crushed fingers. • Apply decals or decorations to sliding glass doors. • Attach nonskid backing to area rugs. • Install a self-latching lock on your basement door. • Put safety gates at the tops and bottoms of stairways. Gates—especially the one at the top—should be well secured so they won't give way when pushed. Stay away from accordion gates that can pinch fingers. • Keep stairs free of clutter. Carpeted stairs are safer. • Install locks on windows that prevent them from opening more than 4 inches (10 cm) to keep crawlers and climbers from falling out.
Living Room and Family Room	• Make sure all furniture is stable and pulled away from windows. • Pad sharp corners of walls, furniture, hearth and fireplace if needed. • Block off fireplaces and radiators with secure screened barriers that won't tip. Be especially careful with hot floor radiators.
Kitchen	• Store knives and sharp utensils out of children's reach. • Cook on your stove's back burners, and keep pot handles turned away from the front of the stove. • Remove stove knobs when they're not in use, or use knob protectors. • Keep small appliances unplugged. Don't let electric cords dangle where they can be grabbed. • Feed and water pets in a room that's not easily accessed by your child. If that's not possible, put the water dish on the counter or near the dog door. • Place chairs and step stools away from the stove and countertops. • Keep a fire extinguisher in the kitchen, and make sure adults and older children know how to use it. • Store cleaning supplies and other hazardous materials in a locked cabinet or one high above the floor.

ROOM	TASK
Bathroom	• Keep the toilet seat lid down and secured with a toilet lock or clamp.
	• Purchase medications with child-resistant packaging, and keep medicines in a high or locked cabinet. (See 43 Organize the Medicine Cabinet.)
	• Install handrails in the bathtub, and place nonskid mats or strips on the bottom of the tub.
	• Use nonslip rugs and bath mats.
	• Protect against scalding with bathtub knob covers. Set the water heater at 120 degrees F (49 C) or lower.
	• Keep the bathroom door shut when it's not in use. Disable the lock so button-loving toddlers will not be able to lock themselves in.
Bedroom	• Follow crib safety guidelines of the U.S. Consumer Product Safety Commission at www.cpsc.gov/tips.html.
	• Make sure the crib mattress fits snugly in the crib.
	• Position the crib away from windows, curtains, lamps and electrical cords.
	• Raise or remove mobiles and other hanging decorations from above the crib when your baby is able to stand up and grab them.
	• Put a nightlight in the room, away from bedding, curtains and other ignitable material.
	• Store toys in open containers. (Small children can get trapped in toy boxes with heavy hinged lids.)
	• Place fire-escape ladders in all second-floor or higher bedrooms. Practice using them with your child. See 464 Formulate a Family Emergency Plan.
	• Install carbon-monoxide alarms and smoke alarms outside all bedrooms.
	• Never put any stuffed animals, blankets or pillows in the baby's crib. All these items are suffocation hazards. Dress him or her in warm jammies under a sleeper instead.
TIP	Many of these steps are also helpful if you have a physically impaired or an elderly person in your home.
WARNINGS	Never use an electric blanket in a baby's crib or a small child's bed.
	Never leave children 4 years and younger unattended around water (bathtubs, pools, ponds—even large buckets). A baby can drown in seconds in just 2 inches (5 cm) of water.

If you can't see the floor of your kids' rooms (or are afraid to open their doors) it's time to take action. Help children organize their rooms in ways that make their space fun to play in and easy to keep clean. Reassure them that putting their rooms in order doesn't mean they have to throw away all their good stuff.

Steps

General

1 Set a good example. Keep your own room organized, and make it a household rule that beds are made every morning and floors picked up every evening. Follow and enforce this rule.

2 Involve your children in setting up their own rooms. Make it easy for them to put away—and later find—their own stuff.

3 Don't worry that the kids' rooms aren't designer showplaces. That's not the goal. Instead, create spaces that encourage them to play, relax and study.

4 Teach children to group similar items together (art materials, cars, puzzles) and how this makes it easier to find things later.

5 Label liberally. See 57 Live Better Through Labeling.

Younger children

1 Establish good habits at an early age. Toddlers love to have jobs to do and can learn to put their toys away.

2 Make the closet kid-friendly by lowering the rod and using kid-size hangers. Use open bins or baskets on the closet floor for socks, underwear and pajamas.

3 Put a wide-mouth laundry hamper near the closet or dresser to keep dirty clothes off the floor.

4 Install rounded (not sharp!) hooks in the closet or on a wall for hanging clothes, backpacks, hats and such. Hang buckets that hold small toys, socks or other little things.

5 Make bed-making easy by using a fitted bottom sheet with a covered comforter instead of the usual sheets and blankets. To make the bed, the child just needs to shake out the comforter and fluff the pillows.

6 Cover part of a wall with corkboard to display your kid's artwork, photographs, certificates and such. Or hang a rope (above head level) between windows and use clothespins to hang artwork. Put a coat of chalkboard paint on one wall and keep a bucket of chalk handy.

Tips

Try to see a child's room from her point of view, even if that means getting on your knees. Hang shelves and hooks where kids can easily reach them.

Use pictures on labels for storage bins and over hooks to help little ones who can't read to put things away.

Keep the toy population under control by letting go of old toys when new ones arrive. See 76 Organize Kids' Play Spaces.

Use open storage bins or clear containers for storage so children can see what's inside.

Use under-bed storage boxes for flat items like board games, puzzles and off-season clothes and shoes.

7 Rotate toys. Put a selection of infrequently used toys in see-through plastic bins and store them in an out-of-the-way place (perhaps the high shelves in the closet) for several months. Label and date the boxes, and switch out some of the toys every few months. Rotate toys between friends and relatives, too.

Teenagers

1 Talk to your teenagers. Show them how organizing their room will improve their lives. They'll have more free time and be less stressed when they know where to find everything. See 1 Get Organized.

2 Set up a desk for homework. Make sure it has a large work surface, proper lighting, storage for supplies, a filing system, a comfortable chair and computer space (see 281 Create a Schedule for Family Computer Use). Also set aside flop space for reading. Make sure both areas have sufficient electrical outlets for the computer, stereo, games and other plug-ins.

3 Get a two-drawer file cabinet that doubles as a side table. It's never too early to teach your children how to store and file their paperwork (see 185 Create a Flawless Filing System). Emphasize that they can design their systems anyway they want—not how you want them to.

4 Put up enough shelves—either bookcases or wall-mounted shelves—to hold all your kids' things: books, music equipment, CDs, videos, stuffed animals, electronics, trophies and lots and lots of odds and ends. Put up a photo wall of corkboard or foam-core panels that they can pin photos, posters and magazine covers to their heart's content.

5 Install a high shelf about a foot (30 cm) below the ceiling on one or more walls to store treasured but infrequently handled collectibles or memorabilia.

6 Put a wide-mouth laundry hamper near the closet or dresser to keep dirty clothes off the floor. Install a basketball net above the hamper to encourage accurate shooting from 3-point range.

7 Mount a full length mirror on the back of the door. This will encourage the cherubs to keep the space behind the door clear and give them a place to check their appearance before entering the world.

8 Respect your teenagers' privacy within the bounds of your house rules. If you promise not to enter their rooms when they're not around, stick to your word.

Who Knew?

Make your child's favorite activity a part of the room's decor. An old hockey stick, a ballet barre or a junk-sale clarinet can be hung horizontally on the wall. Use reclaimed skateboards or snowboards for shelves.

75 | Organize Sports Equipment

Participating in sports often requires you to make a significant investment in gear. In order to get the most out of your sports equipment—OK, just to be able to *find* your equipment when you want it—take advantage of these tricks of the trade and get organized.

Steps

1 Use garbage cans or tall baskets to store hockey sticks, baseball bats, ski poles, oars, lacrosse sticks and other long items. Don't store anything more than twice the height of the container you use, or it might tip over.

2 Look into specialty racks if you have a significant amount of gear. Purchase special wall-mounted racks for multiple pairs of skis, snowboards, bikes, golf bags, fishing poles, hockey gear, baseball bats and more.

3 Keep balls off the ground, accessible and in good shape with mesh bags, wire baskets or duffel bags hung from walls or ceiling. Keep a pump near your equipment so a dead ball doesn't spoil the fun.

4 Put together a duffel bag for each sport—for example, a single bag with baseball gloves, balls, bats, helmet and anything else you need. Toss the entire bag in the car when you head for practice. See 47 Prepare Grab 'n' Go Activity Bags.

5 Hang a set of ropes and pulleys from your garage ceiling and hoist up canoes and kayaks (with paddles or oars inside). Make sure the boats are dry and the storage compartments open before lifting. Hang rowing shells upside down with the ports open. See 147 Store a Boat for the Winter.

6 Gather skateboards and scooters, along with helmets, wrist guards, elbow and knee pads and stash all in a large box in a closet or the garage.

7 Store space-stealing high tops, soccer cleats and in-line skates on a low shelf or lace together and hang on hooks near sports equipment. Insert deodorizing balls to keep the area from smelling like a locker room.

8 Get more specifics from 143 Store Ski Gear, 142 Store Bicycles and Gear and 144 Organize Camping Equipment.

Tips

Make sure your equipment storage area is dry and well ventilated to prevent damage from mold.

See if your local school district sells its old lockers. They're ideal for storing most sporting goods.

Who Knew?

Don't bother storing items that are worn out or need repairs. Repair or replace them—and remember you'll save money if you wait for off-season specials.

Warnings

Remember, water is the enemy. Make sure your gear is clean and dry before you store it—especially for the off-season. Oil your baseball glove, and clean the mud off your cleats. Wash out tents and packs, and let them dry thoroughly.

In some states, wearing a bicycle helmet is the law so…buckle up!

If you're going to be running, biking or walking after dark, make sure your equipment and/or clothing has reflective tape attached.

Unless children's play areas are organized and easy for them to maintain, there's a good chance they'll feel overwhelmed and not want to play there—no matter how many toys they have. Kids like to help, and organizing toys and games is a good activity to do together. Besides helping them take pride in their space, it is an opportunity to learn more about counting, sorting and grouping, as well as sharing—when they donate items they no longer use.

Steps

1 Consider your child's personality and interests. If your daughter likes to paint, prepare an area with paper, paints and an easel and put down a plastic floor cover. If your son likes to have friends over to play board games, put them on a shelf that he can safely reach. See 74 Organize Kids' Rooms.

2 Set up activity centers. A block or Lego area needs a flat surface to build on (a hardwood floor or tabletop) while a game area should contain comfortable seating (floor cushions, beanbags). Set up painting easels on linoleum floors for easy mop-up.

3 Store according to age. Younger children like open bins on low shelves or the floor for easy cleanup and storage. Older children can use drawers, underbed storage, shelves, pegs and pegboards, but items should still be within easy reach.

4 Avoid using large toy boxes as a catchall. What is out of sight rarely gets played with. Sort toys into groups (dolls, dinosaurs, plastic food) and then stash in smaller baskets, bins or boxes.

5 Label everything. Use photos of items (cut from magazines or printed from Web sites) for labeling young children's toy bins. Children that can read can create stickers with a label maker (see Xyron.com), cut words from magazines or print labels from a computer. See 57 Live Better Through Labeling.

6 Have containers around the house for easy pickup and transfer. Even If you have a separate playroom, toys will invade your entire house (and car). Do a quick cleanup each night and take the toys back to the play area for proper storage. This is a great chore for kids. See 17 Streamline Your Morning Routine and 18 Organize a Chore Schedule for Kids.

7 Organize outdoor toys and equipment so you're ready to go at a moment's notice. Use a large basket to store balls, mitts and bats. A bucket can hold sand toys—add sunscreen and you're ready for the beach (see 47 Prepare Grab 'n' Go Activity Bags).

8 Enforce cleanup rules and consequences. Learning to put things away and stay organized takes time and practice (even for grown-ups). Children need adult help to learn new habits, so be consistent with expectations and routines. Remind kids that keeping their play space tidy is not a chore, but a way to make playtime more fun.

Tips

See 73 Make Your Home Safe for Small Children and 264 Blend Families.

Rotate toys and games, and leave out only a reasonable number at any given time. When your child has outgrown a toy or game, give it away.

If space permits, set up a separate play area in the basement or another room to keep your child's bedroom less cluttered. See 87 Turn a Basement Into a Media Room or Playroom.

Put costumes, used scarves, gloves, hats, costume jewelry and other goodies together in a laundry basket so your child and his or her friends can easily play dress-up.

Let your child help. If kids are involved in organizing their own space, there's a much higher likelihood they will maintain it.

Warnings

Don't set up a system that is too hard for your child to maintain. He or she will become frustrated and you'll be back where you started.

Don't organize your child's play space to the point of stifling creativity. Part of the value of play is keeping it open-ended, and combining toys and games in unique ways.

77 Safeguard Your Home Against Allergens

Do you feel healthier when you're outside? Is the air in your house stuffy or stale? Newer houses can be built so airtight that allergens such as pollen, dust mites, mold, and pet hair and dander get trapped inside. The situation actually endangers some people's health. Follow these steps and you'll be breathing easier in no time.

Steps

1 Learn which allergens you're sensitive to, and focus your energy on them. Some advice can be contradictory: For example, mold sufferers should open windows when humidity is low, but that may introduce pollen that aggravates other allergies.

2 Remove wall-to-wall carpeting from your home. Having smooth floors, such as hardwood, tile, vinyl, linoleum or concrete, will help minimize allergens. Don't steam-clean any remaining rugs or carpet—wet padding promotes mold growth.

3 Vacuum regularly. Your vacuum cleaner should have a high-efficiency particulate air (HEPA) filter and bags that seal in dust.

4 Dehumidify the air in your home to between 35 and 40 percent (dust mites and mold prefer over 50 percent humidity). When the air is too dry, however, it can become difficult for some people to breathe, so use a small dehumidifier to remove excess moisture from closets, cabinets and other small, enclosed spaces. Monitor humidity levels with a hygrometer. See 89 Organize the Basement.

5 Clean the ducts in the HVAC (heating/ventilating/air-conditioning) system, and install a high-efficiency low-pressure air (HELPA) filter on the system. Cover vents with filter cloths to filter the air.

6 Make your home a shoe-free zone to reduce tracked-in allergens.

7 Place a HEPA air filter in your bedroom.

8 Shower before you go to bed to remove allergens from your hair. Make sure to run the bathroom exhaust fan during and after your shower, or at least until the mirror clears.

9 Wash your sheets each week in hot water—at least 130 degrees F (54 C)—to kill dust mites. Set your dryer on a high temperature setting for bedding.

10 Put allergen-protective covers on mattresses, box springs and pillows. Seal the zippers on these covers with tape.

11 Clean your refrigerator drip pan every month—it's a breeding pool for mold. See 66 Organize Spring Cleaning.

Tips

Focus your antiallergen work first on the rooms where you spend the majority of your time. For most people, that's the bedroom.

Remove your dry cleaning from its plastic bag and air out the clothes for a few hours before bringing them in the house.

Who Knew?

Adopt a low-allergen pet, such as a poodle, bichon frisé, basenji and some terriers, and sphinx or rex cats. Wash your pet weekly with dander-reducing shampoo and don't let it sleep in your bedroom. Smaller pets (obviously) produce less dander.

Replace plush, stuffed toys with hypoallergenic toys that can be washed in hot water.

Warning

Never use an unvented gas or kerosene room heater in your home.

The typical American family spends close to $1,300 a year on energy in the home, according to the U.S. Department of Energy. A lot of that energy—and money—is wasted. Think green and make your home as energy-efficient as possible.

Steps

1 Insulate your home. The kind of insulation you should install depends on where you live: enter your ZIP code and get recommendations at www.ornl.gov/~roofs/Zip/ZipHome.html.

2 Save up to 10 percent on your energy bill by caulking, sealing and weather-stripping your home.

3 Get an energy-efficient furnace and air conditioner, and a programmable thermostat. Insulate your ductwork so that the heating and cooling you pay for actually reaches your rooms.

4 Install energy-efficient lighting, such as compact fluorescent lightbulbs, in your home. Changing to compact fluorescent lights (CFLs) can save you about $30 per bulb annually. Outdoors, install high-pressure sodium flood lamps.

5 Shop for energy-saving appliances. Old refrigerators, washers, dryers and dishwashers are all energy hogs. Check online at EnergyStar.gov for specific appliance models. Then check with your local utilities, which may offer rebates if you install energy-efficient appliances.

6 Dry your laundry on a clothesline, if you have space to do so (and are permitted). See 62 Organize Your Laundry Center.

7 Tap into the sun's rays for water heating or generating electricity and install photovoltaic panels. You may find yourself selling power back to the utility company. This is called "net metering." Check with local authorities for codes and potential tax breaks and refer to the Database of State Incentives for Renewable Energy at dsireusa.org.

8 Insulate your water heater's hot water pipes to improve energy efficiency. Or, replace it with a new energy-efficient model. Or, look into installing a tankless, on-demand water heater (see GoTankless.com and other sites).

9 Plant deciduous trees on the south side of your house. These will shade your home in the summer and allow the sun to warm the house in the winter.

10 Replace old windows with double-pane models. In colder climates, look for gas-filled low-emissivity (low-e) windows that reduce heat loss. Where it's warmer, choose windows that have spectrally selective coatings because they reduce heat gain.

Continued on next page

Tips

In the summer, open windows in the evening to bring cool air in. Close your windows and drapes during the day to keep the heat out.

Maximize water heating efficiency by removing sediment at the base of your water heater's tank. Adjust burners for the most fuel-efficient and safest combustion (blue flames are good, yellow bad).

Replace dirty air filters to improve air flow and efficiency and to lower utility costs.

Install ceiling fans to circulate heated air trapped high up at ceilings. Doing so will make your home more comfortable and lower your heating bill. A side benefit is reduced condensation at windows and glass doors.

Who Knew?

According to the U.S. Department of Energy, a well-insulated attic is one of the best ways to improve energy efficiency, save money and increase comfort. It will also prevent ice dams from forming.

Compact fluorescent lights now include reflectors, three-way bulbs, globes, dimmers, bug lights, outdoor floodlights and many other styles.

11 Have sun-reflective awnings installed over south-facing windows to reduce the need for air-conditioning.

12 Program certain appliances such as air conditioners, hot water heaters, clothes dryers, swimming pool filters and hot tubs to run during off-peak programs for lower utility costs.

13 Keep the flue closed when your fireplace is not in use. When you burn a fire, open the nearest window an inch (so the fire draws cold air from it, not from the rest of the house) and lower your thermostat to between 50 and 55 degrees F (10 to 13 C).

14 Install a whole-house fan. Open windows on cool evenings and let the fan vent hot air into the attic. Investigate at sites such as QuietCoolFan.com and WholeHouseFan.com.

Warning

Don't attempt to replace windows or add a photo-voltaic system without a proper understanding of techniques, building codes and risks.

---

79 Use Feng Shui to Organize Your Home

Feng shui ("wind and water") is an ancient Chinese art dedicated to using *chi,* or life energy, to its best advantage. *Chi* is said to flow from a home's doors and windows and circulate throughout a house. A lot of feng shui is common sense—you don't need an expensive consult-ant to tell you that a dark room with holes in the walls and piles of clutter can sap your energy.

Steps

1 Read 80 Design a New Home With Feng Shui to learn basic feng shui concepts.

2 Create a flowing path for *chi* within your home. Your front door should open inward, and the entry area should be free of clutter. Make sure that all doors can open fully, that corridors are not blocked, and that your possessions are not stored on the floor.

3 Eliminate clutter and other negative influences (see 37 Conquer Clutter). If an object makes you feel sad, angry or resentful, get rid of it.

4 Patch and paint your walls, doors and other surfaces. Removing imperfections makes *chi* flow more smoothly in your home.

5 Fine-tune the energy in each room by using a combination of five elements: metal (to aid concentration), water (communication), wood (starting new things), fire (passion and intensity) and earth

Tips

The front door is especially important in feng shui. Paint it red, cover its windows with translucent fabric, and make sure the doorbell works.

Carefully placed mirrors, tabletop fountains, lamps and houseplants can improve the energy flow of any home, even oddly shaped apartments.

(stability and commitment). The precise combination of elements depends on what each room needs; consult a feng shui book or practitioner for specific advice.

6 Regularly open windows and doors to improve air circulation and energy flow.

80 Design a New Home With Feng Shui

The perfect time to apply feng shui principles is when you're designing a new dwelling. Creating a balanced environment positively affects the health and success of a home's denizens.

Steps

1 Consider hiring a feng shui consultant to help you correctly interpret the principles. Ask for credentials and references. Find out where the consultant was trained and how many consultations has he or she has done. Ask which feng shui tradition he or she practices.

2 Look for a plot of land that's level and generally rectangular. Avoid jagged rocks or nearby peaks, but rounded hills and forested hillsides are alright, as are creeks, gentle rivers and small waterfalls.

3 Plan a home that's square or rectangular. Odd-shaped or angular buildings have feng shui challenges that are difficult or expensive to undo.

4 Make the building generally symmetrical in shape, and avoid angular protrusions.

5 Include a foyer in the floor plan. Don't have the front door open directly into a room (where *chi* would be permitted to escape), and don't have the front door aligned directly with the back door or large back windows.

6 Avoid floor-to-ceiling windows in bedrooms; these let too much *chi* escape. Don't build narrow, dark corridors, mazelike room arrangements, triangular rooms or steep stairways.

7 Choose smooth surfaces for interior walls. Curved walls and surfaces also encourage positive flow of *chi*.

8 Design a flowing, curvy path to your front door. See 124 Design a Garden Path.

Tip

Avoid designing low or beamed ceilings in your home.

Warning

Serious feng shui practitioners claim you can do real damage to your home and its residents by practicing feng shui without extensive training.

Heart & Home

81 Design Your House

What could be more exciting than moving into a new home? How about moving into a new home that's designed just for you and your family? If this is your situation—lucky you! Here's some advice to make sure the house you design truly is the home of your dreams.

Steps

1 Buy a lot if you don't have one already. Is it a sloping, zero-lot line (where one side of the house sits on one lot line) or a corner lot? The grade, soil characteristics and other factors will all affect which type of foundation you choose (basement, crawlspace or slab). As you begin designing, take into consideration the views, existing trees and other landscape features, as well as the house's planned orientation to the sun.

2 Hire an architect. Highly skilled at integrating the wishes of homeowners with concepts of light and space, architects provide a wide range of services. They'll help you create a wish list, do preliminary or schematic design and design development, prepare construction documents (blueprints), manage the job together with the general contractor, and secure your permits and zoning approvals. Architects are also familiar with local building requirements.

3 Determine the size of the house you can afford to build, keeping in mind the size of your lot. The National Association of Home Builders (nahb.org) has information on the average cost per square foot for new homes in any area. Multiply the square footage of the home you want by the average cost per square foot to get a preliminary ballpark figure.

4 Decide whether your architect will design your home or if you'll acquire readymade plans and then hire a builder who will work from them. Readymade plans will be cheaper, but an architect will capture your personal taste and help you navigate legal and procedural channels.

5 Draw up a detailed, prioritized list of what you want to include in your home (number of bedrooms and bathrooms, kitchen layout, garage size). Which elements are must-haves and which can you live without? Include outdoor features such as porches or decks, gardens and a pool on your list.

6 Consider your family's lifestyle, now and in the future. Do you have frequent overnight guests or entertain large groups? Do you want a home office, a craft room, a media room or a workshop? Do you expect aging parents or returning adult children to be moving in? Should you locate the master suite on the first floor to avoid stairs?

7 Browse home design magazines and shop for house plans, in books and online. Even if you hire an architect for your final project, readymade plans can inspire great ideas. Expect to spend

Tips

See 82 Use Home Design and Planning Software.

If you don't have the money to build your perfect home right now, consider an upgradable house: Leave the second story unfinished or pour a concrete patio where another wing of the house will eventually go. However you proceed, install the electrical, plumbing and heating capacity for your home's eventual size now.

When you orient your house on its lot, consider where the utilities will enter and whether they'll come in overhead or underground.

For ideas on energy conservation, see 78 Prepare for Skyrocketing Energy Costs.

If you're designing a home for people with disabilities, see 84 Incorporate Universal Design Principles as well.

Cut costs by designing shared plumbing (situate the bathrooms back to back, for example), minimizing the use of custom doors and windows, and making sure that staircases don't take unnecessary turns.

Who Knew?

Put the laundry room on the same floor as most of the bedrooms, or put in laundry chutes from bedroom floor to the laundry.

anywhere from $400 to $1,300 for plans, depending on the project size and level of complexity. Order up to eight nonreproducible sets of your final plan—enough to give to tradespeople, contractors and lenders—or one reproducible master set.

8 Pay attention to style. Drive around neighborhoods and take pictures of houses that you like. Collect ideas for paint colors, siding choices, windows, doors, rooflines and other features. Let your architect speak frankly about your list of likes and dislikes to make sure you're not creating a Frankenstein house with a hodgepodge of styles.

9 Be flexible and willing to make compromises as you move forward. Budget, availability of materials and complexity will have an impact on your design.

82 | Use Home Design and Planning Software

Want to release your inner architect and plan your dream home? Software applications can help you design a house, choose paint colors, place your furniture, estimate construction costs and even choose appropriate plants for your future garden. It can also provide 3-D views to help you visualize your finished project.

Steps

1 Decide what sort of software you want. There are different programs for decorating and furniture arranging, landscaping, painting and ground-up home design. Some are available in bundles that have it all.

2 Read the software's system requirements to make sure it'll work on your computer.

3 Take your time learning the software. The best design programs are complicated, and you won't be drawing plans the day you install them.

4 Think about the features that are most important to you. For example, do you want to see a 3-D view of your sketch, build a rough construction budget or add landscaping to your design? Different programs have different features.

5 Measure the lot you'll be building on, if you've already selected it. You'll need the contours of the land as well as its dimensions.

6 Ask paint dealers if they have paint-simulating software. These programs let you apply various color schemes to a digital photo of your house.

83 | Establish Your Home's Space Plan

If your home seems confining, look how the rooms are laid out. Poor arrangement of furniture, plants and other objects can bring traffic flow to a standstill. But applying standard human-dimension guidelines—using some common sense, in other words—can help your home look, work and feel better in no time.

Steps

1 Measure your rooms and draw a floor plan at a scale of ¼ inch (6 mm) to 1 foot (30.5 cm). Note in which direction each door swings and the locations of all windows and electrical outlets.

2 Measure your furniture to scale for each piece, and make paper shapes for them that work with your floor plan.

3 Put your coffee table 15 to 18 inches (38 to 46 cm) in front of the couch. The height of your side tables should be within 3 inches (8 cm) of the couch arm's height. Walkways between the back of the couch and the nearest wall or object should be at least 30 inches (76 cm) wide.

4 Place a dresser that faces a bed at least 42 inches (107 cm) away from it so you can open drawers and still get between the two. Allow at least 24 inches (61 cm) from the side of the bed to the nearest wall or object so you can make the bed.

5 Position a dining table 36 inches (91 cm) from the nearest wall or so it's easy to get in and out of chairs. Hang a light 29 to 30 inches (74 to 76 cm) over the tabletop. Area rugs should project at least 24 inches (61 cm) beyond a table on all sides.

Tip

Use warm, dark, matte colors to make a large room feel smaller. If a room is long and narrow, use warm colors on the shorter walls to bring them forward and make the room appear squarer.

Warning

Avoid tall furniture if a room has low ceilings.

84 | Incorporate Universal Design Principles

There are many reasons to make your home more accessible. Perhaps you have a family member in a wheelchair, or elderly parents who visit frequently. Maybe you just want to make your home work for everyone. No matter the reason, architects no longer think in terms of barrier-free designs; instead, they employ universal design principles to make a house open and attractive for all ages and abilities.

Steps

Whole house

1 Have everything needed for living—bathroom, bedroom, kitchen and laundry—on the main level (without stairs) even if yours is a multistory house. At least one point of entry to the house should be usable without having to go up or down stairs. The door should be at least 32 inches (81cm) wide, preferably 36 inches

Tip

The pitch on a wheelchair ramp should be no greater than 1 in 12 (1 foot of rise in 12 feet of length). A less-steep pitch—from 1 in 14 to 1 in 20—is better. Consult with your local building department for codes in your area.

(91 cm), with a lever-style handle instead of a knob and a flat or beveled threshold no more than ½ inch (1.2 cm) tall.

2 Build interior doors at least 32 inches (81cm) wide with lever-style handles instead of knobs.

3 Pay attention to how lighting is installed throughout the house. Mount rocker-style light switches near doors at a height that a seated person can reach. Install push-button lighting systems for people with severe upper-body disability.

4 Build hallways at least 36 inches (91cm) wide. 42 inches (107 cm) is even better. Keep floors clear, and use nonskid backings on area rugs and runners.

5 Install a telephone and a light switch within easy reach of the bed. Add access to alarm and emergency alert if necessary.

6 Get a front-loading washer and dryer. They're easier for everyone to use and they save energy.

7 Install sturdy handrails on all staircases, and make sure there are light switches for the stairs at both the top and bottom.

8 Install adjustable rods in closets. Clothes can hang at a lower height, enabling people in wheelchairs (and children) to lift hangers off the rod without pulling the clothes down.

Kitchen and bath

1 Install bathroom doors so they open outward—if a person falls in the bathroom, he or she won't block the door. To ensure that everyone will be able to easily use bathrooms, plan for open space of at least 5 by 5 feet (1.5 by 1.5 m), no-scald faucets, grab bars capable of supporting 250 lb. (113 kg), flexible hose shower heads, seating in the bath or shower, nonslip floors and surfaces and lower towel bars.

2 Install lever-style faucet handles in the kitchen and bath.

3 Mount your cooktop at a height of 30 to 32 inches (75 to 81 cm), and make sure that cooks don't have to reach over burners to operate the controls. Use D-shaped handles for cupboards, and install a pullout work surface at a height of 24 to 30 inches (60 to 75 cm).

4 Opt for a side-by-side refrigerator-freezer so food will be at accessible heights.

Who Knew?

Lever-style door handles and rocker-style light switches are great for everyone. Try using a regular doorknob with an armload of groceries and you'll see.

Warning

Pedestal-style (open underneath) kitchen and bath sinks, allow a person in a wheelchair to get close enough to use them easily. But be sure that drains and hot water pipes are positioned to prevent burns.

85 Plan a Remodel

Remodeling is often a costly and stressful experience. But it can also be rewarding, offering a sense of accomplishment, the joy of a newly designed space and an increase in your home's market value. Follow these steps, keep your eyes on the prize and you'll see it through.

Steps

Designing and planning

1 Visit model homes with your camera. Watch decorating programs on television. Prowl home decor stores; pore over remodeling books, magazines and Web sites to get a feel for what you like and what's in fashion. Collect ideas in a folder or binder.

2 Write down everything you'd like to include in your remodel, no matter how outrageous. Divide your list into three categories: must do, want to do and would like to do.

3 Take measurements of the rooms you plan to remodel and draw a rough floor plan. Also take photos from many different angles.

4 Consider the resale value of your house. Overimprove your house, especially in comparison to the neighborhood, and you won't recoup your money when you sell. Kitchen and bathroom remodels typically offer the highest payback; finishing a basement and adding a pool the lowest. A trusted real estate agent can help you decide what projects are worth their ticket price.

5 Decide roughly how much you want to spend. Building costs vary widely from region to region. Your best information may come from friends and neighbors who have remodeled recently. Consult with a banker or a mortgage broker early in the process if your project will require financing. See 231 Organize a Loan Application and 226 Set Up a Budget.

6 Identify architects or designers who are appropriate for your project. Ask friends, neighbors and the building department for references. Call and describe your project in general terms and ask about their design philosophy. Ask what kinds of projects they specialize in. Another option is to hire a design-build contractor, who can take a project through from concept to construction.

7 Narrow down your list of designers and architects to a handful, and schedule interviews at their offices (ask if they charge for this). Show them your idea file, describe what you have in mind and tell them what you plan to spend. View examples of their work, check their accreditations and get names and phone numbers of former clients. Listen carefully and take good notes.

8 Ask the architect or builder you're considering if they have done projects similar to yours. If so, do your best to check them out as

Tips

One online tool for estimating remodeling costs can be found at Contractors.com (click on *Cost Estimator*). But remember that building costs vary widely from region to region.

Make sure your architect or designer enlists the aid of an engineer if your project involves removing walls, adding a second story or altering your home's foundation.

Many contractors, even good ones, have complaints filed against them. If you like a contractor but see complaints in his or her file, ask for an explanation.

Who Knew?

Designers often aren't licensed, so their services may cost less than an architect's, but they may not bring as much training, experience or aesthetic sensibility to your project.

Consider energy efficiency in your plans. Some states and utilities can provide tax breaks, rebates or low-interest loans for energy-saving work.

Include a clause in your contract (if your project requires that you take out a loan) that specifies the contract is valid only if you obtain financing at a particular interest rate.

that will give you a first-hand view of a comparable remodel. Call the homeowners and ask how the work went and if they have any positive or negative comments about how the project went.

Working with contractors

1 Identify several contractors. Confirm that they and their subcontractors are licensed and bonded. Describe your project and ask if they've handled comparable jobs in the past year. Check their availability for your intended time frame and discuss your budget.

2 Narrow the field to those available contractors who impressed you most. Check out their record with local home building organizations, contractor associations or your state's licensing board. Contact the Better Business Bureau (bbb.org) to learn if any complaints have been lodged against the contractor.

3 Ask for names and numbers of current and former customers. Interview them about each contractor's strengths and weaknesses, and ask how the job went. Was the quality of the work and materials what you expected? Was the project completed on time and within budget? During work, did the contractor keep you informed? Did the crew and subcontractors treat your property and family respectfully? Would you hire him or her again?

4 Solicit at least two but preferably three competitive bids (in writing). Contractors will use the architect's blueprints or construction documents to make an accurate bid. If there are significant differences between bids, ask why. A lowball bid won't end up costing the least if you have to replace poor-quality materials or shoddy workmanship.

5 Make sure your contract specifies that the contractor is responsible for building permits, inspections and clearances from the local building department. The contract should also specify a payment schedule and finance charges, if they apply. It should include a start and completion date, set penalties for any delays as well as details on how any cost overruns will be handled.

6 Keep track of subcontractors whenever possible. Get their names and note when they work and what they do.

After construction

1 Make sure all inspections and clearances are complete before you write the final check.

2 Review your homeowner's insurance to make sure you have adequate replacement coverage for your improvements.

3 File any necessary paperwork with your local property tax authority.

Look for a good fit. Ask if you will be treated as a partner in the project. Having a strong rapport and good communication with the architect and contractor will have a tremendous impact on your overall job satisfaction.

Take pictures at every stage of the work. Document (take photos and measurements) where water and sewer pipes, electrical conduits and other infrastructure are located when walls are open.

Warnings

Run if a builder suggests that you serve as your own general contractor or "owner/builder." Under this arrangement you are responsible for the overall job, which may include state and federal taxes, workers' compensation, and other legal liabilities. It may be illegal.

Any changes you decide to make to your plans along the way (typically called a change order) need to be documented in order to ensure that your contractor takes care of them. Whenever you make a decision, be sure that either you or your contractor puts it in writing and signs it. Verbal agreements to fix something offer no legal protection or proof that the request was ever made.

86 | Plan a Multimedia Center

Families don't warm themselves around the hearth anymore. Instead we congregate around our electronics—the television, home theater, stereo and game systems. Unfortunately, it's our job as consumers to put all this gear together, make it work for us and keep it tidy.

Steps

1 Inventory your current gear. Measure your television, and count and measure all your components, consoles and boxes. Give some thought to what you might want to add in the future.

2 Inventory your media, such as DVDs, CDs, video and cassettes, and LPs. See 137 Organize Movies, Music and Other Media.

3 Look at the spot where you want to put your multimedia center. Is it a blank wall, or are there doors and windows you need to work around? How many electrical outlets are there? Is your cable or satellite connection nearby? Take photos and measurements of the area.

4 Shop for furniture to hold your components and media. Bring your inventory notes, measurements and pictures along. When choosing, consider the style of your existing furniture and the way you use your gear (are you constantly disconnecting and replugging, or do you just want to hit the Play button?).

5 Hire an electrician to install an extra electrical circuit (or at least a few more properly grounded outlets) for your media center.

6 Position speakers based on where you watch and listen most frequently. Remember to account for the wires—keep them where people won't trip on them or damage them.

7 Calculate optimum viewing distance from the seats to the television by multiplying the diagonal size of an HDTV screen by a factor of 2.5 to 4. That means you should watch a 30-inch (76 cm) television from a distance of 70 to 120 inches (5.75 to 10 feet, or 1.8 to 3 m). Conventional (analog) televisions should be viewed at twice that distance.

8 Put your media center on casters or easy-sliding pads if it goes flat against a wall. You'll occasionally need to get behind it to hook up wires and make changes.

9 Have the technophile in your household create step-by-step instruction cards telling what combination of buttons to push for basic tasks like playing CDs and DVDs.

Tips

When you have your outlets upgraded, have the electrician run speaker wires inside your walls, too. Electricians have tools and techniques that make this easy.

Many media armoires can be top-heavy, especially if there's a tube-style television on the top. Move such furniture with care, and get help.

Park a basket in front of or on top of your media center for game controllers and remote controls.

Warning

Don't plug extension cords into extension cords or create other Medusa-like electrical configurations. It's a fire hazard (not to mention unsightly).

Say good-bye to that dingy cellar and hello to a home theater or rec room. Being dark, cool and isolated from the rest of the house is now a benefit, so noisy movies and video games won't disturb the peace of slumbering or working residents above.

Steps

1 Read 89 Organize the Basement. Those waterproofing steps apply here, too.

2 Do any needed structural work on your foundation, taking care of drainage or flooding issues as well as earthquake retrofitting, before you finish your basement.

3 Install a vapor barrier, sufficient insulation and electrical wiring (including speaker wire for side- and rear-channel speakers) before you finish your basement walls. Place a bank of six or eight grounded electrical outlets where the entertainment center will go, even if you don't intend to use one immediately.

4 Consider other features such as a ventilation or HVAC system; an intercom; a DSL, T-1 or cable hookup; and soundproofing during the planning stages.

5 Insulate the floor of the main level of the house (the basement's ceiling). This will keep both stories warmer and muffle the sound from the entertainment center. Add soundproofing if desired.

6 Build raised platforms for seating, if your basement will be a home theater and if your ceiling is high enough. Build the platforms strong enough to support chairs and couches.

7 Hang blackout blinds on any basement windows, if you'll use the area for a home theater.

8 Look into indoor-outdoor carpeting or laminate flooring, such as Pergo (pergo.com) or Wilsonart (wilsonart.com). Both are good choices in many basements because they're tough, water-resistant, and easy even for novices to install. Carpeting is warmer on the feet but harder to keep clean.

Tip

Check with building officials to see if you're required to have direct egress (exit) from the basement to the outside in case of fire.

Who Knew?

Take photos of your walls after you've installed wiring but before you've hung wallboard or paneling. They will be helpful later if you need to modify the wiring.

Warnings

Consult your local government and follow all building codes when you remodel your basement.

Pay particular attention to water issues. Nothing beats mold when it comes to spoiling your enjoyment of your new surround-sound media room.

As any curious 8-year-old can tell you, the attic is a cool place to find all sorts of treasures. The rest of us value attics for storing items that aren't needed every day. Just remember not to keep candles, electronics, delicate fabrics, photographs or other heat-sensitive items there: The temperature in an attic can be 40 degrees F (more than 4 C) hotter than the rest of the house.

Steps

Getting it ready

1 Check for signs of rodent infestation. Schedule an appointment with an exterminator to discuss how to get rid of the problem.

2 Nail ¾-inch (2-cm) sheets of plywood or fiberboard between the joists to create a floor, if there isn't one already. Each sheet should span at least three joists to distribute the weight. Make sure your ceiling joists are strong enough to support what you're storing. If there's any doubt in your mind, check with a contractor or engineer.

3 Rig a pull-down staircase or ladder to allow easy access.

4 Install battery-powered lights if the attic isn't wired, and lubricate the attic fan motor and bearings.

Organizing it

1 Read 37 Conquer Clutter and 12 Get Rid of What You Don't Want. Haul out everything that's just collecting dust.

2 Set aside a day and enlist a family member to sort through heirloom treasures. Limit the time you indulge in "remember whens" in order to get through all the items.

3 Store items around the perimeter so that you maintain a clear path to them (see 128 Store Anything). Make sure that nothing blocks air vents or disturbs insulation.

4 Group items together, such as all the seasonal decorations or hand-me-down clothes, so that they'll be easier to locate. See 139 Store Out-of-Season Clothes and 135 Organize Gift Wrap and Seasonal Decorations.

5 Get creative with storage solutions. Install bars between rafters to hang clothes. Hang hooks and build shelving.

6 Cover any stored furniture with old bed sheets to protect it from dust, nicks and sunlight.

7 Post a list of contents tied to a floor plan near the attic door, and update it when you take things down or add more items.

Tip

If you find mice in your attic, plug their entry holes with steel wool. They can't chew through it. An exterminator will have even more tips.

Who Knew?

Ordinary cardboard, paper, metal and wood can deteriorate fabric and should not come in direct contact with textile items. See 140 Store Your Wedding Dress and Other Textiles.

The acid in unsealed cedar chests is especially harmful to cotton, linen and rayon. Use a polyurethane varnish to seal wood that comes in contact with textiles.

Plastic bags and boxes should not be used for storing garments and other cloth items. They seal moisture inside, prevent air from circulating and may give off by-products as they decompose.

Warning

Insulate the attic before you start to use it for storage. Wear long sleeves, pants, a hat and safety glasses when you work with fiberglass insulation and take a hot shower afterward.

Moisture poses the biggest threat to using a basement for storage—you'll face a constant challenge to keeping things dry. These steps will show you how to keep most of the water out so that you can take advantage of an ideal place to stash a variety of household objects.

Steps

Keeping it dry

1   Clean the walls and floor thoroughly with detergent and water (follow that with a diluted bleach solution if mold is present). Fill any pores or gouges with grout or resin filler. Use a wet-dry shop vacuum to remove water afterward.

2   Paint concrete basement walls and floor with a waterproofing sealant, or install a vapor barrier. Look for a sealant that protects the concrete and also blocks soil gases such as radon.

3   Keep the basement floor drain clean and clear of debris. Install a water alarm and a sump pump if flooding is an issue.

4   Put items in waterproof plastic bins if any water remains after taking these steps. Place packets of silica gel desiccant in the bins to further absorb moisture. Raise items off the floor with wooden pallets or plastic crates.

5   Run a dehumidifier in the basement, and empty its pan regularly. (Don't run a dehumidifier unless you have installed a vapor barrier or sealed the concrete, or it will actually draw moisture.)

6   Expect mildew: Choose what you store in the basement very carefully if there is any water or moisture present. Do not store books, papers, photographs, artwork or important documents in the basement. Think twice about storing off-season clothes and quilts there as well—you may rue the day. See 140 Store Your Wedding Dress and Other Textiles.

7   Try to keep the temperature between 60 to 75 degrees F (15 to 24 C) and the humidity between 50 and 60 percent.

Keeping it orderly

1   Install shelving units to store wine, paper towels, canned foods and other items (see 129 Store Bulk Purchases).

2   Label all boxes on the front and sides so you can tell at a glance what's in them (see 57 Live Better Through Labeling). Better yet, use clear plastic storage bins.

3   Install a smoke detector, fire extinguisher and carbon monoxide alarm. Leave space around the fuse box, furnace and water heater to allow easy access.

4   Hang hoses, bicycles and chairs from the ceiling joists. Avoid hanging anything from the pipes, which could damage them.

Tips

If your laundry is in the basement, vent the dryer to the outside (see 62 Organize Your Laundry Center).

Keep a flashlight in a wall-mounted rack near the door for power outages.

Who Knew?

Install roof gutters and downspouts, and grade the soil around your house to channel rainwater away from your foundation.

Homeowner's insurance may not cover damage caused by sewer or drain backups or flooding; so check your policy before you store valuables in the basement.

Wine thrives in basements because of their cool, constant temperature and darkness (see 93 Organize Your Wine Collection).

Warnings

Never store anything in direct contact with bare soil if you have an unfinished space.

Never store flammable liquids in the same basement room as a gas water heater.

Don't run a frost-free freezer in your basement if you have moisture problems.

Are you stumbling over bikes, suitcases, camping gear and boxes filled with assorted junk while your new car sits in the driveway or out in the street? If your garage resembles a rummage explosion, it's time to organize. You may even be able to put your car back in its rightful home—and find that tennis racket that's been missing for two years.

Steps

1 Sort through the clutter. Discard what's broken and sell anything that you're not using. See 1 Get Organized, 12 Get Rid of What You Don't Want and 95 Plan a Yard or Garage Sale.

2 Concentrate on reorganizing the stuff you want to keep. Group like things together. For example, store everything for auto repair in one area, sporting gear in another.

3 Use large stackable plastic bins for small items such as camping gear, craft supplies or hand tools. Buy lockable bins if they contain valuable or dangerous items such as power tools. See 144 Organize Camping Equipment and 133 Organize Craft and Hobby Materials.

4 Attach shelves or cabinets to your garage walls, or put up free-standing units. Store the heaviest items on the lowest shelves. If your garage is barely big enough for the car, hang shelves on all three walls above car-roof height.

5 Hang rakes, brooms, shovels, folding lawn chairs and other flat items on the walls. See 115 Organize Gardening Tools.

6 Hang bikes on hooks from the ceiling along the side of the garage, or over the hood of your car. Install a floor-to-ceiling bike rack if you're storing bikes for the whole team. See 142 Store Bicycles and Gear and 489 Win the Tour de France.

7 Lay ¾-inch (2 cm) plywood in the rafters and create a storage loft. Run a ladder up the wall into the loft for easy access.

8 Build a low storage platform that the hood of your car slides under if you're really pressed for space. Use it to stash stuff in what would otherwise be empty air (unless you're hanging your bikes there).

9 Consider erecting a metal, vinyl or wood shed if you have a yard. Then move tools, gardening supplies and the lawn mower out of the garage. Many home supply stores, such as Lowe's and Home Depot, offer ready-to-assemble kits, or shop online at sites such as ShedShop.com, ShelterWorld.com and ABetter Backyard.net/storagesheds.html.

Tips

When you clean your garage, take everything out and put it in the driveway. Clean, air out and check items for damage, then put it back in.

Avoid the temptation to use your garage to store things until you can put them away properly.

Install adequate lighting in your garage with easily accessible light switches.

Who Knew?

Lay a doormat next to the door of your car. Wipe your feet when you get in or out of the vehicle. Put another mat by the door from the garage to your house, and use it religiously.

Bolt a 2-by-4 to the floor for use as a tire stop. Or hang a tennis ball from the ceiling so that it just hits your windshield when you pull into the garage.

Warnings

Never run cars, motorcycles, snowmobiles, lawn mowers or other gasoline engines in your garage.

Keep gasoline, kerosene, paint thinner and other flammable items in locked, well-ventilated storage separate from the house.

91 | Organize a Toolbox

Every home, no matter how small, needs a set of basic tools. But acquiring tools is really only the first step. You have to know how to use them properly and—just as important—how to care for and store them properly. If you know what tools you have and can access them quickly, you'll be more likely to take on new projects and do quality work. An organized toolbox and clean, cared-for tools will serve you for years, if not decades.

Steps

1 Buy the basics. At minimum, your tool kit should contain a claw hammer, lineman's pliers, needlenose pliers, crescent wrench, large and small screwdrivers (standard and Phillips), a cordless drill with bits, a tape measure, a level, a utility knife, gloves, safety glasses or goggles, and a flashlight.

2 Store small hand tools in a toolbox. Put the ones you use most often on top. Hang additional tools on a Peg-Board mounted in the garage or tool shed. See 92 Set Up a Woodshop.

3 Buy a large toolbox that comes with a smaller one inside. Keep basic tools in the small box in your house, and the rest in the bigger box so you don't have to go to the garage or basement every time a screw is loose. Or, buy a 5-gallon (19 l) bucket and stash your tools in a tool apron that fits around the bucket. (Specialty tools don't have to be immediately accessible.)

4 Keep tools clean and dry—dirt and water are their worst enemies. Rub machine oil onto rusty metal tools, polish them with fine steel wool and wipe clean. Give tools a light coat of machine oil or WD-40 if they're prone to rust.

Tips

Also read 115 Organize Gardening Tools.

A toolbox that doubles as a step stool is a great space-saver for small homes.

Put a piece of cardboard in the bottom of your toolbox to soak up oil and moisture.

Who Knew?

Spend money to get fewer tools of higher quality. They'll last longer, function better and feel much more solid and satisfying to work with.

Warning

Avoid using broken tools (such as hammers with loose heads or cracked handles) and dull saw blades or drill bits. They're dangerous and harder to use.

---

92 | Set Up a Woodshop

Woodworkers, rejoice! You finally have enough room to get your tools out of the toolbox (and shed and car) and set up your own shop. Plan thoughtfully to accommodate all your equipment, but remember: there is no such thing as a dream shop. The perfect setup is one that works just right for you, your projects and your budget.

Steps

1 Glean ideas from other woodworkers about optimal shop layouts and tool configurations. Keep in mind that you can always make adjustments to suit changing needs and to fit in new tools. If necessary, start small and invest in quality tools as you expand.

Tips

Secure Peg-Board hooks with a dab of hot glue or silicone caulk.

Store ladders horizontally so kids aren't tempted to climb them.

Don't forget to leave room for the boom box.

Continued on next page

2 Follow the "rule of plenty." Design as much space, light, ventilation, power, work surfaces and storage in the layout as possible.

3 Build or buy as solid and as well equipped a workbench as you can afford in terms of space and money. The bench is your shop's most important element, so it should suit you perfectly.

4 Organize tools by task in drawers and cabinets, and label them. Put all pliers in one drawer, hammers in another, measuring tools (tape, stick, chalk line, plumb bob) in a third. See 57 Live Better Through Labeling.

5 Mount Peg-Board on open wall space and above the workbench to hold frequently used tools. Outline tools with a permanent marker to make it easy to put tools back in the proper place.

6 Lay out equipment so that you can work easily and safely. To use a table saw, joiner or planer, for example, you need a space that's 18 feet (5.4 m) long and not less than 10 feet (3 m) wide in order to be able to push a full sheet of plywood through. If you have to make do with a small space, buy portable tools that roll into the driveway while you use them.

7 Install plenty of grounded outlets at floor level and along the workbench to minimize overlapping cords and to avoid having to extend cords so far that you're working with no slack. Put in a retractable electric cord that drops from the ceiling for use with hand tools. Install dedicated circuits with sufficient power for high-amperage power tools such as table saws, band saws, drill presses and radial-arm saws.

8 Store all your tool manuals in a three-ring binder. Keep receipts and warranties in an envelope with the manuals. See 100 Manage Warranty Documents.

9 Hang sawhorses from the studs to keep them out of the way. Build a lumber rack to store sheets of plywood.

10 Install task lighting for the workbench and floor tools (such as the drill press and band saw). Make sure the lights shine on the work area and not in your face.

11 Give careful consideration to dust control in your shop. Airborne sawdust can set off—and even explode—smoke detectors so make sure your system collects sawdust and keeps the shop clean. Adequate ventilation will prevent the buildup of fumes and airborne contaminants as well as lower the humidity to keep wood from warping.

12 Paint concrete floors with nonskid epoxy paint. Lay a carpet square at your bench or, better, an ergonomic standing mat to make it more comfortable to work standing up for long periods of time. (Shop Ergoboy.com and other ergonomic specialty stores.)

13 Equip your workshop with a smoke detector, a fire extinguisher and a first aid kit (see 466 Assemble Emergency Kits).

Who Knew?

If you're patient and love the hunt, poke around older pharmacies or typesetting houses for banks of drawers that aren't being used anymore. They're beautiful and well made, and they have infinite numbers of small storage spaces.

For safety, store circular-saw blades in old record album covers. Slit a length of old garden hose to slip over the teeth of handsaws.

Pour a thin layer of linseed oil on top of oil-based paint before you store it. (Don't mix it in.) For latex paints, transfer leftover paint to smaller cans, available at paint stores. Mark the color, room and date on all paint cans. See 145 Store Paint and Other Hazardous Materials.

Buy a 2-gallon (7.5 l) wet-dry shop vacuum and keep it handy in your workshop. Some vacuums will also attach to the dust ports on power tools.

Warnings

Consider putting a keyed electrical circuit in your workshop if you have dangerous power tools and small children.

Unplug power tools and coil up their cords when they're not in use.

Cheaper by the dozen doesn't just apply to doughnuts. If you buy wine by the case, you need to store it—and if you do it right you'll have fine-tasting wines to enjoy for years to come. Many white wines can be stored from two to five years, while red wines will last—and generally improve—for five to 20 years, sometimes longer.

Steps

1 Keep the temperature of your wine closet, refrigerator or cellar between 50 and 65 degrees F (10 and 18 C) for red wines, 45 to 60 degrees F (7 to 15 C) for whites, or as directed by a vintner or wine merchant. Store your white wines closer to the floor and reds higher up. Cooler temperatures generally won't harm wines, but can delay their development.

2 Maintain a relative humidity in your cellar or storage area of about 70 percent for cork health.

3 Store bottles on their sides so that the corks stay in contact with the wine. Keep the area dark, if possible, but definitely out of direct sunlight. Use incandescent lights: Fluorescent bulbs give off more ultraviolet light, which can penetrate bottles.

4 Use untreated redwood for storage bins or racks. It won't deteriorate in cool, humid wine-cellar conditions.

5 Hang identifying tags on the necks so the bottles don't need to be disturbed when you want to know what bottle is what. Keep bottles of the same vintage together as much as possible.

6 Use many small bins rather than a few large ones. Racks that hold individual bottles are ideal.

7 Think strategically when you arrange your cellar. Keep the more frequently used wines by the door, and the long-term investments in the cooler, darker corners.

8 Know what you own and be able to find it quickly. Make a database of your cellar's inventory. Give each wine a location number and listing, including the wine's name, vintage, producer, appellation, vineyard name, region, county, type (red, white, rosé, sparkling), quantity owned, price paid per bottle, value (at latest estimate) and size of bottle (half-bottle, magnum). Add tasting and pairing notes, and keep the file outside of the cellar so you don't have to disturb the bottles to check.

9 Store wine in the garage if where you live doesn't get beastly hot in the summer. Garages tend to be cool, dark and free of ultraviolet light—ideal for wine. See 90 Organize the Garage.

10 Get a freestanding wine refrigerator if your house doesn't have a basement, an appropriate cellar or a garage. A wine refrigerator will hold between 24 and 200 bottles under ideal conditions.

Tips

See 297 Plan a Week of Menus, 328 Set Up a Bar and 322 Impress a Date.

For a complete listing of wines and how long to store each type, consult sites such as CellarNotes.net or Wine.com.

Who Knew?

If you don't have an area with ideal conditions for wine storage, choose a location that isn't subject to dramatic swings in temperature.

If you have a large or valuable collection—and you don't require daily access to it—investigate a wine collection storage service, which will store your wine off site in perfect conditions.

When you buy wine (especially reds) ask the wine shop or winery how long it should age. Make a "Drink in 2010" note in your database so that you drink wines before they start to go downhill.

Warning

Don't store wines in a cabinet above the stove—the heat will kill them in no time.

You don't need to own an estate to have an estate sale. But you do need to know that estate sales differ significantly from garage sales. In an estate sale, you pay a company a fee to manage the event and sell every single item in the home. This is often the best course to choose after a divorce or a death in the family. You don't do any of the actual selling, but there's plenty of work to do to prepare for one.

Steps

1 Create an inventory of the contents of the home, garage, yard and other properties. Make a separate list of important documents, including real-estate deeds, stocks, bonds, insurance papers, bank accounts and personal papers. Locate valuable assets, including jewelry, cash and artwork. Sort through the personal effects and determine how you will dispose of them.

2 Hire a professional organizer to help you with the estate, especially if you live far away or can't invest the time, or if the process is too emotionally difficult. An organizer can help you decide what to keep, throw away, give to relatives or sell, and can suggest places to donate unwanted items. He or she will also inventory the remaining possessions, pack or oversee the packing, and arrange for storage and shipping of household items. See 12 Get Rid of What You Don't Want.

3 Interview at least two estate sale companies. Ask to see a business license and insurance policy. Call recent customers and ask lots of questions. Get a reliability report from the Better Business Bureau (bbb.org). Give each company a copy of your inventory and expect them to inspect the house's contents.

4 Ask what the company estimates you'll earn from the sale, what its fees are (usually a percentage of the gross), what those fees cover and what its timeline is for a sale of property like yours. Get details on what advertising the company will do in advance of the sale.

5 Make sure the company you choose has expertise (on staff or on call) if the estate includes valuable items such as antiques, jewelry or artwork. Reserve the right to get independent appraisals if you're not satisfied with the company's. You'll pay for your own appraisals.

6 Find out if the company policy allows dealers to come in before the sale to buy items. This is not necessarily a problem.

7 Inquire about the company's after-sale procedures. Will it contact a charity to remove items that don't sell? (Make sure you get the tax-deduction receipt.) Will it haul away trash and leave the house empty and broom-clean?

8 Choose a company based on the information you've collected. Get a written contract and make sure it covers all aspects of the

Tips

Make sure that estate sale companies don't charge you for the initial interview and inspection.

Look for a company that can provide lockable show-cases if your estate contains small, valuable items such as jewelry.

Who Knew?

Find out if the sale company will bring leftover items from other sales to your estate sale. This is not necessarily a problem, but many people want to know about it.

sale—when it will take place, what the costs will be, how much advertising will be done, appraisal of special items, and so on.

9 Arrange to get a complete accounting of the sale when it's completed.

10 Sell everything—junk and all—to an auction house or liquidator for the easiest solution. Either will take a percentage of the total sales figure, so there's no out-of-pocket expense for you.

Warning

Stay away from the home during the sale. It's often emotionally difficult to see family heirlooms carried off by strangers.

---

95 | Plan a Yard or Garage Sale

You've been organizing and decluttering like mad; now it's time to get rid of what you've culled. The secrets to a successful garage sale are ample preparation, team organization and sales presentation. Do your prep in advance and relax on the big day while the money rolls in.

Steps

1 Schedule your garage sale far enough in advance that you can place classified ads in city and community newspapers. Hold your sale on a nonholiday weekend, unless you live in a resort town with lots of vacationers. Check the long-range forecast for good weather.

2 Give boxes to everyone in your family a few weeks before the sale. Have each person fill a box or two with things he or she wants to sell (beyond what's already piled in the garage). Let the kids know they can keep the cash from their items.

3 Give your neighbors a courtesy call before the yard sale. They'll appreciate it, and may even have items to add to your stock.

4 Organize your neighbors to hold sales on the same day as yours. An enormous block sale will attract flocks of buyers and generate great foot traffic. Offer to sell stuff for friends and family for a commission.

5 Take out an ad in the paper, and create large, easy to read signs for the neighborhood. Tap into no-cost resources, such as online listings or community newspapers that publish free classifieds.

6 Set and post a starting time, and put out a sign that warns "Early birds pay double"—and stick to it. Otherwise, your doorbell will start ringing at 5 a.m., and the good stuff will be gone before the majority of your customers arrive.

7 Round up volunteers if you expect large crowds. Friends and family may be willing to help in order to get rid of their own junk.

Tips

Save paper and plastic grocery bags for several weeks before your sale.

Pay attention to safety. Don't stretch extension cords across walkways or have sharp knives in boxes with other kitchen tools.

Do provide a live extension cord so buyers can test electrical items.

Continued on next page

8 Scrub, wash, polish and launder anything you plan to sell. If an item needs a simple repair to greatly increase its selling price, do it. Hang clothing on makeshift racks, sorted by size, without cramming too many garments onto the rods. Provide a changing area and mirror.

9 Use masking tape or colored dots and a permanent marker to price everything. Setting up "$1 or less" and "$5 or less" tables or boxes will save you time and attract shoppers.

10 Be realistic when you price things: You may have spent a fortune on that beta VCR, but you'll be lucky to get a quarter for it now. Stay flexible and leave yourself room to bargain down—and remember, the goal is to get rid of stuff. Have a "One thin dime" box to encourage further browsing.

11 Display your merchandise on folding tables (or plywood and saw-horses) to keep it off the ground. And organize your goods: Don't make buyers root through piles of junk to find the gems.

12 Put some real crowd-pleasers up front to entice passing cars. Good looking furniture and large children's play structures make great bait near the curb.

13 Make sure there's plenty of parking. Move your cars if necessary.

14 Spread a rug or blanket on the lawn with a few toys that you're selling. Kids will bond with the toys and demand that their parents buy them.

15 Share your family memories if there's a funny story behind an item. People find it harder to resist buying something with a history.

16 Be cheerful, get people talking and encourage haggling. Many people are reluctant to negotiate but find it's fun once they start.

17 Set up your cash table near the entrance. Have plenty of small bills, change, a cash box, a calculator, pencil and pen, ledger book (to inventory commissions), bags, boxes and newspapers to wrap purchases, and a tape measure. Keep your cell phone close by to call in relief when you need a break.

18 Make sure anything that's not for sale is safely behind closed doors. Protect yourself against theft by displaying small valuables within eyesight and close to the cash box. Keep money in a zipped fanny pack if you're bustling about.

19 Acknowledge a point of diminishing returns. Be ready to slash prices drastically when business drops off. Or donate your leftovers to charity and take a tax write-off.

Who Knew?

Note where you've posted signs on a map, and take them down promptly when your sale is complete.

Opinions vary on whether you should price each item beforehand or negotiate on the spot. Do what feels comfortable and what buyers in your area expect.

Warnings

Stash large sums of money in the house during the sale and keep it locked up tight. Yard sales can be distracting, and bad guys will take advantage of that fact.

Never accept personal checks.

Real-estate agents have a saying: "The way you sell your home is not the way you live in it." That may be true, so try to look at your home through the eyes of a buyer when you're preparing it for sale. The hard part? Keeping the house spotless day after day for prospective buyers who may show up on a half-hour's notice.

Steps

1 Maximize your home's curb appeal. Feed, mow and water your lawn regularly. Plant colorful annual flowers near the door, and make sure you weed and trim the rest of your garden. Wash the windows and pick up any trash.

2 Perform any needed repairs on the interior or exterior of your home. Fix, paint or cosmetically enhance anything that might hinder a sale.

3 Declutter all rooms to make them look and feel larger (see 1 Get Organized and 37 Conquer Clutter). Also, clear out the closets so they look roomier.

4 Clean the oven, stove, refrigerator, exhaust fan and kitchen sink very thoroughly—and keep them clean. Clear the kitchen counters of items you don't use daily.

5 Replace the toilet seat and shower curtain. Clean the bathroom thoroughly and hang fresh towels every day.

6 Send your pets to camp. You love 'em, but your potential buyers may be afraid or allergic (see 77 Safeguard Your Home Against Allergens). Deal with pest problems, such as mice, fleas and flies.

7 Vacuum your carpets, or have them professionally cleaned. Clean and polish all smooth floors.

8 Fix ripped window screens. Replace cracked or broken panes, and make sure all windows open, close and lock smoothly.

9 Patch any holes or cracks in the walls and ceilings. Give them a fresh coat of paint in a neutral color such as off-white. (Be sure you allow enough time for paint to dry so the house doesn't have that fresh-paint smell.)

10 Have your house professionally staged (see StagedHomes.com for local sources). This will cost you, but staging a home aesthetically can shorten the time to sale and boost the bidding.

11 Keep your garage door closed, no matter how spiffed up you keep your garage.

Tips

Consider hiring a professional for yard care or housecleaning until your house sells. The dollars you spend on curb appeal will often come back through a higher sale price.

Some homeowners choose to rent a storage unit while their house is on the market, putting in some of their extra furniture and other belongings. Don't just pile stuff in the garage—buyers will want to inspect that, too.

Put brighter bulbs in all your lamps. Turn them on, even in the daytime, to brighten the house.

Warning

Give up smoking. You probably can't smell it, but your house reeks of smoke. Have drapes, curtains, upholstery and carpets professionally cleaned. If you decide to continue smoking, do it outside—and don't leave an unsightly bucket of butts next to a door.

Moving is a big undertaking, and it often is accompanied by other big ticket events such as starting a new job, changing your marital status or taking on a big debt. Following a logical, orderly series of steps will help keep the move from adding to the pressure.

Steps

Getting ready

1 Decide if you will hire a mover or do it yourself. You'll probably hire a mover if you have lots of heavy things, you've got a bad back or bum knee, you're traveling a long distance, an employer is picking up the tab or your friends are sick and tired of schlepping your stuff.

2 Send change-of-address forms to utility companies, magazines, organizations, friends and family as soon as you know your new address. Close out any accounts you won't need after your move such as library cards and video store and gym memberships.

3 Research the utilities at your new address, including telephone, power, water, television and Internet service. Get a floor plan of the new place to help you decide where to put phones and other plug-ins. Mark all electrical outlets on the plan.

4 Pare down your possessions—moving is a great opportunity to unload unneeded stuff. See 12 Get Rid of What You Don't Want.

5 Empty the refrigerator the day before moving day. Eat up any leftovers, decide what you want to bring with you, and give the rest to neighbors. Unplug the refrigerator and leave the doors open overnight so the moisture can evaporate.

Doing it yourself

1 Pack one room at a time, starting with infrequently used rooms such as guest bedrooms. Use smaller boxes for heavy items such as books, tools and kitchen stuff. If the contents are fragile or must stay upright, mark it on the box. Write three other things on each box: the room, a short description of its contents, and "First Out" or "Regular." "First Out" boxes will be loaded in the truck last, making them available first at your destination. Put the boxes in a garage or family room.

2 Measure your mountain of boxes and your furniture when you're about three-fourths packed. Use this information to rent a truck for moving day. Reserve a hand truck and a large quantity of moving blankets at the same time. If you're moving appliances—especially a refrigerator—reserve an appliance dolly.

3 Close dresser drawers and armoire doors with blue painters' masking tape. It's less likely to damage the finish when it's removed at your destination.

Tips

Most national Internet service providers let you keep your e-mail address when you move from one area to another—but only if you stay with their service.

If you're moving a refrigerator, try to keep it upright. If you must set it on its side, let it stand upright at its destination overnight before plugging it in (to avoid damage).

For long-distance moves, inquire about tracking options so that you can find out where your belongings are. Be sure the mover can guarantee a delivery date.

Contact your insurance agent, banks and creditors, doctor, dentist, pharmacy, and children's current and future schools as soon as you know your arrival date at the new address. Arrange utilities to be turned off several days after you leave your old place, and turned on several days before you arrive at the new one.

Who Knew?

Pack important papers, photos, keepsakes and valuables in their own boxes. Rather than writing "Important Papers and Valuables" on the boxes, strap them closed with colored tape so you can easily identify them.

4 Load the truck carefully. Use as much vertical space as you can: Stand sofas on end, load mattresses and box springs so their long sides are vertical, stand up armoires and tall dressers. Put tall things along the sides; moving trucks have bars or tracks onto which you can tie ropes to keep things vertical. Area rugs should go in after the furniture (so you can roll them out before putting the furniture down in the new place).

5 Put in your boxes, "Regular" ones first and "First Out" boxes last. Put the boxes of important papers and valuables in the trunk of your car, not in the moving truck. If you'll be stopping for any time along the drive, lock the truck with a round, short-shank padlock and make sure your car trunk is locked.

6 Reverse the process at the end. Bring in the valuables (and have someone stay with them in the new place while you unload). If it's been a long day and you're exhausted, just unload the valuables and "First Out" boxes, leaving the rest in the locked truck to unpack later.

Hiring a Mover

1 Call several moving companies, both national and local. Contact the Better Business Bureau (bbb.org) to see if there are complaints against the company. Make sure they're bonded, licensed and insured. Ask for and call all three references to corroborate the mover's professionalism and reliability. Choose a company with excellent customer service.

2 Ask about rates. Be aware of any conditions that will trigger additional costs, such as moves over a certain mileage or goods over a certain weight. Check into any special deals the company offers, and ask whether it gives auto club or senior discounts.

3 Understand how packing options affect the price. For example, if you pack certain goods yourself, can you save some money? Or pack everything yourself with portable containers that are delivered to your home. You pack them, and the company transports them to your new home.

4 Schedule a free on-site estimate if you like what you hear. Bids will vary widely. Get several to find the best deal.

5 Discuss any considerations unique to your move with the estimator. Point out any especially large or fragile items, and ask how they will be handled. Point out issues that affect access, such as staircases, steep driveways or small attics, and be prepared to pay more for complicated moves.

6 Get a signed contract that includes price, pick-up and delivery dates, packing services and mileage, plus policies regarding payment, insurance and guaranteed services. Make sure the contract has a customer-service number on it that you can call with any problems.

Look for free or re-used moving supplies rather than buying new ones: online bulletins boards frequently list boxes, bubble-wrap and other necessities.

Ask what happens if goods are damaged, under what conditions the mover is responsible and for how much.

Warnings

Back up your computer before the move, and pack the backup disks with your valuables.

Be sure you understand how materials affect costs and that it's covered in the contract. Many consumer complaints relate to add-on costs from packing materials such as bubble wrap and boxes.

The kids have moved out, you've simplified your life or you're just tired of having a big house that takes a bite out of your free time (and pay check). Moving to less spacious digs requires a change in lifestyle, but planning makes the transition far more seamless.

Steps

1 Consider the downside of downsizing. You'll give up the comfort and familiarity of your current home—and perhaps your town or neighborhood—and you'll have to contend with the stress, cost and aggravation of moving (see 97 Plan a Move).

2 Look just as frankly at the upside. Your rent or mortgage payment may go down. You may also cut back on some living expenses such as energy costs, resulting in more cash in your pocket. You'll probably have more free time because you'll have less house to maintain.

3 Opt for the simplicity and amenities of condominium complexes or retirement villages. Keep in mind that both have rules and regulations that some people may find restrictive. (On the plus side, somebody else cuts the lawn and cleans the gutters.) Read the fine print and talk to future neighbors before you sign a contract.

4 Measure the dimensions of the rooms you'll be moving into, and measure your current furniture to determine what you'll bring and what you'll need to unload.

5 Take this opportunity to reduce clutter and simplify your life. Get rid of unused stuff and things you won't have room for. See 285 Organize Your Empty Nest.

6 Go through all your treasures and enjoy the trip down memory lane. Then sell the crap. See 95 Plan a Yard or Garage Sale and 12 Get Rid of What You Don't Want.

7 Capitalize on your fresh start to tinker with your systems and get organized. See 1 Get Organized.

8 Determine your storage needs for clothes, kitchen supplies, tools, sports and hobby equipment, pet supplies, vehicles and so on. Make sure there's space for everything in your new place. See 132 Expand the Capacity of a Small Room and 131 Capture More Storage Space.

9 Tally up the money you've made selling your home and all your old stuff. Put most of it to work (see 239 Track Your Investments), then reward yourself with a great vacation. See 405 Plan a Trip.

Tip

Give yourself plenty of time to sort through your things. Do a small section of the house at a time, and don't spend more than four hours a day sorting your stuff.

Who Knew?

If you're selling a house you've lived in for at least two of the last five years, up to $250,000 in profit is tax-free ($500,000 for couples who file jointly). If you move from a home you owned to a rental, you lose income-tax deductions for mortgage interest and property taxes.

Warning

Before making any commitments to a new home, consult a financial adviser to find out all the tax consequences of your move.

While there are advantages to living in a studio or small apartment—such as answering the door without getting out of bed—there are challenges, too. By learning the tricks behind small space living, you'll find that less truly is more.

Steps

1 See 132 Expand the Capacity of a Small Room.

2 Concentrate on making your apartment both attractive and functional. Keep those two concepts in mind in all that you do; you're more likely to keep your place clean and organized if you like the way it looks and works.

3 Consider how you'll use your apartment. Is it just a crash pad for yourself, or will you entertain guests? Do you work at home? Do you have sports equipment or hobby supplies? Define your floor plan and storage options accordingly.

4 Separate your sleeping area in a studio with freestanding screens or bookcases. Paint the back of the bookcase with chalkboard paint and use it for messages and brainstorming, or cover it with fabric and use it as the headboard for your bed.

5 Buy a bed that's designed for small spaces: a loft bed, Murphy bed, sleeper sofa, daybed or futon. These let you reclaim the sleeping area when you're awake. Also look at beds that have storage drawers under the mattress instead of a box spring.

6 Get a drop-leaf table. Fold out one leaf and use it as a desk, fold out both leaves for dinner parties, or fold up the whole thing and push it against a wall when not in use.

7 Look for home office furniture that can fold up and roll out of the way when not in use. If you already have a favorite worktable or desk, put it on easy-rolling casters.

8 Group most of your belongings in one or two areas. More floor space will make your place seem larger.

9 Go ahead—use large furniture in a small space. It can actually make a small space seem larger. Many pieces of small furniture tend to look cluttered.

10 Think vertical. Get 7-foot-tall (2.1 m tall) bookcases instead of the standard 6-foot-tall (1.8 m tall) units, and put baskets of small items and papers on the top.

Tips

Use mirrors to make a small room seem larger.

If your landlord will let you paint, use light or bright colors to enlarge rooms.

Who Knew?

Get creative when confronting a landlord's "no nail holes" rule. Lean very large paintings or prints against walls. Use a freestanding easel to showcase a favorite piece. Get an over-the-door hook, like those used for holiday wreaths, and hang art behind the front door.

Warning

Tall, tip-prone furniture must be secured to the wall in earthquake country. See 105 Prepare Your Home for Nature's Worst.

100 | Manage Warranty Documents

It takes a lot of pricey gizmos to keep a household running these days. Inevitably, some of the them will break, malfunction or need maintenance repairs. When that happens, you need to be able to quickly find the warranty documents.

Steps

1 Read warranties carefully before purchasing something expensive like a car or a large appliance to make sure you understand them. Do some comparisons. Look on sites such as BobVila.com, Law.FreeAdvice.com and OnTheHouse.com.

2 Create a warranty-filing notebook. Purchase a pocket notebook or a binder with plastic protector sheets and organize the warranties and all other product information (such as assembly or operating directions) together by year, type of appliance or area of the house where it's used.

3 Keep track of the following information for each warranty or service contract you acquire: what the warranty covers; when and where you bought the item; the warranty terms; the expiration date; and contact information (phone number, address).

4 Keep warranties and receipts for the life of the product. See 232 Organize Important Documents.

Tip

Buying extended warranties on items like DVD players is a losing proposition. As soon as you walk out the door, their value goes south in a hurry. Better to take it home, hook it up and make sure it works. If not, return it.

Warning

Make sure you understand what terms render a warranty void and who is expected to perform maintenance and repairs.

101 | Manage Home-Improvement Paperwork

They say home is where the heart is. It's also where the leaks, drafts, clogs, funky furnaces and other messes are, too. Keeping home-improvement documents organized and handy will make your life easier should you ever decide to sell your home.

Steps

1 File all home-improvement documents together according to the project or room. Include work orders, contracts, receipts, estimates, and so on. Use expanding file folders, or binders with plastic filing sheets to keep related items together.

2 Keep your own dated notes on each project's progress, along with photos or video footage taken at each completed phase of work. These will be useful if you have a dispute or an issue with a contractor later on. See 85 Plan a Remodel.

3 Retain house-related documents for the minimum length of time.

4 Record in your home inventory checklist: a brief description of each item, the purchase date and price, and a serial number or product code for each item.

Tips

If you have made changes to the original work order, make sure to keep a copy of these changes in your project file.

Make sure any home-improvement contract includes the contractor's contact information, including name, address, phone and fax numbers, e-mail address and license number.

Combining two households is a huge challenge, regardless of whether you're summer roommates or lifetime lovers. When you think about your prized possessions, you've got to figure out how you'll share them with someone else's equally prized possessions. It's not fun or romantic to make lists and agreements, but it'll help you live in peace—maybe even 'til death do you part.

Steps

Roommates

1 Box up and store redundant things.

2 Write an agreement that covers financial responsibility for the rent or mortgage, utilities, insurance and other monthly expenses. Keep it simple but precise. Include what happens if one party becomes unable to do his or her share, and the conditions under which the agreement can be dissolved.

3 Pay special attention to cooking and shopping. Decide if you'll share groceries or if you'll each need your own cupboard space and a way to label your food. Make kitchen cleanups each person's individual responsibility. See 308 Organize Cupboards and Drawers, 306 Efficiently Use the Refrigerator and Freezer and 57 Live Better Through Labeling.

4 Have a frank discussion about house keys, cleanliness, music, children, pets, smoking, alcohol, drugs, overnight guests (including lovers and relatives) and any other area of potential friction. Agree on ground rules and stick to them.

5 Come to an agreement and make compromises when decorating any common areas. Maybe you get to decorate one room or area (or floor), and he or she gets to decorate another.

Soulmates

1 Go through your belongings, choose the best items and eliminate the rest. See 12 Get Rid of What You Don't Want, 97 Plan a Move and 146 Organize a Storage Unit.

2 Set up a joint checking account in addition to your individual accounts, and use it for shared expenses. Or, save receipts and split expenses at the end of the month.

3 Consider selling your individual homes and purchasing a totally new place together so it doesn't feel as if one person is moving in on the other's turf. (This is particularly true if children are involved. See 264 Blend Families.) Or, play it safe and rent both of your homes out until the relationship has proved itself.

4 Make sure both of your signatures are required on checks, and avoid buying hard-to-divide items (such as furniture) from the joint account.

Tips

See 95 Plan a Yard or Garage Sale and 98 Downsize Your House.

As you eliminate redundant items (see step 1), cut each other some slack for duplicate items with sentimental value. Books, music and artwork can't be ruthlessly purged—but it can be stored.

Who Knew?

Divvy up the chores. For some households, it makes sense to alternate (you clean one week, the other person cleans the next). For others, it works better to split up chores (you vacuum and dust, the other person mops and scrubs). Find a system that works for both of you. Or, splurge on a housecleaner: It will keep peace in the family. See 19 Organize Your Chores and 64 Get Ready for the Housecleaner.

103 | Decorate for the Seasons

Henry David Thoreau advised us to "live each season as it passes; breathe the air, drink the drink, taste the fruit, and resign yourself to the influences of each." Tune into the season by periodically infusing your home with seasonal colors, scents and textures.

SEASON	TASK
Spring	• Replace heavy winter draperies with lightweight or sheer cottons. • Accessorize with touches of fresh spring pastel colors—peach, ivory, robin's egg blue and lavender—in accent pillows, bed linens, hand towels and throws. • Add area rugs of hand-woven linen, straw, cotton or bamboo. • Place fresh-cut flowers, such as daffodils, tulips and pansies, around the house. • Use egg-shaped soaps and candles (if spring means Easter to you), put pastel-colored candies in dishes in the living room and use a grass-filled basket of treasures as a dining-table centerpiece.
Summer	• Hang matchstick or silvery white vertical blinds. Keep accessories and collectibles to a minimum; clear, open spaces make a home feel cool and airy. • Brighten the house with saturated colors—cornflower blue, grass green, sunny yellow, fiery red, goldenrod and tangerine—in accent pillows, bed linens, hand towels, throws and accessories. • Put a tabletop fountain on an end table or credenza. Simple plug-in models, available at department stores, create a cool babbling sound. • Add some green plants in terracotta pots, wicker furniture and wind chimes to your decor.
Fall	• Emulate the brisk colors of autumn with orange, gold, olive green, russet or earthy browns, tans and heavy creams in accent pillows, bed linens, hand towels, throws and accessories. • Place a large bowl of apples, pomegranates or pumpkins on the table. Hang husks of native corn on the front door. • Change area rugs to heavier materials, such as wool, sisal or jute. • Accessorize with baskets, dishware shaped and colored like autumn leaves, fruits and vegetables and deep red candles.
Winter	• Bring out indigo, black, brilliant scarlet, green, gold and silver accent pillows, bed linens, hand towels, throws and accessories. • Scent your home with evergreen garlands and wreaths. • Hang heavier-textured curtains made of velvet or damask, and lay a faux bearskin next to the fireplace. • Accessorize with antique toys, fresh poinsettias, and candles.
TIP	Place a few drops of essential oil on a light bulb to scent a room. Rose and jasmine are appropriate for spring and summer, while gardenia and cinnamon evoke fall and winter.

104 | Prepare a Vacation Home for the Off-Season

Your vacation home doesn't need to be a source of worry when it's empty—whether it's a ski cabin that sits idle come May or a beach-front cottage that you close up in November. Perform these tasks and the house will stay snug and tidy until you return next season.

Steps

1 Remove all food from the house to discourage pests. If you must store staples such as sugar, flour or oatmeal in the house, keep them in sealed metal, glass or thick plastic containers.

2 Empty the refrigerator, defrost the freezer, prop open the doors and unplug. Place a box of baking soda or a tub of charcoal briquettes in the refrigerator to absorb odors. Fasten the door open so it cannot shut and trap a small creature or child inside.

3 Tilt your mattresses up against the walls (so air can circulate around them) and cover them with sheets. Cover upholstered furniture with sheets, too.

4 Open all doors (closets, bedrooms) to increase air flow.

5 Pour a 50-50 mix of antifreeze and water into drains in freeze areas. (Check with your sewer company first—they may have a nontoxic alternative.)

6 Drain water from the plumbing system and turn off water at the main line, especially if you're closing a home for the winter. Do this even if you don't expect pipes to freeze, in case a pipe springs a leak.

7 Install a low-temperature thermostat if you plan to keep the furnace running over winter (see Tips). If not, shut off the gas or propane at the main. If the house sits empty during the hottest summer months, you might leave the air-conditioning on with a similar thermostat system.

8 Bring in lounge chairs, umbrellas, grills, toys, garden hoses and other outdoor items (see 147 Store a Boat for the Winter).

9 Trim trees away from the house and clean out the roof gutters. Consider installing screened covers for gutters so they don't clog with leaves if autumn is approaching. Put shutters on windows if necessary.

10 Cover your whole-house attic fan with heavy plastic if the house is idle in winter. Cover outdoor air conditioners, if the manufacturer suggests you do so.

11 Hire a year-round caretaker or a security company to check on your place periodically. Make sure your local contact has keys, can deal with any alarm system and knows how to reach you if there's a real problem.

Tips

In areas with high winter humidity, it's a good idea to leave the furnace on at low temperature, rather than turn it off entirely. This can prevent mold and mildew.

If your vacation place has a satellite dish, disconnect it and bring it inside.

If you get mail at your vacation home, be sure to file a forwarding order before you leave.

105 | Prepare Your Home for Nature's Worst

You're pretty sure that a fire, flood, earthquake, tornado, hurricane or other catastrophe will never happen to your family. But you've got a nagging feeling that you should do *something* to secure your home in case of an unlikely disaster. Putting these quick home-protection fixes into place and using common sense will help you sleep better at night.

Steps

General

1 Put together a basic emergency tool kit, with a wrench, pliers, a hammer, scissors, a knife, a pry bar, matches, a utility knife, heavy work gloves and extra-strength 40-gallon garbage bags. Store essential supplies, such as toilet paper, paper towels, bleach, soap, diapers and personal hygiene products with the emergency kit. Get your family and your neighborhood ready with 464 Formulate a Family Emergency Plan and 390 Create an Evacuation Plan. Also see 466 Assemble Emergency Kits.

2 Insulate your water heater's cold water lines to prevent a burst pipe during freezing weather. Inspect your roof for damaged shingles or flashing and remove debris.

3 Identify local pet shelters or other alternatives to care for family pets if you are forced from your home.

4 Check that your homeowner's insurance is up to date and confirm that the policy covers the full cost of replacing your home, not just your home's cash value, or worse, purchase price.

5 Keep some cash and a copy of important papers, such as identification, wills, insurance policies and financial records, in a portable waterproof and fireproof container. See also 232 Organize Important Documents.

6 Photograph or film all your valuable belongings, and make a separate list that details the visual record. Store copies of both in a safe-deposit box.

For earthquakes

1 Evaluate your house for common earthquake risks. Strap the water heater (and any fuel tanks) to the wall to prevent gas leaks and fire. Anchor bookshelves to walls, and secure pictures and other heavy objects on shelves.

2 Know where the gas and water line shut-off valves are and practice turning them off. Attach a wrench to the valve with a cord so that it's always handy. Know how to turn off the master breaker switch on the electrical power supply.

3 Prepare a supply of nonperishable food and bottled water. Keep in mind that cooking may not be possible.

Tips

Store most of your emergency supplies in a hard-sided suitcase under your bed. That way, you can grab it and get out.

Replace stored water every three months and stored food every six months. Donate any food that's not past its expiration date to your local food bank.

If you store canned food, make sure to keep a can opener with it.

See 223 Prepare Your Business for the Unthinkable.

Go to Ready.gov and RedCross.org for more information on emergency preparedness.

Purchase a stand-by generator (fueled by natural gas or liquid propane) if you run a home-based business or have a medical condition that requires constant power. Costs run from $400 to $4,000.

4 Know where your circuit breakers are, and how and when to turn off your main water and gas valves. Some valves require special wrenches: Get one now and fasten it to the valve.

For fires

1 Buy fire extinguishers for the kitchen, garage and living areas. For general use, look for a combined Class A, B and C rating or buy a different extinguisher based on expected use. Class A is for wood, paper and trash, making it a good choice for bedrooms. Class B is for flammable liquids, and C is for electrical fires, so a combined B-C extinguisher is ideal in the kitchen.

2 Install smoke detectors in the hallways, bedrooms, laundry room, furnace room and anywhere else a fire could ignite. Replace detectors 10 years old or older—sensor chambers become dirty, ineffective or nonoperational even if the button test works.

3 Use a fireplace screen to keep hot embers inside.

4 Have a spark arrestor installed in your chimney.

For floods, wind and rain

1 Put weather-stripping around doors and windows to prevent water from seeping into your home.

2 Install storm doors and shutters or create your own using sheets of ¾-inch (2-cm) plywood cut to fit snugly in each window. Replace an older garage door with a hurricane-rated door.

3 Keep a supply of sandbags handy and ready to fill in you live in a flood zone.

4 Buy several rolls of heavy plastic sheeting (at least 4 mil thick) and a large roll of duct tape to cover broken windows, or to create a "shelter-in-place" in the event of chemical release. Measure and precut the plastic for the windows in your shelter-in-place to save valuable time in an emergency.

Wildfires

1 Clear trees and brush away from your house by at least 30 feet on flat ground and 100 feet down slope.

2 Replace wood shake roofs with fire resistant materials.

3 Attic and foundation vents should be covered with mesh no larger than ¼ inch (.6 cm) to prevent sparks and embers from entering your home.

4 Trim tree limbs so that they are at least 10 feet (3 m) from your chimney. Regularly trim plants and shrubs, promptly remove dead or dying vegetation.

5 See 465 Prepare for an Act of God for more tips.

Warning

If you shut off your gas because of an emergency, never attempt to turn it back on yourself. You can risk a fire or an explosion. Contact your utility company and have a professional turn it back on—for free.

RGANIZE YOUR CONTACTS • GET RID OF WHAT YOU DON'T WANT • SAY NO WITHOUT FEELING GUILTY • BALANCE HOME AND WORK • LI
BAIN • SCHEDULE TELEVISION WATCHING • DESIGN A HEALTHY LIFESTYLE • PLAN TO AVOID JUNK FOOD • CHOOSE A WEIGHT LOSS PLA
EET AN ONLINE DATE • PLAN THE PERFECT DATE • MASTERMIND A BREAKUP • PLAN YOUR SOCIAL CALENDAR • MEET MR. OR MS. RIGH
ORT YOUR SOCK DRAWER • RETURN RENTALS ON TIME • TAKE CONTROL OF YOUR JUNK DRAWER • ORGANIZE THE MEDICINE CABINET
AR CLEAN AND ORDERLY • DEAL WITH A PACK RAT • SELL STUFF ONLINE • ORGANIZE YOUR BOOKSHELVES • CATEGORIZE NEWSPAPER
VE BETTER THROUGH LABELING • ORGANIZE JEWELRY • PLAN YOUR DREAM KITCHEN • CONQUER YOUR CLOSETS • ORGANIZE THE LIN
RGANIZE SPRING CLEANING • KEEP THE FAMILY ROOM ORGANIZED • SET UP A BATHROOM SCHEDULE • ORGANIZE BATHROOMS • ORG
RGANIZE KIDS' ROOMS • ORGANIZE SPORTS EQUIPMENT • ORGANIZE KIDS' PLAY SPACES • SAFEGUARD YOUR HOME AGAINST ALLERG
OUSE • USE HOME DESIGN AND PLANNING SOFTWARE • ESTABLISH YOUR HOME'S SPACE PLAN • INCORPORATE UNIVERSAL DESIGN PF
HE BASEMENT • ORGANIZE THE GARAGE • ORGANIZE A TOOLBOX • SET UP A WOODSHOP • ORGANIZE YOUR WINE COLLECTION • PLAN
TUDIO OR SMALL APARTMENT • MANAGE WARRANTY DOCUMENTS • MANAGE HOME-IMPROVEMENT PAPERWORK • MERGE TWO HOUSE
RGANIC VEGETABLE GARDEN • PLANT A KITCHEN HERB GARDEN • PLAN A BUTTERFLY GARDEN • DESIGN A BIRD GARDEN • DESIGN A C
ORGANIZE GARDENING TOOLS • ADD A POTTING BENCH TO A YARD • SCHEDULE FRUIT TREE MAINTENANCE • LAY OUT A SPRINKLER S
ESIGN A GARDEN PATH • SET UP A COMPOST SYSTEM • WINTERIZE PLANTS • SCHEDULE YARD WORK • STORE ANYTHING • STORE BUL
ND HOBBY MATERIALS • ORGANIZE ART SUPPLIES • ORGANIZE GIFT WRAP AND SEASONAL DECORATIONS • ORGANIZE KIDS' SCHOOLW
OUR WEDDING DRESS AND OTHER TEXTILES • STORE A FUR COAT • STORE BICYCLES AND GEAR • STORE SKI GEAR • ORGANIZE CAMP
HICH COLLEGE IS RIGHT FOR YOU • GET INTO A TOP COLLEGE OR UNIVERSITY • ACE THE COLLEGE ADMISSIONS TESTS • ORGANIZE Y
W SCHOOL • PREPARE FOR THE BAR EXAM • GET A DEGREE WHILE YOU'RE WORKING • WORK AT HOME WITH KIDS • GO BACK TO WO
RGANIZE YOUR JOB SEARCH • PREPARE FOR A CAREER CHANGE • OPEN A RESTAURANT • BECOME A PHYSICIST • BECOME A CONCEF
EALITY-SHOW CONCEPT • BECOME A TALK-SHOW HOST • BECOME A PHOTOJOURNALIST • BECOME A MOVIE DIRECTOR • BECOME A M
LING SYSTEM • ORGANIZE YOUR BRIEFCASE • ORGANIZE YOUR DESK • ORGANIZE YOUR WORKDAY • GET A HANDLE ON E-MAIL • ORG
ALARY REVIEW • CLIMB THE CORPORATE LADDER EFFECTIVELY • ADD A WORKSPACE TO ANY ROOM • ORGANIZE A HOME OFFICE • OR
RAVEL • WRITE A BUSINESS PLAN • SET UP A NEW BUSINESS • CREATE A MARKETING PLAN • AMASS A REAL-ESTATE EMPIRE • POLISH
MPLOYEE • FIRE AN EMPLOYEE • PASS ON A FAMILY BUSINESS • STAY ON TOP OF YOUR SALES GAME • RESTRUCTURE A COMPANY TO
EFEND AGAINST A HOSTILE TAKEOVER • ORGANIZE YOUR OFFICE FOR A MOVE • PREPARE YOUR BUSINESS FOR THE UNTHINKABLE • F
REPARE YOUR TAXES • ORGANIZE A LOAN APPLICATION • ORGANIZE IMPORTANT DOCUMENTS • SAVE FOR PRIVATE SCHOOLING • ORG
LUB • TRACK YOUR INVESTMENTS • SURVIVE BANKRUPTCY • PLAN FOR RETIREMENT • PREPARE A PRENUPTIAL AGREEMENT • CREATE
ONEY • PLAN YOUR FAMILY • BUDGET FOR A NEW BABY • ORCHESTRATE THE PERFECT CONCEPTION • PLAN FOR ARTIFICIAL INSEMIN
AVE • ORDER BABY ANNOUNCEMENTS • ORGANIZE AN INTERNATIONAL ADOPTION • FOSTER A CHILD • ORGANIZE YOUR LIFE AS A NE
OORDINATE A FAMILY CALENDAR • PLAN FAMILY MEETINGS • ORGANIZE HOME SYSTEMS FOR ADD • PREPARE FOR A NEW CAT OR DOC
ACK-TO-SCHOOL • WIN THE HOMEWORK WARS • PLAN A FIELD TRIP • PLAN YOUR CHILD'S ACTIVITIES • PLAN YOUR CHILDREN'S SUM
NLINE • ORGANIZE A GENEALOGICAL SEARCH • PREPARE FOR YOUR CHILD'S DEPARTURE FOR COLLEGE • ORGANIZE YOUR EMPTY NE
DERLY PARENTS' CARE • PREPARE FOR THE DEATH OF A SPOUSE • HELP YOUR ELDERLY PARENTS MOVE • ORGANIZE A HOME MEDIC
ORE TRIPS • SET UP ONLINE GROCERY SHOPPING • ORGANIZE RECIPES AND COOKBOOKS • PLAN THEME MENUS • CREATE EFFECTI
EFRIGERATOR AND FREEZER • ORGANIZE CUTLERY AND KITCHEN TOOLS • ORGANIZE CUPBOARDS AND DRAWERS • ORGANIZE THE P
NCHES FOR KIDS • PLAN PARTY FOODS AHEAD • THROW A DINNER PARTY • FINISH DINNER ON TIME • PULL OFF A LAST-MINUTE PAR
LTIMATE WEDDING CHECKLIST • BUDGET FOR A WEDDING • FIND THE PERFECT WEDDING RING • PLAN AN ELOPEMENT • SET UP A BA
ONOR • EXECUTE BEST MAN DUTIES • HIRE A BAND • HIRE A BARTENDER • PLAN A SHOWER • ORGANIZE THE REHEARSAL DINNER • F
UCCESSFUL SLUMBER PARTY • PLAN A BAR OR BAT MITZVAH • PLAN A QUINCEAÑERA • PLAN A RETIREMENT PARTY • PLAN A FUNERA
ANUKKAH PARTY • ORGANIZE A HOLIDAY CRAFT PARTY • PLAN TO SPEND CHRISTMAS SOLO • PLAN THE PERFECT HOLIDAY GIFT EXC
IE HOLIDAYS • STICK TO YOUR NEW YEAR'S RESOLUTIONS • PLAN THE PERFECT NEW YEAR'S EVE • PLAN A SEDER • PLAN A SPECIA
OOD TREE • ORGANIZE A BICYCLE SCAVENGER HUNT • RUN A SPORTS TOURNAMENT • PUBLICIZE AN EVENT • PLAN AN ORGANIZATIO
AN A CONCERT IN THE PARK • ORGANIZE AN INTERNATIONAL CONCERT TOUR • ORGANIZE A FILM FESTIVAL • PLAN A FUND-RAISING
BUILD A COMMUNITY PLAY STRUCTURE • THROW A BLOCK PARTY • SET UP A NEIGHBORHOOD WATCH • CREATE AN EVACUATION PL
RGANIZE A PROTEST OR MARCH • FIGHT CITY HALL • ORGANIZE A BOYCOTT • ORGANIZE A CLASS ACTION LAWSUIT • MANAGE GROV
CHOOL IN A THIRD WORLD COUNTRY • PLAN A TRIP • PLAN A TRIP WITH CHILDREN • TRAVEL WITH TEENS • BOOK AIRLINE TICKETS •
OTORCYCLE TRIP • PLAN A TRAIN TRIP IN THE UNITED STATES • RIDE THE RAILS ABROAD • PREPARE A VACATION COUNTDOWN CHEC
IGGAGE • LOAD A BACKPACK PROPERLY • PLAN AN ELDERHOSTEL TRIP • ORGANIZE AN RV VACATION • PLAN A TRIP WITH AGING PA
DELY DIFFERENT PEOPLE • PLAN SPRING BREAK • PLAN AN OVERNIGHT GETAWAY WITH YOUR SPOUSE • PLAN A VACATION SEPARAT
OLITICALLY UNSTABLE REGION • GET TRAVEL INSURANCE • GET IMMUNIZATIONS FOR TRAVELING • BOOK AN ADVENTURE VACATION
AN A FISHING TRIP TO ALASKA • PACK FOR A CAMPING TRIP • LEAD A BACKPACK TRIP • HIKE A FAMOUS TRAIL • PLAN A TOUR OF T
IGLISH CANAL TRIP • PLAN A CROSS-COUNTRY AIRPLANE VOYAGE • PLAN THE PERFECT DAY ABROAD • PLAN A VISIT TO THE LOUVF
AN • PREPARE FOR AN ACT OF GOD • ASSEMBLE EMERGENCY KITS • PREPARE FOR SURGERY • PLAN YOUR RECOVERY • SURVIVE A
ING LOST • CONDUCT A SEARCH AND RESCUE OPERATION • PLAN AN INVASION • SURVIVE A POLITICAL COUP • PLAN FOR A TERRC
COME THE PRESIDENT OF THE UNITED STATES • WIN AN ACADEMY AWARD • BECOME AN OLYMPIAN • TRAIN FOR A MAJOR ATHLET

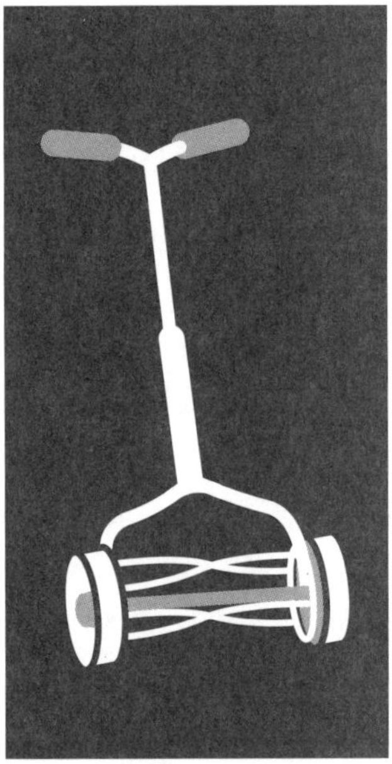

Yard & Garden

People grew organic food for thousands of years—then got "advanced" and started pouring pesticides and chemicals on crops. Simply speaking, an organic vegetable garden is one in which synthetic, manufactured pesticides and fertilizers are never used. The old methods are making a comeback: It all boils down to old-fashioned good sense as opposed to high-tech expertise.

Steps

1 Select a sunny location with well-drained soil. Prepare planting beds first by measuring out a size and length that are convenient. Beds that are about 30 inches (76 cm) wide allow for reaching the middle from either side. Plan lengths to suit the space.

2 Stake out a planting bed or build a frame that is 10 to 12 inches (25 to 30 cm) high to contain and protect the bed soil. This improves drainage and raises the garden's working level.

3 Mix compost into the planting bed about three weeks prior to planting. Compost can come from animal manures or plant material and may be homemade or commercially prepared.

4 Choose varieties of vegetables that are well adapted to your region and known to be disease and pest resistant. Check with your local cooperative extension service for recommendations, and use seed catalogs to identify varieties that are bred to be pest or disease free.

5 Start planting peas, spinach and broccoli once soils are thawed in the spring (or in the fall where winters are mild). These vegetables thrive in cool soils and air and can even survive light frosts. Tomatoes, peppers, corn and squash need heat and do not tolerate frost. Plant them only after soils are thoroughly warm and danger of frost has passed.

6 Encourage beneficial insects such as ladybugs, lacewing flies and hover flies by not spraying broad-spectrum pesticides, by planting the plants that nourish them (such as dill and zinnia) and by releasing purchased insects into your yard. Likewise, provide habitats for toads, birds and bats to live. See 109 Design a Bird Garden and 108 Plan a Butterfly Garden.

7 Water and mulch as needed. Healthy, vigorous plants are somewhat less attractive to some pests, and if attacked are better able to outgrow any damage that they may have suffered.

8 Prevent pests by removing weeds, which often sustain them. Rotate crops every year to avoid pest buildup, and cover susceptible crops with lightweight fabric row covers to exclude pests. Research the crops you're planting so that you can identify their common pests, then strategize how to outmaneuver them. Searching a variety of garden Web sites under "integrated pest management" will provide lots of materials to look over.

Tips

Learn about the USDA's National Organic Standards at www.ams.usda.gov/nop. See ocia.org for information about the Organic Crop Improvement Association.

Time planting to avoid pests. Plant corn early to avoid corn-ear worm; plant broccoli late to avoid cabbage worm.

Who Knew?

Use protective devices, such row covers, cold frames and hot caps, to start your vegetables earlier in the season and extend your harvest beyond the first frost.

Warnings

Avoid choosing shaded, poorly drained, low or soggy spots for your garden. Depending on where you live, you may also need to fence off marauding animals.

Take action against pests when you find them. Hand-picking is an excellent method, or use certified organic control measures starting with insecticidal soap. Light oils and neem—an insecticide derived from the neem tree (check out neemfoundation.org)—are among the many options available.

107 | Plant a Kitchen Herb Garden

Transform your cooking with herbs fresh from the garden. They're not difficult to grow, and creating a garden exclusively for herbs ensures convenient care and easy harvesting.

Steps

1 Pick a sunny site near the kitchen with well-drained soil. Herbs grown in six to eight hours of sun per day have denser, healthier foliage and more intense flavor. Planting herbs in containers works well, too. Work a 4-inch (10 cm) layer of compost into the soil before planting.

2 Choose the herbs you like to use when cooking. In the garden, separate the perennial types from the annuals. This makes maintaining and replanting easier in coming years.

3 Sow anise, coriander, dill and fennel seeds in the garden, as they do not transplant well. Most perennial herbs, including thyme, oregano, chives, French tarragon, sage and rosemary, can be bought as seedlings and transplanted at least 18 inches (46 cm) apart in the garden. Plant others, such as basil, either way.

4 Harvest herb leaves and shoots regularly to encourage dense, fresh growth. For best flavor, cut in the early morning from plants with flower buds just beginning to open.

Tips

Herbs are best divided—and healthy sections replanted—in early spring as new growth begins.

Warning

Mint is invasive and will overtake other plants. Plant it in a bottomless container sunk into the ground. Better still, plant mint in a standard above-ground container.

108 | Plan a Butterfly Garden

Butterflies are attracted to a rich variety of sun-loving plants that bloom over a long season. Bone up on the species common to your area and then invite them to stay by providing food, water and shelter.

Steps

1 Select a warm, sunny site sheltered from high winds. Butterflies need sun to keep warm, and most of the nectar-rich plants they sip from—black-eyed Susan (*Rudbeckia*), aster, joe-pye weed (*Eupatorium*), gay-feather (*Liatris*), butterfly bush (*Buddlea*), purple coneflower (*Echinacea*), butterfly weed (*Asclepias*) and coreopsis—grow best in full sun.

2 Grow plants upon which adult butterflies lay their eggs and caterpillars (the larval stage of butterflies) dine. Each type of butterfly searches for specific plant species among weeds, vegetables, perennials, shrubs and trees. Most caterpillars feed on leaves.

3 Maintain a mud puddle or a patch of moist sand in the garden. You can fill a bowl with wet sand and sink it to ground level. Arrange some flat stones near flowers and at the edge of the puddle for butterflies to bask on and heat up their wing muscles.

Tip

Xerces.org is a good source of information on butterfly gardening.

Warning

Use nontoxic solutions to manage pests in your garden. Pesticides are deadly to caterpillars and butterflies.

Watching birds in your garden and hearing them sing is one of the most pleasurable ways to enjoy nature at home. A well-designed bird garden—one that provides food, water, shelter and nesting places—invites the greatest number and diversity of birds. The key to success is growing a rich mix of plants that are useful to birds.

Steps

Incorporate favored food plants

1 Grow a diverse variety of plants that flower and fruit at different times of year. This provides a continuous supply of food, including flower buds, fruit, nectar and seeds, as well as the insects attracted to plants.

2 Plant a variety of trees. Maples are a good source of buds, flowers and seeds for evening grosbeaks. Pine cones are relished by pine siskins, pine grosbeaks, chickadees, nuthatches and others. Oaks attract a large array of birds, including chickadees, titmice, cardinals, hermit thrushes and woodpeckers.

3 Include several types of shrubs that produce bird-attracting fruit. Some of the best large shrubs for birds are serviceberry (*Amelanchier*), dogwood (*Cornus*), viburnum and chokecherry (*Prunus*). Smaller shrubs are inkberry (*Ilex*), fruit-bearing junipers, currant (*Ribes*) and gooseberry (*Ribes*).

4 Select showy perennials that offer birdseed or nectar for hummingbirds. Examples of the former are California poppy, columbine, purple coneflower (*Echinacea*), coreopsis and goldenrod (*Solidago*). Hummingbird favorites include columbine, red-hot poker (*Kniphofia*), cardinal flower (*Lobelia*), bee balm (*Monarda*), penstemon and salvia.

5 Grow annuals with abundant seeds such as ageratum, amaranth, bachelor's button, calendula, cosmos, marigold, sunflower and zinnia. Let the flowers fade and set seeds.

6 Edge lawns with shrubs that provide leaf litter, where birds such as brown thrashers, towhees and white-throated sparrows can scratch for insects. Plant native grasses to provide seed, and fruit-bearing ground covers such as low-growing forms of bearberry (*Arctostaphylos*) and huckleberry (*Vaccinium*).

Add water for drinking and bathing

1 Provide a consistent supply of fresh water throughout the year. In addition to attracting regular visitors, water lures birds that otherwise may not visit your garden.

2 Add birdbaths with bird preferences in mind. The vessel should be shallow—no more than 3 inches (8 cm) deep—with a gradual

Tips

Add bird feeders to your garden. Supplemental food is not essential to birds, but it increases your garden's power to attract them.

Use nontoxic solutions to rid your garden of pests. Pesticides are deadly to birds. See 106 Prepare an Organic Vegetable Garden.

Who Knew?

Contact your county agriculture extension or type "gardening [your state or region]" into a search engine for more information on choosing plants appropriate to your region.

transition from shallow to deeper water. A roughened surface gives birds a good foothold.

3 Keep water ice-free during winter in northern regions. Use a thermostatically controlled, heated birdbath or a submersible heating element.

4 Add drips or splashes to increase a bath's appeal to birds. Other options include minimisters and drip spouts designed for use in birdbaths, or a commercial birdbath with a built-in fountain.

5 Build a pond or pool that has a shallow area with a nonslip surface for bird access. You can adapt a preformed pool by laying flat rocks at the pool bottom to serve as a landing pad that will elevate birds in deeper water.

Provide shelter and places to build nests

1 Arrange plants so that tall trees tower above lower-growing shade-tolerant trees and large shrubs. Plant shrubs as a bridge from tall plants to flowers and ground covers. Many plants that are good food sources also offer protective cover.

2 Grow evergreens—such as firs, pines, hemlock and spruce— to provide cover from weather extremes year-round. Evergreens offer a place for resting and conceal young birds while providing escape from predators.

3 Plant hedges to provide both protective cover and nesting places. Birds prefer informal, unclipped hedges with a mix of several types of fruiting shrubs.

4 Plant vines on arbors or along a fence. Tangles of grape vines, for example, provide nesting areas and protective cover as well as bark for nesting material used by cardinals, catbirds and purple finches.

5 Incorporate deciduous shade trees into the design. On hot summer days, birds gravitate to the shade provided by maples, oaks, sycamores and the like.

6 Turn prunings and fallen branches into brush piles. Birds seek cover, food and sometimes nesting places in brush. You can place the brush in an out-of-sight corner of your property and construct it from a mixture of deciduous and evergreen branches.

7 Leave a dead tree standing (if it's not in danger of falling). These snags provide nesting cavities for woodpeckers and other birds. Plant a vine at the base of the trunk to dress it up.

8 Add nest boxes to attract cavity-nesting birds, such as chickadees, titmice, nuthatches and wrens. Make sure the boxes are made with the entrance hole and interior dimensions sized for the type of bird you're trying to attract.

Warnings

Choose a safe location for birdbaths. Although some birds prefer baths at ground level, a pedestal birdbath provides some protection from cats. Place baths in the open, away from hiding predators, but near trees and shrubs that offer cover and escape.

Don't use antifreeze in birdbaths to keep water thawed: It will kill birds and other animals.

Dirty feeders with a buildup of old seed can spread diseases among birds. Clean the feeders regularly, using a solution of 1 part household chlorine bleach to 9 parts water.

It's said that gardens grow children, and this is particularly true when a child's first experiences with gardening are fun and successful. Nurturing plants and the sharing the bounty are great confidence builders for budding green thumbs. Indulge your child's curiosity in bugs, worms and sprouting seeds, and offer plants that mature quickly with surprising results. You can also help stimulate interest and a take-charge attitude by including your child in each step of garden planning.

Steps

1 Give your child his or her own small plot or a well-defined section of the larger family garden to encourages a sense of ownership without being overwhelming. A square-yard (or square-meter) garden is a good size for a young child.

2 Talk to your child about where to put the garden. It's an opportunity to share ideas about what plants need to thrive: plenty of sunshine, water and healthy soil. Together, choose a site that is accessible to your child (and the hose).

3 Create a child's garden in just about any shape as long as it includes paths or stepping-stones for easy access to plants. A plot composed of square-foot (or square-meter) planting pockets divided by paths is practical; but a garden shaped like a wagon wheel, with "spokes" dividing the planting beds, works well, too.

4 Plant vegetables that your child loves to eat (or could learn to) and are easy to grow from seed sown directly in the garden. Large seeds, such as beans, cucumbers, pumpkins and zucchini are easiest to plant and sprout quickly. Radishes are the quickest to grow, though seeds are small.

5 Grow dramatic flowers such as sunflowers and zinnias, which have large, fast-growing seeds and produce bold, colorful blossoms. The "mammoth" variety grows to 9 to 12 feet (2.7 to 3.7 m) tall and produces magnificent flower heads loaded with edible seeds. Both require warm soil and full sun.

6 Appeal to all the senses. Include herbs, such as basil and parsley, for garden grazing. Add fragrant plants, such as lemon verbena, rose-scented geraniums and pineapple salvia. Some plants are just for touching, like perennial lamb's ears with its soft, fuzzy leaves and silvery green color.

7 Go to the nursery together to get ideas and choose plants. Include some seedlings, which provide instant gratification and great opportunities to dig holes when transplanting. Sweet cherry tomatoes are a popular choice because they produce loads of bite-size treats that children can pick and eat straight from the garden. In the flower department, snapdragons are favorites because of the flexible dragon's jaw that invites pinching. Let your child choose something new to you, too.

Tips

For a wealth of information on gardening with children, go to KidsGardening.com.

Purchase high-quality, child-size garden tools and teach your child how to use and care for them. Small tools make gardening safer and easier.

Seed catalog companies offer the best selection of seeds for unusual vegetable and flower varieties. Cyndi's Catalog of Garden Catalogs (www.qnet.com/~johnsonj) lists more than 2,000 seeds.

Choose varieties in unusual colors and sizes. "Easter egg" radish seeds produce roots in a mix of red, purple and white. "Munchkins" are pumpkins that mature at 3 inches (8 cm) in diameter. "Purple queen" beans ripen to purple and turn green when cooked.

Warning

Keep pesticides locked up, out of sight and reach of children. Safer still, don't use them in the garden at all.

8 Initiate children's projects to keep things interesting while plants grow. Encourage your child to make a sign for the garden such as "Jeff's Place" or "Patricia's Plot." Construct a scarecrow, paint stepping-stones or build a twig teepee. These and other creative endeavors broaden your child's interest in the garden.

9 Remember that half of the fun is to pick, wash and cook up the bounty. Let your child share the joy of the harvest.

111 Plant a Cut-Flower Garden

Few pleasures in life are so simple as surrounding yourself with flowers, indoors and out. Great satisfaction comes when your vases are overflowing with homegrown blossoms. Spread the joy by sharing summer bouquets with neighbors and friends.

Steps

1 Choose a site with well-drained soil, plenty of sun and easy access to water. Prepare the soil by clearing the garden area of grass and weeds. Work organic matter, such as compost, into the soil. See 106 Prepare an Organic Vegetable Garden.

2 Design the garden for easy care and cutting. Arrange the plants in straight rows or 3-foot-wide (1 m) garden beds. Make paths wide enough for you to walk and work comfortably.

3 Imagine the bouquets you want to create, including colors you love that work with your indoor colors when selecting the plants you'll grow.

4 Plant a mixture of annuals and perennials to have something in bloom at all times. Perennials come back year after year and often bloom early or late in the season. Annuals grow fast and many produce flowers all summer.

5 Combine a variety of flower forms and size. For example, include tall, spiky blooms of bells of Ireland and blazing star; lacy flowers of baby's breath and lady's mantle, and bold, showy flowers such as zinnias and sunflowers.

6 Select plants that have sturdy stems and a long vase life such as lilies, zinnias, black-eyed Susans and snapdragons.

7 Add foliage plants for color and texture. Silver-leafed plants including lamb's ears and lavender are soothing, while the sunny colors of coleus and New Zealand flax add zing to bouquets.

8 Plant bulbs for showy, fragrant color. Cold-loving bulbs such as tulips, crocus, iris, ranunculus and narcissus are planted in the fall for early spring cutting flowers. Many summer-planted bulbs such as gladiolus make stunning additions to tall bouquets.

Tips

To produce abundant blooms, water, fertilize and cut flowers regularly. Cutting flowering stems as they begin to bloom triggers most annuals and some perennials to yield more flowers.

Harvest flowers early in the morning using a sharp knife or floral shears, then place stems in water. For long-lasting bouquets, select buds showing color or freshly opened blossoms.

Warning

Cut daffodils initially release a substance from their stems that will shorten the vase life of other cut flowers. Keep them separate for 24 hours before combining them with other flowers in bouquets.

A shady place to relax on hot days is one of life's simple pleasures. But landscaping in a shady area poses challenges different from landscaping in a sunny spot. Naturally, choosing shade-loving plants is key, but there's a bit more to it than that. The nicest part of the process? After the work is done, you can enjoy your new lush, multi-hued refuge.

Steps

1 Prune overgrown trees and shrubs to let more light through to nearby plants. Remove lower limbs to allow light in from the sides, but hire an arborist to thin a tree's dense canopy (this job can be dangerous and requires experience to avoid harming the tree).

2 Work around tree roots. Some trees that cast shade have large surface roots that compete with smaller plants for water and nutrients, and they get in the way of planting. But digging out or burying roots can kill trees. Consider safer solutions such as planting in the pockets between surface roots and growing plants in containers—which also gives you the flexibility to move plants around as they go in and out of bloom.

3 Add organic matter to shaded soil. Work compost or well-rotted manure into the top 4 to 6 inches (10 to 15 cm) before planting. To grow most plants well, test pH and amend if necessary. If the test indicates soil is acidic, add dolomitic limestone; if it's alkaline, add soil sulfur. Note that moss thrives in acidic, moist and shaded soil and that it's easier to encourage and enjoy than eliminate. (In fact, moss gardening is trendy these days.)

4 Select shade-loving plants adapted to your region. Plants with vibrant flowers are an obvious choice, but also include plants with colorful or variegated foliage that brighten the garden all season. Top-rated choices are coleus, caladium, primrose, some varieties of hosta (also known as plantain lily), coralbells (*Heuchera*) and ferns.

5 Maximize light that is reflected from buildings onto shady surroundings by painting the walls white or a pastel color. Other objects, such as whitewashed fencing and light-colored stone mulch, can also be used to reflect light.

6 In shady areas that are wet, use marsh marigold (*Caltha*), turtlehead (*Chelone*), black snake root (*Cimicifuga*), and spotted dead nettle (*Lamium maculatum*). Where soil is dry, plant white wood aster, barrenwort (*Epimedium*), 'Hermann's Pride' yellow archangel (*Lamium galeobdolon*) and creeping lilyturf (*Liriope*).

Tips

In shaded areas with moist soil and poor air movement, give plants extra growing room. Wide spacing improves air circulation, which reduces disease problems.

After planting, spread a 2- to 4-inch (5 to 10 cm) layer of organic mulch over the soil surface between plants. Organic matter that results from decaying mulch improves the soil.

Warning

Thin, don't "top" or indiscriminately prune a tree. It destroys the tree's shape and stimulates weak new growth that ultimately creates more shade than you started with. Contact a certified and liability-insured arborist if you have a large tree that needs thinning. To find a certified arborist and pruning information, check out the International Society of Aboriculture Web site (www.treesaregood.com).

113 | Design a Dry Garden

A funny thing happens to gardeners that explore the possibilities of a dry garden: They fall in love. And it's no wonder. Dry garden plants are exciting, a tad unpredictable and incredibly diverse. Given their bold color and textures, you can use them as key design elements. If you live in the very dry West and Southwest, live with these plants a season or two and it may happen to you: flat-out xerophytic infatuation.

Steps

1 Choose plants that are adapted to your region. Xerophytes in particular are well adapted to environments with limited water supplies. Native (indigienous) plants or introduced plants stand the best chance of surviving. But non-natives can succeed, too, especially if they're from a similar region.

2 Group similar plants. Among the many well-adapted plants there are still differences. Some need shade, others sun. Some will need less water, others a little more. Moreover, groupings imitate natural plantings, meaning your garden will look more natural.

3 Reconsider your lawn. As lovely as a healthy lawn is, it consumes water like gangbusters. If you are planting one, choose a grass or grass blend adapted to your climate, such as bermuda or buffalo grass. Reduce the size of the lawn by expanding planting beds that surround it. Or eliminate the lawn entirely and replace it with less thirsty plantings, a patio or a deck.

4 Plant ornamental grasses. They're related to the lawn types, but look and grow very differently. Available in various sizes, diminutive to towering, and many colors, all grasses have a naturalistic simplicity and blend beautifully. For instance, combine low growing buffalo grass with deer grass (*Muhlenbergia rigens*).

5 Use African aloes (and their close relatives, the haworthias and gasterias) for showy and dramatic accents. Their red, coral, orange and yellow flower spikes light up the garden throughout the year, especially in late winter and spring.

6 Experiment with yuccas and agaves. Like the aloes, they're notable for their large rosettes of leaves and have tall stalks of white or cream flowers in spring and summer. Agaves, or century plants, offer a dramatic presence in a garden, but especially when their flower spikes emerge like giant asparagus stalks.

7 Plant cacti, the classic dry garden plants. They offer subtle color from spines on stems and pads, while their shorter-lived annuals, such as drought-tolerant California poppy (*Eschscholtzia californica*), come and go around them.

8 Provide dappled shade with trees such as palo verde (*Cercidium*) and mesquite (*Prosopis*). These nonsucculent, drought-tolerant trees and similar shrubs screen, enclose and create a backdrop for the multihued compositions of succulents.

Tip

Make sure the plants you choose can tolerate the minimum temperatures that are common in your area. Check reference books, ask at your local nursery and check with a botanic garden.

Planting at the best time of year means using nature to get your plants established and growing. Where winters are mild, planting in fall is best. Where winters are colder and soils freeze, plant in early spring or late summer.

114 | Plan for a Long-Season Container Garden

Container gardening is great for people who don't have the space or time for a full-blown garden. Stairs and porches make perfect spots for these easy-to-manage gardens. The trick is to make the beauty last so you can long enjoy a striking display in a single container without having to replant. Begin by choosing plants carefully.

Steps

General tips

1 Buy a container large enough to support several kinds of plants with at least one drainage hole. You'll find many options in terra-cotta, plastic, ceramic and wood. Fill three-quarters with a commercially available, lightweight, porous planting mix.

2 Choose an assortment of plants with similar needs for sunlight and water. Include a central upright-growing plant for a sense of permanence and structure—a dwarf Alberta spruce, for example, or, in mild climates, a Japanese aralia.

3 Ring the central plant with smaller plants to create interesting texture, foliage and color combinations. Include plants with a long flowering season, such as a cockscomb (Celosia); those with attractive foliage, such as coleus; and blooming annuals.

4 Soften the edges of the container with cascading plants, such as sweet potato vine, English ivy and lobelia, that hold their form.

5 Keep the display in peak condition with regular care. Provide a continuous supply of moisture and fertilizer. Pinch off fading flowers to encourage plants to continue blooming.

6 Remove annuals as they begin to die, filling in gaps with blooming annuals. Or start fresh with a new burst of seasonal color.

Growing vegetables

1 Choose a deck, staircase or patio that receives at least 6 hours of sun a day. Because soils in containers warm up quicker than garden soil, plants get off to a faster start. If your location is shady you can still grow vegetables. Plant leafy and root crops such as salad greens, radishes, carrots, beets and spinach.

2 Buy containers big enough for the mature root system and water regularly to avoid letting roots dry out. Vegetables grow fast and are set back if stressed.

3 Grow salad greens, radishes, carrots, beets, spinach and bush bean varieties, including 'Frenchie' and 'Provider', from seed. Plant seedlings of tomatoes that don't vine. Plant bush squash, such as 'Gold Nugget' and 'Cream of the Crop', and bush cucumbers, such as 'Bush Pickle'. Peppers and eggplant also grow well in containers.

Tips

In regions where containers can winter out-of-doors, you can plant the container in fall and include spring-flowering bulbs in the mix.

Consider an automated drip watering system to ensure that plants get the water they need (see 118 Lay Out a Sprinkler System).

Who Knew?

To ensure hardiness of container-planted perennials and shrubs outdoors in winter, choose plants suitable to a colder climate, two hardiness zones north of your location.

Leafy and root vegetables (lettuce, carrots) need less light than fruiting kinds (tomatoes, peppers, beans).

Warning

Don't use garden soil for container planting. It's heavy and holds too much water, which can suffocate or drown roots. Garden soil may also introduce pests, weeds, seeds and diseases.

115 | Organize Gardening Tools

A tool is only as good as its accessibility and condition. If you can't find it, or if it doesn't work well, it doesn't matter what it's made of or how much it cost. Organize and store your tools according to their size and how often you use them.

Steps

1   Hang long-handled rakes or shovels, with their heads up, from a parallel set of wooden dowels or similar metal brackets.

2   Buy a carpenter's tool belt or something similar to store and transport hand tools. An apronlike belt that fits around a 5-gallon (3.8 liter) bucket is popular with gardeners and contractors alike.

3   Suspend ladders and tree pruners on U-hooks screwed directly into ceiling beams, or L-brackets mounted on walls.

4   Hang pruning shears, cultivators and seeding tools and more on a Peg-Board, which holds an infinite variety of hooks, brackets and shelves. Outline tools with a marker for speedy replacement.

5   Mount a standard hose hanger—the type made for use in the garden—inside your garage or shed for winter hose storage. Taking the hose inside and away from the effects of sunlight and weather will lengthen its life significantly.

Tip

Remove dirt after each use with a wooden tool or wire brush. Then wipe down metal parts with a light machine or general purpose oil.

Who Knew?

Keep pruning shears sharp by honing blades with a diamond file. High-quality shears have replaceable cutting blades.

116 | Add a Potting Bench to a Yard

For a gardener, nothing is more satisfying then heading outdoors to pot up seedlings; a potting bench makes this easy. The main feature is the worktable, while lower shelves hold supplies like potting soil, pots and miscellaneous tools. The best work centers are designed around the needs of those who use it.

Steps

1   Walk around your entire yard considering possible locations for your potting bench. Obvious spots are exterior walls of the house, shed, garage or fence. Access to a hose, as well as the shed or garage where tools and supplies are stored, offers additional convenience.

2   Decide whether to buy a prebuilt bench, to assemble one from the variety of kits available, or to design and build your own. Use materials that coordinate with or complement your deck or fence.

3   Enhance the usefulness of your potting bench by adding a sink and faucet; bins or storage containers for potting soil and fertilizers; racks for pots; hooks for hanging tools; shelves for small pots and bottles. If possible, allow space to store a garden cart, a bin of potting soil, and trash and composts barrels.

Tip

Coat the completed potting bench with an appropriate exterior stain in order to preserve the wood and match it to its surroundings.

Fruit trees can live for many years and, during their life span, produce hundreds of pounds of fruit. But they need a modicum of care: moist and nutritious soil, pruning, grooming, thinning and protection from pests. How much a tree needs of each depends on the kind of fruit and the season, where you live and, to a lesser degree, the specific variety.

FRUIT	SEASON	WHAT TO DO
Apple	Spring	Spray to prevent scab disease once flowers show color; spray again after petals fall. (Spraying during full bloom may hurt pollinating honeybees.)
	Summer	Water, fertilize; thin fruits, leaving largest ones in each cluster.
	Fall	Harvest.
	Winter	Spray dormant oil in late winter; prune out dead and overly vigorous branches.
Apricot	Spring	Spray to prevent brown rot and shot-hole fungus as flowers open.
	Summer	Water, fertilize; thin leaving three or four fruits per cluster.
	Fall	Prune before winter rains, removing old, damaged branches. Spray before or during leaf fall.
	Winter	Spray dormant oil with fixed copper.
Cherry	Spring	Spray to control brown rot as flowers open and again at full bloom.
	Summer	Water, fertilize; cover trees with netting to keep birds at bay.
	Fall	Harvest; water as needed.
	Winter	Spray dormant oil. Prune out broken and damaged branches.
Citrus	Spring	Water, fertilize, mulch. Prune out damaged and broken branches.
	Summer	Water; fertilize if necessary. Spray with insecticidal soap for aphids or whiteflies.
	Fall	Water and fertilize if necessary.
	Winter	Harvest; protect from frost whenever necessary.
Fig	Spring	Water, mulch.
	Summer	Prune lightly, if at all. Harvest summer crop.
	Fall	Harvest fall crop.
	Winter	Prune lightly if needed.

FRUIT	SEASON	WHAT TO DO
Peach and Nectarine	Spring	Spray during bloom to prevent brown rot. Water, fertilize. Thin fruits to 8 inches (20 cm) apart.
	Summer	Water, fertilize, mulch. Harvest.
	Fall	Spray fixed copper to prevent shot-hole fungus.
	Winter	Spray dormant oil and fixed copper. Prune out half of last season's growth.
Pear	Spring	Spray fungicide just before bloom and again after bloom to control pear scab. Thin fruits to 6 inches (15 cm) apart.
	Summer	Water, fertilize, mulch.
	Fall	Harvest. Water, fertilize.
	Winter	Clean up fallen fruit. Prune to remove one-fifth of last year's growth and damaged branches. Spray dormant oil.
Persimmon	Spring	Water and mulch as needed.
	Summer	Water.
	Fall	Prop branches so heavy crops don't break branches. Harvest.
	Winter	Prune to remove dead and damaged wood.
Plum	Spring	Spray fungicide for brown rot as blossoms appear. Water, fertilize, mulch. Thin fruits to 5 inches (13 cm) apart.
	Summer	Water, fertilize, mulch.
	Fall	Harvest. Water and fertilize. Spray fixed copper to prevent shot-hole fungus.
	Winter	Prune out one-fifth of last year's growth. Spray dormant oil.
TIPS		The Internet if full of good advice, much of it necessarily regional. Type "home garden fruit" into a search engine.
		You can extend your harvest season by keeping trees short by pruning and by planting varieties that bear fruit at different times.
		In a high-density orchard, plums, peaches and nectarines can be planted together as can apples and pears. Cherries go well with everything.
WARNINGS		Never use sulfur or pesticides containing sulfur on apricot trees at any time of year. It is very likely to cause severe damage or even the death of the plant.
		Before spraying any kind of pesticide, read the directions carefully, and take care to prevent the spray reaching non target plants or the neighbor's yard. Remove or cover bird baths or feeders, and patio furniture that might stain.

118 Lay Out a Sprinkler System

If you live where watering is a season-long or year-round affair of hoses and sprinklers, consider a permanent sprinkler system. Whether it's spray or drip, manual or automatic, a customized sprinkler system saves time and possibly even water.

Steps

1 Make a scale drawing of your yard that includes all areas that need watering. Include key features such as the house, driveway and paths, as well as trees, shrubs, planting areas and lawns.

2 Sketch out, with dimensions, all areas that need their own watering schedule and whether they are best served by spray or drip. Drip examples might include the vegetable garden, drought-tolerant shrubs in full sun and drought-tolerant shrubs in shade. Use spray sprinklers for lawn areas or ground covers.

3 Assess how much water pressure and flow is available on a sustained basis from your main water supply. Test a spigot near the supply line that you'll be using. Measure the pressure with a pressure gauge, and measure the flow by counting how many seconds it takes the wide-open spigot to fill a 5-gallon bucket, then divide 60 by the number of seconds, then multiply by 5, the size of the bucket. For example, if it takes 20 seconds to fill the bucket, divide 60 by 20 and then multiply by 5 to get a flow rate of 15 gallons per minute.

4 Figure out how many sprinklers are needed for each area and how much water each sprinkler needs to operate correctly. Add up the amount of water required for each area on your drawing and compare that with the total amount available. If the water supply is sufficient, each area with similar water requirements becomes one circuit, and each circuit is controlled by one valve.

5 Choose between electric valves, which are operated by a timer, or manual valves, which you turn on and off. Inline valves are installed below grade, but require an upstream pressure vacuum breaker to protect household water from backwash. Valves that include an integral antisiphon device must be installed 12 inches (30 cm) above grade.

6 Connect to the water supply via an exterior hose bib, or tap into your water line as it emerges from the meter, whether that's in the front yard or in the basement (in cold climates).

7 Lay out pipes or tubing, dig trenches and, working downstream from a valve, assemble them. Use PVC pipe where soil doesn't

Tips

An automated system can greatly enhance the convenience of a sprinkler system and keep your garden thriving even while you're away.

Plan spray systems so that spray from each sprinkler reaches each adjacent sprinkler. If the site is windy, a slight overlap is a good idea.

Who Knew?

If you live where soil freezes, be sure to install a system drain, or better, a device that permits the pipes to be blown out.

Warning

Check with utility companies before trenching. Call (800) 642-2444. (In Maine, Massachusetts, New Hampshire and Rhode Island, call (888) 344-7233.)

freeze; use polyethylene pipe where it does. Insert **T** connectors and flexible riser pipes where you want sprinklers to be located.

8 Flush dirt from all circuits, cut the riser pipes to length and attach the sprinklers. Operate the circuit, check for leaks or other problems, then refill the trenches.

119 | Plan and Plant a Lawn

Nothing feels as good under bare feet as a lush lawn does. It is incomparable for romping, strolling or simply enjoying your own bit of green earth. Good news: The best method of planting a lawn is a well-known recipe. Follow it for virtually guaranteed success.

Steps

1 Plan the lawn's size and shape, keeping maintenance and watering needs in mind. Lay out your lawn so that you can mow without stopping or backing up. Also make mowing quicker by avoiding sharp curves and corners and including a border.

2 Choose which kind of grass to plant, using your region as a guide. Some grasses, such as Kentucky bluegrass, fescue and ryegrass, prefer cool northern weather. Bermuda, St. Augustine and zoysia prefer hotter southern climates. Tall fescue is popular in areas where the regions merge.

3 Test the soil before planting, then correct it accordingly. Organic matter is usually recommended, and often the acid balance— called pH—needs adjusting with lime or sulfur. Spread a 2- to 3-inch (5 to 8 cm) layer of organic matter over the area and incorporate it 6 to 9 inches (15 to 23 cm) into the soil.

4 Plan and lay out a sprinkler system, especially if you live where the growing season is naturally dry (see 118 Lay Out a Sprinkler System). If you live where summer rainfall is normally abundant, buried sprinklers are optional but convenient.

5 Sow seed if you're planting at the right time of year; late summer or early fall is best. Sowing seed in spring can work, but weed competition will be more severe. Sod is normally a safer choice because you can plant it any time of year.

Tips

Where lawn is harder to grow and mow, such as on slopes and under trees, plant ground cover plants instead.

For recommendations on specific lawn types, rely on local resources such as a cooperative extension, a nursery, or a landscape designer or consultant.

Warning

Where summer-long drought is common and water scarce be mindful of a lawn's prodigious appetite for water. Chose a drought-tolerant grass and minimize lawn area (or eliminate it all together).

120 | Design a New Landscape

Creating the landscape that lives in your imagination is not nearly as complicated as it may seem. Once you divide the process into discrete tasks and put those steps in the appropriate order, you will also more readily see if and at which point you'll need a professional's help.

Steps

1 Collect ideas from gardening magazines and other gardens about your dream landscape. Include major plants you'd like in your landscape, water features such as a pond or dry creek bed, and structural additions such as decks and patios and also built-in barbecue, fences or retaining walls.

2 Obtain a plan of your existing property that includes the property lines and the location of the house, main windows, doors and paths. This plan may be a part of your ownership deed, or available from your city or county building or planning department.

3 Tape tracing paper over your plan to make sketches and notes on. Note key features and accents of your house that you may want to repeat in the landscape. Indicate the garden's shady, sunny, cool, hot, wet and dry spots.

4 Choose key plants, trees and shrubs and finalize your plan, enlisting the help of a professional designer if necessary. Compromise your wish list according to the various limiting factors, whether it's space, time, know-how or budget.

5 Obtain all required permits and locate all underground utilities. Place orders with material suppliers well in advance. Reserve rental tools you'll need, or contract out specific jobs. Order a dumpster bin to facilitate trash removal and demolition.

6 Prepare the site by first removing all unwanted elements, leaving only what is part of the final plan. If heavy equipment will be involved, protect remaining trees and shrubs with barricades around their root zones.

7 Complete any necessary grade changes, resolving any existing or potential water drainage problems in the process.

8 Lay out the primary features of your new landscape, such as a deck or a pond (see 122 Design a Deck or Patio and 123 Design a Water Feature). Then lay out utility lines (including electrical conduit), gas lines and irrigation main lines. Install large-diameter sleeve pipes to accommodate future pipe or wire under or around new permanent structures.

9 Build and complete any new permanent features and plant any large-specimen trees. This is the time you're most likely to need professional help, specialized tools or both.

10 Establish the final grade with a rake or shovel. This is most critical for lawns, or where planting areas join a driveway or path. If planting a sod lawn, set grade ½ inch lower to allow for thickness

Tips

Keep a binder with photos of elements you like such as trellises, arbors, a destination bench or other furniture. Read through the other items in this chapter for ideas on specific gardens and garden elements.

Assess your skills before starting a major project. Seek professional help for projects lasting longer than three consecutive weekends.

Hourly rates for landscape professionals range from $40 to more than $100. Interview several, visit their previous projects, and check with previous clients before hiring.

Aggie-horticulture.tamu.edu/extension/homelandscape has a more detailed description of the landscape design process.

Warning

If you live on or near a hillside, if large amounts of soil are involved, or if drainage issues are significant, hire an an experienced landscape professional or civil engineer.

of sod. Finish the irrigation once all the construction and grading is complete. Test utilities and sprinklers before filling trenches.

11 Plant remaining trees, shrubs and ground cover. Last, plant the lawn, either seed or sod. Once planting is complete, fine-tune the lawn sprinklers and drip system if needed.

121 | Plan an Outdoor Kitchen

Preparing and enjoying meals alfresco—and the pleasures of the casual entertaining it promotes—have become standard elements of gracious living. At one time limited to the South and Southwest, outdoor kitchens and dining rooms are now found all over the country.

Steps

1 Decide whether your outdoor kitchen will be the focal point or simply an accessory of your deck or patio. Take into consideration how much you'll use the kitchen, the quantity and type of space available and if you want a fully functional outdoor kitchen, only a grill or something in between.

2 Minimize the distance between your indoor kitchen and the planned outdoor one. Usually both are used at the same time to varying degrees, so having them in proximity will increase the usefulness of both. A shelf below a sliding window can make both kitchens more functional.

3 Keep the size of the group you'll be entertaining in mind when generating design ideas.

4 Design the kitchen to fit your climate. Wherever winter temperatures typically dip below freezing, all outdoor plumbing will need winterizing. If you live near the ocean, stainless steel will resist the corroding effects of salt-laden air. Where summers are hot, the cook and diners will all need to have shade.

5 Choose equipment to match your cooking style. Many gas-powered grills include side burners that allow for frying, boiling and sautéing. Another popular outdoor cooking option is a wood-fired oven for breads, pizza and roasts. Choose materials wisely and plan for cleaning and tool storage.

6 Check to see if utilities such as plumbing, gas and electricity are accessible at or near the desired area of the outdoor kitchen. Each can be moved or installed, but easy availability of one or the other might determine subsequent choices.

7 Determine how much of the new kitchen you can build yourself and how much expert help you'll need. Usually it's a question of time, experience and tools balanced against dollars. With more of the first three, you can save on the latter, and vice versa.

Tips

As you're laying out your kitchen space, keep in mind that diners need at least 1½ feet (46 cm) between the table and an obstruction—plus room to pull a chair out.

If strong winds or a chilling breeze is common where you live, plan for an appropriate shelter, whether it's a hedge, a fence or a screen.

Warning

To ensure safety, hire a professional to hook up GFCI electrical outlets and to connect gas lines.

Solid structures give a garden a sense of both practicality and perma-nence. Whether you choose a deck or a patio depends on your site and your style. A deck is ideal if your yard is sloped or has poor drainage; it provides a solid, level surface above uneven or soggy soil. A patio, in contrast, requires a level site for the cement, stone or similar pavers.

Steps

General tips

1 Consider your climate, how it affects your use of the outdoors, and what seasons you do and don't spend time outside. Do you need a space that's useful for all seasons or just for summer? Then think of how to improve conditions for that key season where you live. For instance, summer shade is essential in the Southwest, but not in the Northwest. An insect-free screened space makes a deck or patio far more popular in summers wher-ever mosquitoes or flies are abundant.

2 Review the advantages and disadvantages of placing your deck or patio in one area or another. Can the deck or patio capitalize on a beautiful view? Is your property bounded by woods? If pos-sible, design the structure to take advantage of a sunny southern exposure, mature plantings or other standout elements (such as an attractive tree).

3 Make a similar list of your site's liabilities. Is your lot on a steep slope? How much of the lot is exposed to street neighbors, traf-fic or noise? Design a deck or patio that minimizes your yard's special problems and maximizes its advantages.

4 List your family's needs and habits, which reflect the way you live and spend leisure time. Think of how you like to entertain, and for how many people. Keep your cooking style in mind, so that an oft-used barbecue isn't inconveniently placed. Consider pet requirements such as the need to keep a dog confined. Keep this list on hand as you make design, wood and stain choices.

5 Take into account the size and shape of your house, and how it might relate to the size and shape of your deck or patio. A deck or patio can be placed at the entry, rear or side of the house. Possibilities include an interior courtyard, a total wraparound deck or even a rooftop crow's nest.

6 Study how the deck or patio will appear from neighboring prop-erties. Plan for for privacy with fences, screens or plantings.

7 Assess your construction experience and available time so that you can decide if you need to hire a designer, landscape archi-tect, contractor or other professional, or if you will create the

Tips

Make sure imported woods are certified by the Forest Stewardship Council (fscus.org), an international organization that has devel-oped standards for respon-sible forest management.

Keep patio design simple. Limit the variety of materials you use to as few as two, and avoid awkward corners.

Grade patios so that water runs off. Make the edge of the patio farthest from the house 1¼ inch (3.2 cm) lower every 10 feet (3 m).

deck or patio on your own. If you get help, many of the planning choices will be made for you; if you do it yourself, proceed with the following steps.

Decks

1 Plan the deck so it serves as a smooth transition from house to yard—visually as well as practically. Ways to do this include repeating an architectural detail from the house in the deck, and building in benches, tables and storage.

2 Consider pros and cons of various construction materials. Pressure-treated southern pine and hem-fir are most common, treated with CA-B or ACQ respectively (see Warnings). Old-growth redwood and cedar are naturally rot resistant, but supplies are declining and prices rising. Exotic hardwood choices include cambara, ipé, meranti and tauari. (Contact the Forest Certification Resource Center at certifiedwood.org.) Plastic and composite lumber such as Trex (Trex.com) is increasingly available and doesn't require much maintenance, but may be considerably more expensive than wood.

3 Experiment on paper with decking board patterns. Lay planks parallel or perpendicular to the house; alternate plank widths by laying a two-by-four, then a two-by-six and so on.

4 Include plans for railings. All decks that are more than 30 inches (76 cm) above the ground are required by safety codes to have a railing, which must be 36 to 42 inches (91 to 107 cm) high and include balusters 3½ to 4 inches (9 to 10 cm) apart.

Patios

1 Study your site and your house with an eye to materials. Construct the patio with materials that are similar, related to or complementary to those used in your house. This approach will connect your house to the patio, fusing them with a sense of continuity and tradition.

2 Examine your house's design for ideas to mimic in the patio. Look at trim for architectural details, and window and door dimensions for scale.

3 Keep in mind that unlike most decking materials, patio masonry absorbs and reflects much more heat. This may be an advantage or disadvantage depending on your climate.

4 Edge your patio with brick, stone, metal or plastic. Whichever option you choose, use it elsewhere in the garden to link the areas together.

Warnings

Whenever working with pressure-treated wood, wear a dust mask, goggles and gloves. Dispose of (do not burn) scraps and sawdust.

Avoid wood treated with chromated copper arsenate (CCA), which contains arsenic. While no longer distributed to homeowners as of January 1, 2004, some may still be available for sale. Taking CCA's place are two waterborne compounds—alkaline copper quat (ACQ types B and D) and copper azole (CBA-A, CA-B)—sold under the names Preserve, NatureWood and Natural Select. These EPA-approved low-toxicity pesticides have been around for 15 years and resist bugs, mold and rot as effectively as CCA.

A garden pond or fountain needn't be a grand affair. It's the sight and sound of water that counts. A large pond filled with fish and plants is impressive, but a simple bowl with gently moving water may be more appropriate for your garden. However elaborate or simple, water adds life to your garden, and the size and shape of the water feature you desire is limited only by your imagination.

Steps

1 Research your options. Type "water features" into a search engine, or look for ideas in a number of books on the subject, such as *Complete Guide to Water Gardens; Ortho's All about Building Waterfalls, Ponds and Streams; Water in the Garden: A Complete Guide to the Design and Installation of Ponds, Fountains, Streams, and Waterfalls;* and *Sunset Garden Pools: Fountains and Waterfalls.*

2 Decide if you want the water feature to be an accent or the focal point of the garden. Your answer will dictate placement and surroundings (but not size). Options include a pond; a water bowl or pot; and varieties of bubblers, fountains and cascades.

3 Compare the advantages of an in-ground pond to an above-ground one. The former requires excavation but looks more natural. It's also insulated from cold by the soil. Above-ground pools bring the water closer to eye level and provide opportunities for architectural sophistication as well as additional seating.

4 Blend in-ground pools into the landscape. Avoid high spots or places where a natural pond would be unlikely to form. Also avoid the lowest spots, so that your pond doesn't become flooded during storms. And if you're lucky enough to have them, incorporate rock outcroppings into the pond.

5 Sketch out your design and excavation plan. While it needn't be fancy, the more details you can incorporate into the drawing, the more likely the water feature will work out as you intend.

6 Choose between a rigid fiberglass shell, a flexible liner or a concrete (such as Gunite) shell to line your pond. Rigid plastic is the least expensive and easiest to install, but sizes and shapes are limited. Concrete-lined pools are long lasting but may require professional installation. Flexible synthetic rubber liners are easy to work with and the preferred liner for most garden ponds.

Tip

What about adding plants and fish? An empty pond is somewhat simpler at first, but later needs draining and cleaning to prevent algae growth. Ponds with plants and fish can achieve a natural balance and reduce maintenance, but finding that balance can take time. In some cases, a filter is necessary.

Who Knew?

To estimate how much water will be needed to fill your pond, calculate the surface area and then multiply it by the depth to determine the cubic feet. Then multiply by 7.5 to determine the number of gallons.

Warnings

If small children are in your family or nearby, ponds may need to be fenced. Check with your city.

A building permit is likely to be required if the pond is more than 2 feet (61 cm) deep; swimming pool regulations may apply. All electrical systems must be connected to ground-fault circuit-interrupter (GFCI) outlets.

Paths first serve a utilitarian function, making it easy to walk from point A to point B. A basic path directs pedestrians pleasantly and safely, keeping shoes dry in the process. But a well-designed path does much more, inviting, sometimes hiding or revealing views, and stimulating the senses. Paths also add interest to the garden by connecting and unifying unrelated areas.

Steps

1 Lay out the location and shape of the path. All things being equal, people walk in straight lines and will cut across right angle corners. Straight paths are predictable—but paths that disappear around a tree or a corner are more interesting, as well as more natural-looking. If a tree or boulder is in the way, curve your path around it. If a slope is too steep, put in a switchback.

2 Make entry paths about 4 feet (1.2 m) wide so two people can walk side by side. Secondary garden paths, used by one person at a time, are narrower, from 30 to 36 inches (76 to 91 cm) wide.

3 Choose a paving material that is suitable to its intended use. A path that will receive regular use needs to be solid, evenly set and not slippery. The best choices are brick or concrete pavers, poured concrete, cut stones or large stones set close together. Think about what materials would complement your house and its natural surroundings. Stroll through various neighborhoods and thumb through garden magazines to get ideas.

4 Make sure the path won't bog down in water. In order to drain correctly, solid paths of concrete, brick or stone need to slope away from the house at ⅛ inch for every foot of length (1 degree), or ¼ inch per foot of width (2 degrees). Or make the finished path about ½ inch (1.3 cm) higher than the adjacent grade.

5 Excavate a sufficiently deep gravel base to ensure that pavers stay level for years to come. In the South and West, where the ground doesn't freeze, make the gravel base about 4 inches (10 cm) deep. In soils that do freeze, make your base 5 to 8 inches (13 to 20 cm) deep. Confirm with a local supplier.

6 Add a 1- to 2-inch (2.5 to 5 cm) layer of leveling sand over the gravel so that you can nudge a stone or brick slightly until it's in just the right position. If weeds are a likely problem, lay down a layer of landscape fabric over the gravel before adding the sand.

7 Use an edging to hold closely laid pavers in place. Edgings are commonly made of masonry, aluminum or steel.

8 Use low-growing plants such as blue fescue (*Festuca*), candytuft (*Iberis*) or bush germander (*Teucrium*) along path edges to make the transition from path to landscape more graceful. Fill gaps between pavers with green carpet (*Herniaria*), blue star creeper (*Laurentia*), baby's tears (*Soleirolia*) or creeping (or woolly) thyme.

Tips

Consider adding a section of 2-inch (5 cm) PVC piping over the gravel and under the path. Then if you need to run a water or electrical line across the path in the future, you won't have to dig up a section.

Make a path wide enough to accommodate necessary equipment. A lawnmower needs 3 to 3½ feet (91 to 107 cm); a garden tractor, 5 feet (1.5 m) or more.

Warnings

Chose a paving material for primary paths that will provide safe passage during inclement weather. For instance, avoid using slate or marble where rain is common because they are slippery. Where snow and ice are common, consider paving with a rough surface for more stable footing.

Consider drainage even with highly porous gravel paths, taking care to steer them around low spots that routinely flood.

125 Set Up a Compost System

Designing a compost system is more a matter of personal convenience and choice than following a formula. Do nothing at all and compost will still happen. Take an active approach, and you'll have great mounds of leaves, branches, wood chips, manure and so forth melt into a much smaller pile of near perfect fertilizer and soil amendment. Find out for yourself why some people call homemade compost "black gold."

Steps

1 Make compost by combining brown (carbon) and green (nitrogen) materials in roughly equal proportions. Moisten the pile and nature will take it from there. Brown materials include dry leaves, straw and sawdust; green matter includes green leaves and plant parts as well as vegetable waste from the kitchen. This combination of green and brown plus moisture provides the balanced diet microorganisms need to live and, in the process, transform the dead plant parts into compost.

2 Make compost quickly or slowly. The former is *hot* composting, where microorganisms are more active; and the latter is *cold* composting, where they are less active (and so are you). A third approach, called *vermicomposting*, utilizes red wiggler worms to break down organic matter. All three methods produce useful and beneficial compost.

3 Assume your compost will be cold if you just add small amounts to it at a time. Only piles of sufficient mass and moisture that are composed of appropriate materials will allow for the explosion of microorganism populations that results in high temperatures.

4 Make a freestanding compost pile 3 to 5 feet (91 to 152 cm) high and wide so that it has sufficient mass to cook materials in the center of the pile. Situate the compost where there is room for two piles so that you can turn the pile over every two or three weeks.

5 Enclose the freestanding pile in a bin made of hardware cloth wire. Make a hoop about 4 feet (1.2 m) in diameter (which requires 13 feet or 4 m of wire) and 3 to 4 feet (91 to 122 cm) high. Once the pile shrinks, pull the wire up and off the pile, set it to the side, and turn the slumped pile back into the wire hoop.

6 Make a permanent multiple-bin compost system if you have the space, or investigate ready-made models at stores such as Smith & Hawken (smithandhawken.com) and Gardener's Supply (gardeners.com). This would essentially be one long rectangular bin divided into three square compartments. Add fresh material to the bin at one end as it's generated. Once the pile shrinks, turn it into the middle bin. Wait for it to shrink again and then

Tip

Shredding or chopping the raw materials opens more surfaces for microorganisms to work on and thus speeds composting.

Who Knew?

Compost inoculants aren't necessary. Instead, use a small amount of healthy garden soil. It includes all the microorganisms necessary to get your compost started.

again into the last bin to finish. This process can take a week or two or as long as a month, and depends upon the material being composted and other variables.

7 Use a compost bin with a tight-fitting lid and screened base to compost kitchen scraps. The lid and base are needed to exclude rodents and other animals that may learn to use the bin as a food source. Many versions of this type bin are available at nurseries. Some cities give them away to encourage composting.

8 Choose a tumbler-type composter for a clean-looking system that is sealed from pests. Agitate compost by turning a crank.

126 | Winterize Plants

Frost is on the pumpkin, and the summer days of weeding and harvesting are a fleeting memory. But don't shelve the muck boots yet. For northern gardeners, late fall is a critical time to protect plants from hungry rodents and the worst of winter's cold temperatures and drying winds.

TYPE	WHAT TO DO
Trees	Prevent bark-damaging sunscald by shading the southwest side of the trunk or by wrapping the trunk with commercial tree wrap. Young trees or thin-barked trees, including maples, birch, lindens and cherry, are the most susceptible to damage.
	Stop ravenous rodents from chewing on bark in winter by placing a cylinder of ¼-inch (⅔ cm) hardware cloth around the trunk. Leave 1 inch (2.5 cm) between the cylinder and the trunk, extending it 2 to 3 inches (5 to 8 cm) below the ground and 18 to 24 inches (46 to 61 cm) above the anticipated snow line.
Perennials	Cover plants with a loose mulch of straw, pine needles or evergreen boughs after the ground freezes. This protects marginally hardy plants and those that need extra care from severe cold and freeze-thaw cycles that can destroy them. As temperatures warm in the spring, remove the mulch.
Shrubs	Protect evergreens from winter burn, which results in discolored and damaged foliage. Thoroughly water plants before the ground freezes solid. Shield them from sun with an open-top burlap wrap. Commercial antidesiccant sprays may prove helpful.
Lawn	Apply a winterizing fertilizer to promote deep, healthy root growth and build food reserves to speed spring growth. Fertilize when the grass is still green but no longer growing. If the soil is dry, water it to a depth of ¼ to ½ inch (⅔ to 1¼ cm) after fertilizing.
WARNING	Remove tree wrap in the spring so it won't restrict growth or become a haven for pests. Also remove rodent protection circling the tree trunk.

Some garden chores, such as mowing the lawn are routine, and others are infrequent but inevitable. First divide your garden into distinct areas or plant types, then develop a maintenance plan for each. The schedule below serves as a starting point. Once you don't have to consider every option every weekend, your garden will be much easier to manage.

AREA	SEASON	WHAT TO DO
Lawns	Spring	Fertilize with commercial lawn fertilizer according to directions on label. If crabgrass is a nuisance, apply a pre-emergence herbicide in midspring. (If you live where forsythia grows, apply crabgrass preventer when it blooms.)
	Summer	Mow regularly, raising cutting height slightly if necessary to prevent cutting the lawn too low. If a drought extends longer than a week, be sure to water deeply enough to soak 6 inches (15 cm) into soil.
	Fall	Apply fertilizer high in potassium to help strengthen lawn for winter. Seed or overseed lawn if it's weak, thin or headed into winter dormancy.
	Winter	Mow less often and higher where lawns continue growing. Avoid walking on frozen lawns that aren't covered by snow.
Trees and Shrubs	Spring	Refresh mulch, apply organic or controlled-release fertilizer over plants' drip line, water thoroughly. Prune spring blooming shrubs after flowers fade.
	Summer	Keep area around plants weed free, with mulches or cultivation. Shear hedges after flush of new growth; prune faded blooms from spring-flowering shrubs (such as lilacs).
	Fall	Plant most kinds by early fall; mid- or late-fall where hard frosts don't threaten. In cold regions, mulch after soil freezes.
	Winter	Water if rainfall is light. Wrap trunks of young trees to protect them from rodents. In late winter, prune shrubs or trees that flower later in summer (such as crape myrtle, butterfly bush and hydrangea).
Vines and Ground Covers	Spring	Lightly cultivate, renew mulch and fertilize both plant types with organic or controlled-release fertilizer. Thin out overgrown and tangled vines by removing oldest stems to base of plant; cut back and trim edges of ground covers to encourage new growth.
	Summer	Water as needed. Prune spring-flowering vines (such as wisteria) after blooms fade. Groom and trim edges of ground cover beds.
	Fall	Water and lightly fertilize plants to make sure they enter winter in optimum health. Plant ground covers in early fall.
	Winter	Tie vines and climbing roses securely to supports, for preventing winter winds from damaging plants. Mulch after soil freezes.

AREA	SEASON	WHAT TO DO
Flower Gardens	Spring	Plant annual and perennial flowers of all kinds; water; fertilize to get them off to a strong start. Divide crowded clumps of iris and daylilies to improve bloom.
	Summer	Fertilize flowers according to directions on package label, and water as needed to keep soil moist. Pick flowers to enjoy indoors and to promote repeat bloom.
	Fall	Clean up garden and prepare for winter garden, where weather is mild; or for several months of dormancy, where winters are harsh. Cut back perennials to about 6 inches (15 cm) high after blooms fade. Plant spring bulbs; in mild-winter regions, plant winter annuals (such as pansies and primroses).
	Winter	In mild winter areas, fertilize lightly with a nitrate-containing fertilizer (it's active in cold weather). As soon as soil is workable in late winter, plant cool-season annuals (such as pansies, primroses and snapdragons).
Roses	Spring	Prune most roses in early spring, just before growth begins, cutting out old and damaged branches and shortening remaining branches. Watch new leaves for aphids; wash them off with water when or if they appear.
	Summer	Prune off flowers—cutting just above a leaflet, at least a foot (30 cm) below the flower—to enjoy indoors and promote repeat flowering.
	Fall	Leave faded flowers in place and allow seed pods to develop in order to help plant move into dormancy and become more tolerant of cold.
	Winter	Where winter temperatures dip to 10 degrees F (–12 C) or lower, mound soil or mulch over graft union to protect it. Prune to remove dead and damaged branches and to thin center of bush in late winter before spring growth resumes.
Vegetable Gardens	Spring	Prepare planting beds by cultivating and adding organic matter. Plant cool-season crops (such as broccoli and radishes) as soon as soil is workable. Plant warm-season crops (such as beans, corn and tomatoes) after soil is thoroughly warm.
	Summer	Mulch crops with straw or similar material to conserve moisture and cool soil. Harvest frequently to prolong crop.
	Fall	Harvest vegetables before they are cut down by frost (green tomatoes can ripen indoors). Clean up garden residue and add compost to soil. Test soil pH and use dolomitic limestone or sulfur to bring into optimum range of 6.5 to 7.0.
	Winter	In early winter, plant soil-improving cover crop of rye grass where winters are cold; where winters are mild, plant mustard or fava beans.

RGANIZE YOUR CONTACTS • GET RID OF WHAT YOU DON'T WANT • SAY NO WITHOUT FEELING GUILTY • BALANCE HOME AND WORK • LI
GAIN • SCHEDULE TELEVISION WATCHING • DESIGN A HEALTHY LIFESTYLE • PLAN TO AVOID JUNK FOOD • CHOOSE A WEIGHT LOSS PLA
EET AN ONLINE DATE • PLAN THE PERFECT DATE • MASTERMIND A BREAKUP • PLAN YOUR SOCIAL CALENDAR • MEET MR. OR MS. RIGH
ORT YOUR SOCK DRAWER • RETURN RENTALS ON TIME • TAKE CONTROL OF YOUR JUNK DRAWER • ORGANIZE THE MEDICINE CABINET
AR CLEAN AND ORDERLY • DEAL WITH A PACK RAT • SELL STUFF ONLINE • ORGANIZE YOUR BOOKSHELVES • CATEGORIZE NEWSPAPER
VE BETTER THROUGH LABELING • ORGANIZE JEWELRY • PLAN YOUR DREAM KITCHEN • CONQUER YOUR CLOSETS • ORGANIZE THE LIN
RGANIZE SPRING CLEANING • KEEP THE FAMILY ROOM ORGANIZED • SET UP A BATHROOM SCHEDULE • ORGANIZE BATHROOMS • ORG
RGANIZE KIDS' ROOMS • ORGANIZE SPORTS EQUIPMENT • ORGANIZE KIDS' PLAY SPACES • SAFEGUARD YOUR HOME AGAINST ALLERG
OUSE • USE HOME DESIGN AND PLANNING SOFTWARE • ESTABLISH YOUR HOME'S SPACE PLAN • INCORPORATE UNIVERSAL DESIGN P
HE BASEMENT • ORGANIZE THE GARAGE • ORGANIZE A TOOLBOX • SET UP A WOODSHOP • ORGANIZE YOUR WINE COLLECTION • PLAN
TUDIO OR SMALL APARTMENT • MANAGE WARRANTY DOCUMENTS • MANAGE HOME-IMPROVEMENT PAPERWORK • MERGE TWO HOUS
RGANIC VEGETABLE GARDEN • PLANT A KITCHEN HERB GARDEN • PLAN A BUTTERFLY GARDEN • DESIGN A BIRD GARDEN • DESIGN A G
ORGANIZE GARDENING TOOLS • ADD A POTTING BENCH TO A YARD • SCHEDULE FRUIT TREE MAINTENANCE • LAY OUT A SPRINKLER S
ESIGN A GARDEN PATH • SET UP A COMPOST SYSTEM • WINTERIZE PLANTS • SCHEDULE YARD WORK • STORE ANYTHING • STORE BUI
ND HOBBY MATERIALS • ORGANIZE ART SUPPLIES • ORGANIZE GIFT WRAP AND SEASONAL DECORATIONS • ORGANIZE KIDS' SCHOOLW
OUR WEDDING DRESS AND OTHER TEXTILES • STORE A FUR COAT • STORE BICYCLES AND GEAR • STORE SKI GEAR • ORGANIZE CAMP
HICH COLLEGE IS RIGHT FOR YOU • GET INTO A TOP COLLEGE OR UNIVERSITY • ACE THE COLLEGE ADMISSIONS TESTS • ORGANIZE Y
AW SCHOOL • PREPARE FOR THE BAR EXAM • GET A DEGREE WHILE YOU'RE WORKING • WORK AT HOME WITH KIDS • GO BACK TO WO
RGANIZE YOUR JOB SEARCH • PREPARE FOR A CAREER CHANGE • OPEN A RESTAURANT • BECOME A PHYSICIST • BECOME A CONCE
EALITY-SHOW CONCEPT • BECOME A TALK-SHOW HOST • BECOME A PHOTOJOURNALIST • BECOME A MOVIE DIRECTOR • BECOME A
LING SYSTEM • ORGANIZE YOUR BRIEFCASE • ORGANIZE YOUR DESK • ORGANIZE YOUR WORKDAY • GET A HANDLE ON E-MAIL • ORC
ALARY REVIEW • CLIMB THE CORPORATE LADDER EFFECTIVELY • ADD A WORKSPACE TO ANY ROOM • ORGANIZE A HOME OFFICE • OF
RAVEL • WRITE A BUSINESS PLAN • SET UP A NEW BUSINESS • CREATE A MARKETING PLAN • AMASS A REAL-ESTATE EMPIRE • POLISH
MPLOYEE • FIRE AN EMPLOYEE • PASS ON A FAMILY BUSINESS • STAY ON TOP OF YOUR SALES GAME • RESTRUCTURE A COMPANY TO
EFEND AGAINST A HOSTILE TAKEOVER • ORGANIZE YOUR OFFICE FOR A MOVE • PREPARE YOUR BUSINESS FOR THE UNTHINKABLE •
REPARE YOUR TAXES • ORGANIZE A LOAN APPLICATION • ORGANIZE IMPORTANT DOCUMENTS • SAVE FOR PRIVATE SCHOOLING • ORC
LUB • TRACK YOUR INVESTMENTS • SURVIVE BANKRUPTCY • PLAN FOR RETIREMENT • PREPARE A PRENUPTIAL AGREEMENT • CREAT
ONEY • PLAN YOUR FAMILY • BUDGET FOR A NEW BABY • ORCHESTRATE THE PERFECT CONCEPTION • PLAN FOR ARTIFICIAL INSEMIN
EAVE • ORDER BABY ANNOUNCEMENTS • ORGANIZE AN INTERNATIONAL ADOPTION • FOSTER A CHILD • ORGANIZE YOUR LIFE AS A N
OORDINATE A FAMILY CALENDAR • PLAN FAMILY MEETINGS • ORGANIZE HOME SYSTEMS FOR ADD • PREPARE FOR A NEW CAT OR DO
ACK-TO-SCHOOL • WIN THE HOMEWORK WARS • PLAN A FIELD TRIP • PLAN YOUR CHILD'S ACTIVITIES • PLAN YOUR CHILDREN'S SUM
NLINE • ORGANIZE A GENEALOGICAL SEARCH • PREPARE FOR YOUR CHILD'S DEPARTURE FOR COLLEGE • ORGANIZE YOUR EMPTY N
LDERLY PARENTS' CARE • PREPARE FOR THE DEATH OF A SPOUSE • HELP YOUR ELDERLY PARENTS MOVE • ORGANIZE A HOME MEDI
TORE TRIPS • SET UP ONLINE GROCERY SHOPPING • ORGANIZE RECIPES AND COOKBOOKS • PLAN THEME MENUS • CREATE EFFECT
EFRIGERATOR AND FREEZER • ORGANIZE CUTLERY AND KITCHEN TOOLS • ORGANIZE CUPBOARDS AND DRAWERS • ORGANIZE THE
UNCHES FOR KIDS • PLAN PARTY FOODS AHEAD • THROW A DINNER PARTY • FINISH DINNER ON TIME • PULL OFF A LAST-MINUTE PA
LTIMATE WEDDING CHECKLIST • BUDGET FOR A WEDDING • FIND THE PERFECT WEDDING RING • PLAN AN ELOPEMENT • SET UP A B
ONOR • EXECUTE BEST MAN DUTIES • HIRE A BAND • HIRE A BARTENDER • PLAN A SHOWER • ORGANIZE THE REHEARSAL DINNER •
UCCESSFUL SLUMBER PARTY • PLAN A BAR OR BAT MITZVAH • PLAN A QUINCEAÑERA • PLAN A RETIREMENT PARTY • PLAN A FUNER
ANUKKAH PARTY • ORGANIZE A HOLIDAY CRAFT PARTY • PLAN TO SPEND CHRISTMAS SOLO • PLAN THE PERFECT HOLIDAY GIFT EXC
HE HOLIDAYS • STICK TO YOUR NEW YEAR'S RESOLUTIONS • PLAN THE PERFECT NEW YEAR'S EVE • PLAN A SEDER • PLAN A SPECIA
OOD TREE • ORGANIZE A BICYCLE SCAVENGER HUNT • RUN A SPORTS TOURNAMENT • PUBLICIZE AN EVENT • PLAN AN ORGANIZATI
LAN A CONCERT IN THE PARK • ORGANIZE AN INTERNATIONAL CONCERT TOUR • ORGANIZE A FILM FESTIVAL • PLAN A FUND-RAISINC
BUILD A COMMUNITY PLAY STRUCTURE • THROW A BLOCK PARTY • SET UP A NEIGHBORHOOD WATCH • CREATE AN EVACUATION PI
RGANIZE A PROTEST OR MARCH • FIGHT CITY HALL • ORGANIZE A BOYCOTT • ORGANIZE A CLASS ACTION LAWSUIT • MANAGE GRC
CHOOL IN A THIRD WORLD COUNTRY • PLAN A TRIP • PLAN A TRIP WITH CHILDREN • TRAVEL WITH TEENS • BOOK AIRLINE TICKETS
OTORCYCLE TRIP • PLAN A TRAIN TRIP IN THE UNITED STATES • RIDE THE RAILS ABROAD • PREPARE A VACATION COUNTDOWN CHE
UGGAGE • LOAD A BACKPACK PROPERLY • PLAN AN ELDERHOSTEL TRIP • ORGANIZE AN RV VACATION • PLAN A TRIP WITH AGING P
IDELY DIFFERENT PEOPLE • PLAN SPRING BREAK • PLAN AN OVERNIGHT GETAWAY WITH YOUR SPOUSE • PLAN A VACATION SEPARA
OLITICALLY UNSTABLE REGION • GET TRAVEL INSURANCE • GET IMMUNIZATIONS FOR TRAVELING • BOOK AN ADVENTURE VACATION
LAN A FISHING TRIP TO ALASKA • PACK FOR A CAMPING TRIP • LEAD A BACKPACK TRIP • HIKE A FAMOUS TRAIL • PLAN A TOUR OF
NGLISH CANAL TRIP • PLAN A CROSS-COUNTRY AIRPLANE VOYAGE • PLAN THE PERFECT DAY ABROAD • PLAN A VISIT TO THE LOUV
LAN • PREPARE FOR AN ACT OF GOD • ASSEMBLE EMERGENCY KITS • PREPARE FOR SURGERY • PLAN YOUR RECOVERY • SURVIVE
EING LOST • CONDUCT A SEARCH AND RESCUE OPERATION • PLAN AN INVASION • SURVIVE A POLITICAL COUP • PLAN FOR A TERR

Unless you're a practitioner of near-monastic minimalism, it's likely you have a lot of stuff. And much of that stuff needs storage—preferably organized storage. Crammed closets, jumbled drawers, overflowing bookshelves and other storage disasters not only look bad, they sap your time and energy. Getting control of clutter and installing workable storage systems is, in the long run, a gift to yourself.

Steps

1 Assess the way you keep your stuff. Can you find the things you need when you need them? Do items emerge from storage in good shape? What are your biggest storage issues? Once you clearly identify specific problems, you're on your way to finding solutions. See 1 Get Organized.

2 Strive for simplicity with the storage systems you create. Store things as close as possible to where you use them—if you use them frequently. That turkey platter that comes out only on Thanksgiving doesn't need to be on the most accessible shelf the other 364 days of the year. Keep the blender handy if you go into smoothie production every morning.

3 Sort through piles of paperwork and save time and money by finding the right thing at the right time. See 184 Conquer Your Paper Piles and 229 Simplify Bill Paying.

4 Turn closets into allies instead of a no-man's land that things never return from. Add closet organizers to increase capacity while decreasing chaos. Get comfortable with culling and regularly pare down belongings so it's easier to find a place for everything. See 60 Conquer Your Closets and 12 Get Rid of What You Don't Want.

5 Take advantage of the profusion of new containers available both online and in brick-and-mortar stores. From the Container Store to Target, Hold Everything to Home Depot, a wide array of stores offer storage products in every price range. AlwaysOrganized.com, TheHomeMarketplace.com and Improvements.com are just a few of the many Web sites that carry a plethora of storage aids.

6 Browse for storage solutions and continually ask yourself "What else could I store in that?" The hanging shoe holder's pockets could hold a collection of small stuffed animals; the plastic sweater box could store craft supplies; and the acid-free cardboard box designed to protect artwork could preserve vintage linens.

7 Label what you can't see. If you don't want to use clear plastic boxes to store your shoes, at least label the ends so you aren't on a hunt for your sandals when the plane to Hawaii leaves in a

Tips

Keep a storage journal. Whether it's a section or your household organizer or a file on your computer, a list of what storage pieces you need to shop for and what new ideas you'd like to try is a valuable aid to staying organized. It should contain brief notes as to where infrequently used items are stored. A year later you might have forgotten you stowed that turkey platter under the guest room bed. See 265 Create a Household Organizer.

See 57 Live Better Through Labeling.

few hours. Be specific with your labels. Scrawling "books" on a cardboard carton is not enough. "Cookbooks" is better; "Cookbooks: Italian" will make finding a particular volume easy.

8 Decide not to hide. A collection displayed is a collection that doesn't need storage space. Don't reserve wall space just for paintings, photos or a grouping of china plates. If your purses are fabulous, hang them from pegs on the dressing room wall. If you've saved wine corks from every special vintage you ever tasted, pile them in a shallow wooden bowl or in a tall cylindrical glass vase. See 56 End Collection Chaos.

9 Steal ideas from the pros. Retail stores, hotels and restaurants pay designers and stylists to devise innovative and attractive storage solutions. Whether it's wineglasses hung from wooden racks over a bar or a hairdryer stored in a muslin bag and hung from a hook on a hotel sink, clever ideas await your copying.

129 | Store Bulk Purchases

Congratulations! You've survived a Costco run. You now have enough provisions to last for seven years of famine. But where to put it all? Rather than leaving dozens of rolls of paper towels in your car trunk, consider these ideas.

Steps

1 Read 305 Organize Food from Warehouse Stores for tips on storing dry goods and perishable foods.

2 Designate a storage area in the garage, basement, mudroom or pantry and outfit it with metro shelving (heavy-duty wire shelving often found in restaurant kitchens and available at TheContainerStore.com) or large wooden cubbyholes. A wide range of inexpensive, sturdy shelving alternatives are also available at Ikea.com. Label each shelf or cubbyhole so a quick glance reveals which supplies are getting low.

3 Break down big shrink-wrapped packages of paper goods and spread their contents throughout the house. A wicker picnic basket in a bathroom will hold a half-dozen rolls of toilet tissue; most under-sink areas will hold plenty of paper towels or tissue boxes—just make sure there are no drips first.

4 Tuck away cleaning supplies and paper products on a shelf or cabinet in the garage. Refill smaller labeled containers for use around the house.

Tip

Keep a grease pencil handy to label storage buckets or glass jars. See 57 Live Better Through Labeling.

The amount of stuff in your attic, closets and garage may seem overwhelming now. Organize it well and you'll be able to put your hands on whatever you need when you need it. Cruise antique stores, flea markets and salvage shops for storage containers large and small. Kitchen, hardware and office supply

STORAGE SOLUTION	IDEAS
Armoires	Look in antique stores for the walnut and mahogany wardrobes from the 1920s and 1930s, which are just as roomy as the faux-French ones of today and significantly cheaper. Or visit an unfinished furniture store and pick up a unit that suits your needs. An armoire can house not only clothes but a TV, a work station for hobbies, a computer or a compact home office.
Metro Shelving	This heavy-duty chrome wire shelving, often used in restaurant kitchens, provides strong, industrial-looking open storage anywhere. Stack with tools, towels and supplies in the laundry room; plastic toy bins in a child's room; and cookware and bulk food in the kitchen, pantry or utility room.
Baskets	Wicker or wood, open or lidded, large or small, baskets offer storage solutions for every room in the house. Search out the unusual and beautiful to create a beautiful textural display. Stash rolled towels and bathroom supplies, blankets near the couch or fireplace; use for toy storage, shoes at the front door and classy organizers for shelves of all sizes.
Pocket Wall Files	Great not just for the office but also in the kitchen to hold frequently used recipes, takeout menus and receipts. Use in a child's room to keep homework and other school papers organized and easy to access.
Pegs and Hooks	Available in many styles and in wood, chrome, iron and more. Useful alone and below mirrors or shelves. Remove towel bars and install hooks along a bathroom wall to hang enough towels for everyone. Great for kids' rooms so they can hang up jackets and sweaters "all by myself." Pair with a storage bench in the mudroom or entryway.
Bulletin Boards	Think big: Cover the back of a door or a wide stretch of wall with cork, tautly stretched canvas or foam-core panels wrapped in felt. Notes, invitations, photos and all sorts of other miscellany that would jumble a drawer become a colorful collage when organized on a handsome bulletin board.
Ladders	Lean a bamboo ladder against a bedroom wall to display a collection of quilts or scarves. Lay planks across the steps of a painted stepladder in the family room and form shelves for books and magazines.
Piano Benches	Even if you don't own a piano, a reclaimed bench works well in an entryway (with gloves, hats and scarves beneath the hinged lid) or as extra seating in a pinch at party time. Hide magazines, placemats and more inside.
Paint Cans	Buy new paint cans from the hardware store and cover in fabric or wrapping paper. Standing upright, fill with anything from kitchen utensils to garden tools to art supplies. Turned on their sides, cans stack into a pyramid to store mail, jewelry, crayons, shells, seed packets and so on.

stores will also have dozens of storage solutions. And don't forget to shop in your own home, where great pieces may lurk in your attic, basement or spare bedroom. Any item with drawers, shelves or divided space is a candidate for creative storage. Use the ideas below as starting points.

STORAGE SOLUTION	IDEAS
Old Pie Safes	The pierced-tin or wire-mesh fronts that once made these cabinets perfect for cooling pies make them ideal storage pieces for towels and soaps in bathrooms, rustic nightstands or as a corner bar in the living room.
Vintage Suitcases	These nostalgic mementos not only look sophisticated, but store projects, photo albums and other stuff, and stack into charming occasional and bedside tables.
Old Trunks	Though not as easily portable as baskets and suitcases, military or camp trunks provide great storage for extra blankets and quilts in a guest room, a spot to sit in an entryway and stash books within, or in a rear entryway to hold sports equipment, extension cords or boots or bulk supplies. Top one with a large tray to make it work as a coffee or side table.
Salvaged Kitchen Cabinets	Appealingly low-priced at salvage shops, no-longer-loved cabinets become instant storage at floor level or higher in a laundry room or workshop. Or remove doors, repaint the cabinet interiors and use as cubbyholes.
Retail Fixtures	Fixtures that once displayed shirts or sweaters for sale are worth searching for, both in salvage shops and at going-out-of-business sales ("Everything must go! Even the fixtures!").
File Cabinets	Too useful to limit to storing papers, file cabinets can hold caps, gloves and scarves in an entryway, T-shirts or sweaters in a bedroom, or board games and puzzles in a family room. Look for oak pieces in antique shops. Or spray paint a metal model a bright color. Make sure the drawers open and close easily and that locks are disabled so you're not stuck without a key.
Fabric-Covered Boxes	Whether you cover them yourself or buy them already clad, sturdy boxes covered with linen, chintz, denim or silk will organize everything from CDs to old love letters with a stylish note. Buy plenty—just one or two can look like an afterthought, but three, five, seven or more (an odd number makes a better arrangement) become a design statement.
Glossy Gift Boxes	A row of Tiffany-turquoise or Hermès-orange boxes makes a bright display stacked on open shelves while offering labeled homes for documents or bills you need to save, photographs or office supplies.
Garbage Cans	Buy small galvanized garbage cans with lids to serve as stylish out-of-sight storage for large essentials: laundry detergent, pet food, toys, sporting goods, rain boots—even recyclables and kitchen compost.

131 | Capture More Storage Space

Valuable storage potential lurks in nooks and crannies, corners and dormers, wide hallways and the shallow spaces beneath beds. Look carefully at every room and passageway in your home to discover new storage possibilities. Here are a dozen suggestions to spark your creativity.

Steps

1 Choose furnishings with storage in mind. Coffee tables with shelves, side tables with drawers, ottomans with lids that lift to reveal storage space underneath are time-honored ways to sneak additional storage into small rooms.

2 Examine your entryway. If there's room for any furniture, add a chest of drawers, hutch or a sideboard. Mount a trio of long, low shelves along one wall. Fill with covered baskets interspersed with favorite collectibles.

3 Harvest space from your hallways. A wide hallway can fit a drop-leaf table alongside a chair for sitting and sorting (see 7 Deal With a Flood of Mail), or tucked in at the end. See 196 Add a Workspace to Any Room.

4 Put the area beneath a staircase to work. Furnish it with a writing desk and slim chair, build in deep drawers, or outfit the space with shelves. Install lighting to accent collectibles.

5 Hang small, triangular cabinets in a bathroom corner for towels and toiletries. Tall corner cupboards utilize unused space in the kitchen and hallway, too.

6 Add a window seat. Put a cushion over a hinged lid, or leave the area under the seat open and stash magazines, books and throws in deep baskets.

7 Replace your kitchen table with a banquette. Built-in storage benches hide large appliances and bulk supplies. Hang shelves above head height in the banquette area for vases and cook-books. Add a groove an inch or two away from the wall to display decorative plates and platters.

8 Eke out more attic space by framing in a table under the eaves. Don't bother with back legs; just fasten the back side of the table to the studs. Place lightweight items—garment bags, duffels and sleeping bags—on top and stow heavier pieces underneath.

9 Store bedding in plastic bins that slide under the bed. HoldEverything.com, StacksAndStacks.com and other retailers offer a wide range of storage solutions.

10 Build a simple rolling drawer large enough to hold a twin-size mattress and slide it under a child's bed to create a trundle for pals to sleepover. Or, remove the mattress and set up your toddler's train set inside for accessible fun that rolls away.

Tip

Make the area beneath a bed accessible with large, lined baskets on rollers. At the foot of the bed, use a trunk or big rectangular wicker hamper to store extra pillows and other bedding.

11 Mount casters on the bottom of drawers rescued from an old bureau and slide out-of-season clothing, extra blankets, toys and art supplies under a bed.

12 Use a tansu or two to divide a room. These handsome Japanese chests are available in a vast variety of sizes and shapes; all have a multitude of drawers and add considerable storage capacity.

132 | Expand the Capacity of a Small Room

A small space requires a creative approach to storage. Experiment and have some fun before committing to a layout: You can always move furniture pieces back if they overwhelm rather than improve the space, banish table skirts if they create visual clutter rather than curing it, push beds back against the wall. But when an idea works, it can make a small space both look and function better.

Steps

1 Take advantage of the space in the middle of a small room. A pedestal table or oversize ottoman in a small living room may actually make the room look larger while providing a place to pile books and magazines or read the newspaper.

2 Select a great-looking screen to hide unsightly storage cartons or a commercial clothing rack in a closet-deficient room. Elegant Japanese shoji screens partition a room while still letting light through. In a small dressing area, a screen outfitted with fabric pockets on one side will hold stockings, socks, scarves, belts or jewelry.

3 Float a bed away from the bedroom wall to create a dressing area. The back of the headboard creates a new partial wall to place a chest of drawers or other storage piece against.

4 Sacrifice a closet to gain better-organized storage space. Sometimes you can make better use of the square footage a closet consumes by removing the doors and fitting out the space with an entertainment center, a bulletin board and desk, or a pair of chests with shelves hung above them. See 60 Conquer Your Closets.

5 Sew a skirt for a table. Stack puzzles and games beneath a table in the family room or store seldom-used platters and linens in cartons beneath a skirted side table in the dining area. In a bedroom, a round, draped table can serve as a nightstand, concealing a set of hand weights or books underneath, or a large rectangular table can serve as a dressing table with storage space for out-of-season clothes underneath its skirt.

Who Knew?

Purchase ceiling tracks for curtains at a hospital supply store.

Hobbies can result in a tsunami of supplies and equipment. Whether you work on your favorite craft projects in a corner of the kitchen or have the luxury of a dedicated workshop, you'll save your sanity if you organize first and glue, construct, carve, paint, solder, glitter and bead afterward.

Steps

1 Group like items together: all your fabrics, your collection of paintbrushes, your piles of scrapbooking paper. This universal law of storage organization is particularly applicable in the crafts room; once you see the extent of each storage challenge, you can devise a plan to meet it.

2 Explore supply stores. Art supply, office equipment, stationery and hardware stores offer a variety of tackle boxes, towers, taborets and totes useful for organizing craft supplies. Keep scrapbooking paper neat and accessible in stacked in-and-out boxes or in the wire display racks used in stationery stores.

3 Invest in an electric labeler. Using it faithfully will convert plastic shoe boxes, sweater boxes and even three-ring binders into efficient storage for craft miscellany. See 57 Live Better Through Labeling.

4 Panel a wall with Peg-Board and take advantage of all the specialty hooks and brackets available. If sewing is your craft of choice, create a design wall to pin up pattern pieces rather than laying them out on a worktable. Foam core wrapped in flannel, felt or muslin works well. See 63 Create a Sewing Center.

5 Refurbish a flea-market find. Create stylish storage space by using an old card catalog from a library, an oak file cabinet or a Hoosier cabinet (a vintage kitchen piece replete with drawers and bins) to hold craft supplies. An architect's flat files will hold a plethora of patterns or miles of N-gauge track.

6 Convert a computer station or armoire to a mini craft center. The pull-out central shelf designed to hold a keyboard makes a perfect place to keep frequently used tools. Add a clip-on light to a shelf.

7 Remove a closet door to create a space to park rolling carts holding supplies. Fill the top half of the closet with plastic-coated wire shelving to store boxes of materials and supplies.

Tips

A narrow 2-by-2–inch shelf mounted on an easily accessible spot on the wall keeps small containers handy.

Position your worktable in the center of the room rather than against the wall so you can approach a large project from all sides.

Who Knew?

Baby-food jars make good storage containers for tiny pieces or parts. Screw the lid of the jar to the bottom of a shelf for out-of-the-way, spillproof storage.

Warning

Don't store family memorabilia in ordinary cardboard cartons; use archival-quality acid-free boxes. See 53 Organize Your Photos.

Disorganization in an art studio can consume your creative time and sap your energy. Corral your materials and let your studio time be notable for its creativity rather than its chaos.

Steps

1 Top your must-have list with a taboret. This rolling cabinet, designed specifically for art and drafting, keeps a variety of supplies organized and accessible. Available in heavy-duty plastic or hardwood and in a wide range of sizes and prices, these smart carts are the next best things to live apprentices. Some taborets have foldout wings on the top to create more work space; others have pivoting drawers or integrated easels. Shop online at DickBlick.com and at brick-and-mortar art stores.

2 Set up one extra large multipurpose worktable in your studio. Cover it with replaceable, self-sealing plastic so you can cut on it. Regardless what medium you work in, you'll eventually be cutting something. Alternately, buy a large self-sealing cutting mat that slips behind a door when not in use.

3 Find copious storage space in flat files—the stacks of long, slim drawers found in architects' or engineers' offices. They provide superb storage for canvases, paper, mat boards, sketch pads and printing materials. Available in metal or hardwood, the units can be stacked and configured to fit your specific needs.

4 Store different mediums in separate areas if possible. It will help eliminate the tendency to grab your fine needle-nosed jewelry pliers to pull staples out of an old canvas.

5 Keep surfaces and work areas clean. Creative spasms get messy, but make only one mess at a time. There's nothing worse than oil pastel on your worktable getting all over a charcoal drawing, or spray-mount debris destroying a watercolor.

6 Install adjustable, good lighting over all work surfaces. Large, south-facing windows are a boon to any creative endeavor.

7 Hang nylon organizers with clear vinyl pockets. Some have small pockets only for paint tubes, while others add larger pockets for brushes, pens and sketch pads. Designed to hook over a doorframe, they can also hang on a wall hook near your easel. An added advantage: They're easy to hide in a closet if the room has to serve other functions.

8 Stick to a shoestring budget and still create great storage for art supplies. Muffin tins, drawer dividers, silverware caddies, earthenware crocks and plastic storage tubs can all do valuable organizational duty in the studio. Create an art cart similar to the ones teachers use in classrooms. Place casters on a nightstand or a small bookcase to make a movable storage piece.

Tips

Store finished work in acid-free archival boxes before displaying.

Large stackable plastic trays from an office supply store are a cheap alternative to flat files. Keep your eyes peeled for going-out-of-business sales and pick up used flat files on the cheap.

Wooden sketch boxes can hold a large number of paint tubes, colored pencils or pastel chalks in orderly little compartments.

Warnings

Solvents, thinners, adhesives and paint removers are highly toxic: Don't skimp on ventilation equipment and systems. Store your respirator nearby so you won't have to hunt for it. Also see 145 Store Paint and Other Hazardous Materials.

A pile of used rags soaked in paint or solvents can ignite and set your studio on fire. Invest in a fire-safe oily waste can. Resistant to most chemical compounds, the can opens with a foot lever and is ventilated to prevent spontaneous combustion.

Wrapping packages is a pleasure when you have the right supplies organized and at your fingertips. Wrapping your house with lights and other holiday decorations is less of a chore if you can locate the items easily—and find them in good condition, not smashed or cracked. And once the right storage system is in place, you can take advantage of the postholiday sales to stock up for next year.

Steps

Organize wrapping materials

1 Purchase under-the-bed storage plastic boxes specially designed for gift wrap. Look for ones with lift-off inner trays for ribbons, tags, tape and scissors. Consider buying two: one for the major winter holidays, the other for the rest of the year.

2 Dedicate a dresser to wrapping supplies. Lower drawers can hold gifts you've bought ahead (see 357 Organize Gift-Giving in Advance). Label everything (see 57 Live Better Through Labeling).

3 Make the most of minimal storage space by keeping supplies in a large, compartmentalized hanging bag or vertical organizer (available at sites such as StacksAndStacks.com and TheContainerStore.com) designed specifically for gift wrap.

4 Outfit a small closet as a wrapping center. Store rolls of paper in a 5-gallon wastebasket or an umbrella stand. Mount a flip-up shelf on one wall to use as a wrapping surface, keep ribbons and tags in open baskets on low shelves, and hang double-prong hooks on the inside of the door to hold gift bags.

Store seasonal decorations

1 Keep fragile holiday ornaments safe in compartmentalized boxes. Many cardboard units are available in holiday colors, making them easy to spot among other boxes in crowded storage spaces. Also check out vertical seasonal storage towers.

2 Use wreath boxes for storing artificial wreaths, garlands and large bows. Or place wreaths and garlands on clothing hangers. Protect them with plastic bags or, for items too large for standard-size bags, covers made from old pillowcases or sheets.

3 Prevent snarled light strands by storing them in special boxes that come equipped with hanging plastic or cardboard frames to wrap the strands around. Coiling each strand and putting it in its own plastic bag also works well. Store extension cords in the same box as the lights.

Tips

Buy wrapping paper in solid colors. A few colors will work for many different occasions, which means you can buy and store fewer rolls.

Buy a ribbon holder that feeds the ribbons through slits in one side, or make your own from a shoe box and a dowel.

Keep decorations in tubs labeled or color coded for each holiday.

Who Knew?

Wrap thick candles in plastic to keep away rodents. Store them in a wine carton with cardboard dividers.

Store a reminder list with the holiday decorations, telling you what lightbulbs, ornament hooks or other supplies you need to buy early in the season before the stores run out of stock.

136 | Organize Kids' Schoolwork and Artwork

It's never too early to teach young scholars and budding artists the benefits of organization. The task becomes easier if organizing and storing seem like fun. The payoff? Fewer frantic searches for important school papers.

Steps

Set up schoolwork

1 Hang a large bulletin board in the child's room and mark off one section with colored masking tape. Reserve this space for current assignment sheets, reading lists and other important school papers. A metal bulletin board with magnets is the easiest and safest option for younger children since tacks tend to get lost underfoot.

2 Buy a plastic file box or crate in a bright color, along with a set of colored file folders. Take time to teach the child how to choose which papers to keep and file. Start slowly, especially with young children: Choose two folder colors, perhaps one for homework papers and another for notices. Gradually increase the number and specificity of the folders.

3 Invest in an inexpensive label maker when your child grows able to manage more than a few file folders. Kids love gadgets and are more likely to maintain systems they've designed themselves.

Organize artwork

1 Combine storage with display. String a wire along one wall of the child's room and use metal clips or wooden clothespins to create a personal art fair. Rotate pieces out as new ones come in.

2 Add two or three narrow shelves to a section of wall and prop artwork on them. Frame favorite pieces and attach others to foam board with double-sided tape so they're rigid enough to stand up. Or mount acrylic clip frames or shadow boxes at the child's eye level, raising them as the child grows. See 55 Arrange an Art Collection.

3 Store favorite paintings and drawings in an artist's portfolio, and slide under the bed or behind a door.

4 Outfit a bookcase with stackable, clear plastic boxes for all their creations. Labeling the visible ends of the boxes will help the system work. Use a photo or drawing if your child is too young to read. Regularly cull the collection to make room for new pieces.

5 Place picnic baskets, either new or from the flea market, in a corner of the child's room to hold art projects. The hinged lids make it easier to keep things tidy.

Tips

Encourage children to select pieces of artwork and write messages on them to use as greeting cards and wrapping paper.

Pick up a supply of unused pizza boxes. They're the perfect size for a growing portfolio and stack under a bed easily. Mark the outside edge by year and by child.

Today's average household resembles a library with growing collections of CDs, DVDs, digital music files and home movies in a dizzying array of formats. Cataloging and organizing your media will enhance your enjoyment of it and make managing it fast and easy. Digitize your movies, music and photographs, and there's no end to the amount of fun you'll have creating multimedia extravaganzas.

Steps

General tips

1 Sort movies and CDs by type, then by category or genre. If you're not sure what categories to use, visit a video or music store, a library or an online photo archive for some ideas. Sort alphabetically (by artist or title) within categories.

2 Unload items you don't want anymore. Give duplicates to friends, donate them to a library or sell them. Contact a radio station or university to gauge interest in your old record collection. See 12 Get Rid of What You Don't Want.

3 Count or measure your newly sorted and culled collection to make sure you have enough space to store everything. Purchase additional storage shelves, boxes and trays if necessary. You'll find a variety of items ranging from plain boxes to specially designed racks everywhere from Target, Wal-Mart and Home Depot to office supply stores and specialty shops (Ikea, Hold Everything, the Container Store, Staples).

4 Bear in mind that all digital media (music, video footage, photographs) requires software to organize it (known as an asset management system) and adequate storage space.

CDs and DVDs

1 Put address labels on your books, CDs or DVDs if you loan them out. Use 3-by-5-inch cards to track which items you've loaned out, when and to whom.

2 Consider managing your collections on your computer. Simply list items in a word processing file, or catalog them in a spreadsheet to track titles, artists, release years and special features. Better yet, create a database that allows you to search for specific attributes (genre, title). If you have a valuable collection, a computer-generated list is useful for insurance purposes.

3 Update your catalog seasonally, quarterly or whenever you purchase new media or get rid of older items.

Digital music files

1 Choose a listening device for your music (computer, stereo, portable music player, digital audio receiver) before downloading music from an online store or loading songs from your CDs onto

your computer. Different devices require audio files in specific formats, including MP3, AAC and WMA.

2 Download songs for a fee from online stores such as Apple's iTunes (apple.com/itunes) or Napster.com. Search for a song by artist, title, genre and many other options.

3 Take your tunes to go. Portable CD players have long been making way for fast, tough MP3 players with a variety of storage capacities, including the Dell DJ, Samsung Napster and Rio iRiver. Apple's iPod (apple.com) has become invincible in the personal digital music player market. Available on both the Windows and Macintosh platforms, the iPod stores up to 10,000 songs on a 20- or 40-gigabyte hard drive. Coupled with a number of third-party accessories, the iPod has tremendous capabilities:

• It can organize music files into custom albums and playlists. Hook up to a sound system and broadcast your own concert, or play exactly what you want at your wedding without hiring a DJ. Search songs by any number of options, including artist, title, genre and keyword.

• The iPod is not just for music: Download audio books, take notes, record lectures (see 284 Prepare for Your Child's Departure for College). Organize your contact information, and keep appointments with an alarm clock. Download photos directly from your digital camera with the appropriate adapter.

Digital video footage

1 Pull footage directly from your camcorder or camera into your computer. Organize clips in a film-editing application such as iMovie or Final Cut Pro (both available at apple.com). Set up folders for each movie with files for clips, stills and so on.

2 Purchase an external hard drive with as much storage space as you can afford for the enormous files you'll be processing.

3 Save completed movies in a size and format suitable to their intended use and that will work on specific output devices.

Slides and home movies

1 Store slides and Super 8 and 16 mm movies in an area protected from light, humidity and heat; all of which will cause the gelatin in the film to eventually degrade. Take a cue from the pros, who are moving away from the original metal canisters and opting instead for acid-free cardboard boxes.

2 Digitize your home movies and slides to protect them from time and the elements. Even better, once these assets are digital, you'll be able to combine them with digital photographs, and add music and titles. Edit the whole thing into a home movie, then burn DVDs to send to all the relatives.

In order to prevent illegal use of licensed music, online music stores embed rights-management coding directly into their songs. This allows them to be played only on specific devices, and to be burned to a limited number of CDs before listening rights are terminated.

Some new DVD players can record analog VHS footage onto DVDs. Pioneer's DTR-500 makes the transition from analog to digital a snap—and even cranks out VHS copies for your low-tech friends.

The simplest (and cheapest) way to convert those old Super 8 and 16 mm movies is to set up your digital camcorder on a tripod and film the movie as it plays on the screen. Presto! Digital movies. The better the camera, slide screen, light and sound, the better the end result. Digitizing slides is slow and expensive as they have to be scanned one at a time.

Weigh the time needed to input, edit and transform any media into the format you need against the very hefty cost of hiring a professional transfer service.

Warning

If any of your 16 mm or Super 8 movies has a vinegar-like smell to it, immediately isolate that can from the others. "Vinegar syndrome" is contagious and causes film to degrade.

Delicate china, antique and new silver, and lovely old ivory handles on serving pieces or carved figurines will last for generations if carefully stored. Investing in specialized storage materials makes the job easier, but TLC is an equally important ingredient of the preservation process.

Steps

China

1 Hand-wash older china before storing it. Putting china in a dishwasher can cause crazing, fading and damage to metallic trim.

2 Place a cushion between each stacked piece. Stack cups no more than two high to avoid weakening the rims. Purchase premade fabric disks, or use pieces of flannel, paper napkins or even coffee filters. Thin, rubberized matting, available in easy-to-cut rolls, makes excellent drawer or shelf liners for china.

3 Invest in zippered, padded fabric pouches designed for china storage at stores such as HoldEverything.com. Measure your largest plates, bowls and platters before you shop.

Silver

1 Invest in special silver storage cloth impregnated with microscopic particles of silver. These particles lure tarnish-causing sulfur compounds away from your silver. Choose from premade bags, drawer liners or large rolls to cut as needed. Store flatware in wooden chests fitted with slots and lined with treated cloth.

2 Polish silver only just before using it. Don't attempt to keep it party-ready while in storage. Polishing actually removes minute particles of silver, exposing more areas to tarnish.

3 Keep silver pieces in display cases shiny by using protection strips, which neutralize sulfur gases.

Ivory

1 Handle older ivory pieces with care; ivory becomes more brittle with age.

2 Store ivory wrapped in acid-free tissue or cotton in a closed container, such as a zipper-lock polyethylene bag, to help control changes in humidity. High humidity can cause mold and mildew damage, resulting in black spots and surface etching.

3 Keep ivory away from direct sun and heat, and avoid storing next to external walls where fluctuations in heat, light and moisture are more extreme.

Who Knew?

Take out rarely used pieces at least once a year and wash them. This prevents impurities from impregnating the glaze, causing brittleness and even cracking.

Warnings

Never wrap silver items with rubber bands, plastic wrap or bubble wrap, as they all cause sulfide corrosion.

Ivory will turn yellow or orange if exposed to sulfur. Never store it with keratin-based objects such as tortoiseshell.

139 | Store Out-of-Season Clothes

Storing out-of-season clothes properly should protect them from dust, heat, humidity and the biggest threat of all: chomping, chewing, egg-laying bugs. Clothes moths and carpet beetles are the chief villains, the latter being especially evil since they gorge on your garments in both the larval and flying stages. Below is a battle plan for banishing the wicked winged destroyers.

Steps

1 Evict moths from many of their warm, dark homes before they find your clothes. Schedule regular cleaning sessions under furniture, along baseboards, inside closets and around heating vents.

2 Set out pheromone traps to lure clothes moths to an early death. These traps will let you know moths are on the premises and will prevent trapped moths from breeding, but they probably aren't sufficient weapons to win a major antimoth war.

3 Clean clothing carefully before storing it. Although the bugs are most attracted to natural fibers such as wool, down, cashmere, mohair and silk, hungry insects will eat synthetics if they're seasoned with food spills, bloodstains or perspiration. Dry cleaning or washing in hot water will kill pests in all stages.

4 Choose storage containers large enough so clothing doesn't get crushed and wrinkled. Hanging cloth bags will ward off dust and wrinkles, but they aren't airtight enough to contain insect-repellent vapors.

5 Look for tight-fitting, well-constructed cedar chests which make it difficult for insects to get to the clothing. Cedar lumber in closets or chests will lose oils over time and after three years are useless in killing any fabric pest. Mild natural insect repellents, such as cotton balls soaked in lavender or citrus oil, are not very effective and need to be replaced about every three months.

6 Bring out the bigger guns if herbs and cedar don't do the job. Keep in mind, moth repellents containing camphor, naphthalene and paradichlorobenzene may take care of the insects, but they pose a safety risk to people and pets.

7 Store out-of-season, outgrown and still-too-big kids' clothes in containers labeled by age and season. For example, with labels like "toddler, boy, summer," you'll be able to find hand-me-downs or future garage sale items quickly. See 272 Stay on Top of Kids' Clothes.

Tips

See 140 Store Your Wedding Dress and Other Textiles and 141 Store a Fur Coat.

Since clothing resellers buy merchandise only for the upcoming season, sort and store your clothing in bundles labeled for fall to winter or spring to summer. Put a reminder on your calendar to contact a consignment or resale store for an appointment in July and February.

Who Knew?

Freezing also kills pests. Place the infested garment in a polyethylene bag and squeeze out all the air. Place in a freezer chest at -10 degrees F (23 C) for 48 to 72 hours. Let thaw in the refrigerator then bring to room temperature before removing from bag. Repeat the process to make sure all pests have been killed.

Warning

Starch and sizing in stored garments can attract silverfish and crickets.

140 Store Your Wedding Dress and Other Textiles

Embalming your wedding dress, your great-grandmother's handmade quilt, or a valuable old tapestry in one of those cardboard boxes with a cellophane window could be a costly mistake. No fabric should remain folded in a sealed box for years, and cellophane windows can trap damaging moisture. Storing fine textiles is not difficult: Do the job correctly and preserve your precious garments for decades.

Steps

Wedding dress

1 Have the dress professionally cleaned as soon as possible. Some stains, such as sweat, perfume and alcohol, may be invisible at first but will darken with time if not removed.

2 Choose between box and hanger storage. Keeping the dress in a box may prove to be more practical, but hanging the garment in a closet is the best way to prevent difficult-to-remove creases. Purchase plenty of acid-free tissue paper. You'll need it whether you fold or hang the dress.

3 Line an acid-free cardboard box with acid-free tissue paper if you are storing the garment in a box. Lay the hem in the box first and then fold the dress accordion-style, placing crumpled tissue paper between each fold. Stuff the inside of the bodice and sleeves with crumpled tissue. Layer more tissue on top and cover with the box lid.

4 Wrap a wide hanger with cotton batting if you are hanging the garment, then cover it with muslin. Hang the dress and stuff the bodice, sleeves and any deep folds in the fabric with acid-free tissue. Cover the dress with a muslin garment bag and hang it in a cool, dry closet. Take care not to crush it with other clothing.

5 Check the dress's condition each year. If boxed, repack so the folds are in different places; if hung, wash the muslin cover.

Quilts

1 Sandwich the quilt between two clean cotton sheets and then fold the trio accordion-style. Place it on a shelf or in a drawer, but never in a plastic bag or cardboard box. If using a cedar chest, line the chest with acid-free tissue paper to prevent direct contact with the wood's oils.

2 Air out the quilt once a year, but do it inside, as sunlight can fade vintage fabrics.

3 Spread a quilt over a guest bed and then top it with a cotton cover for protection is an easy but safe storage method if your houseguests are careful—and infrequent.

4 Choose a wall away from direct sunlight and hang a quilt from a rack to enjoy.

Tips

Use large storage boxes to minimize the number of fabric folds.

Videotape or photograph valuable textiles for insurance purposes. Store the video in a fireproof box or a safe-deposit box.

Who Knew?

Vintage linens should be hand-washed in hot water with mild soap, rinsed and line dried. If ironing is required, mist with distilled water and iron embroidery on the reverse side. Don't use starch, which is carbohydrate-based and may attract insects.

Light is your linens' enemy: Ultraviolet rays from sunlight and fluorescent lights can damage fibers and cause fading. Low light or darkness are recommended for textile storage. Ask a professional to do the job right.

Tapestries and other valuable textiles

1 Wear cotton gloves while handling antique silk kimonos, wall-hangings and other fragile textiles. Have them professionally cleaned and packaged in acid-free tissue paper, which helps keep fabric from yellowing. Remove any metal rings or hooks before storing. Depending on their shape and size, tapestries and textiles may be stored folded, hung or rolled on cardboard tubes.

2 Roll small items on acid-free cardboard tubes, inserting sheets of acid-free tissue as you roll. Wrap the entire roll in cotton sheeting and tie the ends loosely with cotton twill tape.

Warnings

Never use colored tissue to store textiles. The color can bleed into the fabric.

Don't roll hand-painted textiles, as the paint may crack.

141 | Store a Fur Coat

Giving your fur coat, jacket, stole or hat a summer vacation in cooler climes is one of the best steps you can take to increase its longevity and preserve its value. Store it properly and you'll have a clean, glossy garment when it comes out of hibernation.

Steps

1 Hang fur coats and jackets during the winter season on wide hangers in a closet large enough to avoid crushing garments together. Avoid hanging furs where sunlight could oxidize exposed sleeves or the entire side of a coat.

2 Move furs to a professional storage facility during the warmer months. (Check out sites like Fur-services.com to locate the closest fur storage facility.) An air-conditioned room or a cool basement doesn't offer sufficient protection from moth damage or the drying out of leather. If the leather dries out, it eventually cracks, resulting in excessive shedding of your fine fur.

3 Choose a fur vault for summer storage rather than a dry cleaner's storage room. Look for a vault with circulating air kept at a temperature of 45 to 50 degrees F (7 to 10 C) and a humidity level of 50 percent.

4 Check the terms of the storage company's insurance coverage. Furriers usually offer nominal insurance coverage while your coat is in storage and sometimes make further coverage available for a small fee. Also insure your fur on your homeowner's policy for its replacement value.

5 Have furs cleaned before long-term storage. During the winter months, dust particles sift down through the hairs and settle on the leather, where they absorb the natural oils and hasten the skins' drying and cracking.

Tips

Make sure the facility will take care of minor repairs such as tightening loose hooks and repairing torn lining before placing the furs in storage.

See 139 Store Out-of-Season Clothes.

Who Knew?

Consider having an older fur garment restyled before placing it in storage. When you pick it up in the fall, you'll feel like you're getting a brand-new garment.

Warning

Never crush a fur coat in a plastic bag.

142 | Store Bicycles and Gear

Whether it's your restored Schwinn Sting-Ray with banana seat or the latest carbon-fiber race bike, all pedal-powered machinery has one thing in common: It wants to be used frequently. Extended storage will make it ill-tempered and balky. But there are a few tricks that will keep your two-wheeled friend content during a seasonal layoff.

Steps

1 Oil the chain and sprockets. This is the single biggest problem area for stored bikes. Use a special chain lube, available from a bike shop, or any lightweight machine oil. Spin the pedals and shift through the gears to distribute the oil thoroughly.

2 Wipe the bike down with a rag. Look for dirt caked around the derailleurs, brakes, and bottom bracket (where the pedals attach to the frame).

3 Inspect brake and shift cables for broken strands. If you find any, it's time for a professional tune-up. There's no harm in waiting until next season, but tape a reminder note to the bike.

4 Install large, rubber-coated ceiling hooks in your garage to hang the bike. For a garage with a low ceiling, one hook installed in a corner will hold a bike vertically against a wall.

5 Attach accessory gear, such as your helmet, bike shoes and tool bag, to the bike in a mesh bag so you don't lose it.

Tips

Inspect the tires when you put the bike in storage. If they're cracked or highly worn, take them off the rims and throw them out. When you're ready to take that first ride next season, you won't be tempted to use them.

Cover the bike if it gets direct exposure to sunlight. Ultraviolet rays deteriorate the rubber on the tires, brakes, seat and handgrips.

Warning

Test the brakes when you take the bike out of storage. If you're not sure about them, have a bike shop take a look.

143 | Store Ski Gear

Modern ski gear is extremely durable. It will put up with heaps of abuse before you actually ruin it—but that doesn't mean you can't. Skis slide better, bindings are safer and boots more comfortable when given a few minutes of attention at the end of the season.

Steps

1 Dry off all of your equipment. Wipe the ski bases with a towel. Make sure no water is trapped in any binding recesses. Boots need the soft inner liner pulled out of the hard plastic shell to allow both to dry completely.

2 Wax your skis or have a ski shop do it. Make sure the edges are well covered with wax to keep the metal edges from rusting and prevents the plastic base material from drying out.

3 Remove the spring tension in the bindings. This preserves the springs by allowing them to relax during the summer. Note the tension number on each binding toe and heel piece. All four binding pieces should be set at the same number. Write it on each ski with a felt-tip pen. Using a large screwdriver, turn the

Who Knew?

Ski boots may fit differently after they've been in storage, due to expansion of the soft liner. Wear your boots for an hour or so before your first ski day.

Remember to reset your binding tension at the beginning of next ski season.

Warnings

Incorrect binding adjust-ments increase risk of injury. Don't adjust them if you aren't sure what you're doing.

large screw at the end of each binding piece counterclockwise until the binding tension setting is near the bottom of the scale. (Do not unscrew too far.) Skip this step or get help if you don't have a thorough understanding of how the binding works.

4 Reassemble your boots. Push the liner back into the shell. The tongue should be fully inside the boot, not jammed between the liner and shell. Buckle the boot loosely and store it in a dry place.

5 Stand your skis in a dry closet. If you own multiple pairs, build a rack with a cross piece roughly 3 feet (.9 m) off the floor. Slide single skis in, bindings facing out. If the skis tumble into each other, install pegs 6 inches (15 cm) apart to keep them upright.

Never pile a bunch of garage junk on top of skis. Stay away from wall brackets or hanging pegs that grasp the ski just under the tips and distort their shape.

144 Organize Camping Equipment

If a tent pole falls on your head every time you open your closetful of camping gear, it's time to put it into better order. Organization makes packing for a trip quick work and protects expensive gear. And if you go through your gear after every use, you will be able to take care of what needs repairing or replacing before you hit the trail again.

Steps

1 Empty your entire pack as soon as you get home. Be sure to remove all garbage and food remnants. Hose out tents and packs if necessary and then hang to dry. Turn sleeping bags inside out and also hang to dry.

2 Store down bags and parkas in loose, breathable, cotton sacks. Tight stuff sacks compress the down too much for extended storage. Place these items on the top shelf of a closet where they won't get crushed by heavy gear.

3 Purchase several large plastic storage bins with secure lids. These are great for keeping camp stoves, pots and pans, backpacks, tents and assorted camping gear all in one place and away from rodents, insects and moisture.

4 Fill sealable tubs with supplies, such as a bucket, dish soap, towels, a flashlight, spare batteries, bug spray, sunblock, aluminum foil, garbage bags, rope, string, a first aid kit, propane, a lighter, cooking and eating utensils, plates and bowls, and a tablecloth. Packing for the next trip will be a cinch.

5 Use separate tubs for rock climbing and mountaineering gear. Ropes, carabiners, harnesses, chocks and other technical gear should all go in one place. Keep sunblock, insect repellent, stove fuel and all other chemicals away from this bin. Your life depends on this gear and you need to protect it from anything that might weaken it, including the sun's ultraviolet rays.

Tips

Pay close attention to the washing instructions for your camping equipment and clothing. You don't want to do anything that weakens the material, breaks down insulation or reduces water resistance.

Store stoves and fuel in a different container from the rest of your gear. Sleeping in a bag that reeks of kerosene isn't that fun.

See 447 Pack for a Fishing or Hunting Trip and 449 Pack for a Camping Trip.

Who Knew?

Washing down eventually strips the oil from the feathers. Do it seldomly and never at the dry cleaners. If you must wash your sleeping bag or jacket, use Down Suds or Thunder Down (mcnett.com), which is similar to soap used by down processors.

Paints and potential poisons require careful storage. Caked and dried-out paint can be annoying, but fires or bodily harm from caustic substances pose far more serious concerns. Prevent these problems by following a few simple guidelines.

Steps

Paint

1 Prevent air from contacting the paint surface (and forming a skin) when resealing the can. Cut a circle of wax paper or aluminum foil and float it on top of the remaining paint. Wipe down the rim, then put the lid on very tightly by tapping with a rubber mallet.

2 Brush a line of paint on the can's exterior to show both the level remaining and the paint color. Jot a note on the side with a permanent marker that tells you when and where you bought it and which room it's used in.

3 Pour a small portion of any leftover paint into a Mason jar. When you need to make small touch-ups, you won't have to open and reseal the main container. Label the jar with the paint color or mixing formula, the room it's used in and the date.

Other items

1 Keep gasoline in a tightly sealed, prominently labeled container in a cool location separate from your residence. A detached garage or storage building is far preferable to a basement or an attached porch. Gasoline vapors are invisible and will spread rapidly from room to room if released.

2 Store other hazardous materials (drain opener, rust and lime removers, oven cleaners) in their original containers and out of the reach of children, making sure that the labels are clearly visible. Choose well-ventilated storage areas for materials that might produce vapors and fumes, and never store in the same area as a gas water heater. Keep them away from food, including pet food. Contamination can occur even if the chemical is not in direct contact with the food.

3 Store chemicals out of direct sunlight because some are photodegradable (they break down when exposed to sunlight) and can lose their potency. Keep them at room temperature—some chemicals can release harmful vapors if stored at high temperatures, even if the lid is tight-fitting.

Tips

Read 73 Make Your Home Safe for Small Children.

See 134 Organize Art Supplies for information on disposing of rags soaked in solvents and other toxins.

Warnings

Avoid storing paint in extreme heat or cold—either can damage the paint, and extreme heat plus oil-based paint can lead to a fire.

Never use a food or beverage container for storing hazardous materials. The resulting mistaken identity could be fatal.

Check container labels carefully before discarding; most list specific disposal instructions. Never burn or bury containers that once held hazardous materials.

So your closets are exploding, your basement is bulging and your two-car garage couldn't house a Mini Cooper? Decide if it's worth the money so your extra stuff can dwell in a room with no view. Then organize the off-site storage space, lest said stuff ends up completely out of sight, out of mind and impossible to find.

Steps

1 Analyze whether you really need to pay for more space. Could a thorough weeding out of seldom-used possessions and some reorganizing of your home storage spaces give you the room you need? See 1 Get Organized and 37 Conquer Clutter.

2 Estimate the size of the unit you'll need if winnowing doesn't work. Guidelines are available at Web sites such as www.pspick-up.com/storageneeds.htm.

3 Ask about the rates and availability of units at several locations. Once you select a company, inspect the specific unit you'll be renting to check cleanliness, accessibility, lighting and security measures. Make certain the location is not too far away if you plan to add or remove items often.

4 Get sturdy packing cartons that will stand up to stacking. Box as many of the items you're storing as possible to keep them clean and protected. Use specially designed boxes for mirrors and framed artwork; mark these containers as "Fragile" and store them on their ends, never flat. Stack heavier and sturdier items on the bottom, and lighter and more fragile items on top.

5 Purchase wardrobe boxes for hanging clothing. These make locating items far easier than digging through boxes of folded garments and snarled hangers.

6 Label every carton on both the top and sides with its contents and a box number. Be sure to place the boxes in the unit with the labels facing out. Make a list of the contents and number of each box as you pack it, then transfer this inventory (along with the phone number at the rental unit) to your computer later.

7 Move large pieces of furniture and appliances into the storage unit first. Position the items to use the floor space efficiently. Stack boxes on top of them if possible.

8 Place items you plan to access first or more frequently at the front of the unit. Leave a walkway so you can reach the back of the unit without moving masses of cartons.

9 Thoroughly drain the fuel compartments of any motorcycles, scooters, lawn mowers, chainsaws and other gasoline-powered tools. Brace open appliance doors to prevent mildew from forming inside them. See 147 Store a Boat for the Winter.

Tips

Fill furniture drawers with small items, noting the contents on your inventory list.

Stack a sofa—well wrapped—on end to conserve floor space. Do not place it against an outside wall, where condensation caused by temperature fluctuations might penetrate the wrappings.

Wrap the legs of wood furniture to prevent scratches. In fact, you may want to use drop cloths on all wood pieces.

See 97 Plan a Move.

147 Store a Boat for the Winter

There are numerous methods of storing a boat for the winter, all of them involving some amount of work and misery. A proper storage plan will result in a small amount of misery now rather than a huge amount next spring when you find the boat in ruins. If you don't have basic engine and maintenance skills, you should probably pay a boat-yard to winterize the craft for you.

Steps

1 Begin with the engine, since this is the messiest and potentially most expensive item. Change the oil and filter. You don't want old, dirty oil sitting in the engine all winter.

2 Drain the engine's cooling system. If it's a closed system (like a car's), refill it with the manufacturer's recommended antifreeze and water solution. If it's an open system (one that draws water from outside the boat), flush it with clean water by inserting a garden hose into the intake opening. Drain the system complete-ly by opening the coolant drain(s), located at the lowest point(s) of the system, usually near where a hose attaches to the engine block.

3 Drain the gas out of the tank (if your boat has a carburetor), using the drain screw at the bottom of the bowl. Replace the screw and fill the tank with a fuel stabilizer as directed.

4 Pump the holding tank for bathroom waste as dry as possible. Unless you can easily remove the tank from the boat, you should have a boatyard do this. Treat the tank with a deodorizing solu-tion, available from a boatyard or from marine supply stores such as WestMarine.com. If it's permitted, you may empty the tank in open water if you are far enough out to sea.

5 Remove as much gear as possible from the boat. You don't want life jackets, sails, cushions or anything else left in areas that might collect moisture.

6 Open all hatches and storage lockers if you'll be keeping the boat in a garage. Close all hatches and lockers if you'll be storing the boat outdoors. It's a good idea to spray the bilge, head and lockers lightly with an antimildew product. Put in a dehumidifier if you're storing your boat outdoors.

Tip

Keep small but important items (engine keys, drain plugs, cotter pins) on the boat at all times. Otherwise they are guaranteed to be missing when you need them most.

7 Construct a tarp support system for outside storage. Don't expect your canvas boat cover to keep out heavy rain or snow. An inexpensive tarp, supported above the boat in a steep A-frame to shed snow and rain, works great. A long two-by-four running along the centerline of the boat and supported at each end makes a perfect tarp support.

Warning

Be sure to close all cooling system and hull drains before launching the boat.

148 | Store a Car

Storing a car is not just a matter of park, lock and leave. Nasty problems can develop deep in the innards of a beloved vehicle if you ignore preventive measures. Careful prestorage preparation will keep any car happy during its hiatus.

Tips

Leave a convertible's top up to keep ugly creases from becoming permanent.

For extended storage in a damp climate, investigate car-storage companies that provide storage in special buildings equipped with industrial dehumidifiers.

Steps

1 Fill the gas tank, adding a fuel stabilizer, and then run the car for a while to make sure you've distributed the stabilizer throughout the entire fuel system. Over time, an empty gas tank will rust, and untreated gas can go bad.

2 Add antifreeze to the cooling system even if the car is protected from cold temperatures. The newer coolants have corrosion inhibitors that protect and lubricate the system.

Warning

Heated underground garages are often extremely humid and thus not ideal locations for long-term storage.

3 Change the engine oil and oil filter. Dirty oil can damage the bearings and cause engine rust. Replace the brake fluid, making sure to use the most durable grade. Remove the battery lest it leak corroding acid.

4 Coat all exposed metal surfaces in the engine area with a lubricant spray; remove the distributor cap and spray the contact points lightly.

5 Wash the entire car and apply a good wax. If storage space is damp or humid, place desiccant packs inside the car to keep moisture from damaging the interior. Don't forget the trunk.

0 Set the car up on blocks to get the tires off the ground and prevent flat spots. Drape with a cloth car cover. Heavier is not necessarily better: If the car is stored outdoors, wind can cause a heavy cover to abrade the paint.

RGANIZE YOUR CONTACTS • GET RID OF WHAT YOU DON'T WANT • SAY NO WITHOUT FEELING GUILTY • BALANCE HOME AND WORK • L
GAIN • SCHEDULE TELEVISION WATCHING • DESIGN A HEALTHY LIFESTYLE • PLAN TO AVOID JUNK FOOD • CHOOSE A WEIGHT LOSS PL
EET AN ONLINE DATE • PLAN THE PERFECT DATE • MASTERMIND A BREAKUP • PLAN YOUR SOCIAL CALENDAR • MEET MR. OR MS. RIGH
ORT YOUR SOCK DRAWER • RETURN RENTALS ON TIME • TAKE CONTROL OF YOUR JUNK DRAWER • ORGANIZE THE MEDICINE CABINET
AR CLEAN AND ORDERLY • DEAL WITH A PACK RAT • SELL STUFF ONLINE • ORGANIZE YOUR BOOKSHELVES • CATEGORIZE NEWSPAPER
VE BETTER THROUGH LABELING • ORGANIZE JEWELRY • PLAN YOUR DREAM KITCHEN • CONQUER YOUR CLOSETS • ORGANIZE THE LI
RGANIZE SPRING CLEANING • KEEP THE FAMILY ROOM ORGANIZED • SET UP A BATHROOM SCHEDULE • ORGANIZE BATHROOMS • ORG
RGANIZE KIDS' ROOMS • ORGANIZE SPORTS EQUIPMENT • ORGANIZE KIDS' PLAY SPACES • SAFEGUARD YOUR HOME AGAINST ALLERG
OUSE • USE HOME DESIGN AND PLANNING SOFTWARE • ESTABLISH YOUR HOME'S SPACE PLAN • INCORPORATE UNIVERSAL DESIGN P
HE BASEMENT • ORGANIZE THE GARAGE • ORGANIZE A TOOLBOX • SET UP A WOODSHOP • ORGANIZE YOUR WINE COLLECTION • PLA
TUDIO OR SMALL APARTMENT • MANAGE WARRANTY DOCUMENTS • MANAGE HOME-IMPROVEMENT PAPERWORK • MERGE TWO HOUS
RGANIC VEGETABLE GARDEN • PLANT A KITCHEN HERB GARDEN • PLAN A BUTTERFLY GARDEN • DESIGN A BIRD GARDEN • DESIGN A
ORGANIZE GARDENING TOOLS • ADD A POTTING BENCH TO A YARD • SCHEDULE FRUIT TREE MAINTENANCE • LAY OUT A SPRINKLER S
ESIGN A GARDEN PATH • SET UP A COMPOST SYSTEM • WINTERIZE PLANTS • SCHEDULE YARD WORK • STORE ANYTHING • STORE BU
ND HOBBY MATERIALS • ORGANIZE ART SUPPLIES • ORGANIZE GIFT WRAP AND SEASONAL DECORATIONS • ORGANIZE KIDS' SCHOOLW
OUR WEDDING DRESS AND OTHER TEXTILES • STORE A FUR COAT • STORE BICYCLES AND GEAR • STORE SKI GEAR • ORGANIZE CAMP
HICH COLLEGE IS RIGHT FOR YOU • GET INTO A TOP COLLEGE OR UNIVERSITY • ACE THE COLLEGE ADMISSIONS TESTS • ORGANIZE Y
AW SCHOOL • PREPARE FOR THE BAR EXAM • GET A DEGREE WHILE YOU'RE WORKING • WORK AT HOME WITH KIDS • GO BACK TO WO
RGANIZE YOUR JOB SEARCH • PREPARE FOR A CAREER CHANGE • OPEN A RESTAURANT • BECOME A PHYSICIST • BECOME A CONCE
EALITY-SHOW CONCEPT • BECOME A TALK-SHOW HOST • BECOME A PHOTOJOURNALIST • BECOME A MOVIE DIRECTOR • BECOME A
LING SYSTEM • ORGANIZE YOUR BRIEFCASE • ORGANIZE YOUR DESK • ORGANIZE YOUR WORKDAY • GET A HANDLE ON E-MAIL • ORG
ALARY REVIEW • CLIMB THE CORPORATE LADDER EFFECTIVELY • ADD A WORKSPACE TO ANY ROOM • ORGANIZE A HOME OFFICE • OF
RAVEL • WRITE A BUSINESS PLAN • SET UP A NEW BUSINESS • CREATE A MARKETING PLAN • AMASS A REAL-ESTATE EMPIRE • POLISH
MPLOYEE • FIRE AN EMPLOYEE • PASS ON A FAMILY BUSINESS • STAY ON TOP OF YOUR SALES GAME • RESTRUCTURE A COMPANY TO
EFEND AGAINST A HOSTILE TAKEOVER • ORGANIZE YOUR OFFICE FOR A MOVE • PREPARE YOUR BUSINESS FOR THE UNTHINKABLE •
REPARE YOUR TAXES • ORGANIZE A LOAN APPLICATION • ORGANIZE IMPORTANT DOCUMENTS • SAVE FOR PRIVATE SCHOOLING • ORG
LUB • TRACK YOUR INVESTMENTS • SURVIVE BANKRUPTCY • PLAN FOR RETIREMENT • PREPARE A PRENUPTIAL AGREEMENT • CREAT
ONEY • PLAN YOUR FAMILY • BUDGET FOR A NEW BABY • ORCHESTRATE THE PERFECT CONCEPTION • PLAN FOR ARTIFICIAL INSEMIN
EAVE • ORDER BABY ANNOUNCEMENTS • ORGANIZE AN INTERNATIONAL ADOPTION • FOSTER A CHILD • ORGANIZE YOUR LIFE AS A N
OORDINATE A FAMILY CALENDAR • PLAN FAMILY MEETINGS • ORGANIZE HOME SYSTEMS FOR ADD • PREPARE FOR A NEW CAT OR DO
ACK-TO-SCHOOL • WIN THE HOMEWORK WARS • PLAN A FIELD TRIP • PLAN YOUR CHILD'S ACTIVITIES • PLAN YOUR CHILDREN'S SUM
NLINE • ORGANIZE A GENEALOGICAL SEARCH • PREPARE FOR YOUR CHILD'S DEPARTURE FOR COLLEGE • ORGANIZE YOUR EMPTY N
LDERLY PARENTS' CARE • PREPARE FOR THE DEATH OF A SPOUSE • HELP YOUR ELDERLY PARENTS MOVE • ORGANIZE A HOME MEDIC
TORE TRIPS • SET UP ONLINE GROCERY SHOPPING • ORGANIZE RECIPES AND COOKBOOKS • PLAN THEME MENUS • CREATE EFFECT
EFRIGERATOR AND FREEZER • ORGANIZE CUTLERY AND KITCHEN TOOLS • ORGANIZE CUPBOARDS AND DRAWERS • ORGANIZE THE F
UNCHES FOR KIDS • PLAN PARTY FOODS AHEAD • THROW A DINNER PARTY • FINISH DINNER ON TIME • PULL OFF A LAST-MINUTE PAR
LTIMATE WEDDING CHECKLIST • BUDGET FOR A WEDDING • FIND THE PERFECT WEDDING RING • PLAN AN ELOPEMENT • SET UP A BA
ONOR • EXECUTE BEST MAN DUTIES • HIRE A BAND • HIRE A BARTENDER • PLAN A SHOWER • ORGANIZE THE REHEARSAL DINNER •
UCCESSFUL SLUMBER PARTY • PLAN A BAR OR BAT MITZVAH • PLAN A QUINCEAÑERA • PLAN A RETIREMENT PARTY • PLAN A FUNER
ANUKKAH PARTY • ORGANIZE A HOLIDAY CRAFT PARTY • PLAN TO SPEND CHRISTMAS SOLO • PLAN THE PERFECT HOLIDAY GIFT EXC
HE HOLIDAYS • STICK TO YOUR NEW YEAR'S RESOLUTIONS • PLAN THE PERFECT NEW YEAR'S EVE • PLAN A SEDER • PLAN A SPECIA
OOD TREE • ORGANIZE A BICYCLE SCAVENGER HUNT • RUN A SPORTS TOURNAMENT • PUBLICIZE AN EVENT • PLAN AN ORGANIZATIO
LAN A CONCERT IN THE PARK • ORGANIZE AN INTERNATIONAL CONCERT TOUR • ORGANIZE A FILM FESTIVAL • PLAN A FUND-RAISING
BUILD A COMMUNITY PLAY STRUCTURE • THROW A BLOCK PARTY • SET UP A NEIGHBORHOOD WATCH • CREATE AN EVACUATION PL
RGANIZE A PROTEST OR MARCH • FIGHT CITY HALL • ORGANIZE A BOYCOTT • ORGANIZE A CLASS ACTION LAWSUIT • MANAGE GRO
CHOOL IN A THIRD WORLD COUNTRY • PLAN A TRIP • PLAN A TRIP WITH CHILDREN • TRAVEL WITH TEENS • BOOK AIRLINE TICKETS •
OTORCYCLE TRIP • PLAN A TRAIN TRIP IN THE UNITED STATES • RIDE THE RAILS ABROAD • PREPARE A VACATION COUNTDOWN CHE
UGGAGE • LOAD A BACKPACK PROPERLY • PLAN AN ELDERHOSTEL TRIP • ORGANIZE AN RV VACATION • PLAN A TRIP WITH AGING PA
IDELY DIFFERENT PEOPLE • PLAN SPRING BREAK • PLAN AN OVERNIGHT GETAWAY WITH YOUR SPOUSE • PLAN A VACATION SEPARA
OLITICALLY UNSTABLE REGION • GET TRAVEL INSURANCE • GET IMMUNIZATIONS FOR TRAVELING • BOOK AN ADVENTURE VACATION
LAN A FISHING TRIP TO ALASKA • PACK FOR A CAMPING TRIP • LEAD A BACKPACK TRIP • HIKE A FAMOUS TRAIL • PLAN A TOUR OF T
NGLISH CANAL TRIP • PLAN A CROSS-COUNTRY AIRPLANE VOYAGE • PLAN THE PERFECT DAY ABROAD • PLAN A VISIT TO THE LOUVE
LAN • PREPARE FOR AN ACT OF GOD • ASSEMBLE EMERGENCY KITS • PREPARE FOR SURGERY • PLAN YOUR RECOVERY • SURVIVE
EING LOST • CONDUCT A SEARCH AND RESCUE OPERATION • PLAN AN INVASION • SURVIVE A POLITICAL COUP • PLAN FOR A TERRO
ECOME THE PRESIDENT OF THE UNITED STATES • WIN AN ACADEMY AWARD • BECOME AN OLYMPIAN • TRAIN FOR A MAJOR ATHLET

Education & Career

You're a junior in high school and need to apply to colleges soon. But how do you choose one that's right for you? It's a big decision when you're leaving home for the first time. Remember, academics, while important, are only one aspect of the college experience.

Steps

1 Gather all the information you can on schools and programs that interest you. Ask your high-school counselor for ideas, read college catalogs and visit Web sites such as CollegeBoard.com and PrincetonReview.com to compare schools. Talk to friends and relatives. Investigate traditional colleges as well as alternatives such as studying abroad and enrolling in a trade school, music school or art school.

2 Hire a college admissions counselor for expert, personal attention. It may be money well spent.

3 Examine your motivations if you dream of attending one of the nation's most competitive schools. Read 150 Get Into a Top College or University.

4 Look for academic programs that match your interests. Read books such as *America's Best Graduate Schools* from U.S. News & World Report (available for review and purchase at www.usnews.com). Order course catalogs and visit Web sites such as gradschool.com.

5 Give careful thought to location. You may want to get as far away from home as possible, but will you miss having friends and family nearby? Can you afford out-of-state tuition and transportation home during the holidays? If you're from a big city, you may feel cramped by a small town. But if you're from a small, neighborly town, a metropolitan area may be overwhelming—or just what the doctor ordered. For students who crave a busy social life, city schools can be deceiving since many go their own way come Friday night. Schools in small college towns offer a thriving campus scene, for the sheer reason that there's no where else to go.

6 Weigh the merits of a small school that offers lots of individual attention against a large one with more resources. Many small schools fly under the radar, offering an excellent education and plenty of space available to incoming students.

7 Pay attention to the composition of the student body as well as demographics. Is cultural and ethnic diversity important to you?

8 Choose schools with strong programs in your areas of interest or major if you've already chosen one. Find out how hard it is to get into the classes you need to graduate.

9 Investigate financial aid options. (See 234 Organize Your Financial-Aid Package.)

Tips

When you visit a campus, ask students whether they would attend that school if they could choose again.

Pick up the syllabus for any classes you're interested in. Also keep a copy of the campus newspaper with your notes from each visit.

Almost all applications can be submitted online or can be downloaded from the college's Web site.

For some young adults, taking a year off between high school and college may be an invaluable chance to discover more about their interests, to get experience working, to spend time abroad, or just to grow up a bit more before leaving home. Also look into a national service program through AmeriCorps.com. A year's break will not negatively impact your admission into college.

Who Knew?

Experts say to apply to one to two safety schools, three good matches and one or two reach schools.

Check the National Association for College Admission Counseling site's (nacac.com) Space Availability Survey for openings for qualified students in many schools' freshman and/or transfer classes.

10 Develop an initial list of a dozen or so colleges that interest you. Gather all the information you can and visit the schools while they're in session to get a real picture of campus life, socially and academically. Before you visit, find out when they offer tours and arrange to meet an admissions officer. Bring a parent to listen and take notes, but you should be the one with a solid list of questions. Arrange an overnight stay in a dorm if you can.

11 Get a campus checklist from your high school's guidance office and make a copy for each school. Fill it in during your visit so it will be easier to compare schools when you get home.

12 Find out how much access you'll have to professors and if they or teaching assistants teach most of the classes. Ask about average class size for lectures and labs.

13 Ask students and faculty about the extracurricular activities that interest you. If you're an athlete, meet coaches from your sport and talk to team members. If you're a journalism student, sit in on some classes and see the school newspaper staff in action.

14 Keep your grades up. If you lack the grades or money to get into the college of your choice, attend a community college first. You can save money, improve your grade point average and transfer to a four-year school.

Warning

Don't crowd your campus visits together. A marathon trip to 10 schools will turn every one of them into a blur. Before you visit each campus, schedule a tour and make appointments with admissions and financial aid officers.

150 | Get Into a Top College or University

You've got a blistering GPA, your SAT scores are off the charts, you're captain of your sports team and you still find time to volunteer. But is it enough to grant you admittance to your dream school? While there's no sure-fire recipe to getting into the country's coveted universities, there are things you can do to make yourself an attractive candidate in the eyes of admissions directors.

Steps

1 Work closely with your high-school guidance office. The counselors can help you get into the right classes, pick colleges and chart your course of action. They also write recommendations and communicate with colleges about applications. See also 149 Decide Which College Is Right for You and 152 Organize Your College Applications.

2 Hire a private college admissions counselor if you feel you need extra guidance. Applying to college is a lot of work with a bewildering number of options. An expert helps both students and parents sort through it all, something that over-extended high-school counselors may not have the time or resources to do. He

Tips

Talk to friends, family and alumni who have attended the school of your choice. Work these connections, and ask for recommendations. See 201 Make a Networking Plan.

Find out about scholarship opportunities. Packages are available in sports, music, the arts and other fields.

Keep up the good work in your senior year. College admissions officers don't want to see you slack off.

Continued on next page

or she will make qualified recommendations based your interests, grades and test scores. Contact the Independent Educational Consultants Association (educationalconsulting.org) to find one in your area. If you hire an adviser, be aware that colleges will still direct their questions to your high-school guidance office.

3 Plan out your classes. Ask your guidance counselor to recommend required and elective courses, and the order in which you should take them. For instance, you may need to take geometry as a freshman if you want to advance to calculus by your senior year.

4 Attend summer school to get prerequisite classes if you didn't plan early enough. Admissions officers like students who work hard to catch up. See 280 Choose a Summer Study Program.

5 Take the most challenging course work you can, including advanced placement classes (for which you get college credits). Many admissions officers would rather see you tackle a harder class than settle for an easy one just to get a high grade and look for trends in grades, as well as class rank. At the same time, don't set yourself up for failure by signing up for too many tough classes.

6 Nail your PSATs, SATs and ACT exams. See 151 Ace the College Admissions Tests.

7 Explain yourself if you've scored low on the tests but have a high GPA. Ask your teachers to address the issue in their letters of recommendation. They should stress that your grades are well deserved, and you should do the same in your admissions essay.

8 Get involved in extracurricular activities in your school and community. The number of activities isn't important—admissions committees look for depth rather than breadth.

9 Stay committed to your activities. Begin as a Cub Scout, for instance, and progress on to Eagle Scout. If you can, work your way up to a leadership role—become the editor of the school paper, head church projects or run for class office.

10 Develop a theme that runs through your high-school activities. For instance, if you love art, take painting classes, become a museum docent and volunteer to teach art at an elementary school. Refer to this theme in your application's essay.

11 Plan your summer with college in mind. It looks good to be active and constructive even when you're not in school. Find a camp or college class that fits in with your theme. If you have to pump gas over the summer, turn it into something creative— help improve customer service, for example.

12 Get to know key people at the college you want to attend. Follow through with the college representative who comes to your high school, introduce yourself to a coach or professor and meet an admissions officer.

Who Knew?

Let the admissions office know when you visit the campus, meet staff or talk to alumni. Some colleges track the number of contacts you make to determine how interested you are.

Be aware of the acceptance rates at your top choices. Schools with acceptance rates below 30 percent (for example, Amherst, Williams and Swarthmore colleges can drop below 25 percent) are reaches for anyone who does not have both very strong academics and very impressive achievements. Keep in mind, candidates turned down by top universities quickly take spots at their next choice.

A 4.0 GPA at one high school is not the same as a 4.0 at another. Colleges pay close attention to the quality of the student's high school and the challenging nature of that school's curriculum.

Some high schools have free peer-tutoring programs, or you can pay for a private tutor, a learning center or an online educational service.

Warning

It's tempting to load yourself up with classes and activities, but the stress and fatigue can be counterproductive. Colleges want to see you excel—not spread yourself thin. If you don't know how to slow down, get professional counseling.

Sharpen those No. 2s: Getting into your favorite school is far easier if you get strong scores on the admissions tests. Although plenty of resources are available to help you prepare, your best bet is still to read widely, develop a good vocabulary and challenge yourself in math and science courses.

Steps

1 Discuss with your high-school guidance counselor which tests to take and when. It is recommended that you take the SAT I (Scholastic Aptitude Test, which measures critical thinking) or ACT (American College Test, a content-based achievement test) in the spring of your junior year so there's time to retake it if necessary.

2 Find out which tests are required by your chosen colleges and take the one that better suits your skills. (Most colleges accept both the SAT and the ACT.) Find out if you need to take the SAT II in addition to the SAT I or ACT. Your guidance counselor should have free practice exams.

3 Sign up to take a preliminary test—the PSAT or the PLAN (ACT's preliminary exam) to find out what areas need work before you take the real thing. The PLAN is usually given in the sophomore year; many students take the PSAT in the fall of their junior year.

4 Compare your scores to the average test scores of entering students at your colleges of choice. If your scores are much higher, you may not need to prep for the actual test. Note that a top score of 36 on the ACT equates to a 1600 on the SAT.

5 Develop preparation strategies for the real exams. You have several options with a broad range of price tags. It's debatable how effective the various methods are, but most people agree that prepping boosts self-confidence and sharpens test-taking skills.

6 Buy a study book or software application, make a study schedule and stick to it. This is the least expensive route, but it works only if you're self-motivated and highly disciplined.

7 Take a course. Kaplan.com has offerings for $299 to $350; The Princeton Review (princetonreview.com) offers live online courses for $599 to $699, self-directed ones for $299 to $399, and crash courses for $79 to $99. Smaller companies such as TestU.com offer online courses for $60 and up.

8 Take a classroom course from Kaplan or the Princeton Review. These are expensive (starting at about $599) but are good for students who need structure and motivation. They usually last six weeks, and some come with a money-back guarantee.

9 Hire a private tutor for individual attention. Fees vary from $20 to $200 an hour, but if you need special guidance, it's worth it.

Tips

Visit CollegeBoard.org for SAT information and Act.org for the ACT.

Mom's right: Get plenty of rest the night before a test, and eat a good breakfast.

During the test, answer easy questions first; they carry as much weight as the hard ones. And be sure to pace yourself—don't get hung up on one question.

Can't find a tutor in your area? The Princeton Review (princetonreview.com) can provide you with one.

Who Knew?

The basic fee for taking the SAT is $28.50 and allows you to send your scores to four schools. The basic fee for the ACT is $25 and includes four free score reports.

Students can take Advanced Placement (AP) tests to earn college credit for advanced coursework completed in their high-school years. Each exam costs $80. Check to make sure that your preferred schools accept AP credits before paying for the test.

Warning

Avoid cramming in a lot of memorization before the test. Instead, concentrate on test-taking techniques.

One day you're a high-school junior, happily juggling schoolwork, social life and other activities. Then suddenly you're a senior applying to college, and the balls come tumbling down. The best way to handle all the details and deadlines is to organize everything to a T, beginning the summer before your senior year.

Steps

1 Make a college countdown calendar with important dates such as application deadlines, campus visits and aptitude tests. Review and update the calendar frequently. For a sample calendar, visit the National Association for College Admission Counseling (nacac.com) and go to the section for students.

2 Decide whether you want to apply for early admission, which increase your chances of getting into the college of your choice, but may limit your options. *Early decision* plans allow students to apply early (usually in November) to their favorite school and get an admission decision from the college well in advance of the usual notification date. The catch is these plans are binding—you agree to attend the college if it accepts you and offers an adequate financial aid package. Although you can apply to only one college for early decision, you may apply to other colleges under regular admission. If you are accepted in the early decision plan, you must withdraw all other applications. Usually, colleges insist on a nonrefundable deposit well in advance of May 1. With *early action* plans, students learn early in the admission cycle (usually in January or February) whether a college has accepted them. But unlike early decision, most early action plans are not binding.

3 Narrow your list to the top six colleges of your choice. Experts advise applying to one to two safety schools, three good matches and one or two reach schools. Request applications in the mail or download application forms from the college's Web site.

4 Keep copies of all related correspondence and applications for each college in separate folders. Write down contact names and phone numbers. Document any phone calls and file the notes.

5 Fill out the applications thoroughly, representing all aspects of yourself as fully as possible. Don't just list your extracurricular activities: Offer detailed information, highlighting both accomplishments and contributions.

6 Spend time on your essay—it's one of the most critical parts of the application. Answer the question that's asked, stay focused and use specific examples to illustrate your points. Be creative and show your individuality. Most admissions committees would rather see you take a risk than use a pat formula.

7 Send copies of your completed applications by certified mail, in case you need to prove they went out on time. Call the colleges' admissions offices to make sure they have everything they need.

Tips

Ask for letters of recommendation from teachers, counselors and other people who have a positive view of you. Look for someone connected to the college, such as a donor, a trustee or an alumnus. The letters should be short and to the point. It's your responsibility that the letters arrive on time, so ask for them early.

If a college requires your first-semester grades from your senior year of high school, ask the guidance office to send them. At the end of the year, request that the office send your final transcript and follow up to make sure it's received.

If you're wait-listed, let the college know you're still interested and send a copy of your spring grades.

Have a parent or teacher edit your essay, and use their suggestions to rework it. Before you turn in your final copy, ask someone to proofread it carefully.

Who Knew?

ACT offers fee waivers to students who demonstrate financial hardship; similarly, some schools will waive admissions fees for students with financial need. Ask admissions offices about the options available to you.

Application charges vary widely among different schools and universities, ranging from about $10 (for community colleges) up to $70 (for some elite colleges).

153 | Plan Your Course of Study in College

Graduation day may seem like a long way off, but you have to start charting your course from day one. Every class you take will impact your goal of getting your degree.

Steps

1 Find out what classes are required to graduate, when you must declare a major and what prerequisites must be taken. Also find out how to include studies for a minor.

2 Know how many units you need to take to graduate on time. If you receive financial aid, work on campus or are involved in athletics, you may be required to take a minimum number.

3 Make friends with your adviser. He or she can approve interdisciplinary classes as well as resolve scheduling conflicts. Meet quarterly to stay on track.

4 Avoid overloading yourself with course work. You may need the dean's approval if you exceed the maximum course or credit load.

5 Look into a double major, which fulfills the requirements of two majors within the same degree. To do this, you may need approval of both departments and the deans of the colleges. Also explore interdepartmental majors and double degrees.

6 If you're taking same subject classes in a sequence, try to take them one right after the other. The content will still be fresh in your mind, so you'll have an easier time as you advance.

Tips

Don't load up on one subject such as science or math—variety will keep you sharp. Some colleges limit the number of courses a student can take in a particular subject that you can take.

Register early, especially for popular classes. Online registration is widely available.

Reduce your courseload if you have a special commitment—for example, studying for the Graduate Record Examination (GRE) or completing a thesis—but only if you have enough units to graduate on time.

Balance difficult or time-consuming classes with less-demanding ones as you plan each term.

154 | Organize a Research Paper

A research paper, whether it's for a high-school class or a master's degree, often takes far more work than expected. Get organized and put yourself on a schedule to get it done, step by step.

Steps

1 Clarify the nature of the research paper. For instance, does your professor want you to analyze a problem or defend a position?

2 Define the steps of the project, setting deadlines for each step and noting other requirements, such as a preliminary outline or a rough draft. See 6 Meet Deadlines and 2 Set Priorities.

3 Make a list of topic headers or key words relating to your subject. As you conduct your research, assign each piece of information a key word. When you organize these topics later, they'll form a basis for your outline.

Tips

Ask your professor whether you can read past papers that received good grades to get an idea of what he or she is looking for.

Ask questions as you go. If you've gotten off topic, you want to find out about it while there's still time to change direction.

See 9 Organize Your Thoughts.

Continued on next page

4 Use index cards for your notes or develop a computerized system. Check out software from Onfolio.com or Thomson ISI ResearchSoft (risinc.com), which helps you organize text. Document all sources.

5 Create an initial outline using the topic headers you've gathered. Review with your professor and make necessary adjustments.

6 Block out 30 minutes, an hour, three hours or whatever you need to work on the paper daily. Choose a strategy that works for you, maybe in terms of hours and minutes worked, or perhaps for problems solved or pages written.

7 Write a first draft of your paper and have it critiqued by someone with solid writing experience. Some professors are happy to review first drafts.

8 Find out the required format for your final product. Many professors are particular about what paper stock you use, how you set margins, and the footnotes and bibliography format.

Warning

Plagiarism is a nasty word. If you find the same information in many sources, you don't have to attribute it. But if an idea comes from just one source, you need to credit it.

---

155 | Get Into Grad School

Whether you want to be an engineer or an Egyptologist, graduate school may be a necessary stepping-stone. But getting an advanced degree is a huge investment: Choose carefully to find an academically excellent program that opens career doors as well.

Steps

1 Work in your chosen field for a while to gain experience and knowledge. Job experience with specific applications will help when you apply to graduate schools.

2 Prepare for and take the required test, whether it be the Graduate Record Examination (GRE), Graduate Management Admission Test (GMAT), Law School Admission Test (LSAT), Medical College Admission Test (MCAT) or Dental Admission Test (DAT). See 151 Ace the College Admissions Tests for tips.

3 Investigate graduate programs (see 149 Decide Which College Is Right for You). Order catalogs and visit Web sites such as GradSchool.com to learn about schools that interest you. Make sure you fulfill the entrance requirements. Investigate job placements for students who complete the programs.

4 Talk to the school's faculty members. Find out their background and areas of interest or research.

5 Ask other students for frank feedback on the program, both pros and cons. Find out what support is available to students.

6 Apply. (See 152 Organize Your College Applications.)

Tips

Apply to five or six schools, including some long shots and fallbacks. The average application fee is about $50 per school, which can sometimes be waived for those with limited income.

Get your applications in early to improve your chances of admission. Give your references plenty of notice, too.

Confirm that libraries and labs are well equipped and up to date.

Who Knew?

Graduate schools offer a variety of flexible programs for working people (see 158 Get a Degree While You're Working).

Do you dream of graduating from a top law school? Of being courted by the most prestigious firms even before you get your J.D.? Sounds great, but there's no guarantee you'll be happy at one of these schools. Before you jump in, study the culture to see whether you truly want to attend an Ivy League or comparable school. If you do, apply early, stay on top of the paperwork and show what a valuable asset you'll be.

Steps

1 Attend a college that successfully feeds students into the top law schools (see 150 Get Into a Top College or University). The best bet is to get your undergraduate degree at Harvard, Yale or Princeton, but other colleges are devising ways to make their students attractive to top graduate schools. Pomona College in California, for instance, has upped its success by helping students with interviews, letters of recommendation and more.

2 Strive for a 3.5 or above grade point average (GPA). Be aware that a 4.0 at one school may not be comparable to a 4.0 at a less-competitive school. Admissions directors look at the level of your coursework, too. Major in English/literature, philosophy, history or political science/government. Be able to write well.

3 Take a good look at the law schools you think you want to attend. Harvard, for instance, has a premier reputation and just about guarantees you a big firm job, but will you like the large classes, busy faculty and fellow students? Find out all about highly ranked law schools in *America's Best Graduate Schools* from U.S. News & World Report (www.usnews.com).

4 Understand that good grades aren't enough—you need to ace the Law School Admission Test (LSAT.com). Look into LSAT preparation courses (which can cost upward of $1,000) on Web sites such as PrincetonReview.com and Kaplan.com, and take practice tests. Be aware that effective studying for the LSAT usually takes at least 50 hours. See 151 Ace the College Admissions Tests and 157 Prepare for the Bar Exam for study tips.

5 Take the exam in June or October of the year before you plan to enter law school. In theory, the LSAT is a consistent measure for an admissions officer to compare all applicants with each other. Scores range from a low of 120 to a high of 180. You'll want to score 164 or above to stay in the running. (The national average is about 152.)

6 Register with the Law School Data Assembly Service (LSDAS), which will compile a report about you and send it to any law school you want. The LSDAS report includes your official test scores, transcripts and recommendations, and it's a requirement at nearly every law school approved by the American Bar Association (abanet.org).

Continued on next page

Tips

If you've been out of school for a while, emphasize how your work and other real-life experiences make you a strong candidate.

Before you apply, read *The Paper Chase* by John J. Osborn Jr. and *One L* by Scott Turow.

Who Knew?

The LSAT is not a test of knowledge about the law or other legal matters. So law-related classes (like business law, constitutional law or criminal law) don't necessarily prepare you more effectively for the LSAT than other courses do. Rather, the test is designed to measure reading comprehension, and logical and analytical reasoning, because that's what both law school and the practice of law require.

There's also a writing section of LSAT that's not scored but is sent to law schools when you apply.

The registration fee for the LSAT is $112. Late registrants must pay an additional $56.

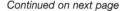

7 Request applications from the law schools you want to attend—you can often download them from the schools' Web sites. To make it easier, start a Web account with LSDAS or buy its CD-ROM so you can electronically access the application of nearly any law school you can imagine.

8 Get all your ducks in a row and submit your application early. By the end of summer, request transcripts and line up letters of recommendation, which you'll need to send to LSDAS. Ask the people who recommend you to be specific about what makes you a great candidate and how you stand out from other students (see 152 Organize Your College Applications).

9 Apply by November of the year before you want enter law school. This is especially important at schools such as Harvard that have rolling admissions. They make a decision on each application as it comes in, and the class starts to fill up as the months go by.

Look into scholarships and other financial aid if the $30,000-plus-a-year price tag makes you shudder. Start searching at Finaid.org. See 234 Organize Your Financial-Aid Package.

Your personal statement may not be as important as your LSAT scores and undergraduate grades, but it may set you apart from everyone else. Let your top choice know who you are, what you believe in and what you hope to accomplish as a lawyer.

157 | Prepare for the Bar Exam

You made it through law school—and that was hard enough. Now comes the bar exam. You want to pass this the first time. If you fail, you can take it again, but statistically, your chances of passing go down each subsequent time you try.

Tips

Contact the National Conference of Bar Examiners (ncbex.org) to find out what subjects are on the multistate portion.

See 151 Ace the College Admissions Tests for more exam-taking tips.

Steps

1 Get the rules and application form from your state's board of bar examiners long before you plan to take the exam. In almost every state, the exam is two days: the one-day multistate bar exam (MBE) portion—200 mind-numbing multiple-choice questions—and a day of essays.

2 Seriously—very seriously—consider taking a bar review course. So many people take bar review courses that the model answer exam reviewers are looking for is invariably in the style taught by these courses. Ask around for the best course in your area. It will be expensive, but now is not the time to pinch pennies.

3 Know what areas you'll be tested on. Your state's bar examiner will tell you which areas of the law you are responsible for knowing for in the essay portion.

4 Start studying the day after graduation. At a minimum, allow eight weeks. Shun your friends, let your personal appearance go and do nothing else but study during this period—consider it your job. Make a timeline listing the subjects you will study each day: constitutional law one day, torts the next and so on. In the beginning, devote a day or more to a single subject. By the end, you should be hitting four to six subjects a day.

Who Knew?

The bar exam is given in July and February and is different in each state.

Download old exams from your state bar's Web site. Study them. If you are not taking a bar review course, you will have to buy sample MBE exams (and answers) from NCBE. Practice on as many tests as you can get your hands on.

You want to advance your career by going back to school, but how could you ever find the time when you're holding down a job? Many colleges and distance-learning programs offer a number of flexible options to help students out. Your employer may even pay for your courses if they're relevant to your job.

Steps

1 Explore colleges, night schools and online programs to find one that meets your needs (see 149 Decide Which College Is Right for You and 155 Get Into Grad School). The range of options will surprise you—in one program, you might study on your own and report to class one weekend a month; in another, you might take summer courses and then write your thesis at home.

2 Talk to counselors at the schools and programs you're considering. Discuss your professional goals, and whether you want to advance in your field or make a career change (see 160 Go Back to Work After a Long Absence and 167 Prepare for a Career Change).

3 Shop around before you commit to a program. Ask professionals in your field about a school's reputation. Compare costs at private and state colleges, as well as distance-learning programs.

4 Decide how much time you can devote to your studies. If you have many other commitments, you may need to take fewer classes over a longer period to reduce stress and increase your chances of completing the program. Ask your boss for a flexible work schedule to fit in with your studies. Make sure to mention how your new skills will benefit the company.

5 Arrange for a sabbatical or use vacation time to take classes (see 162 Plan a Sabbatical). If you can afford it, work part-time.

6 Check out your options for student financial aid. If you ask, your employer might even pitch in, particularly if it adds value to your existing job. See 234 Organize Your Financial-Aid Package.

7 Combine work and school for mutual benefit. For instance, if you do a project or thesis, make the subject applicable to your work (see 154 Organize a Research Paper).

8 Buy the equipment you'll need for school. If your computer is old, you may have to invest in a new operating system to handle specialized software, or a new computer all together; look into educational discounts once you're enrolled. You might need to use the same operating system (Mac or PC) that your school most commonly uses. Some stores offer student discounts, so you may want to wait until you get your student ID.

9 Set aside a quiet place for studying at home. Get help with child and/or elder care so you have time to hit the books. See 159 Work at Home with Kids.

Tips

Your school's guidance counselors can suggest ways to coordinate work and study schedules.

Investigate any online program before you enroll. Check its credentials and affiliations, and how long it's existed. You'll find everything from fly-by-night operations to programs connected to well-respected colleges. UniversityAlliance.com, for instance, is affiliated with several universities, including Villanova, Tulane and Jacksonville.

If you have to drive to school, arrange your classes so you're not hitting rush hour. Carpool if possible.

Setting up a home office so you can work and spend time with your young kids might sound like a dream—the perfect way to balance job and family. If you are the primary caregiver, however, getting any work done while giving your children the attention and focus they need can be a logistical and emotional nightmare. Whether you're planning to work full-time or part-time from a home office or just squeeze a few hours in here and there, you'll need a realistic plan.

Steps

Arranging child care

1   Find child care for the hours you work to avoid neglecting your kids or your job or both (see 263 Arrange Quality Child Care). Hire an in-home caregiver or enroll your child in day care or pre-school. If your job demands fluctuate, consider trading off with other work-at-home parents, so the kids play at your house one day and the other house the next. For a full-time job, on-again, off-again child care won't cut it.

2   Create a plan that covers your child care needs for summertime and holidays as well as during the school year. Also consider before- and aftercare needs in the event you have to attend a meeting and can't pick your kids up on time.

3   Work with your children's schedules—not against them—if you're trying to get work done without additional child care. Set up your hours so that you're working at night while they're asleep and in the daytime during naps and while they're at school.

Creating a balance

1   Keep your office space clean and organized (see 196 Add a Workspace to Any Room and 197 Organize a Home Office). Make sure that your kids know this area is off-limits.

2   Schedule meetings or conference calls for when your children are in school or at day care. If you need to meet with clients, look into shared conference rooms, such as at entrepreneur business centers. Many charge a reasonable monthly fee for a business phone number, professional answering service, mailing address and package receiving.

3   Use your cellular phone, instead of your home line, as your business phone. The kids won't pick it up by mistake or forget to give you messages. And you can deduct it at tax time.

4   Carve out time for your children when you're done with work. Whether it's playtime or dinnertime, make a commitment to your kids that when you're done working, you're done. Resist the seduction of multitasking every possible moment. Make your children your top priority when you're off-duty. They know if you're truly paying attention or just going through the motions.

Tips

Every family needs to find the balance that works for them. Review 14 Balance Home and Work.

Make a list of what you need to do the next day before you turn in for the night (see 3 Write an Effective To-Do List). That way, you can relax and concentrate on the task at hand without being afraid details will fall through the cracks.

Synch your work calendar with the family schedule. See 266 Coordinate a Family Calendar.

If the whole family shares a computer, establish firm rules regarding who's online when. See 281 Create a Schedule for Family Computer Use.

Work out a system with older children to let them know when they need to be quiet. For example, when your work phone rings, the TV volume goes off and any fighting stops.

Who Knew?

Research working from home before you take the plunge. You'll find helpful advice in books such as *Working from Home* by Paul and Sarah Edwards and on Web sites such as WorkingSolo.com and Work-at-Home Moms (wahm.com).

160 | Go Back to Work After a Long Absence

While you took time off to raise a family, care for elderly parents, go back to school or travel around the world, chances are there were major changes in your field's trends and technology as well as at your former workplace. Get up to speed first before you to return to work.

Steps

1 Keep up with your field while you're away. Stay in contact with co-workers and bosses, and meet for lunch or cocktails occasionally. Subscribe to professional journals and keep licenses or credentials up to date. As you get ready to return to work, use the Internet to read up on changes in your profession and discuss them with your colleagues.

2 Start networking at least a year before you're ready to go back to work. (See 201 Make a Networking Plan.) Join a professional organization or a networking group. Talk to friends, family and former work associates who can help you develop contacts.

3 Invest in a career counselor. You'll get the latest information on your industry and the job market in general, work on strategies to maximize what you have to offer and learn how to get the word out about you and your skills.

4 Decide whether you want to go back to the same kind of work or whether you're ready for something new. Your interests and needs may have changed, your capabilities may have expanded or the job you enjoyed years ago may no longer exist due to changing technologies.

5 Sign up for refresher courses and additional training to become more attractive to potential employers. You can study online or enroll in classes at a nearby college to brush up your skills.

6 Create a functional résumé rather than a chronological one that focuses on your skills and not the dates you held previous jobs. Include the skills you have developed goals accomplished— became president of the PTA, for instance, or organized a food drive (see 383 Plan a Toy Drive).

7 Develop a transferable skill, such as sales and accounting, that you can pick up easily after a long absence. Or use your old skills in a new job. If you taught math in your past life but want more flexible hours now, look into private tutoring.

8 Be open to taking a lower position than the one you left long ago. You may consider it a blow to your ego, but you can use it to take advantage of new opportunities in the work place, develop your skill set and get back on track.

9 Hang your own shingle if a 9 to 5 job seems unbearable after all these years away. Become a consultant or start your own business, but be prepared for hard work, long hours and an unpredictable income and benefits. See 204 Set Up a New Business.

Tips

Talk to other people who have gone back to work after an extended period of time off. They may offer practical advice on job hunting, writing résumés and readjusting to the workplace.

Ask yourself whether you want to embark on a demanding career or just get a job you can leave behind at 5 p.m. See 167 Prepare for a Career Change.

Who Knew?

Try temping if you don't know exactly what kind of job you want. You'll get exposure to different work environments while bringing your skills up to date.

161 | Set Up an Internship

An internship is a great way to get your feet wet professionally. You'll make contacts, gain experience and discover whether you like a field before you take a job in it. If you're in the right place at the right time, your internship may even lead to a permanent position.

Steps

1 Identify what you want and need from an internship. What kind of work environment do you like? What skills do you want to use and develop? Do you need to get paid?

2 Look for companies that offer internships in your field. You can find lists at a career or employment office, or visit Web sites such as InternSearch.com and InternJobs.com.

3 Network to find openings (see 201 Make a Networking Plan). Join professional associations, and talk to friends and family members who can help you with contacts.

4 Get in touch with the human resources department of a particular company if you're not sure whether it offers internships. Ask what's available, whether it's full- or part-time and whether it's a paid position. If the company doesn't have an internship program, suggest one.

5 Find out what kind of work you'll be doing day to day. An employer may sound great and project an exciting image, but the actual work could bore you to death. For instance, a love of politics may lead you to an internship in a congressional office, only to find yourself opening mail and answering phones.

6 Send in your application, cover letter and résumé. Tailor them all to the specific internship.

7 Research your prospective employer before the interview. Companies love applicants who have done their homework. Ask questions that show you're in tune with the corporate culture.

8 Bring a well-organized, professional portfolio to your interview— it can help you stand out. Use yours to show off certificates of honor, letters of recommendation or newspaper clippings that detail your accomplishments. Portfolios are a must in any job related to the arts.

9 Ask whether your internship might be a stepping-stone toward a permanent job. Many companies hire interns as a trial period for later employment.

10 Turn in a stellar performance when you land an internship. Show up on time, dress appropriately, ask questions and do your job efficiently. Good work and a positive attitude have helped many interns become full-timers.

Tips

Start looking for internships early. The waiting period can be up to two years for the most selective spots.

If you're a student, investigate internship options at your campus career center. A wide range of situations are available, from short-term summer positions to internships lasting a semester or an entire school year. Some are unpaid positions while others pay a stipend. Have a plan in place to cover living expenses if your internship is a minimal- or nonpaying position.

Ask whether you get credits for internships.

Look for a mentor who will show you the ropes, introduce you to influential people within the company and recommend you for any jobs that open up.

162 | Plan a Sabbatical

Taking some time off is good for body and soul. Whether you tromp through the Amazon rain forest, stay home to write a novel or just play with your kids, you're taking a break from work to refresh yourself and expand your horizons. Careful planning will make it easier to arrange a sabbatical—and to return to work seamlessly.

Steps

1 Start laying the groundwork at least a year before you go on sabbatical. You may need that much time to arrange things at work and plan for your time off.

2 Do some soul-searching. Set up your sabbatical to investigate something you're passionate about—whether you want to take a class, explore all 50 states or build a school in rural Mexico (see 404 Build a School in a Third World Country).

3 Assess your practical needs (see 228 Design a Savings Plan). Once you set your baseline, you'll know how much time you can afford to take off. Find out whether you retain any pay.

4 Use your sabbatical for a positive purpose, not to avoid things you don't like. If you can't stand your job or your boss, these things won't get any better just because you're away from work for a few months. Instead, ask for new duties, apply for a transfer or try to get a different boss. See 167 Prepare for a Career Change.

5 Request your sabbatical, and present it in terms of how it will benefit you and your employer. A cookbook editor would gain tangible skills by attending a cooking school, while a health care worker could learn another language to better serve a multi-cultural population. Your sabbatical can also save money for the company, since they may not be paying you during that time.

6 Be flexible about the time frame—don't ask for six months off at the same time your company plans to launch an important project. Offer to train someone to cover your job while you're gone.

7 Find out whether you're guaranteed the same position when you return after your sabbatical. If you're not, ask whether you're entitled to equivalent work.

8 Schedule regular check-ins during your sabbatical—and leave a way your employer can get in touch with you. This will keep you up on major changes that may affect your job.

9 Stop in at work a few days before you report back to duty. Spend the time catching up with your boss and fellow workers.

10 Give yourself time to fit in when you return. Expect to prove yourself as if you were a newcomer when you return and be prepared to accept new faces and new ways of doing things. On the other hand, don't spend hours talking to colleagues about your time off. They won't enjoy it—and neither will the boss.

Tips

Ask other people who have taken sabbaticals what to do and what to avoid.

Check out Lisa Rogak's *Time Off from Work: Using Sabbaticals to Enhance Your Life while Keeping Your Career on Track* for tips and ideas.

See 160 Go Back to Work After a Long Absence.

Who Knew?

Some businesses offer paid sabbaticals. Find out how they work, and propose one to your boss.

Warning

Don't wait until the last minute to make arrangements or you'll waste precious time off.

Working abroad is like getting paid to travel. You get to live with the natives, soak up local culture and sharpen your language skills. Some lucky people get sent overseas by their employers, while others use creative means to find jobs in the country of their choice. Get all of your paper work in order, since all countries require special permission for foreigners to work in their countries.

Steps

Landing a job

1 Choose a country that interests you. Gather information from that country's embassy and from other people who have lived or worked there. Network at home to find a job in that country (see 201 Make a Networking Plan). If you tell enough people you're interested in working in Japan, for instance, you'll be surprised at how many of them will help you make connections.

2 Pursue foreign work assignments within your own company. This can be the easiest way to go since your employer can guarantee your work permit visa.

3 Go through a work-abroad program if you want a short-term job. Learn about positions on Web sites such as JobsAbroad.com and in books such as *Work Abroad: The Complete Guide to Finding a Job Overseas* by Clayton A. Hubbs.

4 Find work teaching English as a second language (ESL). Some jobs require an ESL degree, others don't. If you have a teaching credential, get a job at an English-speaking international school. Dealing with children from a variety of different countries can be fun and challenging. Also check out 164 Join the Peace Corps.

Getting your paperwork in order

1 If you don't already have one, apply for a new passport ($85) as soon as possible, since it typically takes about 6 weeks to arrive. If you're in a hurry, you can pay an additional $60 and the cost of overnight delivery to receive the passport within 2 weeks. Go to travel.state.gov/passport for more information.

2 Apply for a visa at your nearest consulate or embassy when you've found a job. Bring your passport, passport photos and the employment contract or other documents from your employer. You may also need to show a medical certificate and a criminal record check. For students, visas are fairly easy to obtain. If you're looking for full-time employment, you'll need a work permit visa, which is usually available only through an application placed by the employer offering you the position.

3 Allow plenty of time to get your visa and work papers. It can take anywhere from a few days to six months, depending on the country.

Tips

Check out the Bureau of Consular Affairs (travel.state.gov/visa) for information about getting a U.S. visa.

Check the want ads in English-language newspapers once you've landed. Network the same way you did at home. Call companies in your field to arrange an interview (see 166 Organize Your Job Search).

Many expatriates work as freelance models, photographers and journalists. These jobs sound romantic, but it can be a challenge to work on your own in a foreign country.

Who Knew?

Pay taxes in the country where you work. You don't have to pay U.S. taxes up to a certain income limit, but you should still report what you make to Uncle Sam.

Warnings

Jobs sometimes look great from 3,000 miles away, but they may not stack up when you begin working. You may not have the materials you need, for instance, or your workplace can be dark and dingy. Before you accept a job, contact people already working for the employer for the inside scoop.

If you work abroad without the proper visa, you risk deportation, fines and lack of legal protection.

Travel the world. Help others. And while you're at it, build relations between the United States and other countries. These goals have motivated people to join the Peace Corps ever since John F. Kennedy created the program in 1961. As a Peace Corps volunteer, you work hard under tough conditions for little or no pay, but the rewards are worth it. Here's how to prepare for "the toughest job you'll ever love."

Steps

1 Visit PeaceCorps.org to learn about the mission and philosophy of the Peace Corps, as well as the two-year commitment. Talk to former Peace Corps volunteers to get a realistic idea of what you're in for.

2 Be—or become—a U.S. citizen. You have to be at least 18 years old to apply to the Peace Corps, but there's no upper age limit.

3 Earn a four-year college degree, or develop exceptional skills or work experience in anything from computer science to hydrology to animal husbandry.

4 Submit an application and a health-status form online or through the mail. Specify any medical conditions you have so you end up serving in a country with appropriate health care services. Send in a copy of your college transcript, a résumé and the names of three references. (Urge your references to submit their letters on time. As it is, the application process can take between three and six months.) Once you've sent in your application, go to PeaceCorps.org and click on "Current Applicants" to check the status of your application.

5 Get ready for your interview. Expect to answer both personal and professional questions, and prepare a list of your own concerns.

6 Receive a nomination from your recruiter. This means he or she is recommending you for a Peace Corps program in a certain geographic region, but it's still not a done deal. You need medical and legal clearance—and the final thumbs up from the Peace Corps placement office.

7 Get a complete physical exam, plus dental and vision checkups.

8 Expect to answer questions during your legal clearance about everything from finances to your marital status. The last hurdle you will face is an FBI background check.

9 Receive a formal invitation packet in the mail. You have 10 days to accept or reject it. If you accept, you'll receive your assignment. If you reject the invitation in search of another location, you will get pushed to the back of the line and may not get another invitation depending on what positions are available.

10 Attend your training and orientation in the United States.

Tips

Contact the Peace Corps recruiter in your area if you have questions about the application process.

Read 405 Plan a Trip, 419 Pack for a Trip, 439 Plan a Trip to a Politically Unstable Region and 436 Plan a Trip to a Different Culture.

Who Knew?

Pack light, because you'll need to handle your own luggage. A backpack or light suitcase on wheels is your best bet.

Warning

Get ready for a geographic assignment you might not expect. You can state your preference, but the Peace Corps matches your skills to a country that needs them.

165   Produce a Newsletter

Two simple words sum up a good newsletter—style and substance. An effective piece entices the reader with its attractive design and rewards them with informative, readable content. Whether you target company employees or a more general audience, you want your readers to have an enjoyable—and valuable—learning experience.

Steps

1 Give your newsletter a name people will remember—the shorter, the better. If you want to use more words, turn them into a subtitle. The name could be "Save the Seals," and the subtitle could be "The Monthly Newsletter of the American Society for Seal Preservation."

2 Feature informative content. People want news they can use. Whether you're writing an editorial or a review, back up your opinion with solid facts. Write catchy headlines to grab readers' attention.

3 Keep your articles short and to the point. Your readers are bombarded with information all day long, so write as concisely as possible. And be sure to use everyday language—nobody will spend time decoding technical information or working through dry, stodgy text.

4 Resist the temptation to buy generic, pre-written content. It's usually not interesting, it's hard to verify its accuracy, and you run the risk that your readers will have read it somewhere else.

5 Hire a graphic designer to create a template for your newsletter. It should include simple and attractive design elements, photos, illustrations and graphics, and use clean, readable type.

6 Choose a clear, legible serif typeface for the newsletter's main text and another complementary font for all the headlines. Avoid using an infinite number of distracting vanity fonts. Stay with one type family for headlines, varying the size according to the importance of the copy. Add subheads to break up long chunks of type, and create easy points of entry to the page with sidebars.

7 Find a good editor and a good proofreader. The editor will improve the copy, and the proofreader will catch embarrassing mistakes before you go to press. Your spouse or business partner isn't necessarily the best person for these jobs.

8 Stick to what you can do well. If you can put out only two pages of high-quality design and content, start there. It's better to leave people wanting more than to underwhelm them with mediocrity.

9 Get specific instructions from the printer for delivery of digital files. Most will want all fonts and images included on the CD you'll burn. Some printers will accept e-mailed files, but be sure to ask about specifics. You'll want to discuss details such as ink color, paper selection, turnaround, delivery and more.

Tips

The same basic principles apply to any newsletter, whether it's delivered by e-mail or printed on paper: It needs to be attractive, informative and easy to read.

Use page-layout software such as Quark Xpress (quark.com), Adobe PageMaker or InDesign (adobe.com), or Microsoft Publisher (microsoft.com). Enhance the quality of photos and images with software such as Adobe Photoshop.

Who Knew?

Decide whether you want to mail your newsletter folded and stapled, or send it in an envelope. If you go the fold-and-staple route, leave room for the address and mail permit. Check with the post office for exact requirements.

Develop a style sheet or use a publishing stylebook, such as the *AP Stylebook*, to keep the newsletter consistent. For instance, you shouldn't abbreviate California as "CA" on one page and "Calif." on the next.

Warning

Always ask for a proof before the job runs. Check for typos and color matching, and make sure all the elements (such as photos and illustrations) are there.

Looking for work can be a full-time job in itself. The longer you look, the harder it is to stay positive and focused. To make it easier, organize your search, make creative use of your time, and network, network, network!

Steps

1 Identify your job market by location, industry, company size and job description. Are you willing to move to a new city or state for a job? Are your skills transferable from one industry to another? If you're good at sales, for instance, you can probably sell anything from shoes to software.

2 Read 167 Prepare for a Career Change and research like crazy. Scour the online job boards at Web sites such as Jobs.com and Monster.com. Read professional journals in your field. Take full advantage of the many career guidance books available.

3 Keep careful records of everything, including contacts, dates, interviews and follow-ups. Web sites such as JobFiler.com offer tools to make your search easier. See 10 Set Up a Reminder System and 184 Conquer Your Paper Piles.

4 Post your résumé on job listings sites like Monster.com and in employment centers. Answer newspaper ads and apply for positions online.

5 Hire a professional career counselor to get you on the right path. He or she can help with everything from tuning up your résumé to mastering networking skills to refining goals and expectations (see 16 Set Goals). Ask your librarian or YMCA about free or low-cost career-counseling services or career fairs.

6 Join a job-search group. Members offer one another encouragement and practical tips about the job market.

7 Stay active in the community and keep your work skills sharp. If you're a nurse, volunteer in a neighborhood clinic; if you're a lawyer, help out at a legal aid office.

8 Create an elevator speech. Define what you do and what you're looking for into a soundbite that you could communicate in the time it takes to ride an elevator. Practice it. Tell it to everyone you know and ask if they know someone you could talk to.

9 Turn everything you do into a networking event. (See 201 Make a Networking Plan.) Of course, you'll work the usual places—professional meetings, for instance—but make church gatherings, PTA meetings and parties all work for you. The more people you talk to, the better your chances of making the contacts you need.

10 Create a daily schedule that includes making phone calls, surfing the Web, networking and interviewing. Make sure you get out of the house and see people each day so you don't get burned out.

Tips

If you're shy about networking at first, start with people you know well. As you feel more comfortable, you'll be able to chat with just about anyone. Who knows? The guy in front of you in the grocery store line might be your future boss.

Expand your options. If you're a teacher, for instance, start tutoring or substituting, which may lead to a solid classroom job.

To avoid paralysis and depression, reward yourself for completing tasks.

Changing careers is exciting and fulfilling. It usually involves some personal and financial risk, but that's a small price to pay for a chance to find rewarding work or to completely reinvent yourself. Reduce the risk and increase the rewards by thoroughly investigating your options and carefully plotting your strategy before you jump ship.

Steps

1 Read 201 Make a Networking Plan and 166 Organize Your Job Search for more information on career transitions.

2 Evaluate what's most important to you. (Read 16 Set Goals.) Is it a good income, challenging work or independence? What do you do well and what do you enjoy? If your career fits in with your basic values, you'll like it more and stick with it longer.

3 Ask yourself what you don't like about your current job so you don't end up facing the same issues the next time around.

4 Write down your interests without considering the barrier of skills, education, income and so forth. Try to find intersecting points between your list of interests and desires, and your needs in terms of income and working conditions.

5 Consider what new skills you need to meet your interests, and whether you can realistically obtain those skills. Do you need to go back to school? Can you learn on the job? How much time would it take? Is there something in your current job or skill set that you can use as a bridge to help you acquire the skills for your target job? Can you do volunteer work concurrently to enhance your skills?

6 Explore ways to make your present career more satisfying before you make the leap into a whole new field. Taking a new position or switching employers might be enough of a change. Work with a career counselor to help you figure out your strategy.

7 Draft a plan of action. Include a timetable for writing your résumé, researching jobs and the job market, and going to school for retraining if necessary. See 6 Meet Deadlines.

8 Acknowledge the challenges and obstacles you may face, such as your age, education and financial obligations, and create options.

9 Visit a career or employment center. You can take a battery of tests that evaluate your personality, skills and interests, and suggest appropriate fields. The Myers-Briggs Type Indicator (myersbriggs.org), a standard personality test, and the Strong Inventory (careers-by-design.com or career-lifeskills.com) are popular ways to determine your interests. You can also take career tests on the Internet, but you'll miss the face-to-face interaction with a counselor as you interpret the results. Sometimes

Tips

Craft a résumé that builds on the strengths you developed in the past. If you're switching from teaching to marketing, for instance, emphasize your great communication skills. Be sure to couch these accomplishments in the jargon of your new field.

If you can't afford to give up a well-paying job, scale back your hours and take part-time work in your new field. In time, build up to full-time work in that career.

just talking about what is happening in your life and what you want helps. The tests may complement other activities, but they certainly don't provide all the answers.

10 Work with a career counselor who charges by the hour. Get referrals from friends and co-workers, and make a few introductory appointments until you find a counselor who's tuned in to your job market and your needs and personality. A good career counselor will suggest ways to identify—and snag—your dream job.

11 Pick up one of many other books available on career options such as *What Color Is Your Parachute?* by Richard Bolles. You may find types of work you never knew existed.

12 Learn everything you can about the careers that appeal to you— what training they require, what they pay and whether jobs are easy to find. You can get this information at job fairs and career centers. Ask at your librarian or YMCA about upcoming events— they're usually free or cost very little. Contact professional organizations for a particular field. They usually have helpful newsletters, Web sites, member directories and conferences.

13 Seek out people who work in a field that interests you. Conduct informational interviews to find out how they like their work and what they do day to day. Learn what they did to get started in their career. People generally like to talk about themselves, so ask plenty of questions and listen carefully.

14 When you've narrowed your choices to two or three fields, volunteer or intern in those areas to make sure you enjoy them before giving up the security of your existing job. This will offer you a realistic, nuts-and-bolts feel for the work and let you assess whether that job or field meets your needs. (See 161 Set Up an Internship.)

15 Find out what it will cost to train for your new career, and look into ways to finance it. You may want to stick with your old job while you prepare for the new one. Explore online education, adult classes and other ways to get training without disrupting your current routine or income.

16 Learn about the best ways to land jobs in your field. Networking is crucial—so don't be shy about using your connections, such as alumni organizations and family friends. Talk to anyone who will listen about what you want to do. You never know who will have contacts or will be able to give you helpful input. Also, explore online job sites, newspaper ads and career centers.

17 Develop a support group of friends, families and colleagues. They can offer new ideas, provide encouragement and offer a reality check: "Are you sure you want to be an astronaut?" (See 492 Become an Astronaut.)

Who Knew?

Look into the future for different careers that appeal to you. The Department of Labor's Bureau of Labor Statistics (bls.gov) offers predictions.

Ask a restaurant consultant about opening a restaurant and you're likely to get a succinct answer: "Don't!" The failure rate is high, the costs can soar out of control and the hours are brutal. If you remain convinced that you are the next Alice Waters or Wolfgang Puck, put on your toque, brush up on your knife skills and forge ahead.

Steps

1 Clarify your concept and put all the proposed details—from decor to dessert choices—in writing. If you can't write about them, they need more thought.

2 Investigate the regulatory requirements, both city and state. Prepare for a plethora of paperwork, including byzantine building codes with regulations covering everything from kitchen exhaust systems to interior finish requirements.

3 Find an ideal location. Do a demographic study of the surrounding area. Research the amount of foot traffic and the availability of easy parking. Then negotiate a lease you can afford.

4 Plan your menu early in the game. Kitchen layout and equipment purchases depend on it. Reduce your equipment costs either by purchasing used equipment or leasing new.

5 Find the funds. Write a detailed business plan and consider forming a small private corporation or starting a limited partnership. However much money you think you need, raise more. Many restaurant consultants blame the high rate of new restaurant failures on undercapitalization.

6 Allocate the available space. Remember that in addition to dining and kitchen areas you'll need room for dishwashing, storage, bathrooms and administrative work.

7 Plan the layout for the dining area. Remember to balance your desire for the maximum number of seats with your future customers' desire to shun tables crammed into awkward corners. Also avoid locating tables in the middle of the room like woebegone little islands. "Nestle tables—particularly two-tops—against low divider walls or other architectural features," advises restaurant owner and designer Pat Kuleto.

8 Keep the kitchen layout focused on efficient, safe food preparation. Ensure that there is sufficient light and ventilation, as well as enough space so that cooks, servers and dishwashers are not bumping into one another at the busiest times.

Tips

Plan an advertising and public-relations campaign that begins even before the restaurant opens. Contact the food editor of the local newspaper about doing a "great new restaurant coming soon" story. See 372 Publicize an Event.

Impress upon the wait staff that they should treat each patron as though he or she were the newspaper's restaurant critic.

Read books on planning, designing and securing investment for restaurants. Take a class at a university's hotel administration school. Read *Restaurant Business* magazine (restaurantbiz.com) for strategies and resources.

You'll need to provide your local health department with a list of menu items, as well as how they are prepared, cooking times, refrigeration temperatures and more.

Who Knew?

Decide on the restaurant's overall look. Beware of trendy, contrived design. Patrons may enjoy it for the first visit or two, but then can tire of it quickly. Go for warmth over edginess.

9 Don't neglect the graphics. From the exterior signage to the look of the menus, graphic design plays an important part in a restaurant's overall look.

10 Pay attention to lighting design. Focus dramatic light onto the tables to highlight the food, and complement it with glowing atmospheric light to make the customers look good.

11 Research and develop the menu. Taste-test the recipes repeatedly until the kitchen can achieve consistency. Remember that the food also has to look good on the plate. Plot out your menu-pricing strategy. Have the final menu proofread before sending it to the printer.

12 Decide whether to offer full bar service. Apply for a wine and/or liquor license.

13 Investigate insurance needs thoroughly. Restaurants are simmering stockpots of potential accidents—from fires to floods to food poisoning and a hundred other potential horrors. The National Restaurant Association (restaurant.org) is an outstanding resource for insurance-related information.

14 Select and train the staff. Look for enthusiasm as well as experience. Allow ample training time before the restaurant opens. Remember that the person running the front of the house is as important as the person running the kitchen, and great service is as important a factor in winning customer loyalty as great food.

15 Set up a bookkeeping and accounting system. Establish control over the meal checks. There are dozens of scams that dishonest servers and cashiers can pull; get some expert advice on how to prevent them.

16 Designate a core of trusted employees to supervise storage areas carefully. Stress that they must check in all deliveries and audit the food inventory frequently.

17 Pass your opening inspection by a food safety specialist with your local health department, along with a plumbing inspection. You'll receive a permit to operate, which will be reviewed yearly.

18 Open your doors and welcome hungry diners.

Warning

Be cautious about making coupon offers. They often have a low success rate for generating repeat customers.

Physics is all about the interaction of matter—it focuses on gravity, velocity and other material marvels. While some physicists reach for the stars, others change the way people live on Earth (think of lasers and microwaves). To make a big bang in this field, you have to be loaded with curiosity, intelligence and initiative—and love solving problems.

Steps

1 Earn a bachelor's degree in physics and a teaching credential if you want to teach high-school physics.

2 Get a master's degree in physics if you plan to work in applied or practical physics, conduct research or teach at a two-year college. Explore professional master's degree programs that prepare you for work in the private sector. See 155 Get Into Grad School.

3 Gain experience in other areas such as computer technology if you want to work in applied physics. Many people study physics and then work in information technology fields as software engineers or systems developers.

4 Become a theoretical physicist and explore topics such as the origin of the universe, or work in a practical field developing new materials and equipment. You'll need at least a doctoral degree in physics to work in theoretical research and development. Expect to do postdoctoral work to land a permanent university or government job.

5 Specialize in a subfield such as acoustics or fluids. If you think small is beautiful, pick atomic physics. If your interests are far-reaching, go into astronomy (which some consider a subfield of physics).

6 Look for work in government, commerce or education. You can teach at a university, work for a drug company or find a job at NASA. Some entrepreneurs form their own companies to develop new products and ideas. You can work on everything from electronics and optics to medical and navigation equipment.

7 Slip on that white lab coat—many physicists spend their careers in research laboratories. If you specialize in a field such as nuclear energy, you may need to share bigger, more expensive equipment in a larger team setting.

8 Sharpen your grant-writing skills or find someone else to write those proposals. They're usually essential to keep your work funded.

9 Become an author as Stephen Hawking (*A Brief History of Time*) has done and write about physics.

Tip

Be flexible—specialties sometimes overlap, and you may find yourself switching among them. And you don't have to limit yourself to one science; you can choose a double field such as biophysics or geophysics.

Who Knew?

Physicists earned a median annual income of $85,020 in 2002.

Warning

Expect stiff competition, especially if you want to work in theoretical research. You'll be up against qualified candidates from all over the world vying for a limited number of jobs.

Concert musicians stroll onstage in their gowns and tuxedos and turn in seemingly effortless performances. To get to Carnegie Hall and other prestigious venues, a violinist spends years practicing and rehearses for hours every day. And that's to say nothing of the other challenges, such as auditioning for jobs in a competitive market.

Steps

1 Start young. The famed violinist Yehudi Menuhin began at age 4. Even if you're tremendously talented, it can take years to hone your musical ability and stage presence.

2 Love music—think it, breathe it, dream it. Immerse yourself in a variety of genres even though you'll ultimately focus on classical music. Take private lessons, attend seminars and go to music camps. Get all the experience you can in community orchestras and symphonies.

3 Study at a college or music conservatory, where you'll learn about music theory, composition and performance, and get a degree if you want to teach later. You'll also develop important contacts. Contact the National Association of Schools of Music (nasm.arts-accredit.org) for information about college-level music programs.

4 Intern at a music festival. This can give you exposure and experience playing with a symphony orchestra.

5 Go for auditions even if they're a long shot. You'll get more comfortable with the process and gain composure, which will eventually help you land that coveted spot in a symphony orchestra.

6 Pack your bags. Especially if you're self-employed, you'll most likely be on the road a lot, either looking for work or giving concerts. You may also travel if you work for an orchestra.

7 Keep your day job. Be prepared to work at an outside job along with playing your violin. Many professional musicians have gaps between engagements, so they take part-time jobs to pay the bills. Teaching is one way to remain in touch with the world of music, keep a flexible schedule and earn a steady income.

8 Practice every chance you get. The best performers keep growing and developing new skills to enhance their playing.

9 Hire an agent or a manager if you make it big. You can concentrate on playing the violin while someone else finds you jobs and arranges details.

10 Make sure your wardrobe includes several classic black pieces for performances. Gentlemen, buy a tuxedo. Ladies, start shopping for an elegant gown.

Who Knew?

Musicians often lack health care and other benefits. Many of them join the American Federation of Musicians (afm.org), a group that helps negotiates labor agreements, works to increase benefits and lobbies to raise industry standards.

Salaried musicians earned a median annual income of $36,290 in 2002.

171 | Become a Cowboy

Cowboys cut a hardworking, heroic figure as they moved through the frontier in the 1800s. The frontier has disappeared, but today's cowboys and cowgirls still work hard raising cattle and crops, and riding the rodeo circuit. It's easy to recognize a cowboy—just look for well-worn boots and jeans, an oversize belt buckle and that 10-gallon hat.

Steps

1 Work on a ranch to learn everything you can about cattle. You'll feed the cows, give shots, look for pinkeye, help with calving and much more. Buy a ranch if you can afford it and can handle all kinds of uncertainty, from bad weather to sick cattle to fluctuating markets.

2 Select promising bulls for breeding and rodeo riding. Castrate the others and raise them for meat or for steer wrestling at the rodeo. Decide whether you'll use the females for birthing or beef.

3 Learn some rodeo skills at bull-riding or rodeo school, and develop other skills on the ranch. You rope a calf to give it medicine the same way you rope one to bring it down in the rodeo.

4 Buy cattle feed, or raise your own if your ranch is big enough. If it's really big, grow enough grain to sell to other people. Grass-fed cattle require a pasture consisting of high-energy grasses and clovers.

5 Mend fences and maintain farm buildings and equipment. Learn about machinery—a lot of ranch work, including branding and vaccinating, is now mechanized.

6 Feed and take care of your horses.

7 Be a savvy businessperson. You have to buy grain, sell animals and balance the books.

8 Get someone to watch the ranch while you ride in the rodeo. Many cowboys work their ranches Monday, Tuesday and Wednesday and compete Thursday through Sunday. (Some cowboys are only ranchers, some are only in the rodeo and some do both.)

9 Pay a rodeo entry fee and hope to place high enough to take some prize money home. Top rodeo cowboys earn a good living on the circuit, but many others barely scrape by.

10 Enjoy being outdoors, working with animals and keeping a quintessential American way of life alive.

11 Buy an original Stetson at StetsonHat.com.

Tip

Check out the National Cattlemen's Beef Association at beef.org.

Who Knew?

Get in shape—ranching and rodeo skills take a lot of strength and endurance.

Along with hands-on experience, many ranchers get agricultural-related degrees.

Ranch income varies greatly according to the weather and market prices for crops and livestock, so you have to be prepared for fat and lean times.

172 | Become a Brain Surgeon

The brain, with all its millions of neural connections, weighs just 3 pounds. Cutting one open requires nerves of steel, guts and intellect. If you think you've got the right stuff—and the patience to train for 14 to 20 years—read on.

Steps

1 Ask yourself whether you have what it takes to do the job before you commit to decades of training. Brain surgeons not only need skill, stamina and dexterity, but also have to keep their cool in highly emotional situations. Interview several neurosurgeons.

2 Get into the best school you can (see 150 Get Into a Top College or University) and earn a four-year pre-med degree. Some medical schools require only three years of pre-med studies, but most applicants have a bachelor's or advanced degree. Excel in biology, chemistry and mathematics.

3 Prepare for fierce competition when applying to medical school. Schools look at transcripts, letters of recommendation and Medical College Admission Test (MCAT) scores, as well as extra-curricular activities. Find out from medical students what to expect in your interview with a medical school's admissions committee. See 151 Ace the College Admissions Tests and 155 Get Into Grad School.

4 Go to medical school. (A few schools combine pre-med and medical school into a six-year program, but usually you face four years of undergraduate study and four years of medical school.) In the first two years, you will take classes and begin to examine patients. In the second two years, you will gain real-life experience under the tutelage of practicing physicians.

5 Complete six grueling years of residency in neurosurgery, your chosen specialty. Finally you've attained a paid position. If you're like many brain surgeons, you'll spend another year or two doing advanced study in neuroscience.

6 Pass a licensing exam in any state. Many—but not all—states allow reciprocity, which means you don't have to get licensed again if you move to a new state.

7 Become board certified in neurosurgery. This involves studying for and taking a rigorous professional test. It isn't necessarily required to get a job but may be expected later.

8 Find a job through your professional network. Ask the program director of your residency program to spread the word that you're looking for work. Network at meetings of professional societies and look at the employment ads in professional journals. See 201 Make a Networking Plan.

Tips

Unless you're independently wealthy, look into major financial assistance. Only 20 percent of medical students get through school without borrowing money. (See 234 Organize Your Financial-Aid Package.)

Even after two decades of training, you'll keep studying. To deliver the best care, you need to stay on top of medical advances throughout your career.

Who Knew?

Surgeons earned a median annual income of $255,438 in 2002.

Fifty years ago, half of brain surgeries were fatal. Now it's less than 10 percent.

Warnings

Brain surgery is physically as well as mentally demanding. You need stamina to stand still for hours, performing minute surgical moves.

Expect to pay an outrageously high price for malpractice insurance. Premiums have risen so much in recent years that some surgeons have gone on strike to protest them.

You wear many hats as a rabbi. You have the prestige and responsibility of being a spiritual and civic leader, as well as a scholar and a therapist. You lead religious services; perform bar and bat mitzvahs, weddings and other ceremonies; counsel members of the congregation; and work on projects to better the community at large.

Steps

1 Be Jewish or convert to Judaism. Conversion is a multistep process with different requirements for the different branches of Judaism.

2 Be a good speaker and a good listener. Your success as a rabbi hinges on interacting well with people to gain their confidence.

3 Decide which branch of Judaism you want to serve: Orthodox, Conservative, Reform or Reconstructionist. (Orthodox Judaism ordains only male rabbis.) They feature very different forms of worship and lifestyle, from traditional to quite modern. Format and rituals can even vary within one branch.

4 Get a college degree. Most Jewish seminary programs require it. Your major isn't crucial. Seminaries look for qualities that will make you a successful spiritual leader. They weigh your academic success, volunteer work, psychological makeup and more.

5 Gain substantial life experience. Many lawyers, doctors and business people become rabbis as a second career. They view their religious calling as a way to give back to the community.

6 Complete a four- or five-year seminary program. Each branch of Judaism has its own requirements, but you can usually expect an academic program plus internships and field training. The religious curriculum includes the Torah, Jewish history and Hebrew, and you'll also study psychology, education, public speaking and community problem solving.

7 Graduate as a rabbi with a master's degree in Hebrew letters. Or study longer and earn a doctorate in Hebrew letters.

8 Get hired by a congregation and receive direction from your congregation's board of trustees. Judaism doesn't have a religious hierarchy, so rabbis don't report to a superior such as a bishop or a pope.

9 Expect to start small in your first job. Competition is stiff for large congregations. You can become an assistant rabbi, a leader of a small congregation, a chaplain in the military or the director of a college Hillel center. You can also teach at a college or seminary or work for a Jewish social-service agency.

Tips

Brush up on your Hebrew and Jewish studies before you enter a seminary, or you might spend an extra year there preparing for the regular course of study.

If you need financial aid, seminaries often have loan and scholarship programs. (See 234 Organize Your Financial-Aid Package.)

See 346 Plan a Bar or Bat Mitzvah.

Who Knew?

Rabbis' earnings vary greatly, according to the part of the country, the branch of Judaism and the size and finances of the congregation.

Large cruise ships such as the Queen Mary employ rabbis.

The job description calls for chastity, poverty and obedience, and apparently that's not everyone's cup of tea. In the past 30 years, the number of Catholic nuns in the United States has fallen by about 100,000. But if you're seeking spiritual commitment and the opportunity to provide service to the community, you might be one to boost the numbers.

Steps

1 Be Catholic or convert to Catholicism. Talk to your priest about the steps involved.

2 Do not get married—or divorced. Married women can't become nuns, and the Church frowns on divorce. You may apply if you're a widow, though.

3 Get a college degree. Many religious communities like applicants to have at least a bachelor's degree before they take their vows. See 149 Decide Which College Is Right for You.

4 Find an order, or a religious community, that suits your beliefs and personality. For instance, do you want to be out in the community or do you prefer a cloistered life? (Technically, if you're out in the world you're a sister, and if you're cloistered you're a nun.) A priest or nun at your church usually can point you in the right direction, or check out ReligiousMinistries.com.

5 Look for an order whose work interests you. You'll find everything from beekeeping and winemaking to teaching and family counseling. Benedictine sisters, for instance, work in education and service ministries, whereas Cistercian nuns are devoted to prayer and contemplation. You don't need to be quiet and passive to be a nun—some are antiwar protesters and others lead the fight against AIDS in Third World countries.

6 Contact the vocation director at the community you choose. Spend some time there and ask plenty of questions.

7 Move in for a year or two while you're still studying or working outside if that's an option. This period of residency will give you a good feel for the everyday life of the order you're considering.

8 Go through the novitiate, or training period, which may last another year or two. You'll spend your time studying, praying and deciding whether you really want to become a nun.

9 Take temporary vows of poverty, celibacy and obedience. Depending on the community, these vows may last from one to nine years.

10 Take your final vows. If you made good on your temporary vows, you're ready for the religious life.

Who Knew?

Many nuns don't receive compensation. Nuns who are doctors or social workers, for instance, are paid wages, which support the work of their religious community.

Christianity isn't the only religion with nuns. Many Buddhist women take lifelong vows of simplicity and service.

Want to choose the art that makes your museum the hottest ticket in town? Start by looking, looking and then looking some more to develop your eye. Next, earn a master's degree, land a job at a museum and work your way up to a curator's position. At last you're in prime position to organize a blockbuster exhibition.

Steps

1 Determine the exhibition's theme. Whether you feature a single artist, illustrate an artistic trend or place familiar works in a new context, start with an idea. "Winslow Homer's Paintings" doesn't tell a story. "American Impressions, 1865 to 1925: Prints, Drawings and Watercolors" is an exhibition theme.

2 Choose a date. Factor in considerable lead time, typically two to four years.

3 Seek out supplemental funding—corporate and individual—for both the exhibition and its catalog. Big exhibits cost big bucks but provide impressive opportunities for prestige by association.

4 Plan the catalog and assign essays to experts. Approve designs for other tie-in material, such as banners, postcards, calendars and T-shirts.

5 Allow delivered work to remain in packing materials for 24 hours to adjust to the museum's climate. Do a careful condition report on each piece as it is unpacked. Arrange for additional security guards if needed.

6 Work with the museum's exhibits specialist to design the physical aspects of the installation, including layout and construction of any special display elements such as pedestals, room dividers and temporary alcoves. Arrange for any special lighting needed.

7 Create informational labels for all the works. Great labels go beyond providing basic facts; they answer common questions and help visitors view the artworks with deeper understanding.

8 Identify the most important pieces to illustrate the exhibit's theme. Develop a script about this theme for self-guided tours on cassette or CD, and get a famous person to read it. Interesting art deserves an interesting voice. Check out Antenna Audio at antenna-audio.com.

9 Plan the publicity program. Oversee press releases to send to the art press, both local and national, and to travel publications. Contact a local charity about making the opening party a benefit. See 372 Publicize an Event.

10 Supervise the hanging and placement of the work. Then, just before the preview party, walk quietly around the exhibit—all alone—and savor what you've spent so long creating.

Tips

Plan on earning your degree in fine arts, art history, museum studies or history. See 149 Decide Which College Is Right for You.

Check that your insurance coverage is seamless.

Visit the exhibit several times a week during the busiest hours to see how visitors are responding.

Who Knew?

Consider bringing in one or more guest curators to help with a large, complex exhibition. Additional expertise will enrich the final production.

Make arrangements with other museums to send your exhibit on tour. A touring exhibit not only enables you to share some of the production costs, but also creates publicity for your institution and ensures that your ideas reach a far larger audience.

A great catalog not only sells well during the exhibition, but also can become a museum-store evergreen.

176 | Develop a Reality-Show Concept

As much as everyone says how much they hate them, reality shows are hot and getting hotter all the time. If you think you've got the next "Survivor," follow these steps to see if your idea has legs.

Steps

1 Come up with a million-dollar idea. Think: "Wouldn't it be great if ..." Let your concept sit for a while, then finesse it until it feels right. Decide if it's a half-hour show or a full hour.

2 Outline at least two sample episodes. Writing up additional episode ideas proves the show has legs. They can each be just a few pages long.

3 Develop the treatment. Paint a picture of what the show's all about in a thesis statement. Entice your readers, but make the treatment as straightforward and clear as possible.

4 Identify your audience in the treatment. The single most important element of a successful show is to judge accurately what the market is buying. Is your show the next "Queer Eye for the Straight Guy"? Articulate very clearly which market you're targeting, on which channel, and for which demographic group. For example, say "this is an organizing and makeover show on TLC geared to adults ages 24 to 64."

5 Decide if your idea is a high- or low-concept show. High-concept shows have a twist, a hybrid element that has never been done before. So although surrounding an eligible bachelor with 25 young women who have absolutely no self-respect is not new, abandoning the whole gang in a snow cave with only shotguns to get food and *then* seeing who wins the guy would be. Low-concept means the show is straightforward without a twist, such as "The New Yankee Workshop."

6 Shop your concept around. Since networks won't buy from some Joe Schmoe, pitch your idea to a production company, an agent or even a hot talent (host): If you're peddling better buns in 30 days, you'll want Kathy Smith on board. Make a verbal pitch, but use any visual aids—photos, a short clip that you filmed, storyboards—that would help explain why yours is the next hot show.

7 Take a deep breath if the network decides to develop a pilot: You've made it to the next step. Since the network is a vast animal with many parts, a 10- to 25-minute teaser tape (a pilot presentation) may be filmed to pitch it within the network or to show its syndicators. If a network decides to develop a full pilot, you may be asked to rework it—several times even (and possibly on your own dime).

8 Congratulate yourself if your series gets picked up. Now comes the real work of developing a budget and preparing for production. And ...action!

Tips

The National Association of Television Program Executives (NATPE.org) holds a convention every year. All the program managers attend to see what's new and hot, and decide what to buy. Your pilot presentation may be shown there, as well as to people within the network.

It helps if you have any onboard talent (include photos and bios).

Who Knew?

The most important facet of network programming is advertising. Which companies would most likely sponsor your program or provide product placement? Are there natural product tie-ins? Every reality show has well-placed product endorsements—no matter how great the concept is, the network won't buy it if they can't sell it. Include examples in your pitch.

If the production company or network options your show, it may take three months to a year or more before it's slated in the schedule. You may get paid for this time or not, depending on your contract. During this time, the network may kick it back to you for redevelopment, redevelop it themselves, or pair you with someone on their staff to do the work.

Oprah and Letterman, Howard Stern and Rush Limbaugh. What talk-show hosts have in common is marrying the gift of gab with the ability to glean juicy details from their guests. To get your own show, you can rise through the ranks of broadcasting or enter as an expert in your field. Either way, you need a double dose of confidence and a perpetually quick response.

Steps

1 Get a college degree in journalism and/or communications with coursework in public speaking and drama. See 149 Decide Which College Is Right for You.

2 Attend a private broadcasting school. Before you enroll, ask a variety of broadcasting professionals about the school's reputation. Or apprentice in a training program at a radio or TV station.

3 Work at a campus radio or TV station, or intern at a commercial station to gain experience and develop contacts. See 161 Set Up an Internship.

4 Produce a demo tape to distribute to program directors. Film or record a live performance to showcase your on-air experience and ability to interact confidently with guests.

5 Start out in radio—you have a better chance of getting on the air than you do in TV. Even there, your first job probably will be operating equipment or working as an production assistant, not hosting a show. You'll work behind the scenes—taping interviews, meeting guests' needs and running out for coffee.

6 Expect to begin as an assistant, a researcher or a camera operator if you start out in TV. With luck, you'll move up to an on-air position. Start in a small market to gain experience. You'll do everything from production to fund-raising—and hopefully some broadcasting work.

7 Get some years of experience under your belt and move to a bigger market, where you'll earn more prestige and more money. Your goal may be to work at a radio or TV station in a thriving metropolitan area, but you need a proven track record first.

8 Get on the air first as a guest if you're a specialist in a field such as psychology and want to become a talk-show host. People will fall in love with your wit and wisdom, and you'll go from there. At least, that's how it worked for Dr. Phil and Dr. Ruth.

9 Cultivate mental and verbal flexibility and the ability to ad-lib. You never know who's going to say what on a talk show, and you have to be ready with the right response.

Tips

Don't worry about having the perfect voice for broadcasting. Years ago, it was important because a lot of sound was lost in transmission. With the quality of today's broadcasting equipment, you don't need such a strong voice.

Get ready for odd hours. Even experienced talk-show hosts often work on early-morning or late-night shows.

Focus on radio if your voice scores more points than your face does.

Warning

Start purging the seven "forbidden words" from your vocabulary.

Wanted: Talented individual willing to risk life and limb to get the best picture possible. That's pretty much the job description for successful photojournalists. They need technical know-how and creativity, plus they have to be daring. Great photographers are aggressive enough to get the shot but are also sensitive to the subject.

Steps

1 Invest in good equipment, such as a high-end Nikon or Canon film or digital camera. You'll also need different lenses and flashes or other types of lighting gear.

2 Attend photography or journalism school. Develop your eye, improve your style and technique, and make contacts in the field. It's a good background whether you want to work for a community newspaper or travel the world as a freelance photographer.

3 Get an internship with a magazine or newspaper. This gives you real-life experience and gets you published, and it can turn into a full-time job. Some people have several internships before they find permanent work. See 161 Set Up an Internship.

4 Develop a portfolio that showcases your expertise with a wide range of subjects. It should include everything from one-shot car crashes to photo essays about people's lives. Most newspapers and magazines want to see published work, but a student portfolio may get you an internship or entry-level position. You'll work your way up from there.

5 Learn how to scan prints or download images from your camera, depending on whether you use a film or digital camera. Get training on image editing software such as Adobe Photoshop (adobe.com).

6 Know how to think on your feet. News events happen fast and can pack an emotional wallop. Your ability to stay calm and make quick decisions will greatly impact your success.

7 Go for the best story rather than settling for the easy shot. Just as a reporter would do, look for balanced reporting and seek out opposing viewpoints of the stories you cover.

8 Prepare yourself for physical and mental challenges. You'll carry heavy equipment in all kinds of conditions. You never know whether you'll cover a storm, a robbery or an accident. Some photojournalists work well even in dangerous (sometimes life-threatening) situations and are assigned to cover wars, regional conflicts and other hot spots around the world.

9 Hold up under pressure and get your work in on time. News editors can get pretty touchy when they're on deadline.

Tips

After you gain experience, take a job as a photo editor or teach at a college. Photojournalism is demanding, and you may need a break after spending a long time in the field.

Join the National Press Photographers Association (nppa.org) for seminars, networking and other professional opportunities.

See 53 Organize Your Photos.

Who Knew?

Freelance photographers can submit work to stock photo agencies. These agencies sell customers the right to use your photos and pay you a commission.

Salaried photographers earned a median income of $24,000 in 2002.

The Associated Press (ap.org) offers a highly selective internship program for aspiring photographers.

Warning

Pay attention to detail. Be sure you get your captions right, including names, dates and places. Editors hate to have to print corrections in the next day's paper.

Directing movies is exciting and artistically fulfilling—and it can be a big headache. You direct every step of a movie: auditioning and rehearsing actors, supervising the crew and having the final say on scenery and music. You have to stay on schedule, stay within your budget and stay sane when the cast and crew are melting down. If you can handle temper tantrums and typhoons, you may be the next George Lucas or Steven Spielberg.

Steps

1 Go to college and major in filmmaking (see 149 Decide Which College Is Right for You). According to www.filmmaking.net, the most respected U.S. film schools include the University of California at Los Angeles, the University of Southern California, the American Film Institute and New York University.

2 Move to Los Angeles or New York to get close to the action.

3 Get your foot in the door as an intern or assistant producer on a movie set (see 161 Set Up an Internship). You may not get paid, but you'll gain valuable skills, experience and contacts.

4 Develop your craft, gain as much experience as possible, learn like crazy and work your way up to film editor. When you have some clips to your name and start pulling down a salary, you can begin showing your work to people in the industry.

5 Enroll in a training program for assistant directors, run by the Alliance of Motion Picture and Television Producers and the Directors Guild of America (go to dga.org and click on "Training Program"). You'll get experience handling extras, transporting equipment and making arrangements for food and accommodations. Some companies allow you to shadow a director, which gives you valuable on-the-job training as well.

6 Think small at first. Directing music videos, educational films or commercials is a good way to get experience.

7 Raise money to make an independent film. It's much cheaper than it used to be, thanks to advances in digital technology. Enter your film in festivals and pray you get discovered.

8 Become a well-known actor and step behind the camera to direct your own movies.

9 Become a stage director and make the movie version of your latest hit.

Tips

Study other people's styles but don't copy them. You have to make your own name.

Deal with people respectfully and fairly. People will remember your reputation far longer than they'll remember some of your films.

The job is so multifaceted that directors have to delegate. Hire the most talented, dependable people you can.

Who Knew?

Directors' salaries vary widely according to how many jobs they get each year and how successful their work is. You can always dream about Peter Jackson's $20 million plus a percentage of the gross for a single film.

Warning

Don't go into directing for the big bucks—or even for a consistent income. You might strike it rich one year but then barely make ends meet the next.

It's not enough that you're tall, thin and gorgeous. To make a living as a fashion model, you need to work hard, be lucky, market yourself ruthlessly and watch out for unscrupulous people. And remember, this isn't lifelong work. Even if you hit it big, the typical modeling career lasts only a few years—or until gravity takes its toll.

Steps

1 Start at the right age and have the right body type. If you are female, start as a teenager, be at least 5 foot 8 inches tall and weigh between 100 and 125 pounds. Men often start by their early 20s, are about 5 foot 11 inches and weigh between 140 and 165 pounds.

2 Look for an agency to represent you. Agencies help you find jobs, advise you on your appearance and career, and collect a commission from your earnings. Most agencies are based in New York, but you can find modeling jobs in other cities.

3 Weed out ripoffs such as an agency that hits you with fees before you get work. Many fashion photographers will tell you which agencies take advantage of models. Check with the Better Business Bureau (bbb.org) or the office of your state attorney general. Watch out for agencies that charge high registration fees, photographers who say you need an expensive portfolio and anyone who pushes sex or nudity.

4 Submit professional photographs to the top agencies in the form of 8½-by-11–inch one-sheets, which have a black-and-white professional photograph on one side with your statistics and contact details on the back. The photo should be as simple as possible—wear minimal makeup, use a plain background, dress in a swim suit or other clothing that shows off your figure. Don't invest in a full portfolio; an agency will help you develop that later.

5 Go to an agency's open call. These free events are a great way to get in the door. If an open call isn't scheduled for the near future, ask whether you can stop in to introduce yourself.

6 Enter a model search if it's sponsored by a well-known agency. Fees vary and you don't want to pay a fortune to enter, but model searches can put you in contact with the right people.

7 Go to a modeling convention. These can be expensive to attend, but you'll learn a lot about the field and introduce yourself to several agencies at once.

8 Go to modeling school. Some people doubt whether it's worth the money, but you can gain experience.

9 Register with a Web site such as ModelsAndTalent.com. Model scouts will see your profile and contact you if they're interested.

10 Get a solid education and make plans for a post-modeling future that's based on your brains, not your beauty.

Tips

Hang out in malls or on the beach. Modeling scouts scour teenage hangouts for new talent.

It takes time to break into modeling. Be ready to work at another job while you establish your career.

If you're not young, tall and thin, explore other types of modeling careers. You might become a petite or plus-size model, a senior model or a real-person model for ads and catalogs. Some people are body-part models—for instance, they might have a beautiful neck or hands that look great in jewelry ads.

Who Knew?

Models earned median hourly wages of $10 in 2002. Keep in mind that you probably won't get work every day and many jobs last only a few hours. Supermodels skew the figures, too, with a scant few making up to $40 million a year.

Warnings

Expect a settling-in period when you begin your career, and keep your head on your shoulders. Many models fall prey to shady characters who promise them the world.

Before you sign with an agency, have a lawyer review any contracts to protect you from making a bad deal.

181 | Become a Stunt Person

Whether they're falling off a 10-story building, flipping a Maserati over a car trailer at 70 m.p.h., or delivering a spinning back kick to the villain's head, stunt people make living on the edge look so easy. All that pales in comparison to the hardest parts—getting your union card and landing that first job.

Steps

1 Get into good shape. Many stunt people are accomplished in gymnastics and martial arts.

2 Develop a specialty or two such as high falls, stair falls, car chases, riding horses and fights. Stunt coordinators look for specialists for each job, but it's good to have other skills because you'll most likely break into the field as an all-around stunt person.

3 Take a workshop. You can find specific subjects, such as introductory-level film fights, or classes covering a broad range. For examples, visit StuntsAreUs.com or StuntSchool.com.

4 Create a "one-sheet" to send with your résumé and to have on hand when you meet stunt coordinators. An 8½-by-11–inch one-sheet has a professionally photographed black-and-white head shot on the front. On the back are your basic measurements along with your specialties, certifications (in martial arts or scuba diving, for instance) and union affiliations.

5 Join the Screen Actors Guild (sag.org) or the American Federation of Television and Radio Artists (www.aftra.org). This step is tricky, because you can join only if you're in a SAG or an AFTRA production, and you can only be in those productions if you belong to SAG or AFTRA. One way around this is to find work as an extra and get a voucher that entitles you to union membership. See 484 Become a Movie Star for more tips.

6 Get a copy of the union production list that comes out each month. Mail a letter and your one-sheet to the stunt coordinators on that list. Express your interest in their current project and ask to be considered for the future as well.

7 Hang around movie sets to find out what they're like while you're waiting for your first stunt job. Pick a quiet moment on the set to approach the stunt coordinator. Introduce yourself, then present your one-sheet and résumé—and don't be a pest. If you get a small role in the film, handle it professionally.

8 Remember you're not a big shot when you land that first job. Follow directions and learn from other people. Being a team player is as important as being a talented stunt person.

Tip

Although you're constantly on the lookout for jobs in this field, it's also smart to have an agent. The best way to find a good one is through word of mouth.

Who Knew?

You have to be gutsy but not fearless to succeed in this field. Stunt people need fear to minimize their risk of injury.

The stunt business can be very sporadic, so you'll probably have to hold a job on the side. Waiting tables isn't as exciting as jumping off a cliff, but it'll pay the rent. When they get stunt work, SAG members earn about $500 a day as a base rate—plus extra for every time they repeat the stunt.

Warning

Stunt work is obviously more dangerous than your average desk job. Cuts and bruises are common in everyday film fights, and falls and fires can cause serious injury or death. (See 26 Schedule Doctor Visits.) The best way to protect yourself is to train well, follow safety procedures and not show off.

Imagine being paid to take a European cruise, raft the Bío-Bío or lead treks out of Katmandu. But that's just half of a tour guide's job. You'll also have to take care of every imaginable problem on a trip—and some problems you could never imagine.

Steps

1 Make sure you have solid people skills as well as infinite patience. Be honest about whether you're comfortable being "on" for 10, 12, even 18 hours a day. That's more important than knowing all about art, history or geography.

2 Get trained and certified at a school for tour guides, such as International Tour Management Institute (itmitourtraining.com). Although this isn't essential, these schools may help land a job.

3 Get hired by a tour company. The larger the company, the more work you'll have and the more chance to travel to exotic parts of the world.

4 Sign on with a company headquartered in your own country if you want to go abroad. It's easier than getting a work permit with a foreign company (see 163 Work Abroad).

5 Expect to operate as an independent contractor rather than an employee, especially with smaller companies. Although you'll have to arrange your own insurance coverage, think how much you'll save while you're working and the company is covering your hotel, meals and transportation.

6 Research the area you'll be touring extensively. Companies provide some basic information, but it's good to do homework on your own. You'll have more confidence, and people on your tour will appreciate your expert touch—which may lead to bigger tips and word-of-mouth recommendations from your clients.

7 Be a master of organization—you need to juggle your time and handle details such as getting through customs and finding lost luggage (see 1 Get Organized, 3 Write an Effective To-Do List and 423 Prevent Lost Luggage). You'll be in charge of transportation logistics, accommodations (finding hotels or setting up camp), meals, equipment repairs and maintenance, and more.

8 Stay calm when other people aren't. You have to handle all emergencies, whether a monsoon hits, the bus breaks down, a client has a meltdown or the hotel is overbooked.

9 Plan for a minimum of personal free time on a trip. That's just as well: Once you take care of all the arrangements and everyone else's needs, you'll have very little energy and time to go exploring on your own—or even do your laundry.

10 Be aware that you set the tone of a trip. If you're upbeat and enthusiastic, others will join in and have fun.

Tips

Speaking a foreign language is helpful but usually not necessary, unless you're leading a tour of people from another country where a different language is spoken.

If you have the knowledge or the skills, you can be a specialized guide, leading culinary tours, art history trips and more. Adventure tours are becoming more popular—to get hired as a guide, you need to be good at rafting, climbing or other outdoor activity.

Who Knew?

Depending on the area or country in which they work, tour guides often earn between $8 and $14 an hour.

183 | Organize an Archaeological Dig

If digging through dirt, sifting sand through screens and taking endless photographs of pottery shards sounds like high adventure to you, consider organizing an archaeological dig. You're more likely to find broken bits of artifacts than the lost ark, but meticulous planning will prepare you for discoveries large and small.

Tip

See 402 Save Historic Properties and Landmarks.

Steps

1 Major in anthropology in college and plan to spend six to 12 weeks of your junior or senior year in field school (translation: days and days of digging). Follow with a graduate degree and then a year or so of basic experience (translation: more digging, usually under hot sun or in dense underbrush, for miserable wages). Now you're ready to organize a dig—at least, as long as you're not planning to ask for federal funding, which would necessitate your publishing a thesis and becoming a member of the Register of Professional Archaeologists (rpanet.org).

2 Select a site and develop a research design—a statement of what you are trying to learn, not just what artifacts and features you're looking for. Once you have this, work out a methodology. For example, a study of a Civil War encampment sets out to learn who actually lived there, what they ate and what kinds of weapons they had. The methodology would involve excavating in search of dispersion patterns to locate building footprints, likely walkways, the location of outside gates and so forth, and not just artifacts.

3 Get an adequate permit. Some countries have stringent antiquity laws. In the United States, each state often lists its requirements on its Web site (usually under the subject heading "Historic Preservation"). Some even allow you to download permit applications.

4 Establish the budget and the number of people to involve. Determine if you'll need any experts on site to work alongside students and volunteers.

5 Identify laboratory experts to whom you will send samples, and determine ahead of time their preferred submission procedures. There are labs all around the world certified to do carbon 14 dating, although you may want to send simpler core samples to a soil-testing lab, which can date the age of the soil through context (analyzing the presence of various pollens, for example).

Who Knew?

A complex expedition may require highly specialized professionals such as ceramists (experts on pottery), paleoethnobotanists (experts in the study of ancient plant life) or osteologists (experts in the study of human skeletal remains).

The equipment requirements for even a relatively simple dig are extensive, from pickaxes to dental picks, wheelbarrows to washing buckets, sledgehammers to sieves. Add to this the daily need for bags, notebooks, photo boards, scales, pens, tape and so on, and the difficulty of obtaining supplies in some regions, and you'll soon realize you must meticulously research the equipment list.

6 Survey the area surrounding the excavation zone. Locate sources of water, roads and known current settlements. Arrange housing and food for the entire team. Purchase equipment for the field staff or issue detailed lists instructing participants to bring some of their own tools and supplies.

7 Invest in top-quality trowels. Always choose pointing trowels and margin trowels, not brick-laying trowels. Have them professionally sharpened before the dig and then re-sharpen them with a file in the field. Include flat and rounded shovels. For digging units, use flat shovels to skim off 4 inches (10 cm) of soil at a time; for test pits you want smooth-sided holes, and there's nothing harder than digging a round hole with a square shovel.

8 Design any preprinted forms and field notebooks to use for recording data. Agree on the measurement tables to rely on when recording data. Either metric or English is acceptable, but everyone involved must stick with the chosen scale.

9 Plot a topographical map of the dig site and decide precisely where to dig. Determine a sampling strategy for the digging. It's neither practical nor prudent to attempt to expose an entire site. Set up field squares by running a long line straight north-south and pulling units from it by running other lines to form 3.3-foot (1 m) squares.

10 Assign the field and square supervisors. Field supervisors over-see multiple squares—the areas of excavation within the overall grid. Each square supervisor is in charge of recording everything from the sequence of excavation to an inventory of artifacts found within that square. Instruct diggers to write on every single bag in the field the date, project, provenance, name and what's in it. They must do this every time and never rely on memory.

11 Establish basic procedures for all diggers to follow. For example, a second person should verify any important measurements. It's easier to verify a measurement in the field than it is to try to explain to the lab person why the depth works out to 16 inches above ground level.

12 Plan for publication. The true completion of an expedition occurs not when the workers leave the site, but when the information they've amassed has been assembled in a meaningful way and made available to the world.

Warning

Remind newcomers never to carry sharpened trowels in the back pockets of their pants.

RGANIZE YOUR CONTACTS • GET RID OF WHAT YOU DON'T WANT • SAY NO WITHOUT FEELING GUILTY • BALANCE HOME AND WORK • L
GAIN • SCHEDULE TELEVISION WATCHING • DESIGN A HEALTHY LIFESTYLE • PLAN TO AVOID JUNK FOOD • CHOOSE A WEIGHT LOSS PL
EET AN ONLINE DATE • PLAN THE PERFECT DATE • MASTERMIND A BREAKUP • PLAN YOUR SOCIAL CALENDAR • MEET MR. OR MS. RIG
ORT YOUR SOCK DRAWER • RETURN RENTALS ON TIME • TAKE CONTROL OF YOUR JUNK DRAWER • ORGANIZE THE MEDICINE CABINET
AR CLEAN AND ORDERLY • DEAL WITH A PACK RAT • SELL STUFF ONLINE • ORGANIZE YOUR BOOKSHELVES • CATEGORIZE NEWSPAPER
VE BETTER THROUGH LABELING • ORGANIZE JEWELRY • PLAN YOUR DREAM KITCHEN • CONQUER YOUR CLOSETS • ORGANIZE THE LI
RGANIZE SPRING CLEANING • KEEP THE FAMILY ROOM ORGANIZED • SET UP A BATHROOM SCHEDULE • ORGANIZE BATHROOMS • ORG
RGANIZE KIDS' ROOMS • ORGANIZE SPORTS EQUIPMENT • ORGANIZE KIDS' PLAY SPACES • SAFEGUARD YOUR HOME AGAINST ALLERG
OUSE • USE HOME DESIGN AND PLANNING SOFTWARE • ESTABLISH YOUR HOME'S SPACE PLAN • INCORPORATE UNIVERSAL DESIGN P
HE BASEMENT • ORGANIZE THE GARAGE • ORGANIZE A TOOLBOX • SET UP A WOODSHOP • ORGANIZE YOUR WINE COLLECTION • PLA
TUDIO OR SMALL APARTMENT • MANAGE WARRANTY DOCUMENTS • MANAGE HOME-IMPROVEMENT PAPERWORK • MERGE TWO HOUS
RGANIC VEGETABLE GARDEN • PLANT A KITCHEN HERB GARDEN • PLAN A BUTTERFLY GARDEN • DESIGN A BIRD GARDEN • DESIGN A
ORGANIZE GARDENING TOOLS • ADD A POTTING BENCH TO A YARD • SCHEDULE FRUIT TREE MAINTENANCE • LAY OUT A SPRINKLER S
ESIGN A GARDEN PATH • SET UP A COMPOST SYSTEM • WINTERIZE PLANTS • SCHEDULE YARD WORK • STORE ANYTHING • STORE BU
ND HOBBY MATERIALS • ORGANIZE ART SUPPLIES • ORGANIZE GIFT WRAP AND SEASONAL DECORATIONS • ORGANIZE KIDS' SCHOOL\
OUR WEDDING DRESS AND OTHER TEXTILES • STORE A FUR COAT • STORE BICYCLES AND GEAR • STORE SKI GEAR • ORGANIZE CAM
HICH COLLEGE IS RIGHT FOR YOU • GET INTO A TOP COLLEGE OR UNIVERSITY • ACE THE COLLEGE ADMISSIONS TESTS • ORGANIZE
AW SCHOOL • PREPARE FOR THE BAR EXAM • GET A DEGREE WHILE YOU'RE WORKING • WORK AT HOME WITH KIDS • GO BACK TO W
RGANIZE YOUR JOB SEARCH • PREPARE FOR A CAREER CHANGE • OPEN A RESTAURANT • BECOME A PHYSICIST • BECOME A CONCE
EALITY-SHOW CONCEPT • BECOME A TALK-SHOW HOST • BECOME A PHOTOJOURNALIST • BECOME A MOVIE DIRECTOR • BECOME A
ILING SYSTEM • ORGANIZE YOUR BRIEFCASE • ORGANIZE YOUR DESK • ORGANIZE YOUR WORKDAY • GET A HANDLE ON E-MAIL • OR
ALARY REVIEW • CLIMB THE CORPORATE LADDER EFFECTIVELY • ADD A WORKSPACE TO ANY ROOM • ORGANIZE A HOME OFFICE • O
RAVEL • WRITE A BUSINESS PLAN • SET UP A NEW BUSINESS • CREATE A MARKETING PLAN • AMASS A REAL-ESTATE EMPIRE • POLIS
MPLOYEE • FIRE AN EMPLOYEE • PASS ON A FAMILY BUSINESS • STAY ON TOP OF YOUR SALES GAME • RESTRUCTURE A COMPANY T
EFEND AGAINST A HOSTILE TAKEOVER • ORGANIZE YOUR OFFICE FOR A MOVE • PREPARE YOUR BUSINESS FOR THE UNTHINKABLE •
REPARE YOUR TAXES • ORGANIZE A LOAN APPLICATION • ORGANIZE IMPORTANT DOCUMENTS • SAVE FOR PRIVATE SCHOOLING • OR
LUB • TRACK YOUR INVESTMENTS • SURVIVE BANKRUPTCY • PLAN FOR RETIREMENT • PREPARE A PRENUPTIAL AGREEMENT • CREAT
ONEY • PLAN YOUR FAMILY • BUDGET FOR A NEW BABY • ORCHESTRATE THE PERFECT CONCEPTION • PLAN FOR ARTIFICIAL INSEMI
EAVE • ORDER BABY ANNOUNCEMENTS • ORGANIZE AN INTERNATIONAL ADOPTION • FOSTER A CHILD • ORGANIZE YOUR LIFE AS A N
OORDINATE A FAMILY CALENDAR • PLAN FAMILY MEETINGS • ORGANIZE HOME SYSTEMS FOR ADD • PREPARE FOR A NEW CAT OR DC
ACK-TO-SCHOOL • WIN THE HOMEWORK WARS • PLAN A FIELD TRIP • PLAN YOUR CHILD'S ACTIVITIES • PLAN YOUR CHILDREN'S SU
NLINE • ORGANIZE A GENEALOGICAL SEARCH • PREPARE FOR YOUR CHILD'S DEPARTURE FOR COLLEGE • ORGANIZE YOUR EMPTY N
LDERLY PARENTS' CARE • PREPARE FOR THE DEATH OF A SPOUSE • HELP YOUR ELDERLY PARENTS MOVE • ORGANIZE A HOME MEDI
TORE TRIPS • SET UP ONLINE GROCERY SHOPPING • ORGANIZE RECIPES AND COOKBOOKS • PLAN THEME MENUS • CREATE EFFECT
EFRIGERATOR AND FREEZER • ORGANIZE CUTLERY AND KITCHEN TOOLS • ORGANIZE CUPBOARDS AND DRAWERS • ORGANIZE THE
UNCHES FOR KIDS • PLAN PARTY FOODS AHEAD • THROW A DINNER PARTY • FINISH DINNER ON TIME • PULL OFF A LAST-MINUTE PA
LTIMATE WEDDING CHECKLIST • BUDGET FOR A WEDDING • FIND THE PERFECT WEDDING RING • PLAN AN ELOPEMENT • SET UP A B
ONOR • EXECUTE BEST MAN DUTIES • HIRE A BAND • HIRE A BARTENDER • PLAN A SHOWER • ORGANIZE THE REHEARSAL DINNER •
UCCESSFUL SLUMBER PARTY • PLAN A BAR OR BAT MITZVAH • PLAN A QUINCEAÑERA • PLAN A RETIREMENT PARTY • PLAN A FUNER
ANUKKAH PARTY • ORGANIZE A HOLIDAY CRAFT PARTY • PLAN TO SPEND CHRISTMAS SOLO • PLAN THE PERFECT HOLIDAY GIFT EX
HE HOLIDAYS • STICK TO YOUR NEW YEAR'S RESOLUTIONS • PLAN THE PERFECT NEW YEAR'S EVE • PLAN A SEDER • PLAN A SPECI
OOD TREE • ORGANIZE A BICYCLE SCAVENGER HUNT • RUN A SPORTS TOURNAMENT • PUBLICIZE AN EVENT • PLAN AN ORGANIZAT
LAN A CONCERT IN THE PARK • ORGANIZE AN INTERNATIONAL CONCERT TOUR • ORGANIZE A FILM FESTIVAL • PLAN A FUND-RAISIN
BUILD A COMMUNITY PLAY STRUCTURE • THROW A BLOCK PARTY • SET UP A NEIGHBORHOOD WATCH • CREATE AN EVACUATION P
RGANIZE A PROTEST OR MARCH • FIGHT CITY HALL • ORGANIZE A BOYCOTT • ORGANIZE A CLASS ACTION LAWSUIT • MANAGE GRO
CHOOL IN A THIRD WORLD COUNTRY • PLAN A TRIP • PLAN A TRIP WITH CHILDREN • TRAVEL WITH TEENS • BOOK AIRLINE TICKETS
OTORCYCLE TRIP • PLAN A TRAIN TRIP IN THE UNITED STATES • RIDE THE RAILS ABROAD • PREPARE A VACATION COUNTDOWN CHE
UGGAGE • LOAD A BACKPACK PROPERLY • PLAN AN ELDERHOSTEL TRIP • ORGANIZE AN RV VACATION • PLAN A TRIP WITH AGING P
IDELY DIFFERENT PEOPLE • PLAN SPRING BREAK • PLAN AN OVERNIGHT GETAWAY WITH YOUR SPOUSE • PLAN A VACATION SEPARA
OLITICALLY UNSTABLE REGION • GET TRAVEL INSURANCE • GET IMMUNIZATIONS FOR TRAVELING • BOOK AN ADVENTURE VACATION
LAN A FISHING TRIP TO ALASKA • PACK FOR A CAMPING TRIP • LEAD A BACKPACK TRIP • HIKE A FAMOUS TRAIL • PLAN A TOUR OF
NGLISH CANAL TRIP • PLAN A CROSS-COUNTRY AIRPLANE VOYAGE • PLAN THE PERFECT DAY ABROAD • PLAN A VISIT TO THE LOUV
LAN • PREPARE FOR AN ACT OF GOD • ASSEMBLE EMERGENCY KITS • PREPARE FOR SURGERY • PLAN YOUR RECOVERY • SURVIVE
EING LOST • CONDUCT A SEARCH AND RESCUE OPERATION • PLAN AN INVASION • SURVIVE A POLITICAL COUP • PLAN FOR A TERR
ECOME THE PRESIDENT OF THE UNITED STATES • WIN AN ACADEMY AWARD • BECOME AN OLYMPIAN • TRAIN FOR A MAJOR ATHLE

Business & Work

Are teetering piles of bills, reports, receipts and magazines creating chaos on your desktop, shelves and tabletops? As soon as you get one pile cleared away, does it immediately reappear somewhere else, as though a poltergeist had plunked it there? The fault lies with your system (or lack thereof). Conquer those piles once and for all, step by step, sheet by sheet—no exorcisms required.

Steps

Tackling the piles

1 Deal with new papers first. No matter how high the old piles are, begin by devising a system for the new arrivals.

2 Decide immediately what to do with each piece of paper that comes across your desk. Do not postpone these decisions. Paper piles are messy monuments to a long series of small procrastinations. See 2 Set Priorities.

3 Act on each decision. Pick up that piece of paper and sign it, forward it, scan it, file it or trash it. Decoupage a wall with it, if you like, but don't toss it onto a pile.

4 Use a stepped desktop file if you're determined to keep some papers close at hand. But don't just stuff the file sections with loose sheets. Put them in labeled folders first, then in the stepped file. See 185 Create a Flawless Filing System.

5 Take a deep breath. Once you are faithfully dealing with new papers in a systematic way, haul out all the unfiled, deeply piled older papers and—in either one marathon session or a series of shorter ones—take each ancient sheet through your newly devised system.

Stopping the influx of paper

1 Submit invoices via e-mail attachments. They'll arrive at their destination instantly; you may even get paid more quickly.

2 Use your contact-management program or PDA for storing notes and to-do lists. Retrieving the information is far easier than searching through a snowdrift of scratch pad notes. See 3 Write an Effective To-Do List.

3 Scan business-card information into a contact-management program. If you don't want to invest in a scanner, you'll need to enter information manually—but you'll be richly rewarded for your time when you need to find a contact and can remember only the person's first name or the company's location. See 11 Organize Your Contacts.

4 Limit your hoard of business magazines and journals. Keep only current issues if the publications archive articles on their Web sites. See 52 Categorize Newspaper and Magazine Clippings.

Tips

Label inbox trays so that an assistant can easily make sense of your system and sort papers into them. No assistant? Train yourself to sort your mail or the contents of your briefcase and put papers in the appropriate trays. See 7 Deal With a Flood of Mail.

Use a highlighter to mark pertinent information as you read the mail. Type the highlighted information into your computer, then toss the paper. Print the notes out and work them into your planning calendar or to-do list.

Who Knew?

Get rid of your fax machine. Use a software program to send and receive faxes via e-mail, then only print out what you need to.

Put your printer on a diet. If you are constantly refilling its paper tray, you're printing out too many e-mails and documents. Ask yourself if you need a hard copy before you press the print button.

185 Create a Flawless Filing System

Imagine pulling out a drawer and flipping effortlessly to the desired file within seconds. Only a fantasy? It doesn't have to be. Once you have a working system in place, the filing cabinet of your dreams is within your grasp.

Steps

1 Decide on a system of categorization and labeling. The best way to begin this is to sort the paper piles on your desk into groups; a pattern will scon emerge.

2 Name your file folders with nouns. Choose the ones that first pop into your mind when you need the material. If you think "Background Stuff" rather than "Research Materials," then use the more informal heading. You'll find the file more easily later on.

3 File papers promptly. If you absolutely can't take the time to file a paper immediately, at the very least scrawl a file name on it. This will speed up later sorting and filing.

4 Write the date (month and year) you start a file on its label. This tells you how long you've had it and makes it easier to purge later. If the file gets too fat, just open a second one with the same name but a new date, so you don't end up with overstuffed long-term files.

5 Locate important material quickly by color-coding certain file folders. This works best if you reserve two or three colors for specific file types: perhaps red for "Crisis Pending," green for "Travel Arrangements" and black for "Most Irritating Client." More than three colors become too difficult to remember, which defeats the purpose.

6 Keep your most frequently consulted files in your desk file drawers or in a rolling file holder that fits under the desk or close to it.

7 Devote part of your prime file-cabinet space to a tickler file—an accordion file with numbered daily and monthly slots. Use the daily slots to file date-related papers for the current month, and put longer-range material into the appropriate month's section. See 10 Set Up a Reminder System.

8 Purge your current files, vigorously and without mercy. Limit active files to two drawers. If you start eyeing a third drawer, consider it a sign that you need to go through the main two again and move more material to archives—or the trash can.

9 Establish a purging schedule for archived files. Put papers you are uncertain about discarding in a box and then choose a date for making a final, no-turning-back decision about them. Mark your calendar with the box's execution date. When that day arrives, give the contents one more look and then discard them.

Tip

Store a few empty folders at the front of your most accessible file drawer so creating a new file is easy.

Who Knew?

Store financial records from previous years in storage boxes labeled by the year. Check with the IRS and your firm's legal and accounting departments as to how long you need to keep these. When the time limit is up, feed the contents to the shredder.

Banish the concept of a miscellaneous file from your life. If something is worth putting in a file folder, it's worth putting in a folder that has a specific label.

186 | Organize Your Briefcase

Once you leave your office, your briefcase becomes your portable desk, filing cabinet and supply closet. It deserves an investment of time and thoughtful planning. The dividends will make your work life considerably less stressful and more efficient.

Steps

1 Evaluate your current briefcase. If it's too small, too shabby or lacks sufficient interior pockets and pouches, it's time to shop.

2 Assign sections of the briefcase to hold specific types of folders. Reserve the front for items that require immediate action and a back pocket for background reading, or place folders in the order of scheduled meetings. While the specifics are infinitely variable, the need for some sort of system is fundamental.

3 Sort papers into colored folders by subject matter before stowing them in your briefcase. Digging through a single massive folder while your briefcase is precariously balanced on your lap, an airplane tray or the edge of another person's desk wastes time and fuels frustration. See 185 Create a Flawless Filing System.

4 Designate specific pockets within the case for your PDA and cellular phone. Before closing the briefcase, always check these pockets, and you'll never again leave one of these devices behind.

5 Schedule a regular monthly time to clean out your briefcase. File any straggling papers and business cards, discard worn-out pens and markers, and restock supplies such as notepads and sticky notes, envelopes for receipts and extra batteries.

Tips

Check the battery charge on your phone and PDA if you're leaving the office for an extended time.

Store all the cords you need for chargers and connectors in a small zippered bag.

Who Knew?

Add these six useful items to your briefcase:

• An extra pair of reading glasses in a hard case.

• A small, fully loaded stapler.

• A packet of personalized stationery.

• A book of stamps.

• A compact restaurant guide.

• A cell-phone–battery booster.

187 | Organize Your Desk

Desk a disaster area? Don't just push the piles around; plunge into a full-scale assault on the disarray. Clear off everything except the computer and the phone, then add back essential items one by one.

Steps

1 Begin with an inbox, no more than three sections deep. Assign these to the categories that work best for you: perhaps "Urgent, Current and Background" or "Clients, Prospects and Resources." See 184 Conquer Your Paper Piles.

2 Rely on the calendar on your computer or PDA. If you prefer a paper version, mount it on a bulletin board where it's off your desk and you can see it at a glance.

3 Stash any supplies other than a small pencil cup and a stapler in a single drawer. No one needs more pens, pencils, paper clips, tape or sticky notes than can fit into one drawer.

Tip

Place pictures and other personal memorabilia on a shelf or hang them on the wall. Reserve the prime real estate of your desktop for critical items.

4 Take 5 to 10 minutes at the end of each day to straighten up your desk. Place the files or notes for tomorrow's top-priority project in the center of your clean and organized desktop. Then you're ready for the morning (see 3 Write an Effective To-Do List).

188 | Organize Your Workday

Consider all the hours each day that you devote to your job, from the moment you leave the house in the morning to the relief of opening the front door again in the evening. Are you managing that time wisely? Whip your day into shape by developing a few good habits.

Steps

1 Fine-tune your commute to reduce time on the road as well as stress. If you drive, experiment with alternate routes over the course of a week to determine which is fastest. Tune in to up-to-the-minute traffic news and adjust your route accordingly. Or look into having the information delivered directly to your cellular phone, PDA or GPS unit.

2 Test alternate bus or subway lines if you rely on public transportation. You may need to walk a little more on one end or the other, but the actual commute may be shorter.

3 Stay on top of your electronic inbox. Check e-mail when you arrive, and immediately sort each message into an appropriate folder. Even if you don't have time to deal with the contents of a message or even read it fully, sort it for later action. See 7 Deal with a Flood of Mail and 189 Get a Handle on E-mail.

4 Make your most important phone calls early. You're more likely to catch people at their desks at the beginning of the day.

5 Plan the major portion of your day. Review your to-do list and refresh your memory about scheduled meetings. Then use your paper or electronic calendar to divide the rest of the day into project segments. Even if your time estimates are approximate, they help you focus on how much you can realistically expect to get done. See 11 Organize Your Contacts.

6 Attack the most important projects when your personal energy is highest. For you, this may be first thing in the morning, right after lunch or even later in the afternoon. See 2 Set Priorities.

7 Check your e-mail throughout the day, again sorting it immediately. Read and respond to urgent items, but file the rest away for the time you've already scheduled to handle them.

8 Wrap up the day and prepare for tomorrow. Review your checklist and cross off completed items. Move any pending items to a fresh list for tomorrow (see 3 Write an Effective To-Do List).

Tips

Use calendar software not only for meeting notifications but also to remind yourself of approaching deadlines. See 6 Meet Deadlines.

Dedicate at least one time segment to working on long-term goals, lest your day be consumed with putting out fires.

Don't fall into the trap of eating lunch at your desk and never leaving the office throughout the day. A short walk and some fresh air can revitalize you and increase your afternoon effectiveness.

Who Knew?

Find a hideout. If you work in a cubicle, seek out an empty conference room or a quiet corner of the cafeteria for an occasional escape. You'll be amazed how much faster you can get something done when you're away from your phone and computer, and without the interruptions and noise of an open floor plan.

City transit sites like San Francisco's NextMuni.com can tell you when the next bus will arrive at your stop, giving you time to hustle out the door.

Do you control e-mail or does it control you? While e-mail has become a necessary business and personal tool, it can also disrupt your day and sap your time. Follow these tips for sending, receiving and filing your messages, and you'll make e-mail your servant, not your master.

Steps

Sending

1 Use brief but detailed subject lines. These save the recipient time.

2 Keep messages short and simple. Put all important information in the first paragraph.

3 Call or set up a face-to-face meeting if the information is critical, confidential or time sensitive.

4 Make it easy for people to respond to your messages. Get to the point, and let recipients know what action they should take.

5 Create lists or groups of addresses if you frequently send messages to the same bunch of people. For example, using a family group will ensure that everyone gets exactly the same news at the same time, so nobody is left out of the loop.

6 Avoid overusing or abusing people's addresses. Only send a message when you need to, and don't forward every joke that comes along.

Receiving

1 Set aside certain times of day for answering e-mail, so it doesn't become a constant distraction.

2 Learn to use your e-mail program's spam filter and rules function. For example, rules can automatically file messages from designated addresses in a specified folder, such as weekly airline fare e-mails into a "Travel" folder.

3 Ask people who CC you needlessly to kindly stop doing so.

Filing

1 Create and use folders and subfolders in your e-mail program. You can organize by sender, subject matter, project or any combination that makes sense to you.

2 Empty your deleted mail regularly, or set your e-mail program to do this automatically. Know that even a deleted message can be retrieved and live to haunt you for a long, long time: Never send confidential or inappropriate e-mail from work.

3 Find out if your company's tech department is filing and archiving all messages on company servers. E-mail is becoming increasingly important as evidence in court.

Tip

Back up your e-mail regularly. In corporate environments, the tech department will do this. At home, use your e-mail's built-in backup program; programs like WinGuides Software's Email Saver Xe (about $30 at WinGuides.com) make the task even easier.

Who Knew?

Use encryption when you send personal or sensitive information. Most modern e-mail applications can add encryption; check your program's help file for instructions.

Avoid using all capital letters. In e-mail, capitals are the equivalent of SHOUTING, and are also harder to read.

Dedicate a separate free e-mail account to use when shopping online or participating in message boards. This will help reduce spam and keep your main address private.

Warnings

Invest in virus-protection software and keep it updated.

Don't dump the default folders that came with your e-mail program (such as Inbox or Outbox), even if you don't use them. Deleting them can corrupt the program's database.

The best thing about filing documents on a computer may also be the biggest challenge: You're completely free to create any filing system that works for you. Before all of your files end up piled who knows where, bring order to your hard drive. Think of all the time and energy you'll save every time you need to find a file in the future.

Steps

1 Set up broad-category folders within My Documents (in Windows) or on your hard drive (in a Mac OS). Read 185 Create a Flawless Filing System for suggestions on label names.

2 Set up subfolders within each category. For example, sort financial documents by year or type, and family-related documents by person.

3 Use the computer's sorting function. Put "AAA" (or a space) in front of the names of the most-used folders and "ZZZ" (or a bullet) in front of the least-used ones, so the former float to the top of an alphabetical list and the latter go to the bottom. Or use 01, 02, 03 and so on.

4 Specify the default folder your computer saves files in. This is usually done in the Preferences menu—in Word for Windows XP, for example, pull down the Tools menu to Options, click on the File Locations tab, select Documents, and click Modify.

5 Sort files to suit your needs. Sort by date, for example, to find the file you worked on most recently. (In Windows XP, pull down the View menu, select Arrange Icons By, and choose Modified. Mac users should click on the window they want to sort, pull down the View menu to As List, then select By Date Modified.) Or sort by kind or type to group all spreadsheets, for example.

6 Use meaningful file names for your documents. A file name like Resume is less useful than Resume_Sales_10_2004. Remember not to use slashes, colons, asterisks or any punctuation other than a single period preceding the suffix.

7 Keep refining your filing system so that it works better and better. Rename or rearrange folders, and archive or trash inactive ones. Avoid duplicating folders, particularly those containing photos or other large files; you'll fill up your drive and create confusion.

8 Use the Save As feature when you want to keep an unchanged version of a document. You'll need to specify a new file name, which you can base on the old one or change altogether. This trick from old-school computer geeks is still a good one: Add V1, V2, V3 and so on at the end of a file name to track versions of a document you're modifying over time.

9 Reserve your desktop for items that need immediate attention. When you're done working with them, file them in the proper folder. Try not to store documents long-term on your desktop.

Tip

An organized, hierarchical folder structure helps you when you're backing up your data. (You do back up your files, right?) For example, you can copy all of your financial records by grabbing a single folder. Regularly go through your files and delete those you don't need or burn them to a CD.

Who Knew?

Limit file names to under 15 characters. Shorter names are easier to understand at a glance and also show up in dialog boxes when you're searching for files.

If several people on your team take turns working on any one file, put an asterisk at the end of the file name before you copy it off the server to denote that it is in use. Then raise the version number on the file name and add your initials before the period and three-letter suffix. You have now prevented two people from working on the same file, created a backup, and left a people trail to follow should there be any questions.

Warning

Back up your files. How often depends on how critical your data is and how much work you don't mind re-creating from scratch.

191 | Schedule Appointments Efficiently

An appointment-crammed schedule can take on a life of its own, gobbling up your workdays like a ravenous beast. Tame your schedule by adopting some of the following simple techniques. The secret to success lies in applying them firmly and consistently.

Steps

1 Block out time on your schedule for solitary work. Guard this appointment with yourself fiercely. Make it clear you'll accept no phone calls or pop-in visits. If possible, escape to a solitary spot during this time. Read 188 Organize Your Workday.

2 Deflect excessive requests for your time from co-workers. Ask those who squander your time to submit written proposals, or schedule meeting times with them far enough out so that they might just solve the issues on their own.

3 Allot blocks of time for making and taking phone calls. Avoid phone tag by suggesting these times to callers. Take a list of calls to make when you have a drive of longer than 10 minutes.

4 Cluster out-of-office meetings geographically. Traveling to and from appointments uses up vast amounts of time. See 4 Run Errands Efficiently.

5 Communicate clearly how much time you have to meet with people, and then enforce the finish times. Schedule appointments in your own office back-to-back so the arrival of one person encourages the departure of the other.

6 Keep track of how much of your workweek you devote to appointments. If the amount exceeds 50 percent, evaluate whether other people's agendas are overpowering yours.

Tip

Be realistic about travel time to off-site meetings. Many a schedule has been sabotaged because it didn't factor in heavy traffic or public transportation delays.

Who Knew?

Beware of the phrase "Let's do lunch." Meeting for a restaurant lunch will suck a minimum of 90 minutes from your schedule. Ask yourself whether what you will accomplish will be worth the time invested. Sometimes it will. If you've been trying to meet with your boss for weeks, for example, getting him or her out of the office for lunch may provide uninterrupted, focused time.

192 | Take Control of a Conference Call

A conference call lets you remain at your desk rather than trek off down the hall—or across the country—to a meeting. It also provides a great opportunity to get the opinions and concerns of the entire team heard as long as it doesn't disintegrate into a wasteland of wandering discourse. Investing some time and effort up front will ensure that the call works for everyone.

Steps

1 Volunteer to set up the call so you can assume the role of moderator. Confirm that everyone has both the dial-in and conference-code numbers, as well as the correct time for their zone.

2 Poll the other participants in advance as to the items they want covered in the call. Develop a written agenda with a specific time

Tips

Use a handheld phone on a land line rather than a cellular phone or speakerphone. Your voice will be clearer, with minimal background noise. Use an office where you can close the door to further reduce noise.

allotment for each agenda item. Better yet, e-mail the agenda to all parties before the call.

3 Take charge of gathering and disseminating the printed background material, numbering pages clearly and prominently. Nothing creates conference-call chaos faster than a chorus of "Where are we?" or "I don't seem to have that chart."

4 Refuse to discuss major agenda items until everyone is on the line. Bringing latecomers up to speed on important issues wastes time and irritates those who were prompt.

5 Monitor the clock closely. Be prepared to intervene with "Excuse me, we have to move on—we've run out of time for this topic" or "Let's discuss this topic at another time and report back to the group." Stay polite but firm throughout.

6 End the call with a synopsis of conclusions reached and future actions required. Send out a written summary of these conclusions and action items to all participants promptly.

Who Knew?

If more than two other people are participating in the call, keep a written list of names beside your phone so you can be sure you are getting everyone's input.

193 | Prepare for a Meeting

Meetings that generate more hot air than meaningful decisions are the businessperson's bane. The culprit is often poor planning. Do your groundwork to set up an effective meeting.

Steps

1 Clarify the purpose of the meeting. If you can't figure out what you need to accomplish, you shouldn't be calling a meeting.

2 Prepare an agenda with the focus stated in a single sentence at the top. If someone else is preparing the agenda, contact him or her to add your topics. A first-rate agenda includes not only discussion topics and their time allotments, but also the names of attendees; the location, date and time; and a list of any background material attendees need to bring with them. Circulate the agenda in advance.

3 Make it clear that the meeting will start precisely on time. Establish a reputation as someone whose meetings begin (and end) as scheduled. People will respect you for it.

4 Appoint someone to document a record of decisions made, action items assigned and follow-up strategies agreed upon. Promptly distribute a copy to all attendees.

5 Leave time at the end of the agenda to evaluate the meeting: Did you achieve the objective stated at the start? How can you improve future meetings on this topic?

Tips

Limit the number of attendees. "A meeting called to make a specific decision is hard to keep moving if more than six or seven people attend," writes Andrew Grove in *High Output Management*.

If the meeting is likely to be contentious, consider inviting a neutral facilitator to attend.

Resolve to shepherd the discussion back on track when it wanders, and politely but firmly shut off side conversations.

Warning

Prepare visual aids, but don't drown attendees in slides or flip-chart pages.

Salary reviews can evoke stomach-churning memories of trips to the school principal's office. What many employees don't realize is that sitting in the supervisor's chair at review time isn't a lot of fun either. Whichever side of the desk you find yourself on, make the review process most effective by preparing diligently.

Steps

Giving the review

1 Devote the time required to write out each review in full. Oral reviews aren't worth the paper they aren't written on.

2 Begin by reviewing the employee's job description, then list accomplishments and evaluations. Support your statements— both pro and con—with specific examples. Always survey the employee's subordinates and peers for additional input.

3 Remember that the goal is not just to reveal salary and bonus decisions. The review's most important purpose is to improve the employee's performance by encouraging him to build on his strengths and work on his weaknesses.

4 Give specific examples of the employee's positive impact (on a project, account or team; turning a difficult situation into a positive outcome; making a great sale). Acknowledge excellence and express appreciation for supreme efforts and accomplishments.

5 Suggest specific areas for improvement, but don't overload the number of messages. Target a few key points and make actionable suggestions. If there is a significant gap between performance and expectations, write up a list of specific actions the employee needs to take and have him or her sign it. See 213 Fire an Employee.

6 Give the review to the employee shortly before the meeting so he can read it in private and absorb its major points before discussions begin. Never, however, give it out more than half a day before the face-to-face session.

7 Take time to discuss any plans for the employee to take on a new role or project, and also what specific performance goals need to be met. Listen to any plans he or she might have for additional work or new projects.

8 Have the employee sign the review. This is simply a record that he or she has seen the document, not necessarily that he or she agrees with it in full.

Receiving the review

1 Be well prepared. It's your job to present your case regarding your accomplishments and merit, and to collect data to support it long before the actual review date. Keep a brief journal of projects you've completed and their value to the organization.

Tips

Vow to spend as much time listening during the review as talking, whichever role you're taking.

Stay current on knowledge of salaries in your field and bring that information to the review.

Who Knew?

Vague comments—either positive and negative—do nothing to improve either performance or confidence.

There should be no surprises in a review. If you're not getting adequate feedback on your performance at other times besides your annual review, ask your boss for specific information: "You didn't comment on that report I turned in. It would be helpful if you let me know what you think." If on the other hand you are surprised by something in your review, ask your boss how the two of you can create better lines of communication. Frame such conversations from the perspective of wanting to do your very best work.

Schedule all your subordinates' reviews within a short period rather than stringing them out on the anniversaries of hire dates. By clustering reviews in a short time span, you can rank subordinates as well as rate them.

2 Take a detailed list of accomplishments to the review. This should include quantifiable data such as specific benchmarks achieved that met or exceeded your job description, deadlines made and new ideas implemented. Include e-mail messages, notes or memos from others as backup.

3 Use the review session to ask for compensations besides an increased salary. This can be a good time to request a more flexible schedule, more administrative support or a better benefits package.

4 Practice your pitch with a trusted co-worker before you go into the review to build your confidence and clarify your message.

Warning

Be professional and upbeat during your review no matter how it's going. You're getting valuable insight into the management style of your boss and of the company. If you don't like what you see, now may be the time to consider other options in-house or elsewhere.

---

195 | Climb the Corporate Ladder Effectively

Ascending the corporate ladder takes more than just working longer, harder and smarter. To reach the higher rungs, you must take strategic steps to be noticed—and valued—so someone at the top will reach down and help pull you up.

Steps

1 Go where the growth is, even if this means making a lateral move. The old saying that a rising tide lifts all ships still applies.

2 Build a good network within the company so you'll be alerted of openings before they're announced. Rumors of reorganizations usually seep out early. Pay attention to them and follow up.

3 Interact with managers other than your direct supervisors. The more people are aware of your skills, the better.

4 Take risks. Business columnist Bob Rosner calls volunteering for difficult assignments "the express lane to corporate success." But beware of suicide missions. Analyze whether a challenging assignment is merely difficult or probably impossible.

5 Concentrate on making your immediate supervisor look good. Carry a weak boss on your shoulders if necessary and don't complain about it. Over time, the truth about your contributions will come out.

6 Work with a career counselor to maximize your communication skills and create effective strategy.

7 Keep learning. Whether it's a two-day seminar or a two-year master of business arts program, explore educational opportunities that will increase your skills. Check with your human resources department to see if the company will pay part (or all) of your tuition. See 158 Get a Degree While You're Working.

Who Knew?

Work on your professional profile outside the company. Write for industry publications and speak at professional meetings and industry conferences. Be available to the business press for quotes.

Warning

Don't bury bad news. Bosses hate unpleasant surprises. Be open about a problem, but have a carefully thought-out plan ready to solve it.

An efficient home office doesn't necessarily need to be in its own room. As computers slim down, cellular phones shrink and wireless equipment becomes more prevalent, fitting a work area into a small space gets easier. Cast a creative eye over every room to find a niche for a workstation—one that looks good and functions effectively.

Steps

1 Outfit an armoire—either antique or contemporary—as a combination desk and storage system. Armoires are available in styles and sizes appropriate for every room in the house and may have shelving systems designed for a computer, keyboard and filing system.

2 Mount casters on a tall, backless bookcase to partition off a workspace in a living or family room. Hide files and other work paraphernalia in attractive containers such as lidded wicker baskets or fabric-covered boxes, available at Hold Everything, the Container Store, Pottery Barn and other stores.

3 Commandeer the end of a hallway. If the space is too narrow for a desk, set up a drop-leaf table with a chair alongside it. When you're ready to work, open up the table, pull the chair in front and plug in your laptop. A nearby bookcase can hold supplies.

4 Borrow space from a bedroom, but keep the work area out of sight from the bed so you don't wake up to a pile of papers. Tuck your equipment into an armoire, set a folding screen between desk and bed, or float your bed away from the wall and place the desk behind the headboard. If you're faced with combining guest accommodations and a workspace, a range of options are available for every budget. Opt for furniture that converts easily from sitting to sleeping accommodations, such as a sofa bed or futon, or disappears altogether, as a Murphy bed does.

5 Outfit a multishelf rolling cart with your work supplies for a kitchen too tiny to hold a desk. Store the cart in a pantry or an adjoining utility room. When you're ready to work, roll the cart alongside the kitchen table.

6 Explore your house or apartment for quirky, underused spaces. Fit a cozy office into an enclosed back porch, the nook under a staircase or a guest room closet with folding doors. Make sure there's access to an electrical outlet and phone line.

Tips

See 132 Expand the Capacity of a Small Room. Steal a space-saving idea from the Shakers and use a wall peg to hang a folding chair when it's not in use.

Suspend a curtain from a ceiling track or use a folding screen to give yourself the option of closing off the area when you're done with work.

Who Knew?

Note the office's proximity to phone and cable lines, as well as outlets, before you set everything up. You don't want cables snaking along walls or across floors. Don't forget the surge protector. (See 198 Organize a Home Network.) Also, opt for a desk with a discreet hole in the top so you can corral computer cables and wires underneath.

197 | Organize a Home Office

Even the smallest home office provides an opportunity to establish a space custom-tailored to your personal tastes and work habits. Choose the furnishings wisely and arrange them efficiently to create an office you'll be comfortable and productive in.

Steps

1 Measure the room and make a rough blueprint, including locations of windows, doors, electrical outlets and heating ducts. Cut out paper shapes to scale for furniture and large pieces of equipment so you can experiment with different layouts.

2 Position your desk first. If space allows, an L- or U-shaped desk is ideal. Pair it with a good chair, preferably one that is ergonomically sound. If your chair's height is not adjustable, get a footrest to ease the strain on your back. Add a hinged drop leaf to the shorter end of an L-shaped desk. Flip it up when you need more work space.

3 Use several adjustable task lights in the room rather than relying on a single ceiling fixture. Reducing overhead lighting will cut down on the glare on a monitor's screen.

4 Place a small table (one of the most underrated home office furnishings) alongside the desk. A two-tiered unit is ideal; use the lower shelf for reference material, the upper for a file of items you're currently using. If space allows, place a large table parallel to your desk. You'll find it incredibly useful for laying out research material or large projects in progress. Folding tables are cheap, portable and storable.

5 Track your workflow and arrange furnishings accordingly. Frequency of use is the key to location. Put those things you use most often closest to you and equipment you use less frequently on a credenza or bookshelf. Don't devote prime real estate in your office to a fax machine or copier that you need only occasionally, for instance. See 187 Organize Your Desk.

6 Add a second comfortable chair, along with a good reading light, to the room. It's relaxing to get up from your desk chair occasionally and do some of your reading in a different chair.

7 Set a tiny table—or hang a single shelf—right next to the door to hold outgoing mail. Now you'll never leave the room without the letters and parcels that need to leave with you.

Tips

Mount your computer monitor on a swing arm to save space on a small desktop.

Add a drafting table if you do much drawing or writing by hand. An angled surface for this type of work will reduce pressure on your neck.

Who Knew?

If you tend to cradle the telephone receiver against your shoulder during long conversations, you're inviting neck and shoulder muscle spasms. Keep pain at bay with a headset. When it's not in use, hang it from a small hook attached to the side of your desk.

A hallway just outside the office door can be a good location for a narrow bookcase to hold reference materials or backup supplies.

Add storage space inexpensively by mounting kitchen cabinets from a salvage store on the wall above your desk. Look for cabinets designed to go under the kitchen counter; they're usually more spacious than standard upper cabinets.

198 | Organize a Home Network

You've got a broadband Internet connection to your house or home office—now it's time to hook it up to all your computers and other Internet-ready devices. If you're at all apprehensive about taking on this project yourself, bring in a professional.

Steps

1 Decide how you'll connect your network: wirelessly, via a power line (using your electrical system as a computer network; see Homeplug.org), using Ethernet, or a combination of the above. Most people choose wireless networks. They're the easiest to set up, but present security issues since they can be hacked into.

2 Wander through your house (if you opt for a wireless network), with a wireless-enabled laptop before installation to see what other networks exist in your neighborhood or building. Computers with wireless capability search for wireless networks constantly; a window will pop up and ask if you want to join a network.

3 Decide where you want to place your router, the centerpiece of your network. Locate a wireless router somewhere near the center of your home to provide good coverage for the entire area.

4 Install Category 6 wire if you're installing an Ethernet network, from the router to each location where you'll have a computer or printer, and terminate the wires (put on the connectors).

5 Get a print server for each printer you'd like to put on your network (unless the printer is already network capable). A printer can also be attached to an individual computer and made accessible to other computers on the network using the printer sharing feature in Windows.

6 Find out if your TV, stereo or kitchen appliances are Internet capable. If so, put them on the network and send MP3s and video files from your computer back home—or even operate your appliances from work via the Net. Look into incorporating your home-security system as well.

Who Knew?

You can mix and match equipment from various manufacturers as long as the products employ the same standards. The most common standard for wireless is 802.11g. Equipment labeled 802.11b (or Wi-Fi) will work with 802.11g gear.

A wireless network may work better if you choose a different wireless channel than your neighbors. Check your router manual.

Your router looks at each piece of data traveling on the network and makes sure it goes to the right place. You can connect four or more peripheral devices to most routers.

Warning

Change the default password on your router immediately after configuring it, and enable all security measures such as WEP (Wireless Encryption Protocol) and firewall protection.

199 | Choose the Best Phone System

These days, phone companies are tripping over each other to offer a range of services, via traditional land lines, cellular phones or a broadband Internet connection. There's no one-size-fits-all solution, so choose a combination that's right for you.

Steps

1 Log your calls for a month or two to analyze your calling patterns, the number of minutes you use, and how often you call long distance.

Who Knew?

Cordless phones that use the 2.4-gigahertz frequency can interfere with wireless computer networks, and vice versa.

2 Consider your voice-mail needs. Voice mail that's included in your phone service usually costs a few extra dollars a month. For your home phone, an answering machine may be a more cost-effective option. Either way, you want to be able to access messages easily from any phone line—home, cell or external.

3 Look for packages. Bundling long-distance and local phone service can be good deals if you make a lot of calls from one place, such as a home office. Find out if your broadband Internet provider can bundle telephone and Internet service.

4 Go totally wireless if you're not home much and you don't need a fax, modem or other wire-dependent service. Make sure your provider has good coverage in both your home and workplace.

5 Keep a wired phone around the house for emergencies. When the power goes out, cordless phones go dead because their bases are plugged in, but a wired phone will still work.

Warning

Shop around for a handset. Both Panasonic and V-Tech make nifty combination wired-and-wireless home phones: The wired unit plugs into your phone jack, and the second, wireless handset just requires electricity to work. This is useful when you can't get a wired phone extension where you need it (or in the event of a power outage).

---

200 | Decide on an Accounting System

Business accounting—including payroll—is one of the most complex and confusing areas of business management. To choose the right system for your needs, get good advice and then dig into the numbers.

Steps

1 Consult with a knowledgeable information technology (IT) professional if this is not your area of expertise.

2 Shop for a system based on the size of your business. Systems targeting a small business will work best managing a small payroll (25 to 50 employees). Systems targeting a medium business work best for businesses with up to 250 employees. If you employ more than 250 people, an enterprise-level accounting system is recommended.

3 Inventory your existing database software, as well as the operating system and software of your business network. For example, your creative group may be on Macs while the accounting department is on Windows and your servers are running Unix.

4 Keep projected growth in mind. An accounting system that works in your current business environment may not scale up well if your business doubles in the next five years.

5 Hire an outside payroll vendor if the task is too daunting. Businesses of all sizes outsource their payroll and accounting work to companies dedicated to this service. That may be the best solution if you don't have a full-time, in-house accounting expert. The American Payroll Association's Web site has a listing of firms. Go to americanpayroll.org and click on "Vendors."

Tips

When comparison-shopping for payroll and accounting systems, include your IT person in the decision-making process at the earliest possible stage.

Establish safeguards so that your accounting and payroll information stays private.

Warning

A functional payroll system is essential to any business, no matter how small. There are federal and state laws requiring that you disclose records related to payroll. Failure to do so could result in heavy fines.

You don't have to keep tabs on everyone you've met since grade school to be successful at networking. Some people are social hubs and find networking easy and natural. Others need to make an effort to stay connected with friends and colleagues as well as forge new relationships. Whichever type of person you are, making the most of networking opportunities is critical to business success.

Steps

1 Figure out how to help others without immediately asking them to help you. This is the golden key to networking nirvana.

2 Find ways to put people together whom you think would enjoy or at least benefit each other. They're likely to return the favor.

3 Inventory your existing network. How many people on your list are mere acquaintances? How many would immediately take your phone call? Concentrate on moving pertinent people from the first group to the second.

4 Arrange third-party introductions whenever possible when you target someone new to meet. This doesn't have to be an in-person introduction, which could be an imposition. Often just a brief e-mail message—explaining who you are and what common ground you might share—will plant the seed.

5 Do your homework before approaching someone new, not just about his or her interests but also about how he or she can be a good contact. When someone asks, "How can I help you?" that's not the time to start waffling. Answer with specifics.

6 Join professional organizations directly related to your career goals. Attending meetings, serving on committees and speaking at conferences are all ways to expand your sphere of contacts. See 208 Prepare a Speech.

7 Write memory-jogging hints on the backs of the business cards you collect: where you met the person, mutual colleagues, product names. Follow up with promising contacts as soon as possible, or you risk their forgetting ever meeting you or your forgetting why they seemed so promising.

8 Sift through accumulated business cards and enter the information into a contact-management system. The data entry is time-consuming but infinitely valuable for later search and retrieval. See 11 Organize Your Contacts.

9 Practice listening well. Pay close attention to what people say, and you'll have a better chance of remembering conversation details as well as being able to refer to them later.

10 Identify yourself clearly when making follow-up calls. Don't expect people to remember you merely from your name. To avoid putting them on the spot, immediately supply an explanation of

Tips

Carry a slim, two-section business-card case wherever you go. Keep your own cards in one section and the ones you receive in the other.

Arrive early at functions. The best networking time is prior to the meeting, the meal or the speeches.

Explore social networking communities, such as Friendster.com, Orkut.com and Meetup.com.

Executive-only networking organizations, such as ExecuNet.com, charge a fee but can be another resource if you're looking to advance your career. See also 166 Organize Your Job Search.

Who Knew?

Reconnect periodically with people who have been good contacts in the past. Checking in with people lays a good foundation for future networking. Use a system of alerts on your computer or PDA to remember birthdays, or get a continuous birthday calendar that has months and days, but is not specific to a year.

when or how you met and why you're calling. Keep in mind that people *hate* being embarrassed—so helping them get past an awkward moment is key to a successful conversation.

11 Revive the art of letter writing. A handwritten note always makes a more memorable impression than an e-mail message.

202 Plan Your Business Travel

Business travel can sap your strength and your sanity. You can't control check-in lines, flight delays or the behavior of a bored child in the seat behind you, but you can eliminate a multitude of other problems by incorporating the following ideas into your pre-trip planning.

Steps

1 Collect information in a file folder as soon as you decide to make a trip. Make it the repository for contact names, airline tickets, hotel and car rental confirmations, maps and driving directions, and receipts.

2 Speak personally with the key people you're traveling to meet and get a firm commitment from them. Plan only with assistants and you may end up meeting only with assistants. See 191 Schedule Appointments Efficiently.

3 Create an itinerary and leave a copy at your home base. Factor in jet lag: Whether it's a three-hour difference between coasts or a lengthy overseas flight, the time change and trip fatigue can greatly impact your mental and physical energy. Also scout out restaurants and local attractions on CitySearch.com and other sites in case you have extra time. Read 418 Prepare an Itinerary.

4 Develop a tried-and-true checklist of items to pack. See 420 Pack for a Business Trip.

5 Transfer the contents of your trip-planning file to a large, clear plastic envelope. Place this in the most prominent section of your briefcase (see 186 Organize Your Briefcase).

6 Back up files before you leave your office. Burn a CD of any files you need for your meeting in case of a serious computer crash.

7 Pack a simple meal or buy one at the airport. Airline food is universally abysmal—or nonexistent. You're better off with a bagel with cream cheese from the coffee counter than miserable mystery meat on the plane. In fact, more and more flights don't have food at all, so call the airline ahead of time and ask.

8 Do the best you can to squeeze a workout in. You'll feel better and have an easier time sleeping in different time zones.

Tips

Sign up for pickup service with a rental-car agency or car service. This can save you driving time in each direction. FlyerTalk.com shares numerous additional travel tips.

Get the local access number of your Internet service provider before departure.

Take along a long telephone cord in case the hotel room's phone jack isn't conveniently located. See 412 Arrange Executive Accommodations.

Take advantage of business centers in airports with Internet hookup and wireless areas.

Right before you leave, check that your scheduled meetings are still happening. Bad weather, a business crisis or a personal emergency can disrupt even the best-laid plans. Don't assume that someone will remember to contact you in the midst of a major problem. Leave details— your hotel numbers and schedule—with key personnel in case they (or you) need to change plans.

203 | Write a Business Plan

Business plans can seem like the term papers of the corporate world, but creating one is more than just an academic exercise. In addition to being essential for raising funds from investors, a good business plan can be an effective management tool, providing a guideline for future actions. The following steps can guide you through the process of creating the perfect plan.

Steps

The basics

1 Describe your business mission in the lead section of a two- or three-page executive summary. This sounds obvious, but many plans bury this essential information. Be passionate but factual. Use testimonials only if they are from highly regarded sources.

2 Follow your business outline with a concise description of the market potential and the products or services that will form the core of your business, a description of the management team, and basic financial forecasts and needs.

The body

1 Show the management structure with a simple organizational chart. Point out any gaps in the management team and detail plans to recruit for these positions. Summarize salaries, benefits and stock-option plans.

2 List the board of directors (and any subcommittees) and specify the proposed extent of the board's involvement in key management decisions. See 217 Form a Board of Directors.

3 Indicate locations and facilities, and explain the key administrative functions.

4 Outline the marketing plan in detail. Give an assessment of market potential, an analysis of the competition and the proposed marketing strategies. Be specific about anticipated accomplishments, avoiding vague performance promises. See 205 Create a Marketing Plan.

5 List the operational action plans. Detail major milestones and the timeline scheduled for their achievement. Describe your contingency plans in case conditions change rapidly.

6 Present the financial data. Show how much money is needed in each phase of the business. Describe how you will use the funds, as well as when and how your business will pay back loans. Include an income statement, a cash-flow analysis, a balance sheet and a ratio analysis. Compare projected ratios with industry norms and explain any major deviations. Use visuals such as graphs and flowcharts to clarify the information throughout this section.

Tips

Review examples of actual business plans listed on the Internet. Numerous Web sites provide plans grouped by industry or major service activity.

Aim for 15 to 20 pages, excluding appendixes. Plans intended to woo investors may run even longer; those used primarily for internal planning tend to be shorter.

7 Describe why your product or service is better or more advanced than existing ones. What do you have to offer that your competitors don't? Explain the status of product development, being careful not to use overly technical language if you are presenting the plan to potential investors.

8 Specify the manufacturing data, including plant locations, capital equipment requirements, the size of the labor force, and supply sources, if applicable.

9 Report on methods for hiring, training and retaining employees. Make this a major emphasis if your business is service-related.

The future

1 Project the pertinent portions of the plan over the next two to five years. Changes along the way will be inevitable, but it's a healthy exercise to consider future opportunities and challenges.

2 Hire a skilled facilitator to add an impartial point of view to the planning process. He or she can help you assess your company's strengths and weaknesses, as well as identify opportunities and dangers.

3 Schedule an off-site retreat where the major players can concentrate on the long-range plan without the myriad interruptions of the workplace. See 220 Plan a Company Retreat.

4 Assign an individual advocate from the management team to each long-range goal. These champions should meet on a regular basis to report on successes and failures.

5 Detail the plan monthly for the first year, quarterly for the second and third years, and semiannually for the fourth and fifth years.

The finale

1 End with a summary, delineating the company's unique keys to success as well as a commentary on where it's going.

2 Attach an appendix of backup data. The selection of documents will vary according to whether you're slanting the plan toward potential investors or designing it as an internal road map for company planning. Your appendices might include the following: the résumés, tax returns and/or personal financial statements of management principals; a copy of the franchise contract (for franchised businesses); copies of any real-estate documents (leases, purchase agreements); copies of pertinent licenses; and brief descriptions of supporting external advisers and relationships, such as attorneys, accountants, other investors and lenders.

3 Design a professional-looking cover that incorporates your corporate logo, then create a detailed table of contents.

Warning

Address the challenges of growth and how you'll handle them. Be candid about the company's risks. It would be very damaging if pre-existing risks and problems came to light later.

It can be a long and winding road to opening the doors of a new business. Before you start down that path, map out the route, then buckle your seat belt. The ride may get bumpy, but the prize—a business you've created—will be well worth the pursuit.

Steps

1 Research the business concept to make sure it's viable. This is a crucial step and deserves a significant investment of your time. Assess whether there's a market for your product or service. Analyze whether the business concept addresses your lifestyle goals as well as your financial aspirations.

2 Evaluate the ease of entry into your selected market and the market's potential size. Will it support not only a fledgling business but also a growing one? Consulting with a business adviser in your field can be immensely helpful, but also expensive. Plan your questions ahead of time if he or she charges an hourly rate rather than a flat fee.

3 Seek startup information from the U.S. Small Business Administration (sba.gov) or counseling from a member of SCORE (Service Corps of Retired Executives; www.score.org) if your consulting budget is minimal.

4 Select an attorney and an accountant. With their advice, choose the appropriate legal structure for the business: a sole proprietorship, a general or limited partnership, a corporation, or a limited liability company or partnership. The structure determines many tax and liability factors.

5 Create a detailed timetable of actions to take during the months prior to your start date. Don't panic about the length of the list; just keep checking off each item as you complete it. See 3 Write an Effective To-Do List and 6 Meet Deadlines.

6 Obtain required federal, state and local licenses or permits and ID numbers. Most of these requirements and procedures are listed on Web sites dedicated to specific business types. One of your first applications should be for an EIN (Employer Identification Number) from the Internal Revenue Service.

7 Plan carefully for any environmental, health or safety issues that have an impact on your business. Inspections by the fire department and the board of health may be required.

8 Consult an intellectual property lawyer if your business involves technology products. Apply for any needed copyrights, patents or trademarks.

9 Begin recruiting employees. Remember, a great team brought on board at the beginning will simplify problem-solving later. Hire

Tips

Enroll in a how-to workshop for entrepreneurs early in your startup schedule.

Keep a tight watch on costs during the startup phase. Early bookings may not support much overhead.

See 168 Open a Restaurant.

people for their skills, energy and attitude, not based on friend-ships or family ties. Outsource specialty services such as human resources and accounting until the business can afford full-time employees in these areas. See 212 Hire an Employee.

10 Come up with a great name for the business. Make it short, dis-tinctive and easy to spell. Research your name thoroughly to make sure it's not in use before you register it. Some companies who feel others are infringing upon their name will send a cease-and-desist order and even sue. Once you have the name, hire a graphic designer to create a logo, stationery and business cards.

11 Begin working on a business plan, including an analysis of the known competition. Take care that the plan doesn't depend on everything going right, since problems—even disasters—will arise. Make the plan flexible enough to survive them (see 203 Write a Business Plan).

12 Develop a marketing plan that honestly addresses market size and ease of entry (see 205 Create a Marketing Plan).

13 Secure financing. Beware of underestimating your short-term financial needs (see 209 Prepare a Pitch to a Venture Capitalist and 231 Organize a Loan Application). Once you've set up financing, open bank accounts, set up the payroll system (see 200 Decide on an Accounting System) and arrange insurance coverage.

14 Select a location. Schedule any needed improvements to the physical space. Arrange for service providers, including office maintenance, courier and shipping services, and security.

15 Purchase or lease office equipment and furnishings. If your budget is tight, investigate auctions of everything from used desks and computers to secondhand file cabinets and trash cans. You'll find such auctions listed in newspaper classified sections and on community Web sites.

16 Install communication facilities: phone and fax lines, as well as an Internet connection, Internet service provider and e-mail addresses. (See 199 Choose the Best Phone System.) Allocate funds for communication deposits, which can be hefty. Identify a firm to handle the design and construction of your company's Web site and obtain a domain name.

17 Line up suppliers and place initial orders.

18 Plan a promotional campaign. Join industry organizations and get out there and network. See 201 Make a Networking Plan.

19 Set an opening date. Be prepared for an immense commitment of time and energy—both physical and emotional—in the months ahead and a commensurate amount of satisfaction if all goes well.

Warning

If you are purchasing real estate for the business (as opposed to leasing space), be sure to get an environ-mental inspection and certifi-cate of compliance. The legal defense against civil and even criminal suits when sites are declared hazardous can be astronomically expensive, as can the cleanup process.

205 | Create a Marketing Plan

Marketing success grows out of a good marketing plan. Craft it as well as you can, and then make adjustments as needed. Business conditions can change quickly as markets evolve, new technologies develop or customers go out of business. Your carefully conceived plan will serve as a reliable road map, even when detours arise.

Steps

1 Assess whether you have a marketable product. What's unique about it? Do you know who your customer is, and are you certain your product will meet her wants and needs?

2 Recognize that a marketing plan should establish a clear and specific strategy, including an allocated budget, for the coming year's efforts to identify customers and make effective contact with them. The hours invested in drawing it up will prevent considerable wasted time in future months.

3 Collect background data, including financial and sales reports on current products and lists of target markets, and information on customers and competitors. Survey current customers and collect market research on customers you want to reach.

4 Spell out your overall objectives as fully as possible. Set concrete and measurable goals. If you're not running your own show, get a seal of approval on these goals from senior management before you jump into brainstorming with your co-workers about specific tactics. And even if you are running a tiny startup, don't discount the value of brainstorming with trusted advisers.

5 Set a financial budget. Break down large numbers into more specific ones, such as the investment required to gain one new customer. Large companies should compare projected spending with industry averages for marketing dollars as a percent of sales.

6 Allocate in-house resources. Determine what activities should be outsourced—perhaps Web-site design, direct-mail campaigns or trade-show setups.

7 Create any graphs and charts needed to illustrate important segments of the plan. See 207 Polish Your Presentation Skills.

8 Conclude with an evaluation guideline that includes timelines for reaching specific goals, including new customers identified, orders booked and cost controls achieved. Emphasize what should be accomplished within one year, but include shorter-term benchmarks to track results along the way. Establish a schedule of meetings to evaluate progress.

9 Write the executive overview. Though this is the first section in your finished plan, it's the last one you write, as it's actually a summary. Briefly state the major points of your plan, using bulleted lists and short sentences. Limit it to a single page, but include the most important financial numbers.

Tip

Go off-site for the final sessions of drafting the plan. Getting away from ringing phones, e-mail messages and competing meetings will give you more time for creative thinking.

Who Knew?

Identify the SWOT and the PEST factors for your product and its markets— both actual and potential. Acronyms abound in marketing-speak, but these two actually are helpful for remembering important areas to research: SWOT stands for Strengths, Weaknesses, Opportunities and Threats; PEST for Political, Economic, Social and Technology factors.

Focus on quality over quantity in setting marketing goals. It's far better to achieve three goals—such as improving your company's Web site, identifying a new target market, or increasing your percentage of retained customers—than to spread resources too thin in unsuccessful attempts to reach nine or ten new milestones.

Share major points of your plan companywide. All employees should be aware of the marketing department's vision and goals. Even if your company is small, it's helpful to have clearly defined marketing goals.

The very rich know the way to get richer is by buying and selling real estate, sometimes with a very quick turnover. Plan your conquests well, and maybe some day you'll trump Donald Trump at his own game.

Steps

1 Make sound decisions right from the start. Learn as much as you can before you approach your first deal. Take classes and seminars on investment analysis, real-estate finance and commercial-lease analysis. Now is also the time to get your financial affairs in order.

2 Look for the right properties. Do your research to find what comparable properties are sold and rented for in the location you're considering. The right property attracts the right tenants or buyers, so spend time and effort up front on finding desirable properties. A good rule of thumb is to look for the worst house on the best block, since you can make many changes to a property but you can never change its location.

3 Work directly with a mortgage lender. If you work with a mortgage broker, you add an extra level between yourself and your money, and he or she naturally takes a piece of the financial pie.

4 Get comfortable with risk: Real-estate transactions deal in large sums of money, often borrowed. Become conversant in the language of numbers and focus on increasing property values.

5 Purchase your first investment property. Depending on the location, an existing apartment building or multifamily dwelling (such as a duplex or triplex) is a good choice. Look for properties that are fully leased.

6 Fix up your investment property. This may include everything from exterior paint and landscaping to structural repairs. Take advantage of economies of scale. For example, hire a general contractor to do work on all of your properties for less than he or she would charge for separate jobs. Rent the remodeled units for more.

7 Keep your personal expenses low. Reinvest any profits to increase your holdings.

8 Continue purchasing land and buildings, focusing on acquiring properties with more and more prestigious addresses where demand and price per square foot are always high.

9 Diversify your holdings. Branch out from residential properties to multitenant retail buildings. Rent to credit-worthy, established tenants, and sign longer term leases with rent escalations. Subdivide your properties to create new development and rental opportunities.

10 Gaze upon your empire from your penthouse suite and enjoy the good life. See 500 Die Rich.

Tip

When selecting a mortgage banker, find out if the support staff consists of permanent employees or contract underwriters. Work with permanent employees so you have a team of people who get to know you and your financial dealings over a period of time.

Who Knew?

Turn over the running of your growing empire to a property manager. Yes, it will take a cut of your profits, but you no longer have to worry about doing a landlord's day-to-day chores. Better management practices often result in higher occupancy. Think entrepreneurial, not managerial.

Warnings

Avoid books, videos and seminars that promise millions and require a large payment up front before giving you basic information. The real-estate industry is filled with "get rich quick" cons who want to sign you up for expensive courses that are little more than scams.

Beware of schemes that involve real-estate options. While options are a legitimate financial entity, they are also a common buzzword used by scammers.

Your ability to give persuasive presentations is just one of the skills you need to possess if you want to capture the gold ring on the corporate carousel. As the workplace becomes more complex, the need to communicate ideas effectively grows exponentially. A presentation requires great content, but at its heart, it's a performance.

Steps

1 Research your audience. Knowing the background and interests of the people to whom you'll be presenting helps clarify your content and approach.

2 Think about last things first. Define—clearly and concisely—the results you want from the presentation. Remember that a presentation is a call to action: an appeal for investment, a solicitation of sales or an attempt to have specific information incorporated into future actions.

3 Clarify your story. Define the essence—and the excitement—of your product, project or service. "Getting your story right is the critical factor in making your presentation powerful," says Jerry Weissman, author of *Presenting to Win*.

4 Connect with your audience emotionally—find a hook and introduce it early in the presentation.

5 Stress benefits rather than features. Remember that your audience members care more about positive solutions to their problems than about how the solutions occur. Emphasize how much your solution will cut costs, increase profits or better serve clients, for example, rather than detailing the many steps leading to these results.

6 Arrange a logical flow of content from beginning to ending. The type of structure does not matter—chronological or geographical, modular or matrix; use any form that fits the material. Choose just one, however, and stick to it throughout the presentation.

7 Keep the presentation as brief as possible while still covering the essential material. It's more important to be compelling than to be all-encompassing. Avoid piling on too many details lest you confuse your audience—or put it to sleep.

8 Plan the audiovisual aids. Decide whether to use PowerPoint slides, video clips, flip charts, handouts or a combination.

9 Borrow the storyboard technique from filmmakers. Before creating any slides, write your core ideas on cards or sticky notes. Experiment and rearrange them to get the most persuasive order.

10 Create an ending that circles back to the beginning. Your moments of strongest impact are the first few minutes of a presentation and the last few. Make sure they work together.

Tips

To handle a heckler, try to diffuse the emotion by simply repeating his question in calmer language. Then either answer it or ask the questioner to speak with you later.

Finish your presentation earlier than the time stated on the agenda. You'll feel an aura of gratitude emanating from your audience.

Who Knew?

Hire a coach who's experienced in your business sector to polish your presentation techniques. If your job includes giving frequent presentations, why not spend as much time and effort on improving them as you would on perfecting your golf swing or tennis serve?

Warning

Many presentations rely too heavily on PowerPoint. Be careful that yours does not fall victim to slide-overkill syndrome. Don't let the medium overwhelm the message.

208 | Prepare a Speech

A first-rate speech not only lets you share interesting and important information, but also can help establish you as an expert in your field. Don't skimp on preparation. As you walk to the podium, you'll be grateful for every bit of effort you've invested.

Steps

1 Analyze your audience and the occasion. Plan your speech so it contains specific information that will interest and benefit these particular listeners. See 207 Polish Your Presentation Skills.

2 Choose a key theme. Write this out on a separate piece of paper and refer to it frequently as you research and write your talk. Develop the theme with no more than four or five major sub-points (unless you're writing the State of the Union address, in which case you get to ramble on as long as you like).

3 Write a powerful opening and memorize it so you'll be able to look directly at your audience for the first few minutes. Spend as much preparation time as necessary to create an audience-grabbing beginning. Find an emotional hook to draw people in immediately. News flash: "I'm delighted to be here today" is a yawner.

4 Grab their attention with well-honed quotations for variety and depth, and dramatic statistics.

5 Keep sentences short. This will clarify your message as well as create more frequent pause-and-breathe opportunities.

6 Create a text-marking system that enables you to find your place again after you look up at the audience. Circling a few key words in different-color inks works well. In the margins, write perform-ance reminders such as "Speak confidently" and "Breathe!"

7 Practice with audiovisuals, if you'll be using them, and then practice some more. Have a backup plan, such as printouts in the event of equipment failure.

8 Summarize your key points near the end, but keep them brief. When the end is in sight, the speech should move briskly

9 Close the speech with a call to action, whether it's as specific as "Buy our product" or "Join us in this cause," or as subtle as "Consider me an expert in this area."

10 Time the speech by reading it aloud and edit it if it runs over the allotted time. Keep in mind that after 20 to 25 minutes, even the most attentive listeners may start to drift off. Brief, articulate, memorable speeches always beat long, meandering ones. If your speech is too short, finish with a question-and-answer period.

11 Prepare handouts summarizing key points to give to members of the audience after you speak. Make sure to include your name and contact information.

Tips

Plan your travel time so you arrive at the speech site early enough to familiarize yourself with the podium and microphone.

Borrow a technique from stage actors: Speak from your diaphragm to improve your voice's timbre and pro-jection. Practice helps.

Incorporate the names of specific audience members, if you know any of them, into your speech. These people, at least, will sit up straighter and listen more attentively to the rest of your talk. Just make sure you pronounce their names correctly.

Have a glass of room-temperature water nearby. Ice-cold water can tighten vocal cords.

Toastmasters.org offers tips on public speaking.

Who Knew?

Use strong transitions between ideas, and place internal summaries liberally throughout the text. Bom-barding the audience with a continual stream of new information leads to listener overload.

Warning

Beware of starting with a joke. Too many speech-opening jokes evoke more groans than guffaws.

209 Prepare a Pitch to a Venture Capitalist

Convincing a venture-capital firm to invest in your company is tough, but if the business potential and your management team meet the firm's criteria, it can be done. What's almost as hard as getting the financing is landing the first meeting. Here's what VCs themselves suggest.

Steps

1 Contact the National Venture Capital Association (nvca.com) for a list of venture-capital firms investing in your business sector.

2 Get an introduction. See 201 Make a Networking Plan and search your contacts for a lawyer or accountant who has worked with a venture firm. Cold calls or blind mailings seldom lead to meetings. Other possibilities include an entrepreneur or investor in a venture-backed firm.

3 Enlist an expert as an adviser. A professor or other respected expert in your field can broker an introduction to a venture firm. Willingness to serve on your board would be a bonus, but if the expert won't commit to that, try to get a promise to join an advisory committee. See 217 Form a Board of Directors.

4 Prepare a business plan. This plan is the first thing the venture firm will ask to see, or at a minimum it will want a detailed executive summary, including evidence of an experienced, adaptable management team. See 203 Write a Business Plan.

5 Make certain your plan shows that your business has an expanding market and protection against competitors, also known as barriers to entry. These may be patents or copyrights you hold or intellectual property. Show how you will escalate these barriers as your company achieves success.

6 Distill the essence of your business concept into a 30-second "elevator pitch"—the answer you'd give if someone standing next to you in an elevator asked what makes your business special. Convey your passion—you want to impress the listener with enthusiasm and firm belief in your fledgling company.

7 Attend seminars and panel discussions sponsored by venture capital associations. You'll not only learn more about the participating firms, you'll also find networking opportunities.

8 Enroll in a workshop for entrepreneurs to learn how to perfect your business plan and polish your pitch. Information about these programs is available at BusinessPlanBootcamp.com, SpringboardEnterprises.org and other sites.

9 Prepare for extensive due diligence should you capture a venture firm's initial interest. Meetings will be intense and analysis of the data you present will be rigorous, but if the firm decides to invest in your company, the financial and advisory help can be vast.

Tips

Plan on the process taking at least four to six months from the first meeting with a interested venture firm to receiving the first check.

Identify specific potential customers for your products or services. The VCs will ask for this information, and vague generalities will not satisfy them.

Who Knew?

Explore Pratt's *Guide to Venture Capital Sources.* Published annually, this is a list of active venture firms, along with their locations, investment preferences, contact names and other useful information.

Consider moving to Northern California, Boston or New York. Although there are pockets of venture firms in other parts of the country, the majority of firms are located in these three areas, and most VCs prefer to invest close to home.

Warning

Don't expect the venture firm to just hand over the cash and wish you well. It may demand one or more board seats and stock options, or it may put your company in an "incubator" with some of its other start-ups.

Initial public offerings, or IPOs, were once hotter than a habañero chile, until the dot-com boom went bust and investors got singed. In reality, an IPO is just another way to raise funds for a company. Sure, you can still make your fortune, but successfully executing an IPO also creates a whole new set of investors who also expect to make money on their investments. If you're making the jump from private to public, make sure you get expert help along the way.

Steps

1 Ask yourself if you want to run a public company. You could also create a successful private company and then sell it. As the CEO of a public company, you will spend a great deal of time with investors, analysts and others—and far less time running your business. Can it succeed under those circumstances?

2 Analyze the feasibility of taking your company public. Is it part of a fast-growing area that's popular with investors? Has it already recorded several quarters of profitability?

3 Select a lead underwriter who's enthusiastic about your business. You need audited financials and a good management team to woo the major players in the field. The credibility and experience of your team are crucial for obtaining a top underwriter.

4 Assemble an outside cadre of attorneys, accountants and PR specialists. Since the legal requirements are lengthy and compli-cated, be sure to select attorneys who are experienced in IPO preparation. Their fees will be high, but hiring lawyers who have to learn on your clock will cost even more in the long run.

5 Fill out a registration statement—also known as the dreaded Form S-1. The goal here is registration with the SEC. Your com-pany should be in reporting compliance for at least six months before the S-1 goes out. Be prepared for lengthy question-and-answer sessions with your attorneys as they lead you through the detailed legalese. You'll also need to write a prospectus, which the SEC must approve (see Who Knew?).

6 Prepare a presentation for a road show to meet with prospective investors. The underwriters will make the introductions to investors; your job is to provide an outstanding message. Let there be no doubt: This will be the presentation of your life.

7 Work with the underwriters to determine the best sizing for the offering and the share price. The underwriters need to sell to other brokers, who in turn will sell to their customers.

8 Set a proposed date for the IPO. Pray that a world crisis does not coincide with the selected date.

9 Clear your calendar for the big day. Accept the fact that you and all your employees are not going to do anything that day except watch stock-market reports and drink champagne.

Tip

Hire a presentation coach who's experienced in your business sector. See 207 Polish Your Presentation Skils.

Who Knew?

Your prospectus should include a business description, financial data, management description, business plans, competition analysis and risk factors.

Practice the presentation long, hard and out loud. "Speak the actual words you will use in your presentation aloud, accompanied by your slides," urges Jerry Weissman, author of *Presenting to Win*. Since Weissman has coached hundreds of company road shows, including those of Cisco, Intuit and Yahoo, his advice deserves attention.

Warning

Don't break out the cham-pagne too fast if the first day's stock sales soar; as an insider, you may be subject to a 180-day lockout before you can sell any shares.

211 | Delegate Responsibilities

Do you think your office couldn't get by without you? Sorry—wrong answer. Delegation isn't dumping work on others—it's sharing power and responsibility by assigning others significant tasks along with the authority to achieve them. Don't whip yourself into exhaustion: Polish your delegating skills and make your entire team stronger.

Steps

1 Keep a record for a week of how often you delegate tasks. A low number suggests you should make a conscious effort to delegate more and might indicate that you have difficulty relinquishing control or that you don't trust your people to do a good job. Suppose you come down with a serious illness and cannot come to work—then what? Are your people trained to make the operation fly without you? A good boss sets everyone up for success.

2 Identify tasks to delegate. Define them clearly in your own mind before assigning to others. Map out a flowchart to make sure you've covered the bases (see 9 Organize Your Thoughts).

3 Match subordinates' skills to tasks and make assignments. Explain precisely why you made the assignment choices, always incorporating an element of praise, such as "You're good at details" or "You're tactful with difficult clients."

4 Clarify the nature of the tasks and the expected results. Spending more time on expectations up front will save frustration later. Set clear deadlines for completion so you don't need to constantly ask, "Is it done?" Ask for a report at key stages.

5 Recognize that skillful delegation builds staff proficiency and sends a powerful message that you believe in the people who work for you. As you delegate more, your staff grows more experienced, requiring less briefing and supervision. Best of all, you're boosting their confidence and competence.

Tip

When your staff successfully completes assignments, make sure you share the credit—both upward with your superiors, and downward with those who did the work. Nothing kills morale faster than failing to thank those who worked hard to make something happen.

Who Knew?

Accept that others may take a different approach to tasks than you would, and develop an appreciation for alternate ways of thinking. Let your team members define how they work.

Have an open-door policy and avoid unpleasant surprises by periodically monitoring progress. As Andrew S. Grove writes in *High Output Management,* "Delegation without follow-through is abdication."

212 | Hire an Employee

An old theatrical maxim says that 90 percent of good directing is good casting. Finding and hiring good people will make directing your business easier and more rewarding for all involved. The ideal employees do more than fill vacancies; they bring talents and energy that strengthen the performance of the whole group.

Steps

1 Write a clear and complete job description. List required skills, as well as personality traits and preferred experience. If possible, confer with a person who's already doing the job to make sure you don't omit essential qualifications.

Tips

If the job requires a skills test—such as typing or copy-editing—make sure you have the results before you devote much interview time to a candidate.

2 Write an advertisement based on your wish list. Note which skills and experience are mandatory and which are preferred. Finally, mention a little about your company and the job itself (desirable location, competitive benefits) to encourage replies from qualified candidates.

3 Post your advertisement where job seekers will see it. Choices range from newspapers to online job boards and mailing lists, some of which are industry specific. Specify how you want respondents to send résumés and contact you—by e-mail, fax, phone or regular mail.

4 Sort incoming job queries by immediately putting them in one of three folders: "Don't Interview," "Maybe Interview" and "Definitely Interview." If more than one person will be sorting the first round of applicants, clearly define the desired attributes.

5 Set up interviews. If you find several qualified candidates in the first round, call only those in your "Definitely Interview" pile. If you are not getting a qualified pool of applicants after several weeks, consider rewriting your ad and possibly redefining your mandatory education and experience levels.

6 Interview candidates. Prepare your questions in advance so you can use the interview time wisely. One useful technique is to present a hypothetical (or even real) work problem and see what ideas a candidate can contribute toward a solution. Another possibility is to throw out a startlingly difficult question and see how the candidate handles a curve ball. Rumor has it that for years interviewers at a major West Coast software firm asked candidates: "How much water is contained in all the swimming pools in Los Angeles County?"

7 Sort the annotated résumés and applications in one of two folders: "Second Interview" or "Reject."

8 Schedule the next round of interviews. These should introduce the applicants to other senior-level people at your company. At this level, you need to probe the specifics of résumés. Look out for too many timing gaps in the list of previous jobs and for long-winded, evasive answers to direct questions.

9 Decide on a top candidate after the interviews and thorough checking of references. At this point, references tell the tale. Check facts: Did this person really manage this number of people? Was she actually responsible for the entire region or merely part of it? Probe more-subjective areas: What are this person's greatest strengths? Weaknesses?

10 Make a formal job offer. If you haven't posted the salary up front, have your acceptable range in mind, but let the job applicant name a dollar figure first. This places you in the stronger negotiating position. Applicants know that too.

Don't insist that a candidate have exactly the set of skills the job requires. Instead, look for someone who has demonstrated the ability to learn new skills in the past.

Look for a résumé pattern of ever-increasing responsibilities in better and better companies when interviewing to fill a high-level management position.

Take good notes on your impressions (on the actual résumé or application) as soon as an interview ends.

Mail form letters to the rejected candidates letting them know that the position is filled and thanking them for their time.

Who Knew?

If you expect a flood of responses to an ad, use applicant-tracking software to do the initial culling and sorting. WetFeet.com, MindScope.com and HRMDirect.com are among the many possibilities.

Warnings

It is illegal to ask applicants questions about their age, disability and sexual orientation. Consult with your human resources department or attorney about what is allowable.

A pattern of frequent job changes should raise red flags, a situation one corporate executive describes as "too many jobs, too many excuses."

213 Fire an Employee

Hiring a great employee is exhilarating; firing a bad one can be painful—and fraught with legal land mines. Sometimes you get lucky: The employee, realizing his job is in jeopardy, resigns. If not, the following steps will help make the task less onerous—as well as less susceptible to litigation.

Steps

1 Ask your human resources department to help you with your plan for termination. There is a quagmire of regulations for both union and nonunion employees.

2 Establish an extensive paper trail. Don't sugarcoat the problems in the employee's performance review (see 194 Prepare for a Salary Review). A record of specific warnings and a proposed corrective action plan with the employee's signature should be on file, preferably at least 90 days before the actual firing.

3 Ask an attorney or labor relations specialist to look over the file. Investing time and money on an expert employment attorney before the termination can save agony and the far greater costs of a postfiring lawsuit.

4 Assemble a package of detailed exit information for the employee. Include severance package information and an account of any benefits due.

5 Prepare a list of all company-issued property—from keys and credit cards to computers and cellular phones—to collect from the employee. Back up any important files to which the employee has access and arrange to terminate his or her computer access within an agreed-upon time frame.

6 Have a witness present at the meeting. A third party tends to diffuse emotional outbursts and offers a good defense against a later "he said, she said" dispute.

7 Plan what you're going to say and then stick to your script as closely as possible. If necessary, review your plan with someone from human resources. Get to the point quickly; enumerate the offenses, the warnings issued and the failure to implement the listed corrective actions. Resolve to remain calm even if the employee becomes emotional or combative.

8 Have all waivers and agreements ready to sign. Your best protection against a future lawsuit is a signed release of liability. If possible, make any optional severance pay or benefits extensions dependent on that signing.

9 Remember that any future reference calls about the terminated employee should confirm only dates of employment and salary to avoid possible litigation.

Tips

Prevent leaks about preparations for the firing. Tell only the worker's direct supervisors, the human resources department and any other witnesses attending the termination meeting.

Prepare a list of helpful local resources such as support groups for the departing employee.

Who Knew?

Reevaluate your hiring guidelines to see if they need to be more specific. One firm actually had to put in writing that sleeping on the job was not permitted after some employees claimed, "Nobody said we couldn't!"

Warning

If your business is located overseas, the legal quagmire surrounding terminations is vast. Be certain you get detailed and expert guidance.

Keeping a business in the family isn't for the faint-hearted—even Tony Soprano has his moments of doubt. But while only a third of family-owned businesses succeed under a second generation of ownership, with the survival rate dropping to about 10 percent when the third generation takes over, it remains true that 40 percent of Fortune 500 businesses are family owned. Start now if you dream of passing your firm on to your grandchildren.

Steps

1 Draft a family-business constitution. Include both a future vision for the company and a set of guidelines for handling potential challenges and crises. Bring in a consultant who specializes in family businesses to help—and to referee.

2 Start early. It takes years to devise an effective succession strategy. Form a family council specifically to discuss succession issues. Schedule regular meetings with structured communication between family members. Consider making some of the meetings off-site retreats (see 220 Plan a Company Retreat).

3 Consult with your accountant and lawyer to minimize estate-tax bills. Don't leave your successors with a tax bill so large they're forced to sell the company to pay it. Tax problems rank with family discord as the great destroyers of family businesses.

4 Recognize that management does not have to equal ownership. Some family businesses select one relative to operate the business but split overall ownership among several relatives.

5 Take a realistic look at family members under consideration for succession. Evaluate their education, past career histories, work ethic, strengths and weaknesses. Examine their relationship with nonfamily employees, suppliers and customers.

6 Diversify potential successors' work experiences. Have them work outside the family business for portions of their careers. During their early years in the family business, have them report to supervisors they're not related to. They need to have worked in the firm's lower echelons and not just skipped over the bottom rungs of the management ladder.

7 Develop a training program to groom the chosen successor. Start this at least a year before the final change by gradually increasing his or her responsibilities.

8 Accept the reality that a successor from outside the family may be the best choice for the health of the company. Remember that the survival and prosperity of the business are the ultimate goals.

Tips

Get a financial valuation of your company to facilitate estate-tax planning.

Introduce all potential successors to major customers, legal advisers, suppliers and other important contacts as early as possible in your planning.

Who Knew?

Understand that some conflict among relatives is inevitable. In addition to sibling rivalry, spousal complications often arise. Experts consider these conflicts facts to be dealt with, not insurmountable problems—as long as they are not ignored.

Keep shareholders informed about company performance and major strategic decisions. Surveys show that a large percentage of family firms hold only one or two board meetings a year. Some firms never hold them. Avoid letting rumors foster distrust. See 218 Organize a Shareholders Meeting.

215 | Stay on Top of Your Sales Game

The sales process is a pipeline: You feed prospects in on one end, and then write up the orders when they emerge from the other end. Success depends on funneling the right leads in at the start and then managing them so they don't get stuck and fail to complete the journey.

Tips

Identify internal champions in your customer organizations—individuals committed to your products or services who will help you close sales.

Steps

1 Select a target market and create a focused list of prospects. Qualify each prospect by determining if they have a real need for your product or service, the budget to purchase it and a time-urgent need for its delivery. Only then should you place the prospect in your active pipeline.

2 Establish guidelines as to how quickly you should follow up on leads. Also decide how long you'll allow a prospect to remain in the pipeline. Make a note of the origins of all leads.

3 Set specific goals for the number of completed sales and figure the number of prospects needed to meet those goals. The journey from prospect to confirmed sale can be roundabout, so always have a substantial number of leads in the pipeline to protect against sales slumps.

4 Distribute the best prospects to your sales force. Mark undistributed leads for future follow-up.

5 Measure progress on a regular basis. Track revenue potential, sales calls and closing dates on orders, as well as return on investment from marketing expenditures. Drop prospects from the pipeline if deadlines for specific action items are not met.

6 Consider investing in sales-force automation software. The alerts generated by these programs are particularly helpful in keeping both the sales force and management aware of specific problems and opportunities. SalesForce.com, SalesAction Software (salesaction.com) and iCongo.com are among the many programs available.

Track the histories of former customers who are no longer in the pipeline. They may be good targets for new approaches.

See 201 Make a Networking Plan.

216 | Restructure a Company to Increase Profits

Restructuring a company in the face of declining profits is a tough, no-nonsense operation that requires a willingness to face financial realities and triage difficult decisions. There are ways to not only stop the bleeding, but also heal and strengthen the patient for the future.

Tip

Develop strategic alliances with a limited number of vendors to lower costs.

Steps

1 Consider hiring a turnaround specialist—as either an interim manager or a consultant—to help with restructuring. An outsider often brings objectivity and a fresh point of view.

2 Analyze the extent of the problems. Is the profit picture merely ailing or is it terminally ill? Is the company's core business still financially viable?

3 Develop a restructuring plan and present it to the board of directors, management and employees. It may also be advisable to show the plan to certain outsiders, such as bankers and other creditors, and to major vendors.

4 Start at the top. Replace weak members of top management and the board of directors. Then reduce management layers. Unprofitable companies are often bloated with middle managers.

5 Investigate the possibility of restructuring debts or acquiring bridge loans to finance the restructuring costs.

6 Identify the most profitable customers. These aren't necessarily the biggest accounts. Concentrate on buyers who make few demands on the customer-service department, rarely return products and require only minimal marketing attention to prompt repeat orders.

7 Prune less-profitable product lines and increase financial and employee investment in more-profitable areas. Withdraw completely from unprofitable markets.

8 Close some facilities to reduce overhead. Consolidate divisions to eliminate duplicate administrative functions, and/or sell off underperforming divisions of the company.

9 Lay off employees or reduce some jobs from full to part time. Although this is one of management's most painful tasks, it's often essential for improving the profit picture.

10 Outsource costly services. Paying a flat fee to have selected services performed may reduce expenditures associated with in-house employees.

11 Move part—or all—of the company to another state (or country) to obtain lower employee wages, reduced power rates and/or special tax incentives

12 Form a partnership with another company to share administrative services or technical expertise.

13 Investigate the latest technology for streamlining operations and/or improving products. Autoresponse voice-mail programs can handle phone inquiries. Robotic production components are becoming increasingly sophisticated and cost-effective.

14 Schedule personnel meetings to deal with the questions and concerns of remaining employees. After restructuring, the company's management will need to explain new procedures and financial projections.

Who Knew?

Accelerate the development of products with a high profit potential by shifting supporting resources from less-profitable areas.

Include answers to clients' frequently asked questions (FAQs) on the company Web site and refer to its URL in the company's automated phone system.

217 Form a Board of Directors

Whether you've just formed a nonprofit or incorporated your business, you're required by law to have a board of directors as your governing body. A board's structure and personality varies widely: Do you want a hands-on working board, or big names that lend credibility to fund-raising? Hold casual or by-the-book meetings? The task is to recruit a board that works well with your organization's style and mission.

Steps

1 Specify the board's rules of operation in the corporate bylaws. This document details items such as the number of board members, length of terms, officer positions and meeting conduct.

2 Determine the desired skill set before you begin recruiting. If your corporation lacks financial savvy, recruit an accountant. Plagued by personnel problems? A human resources specialist would make a good addition. Gather a well-rounded board that works effectively toward your organization's goals. See 374 Sharpen the Focus of an Organization.

3 Invite board candidates to the next meeting and see if there is a good fit in person as well as on paper. This also enables candidates to ask questions of the board and confirm their commitment.

4 Ensure that the board stays on track by clarifying its responsibilities. These generally include defining the organization's mission, selecting and evaluating an executive officer, raising funds, and enhancing the organization's public image. Boards are typically required to record minutes of meetings and keep them on file.

5 Establish committees when issues become too complex or numerous for the entire board to handle effectively. Divide-and-conquer strategies can make better use of members' time and expertise. Have at least two members—this can include staff and volunteers—on each committee.

Tips

In some states, you must have bylaws to file for incorporation.

For-profit corporation board members are typically paid, while nonprofit members are usually volunteers.

Find comprehensive nonprofit management information and sample forms at the Management Assistance Program's site (www.managementhelp.org).

Maintain a list of potential board candidates that includes the skills and time commitment they can bring to the organization.

Develop an application template for prospective board members. It should solicit information on the applicant's career history and relevant experience, why he or she wants to join the board, what skills, resources and contacts he or she brings, and any questions he or she has.

218 Organize a Shareholders Meeting

Your company's annual shareholders meeting should be more than a dust-dry occasion for electing directors and dealing with other business matters. The session is also an opportunity for management to tell its story, full of hope and glory, to an audience with a personal financial stake in the outcome. Just be certain to meet all the legal requirements in setting up the session.

Tip

Download templates for meeting notices and proxy cards from Nolo.com. It's far easier to modify a form than to create one from scratch.

Steps

1 Choose the meeting date and related notification dates. (The date may be written into your corporation's bylaws or determined

each year by the board of directors.) Each state requires both a minimum and maximum number of days before the meeting date for notifying shareholders. Ten-day minimums and 60-day maximums are the most common.

2 Set the agenda for the meeting. Important topics include the appointment of directors, approval of audited accounts and approval of the annual budget.

3 Draw up a list of everyone legally entitled to notification. Include each name, address and number of shares held. Reserve the meeting place and prepare the mailing. Along with the official meeting notification, include proxy cards, the agenda and descriptions of major business items to be considered.

4 Get a time estimate of the chairperson's speech. (And hope for everyone's sake that it actually falls within the promised time frame). Prepare informational handouts and any audiovisual aids needed by the chairperson and other speakers (see 207 Polish Your Presentation Skills).

5 Assign someone to keep the minutes. Corporations are legally required to keep written records of all shareholder meetings. Consider outsourcing the extensive task of tabulating the minutes and distributing them to shareholders.

Who Knew?

Make it possible for shareholders to receive meeting materials and background information online. Post a searchable version of the annual report.

Have your attorney review your agenda and mailing to make sure everything is done by the book.

219 | Plan a Company Picnic

Company picnics are more fun to attend than to plan, but turning down the assignment to organize one is rarely a good career move. If the task falls on your shoulders, make the process relatively painless by starting early, staying on top of the details, and having a backup plan in case the rain gods let loose with a deluge on the big day.

Steps

1 Read 2 Set Priorities and 3 Write an Effective To Do List

2 Determine whom to invite: employees only, spouses and significant others, children and/or clients. Dozens of subsequent decisions—from location to menu, entertainment to favors—stem from this first one.

3 Select the date. Avoid days near the beginning or end of a company holiday period, as many people may be out of town. Choose a weekday so employees are not forced to give up their personal commitments to attend a work function.

4 Establish a budget. Take advantage of the fact that unlike most business-related meals (which are only 50 percent tax

Tip

When estimating the amount of food needed, err on the side of too much rather than too little. Late arrivals should not go hungry.

Continued on next page

deductible), costs for food, beverages and entertainment for a companywide picnic are fully deductible.

5 Recruit a committee for each major component, including site selection, food and entertainment. (Remember, a task delegated is a task escaped.) Have committee members gather feedback about the pluses and minuses of previous years' picnics. Read 373 Plan an Organizational Meeting.

6 Research locations, taking into consideration the travel time from employees' homes or the office.

7 Plan the menu with the venue and attendees in mind. If at all possible, have your committee sample the fare ahead of time. Good-quality ice cream bars trump stale cupcakes. Should the proposed baked desserts taste like cardboard, you may be able to arrange for a more palatable alternative from another source. Make sure the menu offers vegetarian options. Too often picnic fare features only hot dogs, hamburgers, fried chicken or bar-becued meats. See 331 Hire a Caterer.

8 Decide on the entertainment, making sure you have activities that appeal to everyone who will be attending. If you can persuade managers to take turns in a carnival dunk tank, you'll have at least one guaranteed crowd-pleaser.

9 Order any party favors well in advance. Special logo T-shirts or baseball caps are always popular, but also consider Frisbees, water bottles, tote bags and beach balls.

10 Create and distribute catchy invitations. A well-planned picnic deserves finer fanfare than a companywide e-mail message. Have the invitation blown up to poster size and displayed promi-nently around the workplace.

11 Set up a Web site about the party and list its URL on the invita-tions. You can post updates, driving directions and answers to frequently asked questions here, saving the organizing commit-tee a lot of effort.

12 Print out a schedule of events and important reminders to hand out to attendees as they arrive at the picnic site.

13 Keep a detailed notebook containing all contracts, menus, publicity material, favor choices, entertainment ideas and any other significant decisions and resources. This will give you an overview of planning—and it will provide an immense aid to the person who handles this job next year.

Who Knew?

There are a number of event directories, often found in wedding guides, such as HereComesTheGuide.com. Type "event venues" into a search engine. Find out if any special insurance or permit is required for your size group. Once you've selected a venue, book your reservation as early as possible.

220 | Plan a Company Retreat

All work and no play would make a retreat dull drudgery, but these off-site sessions can prove to be frivolous (and costly) time-wasters. The trick lies in balancing productive meetings and social merriment. Business goals should be as important as golf scores, and problem-solving sessions as well attended as cocktail parties by the pool.

Steps

1 Start planning early in order to reserve a great site. Many locations are booked a year in advance. Always send someone to check the site in person; brochures and Web sites can be highly misleading.

2 Determine the strategic goals for the retreat (see 16 Set Goals). Whether your goals are team building and morale boosting, creating a long-range plan or plotting the launch of a new product, be specific.

3 Decide whether the entire staff or selected departments should attend and whether attendance will be mandatory. Make transportation as convenient as possible. Arranging carpools is good. Renting shuttles is better.

4 Develop research materials for the working sessions, including background reading and statistical documents. Distribute this information well ahead of the retreat so attendees arrive prepared for meaningful discussions.

5 Appoint an administrative liaison to handle the logistical issues that inevitably arise once everyone arrives at the retreat site. Make sure key personnel have the liaison's cellular phone number. Don't rely on harried hotel clerks.

6 Consider hiring an outside facilitator to act as moderator at key meetings. An unbiased outsider can keep discussions focused as well as lead post-retreat sessions to assess how well the group has implemented ideas and goals.

7 Involve as many attendees as possible in significant roles. Assign them to present specific material at meetings or to lead breakout sessions.

8 Schedule the heaviest work sessions in the mornings. At least part of each afternoon should be free for rest and relaxation.

9 Schedule a specific time at the final work session to document key conclusions reached during the retreat. Don't let this vital step slip away in the flurry of departure preparations.

10 Draw up a detailed evaluation form for attendees' feedback after the retreat. This will make planning next year's retreat considerably easier.

Tips

Establish a firm rule: Mobile phones must be turned off during working sessions.

Schedule one night's dinner at a restaurant other than one connected with the retreat site. Venue variety is the spice of retreat life.

See 374 Sharpen the Focus of an Organization.

Who Knew?

Retreats have as much meaning to those who don't attend as to those who do. Find a way to also show appreciation for the employees who are holding down the fort.

Warnings

Recognize that for some employees, certain vigorous activities—such as wall climbing, rope courses or river rafting—are more of an exercise in terror than a lesson in team building. Make the let's-scare-ourselves-silly sessions voluntary.

Be aware of the effects that a cushy "morale-building" retreat for one team has on all the others who don't attend.

221 | Defend Against a Hostile Takeover

Whether it's Oracle and PeopleSoft, Verizon and Vodafone, or Comcast and Disney, nothing whets the appetite of the financial press more than a hostile takeover bid. If an avaricious company comes hunting for your firm, set the bait with a dose of poison. Here's the potion, as well as some other evasive maneuvers.

Steps

Create a poison pill

1 Formulate a poison pill the hostile buyer won't want to swallow. Also known as a shareholders rights plan, this makes a takeover prohibitively expensive by granting existing shareholders the right to purchase newly issued stock at a greatly reduced price.

2 Establish an exercise price—the amount shareholders will pay to buy additional shares. Include a dilution adjustment factor. Many shareholders rights plans state that the company will issue shares with a current market value of twice the exercise price.

3 Set a redemption price. This is a nominal sum—often $0.01 per right—for which shareholders may redeem the rights before they are exercisable.

4 Set a trigger to launch the shareholders rights plan. For example, have the plan go into effect when someone tries to acquire a certain percentage of outstanding total shares—typically 15 to 20 percent, but sometimes as low as 10 percent.

5 Set a time limit on the plan's terms. Ten years is common.

Put up other defenses

1 Buy back some of your own shares. This is a common defensive measure for both large and small corporations. Of course you'll need to have available capital.

2 Examine your corporate charter. Clauses may exist that provide for removal of directors only for cause or for staggered board terms. The latter make it difficult for the stalking company to eliminate an entire board via a proxy vote and replace it with directors more receptive to the takeover.

3 Research your state's corporation laws, which often include anti-takeover provisions. Consult your attorneys about adding an amendment to your bylaws to make a takeover more difficult.

4 Install a company benefits plan with expensive change-of-ownership provisions.

5 Spin off a fast-growing subsidiary, thus reducing your company's appeal. Be sure to get your attorney's advice on the legality of the divestiture.

6 Enter into a partnership with another company and include a large breakup fee in the agreement. A hostile acquiring company

Who Knew?

Simply put, the stalking company attempts to gain control over its target against the wishes of the latter's management, usually through a stock bid, but sometimes through an attempt to replace the board of directors.

Seek out a white-knight company who is a more acceptable buyer. This is not just fairy-tale talk. In some sectors, 20 to 30 percent of companies stalked by hostile buyers find white knights.

Warning

Beware the poison pill that becomes a suicide pill or "Jonestown defense" if it results in taking on so much debt that it sends the company into bankruptcy.

would then have to pay a significant fee to your partner when purchasing your firm.

7 Respond rapidly and fervently at the first hints of a takeover attempt. The best tactic may be a combination of the above. Many companies, for example, will fight back with both a stock repurchase plan and a spin-off of one or more divisions.

222 Organize Your Office for a Move

Whether it's across the hall, across town or across the country, a smooth office move requires plenty of planning. Start early, keep detailed to-do lists and—to keep your frayed nerves from unraveling—envision a tropical vacation once the move is complete. Until then, the primary goal is to minimize downtime as much as possible.

Steps

1 Read 97 Plan a Move.

2 Interview and hire movers. Set up a timeline for major tasks and communicate it clearly to everyone involved. Obtain any necessary permits as well as insurance quotes for the new space.

3 Inspect the new space and determine the furniture needs and office layouts, as well as locations for any additional electrical outlets and communication connections that need to be installed.

4 Inventory your present office's contents. Be selective about what you move; donate or sell items that won't work well in the new space. Set a budget for additional furnishings and equipment needed. See 1 Get Organized.

5 Apply for new phone and fax numbers as well as Internet access. If you'll be keeping your current phone system, hire an expert to debug it after the move.

6 Order updated letterhead and business cards as well as change-of-address mailers and checks that have the new address printed on them. Update the company Web site. Order keys and access cards, and make sure the security system will be installed and working before the actual move.

7 Set aside the last day before the movers come as packing day, when the whole staff packs up the office. Ask each employee to make a master list of how many boxes she has and what each box contains; she should then give this list to the moving coordinator.

8 Schedule a staff orientation for the new quarters. Have new phone numbers ready to assign and new keys or access cards ready to distribute.

Tips

Schedule a purge-and-shred day shortly before the move to encourage employees to leave behind no-longer-needed papers.

Schedule the move for a Thursday and Friday so you can use the weekend to get up and running.

Work hand-in-glove with your information technology team from the outset to create a seamless transition of servers and all other computer equipment. Take advantage of the opportunity to upgrade and plan for future growth in your systems.

Who Knew?

Prepare visual aids for moving day, including floor plans, positioning labels for furniture and equipment, and directional signs for movers. Reduce moving-day mayhem with a simple system: say, large red labels on items that will be going to an area you've colored red in the floor plan.

Disasters? Not here! No one wants to think about horrendous events that can turn an ordinary business day into the lead story on the evening news. From earthquakes to hurricanes, tidal waves to terrorist attacks, the unthinkable usually remains the unmentionable. Even a minor disturbance like a blackout can shut down an entire operation. No business should risk operating without a disaster-preparedness plan, and every plan should take three basic elements into consideration: human resources, physical resources and business continuity. Start your research at the American Red Cross (redcross.org) and beef up your plan with information from the Federal Emergency Management Agency (fema.gov).

STEPS	SPECIFICS
Make a Master Plan	Senior management, together with human resources, should create a master plan with contingencies in place for evacuating employees, safeguarding company assets, minimizing downtime and recovering after a disaster. Update the plan annually and when company circumstances change. Contact your local branch of the American Red Cross for more information on plans, supplies and training. Among other things, the Red Cross offers a CD-ROM called the *Guide to Business Continuity Planning* offering comprehensive, step-by-step instructions on addressing life safety issues, minimizing interruptions, transitioning back to normal operations, working with public and private agencies, and formalizing the disaster plan.
Back Up Essential Computer Records	A sweeping disaster as dire as a fire or an earthquake, or as mundane as a brownout could leave every computer in your office unusable. Keep copies of the most important computer files, such as customer databases, in a safe off-site location. In addition, because a computer virus could harm not only your office but also your off-site location, keep paper copies of your most crucial documents in both locations. Set up an off-site archiving protocol with your IT team.
Install Emergency Equipment	Install lights that turn on when the main power supply goes out, as well as a sprinkler system.
Set Up Emergency Communication Systems	Put together a comprehensive phone and emergency contact list of everyone involved with your business, from regular employees to part-timers to occasional contractors (off-site IT personnel, freelance designers, the janitorial firm). Distribute the list to all managers.
	Set up a remote voice-mail number that employees can call to hear recorded information if an emergency strikes (for example: "Stay home today; call Friday for an update"). Give this number to all employees.
	Arrange for programmable call forwarding for your main business line. If you can't get to the office or the building is shut down, you'll be able to call in and reprogram the phones to ring elsewhere.
Prepare for Earthquakes	Even in areas where earthquakes aren't likely, it never hurts to take basic precautions. Relegate breakable objects to lower shelves. Anchor bookcases and cabinets. Keep flammable or volatile items (such as cleaning fluids) locked in a closed cabinet. Anchor heavy artwork to the wall. See 105 Prepare Your Home for Nature's Worst, Prepare.org and Ready.gov for more earthquake tips.

STEPS	SPECIFICS
Plan Evacuation Routes	Designate one employee from every floor or work group to act as safety coordinator. Make sure that everyone in your office is aware of all the planned evacuation routes to use in case of emergency. Schedule a fire drill at least twice a year. After each drill, follow up with an e-mail message or company memo reiterating the specifics of the plan and detailing any concerns with the way the drill went, along with suggested improvements.
Post Emergency Phone Numbers in Prominent Locations	Make a list of local and state phone numbers for fire, police, crisis hot lines, utility companies, news outlets, emergency medical care and any other phone numbers you might need in a crisis. Print copies in large readable font, distribute them to all employees and post them in break rooms and throughout the office. Periodically, go through the list and confirm that the phone numbers are still valid.
Establish an Off-Site Meeting Place	In some emergencies, it may be impossible for employees to get into the office. In other cases, there may be great chaos as people try to leave the office. Decide on a nearby location, such as a restaurant or a large parking lot, and tell all employees that this will be your designated meeting place if the office needs to be evacuated in a hurry.
Prepare a First Aid Kit	Have at least one first aid kit on each floor of your office building in a clearly marked location. The Red Cross sells both a personal Safety Tube (it includes a water pouch, dust mask, whistle and six-hour light stick and attaches under a desk or chair); and a Disaster Supplies Kit with items suitable for one person for one day (including a flashlight and batteries, radio, water, first-aid supplies, dust mask, goggles, work gloves, sanitary and personal supplies, poncho, space blanket and whistle). See 466 Assemble Emergency Kits for more information.
Store Nonmedical Emergency Supplies	Because people may be unable to leave the office building for some reason—and remember that you cannot count on properly functioning electricity and plumbing—store a small supply of nonperishable food and bottled water.
Meet With Police and Emergency Personnel	Don't wait until disaster strikes to hear what advice your police and fire department have. Set up a meeting to have an area disaster expert address your company with ideas and encouragement for preparing for emergency situations. Ask your company to offer first-aid and CPR courses, if it doesn't already.
Keep a Manual Cell-Phone Charger Handy	If the regular phones are not working, a charged cellular-phone battery could make the difference between instant communication and complete isolation. You cannot depend on having electricity in an emergency. For less than $30, purchase a portable cell-phone charger, powered by a side crank that you turn manually.
WARNING	Your insurance policy may not cover earthquakes, floods and other situations (such as an act of war). Review your policy and update your coverage to best suit your needs.

It's never easy to watch your business falter. Sales slow down, perhaps one or more major customers take their business elsewhere (or go out of business too)—and there you are, scrambling to keep your company afloat. But with perseverance, a little luck and some vision, you may be able to turn things around—and even grow stronger.

Steps

1 Limit your worrying. This sounds counterintuitive when serious concerns dominate your days (and keep you awake at night), but by allowing yourself to remain in a state of constant anxiety, you're taking energy away from problem solving. Free-floating anxiety saps the imagination. Focus and determination are what you need now. Revisit 16 Set Goals and focus your attention on taking care of critical decisions.

2 Analyze the failure of your current business model. By figuring out why a business is failing, you can often determine the best new direction to take. A consultant can be extremely helpful in this situation, since you may be too close to the situation to understand what went wrong.

3 Assess whether the problem lies somewhere in the supply-and-distribution chain. Compare your pricing structure to that of your competitors. Are you charging too much for your product or service?

4 Ask yourself specific hard questions that apply to your company. Have sales of core products declined dramatically? Has overdiversification drained your resources? Did you attempt too much growth too rapidly? Take a step back and look at your business without emotion.

5 Contact creditors. While you work out a plan to restructure and revitalize your business, attempt to negotiate a payment plan with them (see 227 Get Out of Debt). And remember, when faced with an avalanche of bills, always pay employee salaries first.

6 Reduce your workforce costs. If a reduced workweek or temporary leaves without pay do not cut salary costs enough to save the business, you'll have to consider layoffs. Remember that layoffs will necessitate certain expenditures, including severance pay and insurance costs. Set up clear, nondiscriminatory criteria for choosing which workers to let go.

7 List the pros and cons of taking out a loan. An accountant or financial planner can help you determine if this is an option.

8 Determine if bankruptcy is your best course of action. Because this is such a complex decision, research the subject thoroughly (see 240 Survive Bankruptcy).

Tip

Seek out informational Web sites, such as bankruptcy-law.freeadvice.com and moranlaw.net/struggling.htm, and government agencies for information about bankruptcy options. Helpful books include Grant W. Newton's *Corporate Bankruptcy: Tools, Strategies, and Alternatives* and Thomas J. Salerno's *The Executive Guide to Corporate Bankruptcy*.

Who Knew?

Talk to your landlord to determine if you can move to a smaller, less expensive office space in the same building. This usually proves to be more economical than changing landlords.

Prepare a clear business plan if you decide to apply for a loan. You will need to show precisely how you intend to use the money to solve the company's problems. See 203 Write a Business Plan and 231 Organize a Loan Application.

225 | Dismantle a Business

No one ever started a business expecting it to fail. In these volatile economic times, however, even the best-conceived enterprises may suffer setbacks so severe that they are forced to close their doors. If this happens to you, take these steps to close down operations safely and preserve whatever assets remain.

Steps

1   Identify your assets. These may include intellectual property such as photographs, text, scientific formulas, concepts and products as well as physical inventory such as chairs and computers. Security deposits and rental credits are also assets. Keep this comprehensive inventory available to lenders, lawyers or potential buyers who may request it.

2   Decide if bankruptcy is the best course of action. Not all businesses that shut down must file for bankruptcy. It may be possible to liquidate all assets and close the doors without filing. However, if you choose not to declare bankruptcy, keep in mind that customers or creditors may sue individual officers of the company for money owed.

3   Consult with a bankruptcy lawyer. If you have decided to declare bankruptcy, a lawyer can help you choose which type is most appropriate for your situation. (See 240 Survive Bankruptcy.)

4   List assets for which you (or another individual business owner) are personally liable. For example, you may separate debt secured against a personal mortgage (or on a personal credit card) from company debt when negotiating payment to creditors.

5   Sell office items and liquidate all assets. Doing this yourself has advantages: You know the market and have industry contacts who may want to purchase your stock when you liquidate. However, hire a third-party company if time is an issue.

6   Develop a plan for repayment of creditors to the extent that you are able. Pay trust-fund taxes first; these are the taxes withheld from an employee's paycheck, and they must be paid no matter how old the debt becomes. Second, pay vendors or employees essential to the business's closing process. Third, pay debts for which individuals are jointly liable with the business.

7   Arrange for final tax returns and issuance of W-2s to employees. Offer to write references for employees who are job-hunting.

8   Exchange personal contact information with co-workers and employees with whom you wish to keep in touch. Networking with them may be the path to your next business venture (see 201 Make a Networking Plan and 204 Set Up a New Business).

Tips

Save digital files and hard copies of all business records to avoid losing historical data about your company when your computer hardware is sold or destroyed. Work with your IT team or hire a consultant to make sure all critical files are safely backed up and stored. See 190 Organize Computer Files.

Research the fair-market value of your assets so that unscrupulous buyers don't take advantage of you.

When liquidating assets, keep a paper trail of all attempts to sell them, clearly stating their condition and value and your efforts to find a buyer.

Warning

If possible, avoid securing large amounts of personal debt when growing a business. This can place you in an uncomfortable financial situation if the business goes bankrupt.

ORGANIZED • SET PRIORITIES • WRITE AN EFFECTIVE TO-DO LIST • REMEMBER THINGS EFFICIENTLY • MANAGE YOUR
RGANIZE YOUR CONTACTS • GET RID OF WHAT YOU DON'T WANT • SAY NO WITHOUT FEELING GUILTY • BALANCE HOME AND WORK • LI
GAIN • SCHEDULE TELEVISION WATCHING • DESIGN A HEALTHY LIFESTYLE • PLAN TO AVOID JUNK FOOD • CHOOSE A WEIGHT LOSS PLA
EET AN ONLINE DATE • PLAN THE PERFECT DATE • MASTERMIND A BREAKUP • PLAN YOUR SOCIAL CALENDAR • MEET MR. OR MS. RIGH
ORT YOUR SOCK DRAWER • RETURN RENTALS ON TIME • TAKE CONTROL OF YOUR JUNK DRAWER • ORGANIZE THE MEDICINE CABINET
AR CLEAN AND ORDERLY • DEAL WITH A PACK RAT • SELL STUFF ONLINE • ORGANIZE YOUR BOOKSHELVES • CATEGORIZE NEWSPAPER
VE BETTER THROUGH LABELING • ORGANIZE JEWELRY • PLAN YOUR DREAM KITCHEN • CONQUER YOUR CLOSETS • ORGANIZE THE LIN
RGANIZE SPRING CLEANING • KEEP THE FAMILY ROOM ORGANIZED • SET UP A BATHROOM SCHEDULE • ORGANIZE BATHROOMS • ORG
RGANIZE KIDS' ROOMS • ORGANIZE SPORTS EQUIPMENT • ORGANIZE KIDS' PLAY SPACES • SAFEGUARD YOUR HOME AGAINST ALLERG
OUSE • USE HOME DESIGN AND PLANNING SOFTWARE • ESTABLISH YOUR HOME'S SPACE PLAN • INCORPORATE UNIVERSAL DESIGN PF
IE BASEMENT • ORGANIZE THE GARAGE • ORGANIZE A TOOLBOX • SET UP A WOODSHOP • ORGANIZE YOUR WINE COLLECTION • PLAN
TUDIO OR SMALL APARTMENT • MANAGE WARRANTY DOCUMENTS • MANAGE HOME-IMPROVEMENT PAPERWORK • MERGE TWO HOUSE
RGANIC VEGETABLE GARDEN • PLANT A KITCHEN HERB GARDEN • PLAN A BUTTERFLY GARDEN • DESIGN A BIRD GARDEN • DESIGN A C
ORGANIZE GARDENING TOOLS • ADD A POTTING BENCH TO A YARD • SCHEDULE FRUIT TREE MAINTENANCE • LAY OUT A SPRINKLER S
ESIGN A GARDEN PATH • SET UP A COMPOST SYSTEM • WINTERIZE PLANTS • SCHEDULE YARD WORK • STORE ANYTHING • STORE BUI
ND HOBBY MATERIALS • ORGANIZE ART SUPPLIES • ORGANIZE GIFT WRAP AND SEASONAL DECORATIONS • ORGANIZE KIDS' SCHOOLW
OUR WEDDING DRESS AND OTHER TEXTILES • STORE A FUR COAT • STORE BICYCLES AND GEAR • STORE SKI GEAR • ORGANIZE CAMF
HICH COLLEGE IS RIGHT FOR YOU • GET INTO A TOP COLLEGE OR UNIVERSITY • ACE THE COLLEGE ADMISSIONS TESTS • ORGANIZE Y
AW SCHOOL • PREPARE FOR THE BAR EXAM • GET A DEGREE WHILE YOU'RE WORKING • WORK AT HOME WITH KIDS • GO BACK TO WC
RGANIZE YOUR JOB SEARCH • PREPARE FOR A CAREER CHANGE • OPEN A RESTAURANT • BECOME A PHYSICIST • BECOME A CONCEI
EALITY-SHOW CONCEPT • BECOME A TALK-SHOW HOST • BECOME A PHOTOJOURNALIST • BECOME A MOVIE DIRECTOR • BECOME A N
LING SYSTEM • ORGANIZE YOUR BRIEFCASE • ORGANIZE YOUR DESK • ORGANIZE YOUR WORKDAY • GET A HANDLE ON E-MAIL • ORG
ALARY REVIEW • CLIMB THE CORPORATE LADDER EFFECTIVELY • ADD A WORKSPACE TO ANY ROOM • ORGANIZE A HOME OFFICE • OF
RAVEL • WRITE A BUSINESS PLAN • SET UP A NEW BUSINESS • CREATE A MARKETING PLAN • AMASS A REAL-ESTATE EMPIRE • POLISH
MPLOYEE • FIRE AN EMPLOYEE • PASS ON A FAMILY BUSINESS • STAY ON TOP OF YOUR SALES GAME • RESTRUCTURE A COMPANY TO
EFEND AGAINST A HOSTILE TAKEOVER • ORGANIZE YOUR OFFICE FOR A MOVE • PREPARE YOUR BUSINESS FOR THE UNTHINKABLE • P
REPARE YOUR TAXES • ORGANIZE A LOAN APPLICATION • ORGANIZE IMPORTANT DOCUMENTS • SAVE FOR PRIVATE SCHOOLING • ORG
LUB • TRACK YOUR INVESTMENTS • SURVIVE BANKRUPTCY • PLAN FOR RETIREMENT • PREPARE A PRENUPTIAL AGREEMENT • CREAT
ONEY • PLAN YOUR FAMILY • BUDGET FOR A NEW BABY • ORCHESTRATE THE PERFECT CONCEPTION • PLAN FOR ARTIFICIAL INSEMIN
EAVE • ORDER BABY ANNOUNCEMENTS • ORGANIZE AN INTERNATIONAL ADOPTION • FOSTER A CHILD • ORGANIZE YOUR LIFE AS A N
OORDINATE A FAMILY CALENDAR • PLAN FAMILY MEETINGS • ORGANIZE HOME SYSTEMS FOR ADD • PREPARE FOR A NEW CAT OR DO
ACK-TO-SCHOOL • WIN THE HOMEWORK WARS • PLAN A FIELD TRIP • PLAN YOUR CHILD'S ACTIVITIES • PLAN YOUR CHILDREN'S SUM
NLINE • ORGANIZE A GENEALOGICAL SEARCH • PREPARE FOR YOUR CHILD'S DEPARTURE FOR COLLEGE • ORGANIZE YOUR EMPTY N
LDERLY PARENTS' CARE • PREPARE FOR THE DEATH OF A SPOUSE • HELP YOUR ELDERLY PARENTS MOVE • ORGANIZE A HOME MEDI
TORE TRIPS • SET UP ONLINE GROCERY SHOPPING • ORGANIZE RECIPES AND COOKBOOKS • PLAN THEME MENUS • CREATE EFFECT
EFRIGERATOR AND FREEZER • ORGANIZE CUTLERY AND KITCHEN TOOLS • ORGANIZE CUPBOARDS AND DRAWERS • ORGANIZE THE F
UNCHES FOR KIDS • PLAN PARTY FOODS AHEAD • THROW A DINNER PARTY • FINISH DINNER ON TIME • PULL OFF A LAST-MINUTE PAF
LTIMATE WEDDING CHECKLIST • BUDGET FOR A WEDDING • FIND THE PERFECT WEDDING RING • PLAN AN ELOPEMENT • SET UP A BA
ONOR • EXECUTE BEST MAN DUTIES • HIRE A BAND • HIRE A BARTENDER • PLAN A SHOWER • ORGANIZE THE REHEARSAL DINNER •
UCCESSFUL SLUMBER PARTY • PLAN A BAR OR BAT MITZVAH • PLAN A QUINCEAÑERA • PLAN A RETIREMENT PARTY • PLAN A FUNEF
ANUKKAH PARTY • ORGANIZE A HOLIDAY CRAFT PARTY • PLAN TO SPEND CHRISTMAS SOLO • PLAN THE PERFECT HOLIDAY GIFT EXC
HE HOLIDAYS • STICK TO YOUR NEW YEAR'S RESOLUTIONS • PLAN THE PERFECT NEW YEAR'S EVE • PLAN A SEDER • PLAN A SPECIA
OOD TREE • ORGANIZE A BICYCLE SCAVENGER HUNT • RUN A SPORTS TOURNAMENT • PUBLICIZE AN EVENT • PLAN AN ORGANIZATI
LAN A CONCERT IN THE PARK • ORGANIZE AN INTERNATIONAL CONCERT TOUR • ORGANIZE A FILM FESTIVAL • PLAN A FUND-RAISING
BUILD A COMMUNITY PLAY STRUCTURE • THROW A BLOCK PARTY • SET UP A NEIGHBORHOOD WATCH • CREATE AN EVACUATION PI
RGANIZE A PROTEST OR MARCH • FIGHT CITY HALL • ORGANIZE A BOYCOTT • ORGANIZE A CLASS ACTION LAWSUIT • MANAGE GRO
CHOOL IN A THIRD WORLD COUNTRY • PLAN A TRIP • PLAN A TRIP WITH CHILDREN • TRAVEL WITH TEENS • BOOK AIRLINE TICKETS •
OTORCYCLE TRIP • PLAN A TRAIN TRIP IN THE UNITED STATES • RIDE THE RAILS ABROAD • PREPARE A VACATION COUNTDOWN CHE
UGGAGE • LOAD A BACKPACK PROPERLY • PLAN AN ELDERHOSTEL TRIP • ORGANIZE AN RV VACATION • PLAN A TRIP WITH AGING PA
IDELY DIFFERENT PEOPLE • PLAN SPRING BREAK • PLAN AN OVERNIGHT GETAWAY WITH YOUR SPOUSE • PLAN A VACATION SEPARA
OLITICALLY UNSTABLE REGION • GET TRAVEL INSURANCE • GET IMMUNIZATIONS FOR TRAVELING • BOOK AN ADVENTURE VACATION
LAN A FISHING TRIP TO ALASKA • PACK FOR A CAMPING TRIP • LEAD A BACKPACK TRIP • HIKE A FAMOUS TRAIL • PLAN A TOUR OF
NGLISH CANAL TRIP • PLAN A CROSS-COUNTRY AIRPLANE VOYAGE • PLAN THE PERFECT DAY ABROAD • PLAN A VISIT TO THE LOUV
LAN • PREPARE FOR AN ACT OF GOD • ASSEMBLE EMERGENCY KITS • PREPARE FOR SURGERY • PLAN YOUR RECOVERY • SURVIVE
EING LOST • CONDUCT A SEARCH AND RESCUE OPERATION • PLAN AN INVASION • SURVIVE A POLITICAL COUP • PLAN FOR A TERR

Financial Plans

In an age where consumer spending is high and there's a constant flux of new products on the market, knowing how to budget properly is the key to financial stability. Set long-term financial goals and implement short-term strategies to put you back in control of your wallet. If you're budgeting for an event, the basic concepts still apply.

Steps

Create a personal spending plan

1 Learn how and where you spend your money. Stopping for a beer after work and renting a couple of movies on a Friday night doesn't seem like much, but every expense adds up. Get a small notebook and write down every penny you spend for a few weeks, to start seeing your spending patterns and what your expenses actually are (rather than what you think they are).

2 Create an ongoing spreadsheet listing what you spend, where and when. This will help you track patterns and inconsistencies.

3 Rank your spending priorities from the essentials (food, utilities, mortgage payments, medical costs) to the nice-to-haves (home improvement, vacations) and the luxuries (new car, high-end gadgets, designer clothes). Use what you learned from tracking your expenses to prioritize your spending. See 2 Set Priorities.

4 Factor fixed expenses into your budget, such as your mortgage, tuition or car payment, food costs and tuba lessons. Include annual expenses such as insurance payments and taxes.

5 Pay fixed expenses and bills first and live on what's left. Save up for what you want rather than buying it and then paying it back— with interest. See 15 Live With Less and 227 Get Out of Debt.

Budget for an event

1 Get an estimated head count of attendees and determine how much money you have available to spend.

2 Split the event into components (food, alcohol, entertainment, security, decorations) and prioritize them. Call around and get a range of options and prices for each component.

3 Compare those prices with what you have to spend: If there's a big discrepancy, start slashing low-priority items. Make a cake instead of buying one; hire a DJ rather than a band.

4 Continue paring back until your expenses equal your budget. If you simply can't reconcile the two, make additional cuts or increase the budget and find ways to bring money in.

5 Add money to your kitty by asking for contributions, splitting costs with other people, having volunteers take on critical tasks, or bringing in revenue from outside sources. See 381 Plan a Fund-Raising Event.

Tips

If you keep getting overdraft notices from your bank, it's time to find out why you're not keeping up. Get overdraft protection for your checking account. It's worth a few bucks a month.

Build up an emergency fund to cover repairs, medical bills—or losing your job.

Balance your checkbook and credit-card statements each month. Compare the numbers on your credit-card statement with your receipts.

Notify the credit-card company of any errors as soon as possible. Federal law provides protection from mistakes only if you make notification within 60 days.

See 228 Design a Savings Plan.

Who Knew?

Kick start your new program with a "paperless budget." Hold back a reasonable portion of every paycheck to pay down your debts and force yourself to live on the balance. Then move toward a real spending plan.

If you can't religiously pay off your entire credit-card balance every month, high interest rates and poor impulse control will leave you with enormous debt. Charge only what you must. If, however, you have a solid record of paying off the balance every month, use your credit card to rack up frequent-flier miles or other rewards.

The road to being debt-free begins with an honest assessment of your financial situation. Once you determine where you stand, take steps to turn the tide. Follow these guidelines and you may find ways to accelerate the process of moving from the red to the black.

Steps

1 Control your spending. This is the first step toward fixing money problems. Most people who spend too much are enthralled with the act of buying, not the value of the goods. Question every purchase—what will happen if you don't buy? You might be surprised how little real value most stuff has and how easily you can do without it. See 15 Live With Less.

2 Pay your bills on time. Besides imposing hefty late fees, creditors bump up interest rates for late payments. Pay parking tickets and car registration swiftly to avoid late penalties.

3 Destroy all of your credit cards except one, with the lowest possible long-term interest rate. Leave this card at home and use it only for emergencies. Transfer the debt on your other cards to this remaining card. Carry cash for daily expenses.

4 Get a copy of your credit report from one of the three major credit bureaus: Equifax.com, Experian.com and TransUnion.com. Review your report carefully for accounts or addresses that don't belong to you, creditors who have made mistakes, and companies who have looked at your report without your permission. Report any mistakes to the credit bureau. That means requesting and reviewing a report from the other two bureaus to make sure the mistakes are corrected.

5 Refinance your mortgage at a lower rate. If your credit is already bad, this may not be possible. But if you can get a lower rate, you can apply your savings directly to pay down your debt, or pull extra cash out to take care of it all at once.

6 Sell valuables and use the money to pay off your debt. RVs, cars, boats and other expensive toys should be eliminated. They won't be fun, if they're dragging you into financial ruin.

7 Negotiate a reduction in your annual fee. Finance charges are not the only cost of a credit card—the annual fee can add up to much more than your monthly finance charges. Call your credit-card company and negotiate hard to reduce or even eliminate this fee. Again, threatening to close your account usually gets their attention. Don't bother trying this with cards that are co-branded with airlines or hotels to offer rewards—they will never drop their fee.

8 Call the credit company if, after following all the above measures, you still can't pay your bills. Ask for a lower payoff amount. Credit companies will often work with you in severe cases in order to recoup some of their money. See 240 Survive Bankruptcy.

Tips

Avoid maxing out all your credit limits. If you use 80 percent or more of the credit you have available, lenders will think you are living beyond your means—and you probably are.

Cancel any accounts you don't use. Credit cards you acquired but never use are still considered active.

Who Knew?

Apply occasional windfalls and raises to eliminate outstanding debt.

Warnings

Never use a debt consolidator that advertises aggressively or promises you a quick fix. Often this will plunge you deeper into debt, and it may even damage your credit record more than you already have.

When you're paying off any debt, it's a great idea to know where you stand financially. Specifically, it's smart to recognize any warning signs that might foretell a personal economic plunge. For example, if you have a student loan, three unpaid invoices from your lender is a big red flag that you're not keeping up with your loan payments. Another red flag: Your bank account is consistently overdrawn.

The easiest way to have more money is to manage your finances wisely. That's where a good savings plan comes in. Whether you're saving for your college, a yearlong cruise or retirement, get serious about where you want to be financially and how you plan to get there. Start by creating solid financial goals and figure out how to reach them.

Steps

1 Set specific long-term financial goals. Explicit targets such as "$2,000 into retirement account by August" are more effective than more general targets like "contribute to retirement account."

2 Estimate much you'll need to retire in comfort, based on what you earn—and spend—now. Consult a financial planner for expert advice. See 241 Plan for Retirement.

3 Put raises and bonuses toward debt payments or into savings accounts. If you can live comfortably off your paycheck, then you don't need to live off the extra cash from your raise. Choose the best target for financial bonanzas. The key is making that money work for your financial security.

4 Run with the bulls and bears if you want to move beyond getting ahead and into creating wealth. Yes, you're taking on investment risk with stocks, but you're avoiding inflation risk. And if you have a diversified portfolio, you're spreading your risk. See 239 Track Your Investments and 238 Start an Investment Club.

5 Get cracking and start saving. You'll need to save enough from your 30 to 40 years of working to live for about 20 or 30 years in retirement. When you do ramp up your savings program, overestimate your future needs. It's far better to end up with too much money than not enough. Saving even a little bit more each year can make a big difference in the long term.

6 Fine-tune, buff and polish your savings plan. Understand that how far away you are from retirement plays a large part in how you should invest your retirement money. Historically, there are three stages to a long-term retirement savings plan:

- Capitalization: In the earliest stage of saving (generally up to age 30), the goal is to build up your retirement savings portfolio. In this stage, you can be more aggressive because you have more time to ride out the market's ups and downs.

- Consolidation: This stage (roughly from 30 to 60 years—your peak earning years) makes up the bulk of your savings plan. In this phase, you should balance aggressive investments with tamer ones, thus protecting your existing assets.

- Conservation: This final stage should take place one to three years before you retire. Your investments should aim to preserve your capital. The exact timing of all these should take current market conditions into account.

Tips

Know your credit rating; it's a good barometer on how creditors view you financially. One quick way to do that is to check the three major credit-report companies: Equifax.com, Experian.com and TransUnion.com. Each provides your credit rating report (for a fee) and handles stolen card and fraud complaints.

Remember to take inflation into account in your calculations; it averages about 3 percent annually.

See 500 Die Rich.

Who Knew?

Any Wall Street trader will tell you that it is virtually impossible to beat inflation and generate a decent return without investing in the stock market.

Build a reserve of six months' worth of your annual salary to ride out rough economic times (such as when you lose a job or have a serious illness). When you get paid, pay yourself first: Take 10 percent of your paycheck and stash it in a savings or money market account.

Warning

If you don't have any money at all in your savings account, it's time to examine where your money is going every month. See 226 Set Up a Budget.

Do you use late notices as a reminder to pay your bills? Does your checking account seem to be made of rubber? Irregular bill-paying habits make you a credit risk, and may jeopardize a future car loan, an apartment or even a job. The good news is that with some careful planning and an assertive mind-set, you'll have a bounce in your step—instead of in your checking account.

Steps

1 Designate two days per month to attend to your bills, say the first and the 15th, perhaps on the days you get paid. Make it the same time every month and mark these days on your calendar. If your major bills are due at different times, find out if you can change the payment due date. Sometimes you can do this on the company's Web site.

2 Check your account before you start—you don't want any surprises. Most banks let you access your account balance online, at ATMs or by phone.

3 Devote a corner of the house, preferably quiet and out of the way, to paying your bills. Ideally, you have a special desk for keeping all of your financial records and checkbook. See 184 Conquer Your Paper Piles.

4 Label bills "pending" or "paid." As soon as they arrive, place them in a designated bill file for easy access.

5 Keep a clean checkbook. When you pay a bill, record the bill as "paid" in your checkbook. It reduces the chance of mistakes.

6 Make fast and easy work of your bills with a program like Quicken (quicken.com) or Microsoft Money (microsoft.com/money) to keep tabs on your bills. Set it up to provide automatic reminders of which bills are due. A good software program comes in handy around tax time, since all your bill payment records are in one place (see 230 Prepare Your Taxes).

7 Set up online bill paying with your bank. Most banks let you pay any company or individual in the United States—your credit-card company, the phone company, even your roommate—all from your computer for free or a small monthly fee. Pay multiple bills at once and choose the day when each will be paid. Save the hassle of buying and finding stamps and envelopes.

8 Go completely virtual and receive your bill online from select merchants such as your phone, utility and insurance companies, department stores and so on. Most companies love to see you pay your bills online. In fact, interest rates for some larger bills, such as mortgages and student loans, can be negotiated downward if you pay online.

9 Keep it simple. If you're spending more than an hour a month paying bills, it's time to reassess your plan.

Tips

If you can't pay an entire bill, send a partial payment so you're not marked delinquent.

Thin out your credit cards. If you're juggling four or five cards, that's a red flag on many financial fronts; it likely means you carry too much debt. Close the accounts and cut up all but one or two cards. You'll get fewer bills and your records will be easier to organize. (See 227 Get Out of Debt.)

Who Knew?

Have your mortgage payment deducted from your bank account automatically. Consider switching from a monthly to a biweekly payment plan. Instead of 12 monthly payments, you'll make 26 biweekly payments—and pay down your mortgage much faster.

Warning

Bill payments shouldn't get in the way of building an emergency fund. If you can't stash away three to six months' worth of living expenses and still pay your bills, that's a problem. (See 228 Design a Savings Plan.)

230 | Prepare Your Taxes

You really have to admire the Internal Revenue Service. Any organization that makes tons of money without advertising deserves some credit. For everyone else, April 15 isn't exactly a red-letter day. But with advance planning and organization, tax time doesn't have to be such a grind. Knowing what information you'll need will make the process speedier—and will get your refund to you faster.

Steps

1 Organize your papers and files long before tax time—your system is key to managing your finances. No matter how simple or sophisticated, develop a strategy that you'll actually use. Stay low-tech by just sorting receipts, pay stubs, W-2s and other information into file folders. Or step up to a comprehensive but easy-to-use software program, such as Quicken (Quicken.com) or TurboTax (turbotax.com). See 184 Conquer Your Paper Piles, 185 Create a Flawless Filing System and 229 Simplify Bill Paying.

2 Get a jump on your taxes. If you put it off until April 14, you're more likely to make a mistake, and any tax preparer you work with may not have time to complete your return. Remember, if you file for an extension, you still need to pay up by the April deadline to avoid being assessed penalties and interest.

3 Call in the pros. If you feel overwhelmed just organizing your pay stubs and W-9s, or if your tax situation is complicated (1031 exchange, complex investments, buying or selling a business), hire a professional to do the job right. There are different levels of training required for different designations of tax preparers:

- A certified tax preparer is licensed by the state and is required to take continuing education courses every year.

- An enrolled agent (EA) is certified to represent taxpayers before the IRS (certified tax preparers cannot handle audits). EAs have much more stringent training requirements and are mandated by the IRS to undergo extensive continuing education yearly.

- A certified public accountant is educated in accounting and may specialize in taxes. Be sure to ask.

4 Take advantage of free tax assistance. Download the IRS's Publication 17: Your Federal Income Tax from irs.gov. Known as "the Bible," Pub 17 is a reliable resource for common (and not-so-common) tax payment questions. The IRS has a toll-free TeleTax service at (800) 829-4477, with recorded messages on about 150 tax topics. Have more questions? Call the IRS's 24-hour help line at (800) 829-1040.

5 Glean more tips from the IRS Web site. Download forms, instructions and publications, and find tax law information and answers to frequently asked tax questions. Click on "Site Map," then "1040 Central" to better navigate the mammoth site.

Tips

Save time by filing your return online. The IRS e-file is the fastest and most accurate way to file your tax return. You'll get your refund much faster than paper filers do—as fast as ten days (as opposed to at least six weeks).

For a complete list of financial assets, forms, income data and other information you'll need to bring to your tax preparer, look at sites such as moneycentral.msn.com/tax/home.asp.

Who Knew?

When a mistake is made on your tax return, fix it. Corrections may include a missed deduction, an incorrect interpretation of the law or facts, or simply a late or corrected W-2 or 1099. Cheer up: Amended returns do not have a higher chance of being audited.

A bookkeeper is not allowed to file tax returns on behalf of a client.

Warnings

Double-check your numbers. The most common errors on tax returns are caused by incorrect math calculations and incorrectly entered Social Security numbers. If you are e-filing, these errors will cause your return to be automatically rejected.

The IRS does not hold itself liable for tax information it gives over the phone.

231 | Organize a Loan Application

On the fun scale, applying for a loan falls somewhere between doing your taxes and having minor surgery. Once you get organized, though, the process takes less time than you think. If you need a loan to start or expand a business, the following steps can help you power through the paperwork.

Steps

1 Determine which type of loan you need to apply for: *Working capital* is used to meet immediate, short-term needs (payroll, rent, vendors) that you will repay during the company's next full operating cycle (generally one year). *Growth capital* pays for durable investments that create income (a printing press, a building, a fleet of trucks). These loans are generally paid over a period of not more than seven years. If you're seeking investment capital, the lender will expect you to show how you will increase profits sufficiently to repay the loan in the agreed-upon time frame.

2 Gather the documents you'll need for your loan application. Typically you'll be required to provide a pay stub, an IRS tax return or a W-2 form to prove your income. Pull together bank and 401(k) statements, and of course, any debt and liability documents, such as divorce papers or student-loan statements. You'll need these key documents and information when you apply for a loan:

- Home or work address, phone number and e-mail address.

- Past homes and/or apartments. Go back seven years.

- Social Security number (include numbers for all borrowers).

- Date of birth.

- Contact information for any landlord or lender you've had in the past three years.

- Amount of current mortgage payments, taxes and insurance.

- Pay stubs for the previous two months.

- W-2 forms for the past two years.

3 Check your credit report before you fill out your application, and fix any discrepancies.

4 Go back two years and show a history of payments (credit card, student loan, utility, car) to lenders.

5 Make your loan application tidy and orderly. The condition, completeness and appearance of your loan will reflect on you and affect your chances of getting a loan. Information should be typed, spell-checked and carefully proofed. Add a cover letter for professionalism and style points.

Tips

See 232 Organize Important Documents.

If you're self-employed, make sure to include both your federal and any corporate tax returns over the last two years. Include information on your firm's profit and loss.

Who Knew?

Include all means of income, not just your paycheck stub. Include all bonuses, any outside income (investments, royalties), and government benefits such as Veterans Benefits Administration and Social Security checks.

Warnings

Avoid sending out multiple applications simultaneously. Lenders will check the same credit agencies and will notice an uptick in lender inquiries. Fairly or unfairly, they may smell desperation and give you a thumbs-down.

Keep it real. Don't fudge any information on your application. Banks and lenders don't like liars and they don't like vague generalities. Make sure all your information is accurate and as specific as possible. Verify each line of your application. If you're not sure about a given number, stay on the safe side and underestimate rather than overestimate.

There's not a whole lot of glamour in keeping tabs on your paperwork. But if you want to stay in good fiscal shape, you need to organize your financial records. Consider hiring a pro to get you on the right track—check out cfp.net to find a certified financial planner in your area.

ITEM TO KEEP	WHY	HOW LONG
Tax Returns	The Internal Revenue Service (irs.gov) has up to six years from the date you file to audit you or challenge your returns. Keep copies of tax returns and supporting documents such as receipts for charitable contributions and miscellaneous deductions. There is no statute of limitations on investigations of taxpayers who fail to file or who file fraudulent returns.	Six years.
Investment Records	If your mutual-fund company or stockbroker provides a year-end summary statement of your transactions, shred the monthly reports. Keep a record of all trades, particularly the original price of your stocks and fund shares when you sell. Also save records of all contributions to nondeductible individual retirement accounts, as proof of already having paid taxes on the money.	Keep trade confirmations for a couple of years after sales in case the IRS has questions.
Credit-Card Bills	Review your statements for potential duplicate charges, then shred them when the next bill comes in, unless you are self-employed, in which case file and keep them for tax purposes.	One year.
Bank Statements	File along with canceled checks and pay stubs.	Three years.
Charitable Deductions	Keep receipts and records of donations for tax purposes.	Six years.
Medical Records	Save receipts and insurance payments for dentists, doctors, hospitals and prescriptions. See 289 Organize Medical Records.	Six years.
Home-Related Records	Save all real-estate records and transactions as well as the title and deed to your house. Other records to keep include contracts and receipts for home improvement and repairs, property tax paperwork and warranties. See 101 Manage Home-Improvement Paperwork and 100 Manage Warranty Documents.	Duration of ownership plus seven years.
Vital Statistics	Passports, birth certificates, marriage and divorce papers.	Permanently.
TIP	Consolidate your bank accounts if you have several. You'll see your financial snapshot in one statement; also, many financial institutions offer special pricing and free services when you consolidate your accounts with them.	
WARNING	Do not let strangers see your financial records. Shred any personal papers with your name, address and account numbers. They are gold mines of information for thieves who may want your Social Security number or account numbers.	

Forget about saving for your kid's college tuition. If you're thinking of sending your child to a private school, your timeline just got a lot shorter. These days, private grammar and high schools can cost as much as many universities. You'll need to implement an aggressive savings plan.

Steps

1 Research schools and apply to the best ones for your kids (see 273 Choose the Best Elementary School). Decide if you will send them to private school at the elementary level or wait until high school.

2 Brace yourself for sticker shock. Private schools (K through 12) can run from $10,000 to $20,000 a year. Add any additional costs such as uniforms, lunches, field trips and fund-raisers as well as child care before school, after school, on holidays and during summer breaks. Find out when tuition is due, what sort of payment plans are available, and how likely it is that fees will increase and by how much. Factor all of this into your long-term budgeting plans.

3 Inquire about financial-aid packages at the school of your choice and apply (see 234 Organize Your Financial-Aid Package). Take advantage of aid targeted to specific populations such as single parents, children of color or second children.

4 Determine how your other financial needs, such as saving for retirement, will be affected by the expense of your child's education (see 241 Plan for Retirement). Figure out the minimum you need to save annually for your retirement to determine how much you can spend on your child's education.

5 Consider savings plans that have funds designated for use toward your child's education. For example, a Coverdell Education Savings Account permits a total tax-free contribution of $2,000 per year per child (or beneficiary). Note that educational funds must be used for "qualified educational expenses," which are defined by the IRS (not you). For more information, check out Morningstar.com.

6 Investigate payment protection plans in the event that a parent dies or becomes disabled, or your child becomes seriously ill. This will ensure there will still be funds to pay for your child's schooling to keep his or her education from being disrupted.

Tip

Tell grandparents that they can each give up to $11,000 a year to each grandchild tax-free.

Who Knew?

If your home has appreciated considerably and you can manage your monthly mortgage payments, consider refinancing and using the cash to pay for private school. Only do so if interest rates are low.

Consider waiting until high school to go private. With fewer students in the pipeline, colleges aren't looking as hard at a private elementary school background.

The School and Student Service for Financial Aid (www.nais.org/financialaid /parents) evaluates the factors that determine your eligibility, such as your assets and gross income (taxable and nontaxable). Assets include home equity, business equity, equity in rental or vacation properties, bank accounts and investment accounts (except your retirement nest egg). The SSS also considers how many children you're paying tuition for and what the cost of living is in your area.

The College Board estimates that roughly $68 billion was available to college students in 2000. If you're looking for a way to finance your schooling, apply for as many financial-aid packages as you can—even if you think you're not eligible. Start with the Financial Aid Resource Center (theoldschool.org) and Peterson's helpful college-planning guide (petersons.com).

Steps

1 Seek out grants and scholarships. Sites such as FinAid.org, FastWeb.com, CollegeNet.com and IEFA.org allow you to search massive databases to provide scholarships you're eligible for. Look for scholarships sponsored by local religious institutions, businesses and service organizations like the Kiwanis and the Rotary Club.

2 Gather the necessary documentation (see 232 Organize Important Documents), which typically include:

   • Your Social Security number.

   • Your driver's license number.

   • Your previous year's W-2 tax forms.

   • Any other records of income you earned last year.

   • Your (and your spouse's) previous year's federal income tax return(s)—IRS Forms 1040, 1040A, 1040EZ.

   • Your parents' federal income tax return from last year (if you are a dependent student).

   • Your previous year's untaxed income records: Social Security, Temporary Assistance to Needy Families, welfare or veterans' benefits.

   • Your previous year's bank statements.

   • Your previous year's business and mortgage information; farm records; stock, bond and other investment records.

   • Your alien registration card (if you are not a U.S. citizen).

3 Apply for financial aid prior to being accepted at the schools you are applying to. Ask for financial-aid forms along with your college-admissions applications. Leave yourself some wiggle room: Start your financial-aid discovery process at least six months before starting your school selection process. Designate a file or calendar to keep track of when forms and applications are due.

4 Consider loan packages. If you receive financial aid and it still doesn't satisfy your financial obligations, use a student loan to close the gap. Your best bet might be a federal Parent Loan for Undergraduate Students (PLUS), a federal Stafford loan (salliemae.com) or a private loan from a bank or other financial lender. Check the fine print and make sure interest rates and terms are acceptable before you sign on the dotted line.

Tips

When reviewing financial-aid applications, schools and financial organizations look closely for signs that you can afford to pay for school. Red flags include taking a lump-sum payout or buying a new home the year before you apply for aid.

Pick up a free copy of *The Student Guide: Five Federal Financial Aid Programs* (at studentaid.ed.gov) for sources of federal aid across the United States.

Submit a résumé that places you in the best possible light along with your application.

Don't pay for a service to research scholarships. Online resources and books can deliver equally good results. Doing your own research online and at the library is easy—and free.

Who Knew?

See if your employer has any financial-aid programs. Many civic-minded firms, like Citibank and Microsoft, offer them.

Warning

Grab the U.S. Department of Education's Free Application for Federal Student Aid from the post office or library, at fafsa.ed.gov or by calling (800) 433-3243. It's a shortcut to some of the best financial-aid packages the government offers.

Make no mistake: A college education pays big dividends. Studies show that college graduates earn roughly twice as much as high school graduates. Give your child this opportunity by starting your college savings program today.

Steps

1 Start saving as early as your child is born: The sooner you begin, the more money you'll accumulate. Setting mini-financial goals is as important with a college savings plan as with any long-term savings plan. First calculate how much you will need to save, using your child's age as a yardstick. Then craft an investment plan (get a financial adviser to help), and stick to it like a barnacle on the hull of a ship. See 228 Design a Savings Plan.

2 Invest in higher-risk investments such as growth stocks when your child is very young and time is your ally. You can handle some bumps and pitfalls along the way and still have time to make up ground. Stocks have historically offered the best return on an investment dollar. When college is two or three years off, start to conserve (or "lock in") some of your gains by placing a healthy chunk of your college fund into lower-risk bonds, bond mutual funds or money-market funds.

3 Review financial aid packages for your income level and asset portfolio to estimate a baseline target for savings. FinAid.com and Kiplinger.com offer tools to estimate your contribution. According to the College Board, the current one-year cost of a four-year public college is about $9,000, while the cost of a four-year private college is around $24,000, with a 4 percent annual increase. Use those numbers as a measuring stick to estimate your expected contribution.

4 Launch a college savings campaign. When family members and friends ask what to get your child for birthdays or holidays, ask them to contribute to his or her college fund. Good gifts include Series EE Savings Bonds, stock or mutual-fund shares steered through the tax-friendly Uniform Gifts/Transfers to Minors Acts (UGMA/UTMA), and Coverdell Education savings account (formally known as an education IRA). Cash and checks work just fine, too. Also note that grandparents can pay a child's tuition without any gift-tax penalties.

5 Invest early through one of the many state-sponsored 529 tuition programs to lock in tuition at any college within a certain system (state universities, for example). You can open a 529 plan when your child is born and guarantee tuition fees 20 years from now at today's rates. All profits from a state-sponsored prepaid tuition plan are tax-free as long as the withdrawals are used for a "qualified educational expense" as defined by the IRS. Beware—if you use these funds for an out-of-state school, they may be taxed.

Tips

Look for more tips on SavingsForCollege.com and Morningstar.com.

Capitalize on any tuition-prepayment discounts. Many colleges and universities make it worth your while to pay tuition costs early (in some cases as soon as an infant has a Social Security number), with discount programs of up to 10 percent of the total tuition package.

Who Knew?

Make saving for college a part of your overall household savings plan. It doesn't have to be much; even $50 per month can add up in premium and interest over the years.

Choose your college savings plan wisely. Some allow you to deposit more than $200,000 tax-free, while others limit the amount. Look into how a plan invests its money. Some managers buy mutual funds; others, certificates of deposit. Be sure to get details about how the plan has performed in the past.

A 529 college savings plan is also tax-free and more flexible that its related 529 tuition program (see step 5). It can be applied to any qualified educational program in the United States.

Contrary to what the TV commercials say, not everybody needs life insurance. It protects against lost income—no more, no less. If you don't have dependents or if you are well-off financially, your family may not need an influx of cash when you die. But if they would, find out how to make an educated decision on what kind of coverage you need for how much.

Steps

The basics

1 Calculate how much coverage you'll need. Determine how much your beneficiaries need to live on, and for how long. Losing a loved one is emotionally and financially difficult, and dependents may need a period during which they won't have to worry about money. While two years is an average cushion, some people may want to make sure their beneficiaries are taken care of until they finish college, while others want their loved ones to be set for life. Calculate all expenses for the covered period, including big-ticket items (college, mortgages), as well as living expenses (clothes, food). Then subtract the amount of money you think your beneficiaries will make from salaries and investments (remember, adults may not be able to go back to work right away). By subtracting all their estimated expenses from established income, you'll get a basic idea of how much insurance coverage you need.

2 Analyze what type of coverage best meets your needs. Think of insurance in terms of decreasing protection as you get older. When you are younger and have kids and a mortgage, your family needs protection. As you get older, your kids have graduated and you likely have few or no payments left on your mortgage, so you need less protection.

• *Term* life insurance is the simplest way to go—you pay the premium and are covered for a specific benefit for the period during which you want coverage. When you stop paying, you're no longer covered. Term is a much cheaper option in the long run, and you can invest the money you would have otherwise paid for whole life in mutual funds.

• *Universal* life policies allow you to adjust your premiums as well as your death benefit. *Variable* life lets you choose how to invest the policy's cash value. A portion of what you pay in premiums goes into a cash value, which could increase over time and can be redeemed before your death. Unfortunately, the mortality expense of all cash-value policies goes up significantly after age 60, so that you could be in a situation where your payment goes up drastically or the investment account used to pay your premiums quickly dries up. If you die with a large

Tips

Read 243 Create a Living Trust and 244 Make a Will.

Know the terminology. The *premium* is the money you pay to keep the policy in force. The *death benefit* is the payment to be made upon your death, as dictated by the policy. The *beneficiary* is the person or persons who will receive the death benefit.

The cost of term life insurance has been falling, so you might consider replacing an existing term policy. Check current rates for term life insurance at comparison sites such as Term4Sale.com.

Evaluate whether it makes sense to get an insurance policy on someone else, such as your spouse or business partner, whose death would cause real hardship for you. Insurance policies can be purchased for just about anyone.

cash-value balance, your beneficiary still gets only the face amount, not the face amount plus the cash value.

- *Whole* life insurance has significant drawbacks. First, the premiums are generally far more costly—especially in the early years of the policy, when you're mostly paying commissions rather than building cash value. Second, if you have to cash out the policy early, you may have to pay a surrender charge.

3 Check the ratings. Insurers run the gamut from shaky upstarts to solid, household-name institutions. Most companies are rated for financial strength and claims-paying ability by independent rating agencies. Ratings from A.M. Best, Moody's, and Standard & Poor's are the most often cited.

Borrow against your life insurance

1 "Borrow" money from a cash-value life policy as an absolute last resort. If you own a home, consider an equity line before borrowing from your cash value. With an equity line, your interest is deductible, and you will most often get a better rate than the insurance company is willing to offer.

2 Contact your insurance company if you have no other options and find out how large your cash value is and how much you can borrow. The amount available to you depends on how much cash has accumulated in the policy. That in turn depends on how long the policy's been around, how much you've paid into it and other factors. For example, if you have a $300,000 policy with a cash value of $50,000, your borrowing capability will be based on the $50,000 cash value.

3 Understand that when you borrow against your cash value, you must pay interest on the amount you borrow. The interest you pay does not go into your cash value, as many people think. Instead it goes back into the pockets of the insurance company.

4 Carefully check the terms and conditions of the loan. Some insurance companies restrict how much of your cash value you can borrow and have special payback terms. Make certain that the interest rates are lower than what other loan sources, such as home equity loans, are offering.

5 Withdraw the money. There is no restriction on how you can use the money, as there is with a 401(k) withdrawal, for example. You don't ever have to pay it back, as long as you're willing to have a reduced death benefit for your beneficiaries when you do pass away. But you'll also pay interest on it for the rest of your life. On top of that, any interest you owe on that loan will also be deducted from the payout.

Warnings

If you borrow from a policy that is characterized as a modified endowment contract, you could create a taxable event under certain circumstances.

If you stop paying premiums after eight or ten years when the cash value has risen enough, and then take a loan against it, you may actually have to continue paying annual premiums. Find out in advance if you have this type of premium policy and under what circumstances you'd have to start paying premiums again.

These days, landing in the hospital for even a few days can decimate your savings account. That's why it's extremely important to consider the cost, the benefits, and the extent to which your family's health needs are met when choosing insurance. Research the various plans that are available, and determine how specifically tailored they are to your family's health needs and financial abilities, to decide on a plan that is best suited to your lifestyle.

Steps

1 Sign on with the health insurance provided by your employer: It is likely to be the cheapest option you can find. Your employer's carrier may have more than one option for you to choose from (HMO, preferred). If you're self-employed or if your company doesn't offer insurance, you'll have to search for your own insurance.

2 Assess your needs, taking into account your current use of health care and your medical expenses for the near future, and decide what services are most important to you and your family. Ask about dependents' coverage. Factor in how much you can afford to spend on monthly premiums and co-payments. If you're single and healthy, your health plan needs will be very different from those of a family with three young children.

3 Compare benefits and coverage of key items like monthly premiums, deductibles, co-payments, co-insurance rates, costs for seeing out-of-network providers, preventive care, physical exams, immunizations and the like. Other services that are of interest to your family could include fertility services, mental health coverage, nursing care and long-term care.

4 Ask lots of questions: Are your current providers part of this plan? Do you need referrals for specialist visits? How easy is it to change doctors? What hospitals and facilities can you use as part of the plan? What are the procedures for having emergency room treatment approved?

5 Find out if benefits are limited for preexisting conditions, or if you have to wait for a period of time before you're fully covered. Some plans may completely exclude coverage of preexisting conditions.

6 Research whether there is a fair appeals process available if the company denies treatment, and if these appeals are reviewed by an external, independent agency. Is there a high turnover rate among doctors in the plan? Check if the National Committee for Quality Assurance (NCQA.org) accredits the plan; the Pacific Business Group on Health (HealthScope.org) also offers information on health plans.

Tips

If you're switching plans through your employer, ask when the next open enrollment period will occur. Give yourself at least two months in which to conduct and complete your research of health care options.

If your employer doesn't provide health insurance, investigate professional associations that offer members the opportunity to join a health plan.

Take into consideration any upcoming medical expenses, such as surgery, dental work or a new baby.

Take convenience into consideration: Will you have to file claim forms? How close are doctors, hospitals and pharmacies to your home? How often are you permitted to change doctors? Ask if a telephone nurse advice line is offered, particularly if you have young children who tend to get sick at odd hours.

Who Knew?

Find out if the plan you're reviewing surveys its members to determine how satisfied they are with the services provided. If it does, ask for the information. See how member satisfaction rates. You should also take note of whether the plan offers a toll-free number for assistance. Test it out before you join.

7 Pick a plan that best matches your needs and priorities based on thorough research. Read all materials and call the health plan representative or conduct Internet research to get any information you are missing. Discuss pre-existing conditions and flex-spending plans before making a decision.

8 Investigate long-term care insurance. The rising cost of health care and elderly care can demolish your savings if you are incapacitated for long. The best time to buy it is when you hit your 40s.

Ask your primary care physician how easy it is to get referrals for specialists on certain plans. He or she can also tell you how easy it is to find a specialist, which hospitals and types of preventive care the plan covers, and what the claims and utilization review process is like.

---

238 | Start an Investment Club

If you're interested in investing in the stock market but don't know where to begin, start with an investment club. These clubs allow interested people to learn—as a group—how to invest money and track the results. They're easy and fun to organize, and the knowledge members acquire about investing will prepare them to manage their own portfolios in the future.

Steps

1 Sign up with the National Association of Investors Corporation (better-investing.org). The NAIC has helped individuals start clubs for nearly 50 years. It has loads of useful information, such as manuals for managing clubs and sample agreements, as well as a monthly magazine and tools for studying stocks. The Investment Clubs Guide (investorama.com) can also give you more information.

2 Find and organize your members. Start a club that meets in person or one that convenes online. Spread the word about your intention to start a club as widely as you can. Having something in common is an important fact to consider—draw from family, friends, co-workers and fellow students. Limit the membership to 12 to 15. See 373 Plan an Organizational Meeting.

3 Set a minimum monthly fee that each member is expected to contribute—for instance, $20 to $50. Some clubs set an initial contribution a bit higher to cement each member's commitment to the club. Each member's return is determined by his or her contributions to the club.

4 Make sure all members understand and agree on investment strategies before you even begin. Your club must have a unified purpose—it will not be successful if some members prefer short-term strategies while others want to buy and hold stocks. Every member should expect and want to participate actively in the club's research and responsibilities.

Tip

The Internet also provides countless other resources for investors to learn from and share with each other. *The Wall Street Journal* (wsj.com), CBS Marketwatch (cbs.marketwatch.com) and Motley Fool (fool.com) have message boards and forums.

Who Knew?

NAIC membership is a great first investment for a new club. At $35 annually per club and $14 per club member, it's reasonably priced, too.

Continued on next page

5　Create the club's bylaws or rules. Select club officers and set committees to oversee club activities, serve as a cosignatory, to collect dues and maintain all the financials and tax forms. The NAIC has suggestions for filling these positions in its guide.

6　Determine whether your club wants to work with a stockbroker or go it alone. If you go it alone, check out discount online brokerage houses, such as Charles Schwab (schwab.com) or Ameritrade.com. If you do work with a broker, designate one member to deal with him or her in executing buy and sell orders. Someone needs to take care of bookkeeping; the NAIC-provided guides and software make this job easy.

7　Look for a brokerage house with a good reputation and low trading costs. If all members are investment novices, consider using a broker for the first year or two until you get your sea legs, then switching to a discount broker to go it alone.

8　Conduct and use good research. Use online services, such as Yahoo Finance (finance.yahoo.com), Motley Fool (fool.com) and Morningstar.com. Follow the progress of a particular stock or family of stocks that the club is considering for purchase. The NAIC's guidelines and corresponding software can help you flush out the best stocks to buy. Get as much information about the stocks as you can and make sure all members share this information. Go to the library and reference Value Line reports and Standard & Poor's financial reports.

9　Use your computer. The NAIC sells accounting software for clubs that simplifies record-keeping, as well as investment software that makes it easier to find hidden gems. Find other ideas online. E-mail and chat rooms are great ways of communicating with each other, especially if you are part of an online club.

10　Be patient. It will take a couple of years, based on the ups and downs of the stock market and the economy, to see your investments grow. Members should consider both the club and its investments a long-term commitment, and the club's contract should include some sort of clause and even a small penalty that addresses what happens when someone withdraws funds early. Most clubs work best if members take a buy-and-hold approach to stocks. This means members are committed to buying stock from a solid company with the intent to hold it for five years or longer. This approach rides out the market's ups and downs and keeps trading costs and taxes minimal.

Note that the club must file a partnership tax return each year. Each club must have an employer identification number (EIN) to use when filing its return. You may also have to give the club's EIN to the payer of dividends or other income from investments recorded in the club's name. If your club does not have an EIN, get Form SS-4, Application for Employer Identification Number, from your nearest Social Security Administration office or by calling (800) 829-3676. Mail the completed form to the IRS center where you file the club's tax return.

Warning

It is not a good idea to use a club member's Social Security number as the club's EIN. The IRS may hold that person liable for taxes on any income reported to that number.

Leaving your investments unattended is about as risky as leaving a huge wad of cash on the dashboard of your car while you run into the store. Whether you work with a stockbroker or financial adviser, or you trade on your own, keep a constant, watchful eye on your portfolio to prevent minor mistakes from becoming major financial drains.

Steps

1 Hold on to all paperwork and documents that you get from your stockbroker, mutual-fund firm or financial adviser. When receiving trade confirmations and holding statements, make sure they are accurate. Contact your investment firm if the numbers don't square. See 232 Organize Important Documents.

2 Take good notes. Jotting down comments from your stockbroker or investment adviser whenever you talk to them can come in handy down the road if you have a discrepancy or a problem with your account. Careful record-keeping has jogged a lot of memories on Wall Street over the years.

3 Assign someone to handle your investment documents and make sure to have copies of all documents sent to your proxy. If you're injured, sick or otherwise disabled, keeping careful accounts of your portfolio's performance is more critical than ever.

4 Ask tough questions. If you don't understand your investment statements or you have a problem with some of your portfolio's performance numbers, speak up right away, loud and clear. Don't wait until it's too late to do anything about it and don't be embarrassed by what you don't know.

5 Get cyber-savvy and easily track your investments online with your bank or brokerage house. You may need a personal identification number or other password to gain access to your portfolio online (most fund companies and financial advisers offer such access). The immediate access is invaluable.

6 Review your portfolio at least twice a year; quarterly is preferable. Check to see whether you're on the right path to meeting your financial goals. Assess risks and look closely at how your investment portfolio is diversified. If you're overemphasizing one stock (Wall Street people call that the Enron effect), consider selling some of the stock to balance your portfolio.

7 Meet face to face at least once a year if you're working with a financial adviser or stockbroker. An annual visit where you shake your broker's hand and look him or her in the eye can ensure that you remain a priority. You don't want to be out of sight, out of mind.

Tip

Do due diligence on anyone who handles your money. Remember, Uncle Sam requires stockbrokers, financial advisers and other investment professionals to be licensed and registered. Check out your investment professional with the National Association of Securities Dealers (nasdr.com/2000.asp). Big red flag: Your investment rep isn't listed on the site.

Who Knew?

When you give your financial adviser an order to buy or sell—particularly when it's a big order—make sure the instructions are in writing. You don't want any communications mishaps when your money is on the line.

Warning

If you hold a losing stock in your portfolio for more than one year, get rid of it. Then buy a stock in a similar category (growth, large cap, international) to replace it. A full year is plenty of time for a company to turn its fortunes around. Not only will you get rid of a dog, you'll be thinning out your portfolio and reviewing its performance at the same time.

240 | Survive Bankruptcy

Declaring bankruptcy should be the absolute last resort to keeping your financial ship from sinking. Although it's an emotionally difficult choice to make, the process is relatively simple. You provide the courts with information detailing your income, property, debts and creditors, and the court sends a notice to the creditors to prevent further collection efforts.

Steps

Before you file

1 Read 227 Get Out of Debt.

2 Explore the alternatives to bankruptcy, which include negotiating with creditors to reduce or skip some monthly payments, finding a financial manager, refinancing your home if it has some equity in it, or seeking the help of nonprofit credit counseling groups.

3 Consider filing for bankruptcy if you're paying only minimum amounts on your bills, you can't budget yourself out of debt within five years, you've been notified of foreclosure on mortgages or loans, or you've had a severe financial setback—losing your job or major client(s), a divorce or a costly illness.

4 Understand the serious repercussions of filing for bankruptcy. It is reported on your credit for up to 10 years, and it will take about three years after your bankruptcy to re-establish your credit rating. A poor credit rating can make it tough for you to get a mortgage (or result in higher interest because you are deemed a bad credit risk), to get a small business loan, and to get a car loan, and it's hell if you're involved in divorce proceedings and want custody of your kids. Overall, it should be your last resort.

5 Understand what debts bankruptcy can't get rid of. These include alimony, child support, recent back taxes, student loans, recent large purchases, and fines or penalties of government agencies, as well as debts resulting from malicious and willfully fraudulent acts.

6 Hire an attorney you can trust to help you through the proceedings of bankruptcy. Fully understanding the situation will make it easier and less painful for everyone involved.

7 Find a U.S. bankruptcy court at www.uscourts.gov.

Tip

Only go into bankruptcy if doing so will pay off at least half your debts. Otherwise, you may still have an avalanche of debt awaiting you when you emerge from bankruptcy.

Who Knew?

H. J. Heinz, Walt Disney and chocolate baron Milton Hershey all declared bankruptcy, and they survived.

Warning

Don't assume that your credit report will record your debts declared by bankruptcy. Read it again and make sure—and point out any discrepancies right away to the credit bureau. You'll want a record of debts paid on your credit report to show you've met your financial obligations and are a good credit risk.

After you file

1 Open a checking or savings account right away. Future lenders will want to see that you are capable of handling your money responsibly.

2 Get a credit card to establish some credit. Cards for gas stations are among the easiest to obtain.

TYPE	CONDITIONS AND COSTS	WHO QUALIFIES
Chapter 7	Also known as financial liquidation. Wipes out debts for individuals in six months or less. The property sold to your creditors cannot include portions of equity in your car or home, and exemptions vary by state. The filing fee is $175.	• You are an individual or small business owner with too much debt to file for Chapter 13. • You want to wipe your financial slate clean. • You are willing to give up certain kinds of property for sale to your creditors.
Chapter 11	The filing fee is $800, plus a quarterly fee based on the amount of debt.	• You are a business owner who wants to keep the business running while catching up on debts. • You are a consumer with debts in excess of the Chapter 13 debt limits.
Chapter 12	This is a reorganization option for family farmers.	• Your debts are lower than $1.5 million. • At least 50 percent of your income comes from farm operations. • You own at least 50 percent of the farm operations and 80 percent of the farm assets.
Chapter 13	This option, also known as wage-earner bankruptcy, allows you to pay off all or part of your debts over three to five years by reorganizing your debt-payment schedule. You need to have a stable income with enough money left for debt payments after covering food, shelter and utilities. Before filing, you should make mortgages or loans current so you don't lose your property. The court filing fee is $160.	• You must continue to pay taxes, child support and student loans, which aren't wiped out by Chapter 7. • You have a moral conviction to pay all debts, no matter how long it takes. • You must have secured debts (involving property) of no more than $807,750 and unsecured debts of no more than $269,250.

241 | Plan for Retirement

By 2040, average life expectancy among those who reach age 65 is projected to rise from age 81 to 85 for men and from age 84 to 88 for women, according to the National Center for Health Statistics. While that's good news, it also means that careful retirement planning is more crucial than ever before.

Steps

1 Project your life expectancy (see 295 Make Your Final Arrangements and 499 Live to Be 100 Years Old). Most financial planners use age 85 to 90 as a conservative estimate. The longer you live, the more money you'll need to save.

2 Read 228 Design a Savings Plan. Estimate how much money you will need in retirement. Financial planners recommend that you estimate retirement expenses to be about 80 percent of expenses before retirement. That should allow you to maintain the nearly the same standard of living you now enjoy. If you plan on traveling a lot or want to buy a second home, you're going to have to save about 10 percent more. Figure in 3 to 5 percent for inflation.

3 Calculate a balance sheet to evaluate assets and liabilities you will have accumulated by retirement. Assets are what you own, liabilities are what you owe. Take into consideration retirement plans that don't have the fixed income payout of pension plans, such as 401(k), 403(b), Section 457 plans, profit-sharing plans and IRAs. Don't forget to include income from potential inheritance, and profits that may come from things like selling your home for a less expensive one. See 239 Track Your Investments and 247 Plan Your Estate.

4 Estimate your retirement income sources. Retirement income comes from four main sources: Social Security benefits, pension and retirement accounts, personal savings and investments, and wages from income earned during retirement. Social Security benefits don't kick in until you're 62, and benefits increase if you wait until you're 65. If you do start receiving your benefits earlier, consider investing at least a portion of them.

5 Live modestly. If you work hard toward saving now, you'll achieve your goals of retiring sooner. It may mean making a few sacrifices, but it will pay off in the long run. See 15 Live With Less.

6 Maximize your tax-deferred and tax-free savings opportunities. Take advantage of employer-sponsored retirement plans such as 401(k), 403(b) and 457 plans. You wouldn't pass up free money, so be sure to fully fund any portion of a 401(k) that is being matched by your employer and max out your contribution if you can. If you have savings that exceed the maximum allowable

Tips

Even with limited resources, you can invest through other avenues such as mutual funds. The minimum investment requirement for 900 of the 10,000 funds tracked by Morningstar (morningstar .com) is $250 or less.

It helps to know just how big that check will be. Uncle Sam makes this easy. Check out the Social Security Administration site (ssa.gov).

Complete a retirement planning worksheet to figure out how much you need to save. Investment management firm T. Rowe Price (troweprice.com) has such information; click on "Individual Investing."

Save 10 to 15 percent of your pre-tax household income and the maximum possible in all the retirement planning options available to you. It reduces your taxes today and builds funds for your future.

Who Knew?

If you start investing $100 a month at age 25 in a retirement account that gains 10 percent a year, by 65 you'll have $632,000. But if you wait until you're 35, you'll only take away $226,000.

amount in your employer-sponsored retirement plan, your IRA is just the place to stash it.

7 Invest consistently. Saving a certain amount at scheduled intervals has become easier, in part due to defined-contribution options such as 401(k) plans. These are good start-up investments because your employer automatically deducts the money from your paycheck and often matches your contributions.

8 Fund your traditional or Roth IRA to its maximum. Thanks to recent changes in the tax code, the yearly contribution maximum is $3,000, with the maximum escalating to $5,000 in 2008. The Roth IRA also allows you to withdraw funds early without incurring a penalty—a definite plus when you consider that Social Security benefits may not kick in until your 60s, or later, if Congress pushes out the age limits.

9 Talk to an experienced financial planner about your goals and the best way to reach them. A good financial pro will be able to offer you a second opinion on your plans and offer suggestions on the best strategies for meeting your goals.

10 Take some risks and diversify your stock portfolio. That doesn't mean putting all your money into penny stocks, but it does mean having a greater percentage of your investments in higher-earning equities rather than the more cautious treasury and savings bonds that many people select as they get older. Look carefully at how much of your money goes into the stock of the company you work for. As any Enron employee will tell you, having the majority of your money in one asset can leave you dangerously undiversified.

11 Calculate how long it will take for your investment to double. To figure this out, divide the annual rate of return by 72. At a 7 percent return, your money will double in 10 years and quadruple in 20. Financial gurus call this "the rule of 72."

12 Consider pooling resources with siblings and other family members to buy long-term care insurance for your parents, if they might not be solvent enough to take care of themselves financially should they need elder care. Taking care of your parents can sap your ability to work full-time and can drain your savings.

13 Get your other paperwork in order. See 243 Create a Living Trust, 245 Execute a Power of Attorney, 247 Plan Your Estate and 244 Make a Will.

Rule of thumb: If you don't start saving until you're in your 40s, you'll need to set aside 20 percent of your gross income. If you wait until your 50s, your target will have to be 30 percent. As a last resort, you may have to sell your house and car, get a second job and reduce discretionary spending. The sooner you start saving, the easier it will be to reach your goals.

Somewhere in all of the paperwork you'll sign before you walk out the door of your job may be a form that asks whether you want your accumulated pension to come to you in one big chunk or in monthly payments. Talk this over with your accountant or financial adviser before signing.

Warning

Eliminate credit-card debt. It's the single biggest threat to an early retirement.

242 | Prepare a Prenuptial Agreement

No longer just for celebrities and the ultrarich, a prenuptial is becoming a typical part of planning a wedding. It is a legally binding agreement that describes how assets will be divided between the partners, should divorce or death occur. Consider it a checks-and-balances document that ensures financial well-being for the matrimonial set.

Steps

1 Determine whether you need a prenup. Some instances where one may be advisable include the following:

- You wish to protect your assets and/or those of your children from a prior marriage.
- You are a financially dependent parent.
- You are a business owner concerned about the fact that a spouse is effectively a silent partner in the business (this especially concerns people with professional practices and/or business partners).
- You separately own significant property in a state where a spouse is entitled to a share of income from that property.
- Your future spouse has significant premarital responsibilities, such as child support, alimony or tax obligations.
- You want a written record of the ownership of assets in order to avoid future confusion on the part of creditors or other family members.
- One of you is significantly wealthier than the other.

2 Open a discussion about the prenuptial agreement well in advance of the marriage date. Choose a time and a place to talk where both of you are comfortable. Be open, candid and direct. Listen to your spouse-to-be and invite ideas. Treat it as a collaborative process. Frame the whole concept of a prenup so that both parties feel they gain something from the agreement.

3 Find a good divorce or contracts lawyer to help craft a bulletproof prenuptial agreement. Be prepared to pay anywhere from a few hundred dollars to several thousand dollars for a detailed agreement involving many assets. The entire process should only take two or three weeks.

4 Detail all assets and liabilities and, if possible, any future inheritances.

5 Determine who pays any debts accumulated during the marriage.

6 Specify who gets the house(s) and how you will divide any bank accounts, insurance sums and investment income (including retirement assets)—in other words, who gets what in the event of death or divorce.

Tip

Make sure to draft a prenuptial agreement that is valid in all 50 states. A lawyer can help you with this. See 323 Plan a Wedding.

Warnings

Be careful how you craft your prenuptial agreement. The judge may void documents that are written in a way that can lead to divorce (for example, an agreement that gives a party motivation to leave the marriage for financial considerations).

Be wary of do-it-yourself online prenups. While some companies may be valid, others are fly-by-night firms that will do an inadequate job of writing up your agreement.

7 Note any gifts, assets and belongings that each party is bringing into the marriage.

8 Include an agreement on future alimony and spousal support before you exchange marriage vows.

9 Mention potential death benefits from life insurance, as well as how—and to whom—they will be distributed.

243 | Create a Living Trust

How can you safeguard the wealth that you've earned and pass it on to your heirs? One way is to establish a living trust. This financial arrangement gives someone you choose legal title to your property during your lifetime. This means he or she—not someone the state chooses—will take care of your property should you become incapacitated. Living trusts cost more to create, administer and manage than wills, but they also avoid probate costs, reduce estate taxes, and set up long-term property management. Plus they offer more privacy than wills, keeping your finances out of the courts.

Steps

1 Learn the difference between *regular* trusts and *living* trusts. A trust is a legal arrangement where you give control of your property to a trust and name a trustee and beneficiaries. A living trust differs from a regular trust in that it is created while you're alive, and it allows you to control the distribution of your estate and to transfer ownership of your property and assets into the trust. It also allows your beneficiaries to avoid probate. Many times, living trusts are irrevocable—once you give the money or asset away, you can't get it back.

2 Determine if a living trust is right for you. Consider one if your total estate is valued at $100,000 or more; if you will be subject to estate taxes; or if you have a complicated family situation, such as children from a previous marriage whom you wish to ensure receive their share of your estate. An estate attorney will help you figure out if a living trust is what you need. Key questions to ask include: Am I up to the comprehensive record-keeping duties that come with managing the trust? Do I want to give someone control over my estate if I become incapacitated? Is a will a better option for me?

3 Talk to an experienced estate-planning attorney or a financial adviser. You'll need a lawyer anyway, as most states require that attorneys draft living-trust documents. Ask your local bar association (abanet.org) for a list of reputable lawyers or contact

Tips

Read 244 Make a Will and 242 Prepare a Prenuptial Agreement.

Usually a living trust encompasses a will. (A living trust, however, is not the same as a living will.)

Any living-trust package should have a cancellation form and a copy of your contract or receipt. The receipt must include the date, name and address of the seller and should state that you have a right to cancel.

Check out SaveWealth.com for more information about living trusts.

Who Knew?

The trustor is the person(s) establishing the trust. The trustee controls the trust's assets, and can be the same person(s) as the trustor. The beneficiaries are those heirs named by the trustor who will inherit assets after the trustor passes away.

Continued on next page

LegalMatch.net. When you interview candidates, look for someone with whom you'll feel comfortable working and whose rates are reasonable. Always have the attorney write out any agreements for services and fees.

4 Protect your family's privacy by avoiding probate. Probate is a legal process where a deceased person's will is filed with the local court, and only after all debts are paid off are any remaining assets and property distributed. Probate costs can range from 2 to 4 percent of the total value of your estate. If your estate comes before a judge in court, your will becomes public, and anyone can inspect it. Keep your affairs private with a living trust, and help your loved ones avoid this costly, time-consuming process.

5 Fund your living trust sufficiently. You can use numerous sources, including bank accounts, bonds, stocks, real estate, personal property and life insurance. You simply need to ensure that the title on these assets is retitled with the name of your trust. Also ensure that you transfer any property you own from your name to the trust's name. An estate-planning specialist, ideally a lawyer or a financial adviser, will be able to walk you through it.

Warnings

The AARP does not endorse specific living trust plans. Anyone claiming to have AARP-endorsement is spinning a yarn.

Watch out for scam artists. Check out anyone who claims to be selling estate-planning tools or making arrangements at prices far lower than standard attorney fees. Start by contacting the Better Business Bureau (bbb.org).

244 | Make a Will

Let's face it, it's never pleasant to think about preparing for your death. Unfortunately, not enough Americans do—about half die without a will. Not having a will means the courts distribute your property according to state laws. Protect your family members and assets with a will, and eliminate the stress your loved ones may face if they have to handle your finances without one.

Tips

The number of witnesses required varies by state. A witness should not be a beneficiary on the will.

Be aware that some states seal your safe-deposit box upon death. You can make legal arrangements with a lawyer to restrict the sealing process while you're still alive. But if not, the state can step in while your assets are in probate court. Make sure your loved ones know where to find the will. Leave a copy of it with a note indicating where the original is located (with your attorney).

Steps

1 Consult with an estate-planning attorney to see if you need a simple will or a living trust (read 243 Create a Living Trust). You can write your own, but it may be more easily contested if a disgruntled family member wants to fight it.

2 Check out software such as Nolo Press's Willmaker (nolo.com). In addition to wills, it provides everything necessary to make living trusts, health care directives and financial powers of attorney. (It also tells you when you need professional help.)

3 Organize, organize, organize. Read 295 Make Your Final Arrangements and start working through the details. Outline your objectives, inventory your assets, estimate your outstanding debts, and prepare a list of family members and other beneficiaries. Clearly state everyone's relationship to you in the will. Keep

in mind that you can address items not specifically mentioned in the will with a catchall phrase that states, "I give the remainder of my estate to (name of beneficiary)." Otherwise these items will be distributed in accordance to state law.

4 Include the following elements in your will:

- Your name and place of residence.

- A brief description of your assets. See 232 Organize Important Documents.

- The names of your spouse or partner, children and other beneficiaries, such as charities or friends, as well as alternate beneficiaries in the event that a beneficiary dies before you do. See 236 Buy Life Insurance.

- Specific gifts (car, residence); establishment of trusts, if desired; cancellation of debts owed to you, if desired.

- The name of an executor to manage the estate.

- The name of your children's guardian, as well as an alternative guardian, in the event that your first choice is unable or unwilling to act in that capacity.

- Your notarized signature and witnesses' signatures.

5 Name a guardian for your children. A surviving parent usually assumes the role of sole guardian, but if you are a single parent or if your spouse, parents or family members will not be able to care for your children, name a guardian. He or she must be at least 18 years old.

6 Name an executor to oversee the distribution of your assets as stipulated in your will. Choose a family member, a trusted friend or an attorney. A trust company named as executor can keep your will and execute your wishes after your death.

7 Update your will when necessary. A change in marital status, the birth of a child or moving to a new state should prompt you to review your will. After drawing up any new will, destroy the old one.

8 Consider a living will. This lets your loved ones know what type of care you wish to receive in the event that you become terminally ill. It kicks in when you can no longer express your wishes yourself. Give your family members a signed copy.

Who Knew?

Executors pay valid creditors and taxes; notify the Social Security Administration and other agencies and companies of the death; cancel credit cards and subscriptions; and distribute assets according to the will.

Get ready to pay Uncle Sam. Federal estate taxes are generally due when the net taxable estate is worth more than $850,000 (escalating to $1 million by 2006). Reduce your income (and potential estate tax) by giving gifts during your lifetime. You can also purchase life-insurance policies to pay taxes. Discuss details with an attorney.

245 | Execute a Power of Attorney

If an accident or illness incapacitates you to the extent that you can't make important decisions for yourself, these decisions may instead be made by the courts, the health-care system or financial-service providers. Their rulings may differ drastically from your own wishes. To protect yourself and your family in any contingency, draft a power of attorney—a legal document that allows the people closest to you to make decisions on your behalf in the event that you can't.

Steps

1 Select someone you trust and who has your best interests in mind to act as your power of attorney. Typical charges include your spouse or partner, sibling, adult child or parent. Keep in mind that this person may have access to your bank account, Social Security checks and investment portfolio.

2 Understand the range of decisions someone with POA is authorized to make. He or she can buy or sell your real estate, manage your property, conduct your banking transactions, invest your money, make legal claims and conduct litigation, make gifts on your behalf, and attend to tax and retirement matters.

3 Be clear about the differences between a *durable power of attorney* (DPOA) and a *limited power of attorney* (LPOA). A DPOA carries more authority than an LPOA because it goes into effect if you are not capable of making decisions on your own due to illness or long-term absence, and it carries no specific time frame. It is effective from the date of the document's execution. An LPOA carries less authority and is used for specific needs in nonhealth situations, such as trading authority on an investment while you're out of the country.

4 Appoint an estate or elder-law attorney to take over if you can't identify an appropriate person to act as your power of attorney.

5 Consult an estate-planning attorney or financial adviser to help you fully understand and execute your power of attorney. He or she can answer questions about the powers you are delegating, provide counsel on whom you should choose as your power of attorney, outline this person's obligations, and ensure that your power of attorney meets legal requirements and is correctly executed.

6 Contact the Social Security Administration (ssa.gov) with your new power-of-attorney information.

Tips

Anyone given power of attorney must be a legal adult (at least 18 years of age).

You can always revoke or change your power of attorney if he or she has behaved dishonestly or inappropriately, or if a better candidate has entered the picture (such as a new spouse or a child who reaches adulthood).

Who Knew?

You can appoint more than one DPOA, for example, an estate-planning attorney and a financial adviser.

One of the most important things you can do to help your aging parents is assist in planning their estate. This will clarify their wishes and ensure that they receive the best care possible without placing a heavy financial burden on you and the rest of your family.

Steps

1 Read 247 Plan Your Estate to get the lay of the land. Open up a conversation with your parents. Keep it low-key and relaxed. Start by asking them who should look after their affairs in the event of any medical emergencies. That may pave the way for a dialogue on your parents' financial affairs. If not, spell out the chaos and confusion that could result from not addressing the issue. Be patient, be respectful, and have this conversation in several sessions if necessary to smooth feathers. At a minimum, get names and contact information for their attorney, financial planner, CPA and bankers.

2 Designate a point person for your parents' health-care affairs. Ideally this person is designated by your parents, is objective, and has your parents' best interests in mind. It could be you, a sibling, a family friend or one of their trusted confidants.

3 Have a backup plan. In the event that an estate designee isn't on hand to make a decision, select a second person—ideally one who is equally familiar with your parents' situation.

4 Discuss drafting a living will. Assure them that this document forces medical providers to honor their personal medical choices in the event of a debilitating condition, such as a terminal illness or coma, when they are no longer able to speak for themselves. See 294 Arrange Hospice Care.

5 Designate someone to handle their financial and business affairs. Even if a parent is ill or otherwise incapacitated, the bills don't stop coming in. One option is to draft a durable power of attorney. See 245 Execute a Power of Attorney.

6 Join forces with your siblings or other family members to decide your parents' fate if they have passed the point where they can make their own decisions. Conduct good due diligence beforehand when researching the costs of home care, assisted living, retirement homes and other items associated with long-term health care. See Warning.

7 Craft your parents' estate plan in a way that passes on assets to heirs as easily as possible. A good estate-planning attorney can help. The National Academy of Elder Law Attorneys (naela.org) specializes in parental estates.

Tips

Some estate plans may also be tailor-made for a living trust. That way, if a parent becomes ill or incapacitated, the designated trustee can take over and administer your parent's financial affairs. See 243 Create a Living Trust.

See 295 Make Your Final Arrangements and 349 Plan a Funeral According to Custom.

Who Knew?

If no one is designated, a family member can take over. This scenario is legit in the eyes of the law, absent another guardian. The designee can ensure that appropriate decisions will be made when the parent or parents cannot do so.

Warning

Medicare does not cover long-term care, so you'll have to find long-term health-care options on your own. Encourage parents to purchase long-term health-care insurance if you feel not doing so could eat their entire savings. Or pitch in with your siblings and pay the premiums. Review 237 Choose a Health Insurance Plan.

From castle to condo, your home (together with other assets) is your estate. And as with any asset you own, you have to protect it from taxes, legal claims and other creatures of the night. The best way to do that is by crafting an estate plan that enables you to plan the distribution of your financial assets while you're still alive and kicking, so that after you die, your estate passes on to the people you choose—not to whomever a probate court judge chooses.

Steps

1 Before you launch your estate-planning campaign, take a financial inventory of all your assets—including real-estate and investment holdings, life insurance, household items, bank accounts—and create a record (see 241 Plan for Retirement). Keep a copy of your financial documents in a secure place, like a home safe or a safe-deposit box.

2 Create a net worth statement and update it each year. The statement shows a detailed list of what your assets are, where they are located, and their current value. Create a will and/or living trust to make life much easier for your survivors after you die. Passing on without a will (termed "in testate") spells trouble for those left behind: It can boost legal costs, trigger family squabbles, and leave your loved ones with no control over your assets. Drafting a well-designed power-of-attorney document is also a good idea. See 243 Create a Living Trust, 244 Make a Will and 245 Execute a Power of Attorney.

3 Read 295 Make Your Final Arrangements. Be candid with your family and professional advisers. Keep them in the loop as you plan your estate. Don't assume they'll know how you want your estate distributed.

4 Organize and file key financial documents, such as house deeds, insurance policies and investment documents. Make sure that someone—your spouse, a lawyer, a financial adviser—knows where they are. See 232 Organize Important Documents.

5 Review and update your life-insurance program regularly. Far and away, life insurance is the most cost-effective way to create the cash to pay bills and provide income. (Many insurance policies are "whole life" policies or are packaged in the form of annuities, and can generate investment income that bears watching. See 236 Buy Life Insurance.) If you have an insurance policy, make sure to name both a primary and a contingent beneficiary. Failure to do so could slow payment of insurance money due to your estate.

6 Arrange for legal, accounting and financial advisers to help your surviving family members manage your assets and do post-mortem tax planning.

Tips

Consult a financial adviser or estate-planning attorney.

Note that federal IRS estate-planning tax exemptions will rise from $1.5 million in 2004 to $3.5 million in 2009.

Keep some assets liquid (easily transferable to cash) so your family has cash immediately available to pay bills upon your death.

Who Knew?

Reduce your estate-planning tax burden by gifting up to $11,000 (or $22,000 with your spouse) to any individual you choose on an annual basis. The gift is tax-free and you can gift as many people as you want each year.

Also draft an income statement showing all current income sources and a list of the types of income and amounts that will continue after your death. File it along with a copy of your will.

Warning

If you don't keep estate-planning paperwork up to date, you leave yourself liable to expired insurance or other financial calamities.

Too often young adults learn about debt and the importance of establishing good credit the hard way—by digging themselves out of a hole. Instill the value of saving versus spending and you'll help your child grow up to be a fiscally responsible adult.

Steps

1. Examine your own attitudes and habits about money. Parents are good at preaching, but if you repeatedly waste money, that's what your kids are learning. If you talk about wanting a new digital camera and the next day you run out and buy one, you've sent the message that you can get whatever you want whenever you want it. If, on the other hand, you set up a savings plan to pay for a camera, your kids get a valuable lesson in deciding whether something is important enough to wait for. And when they see you socking money away for it, you've sewn the seeds of wise money management and delayed gratification.

2. Set a good example by creating a spending plan with your spouse. Show kids that setting up a budget doesn't have to be complicated. First, pay yourself: Put aside money to meet your financial goals (savings, emergencies). Then pay your bills. Now divide up what's left to cover food and other necessities—and don't spend more than that. See 226 Set Up a Budget and 228 Design a Savings Plan.

3. Invite your children to participate in financial discussions. When kids are old enough, go ahead and show them how your income gets divvied up into mortgage, food, taxes, bills and clothes. Talk about your own goals—eliminating debt or saving for big-ticket items like a new car, college or a vacation—to prompt contemplation of their own savings goals.

4. Give your kids a weekly allowance. This is money just for being part of the family and taking care of basics, such as picking up toys, making beds and not leaving towels on the bathroom floor. A dollar for every year of age is a good amount. Give kids total control over how they spend their allowance. The whole point is to let them learn from their mistakes.

5. Create opportunities for older children to earn additional money with jobs such as washing the car and mowing the lawn. This is the time to instill appreciation for a job well done and getting paid for your efforts. Teach them that they can get what they want through hard work—not because they are entitled to it.

6. Set up a checking account and give teens a lump sum of money to cover all nonbasic expenses—gas, insurance, clothing, shoes, entertainment, gifts, video games, eating out—for a month. Gradually build up to six months as they gain confidence and competence at living within a budget.

Tips

Give allowance as you would a paycheck: the same amount at the same time every week.

When you go on vacation, give each child a set amount of money to pay for all the extras they want. They'll need to make their cash last the whole trip—and you won't have to hear "Oh, pleeeeeeease!!" (See 406 Plan a Trip with Children.)

Who Knew?

Teach kids that credit-card companies aren't their friend—they're in the business of making money. Credit cards can help you develop good credit and certainly are convenient. If you don't use them wisely and pay them off every month, however, you give control over your life to someone else.

Help your children divide their allowance into long- and short-term savings (about 25 to 35 percent) and charity (10 percent), with the rest for spending. They can pick any charity to support, such as a food bank, an animal hospital or whatever touches their heart.

Kids who feel entitled often have parents who taught them they can have whatever they want whenever they want it. Say "no" and stand firm: They'll still love you and will learn the value of delayed gratification.

GANIZE YOUR CONTACTS • GET RID OF WHAT YOU DON'T WANT • SAY NO WITHOUT FEELING GUILTY • BALANCE HOME AND WORK • L
BAIN • SCHEDULE TELEVISION WATCHING • DESIGN A HEALTHY LIFESTYLE • PLAN TO AVOID JUNK FOOD • CHOOSE A WEIGHT LOSS PLA
EET AN ONLINE DATE • PLAN THE PERFECT DATE • MASTERMIND A BREAKUP • PLAN YOUR SOCIAL CALENDAR • MEET MR. OR MS. RIGH
ORT YOUR SOCK DRAWER • RETURN RENTALS ON TIME • TAKE CONTROL OF YOUR JUNK DRAWER • ORGANIZE THE MEDICINE CABINET
AR CLEAN AND ORDERLY • DEAL WITH A PACK RAT • SELL STUFF ONLINE • ORGANIZE YOUR BOOKSHELVES • CATEGORIZE NEWSPAPER
VE BETTER THROUGH LABELING • ORGANIZE JEWELRY • PLAN YOUR DREAM KITCHEN • CONQUER YOUR CLOSETS • ORGANIZE THE LIN
RGANIZE SPRING CLEANING • KEEP THE FAMILY ROOM ORGANIZED • SET UP A BATHROOM SCHEDULE • ORGANIZE BATHROOMS • ORG
RGANIZE KIDS' ROOMS • ORGANIZE SPORTS EQUIPMENT • ORGANIZE KIDS' PLAY SPACES • SAFEGUARD YOUR HOME AGAINST ALLERG
OUSE • USE HOME DESIGN AND PLANNING SOFTWARE • ESTABLISH YOUR HOME'S SPACE PLAN • INCORPORATE UNIVERSAL DESIGN P
IE BASEMENT • ORGANIZE THE GARAGE • ORGANIZE A TOOLBOX • SET UP A WOODSHOP • ORGANIZE YOUR WINE COLLECTION • PLAN
TUDIO OR SMALL APARTMENT • MANAGE WARRANTY DOCUMENTS • MANAGE HOME-IMPROVEMENT PAPERWORK • MERGE TWO HOUS
RGANIC VEGETABLE GARDEN • PLANT A KITCHEN HERB GARDEN • PLAN A BUTTERFLY GARDEN • DESIGN A BIRD GARDEN • DESIGN A G
ORGANIZE GARDENING TOOLS • ADD A POTTING BENCH TO A YARD • SCHEDULE FRUIT TREE MAINTENANCE • LAY OUT A SPRINKLER S
ESIGN A GARDEN PATH • SET UP A COMPOST SYSTEM • WINTERIZE PLANTS • SCHEDULE YARD WORK • STORE ANYTHING • STORE BU
ND HOBBY MATERIALS • ORGANIZE ART SUPPLIES • ORGANIZE GIFT WRAP AND SEASONAL DECORATIONS • ORGANIZE KIDS' SCHOOLW
OUR WEDDING DRESS AND OTHER TEXTILES • STORE A FUR COAT • STORE BICYCLES AND GEAR • STORE SKI GEAR • ORGANIZE CAMP
HICH COLLEGE IS RIGHT FOR YOU • GET INTO A TOP COLLEGE OR UNIVERSITY • ACE THE COLLEGE ADMISSIONS TESTS • ORGANIZE Y
AW SCHOOL • PREPARE FOR THE BAR EXAM • GET A DEGREE WHILE YOU'RE WORKING • WORK AT HOME WITH KIDS • GO BACK TO WO
RGANIZE YOUR JOB SEARCH • PREPARE FOR A CAREER CHANGE • OPEN A RESTAURANT • BECOME A PHYSICIST • BECOME A CONCE
EALITY-SHOW CONCEPT • BECOME A TALK-SHOW HOST • BECOME A PHOTOJOURNALIST • BECOME A MOVIE DIRECTOR • BECOME A M
LING SYSTEM • ORGANIZE YOUR BRIEFCASE • ORGANIZE YOUR DESK • ORGANIZE YOUR WORKDAY • GET A HANDLE ON E-MAIL • ORG
ALARY REVIEW • CLIMB THE CORPORATE LADDER EFFECTIVELY • ADD A WORKSPACE TO ANY ROOM • ORGANIZE A HOME OFFICE • OF
RAVEL • WRITE A BUSINESS PLAN • SET UP A NEW BUSINESS • CREATE A MARKETING PLAN • AMASS A REAL-ESTATE EMPIRE • POLISH
MPLOYEE • FIRE AN EMPLOYEE • PASS ON A FAMILY BUSINESS • STAY ON TOP OF YOUR SALES GAME • RESTRUCTURE A COMPANY TO
EFEND AGAINST A HOSTILE TAKEOVER • ORGANIZE YOUR OFFICE FOR A MOVE • PREPARE YOUR BUSINESS FOR THE UNTHINKABLE • I
REPARE YOUR TAXES • ORGANIZE A LOAN APPLICATION • ORGANIZE IMPORTANT DOCUMENTS • SAVE FOR PRIVATE SCHOOLING • ORG
LUB • TRACK YOUR INVESTMENTS • SURVIVE BANKRUPTCY • PLAN FOR RETIREMENT • PREPARE A PRENUPTIAL AGREEMENT • CREAT
ONEY • PLAN YOUR FAMILY • BUDGET FOR A NEW BABY • ORCHESTRATE THE PERFECT CONCEPTION • PLAN FOR ARTIFICIAL INSEMIN
EAVE • ORDER BABY ANNOUNCEMENTS • ORGANIZE AN INTERNATIONAL ADOPTION • FOSTER A CHILD • ORGANIZE YOUR LIFE AS A N
OORDINATE A FAMILY CALENDAR • PLAN FAMILY MEETINGS • ORGANIZE HOME SYSTEMS FOR ADD • PREPARE FOR A NEW CAT OR DO
ACK-TO-SCHOOL • WIN THE HOMEWORK WARS • PLAN A FIELD TRIP • PLAN YOUR CHILD'S ACTIVITIES • PLAN YOUR CHILDREN'S SUM
NLINE • ORGANIZE A GENEALOGICAL SEARCH • PREPARE FOR YOUR CHILD'S DEPARTURE FOR COLLEGE • ORGANIZE YOUR EMPTY N
LDERLY PARENTS' CARE • PREPARE FOR THE DEATH OF A SPOUSE • HELP YOUR ELDERLY PARENTS MOVE • ORGANIZE A HOME MEDIC
TORE TRIPS • SET UP ONLINE GROCERY SHOPPING • ORGANIZE RECIPES AND COOKBOOKS • PLAN THEME MENUS • CREATE EFFECT
EFRIGERATOR AND FREEZER • ORGANIZE CUTLERY AND KITCHEN TOOLS • ORGANIZE CUPBOARDS AND DRAWERS • ORGANIZE THE R
UNCHES FOR KIDS • PLAN PARTY FOODS AHEAD • THROW A DINNER PARTY • FINISH DINNER ON TIME • PULL OFF A LAST-MINUTE PAR
LTIMATE WEDDING CHECKLIST • BUDGET FOR A WEDDING • FIND THE PERFECT WEDDING RING • PLAN AN ELOPEMENT • SET UP A BA
ONOR • EXECUTE BEST MAN DUTIES • HIRE A BAND • HIRE A BARTENDER • PLAN A SHOWER • ORGANIZE THE REHEARSAL DINNER •
UCCESSFUL SLUMBER PARTY • PLAN A BAR OR BAT MITZVAH • PLAN A QUINCEAÑERA • PLAN A RETIREMENT PARTY • PLAN A FUNER
ANUKKAH PARTY • ORGANIZE A HOLIDAY CRAFT PARTY • PLAN TO SPEND CHRISTMAS SOLO • PLAN THE PERFECT HOLIDAY GIFT EXC
HE HOLIDAYS • STICK TO YOUR NEW YEAR'S RESOLUTIONS • PLAN THE PERFECT NEW YEAR'S EVE • PLAN A SEDER • PLAN A SPECIA
OOD TREE • ORGANIZE A BICYCLE SCAVENGER HUNT • RUN A SPORTS TOURNAMENT • PUBLICIZE AN EVENT • PLAN AN ORGANIZATI
LAN A CONCERT IN THE PARK • ORGANIZE AN INTERNATIONAL CONCERT TOUR • ORGANIZE A FILM FESTIVAL • PLAN A FUND-RAISIN
BUILD A COMMUNITY PLAY STRUCTURE • THROW A BLOCK PARTY • SET UP A NEIGHBORHOOD WATCH • CREATE AN EVACUATION PL
RGANIZE A PROTEST OR MARCH • FIGHT CITY HALL • ORGANIZE A BOYCOTT • ORGANIZE A CLASS ACTION LAWSUIT • MANAGE GRO
CHOOL IN A THIRD WORLD COUNTRY • PLAN A TRIP • PLAN A TRIP WITH CHILDREN • TRAVEL WITH TEENS • BOOK AIRLINE TICKETS •
OTORCYCLE TRIP • PLAN A TRAIN TRIP IN THE UNITED STATES • RIDE THE RAILS ABROAD • PREPARE A VACATION COUNTDOWN CHE
UGGAGE • LOAD A BACKPACK PROPERLY • PLAN AN ELDERHOSTEL TRIP • ORGANIZE AN RV VACATION • PLAN A TRIP WITH AGING PA
IDELY DIFFERENT PEOPLE • PLAN SPRING BREAK • PLAN AN OVERNIGHT GETAWAY WITH YOUR SPOUSE • PLAN A VACATION SEPARA
OLITICALLY UNSTABLE REGION • GET TRAVEL INSURANCE • GET IMMUNIZATIONS FOR TRAVELING • BOOK AN ADVENTURE VACATION
LAN A FISHING TRIP TO ALASKA • PACK FOR A CAMPING TRIP • LEAD A BACKPACK TRIP • HIKE A FAMOUS TRAIL • PLAN A TOUR OF T
NGLISH CANAL TRIP • PLAN A CROSS-COUNTRY AIRPLANE VOYAGE • PLAN THE PERFECT DAY ABROAD • PLAN A VISIT TO THE LOUV
LAN • PREPARE FOR AN ACT OF GOD • ASSEMBLE EMERGENCY KITS • PREPARE FOR SURGERY • PLAN YOUR RECOVERY • SURVIVE
EING LOST • CONDUCT A SEARCH AND RESCUE OPERATION • PLAN AN INVASION • SURVIVE A POLITICAL COUP • PLAN FOR A TERRO
ECOME THE PRESIDENT OF THE UNITED STATES • WIN AN ACADEMY AWARD • BECOME AN OLYMPIAN • TRAIN FOR A MAJOR ATHLET

Family Affairs

249 | Plan Your Family

It may take a village to raise a child, but it's generally just the parents who are involved in the planning stages. Like every other major life decision, the more thought and planning that go into addressing issues about raising children, the better off your entire family will be.

Steps

1 Evaluate your and your partner's lifestyle for kid compatibility. Workaholics are an asset in the office, but a liability when it comes to spending time with your little one. Discuss values and expectations as well as ways to adjust workloads and travel schedules to bring your focus and energy back home.

2 Try to consciously address feelings of ambivalence about parenthood before age 30. Women and men who start seriously trying until their late 30s often have waited too long. See 251 Orchestrate the Perfect Conception, 252 Plan for Artificial Insemination and 253 Prepare for an In Vitro Fertilization.

3 Start socking money away in savings, money market accounts or whatever gives you the best return. That cute little bottom will completely change your bottom line (see 250 Budget for a New Baby). And it's not too early to think about how to finance private schools—or even college. See 233 Save for Private Schooling and 235 Plan for College Costs.

4 Make sure that your relationship is ready and that both of you want to start a family. Check out what each of you expects from the other after the baby comes. Does the working parent expect to pat the baby and have a glass of wine every night while the stay-at-home parent takes care of the child? Who will get up to do the feedings? How will you handle the stress and conflicts of two very different styles of jobs? If either of you is unsure, resolve these issues in counseling well before you start trying.

5 Cultivate a good support system and practice asking for help. Ideally, you'll want friends who are going through the same thing and whom you can ask questions of, friends to help you install the car seat the first time, friends who will talk to you even in the middle of the night when the baby is crying and you just cannot take it anymore.

6 Discuss what happens after the baby comes. How long a maternity leave will you plan for? Will one of you stay home full-time and care for the baby? How do you choose that person? How will you juggle work schedules if both of you return to work? See 256 Set Up Maternity or Paternity Leave.

7 Start looking at day-care options if neither parent will be staying home. Many of the good programs have waiting lists. See 263 Arrange Quality Child Care.

Tips

Fine-tune communication skills with your partner. Where you may have hours or days to discuss and resolve issues now, after the baby comes it'll be only a few moments here and there.

Make a move to bigger digs if that's desirable. Other attractive amenities include a backyard, good schools and a safe neighborhood.

Who Knew?

A good way to approach parenting is to understand that nothing will ever be the same again. Your relationship with your spouse, your free time, the way you view the world, your relationship to your work—all will be completely different. If you can accept this fundamental truth rather than fight it, you'll be much better off—and so will your kid.

Going from lovers to parents is the single biggest transition any couple goes through. Ease the inevitable friction by discussing some of the harsh realities—midnight feedings, extreme fatigue, changing sexual desire and financial issues—before they become unmanageably difficult.

Children might be priceless, but raising them certainly isn't. A recent survey by the U.S. Department of Agriculture estimated that the cost of raising a child from birth to age 17 is a quarter million dollars for a middle-income family. But you don't have to be a millionaire to raise a family—you just have to create a budget and stick to it.

Steps

1 Get familiar with your spending patterns. See 228 Design a Savings Plan and 227 Get Out of Debt, then clean up your financial act before the new arrival.

2 Ask friends with children what various pieces of baby gear and other necessities cost. See 254 Prepare for a New Baby.

3 Create a list of your current, prebaby expenses (see 226 Set Up a Budget). Once you learn where your money is going, you'll be able to figure out how much of it you can save and reallocate toward baby expenses. If you need to use fertility services such as a sperm bank or in vitro fertilization, add those costs to the equation. See 252 Plan for Artificial Insemination and 253 Prepare for an In Vitro Fertilization.

4 Assume that your household expenses will rise after having your baby, and adjust your budget accordingly. Include essentials like diapers, baby food, clothing, doctor visits, prescription drugs and medicine. Initially, set aside about $200 extra for household bills, and adjust that figure upward as you get a better handle on your monthly budget with baby in tow.

5 Act early to find child care, since many day-care centers have waiting lists. Take the time to do your homework and find the right one for your child and your budget without rushing. See 263 Arrange Quality Child Care.

6 Make sure your home is energy efficient. Conserve water and energy, replace inefficient furnaces and water heaters, and bolster insulation. These measures will help keep utility bills in check despite the larger household.

7 Be cost-conscious about baby clothes. Enjoy the largesse of friends and relatives who happily pass on their children's outgrown clothes. Buy used kids' clothes at deep discounts. Check out manufacturer outlets for bargain buys, and shop during sales and inventory markdowns. See 255 Organize Your Maternity Wardrobe.

8 Start your baby's college fund now. By socking away as little as $50 per month, you can build up a formidable college fund by the time your child reaches 18 years of age. See 235 Plan for College Costs.

Tips

Save for school. Any extra money that isn't needed for bills, debts or regular expenses should be added to savings for your child's schooling.

Leave that convertible on the lot and opt for a solid, dependable, safe family car. (Sigh.)

Factor in one-time charges for essentials like a car seat, a crib, a changing table, a stroller and maybe a new coat of paint in the nursery.

For a breakdown of average prices for baby items, check out surebaby.com/costs.php.

Who Knew?

Food is one of the biggest chunks in your budget. Take measures to reduce food spending—less eating out, more shopping the warehouse stores—to improve your bottom line.

Talk to your employer's human resources person before your baby is born and ask about how your benefits package will change.

Add your baby to your health insurance as soon as he or she is born—it's not automatic.

251 Orchestrate the Perfect Conception

When it comes to making babies, timing is everything. While it might seem like there's nothing more natural than conceiving a child, the reality often ends up being quite a bit more complicated. There's a lot more to consider than just when and where to dim the lights and let the games begin. And there are lots of ways to achieve success, too.

Steps

Staying healthy

1 Get a physical to determine your baseline health. Make a list of questions and issues for your doctor. Discuss any prescription or over-the-counter medication, including vitamins and supplements either of you is taking, to determine if the medication is safe.

2 Review all medical options with your OB-GYN if you need to take the high-tech route. Investigate sperm banks (see 252 Plan for Artificial Insemination). Make an appointment with a fertility or in vitro specialist (see 253 Prepare for an In Vitro Fertilization).

3 Start taking prenatal vitamins well before you conceive and during early pregnancy. Folic acid helps prevent birth defects such as spina bifida, but it works only if taken before and during the first few weeks of pregnancy.

4 Stop smoking—both of you! In addition to being the most preventable cause of babies with low birth weight, smoking is also suspected of contributing to sudden infant death syndrome (SIDS). Smoking can decrease sperm count in men and increase the risk of miscarriage and stillbirth in women.

5 Start exercising regularly if you don't already—but have your doctor sign off on your workout plan first (see 25 Design Your Workout Schedule). You'll build flexibility, reduce stress, increase muscle tone, strength and stamina (a real asset during labor), and protect against back pain in pregnancy.

6 Eat like a mom-to-be. Lay off the junk, especially anything with saturated fats. Eat lots of leafy greens and foods high in calcium, potassium and iron, and low in salt and sugar. See 23 Plan to Avoid Junk Food.

7 Be very clear on this: If you're drinking alcohol or taking recreational drugs, your baby will be, too. Don't. These drugs are passed to the baby through the placenta and adversely affect the baby's development.

8 Cut back on caffeine. Some studies have associated it with increased chance of miscarriage. That daily latte is not your only source of caffeine. Check the labels on tea, soft drinks and chocolate as well.

9 Get lots of sleep and investigate ways to reduce stress in general. Burning the midnight oil is not a fertility-enhancing scenario—

Tips

Find out whether you need any prebaby immunizations, such as a rubella vaccine. If not, you should receive the vaccine at least three months prior to conception.

Talk to your doctor or midwife about ways to enhance your fertility and track your cycle.

After The Act, some doctors recommend propping your hips up on a small pillow and lying still for a minimum 20 minutes to give the sperm time to swim upstream.

See 261 Prepare for Childbirth.

finalize big projects at work, plan a romantic vacation, book a massage at a bed and breakfast. A rested, relaxed body is more likely to conceive than one that is fatigued and stressed out.

10 Investigate all the ways of tracking your cycle, from taking your temperature to checking your mucus. Your body is a gold mine of information; the more you know, the better. Make a chart and start graphing your basal body temperature six months ahead of the ideal conception date to predict when ovulation occurs. Progesterone levels rise as soon as the egg is released, typically resulting in a .5 degree temperature increase.

11 Fine-tune your timing with an ovulation predictor kit. These at-home tests indicate imminent ovulation by showing hormone surges present in the urine.

12 Consider the weather when you're penciling in prime conception dates. Do you really want to be nine months pregnant in August with 100 percent humidity?

13 Count backward to avoid a Christmas birth, for example, or to plan a baby for Thanksgiving when all the relatives are in town anyway. If you have a seasonal job, time your baby's birth for the beginning of the off-season to maximize your maternity leave.

14 Avoid the school-age cutoff date. Children with early fall birth-days end up being either the oldest or youngest in their class because of the September birthday cutoff at many schools.

15 Look at upcoming workloads for both parents. Plan around any major projects, deadlines or trips.

Choosing the gender

1 Increase your chances of getting the gender you want by carefully timing the deed itself. Bear in mind that fresh sperm are viable up to 72 hours inside a woman's body, but frozen sperm peter out after only 24 hours. Optimize your chances of having a boy by having sex or inseminating just a few hours before ovulation. Faster (but shorter-lived) male sperm will be in place when the egg releases. Go for a girl by having sex or inseminating well ahead of ovulation so that the slower female sperm, having out-lived their male counterparts, are in prime fertilizing position.

2 Use the latest technology to aid your chances of selecting a specific gender. When semen is centrifugally spun, it causes a greater number of the X-chromosome (female) sperm to sink to the bottom and the Y-chromosome (male) sperm to float to the top. The preferred sperm is then injected into the uterus.

3 Research an in vitro fertilization technique called *preimplantation genetic diagnosis.* Embryos are created outside the womb, then tested for gender. This method was originally designed to aid couples at risk of having children with inherited gender-specific genetic diseases.

Who Knew?

In order to conceive quickly, some doctors advise stopping birth control pills and having at least three regular periods before you begin trying to conceive.

After age 35, fertility for both men and women starts to decline dramatically, and unfortunately chances of genetic problems for the baby increase as well.

Warning

Women who smoke are 50 to 70 percent more likely than nonsmokers to have a child with a cleft lip and palate.

Tracking basal body temperature doesn't work for many women, particularly those with irregular sleep cycles.

For infertile couples or women choosing to have a baby without a male partner (or on their own), artificial insemination can get the job done. Relatively inexpensive and noninvasive, this is the process of injecting sperm directly into the woman's vagina (an ICI or intracervical insemination) or uterus (IUI or intrauterine insemination). While these methods are not exactly romantic, the wriggling, bright-eyed results are a dream come true.

Steps

1 Talk to your OB-GYN about the procedure's costs, details and any other issues, including guarantees. Get a referral to a fertility doctor if necessary. Ask friends and family for recommendations.

2 Investigate sperm banks (if necessary). Ask your OB-GYN for recommendations, search online and talk to friends or family who have gone through the same thing. Make a list of questions you have and, if you cannot find the answers on the bank's site, call the bank directly.

3 Be aware that sperm is prepared differently for the two different procedures. You'll need to choose IUI or ICI at the time you place your order with the bank.

4 Consider asking someone you know to be a donor if it's a priority that you know your child's father. Tread extremely carefully with a known donor. This scenario has "emotional minefield" written all over it. People's feelings for the baby can change drastically after the birth. There is enormous potential for heartache, distress—even litigation—but also for extraordinarily joyful and creative family connections between all parties.

5 Determine when you ovulate (see 251 Orchestrate the Perfect Conception). If the do-it-yourself route doesn't deliver the goods, talk to your OB-GYN, who may perform blood tests and/or a sonogram to determine precisely when ovulation will occur. Fertility drugs may be called for. Research your options.

6 Choose ICI if you prefer the lowest-tech approach. This procedure—think turkey baster here—can be done at home by yourself, a partner, midwife or close (and about to get closer) friend. The sperm, either fresh or frozen (warmed to body temperature), is simply squirted into the mom-to-be.

7 Opt for an IUI if you need to optimize both time and money. There is a greater success ratio with IUI than ICI inseminations, although they are more expensive. Schedule an appointment for the procedure with your OB-GYN or midwife just before ovulation.

Tips

Plan to be on a flexible schedule. Both parties must be able to drop everything and go to the doctor's office when the moment is right.

Ask your insurance company exactly what procedures are covered. Then check your bank account to confirm that you can cover the costs without blowing your future kid's college fund.

For more information, contact the American Society for Reproductive Medicine (asrm.org).

Who Knew?

Success rate per try (without fertility drugs) is about 4 percent with IUI alone. Adding fertility drugs can raise the chance of success to 7 to 18 percent, depending on the woman's age and health.

Pay particular care to donor selection, sperm testing, and genetic screening issues. If it's relevant to your circumstances, find out about the bank's policy on donor anonymity.

8　Get sperm when the time is right. Ask your known donor to produce a sample, or have the sperm bank deliver the sample to your house or your doctor's office.

9　On the big day, arrive at the doctor's office with partner or liquid-nitrogen tank in tow. Be sure to bring his favorite magazines (wink, wink), because his first and only contribution to this process will be the one he makes in a small sterile cup. If your new best friend is in a large, cold tank, dip the frozen vial into a cup of lukewarm water, then bring it to body temperature by tucking it under your arm for 10 to 15 minutes. Relax. The procedure, very similar to a Pap smear, causes little discomfort.

10　Prepare to spend a minimum of about 20 minutes flat on your back to give the sperm time to reach the egg.

11　Take a home pregnancy test. Many tests on the market today are capable of detecting human chorionic gonadotropin or HCG (a hormone present in women's urine during pregnancy) at very low levels. That means you can get an accurate test result just six to eight days after conception—well before your first missed period. Positive? Congratulations! Negative? Despair not: Fertility experts consider it normal to take a full year to get pregnant.

Warnings

Fertility drugs can have side effects such as weight gain, dizziness and hormonal swings (just like pregnancy).

IUIs involve a small risk of infection.

---

253 | Plan for an In Vitro Fertilization

The science of fertility has come a long way from the first "test-tube babies" of the late '70s. For couples who have not been able to get pregnant using other methods, in vitro fertilization (IVF) is a last resort. In IVF, the egg is fertilized in a petri dish and then implanted in the woman's womb. Couples choosing this expensive procedure—costing upwards of $12,000 for each attempt—realize that the odds of success are against them. Yet, the chance of having a long-dreamed-for child makes it all worth it.

Steps

1　Ask your OB-GYN for a referral to a reputable fertility clinic or get recommendations from friends and family if possible. Research local centers on the Internet.

2　Find out if your insurance covers the procedure. Be prepared to pay, by check or credit card, whatever portion of the procedure your insurance doesn't cover. Ask about financing plans.

3　Get tested for any discernible cause of infertility in both the man and the woman. Men will have their sperm tested for quantity,

Tips

When looking for a fertility doctor, check the Centers for Disease Control Web site (www.cdc.gov), which maintains statistics on infertility clinics' success rates.

Your partner (or a very close friend) will need to become proficient in giving injections.

Be aware that the drugs and the procedure are billed separately.

Continued on next page

motility and morphology (structure). Women will have their hormones tested and will be examined for any other possible cause, such as endometriosis. Other medical issues must be resolved before IVF can begin.

4 Understand exactly what is required while taking daily injections of hormones (such as Pergonal or Repronex), which stimulate egg production in the ovaries. Ask about possible side effects.

5 Speak frankly with both your doctor and your spouse about the likelihood of multiple births. Since more than one viable embryo is implanted at a time to increase the chances that any will survive, there is a high chance that multiple births will result.

6 Discuss the timing of all phases of the procedure with your physician. After the injection phase, the woman's eggs are harvested, fertilized by the man's sperm, and then incubated. The doctor then implants the healthiest embryos into the woman's womb. After the implantation, the woman must be on complete, immobile bed rest for 24 to 48 hours.

7 Inject progesterone daily for the two weeks following implantation to prepare your uterus for pregnancy.

8 Take a pregnancy test. If it's positive—congratulations! Now read 254 Prepare for a New Baby and 250 Budget for a New Baby.

9 Prepare for the possibility of disappointment ahead of time. The success rate of any given attempt ranges dramatically depending on the woman's age. Your financial situation will play a large part in determining how many times you can try. Unsuccessful attempts can be devastating to both of you. Would-be parents can find support and resources at Resolve.org, the national infertility organization.

10 Investigate other options should IVF prove to be unsuccessful. In ICSI, a related procedure, sperm is injected into the egg rather than simply injected into the egg's environs. Couples who have waited too long might consider using an egg donor or a surrogate mother. Adoption is another course of action (see 258 Organize an International Adoption). Couples dealing with the intense emotional storms that infertility issues create can contact Resolve.org for support and resources.

Who Knew?

Although it is unlikely that all the embryos will survive, twins and triplets occur in about one-third of all IVF pregnancies. If more than that number of eggs have been successfully fertilized, the couple, together with their doctor, must decide whether to freeze the extra embryos, discard them, make them available for research, or donate them to another infertile couple.

There's a good reason why you were given nine months to get ready: Not only does having a new baby mean decorating a nursery and buying equipment, it also means preparing for a new life to join yours seamlessly.

Steps

1 Stock the nursery and kitchen with baby-care basics including bottles, nipples, diapers and wipes, as well as a digital ear thermometer, nasal aspirator, baby nail clippers and diaper cream.

2 Organize that tiny, adorable wardrobe by size. Stackable, sliding plastic drawers are great for different sizes and types of clothes.

3 Ask friends with young children for recommendations on what to borrow versus what to buy. You'll be dropping some big bucks on your little bundle—strategic clothing and equipment loans can give significant financial relief. See chart below.

4 Get ready to rock and roll—with baby. If you didn't receive an infant carrier, stroller and car seat at the baby shower, now's the time to research different brands and pick up what you need.

5 Crawl around on the floor to see what needs babyproofing. Read 73 Make Your Home Safe for Small Children.

6 Get your financial and legal affairs in order. Read 250 Budget for a New Baby, 236 Buy Life Insurance, 228 Develop a Savings Plan, 244 Make a Will and 235 Plan for College Costs.

7 Arrange child care if you are going back to work. The right child-care situation takes time to find, and the good places often have waiting lists. See 263 Arrange Quality Child Care.

8 Set up a medical flexible spending account with your employer to use pretax dollars to cover child care and out-of-pocket medical expenses. See 228 Design a Savings Plan.

9 Make meals a few weeks ahead and freeze. See 369 Set Up a Food Tree and 306 Efficiently Use the Refrigerator and Freezer.

Tips

Involve siblings in the preparation process to foster good will toward the new sibling.

If assembly is required with baby gear, do this well ahead of time. Babies are known for arriving ahead of schedule.

Consider bringing in help (your mom, your mother-in-law or a postpartum doula) for a few days after baby is born—especially if you have other children.

Who Knew?

Ask friends and family for recommendations and shop around for a nearby pediatrician whose services are covered by your insurance.

Add the new baby to your medical plan. If both parents have insurance, choose the plan that offers the most comprehensive family coverage, and add the other parent's plan as secondary insurance.

What to Buy	What to Borrow
• Portable crib	• Most clothing for 0–3 months
• Waterproof mattress pad	• Cold-weather jackets, boots
• Diaper pail with airtight lid	• Crib, mattress (unless you're planning on having more than one baby)
• Book to record baby's first year	
• Digital camera or camcorder	
• Diaper bag	• Baby swing, doorway jumper
• High chair	• Infant car seat
• Stroller	• Baby monitor
• Baby backpack	• Front pack or sling

255 | Organize Your Maternity Wardrobe

Feeling comfortable and being sharply dressed for work while your midsection expands faster than the federal budget can be quite a balancing act. Knowing what you have and what you'll need will ease the transition to soon-to-be-mandatory maternity duds.

Steps

1 Arrange your closet so that the comfy elastic-waist pants and skirts, and dresses without defined waists are front and center.

2 Borrow from friends and family who share your sense of style (or your pregnancy timing). Maternity clothes are outgrown long before they're worn out, so passing things on makes everyone happy. Comb secondhand stores, consignment shops and garage sales for more deals.

3 Shop wisely and early, keeping the seasons ahead in mind. If you get pregnant in May, the winter clothes you'll need when you're in the last trimester will be on sale in spring.

4 Choose neutral tones or two or three complementary colors for your maternity clothing staples (pants, skirt, shorts, top). Vary your look with accessories.

5 Buy at least one pair of maternity jeans for everyday wear, and consider a pair of overalls too—the absence of a waistband is exquisitely comfortable. Splurge on one dressy outfit if you have an opportunity to hit the town. Shop MaternityMall.com for a number of maternity options.

Tips

Save money and closet space by leasing more expensive but infrequently worn clothing such as suits and formal wear.

Add pieces slowly. You may go up a clothing size as your pregnancy progresses, especially if you're carrying twins.

Who Knew?

While you're pregnant, buy only one maternity bra at a time since your cup size changes so quickly. Remember that you'll be in one long after the baby's born (if you'll be nursing), so a well-fitting bra is well worth the cost. Be sure to check out the Bravado bra (bravado.com).

256 | Set Up Maternity or Paternity Leave

Having a baby changes nearly every aspect of your life. Be sure to give yourselves time to adjust and enjoy your little one before you rush back to work. The Family Medical Leave Act now enables fathers as well as mothers to take time off after baby's arrival, so take advantage of this once-in-a-lifetime opportunity.

Steps

1 Research your state's laws and your legal rights. Review your contract or employee handbook so you know what you are legally entitled to and how much of it will be paid for by short-term disability, vacation time and/or sick leave.

2 Decide how much time to take off after the baby is born and when it would be best for you to take it. Do you want to work up to the day you rush to the hospital so you can spend all your time with your new baby—or do you want to be home a week before your baby's due date to rest up and prepare?

Tips

If you have to return to work but don't want to leave your new baby in the care of outsiders, stagger your leave with your spouse's so that you take turns staying home, stretching the leave out longer.

During your leave, benefits typically do not accrue, and you cannot contribute to your 401(k) or medical flexible spending account.

3 Examine your finances and decide how much time you can afford to take off. Consider what you can do without to increase that all-important time with your new arrival.

4 Wait until after the first trimester (when the major risk of miscarriage passes) to tell your boss, co-workers and/or employees. Don't wait too long, however—give them as much notice as possible (legally, you must give at least 30 days).

5 Present your boss with a written plan that specifies what you're requesting. Six weeks paid leave? Six months? Part-time upon return? A flexible schedule? Be ready to show him or her how your plan will work successfully for both of you.

6 Know your rights. If your company has 15 or more employees, it is subject to the federal Pregnancy Discrimination Act. This law protects women against being fired, refused a job or denied a promotion merely because they are pregnant.

Who Knew?

In most states, fathers and mothers are legally entitled to up to 12 weeks of unpaid family leave when a baby is born or adopted. By law, pregnant women must be treated in the same manner as other persons with temporary disabilities for purposes of leave as well as participation in benefit plans and health and disability insurance.

257 | Order Baby Announcements

Ooh, baby! New arrival announcements run the gamut from charming homemade cards to photo cards to embossed cards complete with pink or blue ribbons. What you choose will depend on your personal style, budget and how much time you have to devote to the project.

Steps

1 Decide how much you want to spend. This will dictate your options, from paper and printing method to design.

2 Place your order in a stationery store. Pick paper and a type style that suits the mood of the event. Stay with standard sizes and save a bundle; otherwise envelopes have to be custom made. Set it up so that all you have to do is phone in the baby's name and arrival details.

3 Hire a designer to create a custom invitation or announcement if you don't find what you want at a stationer's. He or she will create a unique, elegant or whimsical look to your specifications.

4 Explore printing effects. Traditional engraving, elegant letterpress, and relatively inexpensive thermography are all classy extras. Plain offset printing with black ink is the least expensive option.

5 Go to sites like Walmart.com and Costco.com, which allow you to add a customized message to your baby's photo. Some announcements come as ready-to-mail postcards. The cost is well under $1 per card and takes just a few days to process.

Tips

Order thank-you notes at the same time to match the announcement.

Most baby announcements include the child's first and middle names, date of birth, time, weight and length, and the parents' names.

Print your own announcements from your home printer. Look for software to create photo cards.

While adopting a child is difficult enough, adopting one from another country adds many more layers of red tape. The process is lengthy, emotionally draining and expensive. It's not all dire, though—so long as you find a fabulous agency who will partner with you every step of the way. Be patient and keep a level head.

Steps

1 Prepare financially and emotionally for a lengthy, bureaucratic process that can take from six months to several years (and $8,000 to $30,000) to complete.

2 Talk to friends and colleagues who have completed an adoption. Ask lots of questions about the whole process. Zero in on their choice of agency and find out all the pros and cons. Then do some comparison-shopping online. Narrow your prospects to several international agencies and call them. You're searching for an organization who will partner with you. Look for a good fit, a sense of warmth and trust, a feeling that they're deeply invested in a positive outcome for you and the child.

3 Select an agency. Ask for an information packet and fill out the application forms. Discuss details of the application process, schedule your home study and submit the Immigration and Naturalization Service (INS) forms.

4 Compare host countries. Most agencies feature a chart on their Web site that lists, by country, the ages and genders of available children, their living situation (orphanage, foster care) requirements for parents, the waiting period, travel requirements, adoption fees and so on. Apply to the country of your choice.

5 Prepare for the all-important home study. Typically a three-part process, the home study includes visits from a social worker, gathering of paperwork and attending adoption classes.

6 Carefully consider the age, health and status of the child you are prepared to adopt to ensure a good fit. Make your preferences, abilities and limitations clear to the agency.

7 Choose a child from agency photos or videos. Ask your pediatrician to review the child's file and health records before finalizing your choice. Be prepared for an emotional experience when you receive your final referral—the child who will soon become yours.

8 Travel to your child's country to get your son or daughter—how many times you'll go there varies by country. Bring along a family member or friend for safety, sanity and to help navigate paperwork if you're going solo. It can be a lengthy, expensive and emotionally trying process. See 436 Plan a Trip to a Different Culture.

9 File adoption papers in your child's country and yours. Pick up his or her passport and visa, schedule a medical exam and obtain visa photos. This entire process typically takes two to three days.

Tips

Also see 249 Plan Your Family, 259 Foster a Child, 254 Prepare for a New Baby and 260 Organize Your Life as a New Parent.

Take full advantage of classes offered by your agency or hospital, including attachment and bonding, blending cultures, dealing with the emotional roller coaster, and basic child care.

Complete all paperwork requested by your agency and any other agency or governmental body involved. If you lack a single form, you can be forced to begin anew.

Who Knew?

For information on the regulations and requirements of your adoptive child's country, contact the U.S. Department of State's Bureau of Consular Affairs Overseas Citizens Services Office of Children Issues (travel.state.gov/adopt.html).

Have all documents ready to go: birth and marriage certificates, fingerprints, medical exams, personal references and current passports.

Warning

Institutionalized children from Third World countries often have delays and medical problems. Once you sign the adoption papers, the child's health care is your responsibility.

Foster homes provide at-risk children a temporary, safe place to live until they can be reunited with their families or, in some cases, placed permanently with adoptive families. Some children stay in foster care for days or weeks; some stay for years. Fostering a child is important, difficult and selfless work for little glory and less money. Those who take it on know that every day spent in their care, that child is getting a dose of consistency and love he or she wouldn't otherwise have.

Steps

Before you begin

1 Talk to other foster parents in order to get the lay of the land. Evaluate your situation and desire to parent honestly, especially if you have other kids. The rewards of foster parenting come from watching kids blossom in a household of love and consistent expectations, but it is hard work.

2 Understand the logistical facts of foster care. You will have more appointments than you ever dreamed possible: several visits a week by social workers—sometimes daily, supervised visits to the child's mother or father (or both); and trips to court and to the doctor, psychologist or occupational therapist.

3 Know who the players are. The county often subcontracts out foster care to private agencies who place the kids with families. Check out these agencies' credentials. Ask questions about their track record (is there a pattern of children being removed from care?) and their relationship with your county's department of health and human services.

4 Become a foster parent with the intention of adopting a child (fost-adopt), but carry no illusions that it will be an easy process. Have a candid conversation with the county and ask how long a wait you'll have before an eligible child is placed with you.

Navigating the application process

1 Call the department of health and human services in your county. Get guidelines for becoming a foster parent from the county, not from one of the outside agencies. The county will give you a list of the agencies it works with.

2 Fill in the application with your personal and medical history, and personal and professional references. Indicate the age and type of child (race, gender, language, special needs) you will accept.

3 Schedule an appointment for a required home study and visit by a social worker. You'll typically have three visits: one to inspect the home itself to see that it is safe and suitable, the other two to investigate your psychological background, check that applicants are mentally healthy, complete more paperwork and so on.

Who Knew?

All adults in your home will be fingerprinted for a criminal background check.

Regulations vary from agency to agency. Typically, the child may not share a bedroom with any individual over age 18, and adults cannot move out of their room and onto the couch to make room for a foster child.

Every effort is made by the courts to reunify children with their parents. Before foster children are eligible for adoption, parental rights must be terminated. And biological parents have enormous leeway and a long time to prove themselves fit. It is possible to adopt a foster child, but it's important to be realistic about your chances.

Set up a separate file just for the foster child's paperwork. Keep his or her social worker's and doctor's phone numbers handy in case of emergency. See 185 Create a Flawless Filing System.

Continued on next page

4 Complete 15 to 30 hours of required training in foster parenting skills. Regulations vary by state and agency.

5 Receive your foster parent certification or license.

Preparing your home and family

1 Assess if you are ready to become a foster parent. You will be interviewed by a counselor regarding your own childhood experiences and your family relations. Foster parents can be single, married, divorced or separated, and in some states or counties gay and lesbian.

2 Ask the county for its home-inspection regulations and bring your house up to code before the inspection takes place. Make sure your house is childproof and free of hazards. See 73 Make Your Home Safe for Small Children.

3 Buy any special materials needed for the child (bottles for babies, books for school-age kids). See 254 Prepare for a New Baby and 260 Organize Your Life as a New Parent if your foster child is an infant or young child.

4 Create a room or other special place that your foster child can call his or her own. Start with a cozy bed and a private space for clothes and toys.

5 Enroll school-age children in school.

6 Prepare your children for the arrival of a new foster child. Make sure they understand that this will be his or her home, too, in the days, months, even years ahead. See 264 Blend Families for more tips.

7 Gather the entire family together to welcome your foster child to

Warning

If you can't keep records or are disorganized, don't even consider foster parenting. Filing is a huge part of it.

---

260 Organize Your Life as a New Parent

Your mom has gone home, your spouse is back at work, and you and your baby are bonding beautifully. Things are getting back to normal—except for the fact that you haven't returned your best friend's call from last week, the laundry's overflowing and the fridge is looking pretty bare—again. How will you ever get in front of that 8-ball?

Steps

1 Remember that you and your baby will grow and adapt incredibly quickly. Just as you get used to one phase, you'll be rocketed into another.

Tips

Ask a friend to set up a food tree for you for the month or so after the birth. You'll get short visits and wonderful meals while your friends get a coveted peek at the baby. See 369 Set Up a Food Tree.

2 Practice asking for help. Most friends and family say "call me if there's anything you need!"—and they mean it. You'll do yourself and them a favor by actually asking for what you need. The trick is to figure out what sort of task is best for each person—one may be just dying to hold your baby for an hour while another loves to cook and someone else would happily feed your roses.

3 Be aware that breast-feeding is often not quite as "natural" as you may have expected. If you are having trouble breast-feeding, contact the La Leche League (lalecheleague.org) or a lactation consultant.

4 Turn the phone off and return calls when it's convenient for you. You don't need to be at the whim of other people while you're on a sleep-deprived, 24-hour feeding schedule.

5 Sleep when your baby sleeps. Getting enough rest to be able to function is your top priority. Eating is second. After you get the hang of things, you can start wearing your baby in a front pack or sling while you take care of chores. The baby will be happy as a clam tucked into you, and you'll have both hands to work with.

6 Hire help to do the cleaning and laundry once a week if possible; if not, prioritize housekeeping needs and delegate tasks to other family members.

7 Start an exercise program or pick yours up again once your doctor gives you the go-ahead. Join a yoga class for new moms, walk everywhere (baby in stroller) or join a gym with child care.

8 Join a mom's group for invaluable support from people who are going through exactly the same thing you are. You'll glean more information from other moms than from any baby book and you'll make new friends at the same time. Ask your pediatrician for names, and look at community parenting resources online.

9 Plan for pandemonium when you're least able to handle it. Seasoned parents are familiar with the dreaded witching hours (often 5 to 7 p.m.), when even the calmest babies melt down and cry inconsolably. Realize that this is going to be hands-on baby time, and plan a tag-team dinner with your spouse. See 303 Cook Ahead.

10 Do nothing. When you're overworked or overwhelmed, milk cascading down your shirt, diapers and laundry stacking up—don't deal with anything at all. Simply enjoy being with your baby.

Don't forget that your workload has just doubled while your free time has halved. Recognize you really can't do it all—the Supermom is a myth.

Who Knew?

Buy a headset for your phone so you can get two things done at once. Not only will you be able to talk to people while rocking or changing the baby, but you can also do laundry, the dishes and other tasks.

Warnings

Don't try to multitask complicated chores like paying the bills.

Contact your doctor immediately if you are feeling depressed or even harboring thoughts of harming your lovely child. Don't try to tough it out. Postpartum depression can be severe and frightening, but it can also be treated.

Once, all the preparation a woman did for labor was pack her suitcase. When contractions began, her husband drove her to the hospital, where she was strapped into stirrups and and knocked out cold. Today's mom-to-be is far more in control of her labor destiny. But remember—if you don't know your options, you don't have any. Here are some considerations as you enter the home stretch (as it were).

COUNTING DOWN THE LAST WEEKS

- Finish up at work.
- Buy life insurance (if you haven't already).
- Swim, walk, do prenatal yoga.
- Finalize nursery preparation.
- Cook and freeze meals ahead.
- Buy or rent a breast pump.
- Install the car seat correctly.
- See a movie.
- Get some sleep! (It'll be your last chance for quite a while.)
- Get a pregnancy massage.
- Designate a friend to e-mail and/or phone news of the baby's arrival.

GETTING PACKED

- Birth plan.
- Robe.
- Nightgown (front buttoning).
- Slippers and/or socks.
- Eyeglasses, contacts.
- Lip moisturizer and other toiletries.
- Massage oil or lotion.
- Camera and/or camcorder, film, batteries, tripod.
- Nursing bra and pads.
- Comfy change of clothes.
- Address book, cell phone, recharger.
- Outfit for baby to go home in.
- Blanket, hat, socks or booties.

MANAGING PAIN METHODS

- Drugs (discuss options with your doctor ahead of time).
- Changing positions.
- Acupressure or acupuncture.
- Massage.
- Hypnosis.
- Relaxation and breathing techniques.
- Hot or cold showers.
- Walking.

MAKING A BIRTH PLAN

Specify your preferences:
- Birthing center, hospital or home.
- Circumcise or not.
- Episiotomy or not.
- Epidural or "natural" birth.
- Bank the cord blood or not.
- Shaved or not.
- You want to wear your contacts.
- Your partner wants to catch the baby and/or cut the cord.
- You want to hold the baby immediately after birth.
- You want the baby to stay with you at all times, go to the nursery except for feedings, or go to the nursery only when you're asleep.
- You want to wear your clothes.
- Set up a camera and/or camcorder and tripod; designate who's filming.
- Choose music and level of lighting.

COPING WITH COMPLICATIONS

Prepare yourself for unforeseen circumstances such as:
- Your OB-GYN or midwife is unable to attend the birth.
- Labor needs to be induced: Specify if you prefer pitocin, breast stimulation, breaking the membrane, acupuncture, walking, sexual intercourse.
- An assisted birth is necessary. Specify whether you prefer forceps or vacuum extraction.
- A C-section is necessary. Specify if you prefer to have your partner present at all times, to be able to see the operation, to discuss the type of anesthesia, to be able to film the procedure, and so on.
- You get stuck in traffic.
- Your husband or partner is not able to be at the birth.

CHOOSING YOUR TEAM

- Choose between a midwife, doula, labor coach or OB-GYN.
- Consider having someone there to support your husband or partner.
- Resolve conflicts about who will be present for the birth.
- Decide whether to have siblings present for the birth. If not, set up child care.
- Hire a postpartum doula to provide at-home care.
- Pack a cooler with sandwiches, snacks, fresh fruit and drinks for after the birth. Everyone (but especially the new mom) will be starving.

262 | Stock a Diaper Bag

Your diaper bag is your survival kit and trusted right hand. Keep it well stocked and you'll not only survive shopping trips, restaurants and other excursions (handling head-to-toe blowouts, sudden snack attacks, and boring car rides) in stride, but actually thrive with baby in tow. Include a few extras to handle additional surprises that come your way.

KEY ITEMS	CONSIDERATIONS
Bag Basics	Choose the right bag—not necessarily one labeled "diaper." Microfiber back-packs and plastic-lined handbags can work just as well and keep your sense of style intact. Put the same thing in the same pocket every time so you can locate that pacifier in a hurry. No compartments? Group like items in clear zipper-lock plastic bags.
	Check out hands-free backpacks with attached changing pads.
Diapering Needs	Stock one diaper for every two hours you'll be out, plus a few extras. Pack diaper covers if using cloth diapers. Keep a wad of wipes in a zipper-lock plastic bag or portable container. Take extra plastic bags for dirty diapers or soiled clothes. Include a changing pad and diaper cream.
Feeding Essentials	Stock bottles (one for every feeding time away from home); liquids to put in those bottles; diversions that double as snacks (cereal O's); a snap-on or Velcro bib for secure, cleaner feedings (tie-ons are difficult to tie on squirming infants and are easily pulled off); burp cloths (for babies under six months); a nursing pad (if you are breast-feeding); cooler bags with ice packs for bottles.
Spare Parts	Bring one complete change of clothing per meal away (stored in a zipper-lock plastic bag), including socks, shoes and a blanket.
Road-Trip Toys	Diversions and silence-keepers such as pacifiers and plush or teething toys are essential for everyone's sanity. A bored baby is a dangerous thing.
Health Must-Haves	Flavored teething gel, 30-plus sunscreen (for babies six months and older), Children's Motrin or Tylenol, diaper rash ointment and Benadryl for allergic reactions. Antibacterial wipes for wiping down the high chairs at restaurants.
Other Essentials	Bottles of water and snacks for both of you, single-serving formula packets, disposable breast pads, booties, hat and an extra blanket for discreet public feedings.
TIPS	Keep an extra package of diapers and wipes, and a fresh change of clothes (head to toe) in a zipper-lock plastic bag in your trunk for the inevitable blowout when your bag is empty and you're far from home.
	Replace whatever items you've used each time you return home so the bag is always ready to roll. See 47 Prepare Grab 'n' Go Activity Bags.
	Always carry your pediatrician's phone number and your health insurance card with you. Keep the baby's immunization record in a pocket as well.
	Wise parents keep a book or a magazine in the car for those times when your baby finally falls asleep and can't be moved.

Congratulations! You're expecting a new bundle of joy. Have you got your child care set up yet? Believe it or not, some programs are so popular that parents put their child on a waiting list at conception. Good-quality child care is available in most areas if you're willing to look for it, and there are many options for parents to choose from. Use this primer to find a great fit for your child and your family.

Steps

General tips

1 Decide when you want to put your child in care. Some parents prefer to keep their kids at home as long as possible and don't enroll them in a program until they are around three years of age. Other parents choose to put their children in a child-care setting much earlier. Still others prefer mixing time at home with time in care. Lifestyle and your child's personality will play a role in this decision—social, active children benefit greatly from the stimulation and activity offered in a structured group environment.

2 Ask friends with children, other families and mothers' group members for recommendations. Find out what their experiences have been like. Listen to what excites them and see if your gut tells you the same things would work well for your child. You can also search local parenting Web sites or child-care referral centers, or go to ChildCareAware.org for advice.

3 Consider the available options and decide which type of child care best meets your needs.

Home-based care

1 Check out family day care in your area. Typically, one licensed adult cares for up to six children in his or her home (the number is determined by state law). These situations tend to offer the most flexibility in scheduling, but you'll need a backup if the care provider becomes ill. Family day care is often a good opportunity to expose your child to another language.

2 Give your child the next best thing to Mom or Dad with a nanny. If that's too pricey, sharing a nanny and splitting the cost with one or two other families can make it affordable. Your child will get one-on-one loving care and one or two playmates.

Centers and preschools

1 Draw up a short list of potential care providers and contact them. Ask for brochures or visit their Web sites. Find out if there is space available when you need to enroll or if there is a waiting list. Make appointments to visit providers and show up promptly.

Tips

The National Association for the Education of Young Children (naeyc.org) accredits programs. Contact it for a list of standards as well as recommended teacher-to-child ratios for preschools and childcare centers.

Find more information on choosing child care at ChildCareAware.org.

Ask for and call all references when interviewing potential child care candidates.

Stay involved in your child's care. Volunteer to help out, talk to other parents and foster good communication with all caregivers.

Who Knew?

Weigh the pros and cons of getting child care near your home or office. On the one hand, proximity to work allows for easy lunchtime nursing breaks and a swift reunion at day's end. On the other hand, handling the commute (car seat, crowds, crying) when you and your child are exhausted may be far more stressful than letting him or her stay put for an extra half hour.

2 Review the programs offered by various providers in your area. You'll find ones that offer full-time, part-time and flexible schedules. Consider the amount of structure and the location. Look at staff qualifications and turnaround, teacher-to-child ratios, curriculum, accreditation, discipline strategies and more. If you have an infant, you'll want a high caregiver-to-child ratio. Parents with several children may need a provider that caters to both babies and older kids.

3 Leave your child at home (if possible) for the first visit so you can focus on learning about the program. Bring a list of questions: What is a typical day like? How are behavioral issues dealt with? Are children divided by age? Does your child have to be potty-trained to gain admission?

4 Take a good look at the space. It should be safe, well maintained and cheerful, with separate areas for quiet play and for group activities and plenty of toys. Check the outdoor space. Is there room to run around? Are there climbing structures, a sandbox and lots more toys?

5 Observe how the director and teachers interact with the kids. Are they approachable, flexible and respectful? How do the children respond to them? Is there a lively atmosphere that doesn't seem out of control? Do the kids and teachers seem happy?

6 Use your instincts as a parent and look for a good fit. Some programs have an extended family feeling, while others are more structured and businesslike. Make sure the program and its philosophy are suited to the temperament of your child. A situation may be great for one child but not for another.

7 Review details with the director. Find out what the fees are, what they cover, and how they are paid, including fees for late pickups. Confirm the hours of operation and what days throughout the year that school is closed. Ask how teachers are qualified, what the turnover is, and what the minimum requirements are. Inquire about enrichment such as art, music and field trips. Find out if and how often parents are required to volunteer. Ask if there is a board of directors or other parents you can contact for more information. Call them; they're usually happy to talk to prospective parents.

8 Take your child for a short visit after you've narrowed down your choices. How does he or she respond to the environment?

9 Complete the application process, pay the deposit and set up a plan for entry into the program that will be most effective for your child. Some programs have a well-planned transition both for entering and for moving from one age group to another.

10 Build an alliance with all of your child-care providers. Stay in constant communication to keep abreast of how your child is doing.

Warnings

Schools and centers should fingerprint all employees.

Contact organizations such as TrustLine (trustline.org) to get criminal background checks on any caregiver. Developed in conjunction with the FBI and the U.S. Department of Justice, TrustLine provides authorized screening of in-home caregivers in California. Check with your state for similar services.

More than half of all Americans live in some sort of nontraditional family due to remarriage. While it can be a rocky road, not all blended families necessarily resemble Cinderella's. Merge yours, mine and ours with as few bumps as possible by recognizing how stepfamilies differ from nuclear ones and by having lots (and lots) of healthy communication.

Steps

At home

1 Give each child personal private space. This includes a bed, drawers, closet space, desk and a chair at the dinner table. This is especially important for nonresidential kids.

2 Give each child a caddy for grooming supplies when they share a bathroom.

3 Create a master family calendar that shows who's where when. Mark special events for residential and nonresidential kids. See 266 Coordinate a Family Calendar.

4 Arrange for the stepparent to sign a consent form allowing him or her to authorize emergency medical treatment for all children.

5 Start with a clean slate: To resolve turf wars, it's often easier to just sell the old house and move to one that's new to everyone.

Communication

1 Take classes on stepparenting before the merger. Type "stepparenting resources" or "blended families" into a search engine or contact a child care referral service in your area.

2 Hold regular family meetings to discuss issues as they come up and work out the week's logistics. The structure will be helpful to all kids. See 267 Plan Family Meetings.

3 Talk to your partner about how you want to handle disciplining each other's kids. Ideally you'll parent as a team and be firmly in the same camp when it comes to establishing ground rules, setting limits and defining what's appropriate. At the same time, the stepparent would be wise to follow the biological parent's lead on disciplining style—and when it's possible, leave the disciplining up to him or her.

Part-time kids, full-time kids

1 Accept the fact a blended family will not act or feel like your picture of an "ideal" family. The part-time kids can get jealous of the full-time kids and feel left out. Don't rush to try to create a harmonious family feeling. Be patient—and be creative.

2 Foster an atmosphere of open communication and talk about stuff when it comes up. Strike a balance between having

Tips

Use stepfamily support networks, a licensed social worker, or your church or synagogue as needed to solve problems or find solutions. Contact organizations such as the Stepfamily Association of America (saafamilies.org) or KidsTurn.org.

When discussing your partner's child—or any child—criticize the behavior, not the child.

Make holiday plans far in advance.

Make—and keep—a weekly date night with your spouse. See 434 Plan an Overnight Getaway With Your Spouse.

everyone's feelings heard and doing what needs to be done. Keep it simple and talk to each child at his or her own level.

3 Set up rules and expectations regarding behavior and schedules and enforce them consistently. Your part-time kids may have different rules in their other home, but it's helpful all around when everyone knows what to expect at your house. Insist that everyone speak to and treat one another with respect.

Relationships

1 Plan regular private talks about family issues. Discuss with your new partner or spouse what your mutual long-term goals are. What do you want your part-timers to remember from growing up in their new family (since it won't be about routine and consistency)? Talk about what type of family structure and activities you can both put in place to support those long-term goals. Also see 248 Teach Your Kids About Money.

2 Let kids and stepparents work out differences without your help. They need to learn how to work together within the guidelines you set—and biological parents need to stay out of the middle.

3 Make sure every child feels wanted in your home whether he or she lives there full-time, half-time or just two weekends a month.

4 Make sure biological family members have some time one-on-one time each week, especially at first. At the same time, plan time with your new stepchildren. Kids are often less dramatic if there's no audience to play to.

5 Talk to each other. Tell lots of stories and look at photo albums. Create rituals for this new configuration. Listen to the kids and slowly, patiently develop a common history with them as you grow into a new family.

6 Be as patient as possible, no matter how difficult a phase your new family is in. Don't expect overnight success: It typically takes about two years for a newly blended family to stabilize.

The ex

1 Maintain a civil relationship with your ex and your spouse's. Never bad-mouth the other parent in front of the kids. See 287 Plan an Amicable Divorce.

2 Communicate with the other parent when solving any ongoing problem a child might have. Operating as a team is absolutely in your children's best interests.

3 Establish a visitation schedule and stick to it as much as possible. Don't let your child make plans for days when he or she is supposed to be with Dad or Mom. Inform the ex as far in advance as possible if you do need to change the schedule.

Who Knew?

Let your children take their time when they are deciding what to call their new stepparent. Start at a neutral, conservative place, such as the parent's first name. They can always move to a more intimate name like "Papa [first name]"—or even "Dad"—as their relationship and sense of comfort and security develops over time.

During the beginning stages of a relationship, plan trips and adventures with all the kids on neutral ground rather than inserting part-timers into regular routines on full-timers' turf.

Warning

Recognize common stepfamily traps such as jealousy and resentment when they arise and try not to take them personally.

265 | Create a Household Organizer

Do you feel like your personal life is getting broken down into smaller and smaller fragments: sticky notes, business cards and take-out menus that stuff backpacks, pockets, purses and briefcases? Corral it all with a low-tech but incredibly effective organizer that holds everything anyone in the family needs.

Steps

1 Purchase a large three-ring binder, a dozen or two section dividers with pockets (depending on the size of your family), plastic sleeves and a three-hole punch. All the papers you need to hang onto and find easily at the right moment will go into this binder: Medical forms, school handouts, class schedules, babysitter phone numbers, master occasions list (birthdays, anniversaries), emergency numbers, recommended Web sites, book club ideas and so on.

2 Create section dividers into broad categories: to do; to buy; to fix; schedules; phone and address lists; medical; home repair contacts; and a school file for each kid.

3 Train your family to transfer all the scraps of information that they bring home into the family organizer and to get into the habit of writing down what they need in the appropriate section.

Tips

Tape the emergency phone list on the inside front cover.

Make the binder accessible to everyone at home. If your kitchen has a desk, label the binder clearly "Family Info." The idea is make information readily available to whoever needs it.

Who Knew?

Put time-sensitive papers in your tickler file (see 10 Set Up a Reminder System) with a reminder written in your calendar (see 266 Coordinate a Family Calendar).

266 | Coordinate a Family Calendar

Mondays the kids play soccer, Dad golfs every other Tuesday, and Thursdays Mom works late. How do you keep track of it all? Piece of cake: Create a family planning calendar and message center.

Steps

1 Mount a large, plastic laminated blank wall calendar in the kitchen. Find one with enough space on each day (week and month) to be able to write in a number of different items. Designate one color dry-erase marker for each family member.

2 Teach everyone to write in their appointments, meetings, practice and lesson schedules, book report due dates, social engagements, play dates and activities. Tie this scheduling exercise into your weekly family meeting so everyone stays in the loop. See 267 Plan Family Meetings and 3 Write an Effective To-Do List.

3 Make a rule: No one can make any verbal commitment without first consulting the calendar. And no plan can go on the calendar in ink until confirmed by the driver.

4 Update individual personal calendars with the master family calendar at the beginning of each week.

Tips

See 10 Set Up a Reminder System.

Use colorful stickers as visual scheduling cues to young nonreaders.

Keep a bulletin board next to the calendar to post notes and phone messages.

Who Knew?

Teach your family to write critical to-do items on colored sticky notes and place on the appropriate day. Then you can transfer those notes to your own to-do list.

267 | Plan Family Meetings

Family meetings are a great opportunity to find out what's going on with your gang. They enhance communication and teach kids how to speak up and express their opinions. Meetings also keep everyone working as a team to plan effectively and set goals.

Steps

1 Set a regular meeting time and place when no one has to give up something major to be there—after Sunday dinner is often good. Let phone calls go to voice mail: By keeping this time sacred, you're letting your kids know how important they are.

2 Post an agenda on the refrigerator so everyone can add topics they want to discuss.

3 Let everyone take turns running the meeting. Teenagers or parents can rotate the job of taking notes and what decisions were made. Keep them in a binder for easy reference (see 265 Create a Household Organizer).

4 Set rules for the meeting and write them down. These might include speaking in respectful voices, confining topics to family matters, and how to return to the subject if people get off on a tangent. Make sure the parents follow the rules as well—no interrupting, listen carefully and so on. Establish who's got the floor and set talking limits with an egg timer.

5 Keep the meeting short, positive and fun. Meetings should not be used as opportunities to attack one another. Family meetings will fail if people focus on what's wrong.

6 Start your meeting by offering compliments to each other. Begin with comments like "I loved it when you…" Express your appreciation for each other and teach your children to say thank-you if they receive a compliment.

7 Give each person a chance to speak on each agenda item. Move on to discuss or troubleshoot other issues.

8 Coordinate who will cook meals each night of the week and who will clean up. See 297 Plan a Week of Menus.

9 Finish with a discussion of what's on everyone's calendar for the week ahead. A parent should write everyone's appointments, classes and extracurricular activities on the calendar. This is a good time to resolve any scheduling conflicts. See 266 Coordinate a Family Calendar.

10 Let the leader pick a way to end on a fun note. He or she can decide to have dessert together, turn the meeting into game night, make popcorn and so on.

Tips

See 14 Balance Home and Work.

Even youngsters stand to benefit from a family meeting, so start while they're young.

Hold an annual family meeting to plan for vacations, holidays and special projects.

Family meetings are a good time to rotate chores and give out allowances.

See 16 Set Goals and 248 Teach Your Kids About Money.

Who Knew?

Take children's opinions into consideration, but make it clear that on important matters, parents have the final say.

Setting up systems at home to help a child with attention deficit disorder (ADD) or attention-deficit/hyperactivity disorder (ADHD) manage organizational and focusing challenges makes a world of difference. Creating clearly delineated areas and simple systems for tasks can lessen distractions while maximizing his or her talent and potential.

Steps

1 Discuss your child's condition and treatment fully and openly with his or her teacher(s). Partner closely with them to make sure your child is staying on task at school and not disrupting class.

2 Discuss problem areas at school and mitigate them when possible. For example, if your child is having trouble getting math papers put away and English papers out in time, send labeled folders to put in his or her desk and explain how to use them.

3 Print out or purchase a calendar that your student can take to school and record upcoming and long-term assignments and tests. That way reports don't get pushed to the last minute, resulting in a lower grade. Make a note to check in with your child daily or weekly to budget in the time needed to complete those assignments.

4 Provide a well-stocked desk or table with everything needed for homework, such as pens, pencils, highlighters and notepaper.

5 Create a structured environment with set routines, schedules and bedtimes. Kids with ADD or ADHD need to know what to expect. Show your child how to use calendars, lists and organizers to stay on track both at home and at school, much as adults do.

6 Make eye contact to keep his or her attention focused on you. Keep directions simple and concentrate on only one step or task at a time. Break down the work into 20- or 30-minute segments.

7 Analyze upcoming situations that might trigger your child's condition (a birthday party, a field trip), and strategize to minimize misbehavior. Explain exactly what will happen, what is expected of him or her and what the consequences are for misbehaving.

8 Write down rules, along with specific consequences. Kids with ADD often have trouble connecting actions to consequences, so discipline must immediately follow the misbehavior, even if it's not a good time or place.

9 Encourage appropriate activities or sports. They not only provide a structured outlet for his or her hyperactivity, but also help build essential social relationships.

10 Work with your doctor to develop a treatment plan that works as smoothly as possible into your child's school, social and sports schedule.

Tips

Carefully track your child's height and weight. Some of the stimulant medications can decrease appetite. Discuss any significant changes with your child's doctor.

Make learning interactive, using all the senses. This is especially important for younger children.

Anticipate problematic situations and strategize with your child about how to overcome difficulties and challenges when they arise.

Who Knew?

Don't assume your child has ADD or ADHD. Only a licensed health professional can make this important diagnosis, based on the presence of symptoms in at least two of three lifestyle areas (home, school and/or work/social) before the age of seven years.

Warnings

Environmental changes are not a substitute for medication. Effective management of the disorder requires both. This is not a behavioral disorder (though its symptoms are), but a physiological disorder that can be temporarily corrected through the use of medications that affect how the brain transmits and receives stimuli.

269 | Prepare for a New Cat or Dog

Before you welcome a furry friend into your home, you need to prepare your house—and your family—for the new member. Keeping a pet can be a lot of work and at least a decade-long commitment. Cute kittens and puppies don't just grow up—they eventually turn into old friends who require your love and care into their golden years.

Steps

1 Research cat or dog breeds to decide which one best suits your family's lifestyle and needs. Find out if anyone in your family has cat or dog allergies.

2 Discuss responsibilities and schedules before your new pet arrives. Make written agreements with children requiring them to feed, scoop poop and walk or exercise the animal. Be very realistic about your ability to give a dog the amount of exercise it requires.

3 Set some boundaries and show young children how to handle and talk to their pet. Decide before a paw crosses your threshold exactly where the dog or cat will be allowed (for example, the family room but not the living room) and what it will be allowed to do once it gets there (maybe your furniture is off-limits).

4 Prepare the house and yard. Houses have to be pet-proofed so that the animal won't hurt itself or break something valuable. Keep puppies in a confined space while you're house-training them. Get rid of any toxic plants in your house, and remove or fence in such plants in your yard.

5 Buy food and equipment. A litter box and scratching post should be awaiting kitty at home; bring a collar and leash or a pet carrier when you go to pick up the animal.

6 Decide on the optimum time to bring the pet home. A long weekend would be best. You don't want to pick up a kitten or puppy Sunday night and leave it alone Monday while you work all day and the kids are at school.

7 Line up a vet. Ask friends for recommendations. You'll want to take your new family member in for a checkup right away. It may need additional shots. And puppies will need dog tags; consider having a microchip implanted in case your cat or dog ever gets lost.

8 Sign up your whole family for a dog-training class. It's far easier to teach good habits than to unlearn bad ones—that goes for the dog as well as the humans. Contact your community center or ask friends for recommendations.

9 Avoid surprise pets. Never give or receive a pet on impulse. Both cats and dogs require regular attention, food and exercise and should be chosen by the owner, not by a well-meaning friend or family member. Remember, they'll be with you for their whole life—as long as 20 years.

Tips

The ASPCA suggests that dogs and cats are appropriate pets for children 10 years and older. If your child is younger, consider the pet yours, no matter how many fervent promises your child makes, until he or she is old enough to take over.

House-training your puppy? Buy a large bottle (or two) of Nature's Miracle stain and odor remover, found at most pet stores.

If you live in an apartment, you must have the landlord's permission to get a pet.

Who Knew?

If you get a cat, you need to decide whether it will be indoor, outdoor, or mostly indoor with supervised outdoor time (as in a fenced area or cat run). Outdoor cats are exposed to a lot of dangers (disease, cars, other animals).

Warnings

Do not leave small children unattended with a cat or dog. One or the other might get hurt.

Accidental ingestion of cat feces or airborne fecal dust can infect a person with toxoplasmosis. Pregnant women should never change the litterbox, since the disease can be passed on to and kill the fetus.

Homeschooling is the ultimate way to get involved in your children's education and allows parents to tailor the curriculum to their kids' individual needs. You get to impart your values, share the excitement of learning and spend lots of quality time with your kids. But being their teacher also requires a huge level of commitment, so take a good look at what's involved before you step up to the chalkboard.

Steps

1 Analyze your lifestyle to see how well suited you are for home schooling. Since lessons are so individualized, you'll be able to fit a lot of education into just a few hours each day—but you have to be supremely organized and able to devote your full attention during those hours.

2 Ask other homeschooling parents about the pros and cons of teaching their own children. You can find homeschoolers in your area at homeschoolcentral.com.

3 Contact parents who have tried but gave up homeschooling to get another perspective. A nearby public school may be able to put you in touch with parents in your area.

4 Buy ready-made plans, take online classes, check out software or video lessons, use an "unschooling" approach that teaches through real-life activities or incorporate a mix of all of these.

5 Join a local support group. Some groups study together, go on field trips and take turns teaching each other's children.

6 Ask your school district whether it will provide you with books, materials or other educational support. Some districts allow homeschoolers to attend school part-time and participate in music or sports programs.

7 Create and maintain a comprehensive portfolio for each student, which will provide the basis of assessing your child's academic progress. Keep a daily record of your lesson plans and his or her activities, with specifics such as "English, chapters 6 through 9, *To Kill a Mockingbird.*" Note field trips taken and special assignments completed.

8 Find out what standardized tests (if any) your child is required to take each school year. Keep detailed academic records, including a list of the texts used for each grade level. You may be required to keep these records under state law, and show them if your child decides to enter high school or applies to college.

9 Be aware of college-entry requirements. Most colleges place particular emphasis on standardized test results. Some colleges require homeschooled students (but not other students) to submit a GED score, SAT and ACT scores as well as SAT II scores in multiple tests: English, math, chemistry, foreign language.

Tip

Get new ideas by chatting with other homeschoolers online or subscribing to a homeschooling magazine. Also check out *The Complete Idiot's Guide to Homeschooling* by Marsha Ransom for tips and ideas.

Who Knew?

Research your state's laws that govern homeschooling. For example, in California, parents must establish a private school in their home and complying with the state's private school requirements. Parents who have established a home-based private school cannot be prosecuted for truancy.

If you homeschool children of different ages, they can share some activities but will need separate lesson plans.

If you're not confident about your teaching skills, a satellite school can offer help and guidance. Search online for "homeschool satellite."

Warnings

Critics say homeschooling parents may not be as effective as credentialed teachers. Ask yourself whether you have the patience and personality for it—and whether you can provide a high-quality education.

Homeschooling materials can be expensive. Share with another family or a support group to lower the cost.

271 | Set Up a Carpool

Carpools are virtually mandatory for parent survival. Until scientists clone parents, there's no earthly way you can get one kid to the dentist by 3:45 p.m. and pick up the other one at practice by 4 p.m. But good carpools don't just happen—they take cooperation, trust and planning.

Steps

1 Include only neighborhood families for the carpool. If you have to drive 15 minutes out of your way to pick up a kid, you're defeating the purpose.

2 Work out a schedule for two or three families and stick to it so each family can make plans around the days they don't drive.

3 Give as much advance notice as possible if plans change.

4 Make firm rules for the road: Only the designated driver can pick up the kids; parents cannot run errands with carpool kids in tow; and drivers should not talk on the cell phone while driving.

5 Set ground rules for the kids, too. Everyone has to wear a seat belt; no one under 12 is allowed in the front seat; hands must stay inside the car at all times. Be polite and punctual.

Tips

Meet with the other parents and decide in advance how you'll handle stragglers or misbehavers. Call other carpoolers periodically to touch base and ward off problems.

Adults can carpool, too. Search online for "carpools" to see what's available in your area.

272 | Stay on Top of Kids' Clothes

Kids' wardrobes are difficult to manage because they just keep growing—and growing out of stuff. You're continually donating old clothes, buying new ones, storing out-of-season items—and occasionally finding perfectly acceptable garments somehow lost in the far corner of a kid's closet. Staying on top of all this chaos requires a system.

Steps

1 Go through all your children's clothes and divide them into piles: too big, too small, worn out and just not going to wear. Do this at least twice a year, or when the seasons change.

2 Put clothes away that are still too big. Give away or sell your "too small" or "not worn" piles. Worn-out clothes go in the rag bin.

3 Accept hand-me-downs from friends and relatives happily, but don't take them all. Keep only what your children will wear.

4 Use the same standards for kids' clothes that you do for your own: Buy good-quality, basic coordinating pieces.

5 Organize clothing by activity: school clothes, play clothes, dress-up clothes and sports clothes. That way your child can find things more easily.

6 Put name tags in all garments.

Tips

Install lower clothing rods in closets for young kids.

Think ahead. Buy next year's clothes at end-of-season sales this year.

See 17 Streamline Your Morning Routine.

Public, private or parochial? Montessori or Waldorf? Parents have more educational choices than ever, which is both wonderful and overwhelming. How do you pick a school that helps your child thrive—and that meshes with your educational values? Once you've found the ideal school for your child, all you have to do is get him or her in. As many parents will tell you, this is no easy task.

Steps

Selecting the best school

1 Take a good look at your child's temperament, personality and learning style. You want to find a school, public or private, that builds on his or her strengths. When considering the issue of class size, take into account whether your child is more naturally comfortable in large or small groups.

2 Explore various educational philosophies. Montessori schools, for instance, encourage students to pursue their own interests, while Waldorf schools integrate arts Into the curriculum but frown on using computers and television.

3 Visit schools and talk to teachers, administrators and other parents about that school's academic emphasis. If the curriculum is strong in science but not in art, you may wish to look elsewhere for a school that suits your budding Picasso.

4 Get a written description of the academic goals for each grade. If they're not written out, they may not be sufficiently well developed. Evaluate whether the curriculum will challenge your child. Dig a little deeper into the curriculum and teaching style. Some teachers use broad themes on one topic (dinosaurs, the solar system) to teach lessons in math, science, art and so on. Are students actively engaged in what they're learning? What kind of student work is displayed in halls and classrooms?

5 Look for challenging enrichment programs that encourage creativity and stimulate development such as art, dance, science, music and bilingual language programs.

6 Investigate how well students are doing academically. How does the school measure their progress, and how do they perform on standardized tests? Your school system should publicize each school's test results.

7 Ask what the student-teacher ratio is. Also find out about what kind of help the teachers get in the classroom in terms of the number of aides and parent volunteers.

8 Learn what services are available if your child has a learning disability or other special needs. Investigate the special-education staff, opportunities for individualized attention and the policy on mainstreaming in the regular classroom.

Tips

See 375 Improve Your Child's School.

Ask to see a class in action. A school can look great on paper, but a visit shows you how things actually work.

If your ideal school is an hour away, ask yourself whether it's worth it for your child to spend that much time on the road each day.

Find out what kind of support the school provides for students who fall below grade-level performance standards.

Who Knew?

Money talks at private schools. You can't just offer it outright, but if you have the resources, you can imply that you would love to help support your child's school.

Find out how the school handles discipline. Get a copy of district or school policies.

If there's a child with special needs in the class, find out if extra aides are required, and if so, how many attend that child. It's a sticky issue, but if the teacher's scarce time and resources are being heavily depleted by one student, all the other kids suffer.

Some parents hold their children back a year so they'll test better at the kindergarten level.

9 Ask about family involvement in the school. Schools, often beset by draconian budget cuts, welcome and encourage parent involvement. Find out how much volunteer time is expected and decide if you have that time to give. If you're working full-time, explore other ways besides classroom time that you can volunteer such as write the newsletter and serve on the PTA.

10 Take a look at the condition of the playground, library, classrooms and bathrooms. Is this a place you'd like your child to go to school? Is it a stimulating and creative environment?

11 Step back from the political debate if you're having a difficult time choosing between private and public schools. There's no questioning the value of public education. It is also clear, however, that safety concerns, spiraling class sizes and diminishing resources all detract from a child's education even when the level of teaching and quality of curriculum is very good. The situation is highly variable from district to district and will remain so as long as school funding is tied to property taxes.

Getting your child enrolled

1 Buy or rent a house near your favorite school. In most public-school systems, children must go to the school nearest their home, although others use lotteries for school selection. Children are often allowed to attend a school where their parents work, even if they live in a different district.

2 Enter a lottery to get into a magnet school. These are public schools that specialize in one subject or philosophy or cater to students with special needs. They often attract interested students from all over a school district.

3 Survey the private schools in your area to find the one that's best for your families needs. See 233 Save for Private Schooling.

4 Prepare a speech to deliver at the admissions interview. Make it clear that you've researched the school and explain why you think it's the best fit for your child. Remember: if your child was not accepted at your chosen school, then it wasn't a good fit.

5 Find out what kinds of help the school needs and offer it. Build a reputation as a cooperative parent who will be a great asset.

6 Check up on your application to show your interest. Make it plain that this school is your first choice, but don't be a pest.

7 No matter how good a school is (or isn't), whether it's public or private and how much you're paying to send your child there, every parent needs to fill in the blanks at home. Schools simply cannot do everything, and learning doesn't stop when the bell rings at 3 p.m. Find teaching opportunities at home: Go beyond homework help and make up word games on the fridge or with the dictionary, work puzzles, play chess and visit museums to round out your child's education.

Tell the admissions officer you want to be on the waiting list if your child doesn't make the first cut. Be willing to snap up an opening in the middle of the school year.

Warnings

Don't immediately blame the teacher if your child isn't performing well. Schedule a conference and find out what's going on.

Beware of pressure put on often very young children to perform. Keep your expectations in line with your child's age and abilities.

274 Organize Kids for Back-to-School

Shifting gears from low-key summer schedules to the overdrive of the school year isn't easy. Simplify the transition: Introduce the early-morning wake-up routine a week or two before school starts. Buy school supplies and clothing several weeks ahead. And get the kids in gear as summer winds down by choosing more academic pursuits.

Steps

1 Schedule a doctor visit. Make sure the kids are current with their vaccinations. Obtain a medical release if your child participates in sports programs.

2 Read 271 Set Up a Carpool and start calling other parents.

3 Make child-care arrangements for after school, if necessary. Working parents also need to make arrangements to cover sick days, snow days and school holidays. See 263 Arrange Quality Child Care.

4 Check out your children's school clothes and supplies, and buy whatever they're missing. Make sure everything is cleaned, laundered, mended, hemmed and ready to go.

5 Create a quiet study center for each child. Stock a nearby drawer or shelf with supplies (pencils, erasers, calculator and so on), and give each child a file drawer or bin to contain completed work, tests and ongoing projects. See 275 Win the Homework Wars.

6 Review systems, routines and schedules with the kids. Discuss where to store backpacks, school papers and other gear. See 70 Organize Entryways and Mudrooms.

7 Establish midweek rules. Spell out when kids can use the computer, watch TV or play; be specific when it comes to study hours, bedtimes and wake-up times.

Tips

See 266 Coordinate a Family Calendar.

Make a file for each child with all his or her paperwork (school records, immunizations, birth certificate). See 232 Organize Important Documents.

Create a lunch center in a kitchen cabinet. Gather everything kids need to make their lunches in one place—zipper-lock plastic bags, peanut butter, snacks, thermoses and lunch boxes. See 17 Streamline Your Morning Routine.

Who Knew?

Wean kids from summer sleep cycles by cutting back on late nights and mornings over several weeks.

275 Win the Homework Wars

Much of a child's success in school depends on how well he or she does homework, and that depends largely on his or her time management skills. Teaching a child not only how to get homework done before bedtime but how to plan for short-term and long-term projects—and still have time for a game of tag after school—will create successful patterns for the long haul.

Steps

1 Designate a specific area where your child can do homework without distractions. Equip it with school supplies so he or she doesn't have to be jumping up to get things.

Tips

Homework should review concepts already taught.

Encourage your child to tackle more-difficult subjects first—before he or she gets tired or frustration sets in.

2 Buy your child a homework planner, or create a form on which he or she can record the day's homework for each subject. Check daily that it gets to school—and back—until it becomes a habit. If there's no homework, he or she can learn to write that down, too. A dry-erase board hung in the homework area is also a useful planning tool.

3 Remind your child to double-check his or her planner or homework list before leaving school each afternoon to make sure all textbooks and essential materials are in that backpack. Since this is almost impossible for many younger children, create a colorful matchbox-sized checklist to jog their memory about key tasks (check homework, bring home books, get uniform). Laminate this list, punch a hold in the corner and hang on his or her backpack's zipper-pull.

4 Designate a specific homework time to prevent procrastination. Many parents follow the time-honored rule of requiring all homework to be completed before playtime begins.

5 Map out the day's homework plan together. Foster good time-management skills by helping your child determine how long each subject should take and touching base on how to proceed.

6 Write any long-term assignments on a master calendar at home. See 266 Coordinate a Family Calendar. Help map out a doable strategy to complete these assignments and discuss any additional materials that might be required.

7 Schedule an appointment with your child's teacher at the beginning of each year and ask for guidance about homework. Clarify exactly what you as the parent should be checking for on your child's assignments every night. Since children obviously can't be held to adult standards, precise guidelines such as "underline any misspelled words and give your child a chance to look them up," or "make sure his name is in the top right corner and the title is centered" are extremely helpful.

8 Check on your child periodically to make sure he or she is on task. Encourage your child's questions and don't immediately jump in to solve the problem. If your child gets stuck, ask him or her to explain the problem or assignment to you. Review directions and ask if he or she remembers anything the teacher said to do. If your child is still unclear, share your thinking about how to begin and keep talking until your child starts to get it. Write a note to the teacher explaining the difficulty. Check completed homework and go over any problems or mistakes.

9 Sign any papers or tests and make sure your child packs up his or her backpack that night. The goal is to eliminate as much last-minute stuff as you can so that mornings—and afternoons and evenings—go as smoothly as possible. See 17 Streamline Your Morning Routine.

When reviewing young kids' homework, choose only one thing to look for: Capital letters at the beginning of the sentence, or periods at the end, or apostrophes in their proper place.

For teaching tools and homework help, check out school.discovery.com.

In the first week of school, ask your child to explain the homework system to you (every teacher has one). If he or she doesn't know, ask the teacher for clarification.

Who Knew?

If you find yourself in a homework tug-of-war, look for a homework club or hire a tutor. Tutors are helpful anytime your child is turned off by a particular subject. Sometimes the material is just a bit over his or her head and even a small bit of concentrated attention can turn the situation around.

Depending on what grade your child is in, clarify homework expectations. Ask the teacher that if your kid puts in a solid block of time on an assignment (say an hour) but isn't able to finish it for whatever reason, will that be acceptable?

At some point in your life as a parent, you will be picked to arrange your child's class field trip. It won't matter that you have no experience, did not volunteer and have no interest in arranging field trips. You will be selected because you weren't there. Never fear. You can do this.

TASKS	DETAILS
Choose the Destination	Usually the teacher does this. Or he or she will give you the topic the students are studying so you can research possible sites. Museums, parks and other attractions are accustomed to hosting field trips.
Book a Date	Get on the facility's schedule. Some are booked months in advance. Plan a rain date (or indoor alternative) for outdoor destinations.
Do Your Homework	Ask the facility to send pertinent information and/or papers to be signed to you. Find out: How long will the field trip take? What costs are involved? How should teachers and/or students prepare? Do students need to bring a lunch or snack, or is there a cafeteria?
Scout It Out	Visit the destination in advance if possible to troubleshoot and plan. Where do you park? Is there room for a bus? Do you need parking passes or permits? Do you pay to park? Where's a good meeting area? Where's a good place for lunch? Are there any hazardous areas to keep the kids away from? These are answers the field-trip planner will be expected to know in advance.
Arrange Transportation	Will parents drive students or will everyone take a bus? If reserving a bus is necessary, discuss costs with the school. If parents drive, have their insurance information on record.
Do the Paperwork	About three weeks before the trip, send a packet home with the students that includes the following information: • A letter explaining when, where and how the children are going; appropriate clothing and supplies; whether they need to bring lunch or lunch money (specify how much); and any money required for fees. Also specify what the children should not bring (toys, gum). • A permission slip for the parent to sign and return within three to five days before the outing. The school will have the legal disclaimer necessary for parents to sign. Your job as organizer will be to get one from the administration office, make copies, and get it out to parents in a timely fashion. • Another form asking for volunteers. The teacher will need chaperones (at least one for every four children if they are under age 10; over age 10, one per every six kids) and possibly drivers. Ask one volunteer to be the photographer. Drivers will have to furnish a copy of their driver's license and current vehicle registration. • Circulate a list of volunteers' phone numbers and e-mail addresses to the other parents and the teacher.

TASKS	DETAILS
Prepare the Kids	Get pamphlets, coloring books and other information to acquaint the kids with what they will be seeing or doing on the field trip. Make activity sheets of things they need to look for.
Create a Field-Trip Schedule	Include what the class will be doing when; when and where should the drivers meet; when and where is lunch; when and where to meet for departure back to school. Do the students need to split up into smaller groups to tour the facility? Which chaperone will be assigned to each group?
Bring Identification	If your school does not have uniforms, you need some way to tell which kids belong to your group. Make sure all kids have name tags listing their name, the school's name, and the chaperone's name. Or give everyone a school T-shirt to pull over their clothes.
Set Rules	Go over expectations in class prior to departure. Basic rules include no running, climbing or shouting; stay with your group; and obey your chaperone.
Assign Groups	If a child's parent is driving, she will of course go with her parent. Otherwise, teachers usually determine who goes in what group, mixing problematic children up into a few groups so that no one parent is suicidal at day's end. (Do not assign yourself or a teacher to a group. You need a few free people to troubleshoot and coordinate the groups.) Announce groups to the class at the last minute to reduce begging and whining.
Call the Chaperones	Two or three days before the trip, make reminder calls to volunteers. Ask them to bring their phones along on the field trip. Line up a substitute so you're prepared for last-minute no-shows.
	Make a packet for volunteers (and teachers) that includes:
	• Each driver's name, cell-phone number and which kids are in each car.
	• Directions and/or a map, parking directions; medical and field-trip release slips for each kid in the car.
	• The day's schedule.
TIPS	Enlist an army of volunteers. It's a big job—so if it falls on your shoulders, don't be shy about making calls to other parents to get assistance in planning the event as well as participating on field-trip day. Just getting someone to make phone calls will help.
	Don't overlook the details. One minor miss—say, not asking about whether there's a cafeteria—could leave you with a group full of hungry, unhappy kids and parents and nowhere to buy food.
WARNING	Be sure to count heads throughout the day. Losing a kid seriously undermines your credibility.

277 | Plan Your Child's Activities

Today's kids don't just play outside until dark anymore. They go to piano, soccer, gymnastics—even Mandarin Chinese. Yes, the classes are beneficial and often fill the gap between the last school bell and when parents are done working. Keep your family sane by protecting the balance between crazy schedules and downtime. It's a juggling act air-traffic controllers would be proud of.

Steps

1 Hunt and gather class descriptions, summer camp flyers and schedules all year long. Keep a running file of activities your child is interested in, organized by season.

2 Jot down deadlines for enrollment forms and deposits for those programs or classes you know your child will want to take or those that fill up fast in your personal organizer. Get the paperwork in well before the deadline for signing up.

3 Set limits, for the sake of family finances and sanity. The rule of thumb Is typically two extracurricular activities per child, taking into account your child's age, homework load, and what your other kids are doing. Figure out how your kids will get there and return home, especially if both parents must work full time.

4 Remember that it's not how many different activities your child has but how many times a week he has to do them. Swim team, for example, with five practices a week, is five times the commitment of a weekly karate lesson. Don't be swayed by kids who want to overcommit their time—or yours.

5 Carpool to lighten the taxi load and to allow a bit more flexibility in choosing activities. See 271 Set Up a Carpool.

6 Schedule study time. Things that are on the daily schedule get done; those that aren't, don't. See 275 Win the Homework Wars.

7 Set a bedtime and stick to it. If extracurricular activities push studying into bedtime hours, that's your cue to start cutting back.

8 Make eating together as a family at least three times a week a priority. Don't let work or activities or play dates interfere with this opportunity to regroup and reconnect as a family. See 14 Balance Home and Work.

9 Protect your children's free time as well. Kids are just as overscheduled as their parents—many carry PDAs just to keep track of it all. Children need downtime, time to daydream, time to play—even time to get bored so they are forced to use their imagination to keep themselves entertained.

10 Talk to children age 12 and older about whether they feel comfortable being home alone after school. If so, contact a neighbor that they can call in emergencies—or nonemergencies (see Warning).

Tips

Make sure you read the details carefully. If all the kids in the dance class bring a snack, you don't want your child to be the only one without one.

When the kids tell your their schedule, enter all the class dates, rehearsals and games (and their time and location as well) into your personal organizer and the family calendar (see 266 Coordinate a Family Calendar). Some teams have sites that post changes In the schedule.

Hire a dependable high school or college student to tutor your child or take him or her from school to extracurricular activities.

Web sites that can help kids with homework include SparkNotes.com and HighSchoolHub.com.

Warning

Predators stalk children who are alone and repeat the same daily patterns, so latchkey kids can be easier targets. If your child must go home alone, discuss the lures predators use, and do some role-playing to help your child feel in control. Get your child a cell phone and have emergency numbers, as well as neighbors who are home in the afternoon, automatically set up.

Remember the lazy days of summer? Good. That's your goal for your kids: to create a summer plan that will leave them with the same fun, laid-back memories. Kids can use the summer months to make new friends, pursue a sport or hobby or just have fun at home and in and around the neighborhood.

AGES	CONSIDERATIONS	OPTIONS
Ages 4–9	Children this age usually love going to camp and making new friends.	• Stay home with Mom, Dad or a caregiver. Season with some swim lessons, field trips and play dates. • Go to full- and half-day camps at schools, community centers and parks. Choices include specialty camps (soccer, art, computers) and general camps that offer a little bit of everything. Camps are usually offered in two-week segments. The best ones fill up fast.
Ages 10–12	Kids sometimes feel too old for generic day camps but are too young to be left on their own all day. Consider a camp geared toward a child's love of theater or sports for the best fit.	• Stay at home, with scheduled adventures out every day or so. Kids under age 12 still need supervision, and should not be left alone for long periods of time. Provide structure for the day or else they'll gravitate to the computer or TV. • Look for specialty camps focusing on sports, photography, computers or even circus acts. • Go to local or sleep-away camps. Preteens can learn safe, structured independence, leadership and team-building skills at special-interest camps focusing on horseback riding, crafts or basketball. Some camps fill up in February, so do your research and apply early. Check out organizations such as American Camping Association (acacamps.org) and National Camp Association (summercamp.org). • Enroll in summer school.
Ages 13–15	They are old enough to stay home alone, but prod them to do something. A kid alone all day with nothing to do is a recipe for trouble.	• Stay at home with guidelines on TV and computer use, who is allowed over and for how long, how often your child is expected to check in with you. • Go to sleep-away camp. Teens can work as counselors. There's great appeal in earning some summer cash and being the guy or girl campers look up to. • Enroll in summer school. • Earn cash doing yard work, baby-sitting or tutoring. Volunteer at an animal shelter, senior facility or hospital.
Ages 16–18	All sorts of new opportunities open up once kids get a driver's license.	• Work at the mall or in a restaurant. For intern programs, look to zoos, museums or science centers, or other professions they might like to pursue. • Go on a teen tour across the country or abroad. Type "teen tour" into a search engine. • Enroll in summer school. Kids can catch up or get ahead at their school, another school or even a local university. See 280 Choose a Summer Study Program and 150 Get Into a Top College or University.

Summer camp. What memories! Skinny-dipping in the lake, spying on the boys (or girls) and riding horses for the first time. It's a combination of fabulous fun and homesickness—and for parents, packing your wild child up for the first trip away from home can be bittersweet. Send yours off with everything he or she needs to ease the transition.

Steps

1 Contact the camp ahead of time and ask for a list of recommended clothing and apparel. The camp staffers know the terrain and weather patterns, so they'll have plenty of solid suggestions. Find more tips at the American Camping Association (acacamps.org). Find out if your child needs clothes of a certain color for field trips, religious services or team sports.

2 Begin packing several weeks in advance to avoid last-minute shopping trips or scrambling for a must-have favorite shirt. Your child should help you pack so she knows what she's bringing.

3 Purchase or borrow a large duffel bag (many have wheels now), a traditional trunk or a trunk on wheels.

4 Put your child's name or initials on *everything*—clothes, hat, swim suit, towels—with either a laundry marker or iron- or sew-on labels (available at NameLabels.com and other sites).

5 Pack a small toiletries kit or basket so your child can carry and keep track of essentials such as soap, shampoo, toothpaste, toothbrush, floss, deodorant, comb and brush. Flip-flops for the shower are also a must.

6 Pack sufficient warm clothing. Depending on where the camp is located, even in August the nights can get cold. Include a fleece jacket, a windbreaker, a warm hat and gloves.

Tips

Find out how often clothes are laundered at camp, and pack accordingly. Include an extra pillowcase or laundry bag for dirty clothing.

Ask about camp regulations regarding sending food and money from home.

Warnings

Don't buy a brand-new wardrobe. While one or two new items are fine, camp life can be rough on clothing. Children, especially first-timers, will also find old favorites reassuring when they're away from home.

Send medication in its original container, along with explicit dosage instructions to the camp nurse or health-care facility. A signed medical-release form should accompany all prescription medication. Make sure your child's physician's number is listed.

Clothing	Additional Necessities
☐ Socks, underwear	☐ Towels, sheets, blankets, pillows
☐ Baseball cap	☐ Sleeping bag
☐ T-shirts, long-sleeved shirts	☐ Raincoat or poncho, rain boots
☐ Nice clothes for the big dance, cowboy garb for Western night and so on	☐ Flashlight with extra batteries
☐ Sweatshirts, fleece	☐ Waterproof disposable camera
☐ Comfortable, sturdy shoes	☐ Canteen or water bottle
☐ Tevas or similar sandals	☐ Insect repellent, sunscreen, calamine lotion and lip balm
☐ Bathing suit(s)	☐ Books, games, cards, jacks, diary
☐ Long pants, shorts	☐ Prestamped, preaddressed postcards to write home

Summer schools allow kids to explore topics in more depth in several weeks than they might otherwise do in a whole semester of school. Some are selective, requiring prerequisite classes or minimum subject grades in school. With others, pay up and you're in. To get the most bang for your buck, research carefully—most programs have at least a Web presence to get you started.

AGES	OPTIONS	COMMENTS
Ages 6–12	Day schools	Most schools (private and public) offer classes in everything from computers to creative writing, algebra to French. Strengthen a weak subject or indulge in a favorite.
	Residential programs	Many older children qualify for residential programs at colleges across the country. Kids usually choose one topic to explore in depth for a session lasting two to three weeks. The subject's content should enhance coursework covered at school. Some programs offer more independent study than others. Look for a program that fits your child's personality and needs.
Ages 13–18	Middle schools	Students can take courses not only to strengthen a weak area but also to pave the way for a lighter course load in the fall or to make room for another elective.
	High schools	Sign up for remedial work to boost grades, or work ahead to qualify for advanced placement courses.
	Driver's education	Many cities offer driver's ed courses over the summer. Check www.dmv.org/drivers-ed.php for courses in your area, or take an online course (TeenDrivingCourse.com). Eligibility age varies by state.
	Colleges	High-school students can take courses at many colleges for credit. Some even offer residential programs specifically for high-school students.
	SAT and ACT prep courses	Students get test-taking tips and additional instruction for these crucial exams. See also 151 Ace the College Admissions Tests.
	College admission prep camp	High-school juniors and seniors get an overview of how the college admissions process works. They learn how to write an admissions essay, get letters of recommendation and choose and get accepted at the right colleges. See 149 Decide Which College Is Right for You.
	Live abroad	If living abroad with a host family is your high-schooler's dream, contact Youth for Understanding (yfu.org) and AFS.org (formerly called the American Field Service), among others. Ask about grants or scholarships.

281 Create a Schedule for Family Computer Use

It's not unusual for busy families to jockey for computer time. Kids need the computer for schoolwork; parents need it for work and finances; and everybody wants to surf the Web, play games and e-mail friends. Keep the family peace with some simple guidelines.

Steps

1 Sit down with all computer users in the house and determine who needs the machine, for how much time, and when.

2 Establish a schedule that's fair and sensible. It's better to have fewer, longer time blocks than to change users every 15 minutes.

3 Write out the schedule and post it by the computer. Reevaluate it every few weeks.

4 Use the user-switching feature of Windows XP or Mac OS X to segregate and protect each user's e-mail, bookmarks, applications and documents. User switching can also prevent inexperienced users from corrupting the computer's operating system and preferences.

Tips

Put a kitchen timer next to the computer; it's a good tool for letting users know when their time is up.

A written Internet Use Agreement defines expectations for both parents and children. See safekids.com/contract.htm.

Consider getting an Internet-ready PC (for as little as $400) just for surfing and e-mail.

282 Plan to Keep Your Kid Safe Online

The Internet has significantly increased access to information, but not all of it is suitable for children. Discussing online dos and don'ts with your kids helps you stay involved in their interests. Ensure that your child uses the Internet safely, both at home and away.

Steps

1 Set up the computer in a well-trafficked area in the home so you can keep an eye on your child's Internet use.

2 Discuss ground rules for using the Internet, chat rooms and messaging services. Explain to your child that there are strangers online, just as there are in real life, and that he or she should never give out personal information or agree to meet online friends without your permission.

3 Spend time with your kid online. Ask to see some of the sites he or she visits and to tell you about online friends.

4 Encourage use of kid-friendly sites. Directories such as KidsClick.org, Yahooligans.com and Ask Jeeves for Kids (ajkids.com) feature hand-picked safe and age-appropriate sites.

5 Investigate parental-control software, which blocks access to unmonitored chat rooms and sites with sexual or violent content. NetNanny.com and CyberPatrol.com log and restrict Internet activity, and send an immediate e-mail alert if your child tries to give out personal information or receives solicitations.

Tips

Help your kid set up a safe, spam-free e-mail account at sites such as KidChatters.com, KidMail.net and KidSafeMail.com.

If you agree to meeting an online friend, insist that the meeting take place in a public space and go with your child.

Ask your child's school, after-school care center or club what filtering software is used and under whose supervision.

Warning

Report any unsolicited explicit material that has been sent to your child at CyberTipLine.com.

Tracing your family tree is a treasure hunt: lots of work but plenty of gems to be found. Since the Internet revolutionized research and documentation, you may even uncover relatives you didn't know you had. Keeping all those cousins straight is another feat. Plan well and your tree will bloom.

Steps

1 Download family tree charts and research logs at Ancestry.com and *Family Tree* magazine. Use these to organize ancestor names and important dates.

2 Consider how you are going to record all the information you find before you get too far in. Record and fill in family group sheets, pedigrees and charts all by hand. Or use a computer genealogical program, such as Personal Ancestral File or Family Tree Maker by Reunion (leisterpro.com). These offer you the ability to make backups of your information on a disk.

3 Document the information you find properly. Always copy the title of the book, microfilm reel number, page number, author, publisher, year of publication and whatever else you see on the cover sheet. Also make note of where you got the information, for example, from a LDS Family History Center (familysearch.org), a library, JewishGen.org, EllisIsland.org or the National Archives and Records Administration (archives.gov).

4 Capture interviews with living relatives on video- or audiotape so future generations can hear their words, too. If you shoot digital video, you can copy it without any reduction of quality, and save to a CD or DVD for easy viewing.

5 Create a master tree-type graph, either on paper or electronically, in which you'll insert your ancestors' names and birth, marriage and death dates as you discover them.

6 Print or photocopy all your printed source materials. File in folders labeled by relative's name. Include birth and death dates to distinguish between people with the same name (for example: Block, Anna 1910–1998). You can also file information by family, family line, state or country of origin, or event (birth records, census). You can further break it down into proven and unproven documents. You may want to make separate files for correspondence or event materials, such as wedding programs.

7 Use different-color folders to identify different branches of the family. This will help keep the byzantine paper trail organized.

8 Store all your genealogical information files and tapes temporarily in your filing cabinet and permanently in archival storage boxes for safekeeping. See 137 Organize Movies, Music and Other Media.

Tips

Store fragile documents, photos and tombstone rubbings carefully. See 296 Archive Family Records.

Confirm facts with more than one source whenever feasible.

See 366 Plan a Family Reunion.

Choose a software program that allows simple inputting for record-keeping of all your ancestors and that can print out genealogical charts. This will also make it easy for you to share your information with others.

Who Knew?

Back up your files regularly to safeguard your hand work (see 190 Organize Computer Files). Consider it an inexpensive if somewhat inconvenient insurance policy.

First of all, pat yourself on the back: The fact that you're preparing for this monumental occasion means you've done a spectacular parenting job. The work isn't over, but you and your child can move into the transition phase with confidence.

Steps

Getting your child ready

1 Train your child to handle his or her own laundry well before school starts. The first week of classes is not the time to find out what a red sock does to white shirts, and that you need to take the clothes out of the dryer when they're done so they don't end up all wrinkled.

2 Get your child used to waking up to an alarm without help. He or she needs to develop this skill on their own.

3 Have an open discussion about how you'll handle money and budgeting. By this point, your child should have developed some good money-management skills (see 248 Teach Your Kids About Money and 226 Set Up a Budget). Open a checking account at a branch near campus and discuss how much money you'll put in every month, if any, and what it needs to pay for. Get a prepaid credit card that can't be used if the bearer taps out the balance.

4 Do some advance problem-solving with your child about the roommate situation. Lots of kids talk on the phone or send e-mail to their new roomie before they get to school—but there's no way they can know about each other's lifestyle and habits. Talk about what to do when conflicts crop up. You might encourage your child to bring it up ahead of time: "How do you want to handle it if we have a problem?"

5 Pick up a course catalog (or find one online) to look over with your child. Get an idea of what lies ahead and talk about how to plan the first semester's course load so it's not too hard. See 153 Plan Your Course of Study in College.

6 Help your child sort out transportation on campus. Bikes are key to campus life in most locations—consider buying a clunker (and a lock) to deter thieves. Ask about bike storage facilities.

7 Recommend that your child find out where the student health center is and what services are available (including birth control) before he or she needs them. Keep in mind, it might be a friend or roommate who needs the help.

Care and feeding of your freshman

1 Be conscious about your next phase in parenting. While phone calls help, the absence of day-to-day contact is a huge change.

Tips

Check your health insurance policy to make sure your child is covered.

Suggest that your child talk with his or her roommate about who will bring a microwave, refrigerator and television.

Get the new roommate's cellular-phone number.

Who Knew?

Regularly go over your child's bank statements in the first year and discuss expenses to make sure both student loans and your financial contributions are adequate. Make adjustments accordingly.

Duke University freshmen receive a free Apple iPod, loaded with a campus map, orientation information, schedules and recorded lectures.

Warning

Talk about how you will stay in touch with each other. Will you set up a weekly phone call? E-mail frequently?

2 Expect some friction when your child is home during breaks. She has been living on her own terms, free to come and go, sleep and eat exactly as she wishes. Coming back home means having to ask for the car, eating with the family and not receiving phone calls at all hours. Recognize that both of you are going through a new phase and keep talking. Come to a compromise regarding late nights out and other potential conflicts.

285 Organize Your Empty Nest

Unless they've been there, people don't realize how painful it is when your first (or last or only) child leaves home. This child has been the center of your home and your life for the past 18 years. Remember making the transition to having kids? Dramatic but doable. The transition back will be equally jarring but ultimately as satisfying. Your life is about to get a lot simpler. It's time your systems and setup did, too.

Steps

1 Have a conversation with your fledgling about his or her room. Understand that the room is beginning a transition from belonging exclusively to him to belonging to the whole family, just as that child of yours has grown from belonging exclusively to you to being more and more of his own person.

2 Talk about your plans for the room—moving your computer to his desk, storing craft supplies, using it for guests and so on. See what stuff he is comfortable saying good-bye to.

3 Box up the stuff you've agreed upon, take down the Eminem posters and put on a fresh coat of neutral paint. Now's not the time to turn your hockey stud's room into the frilly Laura Ashley refuge you've always dreamed of. Keep a fair amount of his stuff out—hockey sticks in the corner, sci-fi books filling the shelves— so he feels at home when he comes back.

4 Reward yourself for a kid well done. Get that new leather sofa, now that size 13 feet won't be grinding grit into it every night. Pack up all the mismatched glasses, 20-ounce drink cups and chipped plates and send them on their way (see 95 Plan a Yard or Garage Sale and 12 Get Rid of What You Don't Want). Indulge in a new set of dishes.

5 Make a list of all the projects and things you always wanted to do—someday. That day is upon you. See 3 Write an Effective To-Do List and 16 Set Goals.

Tips

Resist the urge to create a museum of your kids' stuff. You need to think of their needs as visitors to your home, not residents.

Some colleges offer seminars for empty-nest parents. Check it out even if you or your spouse insist you are absolutely *fine,* thank you very much.

Reinvent your household systems now that one less person is involved. See 1 Get Organized.

286 | Plan for Boomerang Kids

The term "boomerang kids" says it all. They leave home—then they come back. With a dicey job market and skyrocketing housing costs, more and more young adults are moving back into their parents' home temporarily. If yours are among them, take these steps to make sure this arrangement is as successful as possible for everyone.

Steps

1 Have a frank conversation with your adult child before she moves back in. Discuss what each of your expectations are. If it's helpful, write up an agreement detailing what was discussed. Include how long the arrangement will last.

2 Discuss lifestyle rules. If, for example, overnight guests of the opposite sex or midnight visitors ringing the doorbell are unacceptable, make that understood.

3 Be mutually respectful of each other's independence and have faith in the good person you raised. Your adult child will make her own decisions about what she'll do and who she'll do it with without asking for your permission. At the same time, you'll want to protect your privacy and independence, too. This may mean getting the sleep you need when you need it, and not getting woken by late calls, cars pulling up, music and so on.

4 Come to an agreement regarding how she will contribute to the household in terms of chores, responsibilities, meal planning, shopping, cooking and cleaning up. Make a laundry schedule so you each have a free machine when you need it.

5 Set up a financial agreement that works for both of you. Include rent, utilities and food contributions.

6 Have a discussion if your child fails to meet her part of the bargain. She may find the arrangement no longer meets her needs, and decide to end it.

Tip

Strike a balance between wanting to make sure your child is actively looking for gainful employment and maintaining a neutral distance.

Enjoy your time together—it won't last forever.

Who Knew?

Hold regular family meetings to discuss what's on everyone's schedules, what nights you'll eat together and any issues that come up. The clearer everyone is about expectations, the easier it will be for all. See 267 Plan Family Meetings.

287 | Plan an Amicable Divorce

Divorce is a painful process for all parties. And if children are involved, the emotional stakes soar. Don't make it excruciating by hitting below the belt and letting hurt feelings rule your head. Take the high road and get it over with.

Steps

1 Talk to a lawyer to understand your rights and how to protect your assets.

Tips

For additional resources, check out DivorceNet.com.

Get counseling if you are overcome with bitterness or anger.

2 Choose your counsel:

- Each spouse hires his or her own lawyer, and the lawyers negotiate the terms. Legal fees average $20,000 to $50,000 per couple.

- Both of you hire a mediator, an attorney who works with both of you to reach an agreement. Hourly fees range from $150 to $300 per hour, and you may resolve the issues in less than 20 hours.

3 Be assertive with your spouse and your lawyer. Decide what you want and need and insist on it. Your future (and your children's) depends on it.

4 Meet with your spouse in neutral locations. Meeting at the home where the two of you lived brings up too many painful memories. And meeting at the ex's new bachelor or bachelorette pad brings up too much painful speculation.

5 Agree with your ex on as much as possible. If he or she makes a good point, say so. He or she might be more inclined to compromise on other things.

6 Nail down all the details in writing. If you both agree on things and it's on paper, you won't have as much to argue about later.

7 Review your goals (see 16 Set Goals) and write down a list of things you've always wanted to do: The day has come to begin your new life. Resist the urge, however, to broadcast your excitement about new loves (both people and activities) lest you sound like you're showing off to your ex. That is not moving on.

8 Don't disparage your spouse to your children. Help them maintain a good relationship with their father or mother. See 264 Blend Families and 288 Make Child Custody Arrangements.

9 Take care of yourself. The more rested you are and the better you feel about yourself, the more rational you'll be with your ex.

10 Use your friends for moral support, but don't keep going over the same complaints. Cultivate new friends and new topics of discussion, too.

11 Think of the kids. Do what's best for them. And that will end up being what's best for you, too.

Warnings

Get expert (legal, financial, emotional) help. Your future is at stake. This is not a DIY affair.

Try your best to keep the divorce out of court. When you go to court, a judge determines your future. You and your ex could probably do a better job.

Children are the most valuable assets in any divorce, and unlike other assets, they cannot be split up and divided. Once, courts automatically gave custody to the mother with visitation rights for the father. Then joint custody was all the rage. The latest legal trend gives primary custody to the parent who's been the primary caretaker. If you want custody, consider these steps.

Steps

1 Be an active participant in your child's life. Courts often consider how much time you spend with your child when they award custody or visitation rights.

2 Keep custody disputes out of court if at all possible. Attempt to work things out with your spouse first.

3 Make a parenting agreement. Nail down as many details as possible to minimize future disputes, including holidays, communication, weekly and summer schedules, pickups and drop-offs, education, religion and medical care.

4 Consider mediation if you can't agree on a custody plan.

5 Never leave the family home and your child if you plan to ask for custody. Possession really is nine-tenths of the law.

6 Avoid disparaging your spouse to your children. Not only does this hurt them, but it could hurt your case in court. Judges often consider whether you are providing a positive situation.

7 Do not prevent the kids from seeing your spouse unless you're ready and able to prove that he or she is an unfit parent. This could result in the kids being taken away from you.

8 If you have a new "friend," keep him or her out of the picture for now. You don't want jealousy affecting your ex's judgment or good will or muddying up the custody waters with the judge.

9 Do not move in with your new lover. Cohabitation will negatively affect your financial settlement and your kids.

10 Commit to providing a stable, loving environment. Your children need your undivided attention and predictability right now.

11 Stick to the schedule that you and your spouse have worked out and avoid asking for changes.

12 Realize that custody agreements can always be changed later as circumstances change. Just do the best you can for your children today.

Warnings

Always consult a lawyer in custody cases. You want expert advice here.

If you ever feel that you or your child is in danger, get help immediately.

If you get joint custody, realize that your ability to move out of state (or even to the next town) may be jeopardized.

Substance abuse, emotional or physical abuse, or abandonment will jeopardize your chances of seeing your child.

Patients or caregivers are often responsible for getting copies of medical records to specialists and consultants. Maintaining an organized copy of your own records—especially if you're ill or have a chronic condition—can literally mean the difference between life and death.

Steps

1 Use a large three-ring binder with dividers to organize the information.

2 Collect all contact information, including doctors' names, telephone numbers, fax numbers and addresses, in one section.

3 Keep a calendar in another section to record all appointments.

4 Maintain a log book for medical phone calls, indicating the person you talked with and when, what was said and what decisions about the course of treatment were made.

5 Keep a separate log of phone calls with your insurance company. Again, log the person you talked with, when, what was said and what follow-up is required.

6 Create a section to record prescriptions: what the medications are, when they were prescribed, who prescribed them, what they are for, and which pharmacy fills the prescriptions.

7 Make a separate section for receipts and financial paperwork, including insurance explanations of benefits (EOBs for short). Keep everything sorted by the date of service.

8 Visit the medical records office of your doctor or hospital on a regular basis to get copies of reports, transcripts and other doctors' records. You will need to show identification, sign a release form (including separate releases for HIV/AIDS and mental health records), and pay a copying fee. File these in reverse chronological order, so the newest record is on top.

9 Visit your medical center's film library if you have imaging studies (such as CT scans, MRIs or X-rays). Get duplicates of films, but realize there will probably be a charge for these. It's often easiest and cheapest to have a radiologist make copies of imaging studies when the images are first made. Be sure to ask.

10 Make extra photocopies occasionally of the most important records and store them with a trusted person.

11 Keep records portable by devoting a briefcase or small rolling suitcase to them. This way you'll be able to take them to all medical appointments.

Tips

Your will should specify that your medical records be given to your biological children. Records provide the best insight into your family's medical history. See 244 Make a Will.

MRIs are often available on a CD for an additional cost.

Warning

There's usually a charge to get medical records photocopied at a hospital or doctor's office. Understand what the cost is before you ask for hundreds of pages of copies.

290 | Plan for Elderly Parents' Care

As your parents enter their sunset years, you want to ensure that their lives are as comfortable as possible—and you want to make sure you aren't saddled with a burden you can't handle. Talk with your parents about their plans and preferences, and ask what arrangements, if any, they've made for their future care.

Steps

1 Help your parents map out their future if they haven't already considered it. List options for varying levels of care that range from independent living arrangements to assisted living to nursing homes. Talk about where they'd prefer to live once they can no longer live alone.

2 Stay on top of the details. Create folders with your parents' pertinent medical, financial and legal information and contacts. See 289 Organize Medical Records.

3 Meet with your parents and their financial adviser. If they don't have one, hire one. Do they have adequate insurance and income to cover their future needs?

4 Review their trusts and/or wills with their lawyer. Are they current? Are they adequate? (See 244 Make a Will.) Ask your parents to sign durable powers of attorney (for health and finances) if they haven't already. This will allow you or someone else in the family to make life-and-death decisions for them if they become incapacitated. See 245 Execute a Power of Attorney.

5 Keep their environment safe. Install safety bars in the bathrooms and ramps and handrails around the house if needed.

6 Determine whether your parents need any help with bills or maintaining the house. Make regular checks of their accounts to make sure things are in order.

7 Look into services available for the elderly, ranging from Meals on Wheels to bus services, even medication reminder services.

Tips

If you are too busy or too far away, you can hire a geriatric-care specialist to help your parents with problems or paperwork.

Find out where their important papers (such as home deeds, wills and powers of attorney) are located. Either store them with your new files, or know where they are so that when the time comes, you can find them easily. See 246 Plan Your Elderly Parents' Estate and 295 Make Your Final Arrangements.

For more information, go to sites such as SeniorCitizens Bureau.com.

Warning

Make sure you have the neighbors' phone numbers. Consider getting your folks a personal emergency response system so that help is a button-push away.

291 | Prepare for the Death of a Spouse

As painful as it may seem, advance planning can help you avoid legal battles and other emotionally exhausting experiences, during one of the most difficult times of your life. If you have children or complicated financial assets, it's even more crucial that you plan now to protect them later.

Steps

1 Get legal advice. Check your wills. Make sure you are each designated to receive all joint property automatically in the event of

Tips

Stay involved in the family finances so that there are no surprises when your spouse dies.

the other's death. If that's not the case, have new papers drawn up and sign them now.

2 Have adequate insurance coverage so your family's lifestyle won't change dramatically. Your kids will be distraught enough with your having to get a second job or move from the home you've all shared for years.

3 Make sure you have a medical power of attorney so you can serve as his or her protector in life-or-death medical situations.

4 Know where your spouse's investment accounts, IRA and other financial paperwork is located. If he or she keeps them at the office, you need to know this.

5 Review all property titles and deeds (for cars and boats) to ensure that both of you are listed as legal owners. Sure, it's a technicality now, but when your spouse dies, it will be a major and legally challengeable issue that your car is in his or her name.

6 Ask your spouse now whether you are eligible to receive benefits from your spouse's company in the event of his or her death. If you're both unsure, bring home the company handbook.

7 Consult with a financial adviser. You're looking for ways to secure your family's financial future.

Make sure your safe-deposit box is listed in both names; if it's under only your spouse's name, you'll need a court order to open it.

Similarly, put bank accounts in both names so they won't have to go through probate.

Read 236 Buy Life Insurance.

Warning

Don't assume anything. The courts won't. Get everything spelled out in writing.

292 | Help Your Elderly Parents Move

There comes a time when your aged parents become too infirm to live independently anymore. Moving out of their home is a wrenching experience for them, as it signifies a loss of independence. Some may worry about losing their beloved pet. Others worry about what will happen to their possessions. Make the transition as smooth as possible for them by handling the details.

Steps

1 Go back to the plans you made together earlier (see 290 Plan for Elderly Parents' Care). Help them choose the best living situation. Depending on their health, that could be a smaller place with no stairs closer to you or another relative, or a nurse-staffed assisted-living community.

2 Help them sort through their belongings. Deliver or mail items they want to give to relatives or friends; store anything they're not sure about, pack up the rest (or hire a moving company) and have it sent to their new home. See 97 Plan a Move.

3 Figure out if there's a way for them to keep a beloved pet — animals provide valuable emotional support. Choose a new place or community that takes pets or bring the pet home with you if they're moving nearby.

Tips

Arrange for them to be near you or other family members if possible. They'll need help if they're living independently, and you'll want to keep close tabs on the care they receive.

Sometimes it's better if your parents are not around to say good-bye to the old homestead. Take them out for the day with the assurance that the movers will handle everything.

The Assisted Living Federation of American offers more information at alfa.org.

293 | Organize a Home Medication Regime

More and more people are taking care of their ill loved ones at home. One reason is that many prescription drugs can be safely administered there. If you find yourself in charge of a complicated medication schedule, you'll find that an organized system is less work overall— and can let you, the caregiver, rest easier and stay well. Additionally, well-organized, clearly documented routines make it easier for caregivers to arrange for respite care.

Steps

1 Analyze the specific requirements of each medication. How often a day does it need to be taken? Should it be taken with food or on an empty stomach? Are there drugs that must be taken prior to it (such as antinausea drugs, which need to be taken before oral chemotherapy)?

2 Write out a schedule that reflects the requirements of all medications. Review the schedule with a doctor or pharmacist for accuracy and for conflicts.

3 Fill all prescriptions at the same pharmacy. This is especially important for patients seeing multiple medical specialists, all of whom are writing prescriptions. Pharmacists have databases that search for drug interactions and other possible complications.

4 Shop for a special pillbox to help you organize medications. There are boxes with several segments for different times of the day (morning, noon, dinner, bedtime), boxes with alarms and boxes with easy-to-read labels for the visually impaired.

5 Never remove the last pill from a bottle until a refill has arrived. then double-check that it's the right medication. Many medications, especially generics, look alike.

6 Get in the habit of rotating your pharmaceutical stock, using the oldest medications first.

Tips

Consider storing your medications in a linen closet. The heat and humidity of a bathroom or kitchen can be hard on pharmaceuticals.

If the patient is easily confused, keep his or her medications securely locked to avoid accidental dosing.

Keep each family member's prescription medications separate from others' in the same household.

Who Knew?

Each Wednesday, check to see if you need to get any prescriptions refilled. This gives you enough time to contact the doctor and pharmacy before the weekend.

Warning

Two people should never share the same medications, even if they have the same symptoms.

294 | Arrange Hospice Care

The final stages of a terminal illness are emotionally and physically devastating to both patients and caregivers. Hospice provides critical at-home care and eases the burden for the whole family as they transition toward death. Knowing when and how to set up hospice care requires much thought and planning.

Steps

1 Determine if hospice care is appropriate. When a life-limiting illness no longer responds to cure-oriented treatments, hospice care can provide comfort and support to patients and their

Tips

Contact the Hospice Foundation of America (hospicefoundation.org) for a list of resource organizations.

families. The patient, family and/or physician can initiate a hospice information or referral call.

2 Know what expectations the hospice will have from the patient and the patient's support system, and what kind of support and training program the hospice has for caregivers.

3 Research insurance coverage and payment options. Hospice care is a covered benefit under Medicare for patients with a prognosis of six months or less, and Medicaid covers hospice services in 41 states. Many private health-insurance policies and HMOs offer hospice coverage and benefits as well. Frequently, hospice expenses are less than conventional care expenses during the last six months of life.

4 Investigate the hospice. Find out if its accredited by a national organization like the Joint Commission on Accreditation of Healthcare Organizations (JCAHO), Medicare certified, and certified by your state, if required. Also check it out with the Better Business Bureau (bbb.org) and/or the state attorney general's office and ask for references.

5 Verify that the hospice's policies and philosophy are a good fit with your family's medical, financial, emotional and spiritual needs. Ask about specialized services, billing procedures, plan-of-care document, designated caregiver requirement, flexibility with balancing the family's other responsibilities and the hospice's procedure for resolving issues. Also pay attention to the general level of concern and competence you observe when communicating with hospice employees.

6 Ask for help. Family members, friends, co-workers, clergy and people who belong to community organizations can all pitch in. Some can help with planning, and others can help with carrying out those plans and giving support.

7 Talk to the hospice about the challenging role of caregiver and find out how they will support you. You will be tending to the patient's constant physical demands, supporting his or her spiritual concerns and helping resolve unfinished business, in addition to dealing with health professionals, family and friends, and taking care of your own needs. Hospice can provide trained volunteers to offer respite care to give family members a break.

8 Be clear and firm about what you want when working with health professionals. Prepare lists of questions and concerns, and have all the information they may need ready when you call.

9 Get help as you and your loved one move into the final stages. Hospice offers a variety of bereavement and counseling services to families before and after a loved one's death. In addition, publications like "Journeys," a monthly newsletter to help in bereavement published by the Hospice Foundation of America, can help during this difficult time.

If the patient is not covered by Medicare or any other health insurance, the first thing hospice will do is assist families in finding out whether the patient is eligible for any coverage they may not be aware of. Barring this, most hospices will provide for anyone who cannot pay using money raised from the community or from memorial or foundation gifts.

Have paper and pencil ready when you call a health care professional, to ensure that you hear the information correctly and don't forget it. See 289 Organize Medical Records.

Warning

Though Medicare covers all services and supplies for the hospice patient related to the terminal illness, in some hospices the patient may be required to pay a 5 percent or $5 copayment on medication and a 5 percent copayment for respite care. Ask about any copayments when selecting a hospice.

Whoever lies beneath the gravestone in Key West, Florida, with an epitaph that reads "I told you I was sick" obviously planned ahead. Most people don't prepare for their own death. Using a "road map" (a guide for executors or survivors) makes simple work of dealing with your demise, and is the final step in a lifetime of careful planning.

Steps

Personal preparation

1 Include your spouse in all your business matters in life so he or she will be able to cope better after your death.

2 Consider leaving notes for your family members in the form of diaries or videotapes. Tell them how special they are to you.

3 Specify how you would like your obituary to read.

4 Make a list of people—family, friends, your banker, stockbroker, attorney, insurance agents—to be notified along with their phone numbers and addresses.

Legal and financial preparation

1 Read 244 Make a Will, 243 Create a Living Trust and 245 Execute a Power of Attorney. Work with a lawyer to draw up these documents.

2 Make sure that your life insurance payout is sufficient to tide your family over until your spouse gets back on his or her feet after your death. See 236 Buy Life Insurance.

3 Keep your list of beneficiaries up to date. Every time you experience a major life change (birth, death, divorce), go down the list and make sure your beneficiaries are still correct.

4 Pick up a road map from the trust department of a bank, a financial planner or an estate attorney. A road map enables those surviving you to handle your affairs as you wish after your death, minimizing confusion and potential rancor.

5 Pour all your vital information—personal and business-related—into the road map. There are sections for personal information, insurance records, account numbers, bank accounts, certificates, securities, safe-deposit box (and key) location, trust fund and tax information, military service details and veterans' benefits.

6 Hire an estate organizer for professional assistance in creating a road map. He or she will help you organize your financial information, clarify your desires and record to whom you want your heirlooms and collections to go—all in the privacy of your home. See 247 Plan Your Estate.

Tips

See 294 Arrange Hospice Care to further understand how to prepare for a terminal illness and death.

Give careful thought to your service. Would you like the ceremony to be traditional and very religious, or a spontaneous, creative memorial? If, for example, family members assume you're a devout Christian but you've had quiet Buddhist leanings for years, clarify your wishes.

Put any favorite sayings, quotes, poems or songs that you would like read at your service in your road map.

Go to FuneralPlan.com for more information on caskets.

The Neptune Society will follow your wishes to have your ashes scattered at sea (with or without family members present), buried in a rose garden or placed in a columbarium.

Who Knew?

What's your life expectancy? Find out at LivingTo100.com.

If you are or were a member of the military, investigate what services are available. Veterans are often entitled to have a military guard, but need to ask for it.

7 Include specific details on what you would like done with your body. Would you like to be buried, cremated or donated to science? What about organ donation?

8 Contact the Neptune Society (neptunesociety.org) if you would like a simple cremation service. Basic cremation starts at $1,300; caskets, urns and other services are extra.

9 Choose a funeral provider. Ask friends for references.

10 Add up how much the funeral and burial will cost if that is your desire. Figure out where you will get the funds and write your instructions clearly in your road map.

11 Buy a casket. Materials range from knotty pine to hardwood, copper, stainless steel and other materials. Decide if you want your casket open or closed during the funeral (some clergy prefer a closed casket). Depending on how rough-and-tumble your exit ends up being, you may ultimately be outvoted.

12 Write down any final comments you would like to make—to your family, community of friends, or the world. This would be the other time where you speak now or forever hold your peace (see also 323 Plan a Wedding).

The laws in most states recognize your right to control your own funeral and cemetery services.

Warnings

Don't get talked into purchasing extras you don't want or can't afford.

Research mortgage insurance so that your home is automatically paid for if you die. Consider similar insurance for other significant properties.

296 Archive Family Records

Your old letters, diaries, Bibles and photographs are your family's history, and time is their enemy. Paper is biodegradable—a process you want to impede if your grandchildren are going to enjoy these documents. Fortunately, thanks to the popularity of scrapbooking, materials to safeguard these documents are easy to find.

Tips

Handle old papers as little as possible.

Clearly label and number your boxes and binders.

See 232 Organize Important Documents.

ArchivalMethods.com is one source for archival storage and presentation products.

Steps

1 Store important papers and books in acid-free, archival-safe boxes or binders. If you use binders, put each document in a polypropylene sheet protector so that you can handle it safely. Make sure any notes and papers you store with the documents are also acid-free. Acids in regular paper and cardboard cause paper to deteriorate.

2 Store newspaper clippings separately from other types of documents as they are highly acidic. Put them in polypropylene protectors laid flat in archival boxes. Make copies of or scan in newspaper clippings because newsprint deteriorates quickly.

3 Store photographs in acid-free, archival-quality boxes in a dark, dry, cool place. They can also be put in albums as long as they are also acid-free and of archival quality.

4 Make a master list of what is in each box so that you don't have to open them (and handle the documents) to find out.

RGANIZE YOUR CONTACTS • GET RID OF WHAT YOU DON'T WANT • SAY NO WITHOUT FEELING GUILTY • BALANCE HOME AND WORK • L
AIN • SCHEDULE TELEVISION WATCHING • DESIGN A HEALTHY LIFESTYLE • PLAN TO AVOID JUNK FOOD • CHOOSE A WEIGHT LOSS PLA
EET AN ONLINE DATE • PLAN THE PERFECT DATE • MASTERMIND A BREAKUP • PLAN YOUR SOCIAL CALENDAR • MEET MR. OR MS. RIGH
RT YOUR SOCK DRAWER • RETURN RENTALS ON TIME • TAKE CONTROL OF YOUR JUNK DRAWER • ORGANIZE THE MEDICINE CABINET
AR CLEAN AND ORDERLY • DEAL WITH A PACK RAT • SELL STUFF ONLINE • ORGANIZE YOUR BOOKSHELVES • CATEGORIZE NEWSPAPER
VE BETTER THROUGH LABELING • ORGANIZE JEWELRY • PLAN YOUR DREAM KITCHEN • CONQUER YOUR CLOSETS • ORGANIZE THE LI
RGANIZE SPRING CLEANING • KEEP THE FAMILY ROOM ORGANIZED • SET UP A BATHROOM SCHEDULE • ORGANIZE BATHROOMS • ORG
RGANIZE KIDS' ROOMS • ORGANIZE SPORTS EQUIPMENT • ORGANIZE KIDS' PLAY SPACES • SAFEGUARD YOUR HOME AGAINST ALLERG
OUSE • USE HOME DESIGN AND PLANNING SOFTWARE • ESTABLISH YOUR HOME'S SPACE PLAN • INCORPORATE UNIVERSAL DESIGN P
HE BASEMENT • ORGANIZE THE GARAGE • ORGANIZE A TOOLBOX • SET UP A WOODSHOP • ORGANIZE YOUR WINE COLLECTION • PLAN
TUDIO OR SMALL APARTMENT • MANAGE WARRANTY DOCUMENTS • MANAGE HOME-IMPROVEMENT PAPERWORK • MERGE TWO HOUS
RGANIC VEGETABLE GARDEN • PLANT A KITCHEN HERB GARDEN • PLAN A BUTTERFLY GARDEN • DESIGN A BIRD GARDEN • DESIGN A G
ORGANIZE GARDENING TOOLS • ADD A POTTING BENCH TO A YARD • SCHEDULE FRUIT TREE MAINTENANCE • LAY OUT A SPRINKLER S
ESIGN A GARDEN PATH • SET UP A COMPOST SYSTEM • WINTERIZE PLANTS • SCHEDULE YARD WORK • STORE ANYTHING • STORE BU
ND HOBBY MATERIALS • ORGANIZE ART SUPPLIES • ORGANIZE GIFT WRAP AND SEASONAL DECORATIONS • ORGANIZE KIDS' SCHOOLW
OUR WEDDING DRESS AND OTHER TEXTILES • STORE A FUR COAT • STORE BICYCLES AND GEAR • STORE SKI GEAR • ORGANIZE CAMP
HICH COLLEGE IS RIGHT FOR YOU • GET INTO A TOP COLLEGE OR UNIVERSITY • ACE THE COLLEGE ADMISSIONS TESTS • ORGANIZE Y
AW SCHOOL • PREPARE FOR THE BAR EXAM • GET A DEGREE WHILE YOU'RE WORKING • WORK AT HOME WITH KIDS • GO BACK TO WO
RGANIZE YOUR JOB SEARCH • PREPARE FOR A CAREER CHANGE • OPEN A RESTAURANT • BECOME A PHYSICIST • BECOME A CONCE
EALITY-SHOW CONCEPT • BECOME A TALK-SHOW HOST • BECOME A PHOTOJOURNALIST • BECOME A MOVIE DIRECTOR • BECOME A
LING SYSTEM • ORGANIZE YOUR BRIEFCASE • ORGANIZE YOUR DESK • ORGANIZE YOUR WORKDAY • GET A HANDLE ON E-MAIL • OR
ALARY REVIEW • CLIMB THE CORPORATE LADDER EFFECTIVELY • ADD A WORKSPACE TO ANY ROOM • ORGANIZE A HOME OFFICE • OF
RAVEL • WRITE A BUSINESS PLAN • SET UP A NEW BUSINESS • CREATE A MARKETING PLAN • AMASS A REAL-ESTATE EMPIRE • POLISH
MPLOYEE • FIRE AN EMPLOYEE • PASS ON A FAMILY BUSINESS • STAY ON TOP OF YOUR SALES GAME • RESTRUCTURE A COMPANY T
EFEND AGAINST A HOSTILE TAKEOVER • ORGANIZE YOUR OFFICE FOR A MOVE • PREPARE YOUR BUSINESS FOR THE UNTHINKABLE •
REPARE YOUR TAXES • ORGANIZE A LOAN APPLICATION • ORGANIZE IMPORTANT DOCUMENTS • SAVE FOR PRIVATE SCHOOLING • ORC
LUB • TRACK YOUR INVESTMENTS • SURVIVE BANKRUPTCY • PLAN FOR RETIREMENT • PREPARE A PRENUPTIAL AGREEMENT • CREAT
ONEY • PLAN YOUR FAMILY • BUDGET FOR A NEW BABY • ORCHESTRATE THE PERFECT CONCEPTION • PLAN FOR ARTIFICIAL INSEMIN
EAVE • ORDER BABY ANNOUNCEMENTS • ORGANIZE AN INTERNATIONAL ADOPTION • FOSTER A CHILD • ORGANIZE YOUR LIFE AS A N
OORDINATE A FAMILY CALENDAR • PLAN FAMILY MEETINGS • ORGANIZE HOME SYSTEMS FOR ADD • PREPARE FOR A NEW CAT OR DO
ACK-TO-SCHOOL • WIN THE HOMEWORK WARS • PLAN A FIELD TRIP • PLAN YOUR CHILD'S ACTIVITIES • PLAN YOUR CHILDREN'S SUM
NLINE • ORGANIZE A GENEALOGICAL SEARCH • PREPARE FOR YOUR CHILD'S DEPARTURE FOR COLLEGE • ORGANIZE YOUR EMPTY N
LDERLY PARENTS' CARE • PREPARE FOR THE DEATH OF A SPOUSE • HELP YOUR ELDERLY PARENTS MOVE • ORGANIZE A HOME MEDI
TORE TRIPS • SET UP ONLINE GROCERY SHOPPING • ORGANIZE RECIPES AND COOKBOOKS • PLAN THEME MENUS • CREATE EFFECT
EFRIGERATOR AND FREEZER • ORGANIZE CUTLERY AND KITCHEN TOOLS • ORGANIZE CUPBOARDS AND DRAWERS • ORGANIZE THE
UNCHES FOR KIDS • PLAN PARTY FOODS AHEAD • THROW A DINNER PARTY • FINISH DINNER ON TIME • PULL OFF A LAST-MINUTE PAR
LTIMATE WEDDING CHECKLIST • BUDGET FOR A WEDDING • FIND THE PERFECT WEDDING RING • PLAN AN ELOPEMENT • SET UP A B
ONOR • EXECUTE BEST MAN DUTIES • HIRE A BAND • HIRE A BARTENDER • PLAN A SHOWER • ORGANIZE THE REHEARSAL DINNER •
UCCESSFUL SLUMBER PARTY • PLAN A BAR OR BAT MITZVAH • PLAN A QUINCEAÑERA • PLAN A RETIREMENT PARTY • PLAN A FUNER
ANUKKAH PARTY • ORGANIZE A HOLIDAY CRAFT PARTY • PLAN TO SPEND CHRISTMAS SOLO • PLAN THE PERFECT HOLIDAY GIFT EXC
HE HOLIDAYS • STICK TO YOUR NEW YEAR'S RESOLUTIONS • PLAN THE PERFECT NEW YEAR'S EVE • PLAN A SEDER • PLAN A SPECIA
OOD TREE • ORGANIZE A BICYCLE SCAVENGER HUNT • RUN A SPORTS TOURNAMENT • PUBLICIZE AN EVENT • PLAN AN ORGANIZATI
LAN A CONCERT IN THE PARK • ORGANIZE AN INTERNATIONAL CONCERT TOUR • ORGANIZE A FILM FESTIVAL • PLAN A FUND-RAISING
BUILD A COMMUNITY PLAY STRUCTURE • THROW A BLOCK PARTY • SET UP A NEIGHBORHOOD WATCH • CREATE AN EVACUATION PI
RGANIZE A PROTEST OR MARCH • FIGHT CITY HALL • ORGANIZE A BOYCOTT • ORGANIZE A CLASS ACTION LAWSUIT • MANAGE GRO
CHOOL IN A THIRD WORLD COUNTRY • PLAN A TRIP • PLAN A TRIP WITH CHILDREN • TRAVEL WITH TEENS • BOOK AIRLINE TICKETS
OTORCYCLE TRIP • PLAN A TRAIN TRIP IN THE UNITED STATES • RIDE THE RAILS ABROAD • PREPARE A VACATION COUNTDOWN CHE
UGGAGE • LOAD A BACKPACK PROPERLY • PLAN AN ELDERHOSTEL TRIP • ORGANIZE AN RV VACATION • PLAN A TRIP WITH AGING PA
IDELY DIFFERENT PEOPLE • PLAN SPRING BREAK • PLAN AN OVERNIGHT GETAWAY WITH YOUR SPOUSE • PLAN A VACATION SEPARA
OLITICALLY UNSTABLE REGION • GET TRAVEL INSURANCE • GET IMMUNIZATIONS FOR TRAVELING • BOOK AN ADVENTURE VACATION
LAN A FISHING TRIP TO ALASKA • PACK FOR A CAMPING TRIP • LEAD A BACKPACK TRIP • HIKE A FAMOUS TRAIL • PLAN A TOUR OF T
NGLISH CANAL TRIP • PLAN A CROSS-COUNTRY AIRPLANE VOYAGE • PLAN THE PERFECT DAY ABROAD • PLAN A VISIT TO THE LOUV
LAN • PREPARE FOR AN ACT OF GOD • ASSEMBLE EMERGENCY KITS • PREPARE FOR SURGERY • PLAN YOUR RECOVERY • SURVIVE
EING LOST • CONDUCT A SEARCH AND RESCUE OPERATION • PLAN AN INVASION • SURVIVE A POLITICAL COUP • PLAN FOR A TERR

GS • SET GOALS • STREAMLINE YOUR MORNING ROUTINE • ORGANIZE A CHORE SCHEDULE FOR KIDS • ORGANIZE YOUR CHORES • NEV
YOUR WORKOUT SCHEDULE • SCHEDULE DOCTOR VISITS • PREPARE FOR COLD AND FLU SEASON • GET A DRASTIC MAKEOVER • ARR
JP • FIND YOUR KEYS • TIDY UP IN MINUTES • CONQUER CLUTTER • ACTUALLY SEE THE BOTTOM OF YOUR PURSE • ORGANIZE YOUR S
E CAR MAINTENANCE • ORGANIZE PET SUPPLIES • MANAGE GARBAGE AND RECYCLABLES • PREPARE GRAB 'N' GO ACTIVITY BAGS • KE
NE CLIPPINGS • ORGANIZE YOUR PHOTOS • ARRANGE PHOTOS AND PICTURES • ARRANGE AN ART COLLECTION • END COLLECTION C
• ORGANIZE YOUR LAUNDRY CENTER • CREATE A SEWING CENTER • GET READY FOR THE HOUSECLEANER • ORGANIZE CLEANING SUF
WAYS AND MUDROOMS • ORGANIZE A DORM ROOM • ORGANIZE YOUR SCHOOL LOCKER • MAKE YOUR HOME SAFE FOR SMALL CHILE
RE FOR SKYROCKETING ENERGY COSTS • USE FENG SHUI TO ORGANIZE YOUR HOME • DESIGN A NEW HOME WITH FENG SHUI • DESIG
LAN A REMODEL • PLAN A MULTIMEDIA CENTER • TURN A BASEMENT INTO A MEDIA ROOM OR PLAYROOM • ORGANIZE THE ATTIC • OF
UL ESTATE SALE • PLAN A YARD OR GARAGE SALE • PREPARE YOUR HOME FOR SALE • PLAN A MOVE • DOWNSIZE YOUR HOUSE • OR
CORATE FOR THE SEASONS • PREPARE A VACATION HOME FOR THE OFF-SEASON • PREPARE YOUR HOME FOR NATURE S WORST • PRE
ARDEN • PLANT A CUT-FLOWER GARDEN • DESIGN A SHADE GARDEN • DESIGN A DRY GARDEN • PLAN FOR A LONG-SEASON CONTAIN
J AND PLANT A LAWN • DESIGN A NEW LANDSCAPE • PLAN AN OUTDOOR KITCHEN • DESIGN A DECK OR PATIO • DESIGN A WATER FEAT
S • STORAGE SOLUTIONS FOR ANY ROOM • THE CAPACITY OF A SMALL ROOM • ORGANIZ
WORK • ORGANIZE MOVIES, MUSIC AND C HRLOOMS • STORE OUT-OF-SEASON CLOTHES •
NT • STORE PAINT AND OTHER HAZARDOUS STORE A BOAT FOR THE WINTER • STORE A CA
APPLICATIONS • PLAN YOUR COURSE OF H PAPER • GET INTO GRAD SCHOOL • GET INTO
ONG ABSENCE • SET UP AN INTERNSHIP • N THE PEACE CORPS • PRODUCE A NEWSLETTEI
BECOME A COWBOY • BECOME A BRAIN S ATHOLIC NUN • ORGANIZE AN EXHIBITION • DEV
ME A STUNT PERSON • BECOME A TOUR G • CONQUER YOUR PAPER PILES • CREATE A FL
TER FILES • SCHEDULE APPOINTMENTS ER NCE CALL • PREPARE FOR A MEETING • PREPAR
E NETWORK • CHOOSE THE BEST PHONE TEM • MAKE A NETWORKING PLAN • PLAN YOUR
TATION SKILLS • PREPARE A SPEECH • PR AN AN IPO • DELEGATE RESPONSIBILITIES • HIRE
OFITS • FORM A BOARD OF DIRECTORS • N A COMPANY PICNIC • PLAN A COMPANY RETF
FAILING BUSINESS • DISMANTLE A BUSINE • DESIGN A SAVINGS PLAN • SIMPLIFY BILL PAY
IANCIAL-AID PACKAGE • PLAN FOR COLLE E A HEALTH INSURANCE PLAN • START AN INVES
T • MAKE A WILL • EXECUTE A POWER OF S' ESTATE • PLAN YOUR ESTATE • TEACH YOUR K
RE FOR AN IN VITRO FERTILIZATION • PREF ATERNITY WARDROBE • SET UP MATERNITY OR I
EPARE FOR CHILDBIRTH • STOCK A DIAPE LEND FAMILIES • CREATE A HOUSEHOLD ORGAN
OL YOUR CHILD • SET UP A CARPOOL • ST HE BEST ELEMENTARY SCHOOL • ORGANIZE KIDS
R SUMMER CAMP • CHOOSE A SUMMER S R FAMILY COMPUTER USE • PLAN TO KEEP YOU
BOOMERANG KIDS • PLAN AN AMICABLE EMENTS • ORGANIZE MEDICAL RECORDS • PLAN
ARRANGE HOSPICE CARE • MAKE YOUR RECORDS • PLAN A WEEK OF MENUS • ORGANIZE
STS • COOK AHEAD • DETERMINE THE SH M WAREHOUSE STORES • EFFICIENTLY USE THE
NTLY USE SPACE UNDER THE SINK • STOV UR COUNTER SPACE • COOK FOR ONE • PLAN H
NNER PARTY FOR YOUR BOSS • PLAN DI PARTY • IMPRESS A DATE • PLAN A WEDDING • C
I PLANNER • HIRE A PHOTOGRAPHER • ACHELORETTE PARTY • PREPARE TO BE THE MAI
YMOON • PLAN A BAPTISM • PLAN A BRI THROW A PARTY • PREPARE FOR HOUSE GUESTS • PLAN A CHILD'S BIRTHDAY PARTY • F

Food & Entertaining

) CUSTOM • PLAN AHEAD FOR A LOW-STRESS HOLIDAY • STAY WITHIN A BUDGET THIS CHRISTMAS • PREPARE A HOLIDAY FEAST • TI
ZE GIFT-GIVING IN ADVANCE • STICK TO YOUR DIET DURING THE HOLIDAYS • PLAN A HOLIDAY OPEN HOUSE • REORGANIZE YOUR LIF
ORGANIZE A HIGH-SCHOOL CLASS REUNION • PLAN A FAMILY REUNION • START A KNITTING CIRCLE • ORGANIZE A BOOK CLUB • SET
HARPEN THE FOCUS OF AN ORGANIZATION • IMPROVE YOUR CHILD'S SCHOOL • PLAN A PROM • ORGANIZE A COMMUNITY THEATER
E A PANCAKE BREAKFAST • PLAN A TOY DRIVE • HOLD A BARN RAISING • ORGANIZE A CHARITY WALK OR RUN • BUILD LOW-INCOM
R-REGISTRATION DRIVE • RUN FOR LOCAL OFFICE • ORGANIZE A PETITION • ORGANIZE A RECALL • GET AN INITIATIVE ON THE BALLC
MUNITY • PRESERVE OPEN SPACE • SAVE HISTORIC PROPERTIES AND LANDMARKS • SET UP A NONGOVERNMENTAL ORGANIZATION
E UNITED STATES • RENT A CAR ABROAD • MAKE HOTEL RESERVATIONS • ARRANGE EXECUTIVE ACCOMMODATIONS • PLAN A CRUIS
AN ITINERARY • PACK FOR A TRIP • PACK FOR A BUSINESS TRIP • PACK FOR A WEEK IN ONE CARRY-ON • PACK A DAY BAG • PREVEN
E A SAILING TEAM • PLAN A SAILBOAT CRUISE • PLAN A BICYCLE TRIP WITH A TOUR COMPANY • TRAVEL ABROAD • PLAN A VACATION
OUSE • PLAN A TRIP TO A DIFFERENT CULTURE • FORAGE ABROAD • MAIL PACKAGES BACK TO THE UNITED STATES • PLAN A TRIP TO
ROAD • PLAN A CLIMB OF MOUNT KILIMANJARO • PACK FOR A SAFARI • ORGANIZE A HUNTING TRIP • PACK FOR A FISHING OR HUN
S • ORGANIZE A BACKCOUNTRY SKI TRIP • ORGANIZE A CAR RALLY • PLAN A WHALE-WATCHING TRIP • PACK FOR A VOYAGE AT SEA
DNEY HARBOUR BRIDGE • PLAN A TRIP TO NEW ORLEANS FOR MARDI GRAS • PLAN A DAY AT DISNEYLAND • FORMULATE A FAMILY E
YOU'RE ALONE • SURVIVE IF YOUR CAR BREAKS DOWN • DEAL WITH AMNESIA • FIGHT AN EBOLA OUTBREAK • FIGHT A FOREST FIF
CUE A HOSTAGE • OUTSMART PIRATES • DELIVER A BABY • MAKE AN EMERGENCY LANDING • MAKE A JAIL BREAK • BECOME A MOV
TOUR DE FRANCE • RUN A MARATHON •

297 | Plan a Week of Menus

It's the million-dollar question: What's for dinner? When you plan ahead, there's no need to stare with glazed eyes into the refrigerator hoping for divine inspiration. Make grocery shopping a snap, eat more satisfying meals and always know what's for dinner—with just a little advanced planning.

Steps

1 Set aside time to plan your menu. Saturday or Sunday afternoons are a good time to think about the week ahead. If you stick to a routine, you're more likely to be successful in continuing with your menus.

2 Check your family's weekly schedule to find out how many nights and eaters you need to plan for. See 266 Coordinate a Family Calendar.

3 Match the time needed to prepare specific dinners to your family's schedule: On lazy Sundays you'll have time for a slow-cooked pork roast while jam-packed Wednesdays might mean throwing stew ingredients into a crock pot before leaving the house in the morning. Some nights, you may only have time to pick up a pizza between shuttling the kids from practice to piano lessons.

4 Be realistic: On weeknights, plan quick and easy meals that can be prepared ahead or cooked quickly. Simple meals can be delicious—such as goat cheese and herb omelets or angel hair pasta with olive oil, fresh tomatoes and Parmesan cheese.

5 Build dinners around tried-and-true recipes for the least resistance from picky eaters. You don't need to reinvent the wheel every time you sit down to plan your menus.

6 Focus on the main dish first: grilled fish, broiled steaks, marinated pork tenderloin, roasted chicken or pasta primavera. Build in salads and side dishes to round out the meal.

7 Try at least one new dish each month—it might become your family's next favorite. Use family dinners as a menu-testing laboratory and cultivate adventurous eaters.

8 Get inspiration for new recipes from cooking magazines, cookbooks, your newspaper's weekly food section or Web sites such as Epicurious.com and Williams-Sonoma.com. Check out software, such as the one from LivingCookbook.com that has a meal-planning calendar that accesses your saved recipes.

9 Scan the advertised specials in the newspaper and incorporate budget items into your weekly menu. Find a deal on filet mignon? Make that the star of your menu one night.

10 Take inventory of your pantry and fridge for any produce or perishable items that need to be used. Incorporate them into your menus.

Tips

Keep an envelope of take-out menus in your household organizer for easy reference—even staunch menu planners need a break sometimes. See 265 Create a Household Organizer.

Use sticky notes to mark intriguing recipes in your cookbooks. When you're stuck, you can always crack one open for easy inspiration. See 300 Organize Recipes and Cookbooks.

Before heading to the market, chop up leftovers for fried rice. Steak or chicken, veggies, frozen peas and green onions can be sautéed with soy sauce and cooked white rice—stir in an egg to bind it together and a dollop of oyster sauce for an authentic zing.

Keep a quick meal on hand for nights when you're not in the mood to cook. After all, you can whip up spaghetti with jarred sauce in less than 15 minutes. (See 309 Organize the Pantry.)

Stock up on frozen vegetables such as peas, corn, spinach, green beans and julienned bell peppers—they're just as nutritious as fresh ones, and they make last-minute cooking a snap. (See 306 Efficiently Use the Refrigerator and Freezer and 303 Cook Ahead.)

11 Spice up your die-hard dinners. Try fajitas instead of burgers, couscous instead of white rice, bok choy instead of broccoli or Indian-spiced ground beef instead of meat loaf.

12 Behold the humble casserole. It's not the most glamorous entrée, but for a no-fuss meal—be it Mexican tortilla, shepherd's pie or homemade mac and cheese—it's tasty, it can be assembled in advance, and it doesn't need a side dish, except perhaps a simple salad. Freeze the remainder for a quick meal later in the week.

13 Plan for speedy leftovers. For instance, grill extra chicken breasts on Monday for a quick chicken Caesar on Wednesday. Poach additional salmon on Tuesday for easy omelets with chives and goat cheese on Thursday. Triple a recipe of black bean chili— use the leftovers to top baked potatoes the next day and freeze the rest. Check out sources such as RealSimple.com for more multiple day recipes.

14 Store your weekly menus in your computer, or in a file folder or three-ring binder that you keep in your kitchen. That way, you can easily access old meals that were a hit.

Instead of spending precious minutes to bake a dessert (who has the time?), stock no-cook sweets such as frozen yogurt and sorbet. One night a week, when time allows, treat your clan to an easy homemade apple crumble or store-bought pound cake topped with berries and whipped cream.

Post your menu on the refrigerator or kitchen bulletin board and your family can always have the answer to "What's for dinner?"

298 | Organize Grocery Store Trips

There are two types of supermarket shoppers: Those with a game plan and those who meander from the produce department to the freezer aisle and back again for that forgotten bunch of celery. Efficient shopping all starts with a foolproof list, good timing and steely focus.

Steps

1 See 302 Create Effective Shopping Lists.

2 Review your list one last time before you head out. Does it have the items you need for the week's menus and to restock staples?

3 Check advertisements for sales, clip the appropriate coupons, and attach them to your list. Don't forget the membership card that entitles you to extra discounts.

4 Have a snack: You'll cut down on SSS (starving shopper syndrome) and impulse buys at the checkout line. See 24 Choose a Weight Loss Plan.

5 Shop first thing in the morning, if possible. It's the least crowded time. Your trip will be less hectic, and bargains easier to spot.

6 Ask questions. Employees are there to help and can cut down on time spent pinballing around the store.

7 Start with produce and dry goods and end with meats, seafood and other perishables.

8 Stick to your list—it will help you save time and money.

Tip

Double-bag meats and seafood so they don't contaminate other foods.

Who Knew?

Meat serving sizes: 6 ounces (185 g) per person for dinner and 4 ounces (125 g) per person for lunch.

299 | Set Up Online Grocery Shopping

When your life hinges on split-second timing, stopping at the store doesn't always make the cut. And if you have young children, it's sometimes not even possible. Save yourself the headache and shop online. With the click of a mouse, your goods will be delivered painlessly to your door.

Steps

1 Find a service that delivers to your neighborhood. Contact your local supermarket to see if it offers delivery. Or type "online grocery service" into a search engine for regional services such as Peapod.com. Then type in your ZIP code to make sure you're in the delivery area. Outside the service area? Netgrocer.com ships groceries by FedEx.

2 Set up an account. You'll need to supply an address, daytime phone number and e-mail address, and set a password. Find out if there's a delivery cost or a minimum order.

3 Start shopping. Grab your master shopping list (see 302 Create Effective Shopping Lists) and set up an online shopping list, too. The time you spend upfront you'll save each time you shop. Use the site's search engine to find particular items or browse by department (dairy, produce, deli). Check the home page for weekly specials.

4 Think strategically. This is a great way to buy cases of soda and beer, big boxes of laundry detergent and household cleaners, a three-month supply of toilet paper or paper towels, jumbo packs of diapers and infant formula, or any other bulky or heavy items you don't want to lug in and out of your car.

5 Stock up on goods you can't find at your neighborhood market. NetGrocer.com carries a nice array of kosher foods (even kosher pet food), and EthnicGrocer.com has hard-to-find items such as spicy red Thai curry. Schwan's (schwans.com), which has been delivering foods for 50 years, offers full frozen meals.

6 Scan your order to verify that you've selected the correct items. When you've used the service a few times, you'll be able to click through past orders to make sure you're not forgetting anything. Several services allow you to add items from previous orders to your current order.

7 Select a delivery time and day. You'll get several options of delivery windows, usually in two- or three-hour time chunks. Plan ahead: Some services will deliver the next day, some within 3 to 7 days via FedEx.

8 Check out. Enter any promotional codes you've received, coupon codes and, if applicable, your frequent shopper number. Review your order (and approve any suggested substitutions) and pay using your credit card.

Tips

Check to see if you can earn airline miles or points toward your store's rewards program for shopping online.

If you can't get good organic and seasonal fruits and vegetables in your area, or you'd like them delivered fresh to your doorstep, sign up for produce delivery online at DiamondOrganics.com, DannysOrganic.com or PlanetOrganics.com. Some sites also deliver beef, cheese or flowers. Look into delivery services from local farms at your farmers' market as well.

When your groceries are delivered, check out the produce and any substitutions before the driver leaves, to make sure it's to your liking. You can give the driver unwanted items to return to the store (and credit your account), which saves you a trip to make returns.

Who Knew?

Have it your way. Enter in special requests, for example: "Buy the bananas green so they ripen at home." If a service can't fill your order, it will typically contact you via e-mail ahead of time.

When ordering items in bulk (such as apples), note the unit: Some items are sold by count, others by the pound.

300 | Organize Recipes and Cookbooks

You've got recipe boxes full of family favorites, folders of torn out pages from food magazines, newspaper clippings and a computer of downloaded recipes from your go-to cooking site. How can you make sense of it all? While there is creative satisfaction in thumbing through your collection—not to mention the emotional tug from seeing Grandma's handwriting on her famous cookie recipe—it's time to bring this conglomeration to order.

Steps

1 Preserve your handwritten family recipes, which will become heirlooms for generations to come, by laminating them. This is an inexpensive way to protect against food smudges and torn edges.

2 Sort all your recipes into categories, such as appetizers, salads, side dishes, meat, fish, poultry, pasta, vegetarian entrées and desserts. Throw out any recipes that are incomplete or illegible or that have lost their appeal.

3 Invest in large three-ring binders that will fit your recipes. Insert subject dividers labeled with your categories and plastic page protectors that will hold your recipes (two per page, one for the front and one for the back).

4 Refine the categories in your recipe binders according to how you cook: For example, if you're vegetarian there's no need for a meat section. If you've got a sweet tooth, divide your dessert recipes into cookies, cakes, pies and tarts. If you entertain, make a section for cocktails and hors d'oeuvres.

5 Tackle your recipe cards: Instead of jamming them into a card file, add them to your binder. Get clear page inserts that accommodate index cards (these will fit standard-size recipe cards) or use double-sided tape to attach cards to a piece of paper (then slide the paper into a page protector and add it to your folder).

6 Digitize your collection with recipe software if you have the time and energy. You'll need to input all your recipes by hand (unless you already have some saved to your computer), but you'll be able to easily search your collection, export shopping lists, create weekly menus and run nutritional analysis. Check out programs such as Cook's Palate (cookspalate.com), LivingCookbook.com and AccuChef.com.

7 Clean up your cookbooks. Arrange them by topic (Italian, soups, desserts) instead of by author or title. Donate the books you don't use. When you try new recipes, mark the book with notes ("add olive oil last" or "too dry") that will help you in the future. See 51 Organize Your Bookshelves.

Tips

As an alternative to the three-ring binder, use photo albums with self-adhesive pages to store your recipes. The downside is they're slightly more expensive than binders and typically won't hold as many recipes. An accordion file will hold plenty of recipes, but it can get messy and bulky.

Store a few of the reference cookbooks you use most often (*The Joy of Cooking*, for example, or *The New Basics*) on a shelf in your kitchen. If you're short on space, tuck away the rest of your cookbooks in a den or bookcase. You can get to them to brainstorm or research recipes.

Who Knew?

If you don't have a laminator, use plastic sandwich bags to seal away recipe cards.

Themed menus can bring focus to your dinner party and add spark to your family dinner. When you step outside your comfort zone to create a themed dinner for your guests, don't stop at the menu. Complete the transition with cocktails, hors d'oeuvres, decorations and music.

THEME	MENU	DRINKS	EXTRAS
French Bistro	Frisée salad topped with crispy prosciutto and poached egg, coq au vin with crusty bread and tarte Tatin for dessert.	Pernod or pastis and plenty of French wine in little glass tumblers instead of wineglasses.	Edith Piaf's "La Vie en Rose" and other French music.
Caribbean	Slow-cooked pork in a lime marinade, white rice, black beans and fried plantains.	Mojitos and caipirinha.	Cuban cigars.
Greek	Moussaka (ground beef casserole with a creamy sauce), Greek country salad (called horiatiki), gigantes (white beans) drizzled in olive oil and sprinkled with fresh oregano.	Ouzo (licorice liqueur) and retsina (wine), thick espresso served in tiny cups.	Serve a cake baked with a lucky coin (Greek or Italian bakeries will make these to order). The guest who gets the piece with the coin will have good luck for the year to come.
Indian	Chicken tikka masala; lamb curry; fried okra with cumin, turmeric and coriander; and basmati rice with peas and onions.	Mango lassies.	Jewel-colored cushions, henna appliqué tattoos and strands of red and orange marigolds.
Italian	Caprese salad (tomato, fresh buffalo mozzarella and basil), a pasta course (creamy tagliatelle with peas or linguini with tomato sauce) and veal scallopine. Risotto pudding for dessert.	Prosecco (wine), negronis and bellinis for cocktails.	Opera music.
Japanese	Edamame, miso soup, tuna and veggie maki sushi and teriyaki chicken. Follow with green tea ice cream.	Sake, green tea, Japanese beer.	Sit on tatami mats or cushions around a coffee table.
Latin	Shrimp and fish ceviche, grilled chicken with tomatillo sauce, beef picadillo, vegetable empanada and grilled pineapple skewers with coconut ice cream for dessert.	Pisco (Peruvian grape brandy) sour.	Latin jazz, Afro-Cuban All Stars, Compay Secundo in the background.

THEME	MENU	DRINKS	EXTRAS
Provençal	Artichoke and fava bean crostini, leg of lamb crusted with mustard and herbs de Provence bread crumbs, tomatoes provençal and potato and fennel au gratin. Finish with a fig tart for dessert.	Acidic white wines and fruity reds.	Small bowls of lucques green olives and glasses filled with rosemary breadsticks on the table.
Southern Barbecue	Barbecue beef brisket, pork ribs and chicken. Corn bread, black-eyed peas, collard greens, and peach cobbler or apple brown betty for dessert.	Lemonade with a splash of vodka.	Bright red tablecloths, gingham napkins and hay bale seating.
Spa	Nonfat gazpacho, salmon with no-cream sorrel sauce and grilled asparagus drizzled with balsamic vinegar. Tropical fruit parfait with nonfat yogurt for dessert.	Fruit smoothies or fresh limeade with sprigs of mint.	Give guests recipes so they can recreate your healthy meal at home.
Spanish Tapas	Green olives and manchego cheese to start, seafood paella, tomato and roasted pepper gazpacho and tortilla (an omelet of eggs, potatoes, salt and olive oil. Additional ingredients may include peppers, onions, tuna, anchovies, artichokes, asparagus, and mushrooms). Follow with flan for dessert.	Sangria or rioja wine.	Provide small cocktail plates instead of full-size dinner plates.
Tex-Mex	Guacamole and chips to start, crispy pork carnitas and carne asada, Mexican rice and whole pinto or black beans.	Margaritas, tequila sunrise.	A candy-filled piñata; anything by Selena or Los Lobos in the background.
Wine Lovers	Start with a fish course (salmon with pesto cooked in phyllo) paired with a Chardonnay or white Burgundy. Then filet mignon with Bordeaux sauce, mustard greens and potato au gratin. Serve a cheese course with a sweet Riesling or other dessert wine to finish the meal.	Wine, of course. Pair a different varietal with each course, starting with the lightest white and ending with a red for the main course. Include dessert wine.	Grape clusters and baskets of dried fall leaves on the table. Choose a different wine-growing region or country and base your menu and decorations on that.

Do you dart around the grocery store like a chicken with its head cut off? Invest the time to organize your shopping list, and every trip to come will be a breeze. The most effective lists are based on the layout of your supermarket.

Steps

1 Set aside a distraction- or child-free hour and take a clipboard to your grocery store. Map out the store's floor plan, aisle by aisle, listing the products stocked on each aisle.

2 Go home and set up a master list on the computer based on the floor plan. Fit your list onto a single page using one column for each aisle. You don't want to hassle with stapling papers and sorting printouts.

3 Make space for quantities before each item; you can fill those in before each shopping trip.

4 Include boxes or bullets next to each item so they can be checked off as you put them in your cart.

5 Underline regular purchases for each aisle. For instance, if you buy skim milk or crackers every week, underline it—you can always cross items off the list if you don't need them.

6 Check your pantry and refrigerator for specific staples such as rice wine vinegar. Add them to the template.

7 Consult your weekly menu (see 297 Plan a Week of Menus) to pencil in ingredients you'll need for nightly dinners.

8 Leave plenty of blank lines for additional items to add as needed.

9 Test your list and make any edits to the master template. Aim for a fluid trip from one end of the store to the other.

10 Print several copies of the master and keep them in your household organizer.

11 Post your weekly shopping list in your kitchen, where the hungry masses can see it. Train them to highlight items that need replacement. See 3 Write an Effective To-Do List and 265 Create a Household Organizer. Add anything you'll need to buy as soon as you notice you're running short.

Tips

Make and post a separate list for discount warehouse chains that includes paper products, cleaning supplies, vitamins and anything else you regularly purchase. See 129 Store Bulk Purchases.

Create a seasonal shopping list of farmers' market produce.

Download lists to your personal digital assistant and check off items as you go.

Who Knew?

Some stores have maps. Ask the store's manager or a checkout clerk for one to base your master shopping list on.

There are dozens of shopping lists available online. Do a search for "grocery shopping list" and select one that fits your needs. You can edit and rearrange it as needed.

At the end of a busy day wouldn't you rather have more time to spend with your family or friends than face a bare table without a moment to spare and the faintest idea of what you'll prepare for dinner? Utilize your freezer and do prep work ahead of time for more enjoyable evenings and no-stress meals.

Steps

1 Start a new mantra: Your freezer is your friend. Side dishes, entrées and desserts freeze well and can be reheated for ultra-easy cooking.

2 Plan your menus and do your shopping (see 297 Plan a Week of Menus) and then chop, julienne or dice any of the ingredients you'll need for the week ahead. Prep work is the real time thief in the kitchen.

3 Make stocks or soups up to a week ahead and store them in the refrigerator; or freeze extras in 2-cup rations for future use.

4 Stock your fridge with a few days worth of essentials: Using your food processor's chopping blade (or a knife), chop three yellow onions and six to eight garlic cloves and store separately in zipper-lock plastic bags in your refrigerator. (For recipe purposes, one small garlic clove is roughly 1 teaspoon, and half an onion is roughly 1 cup chopped.)

5 Make extra waffles, pancakes, biscuits, muffins or scones on lazy weekend mornings to freeze. During the week they can be toasted for a fast, delicious breakfast.

6 Double (or triple) your recipe for pasta sauce and freeze family-size portions for easy lasagna, baked ziti and spaghetti.

7 Slightly undercook pasta, vegetables and rice for frozen casseroles or entrées. They will continue to cook when you reheat the entrée.

8 Freeze batches of appetizers for easy entertaining. Make individual portions of empanadas, phyllo spinach triangles or miniquiches and freeze them in a single layer on baking sheets. Once they're firm, transfer them to labeled zipper-lock plastic bags.

9 Fill pie tins with pastry dough, and wrap and freeze for up to a month. They can be filled and cooked the day before you need them. See 315 Plan Party Foods Ahead.

Tips

For fresh lemon juice (for salad dressings, desserts or sauces), juice five to 10 lemons into a glass jar, seal and refrigerate. The juice will keep for about two weeks.

See 302 Create Effective Shopping Lists.

Who Knew?

To reheat frozen foods, thaw overnight in the refrigerator. Bake according to the recipe; if still slightly frozen in the center, add about 10 to 15 extra minutes to the baking time.

Fish should always be cooked fresh. Meats, unless they're a casserole ingredient, should be sautéed or grilled at the last minute.

Warning

Store foods correctly. Foods that oxidize (turn brown), such as apples and avocados, should be chopped and used at the last minute. Custards and curds should be covered with plastic wrap touching the surface so they don't develop a film on top.

304 | Determine the Shelf Life of Foods

When you get around to cleaning the cobwebs out of your pantry and wiping the mystery spills from your refrigerator, you're bound to come across some scary science projects. To determine what's perfectly fine and what's petrified, follow this guide.

Steps

1 Remember that not all foods are created equal: Depending on the quality of the food when you purchased it, and how it has been stored (temperature, packaging), foods may deteriorate more quickly or last longer.

2 Know your terminology. "Best if used by" is not a "purchase by" or safety date; it's an estimate for how long the food is expected to retain its flavor, texture and freshness.

3 Follow expiration dates on foods—they mean what they say. Throw out anything in your pantry or refrigerator that's expired. Give yourself some leeway with "sell by" dates. You don't have to throw out the rest of the milk that morning. Your nose knows: If it still smells fine, you can drink it.

4 Check packaged and boxed foods for the bar code, which is not easy to decipher. It may be coded by month, day and year, such as YYMMDD or MMDDYY. Or it may be coded using Julian numbers, whereby January 1 would be 001 and December 31 would be 365. In even more convoluted codes, letters A through M (omitting the letter I) are often assigned to the months, with A being January and M being December, plus a numeric day, either preceded or followed by the numeric year.

5 Be aware that canned foods lose from 5 to 20 percent of their nutritional content each year, depending on length of storage and temperature. Store all canned foods in a cool, dry, dark place (less than 70 degrees F (21 C) is preferred; 50 degrees F (10 C) is optimal). Try to use up canned foods within a year—rotate older ones in front of the shelf and the newer ones in back.

6 Store raw meat (beef, lamb, veal, pork) for up to five days in the refrigerator; four to twelve months in the freezer. Poultry and ground meats can be kept in the fridge for up to two days before cooking and one to four months in the freezer. For a comprehensive list of how long foods can be safely stored, see sites such as www.foodsafety.gov and pastrywiz.com/storage.

7 Package foods correctly to lengthen their storage life. Use airtight containers in the fridge and freezer. Cool foods before freezing. Reduce freezer burn by wrapping foods in plastic wrap and then sealing in an air-tight zipper locked plastic bag.

Tips

Use up leftovers within four days. Mayonnaise-based sauces and dressings should be used within two to three days. Refrigerate what you'll use for the next day or two, and freeze the rest for up to four months.

Examine which foods you toss because they don't get used up. Are you over-buying? Update your master shopping list to save time and money.

Once you open foods, the dates become moot if the contents are perishable. Use foods as quickly as possible after opening.

Who Knew?

Food frozen at 0 degrees F (-18 C) will be safe to eat indefinitely, but the quality, nutrient level and flavor will deteriorate.

Food dating is not required by U.S. law, except on baby food and infant formula.

Flour and other dry goods can be frozen.

Warning

Don't buy canned foods that are dented, oozing or damaged. Aluminum can leak into foods.

Organize Food from Warehouse Stores

You've smugly patted yourself on the back for how much cash your recent shopping spree saved you. But unless you have a restaurant-size walk-in refrigerator, those flats of yogurt and vats of hummus could quickly end up in your loss margin. Divide and conquer the goods for money well spent.

Steps

1 Shop discerningly and be willing to just say no. Perishable items, such as gallons of milk or huge packets of lunch meat, aren't a good idea if your family won't consume them within a few days.

2 Divvy up the receipt as well and the contents of individually packaged items with a friend. It's difficult to share a big squeeze bottle of mustard, but you can each take home one loaf of bread or box of cereal from a double pack. And if you'll never get through 10 pounds of strawberries in a few days, split the flat in two.

3 Unpack frozen goods. Break up portions and package them into family-size chunks so you don't need to defrost the whole pack-age for one meal. Rotate the goods in your freezer so the older items get used first; put newer purchases in the bottom or back.

4 Tackle the bakery goods. Breads, muffins, English muffins and croissants all freeze well. Divide the contents into meal-size portions, seal in airtight plastic storage containers or zipper-lock plastic bags. They can go straight from the freezer to the oven.

5 Divide the dry goods into smaller containers. Flour, sugar, baking soda and rice will stay fresh in a cool, dry cupboard sealed in air-tight containers. Use the bottom of a linen closet or out-of-the-kitchen space to store that mammoth bag of pancake mix or sugar (sealed in plastic containers or bags) and just refill contain-ers when necessary.

6 Take unopened soda, water bottles, olive oil or vinegar bottles, and other food items that can remain at room temperature and store them out of the kitchen until you need to replenish supplies or refill containers.

Tips

Set up one storage area or shelf for extra dry goods, food and supplies so you don't waste time hunting for replacements.

Use low plastic storage con-tainers designed to fit under beds to tuck away extra dry food and supplies.

If you buy large canned goods and only need half, don't store the remainder in the aluminum can. The metal can leech into the food. Move the contents to an airtight container or zipper-locked plastic bag.

See 129 Store Bulk Purchases.

Who Knew?

If possible, avoid warehouse stores on the weekends and the days leading up to major holidays. Shop right when the store opens or an hour or two before closing during the week to skip the crowds.

Who knows what radioactive waste lurks in the depths of many of the country's refrigerators and freezers. The circa-1990 condiment collection and the frozen mystery meat are just the beginning. Perform a clean-out to maximize (and disinfect) your cold-storage space.

Steps

1 Remove all the food from the fridge and freezer. While you're cleaning, store perishables and frozen foods in an ice chest.

2 Throw out anything you can't remember buying or that has expired. See 304 Determine the Shelf Life of Foods.

3 Wash the shelves, door and trays of the refrigerator and freezer with warm, soapy water.

4 Defrost and remove the frost that accumulates on the roof and sides of the freezer. If it's more than ¼-inch (⅔ cm) thick, think about switching to a no-frost freezer. Frost buildup increases the amount of energy needed to keep the motor running.

5 Throw out the ice: The chunks at the bottom of the tray may have been resting there for years. Clean out the tray with warm soapy water, fill and return it to the freezer.

6 Create sections in the freezer for well-labeled (date purchased, item and amount) meats, fruits and vegetables, convenience foods and desserts.

7 Pull older items out of the freezer after a big shopping run. Put the newer items in the back, moving the older ones to the front so they get used up. In the refrigerator, keep perishables front and center where you'll see them.

8 Store foods in designated spaces inside your fridge or freezer so you don't spend time hunting down ingredients—and your spouse will always have the answer to "Honey, where's the butter?"

9 Keep like items together: condiments in the door; soda, beer and wine on a top shelf; and yogurt, cottage cheese, hummus and snacks at eye level.

10 Stash meat, seafood and poultry in the middle back of the refrigerator, the coldest spot in the house.

11 Cover liquids and wrap foods stored in the fridge. Uncovered foods release moisture (and get dried out), causing the compressor to work harder.

12 Sweep through your fridge once a week. Throw out any leftovers that won't be eaten, get rid of perishables that are past their prime and wipe down any spills.

Tips

Don't stand in front of the refrigerator with the door open. It wastes energy and brings down the temperature of your food (which, if done repeatedly, can cause food to spoil prematurely).

Set the refrigerator's temperature between 38 and 42 degrees F (3 to 5 C), and the freezer between 0 degrees F (-18 C) or lower. Use your own thermometer for this, as the fridge's dial may not be correct.

Who Knew?

A humming refrigerator is driving up your electricity bill. Dirty and dusty condenser coils are likely to blame. See 66 Organize Spring Cleaning.

Check to see if you have a power-saving or a summer-winter switch. Many refrigerators have a small heater (yes, a heater!) inside the walls to prevent condensation buildup.

Warning

Ditch the extra fridge or freezer in the garage. The electricity it's using—typically $130 a year—costs far more than the six-pack or two you've got stashed there. Or unplug it until you need it for your next big bash (see 342 Throw a Party).

307 | Organize Cutlery and Kitchen Tools

Knives, odd baking tools and barbecue gadgets can quickly wreak havoc on your kitchen's carefully constructed organization system. Put these tools where they belong—and where you won't forget that you even own them.

Steps

1 Edit your collection: Throw out or give away that rusty serrated knife, the apple peeler you've never used and the caked-with-grease grill brush.

2 Keep knives in a knife block, on a magnetic strip on your wall (unless you have young kids) or covered with plastic blade protectors in a drawer.

3 Store the tools you use often (can opener, vegetable peeler, measuring spoons) in your silverware drawer, where you can get to them easily.

4 Keep lesser-used cutlery and tools (boning knives, oyster shuckers, cherry pitters, meat tenderizers) in a covered plastic container tucked inside a drawer. Tape a list of what's inside to the top of the lid. See 57 Live Better Through Labeling.

Tips

See 73 Make Your Home Safe for Small Children.

Store spatulas, wooden spoons, tongs and other frequently used utensils in a canister by your stove—they'll be in arm's reach and will free up valuable drawer space.

Who Knew?

Make sure your knives are completely dry before you store them in butcher blocks. Bacteria can form from droplets of water left on the blades after washing.

308 | Organize Cupboards and Drawers

Americans follow blithely along with ads and commercials exhorting us to buy, buy, buy. If your kitchen is a showcase of Home Shopping Network excess, follow these tips to give it some breathing space.

Steps

1 Clear out cupboards and drawers, and wipe them down. Throw out anything that is broken or chipped. Donate duplicates, duds or unused gadgets. See 12 Get Rid of What You Don't Want and 49 Deal with a Pack Rat.

2 Store pieces you rarely use, such as china, chafing pans, seasonal serving platters or underused appliances, outside the kitchen. See 138 Store China and Family Heirlooms.

3 Group remaining items in like piles. Serving platters can be stacked (place a paper towel in between to cushion); bowls or pots and pans can be nested within each other. Keep loose items such as tea bags in clear containers or tins to keep them fresh.

4 Install under-shelf hooks for mugs, with plates directly underneath.

5 Use lazy Susans or shelf organizers to keep all items in sight and within reach.

Tips

Sort through the plastic storage containers and throw out incomplete sets. Store the lids in a basket and nest the containers.

Mount Peg-Board to hang pots, pans, baking equipment and utensils. Paint it to match your walls. See 311 Stow Pots and Pans.

Get stacking drawer organizers. Store rarely used utensils—apple corers and pastry blenders—on the lower level.

309 | Organize the Pantry

You don't have to go as far as alphabetizing the spice rack, but a well-organized pantry simplifies meal planning, preparation and food shopping. From casual suppers to elegant dinner parties, you'll find planning a snap with an easy-to-navigate pantry.

Steps

1 Pull staples from wherever they lurk and pile them onto a table. Discard anything that is stale, spoiled or expired (see 304 Determine the Shelf Life of Foods.) Haul the edible but unwanted items to your local food bank. Repeat every six months.

2 Wipe down the shelves and walls. Install new shelving, hooks or wall-mounted wire organizers for canned goods and spices.

3 Use canisters to hold dry goods such as flour and sugar, and label them with their contents. Small items, such as teabags, dried fruit or bouillon, should go into small plastic bins or baskets.

4 Put spices on a lazy Susan on a shelf or a wall-mounted rack on the inside of your pantry door. Move your bulky bottles of olive oil, vinegar, soy sauce and teriyaki to a lazy Susan, too, so they'll be easier to reach. See 308 Organize Cupboards and Drawers.

5 Group like items together: pastas, rice and lentils on one shelf; canned vegetables on another, keeping all the cans of crushed tomatoes, black beans and so on in a row (newer ones in back).

6 Label the shelves—"Crackers and snacks," "Cereal," "Canned fruits"—to keep things in their proper place. See 57 Live Better Through Labeling.

7 Purchase other handy space savers to corral goods: stacking containers, caddies to store foil and wax paper, and sturdy baskets for onions, garlic and potatoes. See 128 Store Anything.

Tips

Buy backups of staples so you always have an extra jar of pickles and mayo on hand for emergency tuna sandwiches. When you break into a backup, be sure to add it to your list and replenish (see 298 Organize Grocery Store Trips).

If you have school-age children, create a snack shelf of parent-approved treats ready for the taking.

Who Knew?

Paint the inside of your pantry white: It will make it brighter and easier to find what you're looking for. Or add a closet light or self-sticking battery-operated light available at hardware stores.

Square containers take up less space than round ones because they fit more efficiently on shelves.

310 | Efficiently Use Space Under the Sink

Call it the black hole. All those scouring pads, soaps and plastic bags under the sink waste space and may never see daylight, even when they're needed. Drippy pipes don't make it easier. Help is on the way.

Steps

1 Clear everything out from under the sink—top to bottom. Scrub the area thoroughly.

2 Discard rusty or crusty items. Old products may no longer work well because the chemicals degrade over time. Dispose of household hazardous waste safely (see 46 Manage Garbage and Recyclables).

Tips

Don't store paper towels under the sink—in the event of a leaky pipe or bottle of dish soap, they'll be ruined.

See 145 Store Paint and Other Hazardous Materials and 65 Organize Cleaning Supplies.

3 Group together the items you use every week: dish soap, garbage bags, scouring pads, rubber gloves. Make another pile of less frequently used items (ant spray, silver polish) and find a new, safe home for them in the hall closet or the garage. Gather household cleaners together in a caddy or basket. See 73 Make Your Home Safe for Small Children.

4 Shop at stores such as Stacks (stacksandstacks.com), Target (target.com) and The Container Store (thecontainerstore.com) for a wide range of useful organizers, including plastic wrap box organizers, slide-out stack units, sponge holders and slide-out garbage can holders.

5 Install a special under-the-sink shelf system that will add more storage space. These expandable shelves can be adjusted to fit around bulky kitchen pipes and keep air circulating.

Who Knew?

Use a glass jar with a lid to store cooking oil and grease you don't want to toss down your pipes; when it's full, screw on the cap and throw it in the trash.

311 | Stow Pots and Pans

You use pots and pans every day, but they often end up in an awkward, towering heap. They are bulky and heavy, don't always nest well, and may have handles of varying shapes and sizes.

Steps

1 Pull out all your pot and pans (including woks, roasting pans and steamers), along with their lids. Throw out anything that's gouged, nicked or burned beyond repair, including nonstick pans if the coating is peeling. Toss aluminum pots immediately: The metal they leach into cooked foods and liquids has been associated with Alzheimer's disease.

2 Scan your kitchen: Does it make sense to return the pans to their drawer or cabinet, or do you need the space for other appliances? Free up space by installing a wall- or ceiling-mounted pot rack or a Peg-Board outfitted with hooks.

3 Make cabinets that house pots and pans more efficient by installing a deep, slide-out drawer. Nest pots and pans as much as possible. Start with the roasting pan on the bottom, then stack pots followed by frying pan.

4 Target a shallow drawer for the lids. Or, organize them in a lid rack (available at organizational and hardware stores) or a long, thin plastic basket that will fit in your drawer or cabinet.

Tips

To protect the coating on nonstick pots and pans, set a paper plate inside each when you nest them with others.

To clean out pots that have burned bits of food stuck to the inside, fill the pot or pan with water and a small drop of dishwashing liquid. Boil on the stove for 10 minutes and scrub the pot.

Store less-used cookware out of the way, such as above the refrigerator or on a baker's rack.

312 | Make the Most of Your Counter Space

Does your kitchen feel more like a ship's galley than a gourmet retreat? Look to your drawers, cupboards and walls to free up valuable kitchen countertop real estate.

Steps

1 Start by clearing off your counters and scrubbing down.

2 Determine the items you use several times a week, such as the toaster and coffeemaker. Keep those things out.

3 Think of your countertops as triangles of work space: Keep your knives and chopping boards in the same area, and store your cooking utensils to the side of your stove for quick and easy meal preparation.

4 Opt for smaller, sleeker appliances to grace your countertops—they'll take up less room now and will be easy to store later. Identify the appliances you don't use often, and stow them in a drawer or cabinet space.

5 Mount a toaster oven, microwave, paper towel holder or an electric can opener under your overhead cabinets.

6 Incorporate a rolling butcher block island into your kitchen if possible. It may add not only more storage space, but a cutting board and utility areas as well.

7 Designate one area for paperwork, notes and mail that ends up on the counters. Instead use your tickler file (see 10 Set Up a Reminder System) or "file," "do" and "pay" boxes. See 7 Deal with a Flood of Mail and 184 Conquer Your Paper Piles.

Tips

See 311 Stow Pots and Pans.

If you have a collection of bulky appliances you rarely use (ice-cream maker, pressure cooker, bread maker), invest in a baker's rack. Or stash them outside the kitchen (the top shelf of the linen closet, the garage) or above the refrigerator and bring them out as needed.

If you have space, add a small center island that has storage underneath.

Are your dish towels in a soggy heap on the counter? Stow them away with a towel hook or bar in the cupboard under your sink.

313 | Cook for One

Cereal again? It can be daunting to cook real meals for yourself. With a little preparation and advance planning, though, you can break away from ramen and scrambled eggs and truly eat well.

Steps

1 Break up packages of meat into one-meal portions and freeze.

2 Incorporate semiprepared foods, such as frozen chopped vegetables, minipizza crusts (if there are two in the package, freeze one) or quick-cooking boxes of grains and rice.

3 Free yourself from recipes—they're usually scaled to four or more. Experiment with dishes that rely on a few key ingredients: grilled fish topped with store-bought fruit salsa, or a chicken breast with carmelized onion and a drizzle of balsamic vinegar.

Tip

Reinvent leftovers: Roll up cooked chicken in a tortilla with cheese, avocado and salsa. Or sauté wilting vegetables and leftover meats with cooked rice, soy sauce and a scrambled egg to make "clean out the fridge" fried rice.

4 Buy individual cans of stock-based soup, such as vegetable or minestrone, and spruce it up by tossing in leftover vegetables (zucchini, bell peppers, onion, tomatoes) and meat.

5 Indulge in easy frozen entrées from time to time, but pair that chicken pot pie with a green salad or steamed broccoli.

314 | Plan Healthy Lunches for Kids

Making sure that your carefully prepared lunch doesn't get ignored or ditched in the trash can is a tricky feat. Here's how to avoid those expensive, high-fat, premade lunches, and give your kid a meal that will make him or her the envy of the cafeteria.

Steps

1 Get input from your children about what they want. They'll be more likely to eat what they choose (except nutritional zeros like chips and soda of course).

2 Prep the lunches as you're making dinner the night before. You'll be more creative and less frazzled in the evening. Save some chicken breast for salad with red grapes and celery, a slice of meatloaf for a sandwich, or cooked vegetables for pasta salad with Italian dressing. See 17 Streamline Your Morning Routine.

3 Strive for balance. Healthy lunches should have a complex carbohydrate such as whole-grain bread or pita, a source of protein (peanut butter is fine), at least one serving of fruits or vegetables and one source of dairy (string cheese, yogurt, cottage cheese or milk).

4 Get creative: Use cookie cutters to carve sandwiches into fun shapes or include the fixings for "ants on a log"—aka peanut butter and raisins on celery.

5 Sneak in fresh vegetables and fruits. While your child may leave a whole apple untouched, she may love diced apples in her chicken salad sandwich.

6 Introduce new foods gradually, pairing them with your child's favorite snacks. For example, if he loves carrots with ranch dressing, slip in some cucumber and zucchini slices as well.

7 Indulge in desserts, but don't go overboard. Rice crispy treats are low fat, oatmeal raisin cookies pack a nutritious punch, and puddings and Jell-O come in low-sugar and low-fat varieties. You don't want to deprive your children, but you also don't want them to be high-wired on sugar or falling asleep in class from a heavy, rich treat.

Tip

At the beginning of the week, boil a dozen eggs to use in egg salad, tuna salad or as a healthy late-afternoon snack.

Who Knew?

Wrap a frozen juice or drink container with a paper towel to keep the condensation from getting the rest of the lunch moist—your child can then use the damp paper towel to clean sticky fingers and faces.

Don't get stuck in a rut: If your child ignores her sandwiches, try stacking cheese and salami on whole-grain crackers instead; swap the peanut butter and jelly for pita with hummus or cinnamon-raisin bagels with cream cheese and jelly.

Add a favorite healthy snack, such as grapes, granola bars, trail mix or string cheese, for an afternoon pick-me-up.

| **Plan Party Foods Ahead**

If you'd rather be having a relaxed glass of wine than sweating over the hors d'oeuvres, cook party foods that need just a little assembling and warming up in the oven. The best party foods can be eaten standing up with no silverware. For a two-hour party with 12 guests, you should have roughly 130 pieces of hors d'oeuvres. Sounds like a lot, but it goes fast. Quick tip? Costco.

HORS D'OEUVRE	WHEN TO PREPARE	HOW TO COOK AND SERVE
Savory empanadas, feta and spinach phyllo triangles, dumplings and miniquiches	Assemble uncooked on cookie sheets up to a month ahead. Freeze in airtight plastic bags.	Move from the freezer to oven and serve warm.
Strattas or frittatas with eggs, ham or sausage, gruyere and herbs	Cook up to a month in advance. Remove from oven before they brown, let cool, wrap and freeze.	Warm in a 350-degree F (180 C) oven and cut into bite-size pieces.
Firm polenta	Make a couple days ahead and cool in one even layer in a pan. Cut into bite-size pieces.	Serve topped with sun-dried tomatoes, fresh basil and a drizzle of olive oil.
Skewers or brochettes of meats	Marinate and assemble up to two days in advance. Refrigerate.	Grill a few hours before the party and reheat in a 350-degree F (180 C) oven.
Other skewers: colorful fruit; tomato, basil and mozzarella; tofu or vegetable	Assemble the day before a party. Store in large plastic bags in refrigerator.	Refresh with a drizzle of olive oil and salt (or mint and sugar for the fruit).
Hummus, white bean dip, eggplant spread or roasted pepper tapenade	Puree up to 3 days before and refrigerate.	Serve in bowls.
Soft focaccia filled with pesto, prosciutto, goat cheese or other savory fillings	Assemble the morning of the party and refrigerate.	Cut into small square pieces for minisandwiches.
Pita chips and crostini	Toast the day before and store in an airtight container.	Serve in big bowls.
Mushrooms stuffed with spinach and Parmesan	Stuff the day before the party and refrigerate.	Pop in the oven an hour before the guests arrive.
Crudités	Chop vegetables and make a yogurt or sour cream-based dip the day before. Refrigerate.	Serve chilled.
TIPS	A couple days in advance, pull out and wash your serving trays, napkins, containers or cups for used skewers, bowls for olive pits and any other party supplies. Label everything for last-minute ease. Hire a student or server to pass the hors d'oeuvres and refill the trays and platters.	

316 | Throw a Dinner Party

Do you lie awake the night before a dinner party frought with anxiety? What if they don't come? What if the food is lousy? What if they have a horrible time? Quell those misgivings with a streamlined plan.

Steps

Party basics

1 Choose a cause for celebration. It will set the tone and anchor all the elements of your party. See 342 Throw a Party for more tips.

2 Select a date. Make it easy on yourself and pick a day and date that gives you enough time to prepare without being rushed.

3 Choose a style—an informal gathering with a few friends, a backyard picnic for the team, a low-key cocktail party for 20 or an elegant fund raising dinner for 50. The reason for the party and its style provides the structure for all other components to hang on.

4 Compile the guest list and send out invitations. Casual affairs need a few days to a week's advance notice by phone or e-mail, while written invitations to formal dinners might be mailed a full month ahead.

5 Create the desired ambience. Whether it's simple candlelight or more ornate decorations, everything from your table settings and decorations to the menu and music will set the tone.

One week ahead

1 Create the menu. Instead of immediately searching cookbooks for recipes, begin by thinking about what flavors, tastes, textures, colors and sensations would complement each other. Visit a farmers' market and taste what's fresh, in season and delicious. Keep balance in mind: If you're having cheese tortellini, don't serve cheesecake for dessert and overload on dairy and heavy creamy textures. And last, be realistic about how much time you have to prepare before choosing your recipes. See 301 Plan Theme Menus, 315 Plan Party Foods Ahead and 303 Cook Ahead.

2 Start thinking about how you'll arrange seating (see 320 Plan Dinner Party Seating).

3 Hire help or rent supplies from a party rental store. Consider getting extra plates or silverware, bar glasses and linens, as well as serving help, a caterer and a housekeeper to clean up after. See 331 Hire a Caterer and 336 Hire a Bartender.

Two days ahead

1 Polish the silver, wash the stemware and iron the tablecloths. When you set the table, pay attention to details. Arrange flowers

Continued on next page

Tips

Prevent logjams by setting up the bar away from the buffet table.

Get out the platters or dishes you'll use to serve the food. Label them with sticky notes so you're sure you have enough serving dishes for everything on the menu.

Remember—you want your guests to be relaxed and have a great time. Cue the mood by relaxing and enjoying yourself, too.

Who Knew?

A manageable dinner party size is 6 to 12 guests. Consider how many can sit at your table without bumping elbows.

in dramatic side-table displays or individual vases at each place setting. Tuck a sprig of lavender into crisp, cloth napkins; float candles in a bowl of water; craft simple but classy name cards. Centerpieces can be anything from a simple bowl of lemons to a beautiful floral arrangement (see 103 Decorate for the Seasons).

2 Select dinner music that enhances your ambience and is well matched to the menu.

3 Choose wine for the meal. Go to Wine.com for tips about pairing wines with foods. One type of red and one white will suffice. Figure two to three glasses per person when estimating how much to buy—one bottle holds roughly four glasses.

Party time!

1 Mastermind the mingling. Create conversation corners in your cocktail area. Instead of one marooned chair, think huddles of chairs. Seat guests with similar interests next to each other.

2 Enjoy yourself. Have fun and relax—it will be infectious and will set your guests at ease.

3 Pay attention to cues that the party is wrapping up, including ignored wineglasses, yawns and nervous comments about babysitters. Graciously thank your guests for coming and help them gather their things.

4 To get people moving out the door, drop subtle hints ("Does any-one need a last cup of coffee?"). If all else fails, start clearing up glasses and dishes.

5 Celebrate sweet success. Once you've done a load of dishes, kick off your shoes, settle back with a last glass of wine, and enjoy rehashing with your spouse or co-host.

Who Knew?

To remove red wine stains, blot up as much as possible with an absorbent cloth. Saturate the stain with club soda. Later, apply a paste of three parts baking soda to one part water. Let dry, then vacuum.

Do your shopping three to four days in advance, except for vegetables, fresh fish and flowers.

Consider shopping online for your groceries, flowers and wine—many food delivery sites sell all three. See 299 Set Up Online Grocery Shopping.

317 | Finish Dinner on Time

It's a race against the clock. Your chicken roasts for 60 minutes and the spinach sautés for 15, the salad gets chopped and dressed, and the apple cobbler needs to be baked. How do you get dinner on the table and have everything remain warm? Get organized, make a timeline and use a kitchen timer to stay on top of your game.

Steps

1 Read (don't skim) the recipes ahead of time from start to finish.

2 Use the preparation time stated in the cookbook as a rough estimate only. Then make notes in the cookbook's margin,

Tip

Invest in a digital kitchen clock with multiple timers, available at cooking stores. You can set the timer for three to four different dishes simultaneously.

estimating the time you'll need to prep the food (washing greens, chopping veggies, measuring liquids) and cook it on the stovetop or in the oven. For example, 1 minute to brown the garlic, 5 minutes to soften the onions and 10 minutes for the spinach to wilt is 16 minutes total cooking time

3 Add the estimated number of minutes to finish the dish once it's been cooked—for example, letting the meat rest for 5 minutes before carving it.

4 Work backward from when you want dinner on the table to determine when you need to tie on the apron. If you need an hour of prep time for all your recipes and an hour of cooking time, you should start dinner at 5 p.m. in order to eat at 7 p.m.

5 Select appropriate pots, pans and cookware.

6 Write a cooking timeline of what to start when, using the notes in the margin of your recipes (don't include prep work, it should already be finished). As a sample timeline, boil water for couscous at 5:30 p.m.; sauté spinach at 5:45 p.m.; put fully dressed chicken in oven at 6 p.m. Cobbler goes in the oven at 7 p.m. and will be ready to eat warm for dessert at 8 p.m.

7 Gather what the French call *mise en place*, or "everything in place." Just like cooking shows, for which everything is perfectly diced in little bowls, you should have all your ingredients chopped and measured before you even think of turning on those burners. This is the most important step to make cooking organized and timely.

8 Complete your *mise en place* as far ahead as possible if you're planning for guests. Chop vegetables, measure liquids and assemble desserts a day or two ahead. See 303 Cook Ahead and 315 Plan Party Foods Ahead.

9 Start cooking. Notice how this comes way down at step 9? It's important to get everything chopped and measured, write your cooking timeline and gather appropriate cookware before you start frying.

10 Warm up dinner plates slightly in a 200-degree F (95 C) oven— it's a restaurant trick that helps food stay warm on the plate. Use warming trays to keep items hot while they're on the table. Or, zap dishes in the microwave for a minute to warm them if necessary.

11 Practice: Use timelines for casual family meals as well as dinner parties, and soon getting plates done simultaneously will become second nature. See 316 Throw a Dinner Party.

Who Knew?

Don't choose recipes with dozens of ingredients to chop, mince and dice if you don't have time to prep. Or, buy a food processor to shave off half the time.

If you're entertaining, pull out and clean serving trays and platters a couple days ahead and tag them with sticky notes labeling what dish they'll hold.

318 | Pull Off a Last-Minute Party

Friends just called to say they're in town, you just landed a promotion or maybe just the movie was sold out. Whatever the occasion, be quick on your feet to pull off a fabulous spur-of-the-moment fête.

Steps

1 Stock a range of party staples that can become an instant feast. Pasta is easy and quick—and almost everyone has an extra box in the cupboard. Other basics include balsamic vinegar and olive oil, Parmesan cheese, canned whole tomatoes, jars of pesto, sun-dried tomatoes, crackers, chips and jars of salsa, soy sauce and rice wine vinegar (for easy dipping sauces), boxed cake mixes and ice cream.

2 Stock extra wine, champagne and beer, hard alcohol and mixers. You can blend margarita mix and tequila with ice in seconds.

3 Give them something to snack on: You should always have nuts and olives at the ready. Then put out crackers, chips and salsa, raw veggies and ranch dressing, or quesadillas cut into thin strips.

4 Fire up the grill. People can catch up outside while you make appetizers (grilled bread with mozzarella and fresh basil), dinner (salmon, kebabs, portobello mushroom burgers) and even dessert (grilled peaches with vanilla ice cream).

5 Let your guests assemble and serve their own meals from food bars with mashed potato fixings and chili, build-your-own burritos or ice-cream sundae ingredients.

6 Buy a roasted chicken for an impromptu dinner party and pull together easy side dishes: smashed boiled red potatoes (skins on) with herbed goat cheese mixed in, a green salad and the frozen green veggie of your choice cooked with a little butter and salt.

Tips

Create mood lighting; glaring bright lights can kill any party. Turn off overhead lights, light some votive candles and turn on low table lamps.

Chocolate chips can be melted in a microwave and drizzled on top of vanilla ice cream.

Who Knew?

If you're serving takeout and passing it off as homemade, sauté an onion and a few garlic cloves on the stovetop over low heat. The whole house will smell like some serious home cooking.

Make use of your grocery store's convenience foods such as prepared fruit trays, bagged salads, deli potato salad and marinated and assembled kebabs from the meat counter.

319 | Throw a Dinner Party for Your Boss

Entertaining at home is stressful enough, but throw job security into the mix and the stakes go way up. Time for an attitude adjustment—there's no need to dread this day. Plan ahead and keep in mind that the bottom line for your guests—and yourself—is to have a great time and enjoy the relationships you are building.

Tips

Pick a weekend night so you don't have to work all day and host a dinner that night.

See 317 Finish Dinner on Time.

Steps

1 See 316 Throw a Dinner Party.

2 Clarify the purpose. Is this a working dinner, or a relaxed gathering of co-workers? Is your boss flying in from the out-of-state

headquarters or just driving down the road? Your reason will dictate who comes and how you set up the party.

3 Determine the guest list. Keeping in mind how many people will comfortably fit at your house, invite confident, interesting and lively colleagues and friends who complement your boss's interests or share similar passions, such as golf or travel.

4 Learn your boss's food likes, dislikes, allergies and latest diet, before you plan the menu. See 301 Plan Theme Menus, 303 Cook Ahead and 315 Plan Party Foods Ahead.

5 Plan seating. It prevents an awkward moment when guests must choose who to sit with. See 320 Plan Dinner Party Seating.

6 Set up an open bar (see 328 Set Up a Bar) or arrange open bottles of wine on a side table with ample glasses so guests may serve themselves. Or mix a signature drink for the evening, such as blended mojitos or a classic cocktail. As the host, keep your consumption in check.

7 Keep in mind that the ultimate goal of your dinner is that your guests enjoy themselves. Be sincere, have fun and relax.

Splurge on a caterer. If there was ever a time to be free from cooking responsibilities, this is it. See 331 Hire a Caterer.

Warning

Do not download on your boss, whine about a project or deadline, or otherwise abuse his or her willingness to join you for dinner. If you do, rest assured that you've just had your last party for your boss.

320 | Plan Dinner Party Seating

Diplomatic careers have advanced and derailed over a simple thing like dinner seating. Think of yourself as the ambassador of the table and set up the seating to maximize your guests' enjoyment.

Steps

1 Write your guests' names on place cards.

2 Put yourself in the seat closest to the kitchen for quick getaways. Move clockwise around the table to map out the rest of the guests. Don't sit the hosts next to each other—spread them out to better cover the dinner table territory.

3 Consider conflicting political affiliations, career connections, activities and athletic pursuits or travel interests when seating guests. Spark the conversation with introductions such as "John, have you met Sally? She just got back from the same area of Thailand you visited last year."

4 Rotate. Have two people from each table move to another table for dessert and coffee. If you've got one long table, ask every third person to take his or her wineglass and fork, and rotate between courses (when plates are cleared anyway).

5 Set up a buffet and let your guests sit wherever they want.

6 Manage troublesome, loud or contentious guests by giving them a job to do: mix drinks, help in the kitchen or serve appetizers.

Tips

Place low-maintenance guests to your right and left. You'll be away from the table from time to time and need to make sure your companions will be comfortable without you there.

Seating charts can be done a day or two in advance or as soon as you have your RSVPs. You don't want to be playing musical chairs on the night of your dinner party.

Who Knew?

It's a time-honored custom to separate couples so that they mingle with other guests.

321 | Plan an Outdoor Party

Whether you're hosting a summer pool party, a football tailgater in the fall or a winter excursion and picnic on snowshoes, entertaining outside is fun, different and exciting. Serve plenty of food and drink, bring all the necessary gear—and don't forget the sunscreen!

Steps

1 See 342 Throw a Party and 316 Throw a Dinner Party.

2 Establish the tone when you set the table and put up decorations. Use crisp linens and fresh flowers for an elegant garden luncheon party, jaunty bandanas for a barbecue rib bash, and sand pails and seashells for a beach party.

3 Ply your guests with plenty of fluids: Lemonade and mint iced tea for a summer garden party, buckets of icy beer for a clambake on the beach or rich, hot chocolate and mulled wine for a holiday party. See 359 Plan a Holiday Open House.

4 Make your guests comfortable. Keeping age and ability in mind, provide blankets and cushions or portable tables and chairs. Look into folding camp chairs at stores such as REI.com.

5 Set up a changing room for your pool party, with extra towels poolside. If it's a big group that includes children, hire a lifeguard.

6 Decorate with team colors, flags and pom-poms for a tailgate party, pails and shovels, umbrellas and beach balls for a clambake; or cactus and western gear for a barbecue.

7 Feed everyone family-style. Set up a buffet on a picnic table and let guests serve themselves. If you're entertaining at home, position the table near the kitchen for easy transport and serving.

8 Choose foods that travel well if you're going farther than the backyard. Salads are perfect for feeding crowds: classic potato, pasta, turkey with dried apricots and walnuts, cold tofu with shiitake mushrooms and napa cabbage, and wild rice or tabbouleh.

9 Bring on the fun with a football, Frisbee or volleyball set. Start a game of croquet, lawn bowling or softball. The kids will love sack races and an egg or water balloon toss. For pool or beach parties, provide air mattresses, boogie boards, fins and goggles.

10 Turn up the tunes. Hire a musician for an hour or two, or provide plenty of CDs and a boom box (don't forget extra batteries).

11 Find a spot for the table with the right mix of sun and shade, sheltered from the wind if possible. Create shade in open areas by setting up umbrellas, pitching open-walled tents or building makeshift "forts" of blankets attached to chairs or trees.

12 Make reservations well in advance for national and regional parks or campsites, especially for three-day weekends and major holidays. If no reservations are accepted, ask a relative or friend to stake out the site early and partition your area with ribbons.

Tips

Staple-gun paper tablecloths to tables if it's windy. Anchor cloth corners with stones, pinecones or seashells.

Check to make sure you're fueled up with lighter fluid, charcoal or a full tank on your gas grill.

Pack plates, napkins, silverware and cups as well as serving spoons, garbage bags, a corkscrew and bottle opener.

Separate beer, wine and nonalcoholic drinks into three separate coolers or iced buckets so that guests don't have to fish for their drink of choice.

Bring extra toilet paper, moist towelettes to wash hands. If there isn't a bathroom or port-a-potty at the site, rent one.

Rent portable gas heaters.

Who Knew?

Do double duty with centerpieces of citronella votives— you'll have light, protection from bugs and a cozy centerpiece all in one.

People tend not to eat or drink as much when the weather is either extremely hot or bitterly cold or windy. Move your party indoors if that's an option—physical discomfort will trump fun every time.

13 Prepare for less-than-ideal conditions. Pack insect repellent, extra sunblock and hats; or extra coats and sweaters. When the sun goes down in the mountains, desert or at the beach, it can get bitterly cold in no time—particularly if there's any wind.

14 Scout the parking situation in advance and clearly designate where guests should park their cars. Hire a van or bus to shuttle guests to and from remote spots or those where parking is difficult.

15 Light up the party if it goes into the evening. String lights or Chinese lanterns from trees to create a festive glow at a park or stick tiki torches in the sand at the beach. Votive candles in paper bags weighted down with sand (luminaria) cast a lovely glow on paths and in seating areas.

Warning

Food should not sit out for more than a couple of hours, even less if it's hot. And to ensure food safety, use coolers with plenty of ice to keep foods chilled while you're en route.

322 | Impress a Date

Ready to let your domestic diva or Renaissance man take center stage? Tie on that apron and start cooking. A quiet home-cooked dinner for two, with a little style and sizzle thrown in for good measure, can turn up the heat just when you need it.

Steps

1 Read 316 Throw a Dinner Party and get to work. Cook ahead as much as possible, have the house clean, table set and music lined up in the CD player so you're relaxed.

2 Ask your date tactfully if he or she has any food preferences. Stay away from fish unless you're grilling it outside—you don't want your house and clothes reeking of trout.

3 Pop a cork—champagne, Prosecco and other bubbly drinks aren't just for big events. Start off the evening with a little toast to the night ahead.

4 Think aphrodisiacs (if not now, then when?). Set up a sumptuous finger feast with caviar, oysters, lobster, figs, mango and artichoke leaves dipped in butter. If your date is an outdoor lover, pack your feast in a basket and head to the beach or a quiet, scenic park. See 321 Plan an Outdoor Party.

5 Start with soups or savory tarts—they're more unusual and impressive than your typical green salad.

6 Try a cheese course before dessert, paired with thin slices of baguette, toasted nuts with a drizzle of honey and olives for a sophisticated touch.

7 Finish it off with a chocolate fondue or flourless chocolate cake. Chocolate, unlike whatever follows, is a "sure thing."

Tips

Get a meat thermometer that reads in doneness rather than temperature, for example, "well-done steak" will be easier to comprehend than 170 degrees F (77 C).

See 251 Orchestrate the Perfect Conception.

If you're pressed for time, or you're a wreck in the kitchen, buy prepared food from a high-end market and plate it up at home. Or get takeout to serve as appetizers, such as sushi or spring rolls. Find a little French bakery where you can pick up a delicious dessert.

RGANIZE YOUR CONTACTS • GET RID OF WHAT YOU DON'T WANT • SAY NO WITHOUT FEELING GUILTY • BALANCE HOME AND WORK • L
GAIN • SCHEDULE TELEVISION WATCHING • DESIGN A HEALTHY LIFESTYLE • PLAN TO AVOID JUNK FOOD • CHOOSE A WEIGHT LOSS PL
EET AN ONLINE DATE • PLAN THE PERFECT DATE • MASTERMIND A BREAKUP • PLAN YOUR SOCIAL CALENDAR • MEET MR. OR MS. RIGI
ORT YOUR SOCK DRAWER • RETURN RENTALS ON TIME • TAKE CONTROL OF YOUR JUNK DRAWER • ORGANIZE THE MEDICINE CABINET
AR CLEAN AND ORDERLY • DEAL WITH A PACK RAT • SELL STUFF ONLINE • ORGANIZE YOUR BOOKSHELVES • CATEGORIZE NEWSPAPER
VE BETTER THROUGH LABELING • ORGANIZE JEWELRY • PLAN YOUR DREAM KITCHEN • CONQUER YOUR CLOSETS • ORGANIZE THE LI
RGANIZE SPRING CLEANING • KEEP THE FAMILY ROOM ORGANIZED • SET UP A BATHROOM SCHEDULE • ORGANIZE BATHROOMS • ORG
RGANIZE KIDS' ROOMS • ORGANIZE SPORTS EQUIPMENT • ORGANIZE KIDS' PLAY SPACES • SAFEGUARD YOUR HOME AGAINST ALLERG
OUSE • USE HOME DESIGN AND PLANNING-SOFTWARE • ESTABLISH YOUR HOME'S SPACE PLAN • INCORPORATE UNIVERSAL DESIGN P
HE BASEMENT • ORGANIZE THE GARAGE • ORGANIZE A TOOLBOX • SET UP A WOODSHOP • ORGANIZE YOUR WINE COLLECTION • PLAI
TUDIO OR SMALL APARTMENT • MANAGE WARRANTY DOCUMENTS • MANAGE HOME-IMPROVEMENT PAPERWORK • MERGE TWO HOUS
RGANIC VEGETABLE GARDEN • PLANT A KITCHEN HERB GARDEN • PLAN A BUTTERFLY GARDEN • DESIGN A BIRD GARDEN • DESIGN A (
ORGANIZE GARDENING TOOLS • ADD A POTTING BENCH TO A YARD • SCHEDULE FRUIT TREE MAINTENANCE • LAY OUT A SPRINKLER S
ESIGN A GARDEN PATH • SET UP A COMPOST SYSTEM • WINTERIZE PLANTS • SCHEDULE YARD WORK • STORE ANYTHING • STORE BU
ND HOBBY MATERIALS • ORGANIZE ART SUPPLIES • ORGANIZE GIFT WRAP AND SEASONAL DECORATIONS • ORGANIZE KIDS' SCHOOLV
OUR WEDDING DRESS AND OTHER TEXTILES • STORE A FUR COAT • STORE BICYCLES AND GEAR • STORE SKI GEAR • ORGANIZE CAMF
'HICH COLLEGE IS RIGHT FOR YOU • GET INTO A TOP COLLEGE OR UNIVERSITY • ACE THE COLLEGE ADMISSIONS TESTS • ORGANIZE \
AW SCHOOL • PREPARE FOR THE BAR EXAM • GET A DEGREE WHILE YOU'RE WORKING • WORK AT HOME WITH KIDS • GO BACK TO WC
RGANIZE YOUR JOB SEARCH • PREPARE FOR A CAREER CHANGE • OPEN A RESTAURANT • BECOME A PHYSICIST • BECOME A CONCE
EALITY-SHOW CONCEPT • BECOME A TALK-SHOW HOST • BECOME A PHOTOJOURNALIST • BECOME A MOVIE DIRECTOR • BECOME A I
LING SYSTEM • ORGANIZE YOUR BRIEFCASE • ORGANIZE YOUR DESK • ORGANIZE YOUR WORKDAY • GET A HANDLE ON E-MAIL • ORG
AIARY REVIEW • CLIMB THE CORPORATE LADDER EFFECTIVELY • ADD A WORKSPACE TO ANY ROOM • ORGANIZE A HOME OFFICE • OF
RAVEL • WRITE A BUSINESS PLAN • SET UP A NEW BUSINESS • CREATE A MARKETING PLAN • AMASS A REAL-ESTATE EMPIRE • POLISI
MPLOYEE • FIRE AN EMPLOYEE • PASS ON A FAMILY BUSINESS • STAY ON TOP OF YOUR SALES GAME • RESTRUCTURE A COMPANY T(
EFEND AGAINST A HOSTILE TAKEOVER • ORGANIZE YOUR OFFICE FOR A MOVE • PREPARE YOUR BUSINESS FOR THE UNTHINKABLE • I
REPARE YOUR TAXES • ORGANIZE A LOAN APPLICATION • ORGANIZE IMPORTANT DOCUMENTS • SAVE FOR PRIVATE SCHOOLING • ORC
LUB • TRACK YOUR INVESTMENTS • SURVIVE BANKRUPTCY • PLAN FOR RETIREMENT • PREPARE A PRENUPTIAL AGREEMENT • CREAT
ONEY • PLAN YOUR FAMILY • BUDGET FOR A NEW BABY • ORCHESTRATE THE PERFECT CONCEPTION • PLAN FOR ARTIFICIAL INSEMIN
EAVE • ORDER BABY ANNOUNCEMENTS • ORGANIZE AN INTERNATIONAL ADOPTION • FOSTER A CHILD • ORGANIZE YOUR LIFE AS A NE
OORDINATE A FAMILY CALENDAR • PLAN FAMILY MEETINGS • ORGANIZE HOME SYSTEMS FOR ADD • PREPARE FOR A NEW CAT OR DO(
ACK-TO-SCHOOL • WIN THE HOMEWORK WARS • PLAN A FIELD TRIP • PLAN YOUR CHILD'S ACTIVITIES • PLAN YOUR CHILDREN'S SUN
NLINE • ORGANIZE A GENEALOGICAL SEARCH • PREPARE FOR YOUR CHILD'S DEPARTURE FOR COLLEGE • ORGANIZE YOUR EMPTY N
LDERLY PARENTS' CARE • PREPARE FOR THE DEATH OF A SPOUSE • HELP YOUR ELDERLY PARENTS MOVE • ORGANIZE A HOME MEDIC
TORE TRIPS • SET UP ONLINE GROCERY SHOPPING • ORGANIZE RECIPES AND COOKBOOKS • PLAN THEME MENUS • CREATE EFFECT
EFRIGERATOR AND FREEZER • ORGANIZE CUTLERY AND KITCHEN TOOLS • ORGANIZE CUPBOARDS AND DRAWERS • ORGANIZE THE F
UNCHES FOR KIDS • PLAN PARTY FOODS AHEAD • THROW A DINNER PARTY • FINISH DINNER ON TIME • PULL OFF A LAST-MINUTE PAF
LTIMATE WEDDING CHECKLIST • BUDGET FOR A WEDDING • FIND THE PERFECT WEDDING RING • PLAN AN ELOPEMENT • SET UP A BA
ONOR • EXECUTE BEST MAN DUTIES • HIRE A BAND • HIRE A BARTENDER • PLAN A SHOWER • ORGANIZE THE REHEARSAL DINNER •
UCCESSFUL SLUMBER PARTY • PLAN A BAR OR BAT MITZVAH • PLAN A QUINCEAÑERA • PLAN A RETIREMENT PARTY • PLAN A FUNER
ANUKKAH PARTY • ORGANIZE A HOLIDAY CRAFT PARTY • PLAN TO SPEND CHRISTMAS SOLO • PLAN THE PERFECT HOLIDAY GIFT EXC
HE HOLIDAYS • STICK TO YOUR NEW YEAR'S RESOLUTIONS • PLAN THE PERFECT NEW YEAR'S EVE • PLAN A SEDER • PLAN A SPECIA
OOD TREE • ORGANIZE A BICYCLE SCAVENGER HUNT • RUN A SPORTS TOURNAMENT • PUBLICIZE AN EVENT • PLAN AN ORGANIZATIC
LAN A CONCERT IN THE PARK • ORGANIZE AN INTERNATIONAL CONCERT TOUR • ORGANIZE A FILM FESTIVAL • PLAN A FUND-RAISING
BUILD A COMMUNITY PLAY STRUCTURE • THROW A BLOCK PARTY • SET UP A NEIGHBORHOOD WATCH • CREATE AN EVACUATION PL
RGANIZE A PROTEST OR MARCH • FIGHT CITY HALL • ORGANIZE A BOYCOTT • ORGANIZE A CLASS ACTION LAWSUIT • MANAGE GRO'
CHOOL IN A THIRD WORLD COUNTRY • PLAN A TRIP • PLAN A TRIP WITH CHILDREN • TRAVEL WITH TEENS • BOOK AIRLINE TICKETS •
IOTORCYCLE TRIP • PLAN A TRAIN TRIP IN THE UNITED STATES • RIDE THE RAILS ABROAD • PREPARE A VACATION COUNTDOWN CHE(
UGGAGE • LOAD A BACKPACK PROPERLY • PLAN AN ELDERHOSTEL TRIP • ORGANIZE AN RV VACATION • PLAN A TRIP WITH AGING PA
'IDELY DIFFERENT PEOPLE • PLAN SPRING BREAK • PLAN AN OVERNIGHT GETAWAY WITH YOUR SPOUSE • PLAN A VACATION SEPARAT
OLITICALLY UNSTABLE REGION • GET TRAVEL INSURANCE • GET IMMUNIZATIONS FOR TRAVELING • BOOK AN ADVENTURE VACATION
LAN A FISHING TRIP TO ALASKA • PACK FOR A CAMPING TRIP • LEAD A BACKPACK TRIP • HIKE A FAMOUS TRAIL • PLAN A TOUR OF T
NGLISH CANAL TRIP • PLAN A CROSS-COUNTRY AIRPLANE VOYAGE • PLAN THE PERFECT DAY ABROAD • PLAN A VISIT TO THE LOUVE
LAN • PREPARE FOR AN ACT OF GOD • ASSEMBLE EMERGENCY KITS • PREPARE FOR SURGERY • PLAN YOUR RECOVERY • SURVIVE
EING LOST • CONDUCT A SEARCH AND RESCUE OPERATION • PLAN AN INVASION • SURVIVE A POLITICAL COUP • PLAN FOR A TERR(
ECOME THE PRESIDENT OF THE UNITED STATES • WIN AN ACADEMY AWARD • BECOME AN OLYMPIAN • TRAIN FOR A MAJOR ATHLET

Celebrations & Events

Congratulations on your engagement! Whether this is your first trip down the aisle or the second (or third), any wedding requires an incredible amount of preparation, planning and big bucks—just one reason some brides and grooms opt to marry at city hall. If you and your betrothed vow to tie the knot with a wedding that'll wow your family and friends, say "I do" to the following planning advice.

Steps

Every wedding

1 Choose a date. Consider all factors, including venue availability, work schedules, family commitments, travel plans of friends and family, holidays and preparation time. Some venues and vendors give discounts for weddings on nontraditional days such as Friday and Sunday. Also think about when you want to hold the wedding; a morning or afternoon reception may be cheaper than the typical Saturday night. Off-peak times of the year, such as after the holidays, may also be discounted.

2 Decide on the size and type of wedding you'd like. Your dream wedding may be entirely different from that of your betrothed. Discuss the desire for a formal or casual event, the ideal location, how many people you'd like to invite (and who they are), as well as family expectations. If you have an elegant evening wedding in mind and your partner thinks a luau on the beach would be perfect, keep talking until you close the gap.

3 Set a budget. When looking at options and making choices, bear in mind: Who's paying? What can they can afford? How formal will it be? See 325 Budget for a Wedding.

4 Select a venue. Find out if there will be another event at the same time as yours. Ask if you can hire an outside caterer.

5 Choose an officiant. Find someone whose beliefs resonate with yours. Select from a wide range of religious officiants, a judge or justice of the peace—or have a friend do the honors (see Tips).

6 Decide if you want attendants. Choose them early so they can help you (see 333 Prepare to be a Maid of Honor and 334 Execute Best Man Duties). Let bridesmaids and groomsmen know how much you appreciate their accepting this important and costly role in your wedding.

7 Create the guest list based on the venue's capacity limit and your budget. Get additional names from both sets of parents and divide the list into must-have people and those you hope to fit in. Get a firm quote from the caterer before the final cut so you can trim names if the budget requires it (see 331 Hire a Caterer).

8 Order a cake. Browse bridal magazines, get references from friends and call around. Schedule a complimentary tasting

Tips

Purchase a binder or a large expanding file and create a section each for the officiant, gown, reception, caterer, florist, photographer, bridesmaids, maid of honor, best man and so on. Stash phone numbers, business cards and records of key phone conversations in the appropriate pockets.

Hire a wedding planner, especially if you're pressed for time or feeling over-whelmed (see 329 Hire an Event Planner). But don't be a control freak. Let him or her do the job you're paying for.

Ask the venue coordinator for a list of preferred vendors to make your search easier.

All-inclusive resorts make getting hitched easy with budget-friendly packages and on-site wedding planners to help every step of the way.

Create dramatic lighting for evening weddings by stringing lights through trees and placing candles, luminaria and torches all around.

Plant flowers six weeks earlier so they're in full bloom on the big day.

Who Knew?

At the Universal Life Church (ulc.com), you can fill out a form online, pay $12 and presto! You're an ordained minister. (Laws vary by state.)

session with your top two choices. Expect to pay $2 to $15 (or more) per slice.

9   Work with a florist to select your flowers, including centerpieces. Keep in mind that flowers are more expensive and are in limited availability during the winter.

10 Hire someone to capture the big day on film. Whether you want movies or black and white, color or digital pictures, find a professional videographer or photographer. See 330 Hire a Photographer.

11 Buy your wedding gown, either off the rack (with alterations) or from a dressmaker. Expect custom-made gowns to require up to several months for fittings. Coordinate shoes, stockings, veil and headpiece.

12 Order custom invitations or design and print your own.

13 Send out a "save the date" notice at least six months in advance for people needing to make travel and hotel arrangements, or if it's a holiday weekend. Include a list of contacts for lodging and car rentals.

Outdoor weddings

1   Check out *The Complete Outdoor Wedding Planner* by Sharon Naylor for tips on how to handle all the outdoor details.

2   Select shoes and a dress style (for brides and attendants) that will work in any weather. Stay away from long trailing hemlines that would be ruined by mud or even damp grass. Choose a warm wrap for yourself and your bridesmaids to throw on as the evening temperatures drop.

3   Determine how many chairs, tables, linens, portable toilets and gas heaters you'll need to rent. Expect your caterer, band and photographer to build in additional costs to transport food and equipment to remote or out-of-the-way locations.

4   Keep the comfort of your guests foremost in mind. Situate chairs so they don't face directly into the setting sun. Consider rigging a shade-cloth awning if your nuptials are planned for a hot sum-mer day.

5   Use a microphone in any group larger than 25 people, or your guests may not be able to hear the "I do's." Test wiring, acoustics, wind distortion, extension cords and speakers ahead of time.

6   Keep the ceremony itself short and sweet. Don't ask guests to survive a long ceremony while braving the elements. Be prepared for any weather. Have plenty of umbrellas and raincoats if there is any possibility at all of rain. Take a deep breath should rain or snow delay the arrival of guests, officiants and vendors.

Make sure there's an easy and accessible way for elderly or disabled guests to get to the ceremony site.

Bear in mind that sunset ceremonies, while gorgeous, are often difficult to view and to photograph. The bride and groom are often backlit, and the photographs show all the guests screening their eyes with their programs.

Find out if you need a permit to hold your wedding on the beach. Or choose to have your wedding on the beach fronting a resort or restaurant.

Warnings

It's a fact that whoever pays for the wedding exerts a fair amount of control over the process. If that is the bride's parents, the mother of the bride should be consulted. A delicate balancing act between mother's and daughter's wishes? You bet.

Be extremely considerate when you're borrowing a house or garden for your wedding—the generous offer adds considerable expense, time and anxiety to the owner's life.

Put together a solid plan B in case of bad weather. Select a venue that has an indoor alternative, like a museum, a hall or even a barn. Look into renting tents or large awnings.

You've set the date. You're ecstatic. You've told all your friends. Panic creeps in as you realize everything you have to do to pull this wedding off. Break it down into simple steps, and you'll get it done.

12–6 months before

- Announce engagement.
- Decide on date and time.
- Decide on style of wedding.
- Start idea scrap book.
- Establish budget with families.
- Book ceremony, reception location.
- Book the officiant.
- Decide on number of guests.
- Choose attendants.
- Book caterer, musicians, florist.
- Book photographer.
- Book transportation.
- Choose and order wedding dress.
- Set up gift registry.

6–3 months before

- Choose wedding rings.
- Choose and order groom's attire.
- Order attire for male attendants.
- Arrange dress fittings for gown.
- Confirm bridesmaids' dress orders.
- Order invitations and other stationery.
- Write personal vows and readings.
- Order wedding cake.
- Plan rehearsal dinner.
- Choose attire for rehearsal dinner.
- Book room for wedding night.
- Book honeymoon.
- Reserve blocks of rooms for guest accomodations.

3–1 months before

- Complete guest list.
- Address and send wedding invitations.
- Choose music and playlist.
- Draw up seating plans.
- Reserve rental items.
- Purchase wedding favors for guests.
- Order final flower arrangements.
- Organize delivery of wedding cake.
- Book hair stylist and makeup artist.

1 month before

- Choose gifts for attendants.
- Pick up wedding rings.
- Choose presents for each other.
- Confirm all services.
- Discuss music with musicians.
- Send wedding-day schedule to all service providers.
- Send invitations for rehearsal dinner.
- Attend final fitting of wedding gown.
- Have hair styled as trial run.
- Arrange for blood tests, if necessary.
- Borrow items for wedding.
- Organize cake table decorations.
- Give photographer required photo list.
- Get paperwork in order.
- Confirm honeymoon reservations.
- Write thank-you notes.

2 weeks before

- Obtain marriage license.
- Prepare announcements.
- Arrange final cleaning and pressing of wedding attire.
- Write place cards for reception.
- Arrange transportation from reception to wedding-night location.
- Make list of wedding day needs.
- Buy traveler's checks for honeymoon.
- Send schedule to wedding party.
- Order birdseed, petals or confetti.
- Ask maid of honor to follow up on missing RSVPs.
- Write more thank-you notes.
- Create ceremony program.

1 week before

- Pick up gifts for attendants.
- Discuss seating with ushers.
- Confirm final guest numbers and seating arrangements with caterer.
- Practice toasts and speeches.
- Break in wedding shoes.
- Attend rehearsal and rehearsal dinner.
- Place fees in envelopes for services.
- Get manicure/pedicure.
- Confirm final details with vendors.
- Arrange for attendants to take care of wedding attire after reception.
- Pack for honeymoon.

Wedding day order of events

- Hair is styled.
- Bride, groom and attendants get dressed.
- Transportation for bride and bridesmaids arrives.
- Transportation for groom arrives.
- Groom leaves for ceremony.
- Bridesmaids leave for ceremony.
- Bride and her father (or escort) leave for ceremony.
- Guests arrive for ceremony.
- Ceremony begins.
- Ceremony ends.
- Wedding party arrives at reception.
- Photographs are taken.
- Guests arrive at reception; receiving line begins.
- Music begins.
- Food is served.
- Speeches and toasts.
- Cake is cut and served.
- Bride and groom depart.

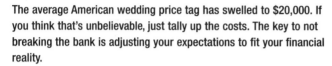

The average American wedding price tag has swelled to $20,000. If you think that's unbelievable, just tally up the costs. The key to not breaking the bank is adjusting your expectations to fit your financial reality.

Steps

1 Determine if anyone else will be pitching in to pay for the wedding. Traditionally, the bride's parents pay for the ceremony and reception. These days you'll often find the groom's family offering to cover part of the costs, such as the bar tab or rehearsal dinner. Remember, though, the more people are footing the bills, the more they feel they are entitled to their say. Many couples save up to pay for their own wedding and sidestep all the trouble.

2 Create a budget. Figure that the reception will eat up about 50 percent. Music, photography and flowers each take up about 10 percent. The remaining 20 percent goes to everything else — dress, tuxedo, invitations, hotel, limo and so on. See the chart below for suggested contributions.

3 Get creative with where you can cut back. Cull your guest list, starting with kids, colleagues and dates of single guests. Use less-expensive thermography instead of engraving invitiations. Find out if a club or museum that you belong to offers a reception discount for members. Borrow the gown or rent the tuxedo.

4 Open an interest-bearing checking account exclusively for wedding expenses. Sock away as much as you can during the engagement. Although the final bills are usually not due until the week of the wedding, be prepared to place down payments with the band, photographer, caterer and venue. Don't forget tips.

Tips

Enlist the help of an online wedding-budget planner such as TheKnot.com. Also check out wedding-budget software.

Who Knew?

Purchase alcohol at a wholesale beverage store rather than through the caterer. Keep in mind that most caterers may charge a modest corkage fee.

Read 226 Set Up a Budget.

Warning

There are places to skimp, and places where cutting costs is a big no-no. For instance, don't have a cash bar. If you can't afford a full bar (alcohol is a big chunk of change in any wedding budget), consider limiting the bar to wine and beer.

The Bride and Her Family	The Groom and His Family
• Stationery	• Bride's engagement and wedding rings
• Newspaper announcements	• Rehearsal dinner
• Engagement party	• Marriage license
• Ceremony costs	• Groom's attire
• Bride's attire	• Bouquets, boutonnieres and corsages
• Gifts for bride's attendants	• Gifts for the groomsmen
• Groom's wedding ring	• Transportation to the ceremony for the groom and his attendants
• Photography	• Transportation for the entire wedding party after the ceremony
• Transportation to the ceremony for the bride and her attendants	• Accommodations for groomsmen
• Reception costs	• Honeymoon
• Accommodations for bride's attendants	
• Bride's trousseau	

326 | Find the Perfect Wedding Ring

The rings you slide on each other's fingers on your wedding day will be a lasting reminder of its promise and joy. Choose a ring you'll cherish for the rest of your life.

Steps

Diamonds

1 Study styles. The traditional solitaire—a single diamond held aloft by prongs—is the most popular. Bezel settings (in which a slim border of platinum or gold surrounds a smallish diamond) can make the gem look bigger. The anniversary style is a row of diamonds or a diamond flanked by sapphires or emeralds.

2 Become fluent in the four Cs—the international language of diamonds: carat weight, color, clarity and cut.

- Diamond weights (not sizes) are measured in metric carats. Jewelers should disclose precise amounts and ranges.

- Letters represent colors ranging from D (colorless, very rare and most desirable) to Z (light yellow or brown and less desirable). Grades vary. It's also a matter of taste. Winter-white diamonds look best with platinum, warmer shades with golds.

- Clarity measures *birthmarks*—internal flaws are called *inclusions,* external ones *blemishes.* Grades include FL for flawless, VS1 for very slightly included, and I3 for included.

- Seek out a cut that maximizes brilliance, fire and sparkle.

3 Ask for an independent grading report—your diamond's detailed genealogy. Don't buy a costly stone without one, since it's your guarantee that you're getting what you've paid for.

4 Take a valuable diamond to an independent appraiser. If necessary, buy it first, but only with a written, unconditional money-back guarantee allowing you a few days to have it appraised.

Precious metals

1 Look for marked jewelry. While gold need not by law carry the karat marks (not to be confused with carat, the weight measurement for diamonds) that define its level of purity, virtually all reputable stores sell only marked gold. If it is karat-marked, law dictates that it also be stamped with a hallmark, which shows that the manufacturer stands behind the karat mark's accuracy. The country of origin is also often noted.

2 Buy gold in a range of colors and levels of purity. The higher the karat rating, the more pure gold is in a piece and the richer the color (and the softer the item). See chart, next page.

Tips

Shop at a jewelry store that makes you feel good. Trusting the jeweler, and subsequently the advice and jewelry he or she offers, is very important.

Ask your jeweler for a free copy of the industry's helpful diamond-buying booklet or contact the Gemological Institute of America (gia.edu).

Who Knew?

Buy only from a reputable retailer who will accept returns—preferably one affiliated with the Jewelers Association or another professional trade association.

Your jeweler can have a unique report number laser-inscribed on your diamond's outer edge. If you ever have it resized or professionally cleaned, you can make sure you're getting your own diamond back. Grading reports and identification numbers also serve insurance purposes.

Establish a relationship with a reputable jeweler who will be able to resize, clean, remount and engrave your jewelry over the years.

3 Step up to platinum, the rarest, purest and heaviest precious metal. Almost double the weight of 14-karat gold, platinum is incredibly dense but also very soft.

KARAT	PERCENTAGE GOLD	DESCRIPTION
24k	100 percent pure gold	So soft that it is not often used for jewelry.
18k	75 percent gold, mixed with copper or silver	More "lemony" in tone, strong enough for rings.
14k	58.3 percent gold	Lightly reddish hue comes from added copper alloys, which also lend it durability.
10k	41.6 percent gold	Less than 10-karat gold can't legally be called or sold as gold in the United States.

327 | Plan an Elopement

No longer strictly for couples who decide to marry on the spur of the moment or need to (ahem) rush things along, elopements are increasingly favored by those who want a simple wedding ceremony. Perhaps the two of you covet privacy and prefer not to be the center of attention at a lavish wedding, or are on a shoestring budget. Whether your destination is a chapel in Vegas, the steps of city hall or a quiet mountaintop, even a speedy tying of the knot takes some planning.

Steps

1 Decide if you'll take the plunge in complete secrecy or in relative simplicity with a small group of friends and relatives.

2 Set your budget for the event, then decide on a venue. Agree on a destination you both enjoy or have always wanted to visit. Or just head to city hall.

3 Find out if your state requires a blood test or a physical examination before marriage (only a few still do). Tests are intended to show whether either party is infected with a venereal disease. Many states also have waiting periods before marriage. Check with the county clerk.

4 Find an officiant to perform your ceremony. He or she will often be able to make recommendations for hotels, caterers, bakers and florists.

5 Hire a photographer or videographer to capture on film even the speediest of nuptials. See 330 Hire a Photographer.

6 Exchange your vows and let the honeymoon begin!

Tips

If you choose to elope at a resort, plan to marry during its off-peak season for the best deals.

See 325 Budget for a Wedding and 242 Prepare a Prenuptial Agreement.

Who Knew?

Keep in mind that the officiant must be able to issue the marriage license in the city and county where he or she is registered.

Some photographers will charge you by the roll and simply hand you the undeveloped film after it's shot. You handle the printing yourself for far less than the cost of standard wedding packages.

A well-stocked bar can elevate any party to a classy soirée. Give your thirsty guests a palette of cocktail ingredients to choose from. If you're no mixologist, read 336 Hire a Bartender.

LIQUOR

Essentials	Extras
Amaretto	Apricot brandy
Anisette	Chambord
Bourbon	Crème de cacao
Brandy	Crème de cassis
Gin	Crème de menthe
Grand Marnier	Midori
Irish cream liqueur	Peach schnapps
Kahlúa	Peppermint schnapps
Rum, dark or spiced	Sambuca
Scotch	
Tequila	
Triple sec	
Vermouth, sweet and dry	
Vodka	
Whiskey, Canadian and Irish	

MIXERS

Essentials	Extras
Bitters	7-Up
Club soda	Grenadine
Coffee	Ice cream
Cola	Half and half
Cranberry juice	Milk
Ginger ale	Sweet-and-sour mix
Grapefruit juice	Sweetened lime juice (Rose's brand)
Lemon juice (fresh)	
Lime juice (fresh)	
Orange juice	
Pineapple juice	
Sugar	
Tabasco	
Tomato juice	
Tonic	
Water	
Worcestershire sauce	

GARNISHES

Essentials	Extras
Celery	Crystallized sugar
Cocktail onions	Maraschino cherries
Cocoa powder	Mint (fresh)
Horseradish	Pineapple
Lemons	Raspberries
Limes	Strawberries
Martini olives	Whipped cream
Nutmeg	
Oranges	
Pepper	
Salt, coarse and fine	

GADGETS

Essentials	Extras
Bar towels	Coasters
Blender	Cocktail picks
Bottle opener	Cocktail napkins
Cocktail shaker	Cocktail umbrellas
Corkscrew	Stirrers
Glasses (highball, cocktail, martini, margarita)	
Ice bucket and tongs	
Jigger	
Lemon reamer and zester	
Margarita pitcher	
Strainer	

With a skilled event coordinator in your corner, you'll be able to throw a corporate picnic for 100 people, an intimate dinner party or a country wedding—without breaking a sweat. Replace panic with peace of mind and enjoy the festivities.

Steps

1 Base preliminary logistical decisions on your budget: number of guests, atmosphere, location, date and time, food (buffet, sit-down meal, cocktail party, box lunches) and degree of formality. Give yourself six to nine months of lead time when planning a large event. See 324 Create the Ultimate Wedding Checklist.

2 List those tasks you want taken off your shoulders. A pro can plan budgets, rent audiovisual and other equipment, scout venues, hire and manage live music, manage guest lists, arrange decorations and valet parking, handle airline and hotel bookings for out-of-town events or guests—even hire portable rest rooms.

3 Consult local wedding and business reference guides, and ask for referrals from friends, colleagues, caterers, and local hotels and businesses for event planners, consultants or coordinators.

4 Interview likely prospects. To find out if they're experienced in the kind of event you're throwing, ask how many events they've produced, what kind, for what size group, and what made these events special. Discuss what aspects of your event they will assume control over. A good planner should also be able to offer creative ideas to suit any budget.

5 Discuss whether you will be billed by the hour, by the event or as a percentage of the total budget. Ask if package prices are available. Explain in detail what you want the coordinator to do, then ask for a quote in writing. Ask what he or she can do to reassure you that costs won't run over, at least not without your prior agreement.

6 Query the coordinator to see how he or she would handle potential catastrophes such as the caterer running out of food, the DJ not showing up, or a sudden downpour drowning out an outdoor event.

7 Ask if you can drop by one of the planner's events in progress. Request contact details of previous clients and call them to ask about their experience with that particular event coordinator.

8 Spell out the project's scope in detail. Describe the planner's responsibilities and delineate all payment information in a written, signed agreement.

Tips

See 226 Set Up a Budget.

Your coordinator should inquire about local noise ordinances.

Hire a licensed, insured company for major events. See 381 Plan a Fund-Raising Event.

Remember that well-connected professionals can save you money by passing on discounts and perks they get from vendors and banquet managers. And since they're experienced with service-provider contracts, arrange for them to handle all the negotiations, notifying you of any hitches or price increases. Do your homework first so you are familiar with acceptable price ranges. See 5 Hire a Professional Organizer.

Your wedding day. Your baby's first portrait. A four-generation reunion. Whatever the event, you want the moment beautifully captured on film. A professional photographer will offer a total package: proofs, prints, matting and albums. Don't scrimp on the person you choose— you can't reshoot the event!

Steps

1 Start interviewing photographers as soon as you have the time and location of the event nailed down.

2 Choose a photographer who specializes in the type of event you're holding, such as weddings, family portraits or corporate head shots. Ask for references and get recommendations whenever possible. Your venue may also have a list of preferred vendors. Use the Yellow Pages as a last resort.

3 Ask to see samples of their work that are similar to what you want. Look for relaxed expressions and posing, and watch out for stiff, cookie-cutter staging. Great pictures look natural and easy. Also ask to see photos of a complete wedding in a real proof book. This will give you an accurate idea of what to expect.

4 Trust your instincts. Do you get a good feel from the photographer? Does he or she listen to what you really want? Could you work well together?

5 Ask how long he or she has been in business and get a sense of his or her level of professionalism. You want someone who dresses and acts sharp to shoot your event. Also find out if you'll be paying for an assistant.

6 Specify if you want color or black-and-white pictures, or both. The latter will require the photographer to bring two cameras, each loaded with different film. Ask about sepia tones and other special effects.

7 Inquire if digital photographs are an option. If so, find out if you will view the pictures as paper proofs, as contact sheets or on a CD. Some photographers put up a Web page so clients can proof their pictures online.

8 Ask how long it will take to see the proofs, whether you get to keep them, how reprints and enlargements will be handled and what they cost. Inquire about bulk discounts on large orders and the possibility of ordering prints online.

9 Review the contract and button down all the details. All terms should be specified, including the deposit, cancellation and refund policies.

10 Touch base in the weeks prior to your event to finalize all the details. Give the photographer a list of people (with descriptions) you definitely want photographed.

Tips

If your event will be photographed digitally, look at a printout of a sample photograph to make sure you're satisfied with the quality.

Check out the studio if you are having portraits taken. Look for a place to change clothes if you care to, as well as comfortable ambient temperature. You want to be very comfortable in the studio in order to take a relaxed photograph.

Warning

Try to get a read on whether the photographer is intrusive, bossy or arrogant. An event that is dictated by the photographer can be a miserable affair for everyone.

When planning a big event, the last thing you want to go wrong is the food. The tablecloths may not match perfectly and the bartender may not know how to make a Mojito, but the food—good or bad—will be what guests remember. Finding the right caterer will make your life easier and ensure your party's talked about for all the right reasons.

Steps

1 Start your search as soon as you have the date and venue nailed down. Get a list of preferred caterers from your venue or ask friends for recommendations. If you loved the food at a party or event, ask the host for the caterer's number.

2 Create a budget based on what you want to pay per head for food and beverages, and go over this with prospective caterers. (See 325 Budget for a Wedding.) High prices don't necessarily guarantee quality. Some famed caterers resort to premade sauces, while many small operators make everything from scratch using fresh ingredients.

3 Flip through the caterer's portfolio of color photographs. Look at the presentation of individual dishes, table designs and buffet spreads. Does the food look beautiful and delicious?

4 Get phone numbers of previous customers and ask them if they were satisfied with the caterer.

5 Ask for sample menus that fit your budget. The caterer will create a tasting for you. Besides evaluating the dishes' flavor, you'll be able to gauge his or her desire to please you with additional special requests. Are vegetarian or low-fat dishes offered? A larger caterer may offer more dishes to sample, but this isn't the most important issue. Just make certain the company can handle the total number of guests, even if it has to outsource some tasks.

6 Expect to be charged per person for food, ranging from $10 to $100 per head depending on the event. Beverages, furniture rental or linens may be priced separately. Ask for an estimate on the rates for servers, bartenders and cleanup crew. A six-hour affair might stretch to an eight-hour bash, and the caterer must keep paying the staff until the last guest leaves.

7 Review the venue with your caterer, who will want to see the kitchen facilities and space where guests will mingle and dine. Make sure that he or she surveys the space carefully and plans the positioning of food and beverage tables to optimize traffic flow. This is crucial to arranging serving and dining tables.

8 Determine who will provide or rent tables, chairs, centerpieces, tent, glassware, utensils and linens. Also confirm the number of wait staff, their dress code, taxes, gratuities and payment schedule. Have all agreed-upon details written into the contract.

Tips

Clarify the dress code for servers and staff. The bistro look—a neat white shirt, black tie and pants, and an apron—has overtaken the tuxedo look, although you can request formal wear if you wish.

Some caterers will act as a coordinator on the day of the event. Even if you don't have your caterer take on this role, provide it with an event timeline.

You are expected to tip the caterer 15 to 20 percent after the event.

Who Knew?

Ask your caterer and the venue if you can bring in your own alcohol—this can save you a bundle. Buy from a discount beverage store that will let you return unopened bottles.

Warnings

Some function halls or hotels won't allow you to bring in outside caterers.

If the caterer is not insured and bonded, you're taking a big risk.

You would be right to worry if a caterer doesn't ask lots of questions about what you like, love and hate, and about your ideas and goals for the event. A lack of curiosity sends up a red flag that you're in for generic, impersonal service.

332 Plan a Bachelor or Bachelorette Party

Nights of drunken debauchery are so yesterday. Today, there are many more imaginative and tasteful ways to celebrate the bride's and groom's last days of singlehood. Find out what he or she actually wants before planning the party, and tailor the fun accordingly.

Steps

1 Invite the entire wedding party, close friends and relatives. Don't forget to include your future in-laws.

2 Consider how much money you can spend and who will chip in. Family and friends who are already investing heavily in the wedding itself, traveling to it and buying gifts, will greatly appreciate it if you keep the costs down.

3 Set a date. Traditionally, the bachelor and bachelorette parties are held several weeks before the wedding. However, if many out-of-towners will be attending, hold both events the same weekend to make it easy for invitees. Steer clear of blowout parties the night before the wedding—no bride or groom wants to be hung-over at the altar.

4 Plan something that's appealing, simple, easy and brief. While the trend these days is toward elaborate weekend-long events at a spa, in Las Vegas and so on, the cost and time commitment may be too much for many to bear. Plan a dinner at someone's home, get tickets to a game, play a round of golf together or dine in the private room of a restaurant.

5 Arrange designated drivers, a limo service or taxis to make sure everyone gets home safely if people will be drinking at the event.

Warnings

If the bride and groom doesn't want to overdrink, don't make her or him do so.

Don't expect people to fly out for both the wedding and the bachelor party.

333 Prepare to Be the Maid of Honor

The good news is you've been asked to be the maid or matron of honor. You are truly honored to be chosen—your friendship has passed the test of time. The bad news is you've been asked to be the maid or matron of honor. It's a big job and the pressure's on. Don't worry, though—good friends always rise to the occasion.

Steps

1 Start saving. You'll be shelling out big bucks on your dress, shoes, shower and bachelorette gifts, airfare and hotel costs.

2 Talk to the bride and see what she has in mind. Ask what her expectations are up front and how she would like you to help her. Ask what kind of shower she would like and whom she would like to invite.

3 Get the measurements of the other bridesmaids to the bride when she needs them for the dresses.

Tip

Donate bridesmaids' dresses to charity after the wedding, if they won't be used again. Some organizations, such as Fairy Godmothers Inc. (fairygodmothersinc.com), collect dresses to distribute to girls who cannot afford a prom dress.

4 Keep in touch with the bride about RSVPs. Offer to contact invited guests who haven't responded by the requested date. Also offer to mediate between bickering family members or friends.

5 Send frequent e-mail messages to update the bridesmaids as well as the bride. If nothing else, it'll reassure her that you're on top of things.

6 Plan the bridal shower and bachelorette party (see 337 Plan a Shower and 332 Plan a Bachelor or Bachelorette Party).

7 Help the bride get dressed on the big day.

8 Toast the bride and groom (if you want—the best man usually does this).

9 Point out key people to the photographer to make sure the bride gets photos of everyone she wants.

10 Arrange for safe delivery of the wedding gifts.

11 Make sure the bride and groom get something to eat and drink during the reception. Offer snacks and water before the ceremony.

Who Knew?

Put together a bridal emergency kit for the wedding. Include an extra pair of stockings, tampons, dental floss, toothbrushes and toothpaste, breath mints, hair spray, tissues, needle and thread, stain remover, small scissors, nail polish in her chosen color, aspirin, lip gloss, ibuprofin, bottled water and an energy bar.

---

334 | Execute Best Man Duties

There's a lot more to being best man than planning the bachelor party and standing next to the groom. In large part, you will perform many of the wedding tasks so the groom doesn't have to worry about them, and help out your brother or friend at a time when he needs you most.

Steps

1 Start saving. You'll be paying for your tuxedo, the bachelor party and gifts, as well as airfare and hotel costs.

2 Consult with the groom about the attire for the male attendants. Arrange for all groomsmen's tux rentals, including their measurements. You'll also be in charge of returning them.

3 See 332 Plan a Bachelor or Bachelorette Party.

4 Prepare a sentimental or funny toast for the rehearsal dinner and reception. If you're shy, simply ask everyone to raise their glasses to the couple's happiness and new life. Be a class act: Don't humiliate the groom or the bride.

5 Take charge of the getaway car. Make sure it arrives on time, and decide if and how the groomsmen will decorate it.

6 Keep the groom calm before the ceremony. Give him water or anything else he needs. Humor helps.

7 Lead the groomsmen in ushering guests into the church and bridesmaids down the aisle.

Tips

Check out AfterHours.com for a cheat sheet on selecting tuxedos.

Keep an eye out for female guests—young and old—who may be in need of a dancing partner. Ask them to join you in a dance.

335 | Hire a Band

Nothing gets a crowd moving like great live music. From a string quartet at a brunch to a rockin' band at a prom, here's what you need to know to start your event off on the right note.

Steps

1 Decide what type of band you want to hire and start searching for one as soon as you know the date and location of the event. Get recommendations from friends, newlyweds and event planners. Look in the phone book for booking agents.

2 Check with your venue for any noise or space restrictions. Ask the manager what size band has worked best in the past.

3 Listen to tapes, watch videos, or—even better—go listen to the band play. Note how the musicians interact with the audience and the variety of music they play.

4 Tell them what type of music you want played, such as swing and jazz. Ask to see their playlist and note any songs you definitely want played and those you want nixed. For weddings and proms, let them know what *your* song is. Find out what type of music they'll play on the sound system during breaks.

5 Make a contract that includes dates, setup and finish times, breaks, musicians, emcee duties, clothing, equipment, food, rates, deposits, and cancellation and refund policy.

Tips

Hire a band that has played your type of event before— they will be familiar with the flow of events and can serve as emcees.

See 137 Organize Movies, Music and Other Media and consider using your iPod instead of hiring a band or DJ.

Who Knew?

If the band doesn't have a song you want on the playlist, ask if they'll learn it.

A band's fee is usually based on a four-hour minimum. As a point of reference, expect to pay from $3,500 to $5,500 for a seven-piece band; tipping is not expected.

336 | Hire a Bartender

An experienced bartender can be a party-planning asset in more ways than one. Go with a pro and know the thirsty hordes at your event will be in good hands.

Steps

1 Get recommendations from friends, caterers or party planners. If your search comes up short, go online to find an agency.

2 Ask if the bartender has his or her own bar kit. Pros travel with their own wine opener, pour spouts, cocktail shaker, strainer, long-handled spoon, towel and knife for cutting garnishes. You're expected to provide a blender, beverages, glasses and ice.

3 Test expertise. Good bartenders know major mixed-drink recipes by heart. Ask how many years of experience the bartender has and of what kind.

4 Quiz them on how they set up their bars and how they cope with nonstop drink demands and empty glasses and bottles. They should be in command of their work space, trash containers, and supply of glassware and beverages.

Tips

Good bartenders ask about guests' ages and tastes, and know which drinks different groups favor. For example, a bar mitzvah calls for a different approach than a retirement roast.

An experienced bartender can help you calculate how much and what alcohol you'll need (see 328 Set Up a Bar).

Warning

Avoid novices or anyone fresh out of bartending school.

Expectations abound! Whether it's an imminent wedding or a baby who's due, showering your loved one with congratulations and gifts is an honor and a delight. And now that showers for couples are gaining in popularity, you fellows aren't getting off the hook.

Steps

1 Determine if your friend actually wants a shower. If it's a second marriage, a couple may want to forgo the party. Parents-to-be may not want a baby shower until after the bundle of joy arrives.

2 Consult with your friend to see what showers are planned. Oftentimes multiple showers are given, and you don't want to duplicate themes and/or gifts. If more than one shower is planned, avoid overlapping the guest lists—although family members can certainly be invited to more than one shower.

3 Enlist the help of anyone who shows interest in planning the shower and has the time, or choose a co-host. A shower can be a daunting—and occasionally expensive—task to undertake alone.

4 Pick a date as far in advance as possible to accommodate far-away invitees. If guests are mostly local, shorter notice is fine.

5 Set the budget and come to an agreement with your co-hosts about how to divvy up costs. If funds are limited, hold a cozy shower at the host's home. Deeper pockets can consider hosting the event at a hall or restaurant—even a spa or resort. See 226 Set Up a Budget.

6 Brainstorm theme ideas, keeping in mind the honoree's preferences. If she hates spicy food, for instance, you certainly don't want to hold her shower in a Thai restaurant. How about an afternoon tea party? Be creative. Decide whether to make the shower a surprise or not. If it's not, ask the guest(s) of honor for input on their preferences.

7 Prepare the guest list. Mail the invitations. Include registry information and request RSVPs a few weeks before the event.

8 Decide on the menu. If you're holding the shower at a restaurant, this will be easy. If it is a home shower, decide whether you want to cater the affair, cook yourself or go potluck. Keep any special food preferences in mind. See 342 Throw a Party.

9 Plan the entertainment. Will you play games, provide live music or play CDs in the background? Make sure the guest of honor *wants* to play games before you arrange any.

10 Confirm all reservations and RSVPs a week before the shower. Buy food and decorations and begin cooking anything that you can prepare in advance and freeze (see 315 Plan Party Foods Ahead). The day before the shower, pick up and arrange the flowers, set the tables and address any other final details.

Tips

Ask the guest if he or she would like to open the gifts in front of the guests or later. Pick someone to write a list of gifts and givers if they are to be opened at the event.

Decide whether to make the shower a girls-only event or a coed affair. While coed showers are very trendy, a traditional bride or mom-to-be may want to go with a female-only fling.

Counter with a mens-only shower to fete the new father. Forget pastels—serve up steaks, deli platters and beer.

Who Knew?

Traditionally everyone who is invited to the wedding should also be invited to a bridal shower; a baby shower list is less formal.

338 Organize the Rehearsal Dinner

The rehearsal dinner is a fabulous evening for the bride and groom's closest family and friends to enjoy a meal together, relax after all the wedding preparations and toast the lucky couple. Traditionally, the rehearsal dinner is held the night before the wedding and immediately following the rehearsal—when love is in the air and the wedding anticipation is building.

Steps

1 Determine who will pay for the dinner and how much to spend. Traditionally the groom's family acts as host, but these days anything goes. See 325 Budget for a Wedding.

2 Select an appropriate venue. A private dining room in a restaurant is a popular choice. You could also host the dinner on a yacht, in someone's backyard or at the beach.

3 Invite both families, all of the attendants and close friends, as well as guests who have traveled a great distance to attend the wedding.

4 Remind the best man and the groom's dad that it is customary that they toast the couple first. After they have done so, anyone can offer up a toast. You might follow this order, but keep the toasting under control:

• The best man toasts the bride.

• The bride toasts the groom.

• The groom toasts the bride.

• The groom toasts the bride's mother.

• The bride's father may toast the groom's parents.

5 Present thank-you gifts. Typically, the bride and groom give gifts to the maid of honor, bridesmaids, best man and groomsmen at the rehearsal dinner. Express your appreciation in short but sweet speeches as you hand out each gift, or opt to present gifts privately.

Tips

Show home movies or videos of the groom and bride as kids. Or create a photo collage of the two over the years.

See 208 Prepare a Speech.

Who Knew?

Invent a cocktail for the couple. Get together one evening before the rehearsal dinner with some of the other attendants, and mix up different ingredients for a signature cocktail. Create a name for the cocktail (based on the couple, of course), and ask the bartender to mix up drinks for everyone.

Warning

If there are divorced parents in the mix, things can get especially saucy at the rehearsal dinner, because it is typically an intimate affair with not much breathing room available. Take extra care to arrange the seating so that all of your guests are comfortable.

Choosing a honeymoon destination bears some similarity to selecting a mate. You shouldn't decide haphazardly, and what looks good on paper isn't always so. You want the perfect getaway, but you've learned by now that perfection is elusive—even your Prince or Princess Charming has faults (not that you can remember any just now).

Steps

1 Sit down with your spouse-to-be and make a list of things that are essential (tropical setting, surfing) and what you can live without (beachfront condo). Discuss whether you'll take off for the honeymoon immediately following the wedding or whether to postpone it a few days, weeks or longer.

2 Surf the Web and scan travel magazines for destination ideas.

3 Agree on a honeymoon that suits both of your personalities. Hedonistic hammock-dozers and lovers of *la dolce vita* will swoon for a beach resort in the Caribbean, Hawaii, Fiji or Tahiti. Exotic dreamers who love to scuba dive and snorkel will flip for the Seychelles and Palau. Fun-in-the-sun personalities will be drawn to resorts, where you can go from a pool to the golf course to a reggae-blaring beach bar to the spa and back to the pool again. Or fly to a cosmopolitan European city that has a great restaurant and theater scene. If a sprig of forsythia, wooded strolls and a vintage bottle of wine stirs your souls, a country inn in New England or Napa Valley has newlywed written all over it.

4 Talk about how you'll pay for the honeymoon and, if it's necessary to save up for it, how you'll go about that (see 228 Design a Savings Plan). Check out honeymoon registry sites such as HoneyLuna.com for more ideas and help.

5 Pick a package. A travel agent will be wired into the latest and greatest land, air and car packages, which cost less than booking accommodations, flights and car rental separately. A typical Hawaiian or Caribbean honeymoon package might include a cocktail greeting, a champagne breakfast, a dinner at the resort, and complimentary golf cart and greens fees, all for one price.

6 See 405 Plan a Trip and put your official documents in order, including passports or visas. Purchase travel insurance, if you're not already covered by your credit card or insurance. If you are going abroad, exchange a few days' worth of currency before you leave. If you're going off the beaten path, make sure your vaccinations are up to date (see 431 Travel Abroad).

7 Pack for the honeymoon well before the wedding. There's plenty on your plate already. See 419 Pack for a Trip and 417 Prepare a Vacation Countdown Checklist.

8 Make arrangements for transportation to and from the airport and to have your home and pets cared for in your absence.

Tips

If you need new luggage and travel essentials, add these items to your bridal registry.

Enlist the services of a travel agent. A good agent will spend time with you to find out your preferences and advise you accordingly.

Now is the time to use those miles for upgrades to first class.

Who Knew?

Many couples take their honeymoon months or even a year following the wedding for various reasons—they may have just started a new job, or they may be in school and have to wait until the semester is out.

Even the most expensive and luxurious hotel room won't be worth much if you have a view of a parking lot or garbage dumpsters. Yes, you'll have to pay more for a room with a view, but consider it money well spent.

Warning

If the bride is taking her husband's name and uses her new name on the airline tickets, take the marriage license along for proof. You don't want to risk being turned down at the airport for having a different name on your driver's license.

340 | Plan a Baptism

A new baby is cause for celebration. A baptism (also called a christening) is when a family and the church officially welcome the infant into the Christian religious life. Until the fourth century, adult baptism was the norm. Today, the initiation is performed most often on infants, but also on older children and adults. A naming ceremony celebrates the birth of a child without religious overtones.

Steps

1 Decide if you will have a religious baptism or a nonsecular naming ceremony.

2 Choose the location. Either occasion can take place in a church, a home or even a garden.

3 Call your church if you have chosen to baptize your child. Make contact well before birth or in the later stages of an adoption and inquire about the church's guidelines. Register your child and also yourselves if you aren't already registered.

4 Ask the following questions:

- Does the church set certain dates aside for baptisms, or can you request a date? Do the dates differ for adult baptisms?

- Will the church provide a bib or cloth to drape over the child for the ceremony?

- Must the child (or adult) wear a gown and must it be white in color (to symbolize purity)?

- Will the officiant fully immerse the child in the water or will he or she pour or sprinkle water over the child's head? (If the child will be immersed, ask if you need to bring a towel.)

5 Choose the child's godparents. Godparents should be faithful individuals who are ready to embrace the responsibility of being a part of that child's life for the rest of his or her life. Pick one man and one woman who will be good role models. Consider relatives—even grandparents—who have a blood relationship with the child and have kept their faith over the years. Close friends are also appropriate choices.

6 Meet the priest, minister or clergy who will be conducting the ceremony to prepare for the baptism. Discuss what will happen —he or she will likely require that you attend a class.

7 Plan a simple party to take place immediately following the baptism or naming. You can hold the party anywhere (a restaurant, home, church hall), as long as it isn't a boisterous spot.

Tips

Ask the priest's or minister's approval to use a video camera.

Some churches allow parents to take the baptism class before the child is born; ask your church.

Who Knew?

Adults are generally immersed fully in the water (clothed), while children and infants usually have water sprinkled on their heads.

Ask your parents or grandparents if they have a christening gown in the family that you can use and pass down. Traditionally, both sexes wear infant christening gowns, although suit- or romper-style christening outfits for boys are becoming more popular.

341 | Plan a Bris

Mazel tov! You have a beautiful boy—and eight days to plan a bris (also called a Brith Milah), when the baby is circumcised and receives his Hebrew name. A bris is one of the rare Jewish life-cycle rituals that can be performed on Shabbat or even High Holidays. Don't forget the bagels and lox!

Steps

1. Choose a *mohel* to perform the ritual circumcision. Ask for a recommendation from your rabbi, cantor or Jewish friends who have boys. You can even find listings on the Internet. You should line up a mohel well before the birth (if you know the sex).

2. Ask candidates the following questions:

   - Will you be available a week after the baby's due date?

   - How many years have you been a mohel, and how often do you perform the bris (is it a part-time or full-time job)?

   - What is your training? Are you also a rabbi or physician? Do you have a current medical license and board certification? Are you a member of a national organization representing the *mohelim*?

   - Do you use anesthesia? How do you sterilize your instruments? What technique do you use to perform the circumcision? How do you prepare the baby for the procedure?

   - Do you restrain the baby? If so, how?

   - What is your fee?

   - Can you supply references?

3. Get the mohel's clearance that the baby is healthy enough for the bris. Sometimes the pediatrician will intervene and say the baby is too sick or weak. Under these circumstances you can postpone the bris until the baby is well enough.

4. Select a place to have the ceremony. Hold it in your synagogue as part of the daily morning services, or have it in your home. If there are health considerations, the mohel might opt to do the circumcision in the hospital.

5. Spread the word. The only people required to attend are the parents, the baby, the mohel, and the *sandek*, who is most often the baby's grandfather and who is responsible for holding the baby during the circumcision and when he receives his Jewish name.

6. Decorate the house or synagogue with flowers and candles.

7. Hire a caterer or rely on friends and family to bring food. Even if you don't observe kashruth (the Jewish dietary laws), make sure to serve foods that will accommodate the rabbi's and mohel's preferences. Fruits, vegetables and fish are always safe choices.

Tips

If you will be holding the Brith Milah at your home, provide yarmulkes (skull caps) for all the men, even non-Jewish ones.

Ask the mohel if it's alright for both men and women to participate in the ceremony and what part non-Jews can play.

Ask a special guest to make the *hamotzi* (blessing over the bread) before the meal begins.

Take plenty of pictures and video (if the mohel and rabbi approve).

Who Knew?

A bris is usually held in the morning of the eighth day after the baby's birth. For example, if your son was born late Tuesday night, you might schedule his bris for Wednesday morning of the following week.

Traditionally, people aren't invited to attend a bris, but are notified and encouraged to come. You won't have a lot of advance notice, so it's usually best to use word of mouth, a phone tree and e-mail.

Whether you're inviting the entire neighborhood for cocktails, celebrating your child's birthday or planning a fête for 50, throwing a great party requires panache and lots of planning. As host, your task is to create a mood—relaxed, elegant, festive or wild—that carries through every aspect of the party.

Steps

1 Find a reason to celebrate. Whether it's a holiday, a special occasion, an achievement, a big announcement, a new endeavor, a job well done or a journey completed, the reason you're partying will set the tone. See 316 Throw a Dinner Party for more ideas.

2 Pick a date that allows ample preparation time. Consider catering, decorating and entertaining needs when choosing the date.

3 Decide on a guest list. Take into account the size of your dining table, party area or rented venue. For cocktail parties, you'll need 4 to 5 square feet of space per person. Expect 70 to 80 percent of invited guests to show up for a large event.

4 Spread the word with flair: Invites that reinforce your theme add an exciting buzz. For example, attach potluck invites to inexpensive potholders if guests are expected to bring a dish. Specify the dress code (if there is one).

5 Determine the party's tone and style (celebratory, elegant, themed). Keep in mind the time of year, what you're celebrating, and how formal or casual you'd like it to be.

6 Plan your menu a week in advance. Consider flavors and combinations that reinforce your theme. What you serve is almost always determined by what's in season. Read 301 Plan Theme Menus, 315 Plan Party Foods Ahead and 316 Throw a Dinner Party for more ideas.

7 Consider serving beer and wine, plus one cocktail you can pre-mix in batches, such as margaritas or sangria. Hire a bartender if your group is larger than 30 and you're serving cocktails, wine and beer. (Three to four drinks per person for a two- to three-hour party is standard.) See 328 Set Up a Bar and 336 Hire a Bartender.

8 Spread out the food and drinks so there's a smooth flow to your party. If you don't want people in the kitchen, direct the traffic to other rooms—an outdoor bar, for example, or put most of the food in the living room. Hire servers to pass hors d'oeuvres.

9 Buy a few yards of colorful silk or other bright, textured fabric. Use it as a table runner or wrap it around the middle of the table for a splash of color. See 103 Decorate for the Seasons.

10 Enjoy yourself and your guests. Fun is contagious: Relax, pour yourself a drink, eat—and have a good time.

Tips

See 344 Plan a Child's Birthday Party and 388 Throw a Block Party.

Most people end up in the kitchen because that's where the host is. Do the prep work ahead of time so you're not stuck by the stove.

Label dishes so that guests with food allergies or on restricted diets will know what's in them.

Who Knew?

Give neighbors a head's up several days in advance. If your guests stayed late, the party got noisy or street parking became a nightmare, stop by your neighbors' house the following morning with extra dessert, flowers or a bottle of wine.

If guests are bringing food, ask them to cook their dishes ahead of time. You won't have time or space for a gaggle of chefs to finish off their contributions in your kitchen.

Display a bar menu so guests know what you're pouring, especially if you're featuring a sensational signature drink.

If you're throwing a potluck, firm up food assignments when guests call to RSVP—that way you won't have duplicates or an over-abundance of one course.

343 | Prepare for House Guests

You love having your friends and family visit, but getting the house ready is a ton of work. You'll need to strip the beds, scrub the bath and put out a welcome mat—and that's all before they arrive. There are ways to make it easier on yourself, though—in fact, you may actually hate to see them go.

Steps

1 Get ready ahead of time so your guests feel welcome instead of in the way. Clean the house and clear the clutter from your guest room (see 37 Conquer Clutter). Fresh flowers, candles and chocolates are all thoughtful, welcoming touches.

2 Make an extra set of house keys for your guests so they can come and go as they please. Not only is this a generous gesture, but it will free you up.

3 Buy an inflatable air mattress to supplement sleepovers. They're inexpensive, comfortable and can be re-inflated at the touch of a button. Well before guests arrive, inflate the mattress outside and let the smell leach out. Lie down and check for leaks.

4 Place a basket of sample-size shampoos, soaps and lotions near a stack of fresh towels for guests' convenience.

5 Set up a small television (with headphones) in the guest room in the event that your guests have trouble sleeping or wake much earlier than the rest of the household. Include some books and magazines.

6 Draw up a map of your neighborhood and environs, pointing out points of interest. Purchase a guidebook and flag any special places or activities your guests would be interested in.

7 Provide a surface or suitcase rack where guests can open their luggage so they don't have to spread out their belongings all over the floor. Clear out part of the closet and provide hangers.

8 Give guests the grand tour. Point out where glasses, dishes and silverware are kept, as well as tea, coffee, cereal and doughnuts. Encourage early risers to help themselves.

9 Put the coffeemaker on a timer to start up in the morning, or get it ready to go with a flip of the switch (see 17 Streamline Your Morning Routine).

10 Let guests know what to expect as far as household schedules are concerned. Clarify when people get up and go to bed, and mention any special events that are in the works to minimize miscommunications. See 68 Set Up a Bathroom Schedule.

Tips

Make your guests as self-reliant as possible. They'll appreciate the freedom and you will, too.

Fill in guests on the rules or procedures of the house—for instance, they need to be careful when opening the door not to let kitty escape.

Who Knew?

If you can't comfortably host guests in your house for whatever reason, offer to help make them reservations at a nearby hotel.

344 | Plan a Child's Birthday Party

The excitement of a child's birthday party builds to a feverish pitch as the big event approaches, but sometimes chaos and budget overruns do too. Keep things happy and peaceful by making your game plan well ahead of time—and sticking to it.

Steps

1 Set a party budget to cover the entire affair—from food, decor and party bags to room rental or hiring an entertainer. Estimate the number of guests; use a cost-per-guest figure to help determine your venue, entertainment and food options.

2 Remember that your child doesn't need an over-the-top party to have fun. Depending on his or her age, a picnic in the park can be just as much fun as an expensive party at a climbing gym.

3 Give your child several party options and themes to choose from. Describe what comes with each so he or she will know the benefits and drawbacks before choosing. Keep it simple.

4 Set a party time to best suit your child. Work around nap times for the four-and-under set; weekend mornings or afternoons for school kids; Friday or Saturday night for preteens or teens.

5 Confirm the time, date and place (with a deposit if necessary). Ask what you'll need to supply, what the venue will provide, how early you can arrive to set up and when you're required to leave.

6 Come up with ways to incorporate games and activities with party favors. Small, wrapped gifts discovered in a treasure hunt or piñata, or a gingerbread house proudly brought home after a decorating party, become tangible memories of the party instead of an expected payoff. Test-drive all activities with your child and plan extras in case something doesn't pan out.

7 Create invitations at home with your child on the computer to add personal pizzazz. Include an ending time and an RSVP date, and, for kids under three, specify whether you'd like parents to stay.

Tips

See 342 Throw a Party.

Shop for food, decorations, party bags and fillers three days ahead.

Take a photo of your child with his or her prized toy du jour on each birthday. Kids love looking back at their favorite things.

If the party's at home, block out the morning or afternoon the day before the party (and after) for cleaning and decorating the party areas.

Who Knew?

Check the party date with the parents of your son's or daughter's best friends before finalizing it.

Send invitations by mail three weeks before the party. Invites via backpacks are a bad idea even if the whole class is invited. The invitations inevitably end up covered in juice and are discovered two weeks after the affair.

345 | Plan a Successful Slumber Party

It's a red-eye reality of parental life—kids love slumber parties. If you value peace, quiet, and a bit of sleep at night, invite nice kids, plan some great activities and make the ground rules clear.

Steps

1 Invite six guests tops, and even numbers whenever possible so there's never an odd boy or girl out. Skip sleepovers for kids under age six to increase the odds that you'll be snoozing at midnight instead of placing a phone call for a homesick child.

Tips

Stay within earshot of the kids at all times.

Give guests a home tour and a flashlight to prevent frantic 3 a.m. searches for the bathroom.

2. Ask guests to arrive with a sleeping bag and pillow in time for a no-fuss dinner (pizza, pasta). Designate a pickup time, such as 10 a.m., after a hearty breakfast.

3. Prepare activities suitable for a group of excited kids. Rent plenty of movies, pull out group games, or plan a simple craft project the kids can take home.

4. Ask a birthday child if he or she is OK with a sibling joining the party. If not, set up an alternate activity for the left-out sibling, such as a play date or sleepover. Or, plan an evening's activity (games, a family movie), that will keep him or her with you—and out of the way of the other kids.

5. Give your child the good-host talk before guests arrive. If TV's OK, discuss how long and what they can watch, and set an appropriate lights-out time. Remind him or her that solitary pursuits, such as computer games, prevent interaction instead of encouraging it. Suggest board games or outdoor play instead.

6. Tell your guests what your house rules are and let them know that you expect everyone to follow them. This should include explaining what rooms (such as yours) are out of bounds, as well as any limits on phone, stereo and computer use.

Let the kids know when the adults are going to bed and make sure they understand that you expect them to dial down the volume accordingly.

Who Knew?

Never forget that while other children are in your home, their safety is your responsibility. Act accordingly.

Get emergency contact information from parents, such as a cellular phone or restaurant number, for that evening, during the night and in the morning. Ask about any food or pet allergies.

346 | Plan a Bar or Bat Mitzvah

Mazel tov! Your child, who probably still watches cartoons and is years away from getting a driver's license, is considered by the Jewish tradition old enough to become a full member of the congregation. Preparation for the big day, which includes learning to chant a passage from the Torah in Hebrew, starts long before the child turns 13.

Steps

1. Enroll your child in Hebrew school, if he or she isn't already in it. These classes are usually affiliated with a synagogue, and some require up to five years of study before the bar mitzvah.

2. Secure a Friday night or Saturday morning with your synagogue. (Sometimes you need to do this several years in advance.) Formal training—learning the *haftarah* portion for that day— will start about six months before the event.

3. Work with your child to choose a venue. The reception may take place at the synagogue directly following the service, or it can be later at another location, such as a hall or restaurant.

4. Talk to your son or daughter about what kind of party he or she wants to throw, including decorations, band or DJ (see 335 Hire a Band), and favors. Make sure they understand your budget limits.

Tips

Get help if you need it. Read 329 Hire an Event Planner.

Search online for "bar mitzvah expo" to find one in your area to get ideas from.

Help your child select a charity to which he or she will donate gift money.

Order yarmulkes monogrammed with your child's name and the bar mitzvah date.

Who Knew?

Yes, there actually is bar-mitzvah–planning software out there.

Continued on next page

5 Write up the guest list. The child usually invites his or her Hebrew-school class as well as friends from regular school. Parents invite family, friends and business associates. Order invitations and mail them six weeks before the event.

6 Choose the menu. If the service is on Friday night, a meal and celebration will follow. If it's on Saturday, you may also be responsible for the previous night's Oneg Shabbat (a buffet of treats to welcome the Sabbath). If you don't have a kosher caterer, offer a fish or vegetarian alternative for the rabbi, cantor and other observant guests. See 331 Hire a Caterer.

7 Arrange for photos of the service and reception (see 330 Hire a Photographer). In some synagogues, photographs may only be taken before or after Shabbat.

8 Hold a complete rehearsal several days before the event in the sanctuary with the rabbi and the cantor. The rabbi will go through the service and your child will practice reading from the *bimah*.

For out-of-town guests, provide travel information and numbers for local hotels and car-rental agencies with the invitation. Consider sending a save-the-date postcard to these folks as soon as you determine the date of the event.

Give relatives advance notice if they will be saying the blessing over the bread or wine, or will be called to the *bimah* (the platform that contains the podium) to chant an *aliyah* (a reading from the Torah).

347 | Plan a Quinceañera

In many Hispanic traditions, a girl's 15th birthday is celebrated with a gala quinceañera party. While this deeply religious event which cements the bonds of family and culture once signified that she was eligible to marry, today it means she's ready to date.

Who Knew?

Rent a banquet hall or hotel ballroom or just set up tables and chairs in an orchard.

The origins of quinceañeras date back to the arrival of Spaniards in the 1500s in South American when Christianity started blending with Aztec culture. Quinceañeras are popular in Cuba, Mexico, Puerto Rico, Central and South America as well as the United States.

Godparents are considered special guests whose counsel is important in this time of emotional and spiritual reverence. A special token of appreciation from the guest of honor to her padrinos is appropriate during the reception.

Steps

1 Understand that the heart of a quinceañera is a thanksgiving Mass for the extended family, rich in traditional rites. An elaborate party follows with food and dancing for friends and family.

2 Set a budget. Godparents (*padrinos*) may help by sponsoring elements of the party—the dress, the band, party favors, the bar, the cake and so on. The guest list, food and level of opulence will all depend on available finances.

3 Choose a venue at least several months ahead of the party, and decide on a menu (see 331 Hire a Caterer). Get your daughter's input when choosing the music (see 335 Hire a Band), or buy a compilation of Quinceañera songs on CD. Order invitations.

4 Buy a full-length, frilly, pastel ball gown for your daughter. She may also receive traditional gifts such as a tiara, bracelet, ring, earrings, a necklace with a cross, a Bible and a rosary. (Shop online at Quinceanera-Boutique.com and others for gift ideas.)

5 Have your daughter select her court from close friends and family. Traditionally seven *damas* (female attendants) and seven *chambelanes* (male attendants) are included. The young man who accompanies the celebrant is called the man of honor.

348 | Plan a Retirement Party

Hard work may be its own reward, but throwing a party is much more fun. Celebrate a long-term employee's efforts with a retirement party that signifies unique contributions and special relationships. Prepare your toast, raise your glass and send your co-worker off in style.

Steps

1 Consider the honoree's preferences. Does he or she prefer not to be singled out? Then something low-key and elegant might be appropriate. People who love to be the center of attention are perfect candidates for a roast.

2 Create a budget. Nail down costs for the venue, food and drinks, and entertainment.

3 Come up with a theme that highlights the retiree's interests, including hobbies, activities and passions. For instance, if he or she always seemed to call in sick on opening day, organize a ball-game party with tickets, banners, music and food. Arrange for his or her grandchild's little league team to come sing "Take Me Out to the Ball Game."

4 Plan a roast. Meet with other co-workers and brainstorm jokes and comments on the office politics. The key to a successful roast is selecting the master of ceremonies. He or she must be comfortable working a crowd—and articulate. A roast may not be not tightly scripted, so the emcee must be adept at ad-libbing.

5 Keep in mind that simply offering heartfelt appreciation for some-one may be the best accolade of all. Start a round of toasts where guests can tell the honoree what he or she did that changed their life.

6 Choose a venue, again depending on the retiree's preferences. Would he or she prefer a small or large affair, a traditional evening or an out-of-the-box celebration? Some possible loca-tions include hotels, art galleries, restaurants, country clubs, yacht clubs, American Legion halls, a historic mansion or a casi-no. Take a more intimate group on a sunset cocktail cruise.

7 Put up decorations that highlight the guest-of-honor's life and accomplishments. Display awards, trophies and photos. Create table centerpieces, each of which focuses on one of his or her interests: golf, classic cars, music, gardening, skiing and so on.

8 Hire a videographer or photographer to record the festivities. Encourage guests to toast—or roast—the retiree on camera and present the video to the retiree at the evening's end. See 330 Hire a Photographer.

Tips

Invite mystery guests: a former co-worker from years back or a first boss. Keep it relevant to the job.

Have a guest book available for guests to sign, reminisce about old times and send good wishes for the future.

Who Knew?

While gifts aren't typically given, you could ask guests who want to bring one to select a gift that revolves around the theme, or ask for donations to a charity or organization close to the retiree's heart. Or include the gift in the price of the ticket.

349 | Plan a Funeral According to Custom

Many modern funeral rituals have their roots in ancient traditions. Whatever beliefs your loved one held, and even if they are different from the rest of the family's, a dignified send-off provides comfort within a sense of tradition for the living while honoring the departed.

TYPE OF FUNERAL	WHAT TO EXPECT
Protestant, Lutheran, Methodist, Presbyterian and Episcopalian	• The funeral takes place within three days of the death. A visitation period at the funeral home prior to the service is standard. Guests visit only briefly to pay their respects to the family. Traditional funerals include readings from scripture, hymns and a sermon. Close friends and family offer eulogies. • Guests should dress respectably. Black is traditional, but other dark colors are acceptable. • Invite family and friends to gather at a reception immediately after the funeral. Ask friends to bring food, or have the reception catered.
Jewish	• "Bury me before sundown on the day I die," states Jewish tradition. Funerals are held as soon as the family can assemble, usually within 24 hours. The body is wrapped in a white sheet, or *kittel*, and buried in a closed casket made of pine. • The rabbi will conduct the funeral and will arrange a private time for family members to bid farewell to the deceased before the funeral. The service itself is usually a short and simple graveside one. Typically, funeral-goers wear formal clothing in subdued colors. Men must wear a yarmulke. If the service is Conservative, women must cover their head. In Orthodox services, women must cover their arms and their legs to the knee. Non-Jews are not allowed to wear symbols of other faiths. In lieu of flowers, it is traditional to remember the deceased with charitable gifts *(tzedakah)*. • The family sits in mourning, or *shivah*, for seven days and receives visitors. Guests usually bring food. Among other rituals, family members wear a small torn black ribbon on their clothes to show that a loved one has been ripped from the fabric of their lives.
Roman Catholic	• Contact the priest at the church to discuss the wake and funeral. Typically, a wake—the period of time when the deceased's body can be viewed at the funeral home prior to the funeral at the church—is held the second day after a person has died. Wearing black is customary. • The funeral is held the third day after the person has died. It is often celebrated as a mass. The priest reads from the Scripture, leads prayers and administers Holy Communion. Non-Catholics should stand when Catholics do, but are not required to kneel, sing or say the prayers, nor take Holy Communion.
Hindu	• Hindus believe that the soul is reincarnated upon death. Funerals are traditionally held before the sun goes down on the same day and are typically conducted by the firstborn son who offers prayers from the entire family. • The body is wrapped in a shroud and cremated, sometimes on a pyre. The Hindu faith dictates that the ashes must be washed or placed into a holy river for their final cleaning. Family and friends gather afterward for a meal. The mourning period lasts for 13 days, during which friends visit the family.

TYPE OF FUNERAL	WHAT TO EXPECT
New Orleans Jazz	• Since jazz was born in New Orleans, celebrated musicians and regular citizens alike have jazz bands playing at their funerals. • The band meets at the church or funeral parlor. After the service, the band leads a funeral procession slowly to the cemetery, playing solemnly. When interment ceremonies are complete, and after the band has reached a respectful distance from the site, it begins to play again—this time loud and clear, playing lively tunes such as "When the Saints Go Marching In." • You don't have to live in New Orleans to have a jazz funeral. Jazz lovers around the country may request a jazz band to play at their service.
Tibetan Sky Burial	• In this extraordinary ritual, Tibetan lamas cut up the body (flesh into meat chunks, organs into pieces, bones smashed and broken) and offer it to the vultures, which in turn carry the soul to heaven. It's illegal in the United States, and in Tibet, foreigners are not allowed (except in special circumstances) to even witness a celestial burial.
Buddhist	• Buddhists believe that upon death the spirit reincarnates into the next life, and funerals celebrate the soul of the deceased as it makes its ascent from the body. Most Buddhists prefer cremation. The family dresses in white, but guests typically wear black. • A first service is held at the person's home within two days of a death. • The second service is held at a funeral home up to five days following the death and is traditionally performed by monks. The funeral involves chanting and individual offerings of incense. Guests do not usually participate. • The final service is held seven days after the burial or cremation to create positive energy for the deceased as he or she travels to the next stage of reincarnation. This service is often held in a temple.
Islamic	• Funerals take place as soon after death as possible, usually on the same day. Services are held in a mosque. All attendees remove their shoes and sit on the floor—women must sit separately from the men and are required to wear loose clothing and a veil or scarf. • The service is brief and consists of ritual chanting and recitation from the Koran. Afterward, mourners file past the body and pay their last respects. A short ceremony takes place at the burial grounds and then the mourners return to the mosque for more prayers. Later, a meal is served at the mosque.
State	• If you are a sitting president or vice president of the United States, it is customary within the first year in office to be asked to start planning your own funeral, and to keep updating it regularly for the rest of your life. • The Military District of Washington oversees presidential funerals; many of the rites are dictated by military and historic custom.
Military	• At no cost to the family, burial benefits include a gravesite in any of the 120 national cemeteries with available space, opening and closing of the grave, perpetual care, a government headstone or marker, a burial flag and a Presidential Memorial Certificate. Cremated remains are buried or inurned in national cemeteries in the same manner and with the same honors as casketed remains.

350 | Plan Ahead for a Low-Stress Holiday

Every adult's fantasy for the month of December? A seamlessly organized and enjoyable holiday season where there's plenty of time for everything. The reality, of course, is that the holiday season is chaotic: chock-full of frenetic shopping trips, party planning and a packed calendar of events. Here are some stress-busters that will allow you to actually enjoy the spirit of the season and all the merrymaking—without the January hangover.

Steps

1 Shop when no one else does. Take off a midweek morning and shop the malls when they open. Or don't shop at all. Make certificates for friends and family entitling them to a movie, dinner or other treat with you whenever they wish. Shop online day or night.

2 Make room for your new purchases. Purge worn or broken decorations and loosen your grasp on holiday items with sentimental value that stay in storage, year after year. See 1 Get Organized and 12 Get Rid of What You Don't Want.

3 Set a budget for how much you can spend on the holidays, including gifts, wrapping paper, decorations, postage, food and parties. See 351 Stay Within a Budget This Christmas.

4 Prepare your kids for the types and quantity of gifts they'll be getting (translation: no pony). Find ways to de-emphasize the commercialism for your family. Collect food and blankets for the needy, wrap gifts for children in the hospital, help out at a soup kitchen and so on. See 383 Plan a Toy Drive.

5 Prepare as much food ahead of time as possible. Cook or bake dishes a couple of weeks out and freeze them. Also, buy liquor and beverages during sales to avoid waiting in hour-long lines right before the holidays. See 352 Prepare a Holiday Feast and 315 Plan Party Foods Ahead.

6 Splurge on a cleaning service or rental dishes. Two of the biggest headaches of a holiday dinner are cleaning up before people arrive and cleaning up after they leave. If you have any extra money, hire a service to clean your home. Think about renting dishes: When dinner is finished, you just put the dirty plates in crates and return them to the rental service. See also 64 Get Ready for the Housecleaner.

7 Relinquish control and ask for help. One of the biggest mistakes people make at this time of year is thinking they have to do it all themselves. When someone offers to bring dessert, say yes. If you're stressed about getting dinner done before the party, ask someone to set the table or peel the potatoes (see 317 Finish Dinner on Time). No one expects you to be a hero—except perhaps yourself.

Tips

Get enough sleep. Nothing is worse than sleep deprivation during a stressful period like the holidays. If that means skipping out on a party early, do it.

Bear in mind that alcohol can disrupt your sleep—just when you need it most. You might want to keep tabs on your intake levels.

Make holiday visitation arrangements for your children with your ex-spouse long before the holidays to avoid stress and conflict during an already emotionally and physically loaded time. See 288 Make Child Custody Arrangements.

8 Set a deadline—say, December 15 (some people finish as early as December 1)—to have your shopping and wrapping done. You'll have time to kick back, relax and enjoy the season. If you leave all your running around until the last minute, you'll miss the essence of Christmas or Hanukkah (not to mention experiencing headaches and panic attacks). Volunteer your family to help.

9 Learn to say "no" to overnight guests if your home isn't big enough or you have too much on your plate. See 13 Say No Without Feeling Guilty.

10 Research charities to which you'd like to contribute, long before the holiday season gets under way. Many need assistance year round.

Who Knew?

Read 331 Hire a Caterer. You don't have to have him or her cater the whole affair. For example, ask the caterer to just cook the main dishes and supply a cleanup person, and you'll take care of dessert.

351 Stay Within a Budget This Christmas

The holidays seem to grow more expensive each year. Holiday decorations become increasingly elaborate and plentiful, and your naughty-or-nice list has expanded exponentially. What's a Santa to do? Make a list, check it twice—and read on.

Steps

1 Kick off your Christmas budget plan in January. Not only will you be able to take advantage of post-holiday sales, but you'll have all year to make your spending plan work. See 228 Design a Savings Plan and 226 Set Up a Budget.

2 Squirrel money away month by month. Open a Christmas Club account or have your bank or credit union regularly transfer a designated amount (such as $25 or $50) into a dedicated savings account. Setting up an auto-transfer after each paycheck makes it easy. See 227 Get Out of Debt.

3 Do your Christmas shopping year-round. Take a master shopping list with you wherever you go. Include the recipient's name, a gift idea and a price range. See 357 Organize Gift-Giving in Advance.

4 Do your homework online. Even if you don't actually buy the gift on the Internet, you can comparison-shop while sniffing out the best deals. Then visit the store with the best price.

5 Seek out online deals. Sometimes major stores offer discounts on online purchases. Check out Web sites regularly, as prices and offers change often during the weeks leading up to Christmas.

Tips

Take care of friends and relatives with a single holiday gift project. Instead of popping $10 to $20 on a number of small presents, make a gift from your kitchen. See 354 Organize a Holiday Craft Party and 356 Plan the Perfect Holiday Gift Exchange.

Many people don't need (or want) more stuff. Instead, give them the gift of your time—to take them out to dinner, run errands or fix little things around their home.

Food defines holiday get-togethers. Thanksgiving wouldn't be the same without turkey and stuffing, and crispy potato latkes during Hanukkah are mandatory. As your calendar books up during the holiday season, it helps to start the preparations well ahead of time.

Steps

1 Prepare the menu a couple weeks in advance. Thumb through magazines, favorite cookbooks and one of the many books focusing on gracious entertaining such as Williams-Sonoma's *Entertaining*. Surf the Internet for tempting ideas. Call your grandmother and ask for her famous brisket recipe. See 316 Throw a Dinner Party.

2 Spread the word. Call or e-mail relatives and guests several weeks in advance to find out who can come, who has to stay at school and who is feasting with their in-laws this time around. Tell them what time to arrive and what dish to bring.

3 Stock up on nonperishable essentials (canned chicken broth, butter, olive oil, canned pumpkin pie filling, beans, wine, sparkling water). Order meat or turkey from the butcher and fish or seafood from the fish market one month in advance.

4 Make your meal a feast for the eyes, too. Wash or dry-clean tablecloths and linen napkins. If you don't have tablecloths, buy a few yards of bright fabric to cover the table, and don't worry about sewing hems—no one will notice. Polish silverware and serving dishes. Buy tapered candlesticks and fresh flowers for a table centerpiece, or fill a beautiful bowl with gourds or the fruits of the season—mandarin oranges, lemons or apples. Tie colorful ribbons around the back of each chair. Set the table one or two days in advance.

5 Prepare and cook as much as possible in the days leading up to your feast. Peel and chop vegetables. Make stuffing a day or two before and keep covered in the refrigerator. Make and freeze appetizers such as empanadas, spanakopita, miniquiches or dumplings. Cakes and cookies can be baked in advance and frozen, as can casseroles. See 303 Cook Ahead and 317 Finish Dinner on Time.

6 Determine if you have enough tables, chairs and serving dishes. Rent tables and chairs if you won't have enough—and even dinner and dessert plates to ease cleanup. Most rental companies let you return them unwashed.

7 Set up an out-of-the-way table for the kids (along with aprons and a willing adult to supervise), equipped with egg-dyeing supplies, wooden dreidels to paint, construction paper and popsicle sticks to make turkey puppets, or oranges to decorate with cloves for holiday mementos.

Tips

Borrow, buy or rent chafing dishes to keep buffet food warm.

Place large pitchers of water (filled with fresh mint and lemon for color and flavor) and wine bottles on the table so guests can refill their own glasses.

No matter what the holiday or event, it's thoughtful to offer several dishes to accommodate various dietary needs, whether guests are vegetarians, are cutting calories or have food allergies.

See 103 Decorate for the Seasons.

Introduce traditions from other cultures. Bake colomba, an Italian Easter bread; mix Scandinavian glögg for holiday toasts; or make a German turkey stuffing with sweet breads, raisins, cinnamon and nutmeg.

Warning

If your turkey or other meat is frozen, check the thawing instructions. A large turkey or roast can take several days to thaw. Go to sites such as Butterball.com and Beef.org for all the juicy details. Pay particular attention to safe food handling.

Hanukkah, the eight-day celebration beloved by Jewish families, begins on the 25th day of the month of Kislev in the Hebrew calendar (the exact dates in November or December vary each year). Families light candles each evening at sundown while reciting blessings, and eat traditional foods and give small gifts.

Steps

1 Decorate your house in blue, white and silver, the traditional colors of Israel. You'll also want to display time-honored Hanukkah items, such as chocolate *gelt* (Yiddish for money) and dreidels (tops for an ancient gambling game).

2 Set up the menorah. This special candelabra has nine branches, one for each night plus one at a different height to hold the *shamas* candle. The *shamas*, which means "servant," is lit with a match and used to light all the other candles on the menorah.

3 Say the blessings. There are three significant blessings to speak during the eight days. Print them and keep them in a special book to open during the lighting of the candles. Print out the words to the traditional Hanukkah song "Maoz Tzur" (translation: "Rock of Ages").

4 Prepare the menu. The centerpiece is always the potato latkes fried in oil (representing the oil found in the temple); serve with applesauce and sour cream. In Israel, Jews feast on *sufganiyot* (jelly doughnuts).

5 Give inexpensive but thoughtful gifts, one for each of the eight days. Some families who will spend only one of the eight days together choose to buy one present to exchange that night. A gift exchange is also popular (see 356 Plan the Perfect Holiday Gift Exchange).

6 Play the dreidel game. The dreidel, a four-sided top, is the centerpiece of an easy game that uses coins or nuts for betting. The Hebrew letters carved or painted on each side correspond to what the player must do: *nun* (do nothing), *he* (take half of the kitty), *gimel* (take the kitty), and *shin* (lose what you bet). Ante up!

Tip

Shop for menorahs at boutiques, craft fairs, museum shops or Judaica stores.

Warning

Although you can't leave candles unattended, it's forbidden to blow them out. Wise Jews place menorahs in the sink if they need to step away.

354 Organize a Holiday Craft Party

Nothing kicks off the holidays better than great company, a glass of mulled wine and the chance to whip up a batch of fabulous home-made presents. Turn up the music and let the (reindeer) games begin!

Steps

1 Select a date early in the season before people get booked up. Set it up as an all-day event so guests can drop in on their way to other holiday functions. See 359 Plan a Holiday Open House.

2 Send out invitations a month in advance. Ask guests to bring evergreen branches (for wreath-making), a dish to share and any project they wish to make.

3 Decide which projects you want to make. Pore through magazines, surf sites such as MarthaStewart.com and steal ideas liberally for easy, quick projects.

4 Set a budget for materials, ingredients and decorations based on a projected head count. If you're watching your own bottom line, include something in the invitation along the lines of "Please contribute $20 per person for materials." Or assign each guest a project and ask him or her to bring materials for 12 people.

5 Start purchasing materials and supplies months in advance to take advantage of good deals. Keep your supplies list with you and check items off as you find them. See 351 Stay Within a Budget This Christmas and 357 Organize Gift Giving in Advance.

6 Earmark a set of shelves in the garage or a spare bedroom to stash your supplies. Tape a copy of your master list to the shelf and check off items as you purchase and store them.

7 Set up stations for each project. In order to give everyone plenty of room to work in, put stations in various rooms on the main floor. Stock each work area with ample materials and supplies (scissors, glue guns).

• For cooking projects, fill large (labeled) mixing bowls with the main ingredients and add a serving spoon to each. Have pounding tools (plastic-wrapped flashlight, food can), cellophane packets and boxes of canning jars nearby for speedy assembly. (See chart for recipes.)

• For craft projects, ask one guest at each station to show newcomers how to do that particular project. Stow additional materials for each project under the table.

• Set up a separate station for making labels and wrapping packages. Stock with raffia, holiday-patterned fabric cut in circles (for layered jar lids), boxes and bags for hauling loot home, blank tags, a hole punch, gift wrap, ribbon, tape, glue and scissors.

8 Make your gifts one of a kind with handmade or personally designed gift tags. Incorporate a digital photo of your kids or of

Tips

If you hold an annual event, incorporate some new ideas into the mix along with old favorites.

Keep projects simple enough for even noncrafty people to participate.

Stand evergreen branches in water in a tub or garbage can outside.

the finished project on the front, put any instructions on the reverse, and add a personal message inside. Print out as many as you have need for.

9 Assemble fast and easy gifts from the kitchen that your friends and family can cook months after the holiday feasting has tapered off. See below for two layered "mix in a jar" recipes guaranteed to bring a smile to the face of anyone on your list.

MIX IN A JAR	YOU ASSEMBLE THE INGREDIENTS . . .	. . . AND THE RECIPIENT COOKS IT
Winter Bean Soup	1 cup each of great Northern white, kidney, black, pinto and lima beans ½ teaspoon basil ½ teaspoon thyme 1 tablespoon parsley 1 bay leaf Layer beans in a 1-quart wide-mouth canning jar. Wrap basil, thyme, parsley and bay leaf in cellophane to create an herb packet to include in the jar. Tape securely. Cut a round piece of fabric to tuck under the screw-top part of the canning lid. Make a festive label with cooking instructions (right) on the reverse.	¼ cup olive oil 2 cups onion, chopped 2 cups celery, chopped 3 cloves garlic, minced 8 cups chicken broth 12 ounces ham, turkey or chicken, chopped 2 cups tomatoes, diced Empty jar into large bowl, reserving herb packet. Soak beans overnight; wash and sort. Heat oil in large pot. Sauté onion, celery and garlic. Add broth, meat, tomatoes and beans. Add contents of herb packet. Bring to a boil. Cover and simmer for three hours, stirring frequently. Add water if the soup becomes too thick. Add salt and pepper to taste. Makes more than ½ gallon.
Chocolate Chip Cookies	½ cup sugar ½ cup pecans, chopped 1 cup semisweet chocolate chips 1 cup firmly packed brown sugar 2½ cups flour mixed with 1 teaspoon baking soda and ¼ teaspoon salt Layer the ingredients in the above order in a 1-quart wide-mouth canning jar. Press each layer firmly in place (the base of a flashlight or food can wrapped in plastic works great) before adding the next ingredient. Cut a round piece of fabric to tuck under the screw-top part of the canning lid. Make a festive label with cooking instructions (right) on the reverse.	1½ sticks very soft butter 1 egg, slightly beaten 1 teaspoon vanilla Empty cookie mix into large mixing bowl. Blend mix thoroughly with fingers. Add butter, egg and vanilla and mix until completely blended. Drop by spoonfuls onto greased cookie sheet. Bake at 350 degrees F (176 C) for 13 to 15 minutes. Let cool. Makes 24 cookies.

355 | Plan to Spend Christmas Solo

Spending Christmas by yourself? There can be any number of reasons, and maybe, just maybe, visions of sugarplums are not your thing. Take time to set up a blissful, rewarding year-end interlude and start off the New Year relaxed, calm—OK, fine—even smug.

Steps

1 Create a wish list of how you would like to spend the holidays.

2 Express your desires to friends and family. Oftentimes people simply assume that everyone has plans and don't think to ask. Sometimes knowing you have an invitation to spend the holidays at a friend's home makes it feel all right if you ultimately decide to curl up with a book or watch a favorite movie by yourself.

3 Jump on a plane. Plan and book your trip in advance for the best rates. Experience a different holiday mood and look. If you live in a cold climate, this might be the year to celebrate the holidays in a warm-weather spot. If you live in a warm area, why not go skiing or celebrate in a destination where a white Christmas is guaranteed? See 405 Plan a Trip.

4 Hang out with other poeple who don't celebrate Christmas.

5 Volunteer at a children's hospital or the pediatric ward of a local hospital to deliver presents from Santa. Dress the part.

6 Contact a local senior-citizen center or assisted-living home to see if there are any folks who will be spending the holidays alone. Ask if you can visit them—and even take a picnic lunch.

7 Pick up your hammer and contact an organization like Habitat for Humanity (habitat.org). Many of these organizations host volunteer trips to Third World countries during holiday breaks (because many of the volunteers are students and teachers). See 404 Build a School in a Third World Country and 386 Build Low-Income Housing.

Tips

Use Christmas Eve or Christmas Day as a travel day if you're going on vacation. You'll avoid the crowds.

If you decide to travel to a vacation spot, make sure it is not a hotel or destination that shuts down tight for Christmas. There's a big difference between solitude and isolation.

Warning

You may enjoy your solo holiday so much, you'll want to avoid large family holiday gatherings in the future. Don't get too used to it.

356 | Plan the Perfect Holiday Gift Exchange

Gift-giving comes with an enormous price tag—figuratively and literally. You may worry: Is the gift appropriate? Is it too expensive or too cheap? A creative approach to keeping costs down is a gift exchange (popular with large families and office groups).

THE EXCHANGE	THE SCENARIO
Secret Santa	• Determine who gets whom. Have someone draw everyone's name from a hat, then make the master list. Encourage family members and employees not to discuss whom they have. As people open their gifts, they'll guess who their Secret Santa is.
	• Set a monetary limit on gifts. A suggested amount for companies is $10 to $20; among families it can range from $10 to any amount that's chosen.
	• Enjoy shopping for just the right gift for your Secret Santa.
White Elephant	• Set up the party as you would a Secret Santa event.
	• Go through your closets and dig out unloved treasures, retail disasters and plastic monstrosities. Bob the Big-Mouthed Bass singing "Take Me to the River," dancing Santas and kung fu rodents are perennial white-elephant favorites.
	• Wrap your elephant beautifully to encourage all those suckers to take your bait. The uglier the gift, the better you need to wrap it.
	• Hand out slips of paper with numbers on them to assign the order in which gifts are chosen. Explain that each person can either choose a wrapped present, or take something another person has already opened. If that happens, that poor soul has to brave the gift pile again.
	• Enjoy all of the pleasure of giving and receiving with absolutely none of the stress.
	• Unwrap the gift you got stuck with and put it away for next year.
Cookie Swap	• Set the date for your cookie exchange early, before holiday schedules become too hectic. Invite four to ten bakers to participate, and ask each to bake a dozen cookies for every other person. The more guests, the greater the variety and quantity of cookies you will receive. But keep in mind that the more people you invite, the more cookies each person will have to bake.
	• Have guests bring an empty container for taking cookies home. Request that your bakers bring their cookies in disposable containers so there will be no confusion or worry if they are not returned.
	• Set up cookie swaps for other occasions, such as birthdays or anniversaries. Not only is it a wallet-friendly idea, but chances are there won't be as much competition from other cookie bakers as during the holidays.

357 | Organize Gift-Giving in Advance

Birthdays, holidays, graduations, anniversaries, Mother's Day, Father's Day—so many reasons to spoil your friends and family, and somebody's got to do it. The beauty of planning ahead is that you don't rush into buying any old thing and you're not stuck without the perfect gift on someone's big day.

Steps

1 Get out your calendar and datebook at the beginning of the year, and enter all birthdays, anniversaries and graduations. Or program your personal digital assistant (PDA) with these dates. See 3 Write an Effective To-Do List and 266 Coordinate a Family Calendar.

2 Create a separate list for all your people for each of these occasions. Next to each name, write gift ideas (if you have any) and a monetary limit.

3 Take advantage of sales throughout the year. Keep your gift list in your wallet and check off items as you spy just the right thing.

4 Go in on a fabulous, overpriced gift with other siblings or friends to stay within your budget.

5 Buy birthday, sympathy, anniversary and graduation cards in bulk. Often stationery stores offer two-for-one specials and other deals. Buy boxes of blank cards to have on hand.

6 Designate a closet or space in your home for the gifts that you buy during the year so you can remember where they are months down the road.

Tips

Collect souvenir gifts when traveling throughout the year.

Recycle gifts that you received and either don't want or won't be able to use. Designate a storage place for unused presents that you can pass on to others for birthdays or other occasions. Note who gave you the gift so you don't give it back to that person.

See 356 Plan the Perfect Holiday Gift Exchange and 351 Stay Within a Budget This Christmas.

You and your kids can create homemade cards with craft kits or software programs.

358 | Stick to Your Diet During the Holidays

Way to go, slim! You shed enough pounds to strut your stuff during the summer. But here come the holidays. Turkey with all the trimmings is just a prelude to cookies, candies and fruitcakes. Enjoy the season's temptations in moderation—armed with a solid game plan.

Steps

1 Drink a large glass of water and eat a savory snack—some protein, a little fiber—before you go to a party. If you're not famished, you won't be compelled to eat everything in sight.

2 Offer to bring a vegetable platter to the party—in fact, insist on it. That way you know there will be something diet-friendly that you can nibble on. But don't bring just any old vegetable platter. Make something you especially love and don't normally eat so you'll feel like you're celebrating, too. Bring a delicious but low-fat dip to accompany your crudités.

Tips

Cut yourself some slack. Plan to maintain your weight rather than lose any pounds during the holidays. Just try not to put on any extra.

Take into account that alcohol is high in calories.

See 24 Choose a Weight-Loss Plan.

3 Pair parties with workouts. Indulge in some foods you wouldn't normally eat, then offset the added calories with a pumped-up exercise routine. As you block out your calendar with cocktail parties and eggnog tastings, write down what your matching aerobic workout will be. Put your money where your mouth is and buy several sessions with a personal fitness trainer to keep yourself on track.

4 Have salad first if you're eating at a restaurant. Ask for dressing on the side. Dip just the tines into the dressing before stabbing a forkful—you'll get all the flavor and hardly any sin. Ask the waiter to box up half your entree before it leaves the kitchen for you to enjoy at another time.

Warning

Shopping malls and food courts make it all too easy to pick up a quick snack, usually high in fat, carbs and calories. Shop on a full stomach.

359 Plan a Holiday Open House

One of the most enjoyable holiday gatherings is the drop-in-when-you-want party—ideal for busy guests as well as party hosts. Open houses often come with lower expectations (guests don't expect a gourmet meal and can leave without fuss) and a casual, festive mood.

Steps

1 Set a date that is as far out from Christmas and Hanukkah as possible before calendars book up. Set an ending time as well, or folks may drop by expecting the party to be in full swing while you're in the middle of cleanup.

2 Set the mood and level of formality. Will you hire a bartender and servers and offer a catered menu of gourmet goodies? Or do you prefer a casual, self-serve buffet with 6-foot heros and a cooler full of drinks? Keep size in mind—do you want a small gathering of friends or a hey-stop-by-for-a-drink affair for the masses? See 342 Throw a Party.

3 Create the menu. Time is valuable, especially at this time of year, so consider hiring someone to help with the food. See 315 Plan Party Foods Ahead.

4 Be aware of your guests when you plan entertainment. A non-secular holiday open house makes guests from many different backgrounds comfortable. If you celebrate Christmas, it's fine to have a tree and decorations. Save caroling and other traditional Christmas rituals for a caroling party, when guests expect it—or risk offending people of different faiths.

5 Set up a corner (away from ornaments and decorations) with toys and trains for young children to play with. Their parents will be grateful that their kids are happily occupied—then they get to have fun, too.

Tips

Invite kids from the high-school jazz band to play some holiday tunes.

See 354 Organize a Holiday Craft Party and 331 Hire a Caterer.

360 Reorganize Your Life After the Holidays

You did it. Ribbons are slung everywhere, there's wax all over your good tablecloth, and the fridge is bursting with delectable leftovers. And now? Time to get your life on track again—regroup, catch up, resurrect routines and start good habits. But first, pour yourself another cup of coffee and relax. You've earned it.

Steps

1 Get immediate closure by writing your holiday thank-you notes.

2 Fine-tune your storage system for your tree trimmings and other holiday decorations. See 135 Organize Gift Wrap and Seasonal Decorations.

3 Plan your budget for the upcoming year. See 228 Design a Savings Plan.

4 Kiss that sugar high good-bye. Toss or freeze sweets, look lustfully at those leftover mashed potatoes one last time, and stock up on healthy food. Getting back to eating right is one of the quickest ways to feel on top of your game again. See 297 Plan a Week of Menus and 298 Organize Grocery Store Trips.

5 Get your exercise program back on track if you're kicking yourself for not getting to the gym over the holidays (see 25 Design Your Workout Schedule). It can be hard to get the momentum going, but the minute you start working out again, you'll feel better. Exercise also strengthens the immune system, helping your body resist viruses that are particularly virulent during the winter months (see 27 Prepare for Cold and Flu Season).

6 Tinker with your priorities to make sure they're still working for you. Find ways to bring your life back into balance. Create new (or bring back) family traditions, such as game night every Sunday or movie-and-pizza night on Friday evenings.

7 Designate a night for putting holiday photos in albums and frames or burning digital photos onto CDs. See 53 Organize Your Photos.

8 Set up a toy-storage system or you'll find that half the new toys are broken or have missing parts by Valentine's Day. Enlist your kids on this project. Ask them to make a pile of toys to give away. See 74 Organize Kids' Rooms and 12 Get Rid of What You Don't Want.

Tips

Make it a family resolution for everyone to clean out his or her clutter. See 37 Conquer Clutter.

Read 227 Get Out of Debt if the holidays took an extra-big bite out of your finances.

361 Stick to Your New Year's Resolutions

New Year's resolutions can be both troublesome and rewarding. Many people make them, but few make a real committment to them. Before you put the champagne on ice, spend some time pondering exactly what you hope to achieve in the year ahead and how you plan to do it.

Steps

1 Be very specific about your resolution. Don't say: "I want to lose weight." Do say: "I want to lose 5 pounds a month so that I look *hot* in my new swimsuit on the fourth of July." Make realistic, measurable goals and write them down. See 16 Set Goals.

2 Limit the number of resolutions you make. It's better to do one thing well than several things poorly (or not at all).

3 Post your list in a visible place to serve as a reminder and encouragement to yourself. It will also allow other people to see your resolutions and provide support. If you want to keep your resolutions private, record them in a journal.

4 Enlist the support of your friends and family. If you're lucky, they'll have similar goals and you can work on your resolutions together. Encourage people to be helpful and supportive.

5 Take action immediately. Make important appointments with a doctor, dietitian or counselor. Sign up for a gym membership or buy any equipment you need.

6 Practice new behaviors that encourage success. If you want to stop smoking, don't hang out in smoke-filled bars or casinos. If you want to lose weight, don't bring desserts, junk food, candy or ice cream into the house. Limit your exposure to people who are likely to encourage resolution-breaking. There's a reason parolees aren't allowed to hang out with known criminals— they're a bad influence. Surround yourself with good ones.

7 Set incremental goals and reward yourself for partial successes. If you're working on saving more of your income, for example, reward yourself with a small splurge at each significant step. Each time you squirrel away another $1,000, take yourself to a favorite restaurant or get a massage. See 228 Design a Savings Plan and 500 Die Rich.

8 Substitute a good habit for the bad one you want to break. If your goal is to eat less junk food, find a healthy food you love. See 23 Plan to Avoid Junk Food. If you want to spend more time with your family, establish a special time during the week when everyone is together.

Tips

Visualize success. Create a mental picture of the new, improved you. Focus on this image when you're tempted to blow off your goal.

Stay positive. If you slip up one month, just let it go and get back on track.

See 501 Be Happy.

Some people might argue that there's no such thing as the perfect New Year's Eve. Another party with 100 of your closest friends, all sloshed and wearing funny hats? Or stay home and watch that ball drop again? Neither! Your first resolution is to ring in the New Year with style and fun. Here are a range of options to suit almost anyone.

Steps

1 Plan games: Have everyone write down his or her resolutions on a slip of paper (no names), toss them into a hat, and randomly read them aloud. Everyone has to guess which resolutions belong to whom. Hire a bartender and serve exotic cocktails. Cater the affair with gourmet food: caviar, lobster, beef Wellington.

2 Get out your calendar. If you plan it right—9½ months in advance—you might give birth to the first baby born on New Year's Eve. See 251 Orchestrate the Perfect Conception.

3 Celebrate New Year's twice by crossing a time zone. Escape to the South Pacific and be one of the first to see in the New Year (timeanddate.com/counters/firstnewyear.html).

4 Make some money. There are many one-off casual jobs available on New Year's Eve and New Year's Day. Often the people working have access to some of the best parties and get great vantage points to see live musical acts and of course, the fireworks—and they're paid good money to experience it all!

5 Run into the New Year. Get an early start on your New Year's resolution to get fit, and join one of the many fun runs beginning at around 11:45 p.m., New Year's Eve. Each year the New York Road Runners organizes a 5K midnight race in Central Park (nyrr.org). Many towns and cities host midnight races—check with your running group to find out if there is one in your area. Distances range from 1 to 4 miles, and there are also fun runs for kids in the late afternoon. If you don't run yourself, go and cheer on the racers. See 490 Run a Marathon.

6 Keep it simple and attend a midnight church service.

7 Celebrate First Night, a family-friendly, community-based alternative to traditional New Year's Eve parties. Starting in Boston in 1976, First Night celebrates creativity and cultural diversity through its New Year's Eve festivals of the performing and visual arts. The alcohol-free festivals include dancing, theatre, film, poetry and fireworks displays. First Night festivals are held in over 100 cities in the United States, Canada, the United Kingdom and New Zealand. Visit First Night International (firstnight.com).

8 Celebrate the four-day festival, Hogmanay, in Edinburgh, Scotland. Watch the torchlight procession and march of 1,000 pipers, then join Europe's biggest New Year's street party (www.edinburghshogmanay.org).

Tips

If you'll be throwing a party at your home, make sure guests who are drinking have a designated driver in their group. Give numbers of cab companies to all guests and offer to pay the fare.

See 336 Hire a Bartender.

Check out New Year's celebrations around the world online (earthcam.com).

Learn the words to *Auld Lang Syne* at the Robert Burns Federation's Web site, worldburnsclub.com.

Who Knew?

Strip down for the annual New Year's Day Polar Bear Swim in your area. Type "polar bear swim club" into a search engine.

Passover is celebrated in a festive meal called a Seder, during which the exodus of the Jews from Egypt is in a sense reenacted. Passover is perhaps the most important holiday for creating lasting and warm Jewish memories for all guests, young and old. Seder means "order," and in celebrating this holiday you'll need to follow specific procedures, as spelled out in a book called the Haggadah.

Steps

1 Determine your guest list of family and friends. Non-Jewish friends are also invited to share in the festivities. In fact, you are encouraged to invite non-Jews, to remind yourself and your kin that you were once strangers in the land of Egypt.

2 Decide on the day you'll hold your Seder. Passover lasts eight days, and many Jews attend several Seders during that time. The first night of Passover is the most celebrated. Consult with friends and relatives before choosing a date for your Seder.

3 Create the menu. Guests share traditional foods and drink at Passover, including beef brisket, roast turkey or chicken, gefilte fish, hard-boiled eggs, candied carrots, potato kugel, salad, and chicken soup with matzoh balls. Pork is forbidden, of course, as is leavened bread, symbolizing the fact that the Jews had to leave Egypt so fast that they didn't have time for the bread to rise. You should also empty your kitchen of all foods forbidden during Passover, including bread, cakes, biscuits, crackers, cereal, wheat, barley, oats and rye.

4 Buy items for the ceremonial Seder plate, including *matzoh* (unleavened bread), *karpas* (fresh parsley), *maror* (bitter herbs, usually horseradish), *charoset* (an apple, nut and honey dish), a lamb shank bone, and a roasted egg. You'll also need kosher-for-Passover wine, enough for each person to drink four glasses.

5 Choose your Haggadah reading. Your selection will depend on your guests. If children will be present at your Seder, select a child-friendly Haggadah. Or use a traditional Haggadah passed down through the generations.

6 Prepare the table, making sure you have enough seating (you'll need an extra seat for Elijah, the Prophet, just in case he decides to come back and herald the messianic era). Place a small ornamental pillow at the left arm of the Seder leader's chair. A traditional Seder table includes several small dishes of salt water (all participants dip greens into this), and a dish and towel in which the leader may wash his or her hands.

7 Encourage everyone to participate in the Seder by singing songs and taking turns as the leader.

Tips

Purchase Passover coloring books and videos (there's even a Rugrats Passover video) to entertain and educate the younger ones.

If you will be having a lot of people at your Seder, you may want to ask each guest to bring a dish.

Who Knew?

The youngest attendee is traditionally responsible for asking the four questions of Passover: Why do we eat only matzoh and no bread on this night? Why do we eat bitter herbs on this night? Why do we dip our food into salt water two times on this night? Why do we recline when we eat on this night? (Don't worry—it's all in the Haggadah.)

You don't have to be Colin Cowie, party planner to the stars, to throw a great bash. Be an opportunist and plan your party around a big event such as the Super Bowl, Mardi Gras, the Fourth of July or the Academy Awards—and let the occasion inspire you.

EVENT	INVITATIONS	SETTING	MENU
Super Bowl (last weekend in January)	Could be in the form of a ticket—substitute "Kickoff" for "Time" and "Stadium" for "Address."	Have a pregame tailgate party in your driveway or yard. Fire up the grill and serve steak sandwiches, brats and burgers. Have a stat sheet for interested takers. Set up the betting pool during the pregame show with a minimum wager.	Buffet style works best. Think finger foods: deli platters, nachos, jalapeño poppers, and veggies and dip. Have a big pot of chili on the stove. Serve beer and soda.
Mardi Gras (47 days before Easter Sunday; falls somewhere between February 3 and March 9)	Incorporate the colors of Mardi Gras: Purple represents justice, green represents faith and gold represents power. Include confetti inside the envelope. See 462 Plan a Trip to New Orleans for Mardi Gras for more inspiration.	Transform your home into Bourbon Street, New Orleans, with lots of glittery lights, balloons and vibrant color. Voodoo is a big part of the New Orleans mystique—hire a fortune-teller or tarot-card reader. Weave the Mardi Gras colors of purple, green and gold throughout your home in the form of tablecloths, napkins, ribbons, candles, strings of lights, coins and beads. Set the mood with Preservation Hall–style jazz or zydeco. Have hats, masks and lots of beads on hand. Designate the costume winners the party's king and queen with capes or crowns.	Channel Emeril Lagasse and serve bayou-inspired food such as crab cakes, steamed crawfish and lots of spicy goodies like Cajun sausage. A must is a "King Cake" and the Mardi Gras hurricane, a concoction of rum, grenadine and passion-fruit juice (mixes are also available). For dessert, chicory coffee and beignets (deep-fried pastries) will have guests thinking they're in New Orleans' famed Café du Monde.

EVENT	INVITATIONS	SETTING	MENU
The Academy Awards (end of February)	Make the invitations glamorous, darling. Include Oscar ballots for guests to cast their votes at the party—including for best- and worst-dressed actors (see 486 Win an Academy Award). Raise the glam factor a notch and make it a black-tie–optional affair. Air kiss, air kiss.	Roll out the red carpet—from your front door to the driveway or street (you can use a roll of red paper). Take Polaroid pictures as guests strut their stuff, and hand out the photos at the end of the party as souvenirs. Whether you decide on a buffet or sit-down affair, use your best stuff—china, linens, vases. Play music from the soundtracks of nominated films.	Incorporate food from nominated movies. Serve decadent, celebrity-worthy nibbles such as caviar, chocolate truffles and, of course, champagne.
Cinco de Mayo (May 5)	Cinco de Mayo commemorates Mexico's victory over the French army at the Battle of Puebla in 1862. (It is not, as many people think, Mexico's Independence Day—that's on September 16.) Make invitations in the colors of the Mexican flag, red, white and green, or in the shape of a traditional Mexican symbol, such as a cactus or a sombrero. Attach a dried chili pepper to a recipe.	Decorate with red, white and green balloons, streamers and Mexican crepe-paper flowers. Make or buy a colorful, candy-filled piñata. Use bright flowers or cactus plants as centerpieces. Play Latin music or hire a mariachi band. Get your guests up to do the Mexican Hat Dance, or host a samba, cha-cha or tango contest.	Prepare a traditional Mexican buffet. For appetizers, serve tortilla chips, salsa and guacamole, followed by a mango-orange salad with jalapeño dressing and lime-tortilla soup. Let the guests build their own fajitas, tacos or enchiladas with rice and black beans on the side. Wash it all down with Pacifico or Dos Equis beer, sangria and margaritas.
Fourth of July	Create an invitation in the shape of a flag. Borrow from the Preamble: "We the people of 12 Maple Lane, in order to form a more perfect celebration, do invite you…"	Plan to have your party outdoors, but consider renting a tent as a rain backup. Post red, white and blue streamers and balloons. Set up a baseball game or play horseshoes. Have a taffy pull and run a three-legged race.	Keep the Americana theme alive with barbecued chicken, hot dogs and hamburgers, corn on the cob, apple pie, watermelon, iced tea and lemonade. Get fancy and do a lobster bake. Or ask guests to bring a favorite patriotic dish.

So you've been crowned organizer of your class reunion. Sure is different from homecoming queen or king, isn't it? It's time to celebrate life's successes and renew old acquaintances. It's also time to start losing the pounds, covering the gray and planning a reunion to remember.

Steps

1 Form a committee (see 373 Plan an Organizational Meeting). First try contacting the class officers from your year. Then find local classmates. Assign one person to keep track of the master list and update it as responses come in. Delegate other tasks such as securing the site, maintaining the budget, invitations, food, music and decorations to other committee members.

2 Develop a detailed budget. You'll need to figure out how much each attendee will pay in order to cover the venue deposit, printing and mailing of invitations, and long-distance phone calls.

3 Start sleuthing. Call your high school to ask if it has contact information. Use Web sites like Classmates.com, Reunion.com and Switchboard.com. Send out an SOS e-mail message asking for the whereabouts of missing classmates. Check phone books on the Web or in libraries. Call local alumni from other classes. Check your yearbook for people's full and maiden names.

4 Shop for a venue. Find out if a favorite hangout from back then is still operating. Contact clubs or banquet halls. Ask what's included and shop around. Inquire about discounted rates at hotels for families of alumni attending the reunion.

5 Select a date and start publicizing the reunion as early as possible so attendees can make travel plans (see 372 Publicize an Event). Thanksgiving and summer reunions allow alumni to plan their vacations accordingly.

6 Decide how the event will be structured. It can be anything from a one-night banquet to a weekend-long event. Some classes host an informal cocktail party on Friday night, a sit-down dinner on Saturday night, and a Sunday family barbecue.

7 Set up an account at a bank or credit union with two people required to sign for transactions. If you have a large number of attendees or an expensive reunion paid for in installments—a cruise, for instance—this is a must.

8 Decide to go with a band or a DJ, then shop around and book one. If you recall a good high-school band, ask those alumni if they'll play a couple of tunes. See 335 Hire a Band.

9 Ask classmates for information about their lives (including contact information). Compile it all into a booklet and mail this out to alumni before the reunion so they can be ready to pounce on old friends as soon as they walk through the door.

Tips

Invite a mystery guest—maybe a student who became a celebrity, or a stand-out teacher.

Hire a professional reunion planner who can take your event every step of the way, from locating classmates to contacting local media to hiring the band. Contact the National Association of Reunion Managers at Reunions.com.

Make the invitations fun, incorporating your school mascot or prom song. (Still know all the lyrics to *Hotel California*, don't you?)

Create collages from yearbook photos and newspaper articles (on microfiche at your library) to transport classmates back in time.

See 226 Set Up a Budget.

Warning

Be prepared to recognize your friends' parents. That's right—your friends now look exactly like their parents did when you were in high school. Don't laugh, pal—you're in the same boat.

Genealogy has exploded in popularity these days, and reuniting family members can be both exciting and perhaps a little daunting. If your family is small, it can be a lovely backyard gathering. If your clan has a tartan named after it, think bigger.

Steps

1 Call around and get people interested. Don't give up if your idea for a family reunion doesn't meet with enthusiastic applause right away, particularly if cross-country travel is involved. Assemble a team of people drawn from different branches of the family to spread out the work.

2 Determine what kind of reunion you'll hold. Opt for a weekend affair at a resort or campground, or a one-day barbecue at a local park. The party doesn't have to be lavish—it's all about re-establishing connections and making new memories.

3 Poll the relatives to narrow down optimal dates. Summer or holidays are usually best as kids are out of school. Choose a date as far in advance as possible so everyone has a chance of making it. If you're considering a resort, ask for off-peak and group rates.

4 Create a menu or decide how food will be handled. See 301 Plan Theme Menus and 321 Plan an Outdoor Party.

5 Discuss money issues and set a budget. Some family members who live far away might not be able to swing the airfare. Talk to other family members about chipping in—maybe you can make the ticket a birthday present.

6 Make sure everyone's accounted for and has a place to stay. Send out a save-the-date notice six months (or more) in advance for people needing to make travel, hotel and car arrangements, or if it's a major holiday weekend. Include a list of options, along with phone numbers for lodging and car rentals.

7 Trace your roots to create a family tree that you can pass out at the event. Software programs such as Reunion (leisterpro.com) can help you do this, as well as Web sites (genealogy.com). See 283 Organize a Genealogical Search.

8 Ask relatives to send their life stories and a digital photo (or two) ahead of time, and compile a family history book to hand out at the reunion.

9 Take photos of each family member on reunion day, and create a family history book to give to the matriarch or patriarch. Consider various formats for reproduction, including copied and bound printouts, or a slide show saved to a DVD, CD or videotape.

Tips

Disney's Magical Gatherings (disneyworld.com/magical gatherings) helps you plan reunions at a Walt Disney World resort. This online tool can help you chat with your group, vote on things you want to do and plan your itinerary. See 463 Plan a Day at Disneyland as well.

A perfect time to hold a family reunion is around a milestone—for example, Grandma's 80th birthday or Mom and Dad's 50th wedding anniversary.

See 432 Plan a Vacation for Wildly Different People.

Who Knew?

Plan activities for kids. The adults will have a blast reminiscing and catching up with their relatives. But the kids will need more structure—and in most cases won't know each other. Set up games like a scavenger or treasure hunt (with clues to get kids to know their cousins), whiffle ball, baseball, sack races and water balloons.

See 388 Throw a Block Party for tips on handling large groups.

RGANIZE YOUR CONTACTS • GET RID OF WHAT YOU DON'T WANT • SAY NO WITHOUT FEELING GUILTY • BALANCE HOME AND WORK • L
GAIN • SCHEDULE TELEVISION WATCHING • DESIGN A HEALTHY LIFESTYLE • PLAN TO AVOID JUNK FOOD • CHOOSE A WEIGHT LOSS PL
EET AN ONLINE DATE • PLAN THE PERFECT DATE • MASTERMIND A BREAKUP • PLAN YOUR SOCIAL CALENDAR • MEET MR. OR MS. RIG
ORT YOUR SOCK DRAWER • RETURN RENTALS ON TIME • TAKE CONTROL OF YOUR JUNK DRAWER • ORGANIZE THE MEDICINE CABINET
AR CLEAN AND ORDERLY • DEAL WITH A PACK RAT • SELL STUFF ONLINE • ORGANIZE YOUR BOOKSHELVES • CATEGORIZE NEWSPAPER
VE BETTER THROUGH LABELING • ORGANIZE JEWELRY • PLAN YOUR DREAM KITCHEN • CONQUER YOUR CLOSETS • ORGANIZE THE LI
RGANIZE SPRING CLEANING • KEEP THE FAMILY ROOM ORGANIZED • SET UP A BATHROOM SCHEDULE • ORGANIZE BATHROOMS • ORG
RGANIZE KIDS' ROOMS • ORGANIZE SPORTS EQUIPMENT • ORGANIZE KIDS' PLAY SPACES • SAFEGUARD YOUR HOME AGAINST ALLERG
OUSE • USE HOME DESIGN AND PLANNING SOFTWARE • ESTABLISH YOUR HOME'S SPACE PLAN • INCORPORATE UNIVERSAL DESIGN P
HE BASEMENT • ORGANIZE THE GARAGE • ORGANIZE A TOOLBOX • SET UP A WOODSHOP • ORGANIZE YOUR WINE COLLECTION • PLA
TUDIO OR SMALL APARTMENT • MANAGE WARRANTY DOCUMENTS • MANAGE HOME-IMPROVEMENT PAPERWORK • MERGE TWO HOUS
RGANIC VEGETABLE GARDEN • PLANT A KITCHEN HERB GARDEN • PLAN A BUTTERFLY GARDEN • DESIGN A BIRD GARDEN • DESIGN A
ORGANIZE GARDENING TOOLS • ADD A POTTING BENCH TO A YARD • SCHEDULE FRUIT TREE MAINTENANCE • LAY OUT A SPRINKLER S
ESIGN A GARDEN PATH • SET UP A COMPOST SYSTEM • WINTERIZE PLANTS • SCHEDULE YARD WORK • STORE ANYTHING • STORE BU
ND HOBBY MATERIALS • ORGANIZE ART SUPPLIES • ORGANIZE GIFT WRAP AND SEASONAL DECORATIONS • ORGANIZE KIDS' SCHOOLW
OUR WEDDING DRESS AND OTHER TEXTILES • STORE A FUR COAT • STORE BICYCLES AND GEAR • STORE SKI GEAR • ORGANIZE CAMP
HICH COLLEGE IS RIGHT FOR YOU • GET INTO A TOP COLLEGE OR UNIVERSITY • ACE THE COLLEGE ADMISSIONS TESTS • ORGANIZE Y
AW SCHOOL • PREPARE FOR THE BAR EXAM • GET A DEGREE WHILE YOU'RE WORKING • WORK AT HOME WITH KIDS • GO BACK TO WO
RGANIZE YOUR JOB SEARCH • PREPARE FOR A CAREER CHANGE • OPEN A RESTAURANT • BECOME A PHYSICIST • BECOME A CONCE
EALITY-SHOW CONCEPT • BECOME A TALK-SHOW HOST • BECOME A PHOTOJOURNALIST • BECOME A MOVIE DIRECTOR • BECOME A
LING SYSTEM • ORGANIZE YOUR BRIEFCASE • ORGANIZE YOUR DESK • ORGANIZE YOUR WORKDAY • GET A HANDLE ON E-MAIL • ORG
ALARY REVIEW • CLIMB THE CORPORATE LADDER EFFECTIVELY • ADD A WORKSPACE TO ANY ROOM • ORGANIZE A HOME OFFICE • OF
RAVEL • WRITE A BUSINESS PLAN • SET UP A NEW BUSINESS • CREATE A MARKETING PLAN • AMASS A REAL-ESTATE EMPIRE • POLISH
MPLOYEE • FIRE AN EMPLOYEE • PASS ON A FAMILY BUSINESS • STAY ON TOP OF YOUR SALES GAME • RESTRUCTURE A COMPANY T
EFEND AGAINST A HOSTILE TAKEOVER • ORGANIZE YOUR OFFICE FOR A MOVE • PREPARE YOUR BUSINESS FOR THE UNTHINKABLE •
REPARE YOUR TAXES • ORGANIZE A LOAN APPLICATION • ORGANIZE IMPORTANT DOCUMENTS • SAVE FOR PRIVATE SCHOOLING • ORG
LUB • TRACK YOUR INVESTMENTS • SURVIVE BANKRUPTCY • PLAN FOR RETIREMENT • PREPARE A PRENUPTIAL AGREEMENT • CREAT
ONEY • PLAN YOUR FAMILY • BUDGET FOR A NEW BABY • ORCHESTRATE THE PERFECT CONCEPTION • PLAN FOR ARTIFICIAL INSEMIN
EAVE • ORDER BABY ANNOUNCEMENTS • ORGANIZE AN INTERNATIONAL ADOPTION • FOSTER A CHILD • ORGANIZE YOUR LIFE AS A N
OORDINATE A FAMILY CALENDAR • PLAN FAMILY MEETINGS • ORGANIZE HOME SYSTEMS FOR ADD • PREPARE FOR A NEW CAT OR DO
ACK-TO-SCHOOL • WIN THE HOMEWORK WARS • PLAN A FIELD TRIP • PLAN YOUR CHILD'S ACTIVITIES • PLAN YOUR CHILDREN'S SUM
NLINE • ORGANIZE A GENEALOGICAL SEARCH • PREPARE FOR YOUR CHILD'S DEPARTURE FOR COLLEGE • ORGANIZE YOUR EMPTY N
LDERLY PARENTS' CARE • PREPARE FOR THE DEATH OF A SPOUSE • HELP YOUR ELDERLY PARENTS MOVE • ORGANIZE A HOME MEDIC
TORE TRIPS • SET UP ONLINE GROCERY SHOPPING • ORGANIZE RECIPES AND COOKBOOKS • PLAN THEME MENUS • CREATE EFFECT
EFRIGERATOR AND FREEZER • ORGANIZE CUTLERY AND KITCHEN TOOLS • ORGANIZE CUPBOARDS AND DRAWERS • ORGANIZE THE F
UNCHES FOR KIDS • PLAN PARTY FOODS AHEAD • THROW A DINNER PARTY • FINISH DINNER ON TIME • PULL OFF A LAST-MINUTE PAR
LTIMATE WEDDING CHECKLIST • BUDGET FOR A WEDDING • FIND THE PERFECT WEDDING RING • PLAN AN ELOPEMENT • SET UP A BA
ONOR • EXECUTE BEST MAN DUTIES • HIRE A BAND • HIRE A BARTENDER • PLAN A SHOWER • ORGANIZE THE REHEARSAL DINNER •
UCCESSFUL SLUMBER PARTY • PLAN A BAR OR BAT MITZVAH • PLAN A QUINCEAÑERA • PLAN A RETIREMENT PARTY • PLAN A FUNER
ANUKKAH PARTY • ORGANIZE A HOLIDAY CRAFT PARTY • PLAN TO SPEND CHRISTMAS SOLO • PLAN THE PERFECT HOLIDAY GIFT EXC
HE HOLIDAYS • STICK TO YOUR NEW YEAR'S RESOLUTIONS • PLAN THE PERFECT NEW YEAR'S EVE • PLAN A SEDER • PLAN A SPECIA
OOD TREE • ORGANIZE A BICYCLE SCAVENGER HUNT • RUN A SPORTS TOURNAMENT • PUBLICIZE AN EVENT • PLAN AN ORGANIZATIO
LAN A CONCERT IN THE PARK • ORGANIZE AN INTERNATIONAL CONCERT TOUR • ORGANIZE A FILM FESTIVAL • PLAN A FUND-RAISING
BUILD A COMMUNITY PLAY STRUCTURE • THROW A BLOCK PARTY • SET UP A NEIGHBORHOOD WATCH • CREATE AN EVACUATION PL
RGANIZE A PROTEST OR MARCH • FIGHT CITY HALL • ORGANIZE A BOYCOTT • ORGANIZE A CLASS ACTION LAWSUIT • MANAGE GRO
CHOOL IN A THIRD WORLD COUNTRY • PLAN A TRIP • PLAN A TRIP WITH CHILDREN • TRAVEL WITH TEENS • BOOK AIRLINE TICKETS •
OTORCYCLE TRIP • PLAN A TRAIN TRIP IN THE UNITED STATES • RIDE THE RAILS ABROAD • PREPARE A VACATION COUNTDOWN CHE
UGGAGE • LOAD A BACKPACK PROPERLY • PLAN AN ELDERHOSTEL TRIP • ORGANIZE AN RV VACATION • PLAN A TRIP WITH AGING PA
IDELY DIFFERENT PEOPLE • PLAN SPRING BREAK • PLAN AN OVERNIGHT GETAWAY WITH YOUR SPOUSE • PLAN A VACATION SEPARAT
OLITICALLY UNSTABLE REGION • GET TRAVEL INSURANCE • GET IMMUNIZATIONS FOR TRAVELING • BOOK AN ADVENTURE VACATION
LAN A FISHING TRIP TO ALASKA • PACK FOR A CAMPING TRIP • LEAD A BACKPACK TRIP • HIKE A FAMOUS TRAIL • PLAN A TOUR OF T
NGLISH CANAL TRIP • PLAN A CROSS-COUNTRY AIRPLANE VOYAGE • PLAN THE PERFECT DAY ABROAD • PLAN A VISIT TO THE LOUVR
LAN • PREPARE FOR AN ACT OF GOD • ASSEMBLE EMERGENCY KITS • PREPARE FOR SURGERY • PLAN YOUR RECOVERY • SURVIVE
EING LOST • CONDUCT A SEARCH AND RESCUE OPERATION • PLAN AN INVASION • SURVIVE A POLITICAL COUP • PLAN FOR A TERRO
ECOME THE PRESIDENT OF THE UNITED STATES • WIN AN ACADEMY AWARD • BECOME AN OLYMPIAN • TRAIN FOR A MAJOR ATHLET

SS • SET GOALS • STREAMLINE YOUR MORNING ROUTINE • ORGANIZE A CHORE SCHEDULE FOR KIDS • ORGANIZE YOUR CHORES • NE
YOUR WORKOUT SCHEDULE • SCHEDULE DOCTOR VISITS • PREPARE FOR COLD AND FLU SEASON • GET A DRASTIC MAKEOVER • ARR
JP • FIND YOUR KEYS • TIDY UP IN MINUTES • CONQUER CLUTTER • ACTUALLY SEE THE BOTTOM OF YOUR PURSE • ORGANIZE YOUR
E CAR MAINTENANCE • ORGANIZE PET SUPPLIES • MANAGE GARBAGE AND RECYCLABLES • PREPARE GRAB 'N' GO ACTIVITY BAGS • KE
INE CLIPPINGS • ORGANIZE YOUR PHOTOS • ARRANGE PHOTOS AND PICTURES • ARRANGE AN ART COLLECTION • END COLLECTION C
• ORGANIZE YOUR LAUNDRY CENTER • CREATE A SEWING CENTER • GET READY FOR THE HOUSECLEANER • ORGANIZE CLEANING SU
WAYS AND MUDROOMS • ORGANIZE A DORM ROOM • ORGANIZE YOUR SCHOOL LOCKER • MAKE YOUR HOME SAFE FOR SMALL CHIL
RE FOR SKYROCKETING ENERGY COSTS • USE FENG SHUI TO ORGANIZE YOUR HOME • DESIGN A NEW HOME WITH FENG SHUI • DESI
PLAN A REMODEL • PLAN A MULTIMEDIA CENTER • TURN A BASEMENT INTO A MEDIA ROOM OR PLAYROOM • ORGANIZE THE ATTIC • OF
FUL ESTATE SALE • PLAN A YARD OR GARAGE SALE • PREPARE YOUR HOME FOR SALE • PLAN A MOVE • DOWNSIZE YOUR HOUSE • OF
CORATE FOR THE SEASONS • PREPARE A VACATION HOME FOR THE OFF-SEASON • PREPARE YOUR HOME FOR NATURE'S WORST • PR
ARDEN • PLANT A CUT-FLOWER GARDEN • DESIGN A SHADE GARDEN • DESIGN A DRY GARDEN • PLAN FOR A LONG-SEASON CONTAIN
N AND PLANT A LAWN • DESIGN A NEW LANDSCAPE • PLAN AN OUTDOOR KITCHEN • DESIGN A DECK OR PATIO • DESIGN A WATER FEA
S • STORAGE SOLUTIONS FOR ANY ROOM • THE CAPACITY OF A SMALL ROOM • ORGANIZ
TWORK • ORGANIZE MOVIES, MUSIC AND O   IRLOOMS • STORE OUT-OF-SEASON CLOTHES •
NT • STORE PAINT AND OTHER HAZARDOUS   • STORE A BOAT FOR THE WINTER • STORE A CA
E APPLICATIONS • PLAN YOUR COURSE OF   CH PAPER • GET INTO GRAD SCHOOL • GET INTO
ONG ABSENCE • SET UP AN INTERNSHIP •   N THE PEACE CORPS • PRODUCE A NEWSLETTE
BECOME A COWBOY • BECOME A BRAIN S   ATHOLIC NUN • ORGANIZE AN EXHIBITION • DEV
ME A STUNT PERSON • BECOME A TOUR G   G • CONQUER YOUR PAPER PILES • CREATE A FU
ITER FILES • SCHEDULE APPOINTMENTS EF   NCE CALL • PREPARE FOR A MEETING • PREPAR
IE NETWORK • CHOOSE THE BEST PHONE   TEM • MAKE A NETWORKING PLAN • PLAN YOU
TATION SKILLS • PREPARE A SPEECH • PR   AN AN IPO • DELEGATE RESPONSIBILITIES • HIRE
OFITS • FORM A BOARD OF DIRECTORS • C   AN A COMPANY PICNIC • PLAN A COMPANY RET
FAILING BUSINESS • DISMANTLE A BUSINE   • DESIGN A SAVINGS PLAN • SIMPLIFY BILL PAY
NANCIAL-AID PACKAGE • PLAN FOR COLLE   E A HEALTH INSURANCE PLAN • START AN INVE
ST • MAKE A WILL • EXECUTE A POWER OF   S' ESTATE • PLAN YOUR ESTATE • TEACH YOUR
RE FOR AN IN VITRO FERTILIZATION • PREF   ATERNITY WARDROBE • SET UP MATERNITY OR
REPARE FOR CHILDBIRTH • STOCK A DIAPE   LEND FAMILIES • CREATE A HOUSEHOLD ORGA
OL YOUR CHILD • SET UP A CARPOOL • S   HE BEST ELEMENTARY SCHOOL • ORGANIZE KID
OR SUMMER CAMP • CHOOSE A SUMMER S   R FAMILY COMPUTER USE • PLAN TO KEEP YOU
BOOMERANG KIDS • PLAN AN AMICABLE   EMENTS • ORGANIZE MEDICAL RECORDS • PLAN
• ARRANGE HOSPICE CARE • MAKE YOUR   ECORDS • PLAN A WEEK OF MENUS • ORGANIZ
ISTS • COOK AHEAD • DETERMINE THE SH   M WAREHOUSE STORES • EFFICIENTLY USE THE
ENTLY USE SPACE UNDER THE SINK • STO   UR COUNTER SPACE • COOK FOR ONE • PLAN
DINNER PARTY FOR YOUR BOSS • PLAN DE   PARTY • IMPRESS A DATE • PLAN A WEDDING •
ENT PLANNER • HIRE A PHOTOGRAPHER •   ACHELORETTE PARTY • PREPARE TO BE THE MA
EYMOON • PLAN A BAPTISM • PLAN A BRI   GUESTS • PLAN A CHILD'S BIRTHDAY PARTY •

Community Works

O CUSTOM • PLAN AHEAD FOR A LOW-STRESS HOLIDAY • STAY WITHIN A BUDGET THIS CHRISTMAS • PREPARE A HOLIDAY FEAST • T
IZE GIFT-GIVING IN ADVANCE • STICK TO YOUR DIET DURING THE HOLIDAYS • PLAN A HOLIDAY OPEN HOUSE • REORGANIZE YOUR LIF
• ORGANIZE A HIGH-SCHOOL CLASS REUNION • PLAN A FAMILY REUNION • START A KNITTING CIRCLE • ORGANIZE A BOOK CLUB • SE
SHARPEN THE FOCUS OF AN ORGANIZATION • IMPROVE YOUR CHILD'S SCHOOL • PLAN A PROM • ORGANIZE A COMMUNITY THEATEF
IZE A PANCAKE BREAKFAST • PLAN A TOY DRIVE • HOLD A BARN RAISING • ORGANIZE A CHARITY WALK OR RUN • BUILD LOW-INCOM
TER-REGISTRATION DRIVE • RUN FOR LOCAL OFFICE • ORGANIZE A PETITION • ORGANIZE A RECALL • GET AN INITIATIVE ON THE BALL
MMUNITY • PRESERVE OPEN SPACE • SAVE HISTORIC PROPERTIES AND LANDMARKS • SET UP A NONGOVERNMENTAL ORGANIZATION
HE UNITED STATES • RENT A CAR ABROAD • MAKE HOTEL RESERVATIONS • ARRANGE EXECUTIVE ACCOMMODATIONS • PLAN A CRUIS
E AN ITINERARY • PACK FOR A TRIP • PACK FOR A BUSINESS TRIP • PACK FOR A WEEK IN ONE CARRY-ON • PACK A DAY BAG • PREVE
IZE A SAILING TEAM • PLAN A SAILBOAT CRUISE • PLAN A BICYCLE TRIP WITH A TOUR COMPANY • TRAVEL ABROAD • PLAN A VACATIO
IOUSE • PLAN A TRIP TO A DIFFERENT CULTURE • FORAGE ABROAD • MAIL PACKAGES BACK TO THE UNITED STATES • PLAN A TRIP TO
K ROAD • PLAN A CLIMB OF MOUNT KILIMANJARO • PACK FOR A SAFARI • ORGANIZE A HUNTING TRIP • PACK FOR A FISHING OR HUN
IKS • ORGANIZE A BACKCOUNTRY SKI TRIP • ORGANIZE A CAR RALLY • PLAN A WHALE-WATCHING TRIP • PACK FOR A VOYAGE AT SEA
YDNEY HARBOUR BRIDGE • PLAN A TRIP TO NEW ORLEANS FOR MARDI GRAS • PLAN A DAY AT DISNEYLAND • FORMULATE A FAMILY
F YOU'RE ALONE • SURVIVE IF YOUR CAR BREAKS DOWN • DEAL WITH AMNESIA • FIGHT AN EBOLA OUTBREAK • FIGHT A FOREST FIF
SCUE A HOSTAGE • OUTSMART PIRATES • DELIVER A BABY • MAKE AN EMERGENCY LANDING • MAKE A JAIL BREAK • BECOME A
E TOUR DE FRANCE • RUN A MARATHON • LEARN TO FLY • BECOME AN ASTRONAUT • LIVE OFF THE LAND • END WORLD HUNGER •

367 Start a Knitting Circle

Hooked on knitting? You're not alone—it's the latest craze. Invite your friends to join you while you knit one, purl two, and spin yarns. Even teens are getting into it—boys as well as girls. It's neither expensive nor difficult to learn, and you get to wear the fruits of your labor.

Steps

1 Decide how many members you want in your club. See 368 Organize a Book Club.

2 Set a date, time and place to meet (see 373 Plan an Organizational Meeting). Call friends and place flyers in yarn or fabric stores as well as the library.

3 Decide if you'll open the group to novices or only to seasoned knitters. New knitters will need instruction; consider pooling money to hire an expert from a yarn store. Or, call a senior center or nursing home to see if someone is interested in giving lessons and pointers.

4 Make the first meeting an informal organizational one at which you determine all logistics. Establish the club's policies, including who will be responsible for refreshments (nothing sticky!), if guests and children are allowed, and whether meetings will be woven around a theme, such as knit-a-scarf night.

Tips

Ask a yarn store if it will sell knitting supplies and yarn to your group members at discounted prices.

Have all the members knit a scarf or mittens to donate to a homeless shelter or an armed services unit.

368 Organize a Book Club

The read on book clubs is that they're hotter than ever, thanks in part to Oprah. There are even radio- and Internet-based book clubs that let you share your thoughts with readers around the world, as well as mother/daughter groups and clubs for couples.

Steps

1 Decide how big you want the club to be and the criteria you'll use to pick members. Important factors include: Will they show up consistently? Are they likely to read the book? Are they intelligent and opinionated? Do they have a sense of humor?

2 Discuss how you'll choose the books. Some clubs select titles for an entire year. Others pick their next book at each meeting. Will the host pick the book or will members vote? Will you read only paperbacks or only books available online? Strictly classics? Will you prohibit best sellers? You might pick a genre and period, such as 18th-century English literature, for the entire year. BookmarksMagazine.com can get you started.

Tips

Invite an author to speak at a meeting.

Food, of course, is key to your club's success. Decide if the host will provide the food or if meetings are potluck. Bring food inspired by the book: sushi if you've read *The Life of Pi*; dim sum for *The Joy Luck Club*; brats, curly fries and beer for *Moneyball*.

3 Figure out logistics. Will you meet once a month, at the same day and time? If someone can't make it, or the date needs to be changed, will this be communicated by phone or e-mail?

4 Determine the discussion format. Will the host lead the group or will there be an informal exchange of ideas? Will you take turns offering feedback or will it be a casual free-for-all? Will the first half-hour or so be set aside for dishing (and eating)? Will some-one research the author, period and subject matter? Set ground rules, including how to get the group back on track if it digresses.

5 Get serious. If your book club has degenerated to a gossip fest, hire a professional facilitator to lead the discussion, provide background information and choose the next book. Ask a book-seller or librarian for references, or look up the Association of Book Group Readers and Leaders based in Illinois. Sure, the pros are pricey, but you're guaranteed an insightful and informa-tive discussion.

Warning

Remember that book clubs are extracurricular activities. If personality clashes are taking the fun out of it, quit and start a new one.

---

369 Set Up a Food Tree

Whether a dear friend is having surgery or is expecting a baby, setting up the delivery of hot, delicious meals is a thoughtful gesture that's always appreciated—and a piece of cake to set up.

Steps

1 Ask the potential recipient if he or she is interested in a food tree. Find out about any food allergies and likes and dislikes, and ask how they'd like have their meals delivered: Would they prefer people to just leave meals at the door, come in for a short visit, or sit down and join the family for dinner?

2 Ask friends and family if they would like to join the food tree. Most people are delighted to be able to help in such a funda-mental, nurturing way.

3 Set up a two-week schedule after giving people the chance to choose which day of the week they prefer. Since leftovers can be abundant, schedule deliveries for every other day.

4 Create a simple meal when it's your turn. Keep their tastes in mind. Just because you think your cheesy broccoli casserole is the bomb, doesn't mean the family you'll be feeding does.

5 Deliver your meal and know that you've made someone very happy. For bonus points, slip into the kitchen and do the dishes.

Tips

Label all containers so it's easy for your friend to return them to the right people. Also, ask volunteers to include heating instructions.

Mark which items can be frozen for savoring at a later date.

One option is to hire a caterer or restaurant to prepare and deliver food.

Faraway friends and family can order meals from nearby restaurants, or search online for companies that deliver food via overnight mail. See 299 Set Up Online Grocery Shopping.

370 | Organize a Bicycle Scavenger Hunt

This hunt is tons of fun, burns calories and is a great way to spend the day with good friends. Cyclists peddle to specified locations, find a clue or solve a challenging riddle, and then ride on to the next destination. Glean ideas from 454 Organize a Car Rally, and you're off!

Steps

1 Decide whether your scavengers will compete individually or in teams. If you're expecting lots of children and teens, it's safer if participants ride in teams.

2 Map out your route according to the fitness level and age of participants. Remember that the scavenger hunt is supposed to be fun. Avoid steep hills and busy roads and intersections, and include safe places to stop and rest.

3 Get creative when you write the riddles. They should be clever enough to be challenging but not impossible to solve. Use landmarks (a statue or historical building) and natural features (rivers, parks and vista points) to add interest and local flavor.

4 Celebrate the finish with a barbeque bash and prizes for all. See 321 Plan an Outdoor Party.

Tips

Cyclists should wear helmets and bring water, sunblock and sunglasses. See 430 Plan a Bicycle Trip with a Tour Company and 142 Store Bicycles and Gear.

Encourage cyclists to rent tandem bicycles (built for two) for extra fun.

Warning

Make sure at least several participants have cell phones as well as first aid and tire repair kits.

371 | Run a Sports Tournament

Golf, tennis and swimming are popular tournament sports—whether their goal is to raise money for charities, attract serious contenders or just have fun. If you've been crowned the tournament director, key tasks will be to secure the venue, set the budget, organize a simple sign-up process, publicize the event and enforce the rules to ensure a smooth-running event.

Steps

1 Determine whether your tournament will benefit a charity. If so, mine tips from 381 Plan a Fund-Raising Event. Hit up sponsors to donate refreshments, trophies and giveaways such as sunscreen, visors, balls and sweatbands.

2 Form an organizing committee to select the judges, create the brackets and lay down the rules (see 373 Plan an Organizational Meeting). Purchase software for automatically tracking tournament results (type "tournament tracking software" into a search engine). Or, take the low tech route and buy a chalkboard or white board with erasable markers.

3 Publicize your tournament in newspapers and at other sports events and fitness clubs. See 372 Publicize an Event.

4 Buy trophies or prizes to hand out at the awards ceremony.

Tip

Contact the athletic directors at schools and colleges. Ask them to spread the word and to suggest students who might like to volunteer. See 385 Organize a Charity Walk or Run for more ideas.

Warning

If your tournament is held in summer's blazing heat, schedule competition early or late in the day so that participants won't suffer.

SPORT	WHAT TO DO
Tennis	• Determine whether the tournament will be played indoors or outdoors, on hard courts or clay. If you are playing outdoors, schedule playing times to allow enough daylight for the entire tournament. Otherwise, find a venue with lighted courts.
	• Decide how the tournament will be structured. Singles or doubles? Mixed or not? By age or gender? Single or double elimination? Round robin? Will players be separated by skill level (see nsta.org for guidelines)? How will a win be determined? How will tie breakers be structured?
	• Provide players with new balls for play. Have extra cans on hand.
	• Hire USTA-approved referees and umpires for high-level tournament play.
Golf	• Schedule your event for when Mother Nature tends to be at her kindest: Good weather is key to a successful golf tournament.
	• Contact officials at a local golf course (public or private) for permission to use their course and carts.
	• Determine the tournament format. Check the United States Golf Association site (usga.org) for rules of the game. Will you rank by handicap? Will trophies be awarded to those who play the best game of golf rather than make lucky shots? If so, you might also include par 3 games and other contests at which participants can win small prizes such as golf balls, visors and tees.
	• Contact a youth golf league to inquire about volunteer caddies.
Swimming	• Contact a public or school pool facility and discuss the possibility of using their venue. Also consider private clubs, which usually have one day a week that they rent out their facilities. Expect insurance to be an issue.
	• Make safety your top priority and inspect the facility for broken equipment. Plan for crowd control. Appoint a safety marshall to supervise warm-ups and competition. Hire certified lifeguards to work the tournament.
	• Get a copy of the USA Swimming Meet Director's Handbook at usaswimming.org. Originally written as a guideline for hosting a national-level competition, the handbook also applies to swim meets run at the local level. It will include necessary announcements, such warm-up procedures, lane assignments, not entering the water feet first, and no racing starts or dives during the warm-up period.
	• Determine the structure the tournament. Set the types of races, distances and ages or skill levels. Consider alternate structures, such as relay races. If you're considering an aquatic fund-raiser, organize a swim-a-thon, where swimmers collect pledges for the number of laps they swim at the tournament.

In this day of information overload, you have to know the rules of the game to get your event or cause noticed. Any public relations pro will tell you that publicity is a cheaper and more credible way to spread the word than advertising. And the best publicity of all? Word of mouth: When friends start telling friends, suddenly your event is *hot*.

Steps

1 Determine your primary goal. Do you want people to attend an event? Purchase your product? Make a contribution? Once your goal is clear, make sure all of your publicity materials support it. See 16 Set Goals and 374 Sharpen the Focus of an Organization.

2 Identify and research your target audience. These are the people who will respond most positively to your message and provide valuable word-of-mouth buzz. Avoid the trying-to-reach-everyone syndrome, which will only water down your message.

3 Create a Web site. Find a college student or designer who's just starting out to create (and maintain) the site pro bono or on the cheap. Keep the design and navigation simple, and have someone outside your organization test the site and provide feedback. Approach similar sites and set up reciprocal links.

4 Write a one-page press release with a great hook. Capture the reader's attention with a compelling title and first paragraph, but avoid writing it like an ad. Cover the five Ws—who, what, when, where and why. Include your contact information and Web site.

5 Prepare a media kit. Include the press release, organizational information, logo, black-and-white print-ready photographs, copies of articles about your event or organization, testimonials from celebrities or past attendees, and a business card. Write a brief, personal letter to the media contact, and put it all in a folder.

6 Distribute your media kit to the right people. For a local event, start with your hometown newspapers, magazines, news programs and radio stations. Take the time to find the person who reports on your type of event or organization. You can almost always get it into calendar listings if you meet the deadline. For larger scale distribution, enlist a professional service such as PR Newswire (prnewswire.com).

7 Get friends, family and anyone interested in your cause to post flyers or leave postcards at cafes, stores and libraries. Ask them to wear a hat or T-shirt or carry a tote bag with your logo on it.

8 Use the Net to spread the word quickly and inexpensively. Send e-mail notices and newsletters that are easily forwarded to others stating specifically what you want recipients to do. Connect with like minds through blogs and discussion groups or become part of a networking group. Check out Friendster.com, MeetUp.com, Tribe.com and Ryze.com.

Tips

Also read 373 Plan an Organizational Meeting.

If you're not a good writer, find one. Hire a professional or enlist a competent volunteer to ensure that your materials get the attention they deserve.

Rehearse any key points with a friend or colleague if you're asked to do an interview or appearance.

Who Knew?

Call media contacts and ask if they prefer press releases sent via e-mail, fax or snail mail. They almost always have a preference, and if it's e-mail, you save time and money. Ask for digital format specifications (size and resolution) before you send logos or photos.

Invent a catchy name or slogan for your event that the press and participants will remember. Include an inexpensive giveaway in your press kit, like a magnet, pen or water bottle with your logo and contact information.

Warning

Be a professional. Return phone calls and e-mails promptly and provide requested information. Failing to do so could sabotage your organization's reputation and future publicity efforts.

Plan an Organizational Meeting

The cause is grand, the group enthusiastic, and you may even have a deadline established. Now how is all the work going to get done? The first meeting can make the difference between sizzle and fizzle. Use this time to map out a plan, get people moving in the right direction and keep lines of communication open.

Steps

Setting up the meeting

1 Prepare for an efficient meeting by doing some preliminary fact-finding. Establish who the core members of your group are and get their contact information, best days and times to meet, list of skills and interests and how much time they can commit. From this list, select a meeting date. See 193 Prepare for a Meeting.

2 Call the meeting to order and begin by having an informal discussion of why each person is there. Once you've established what the group's vision is, you can create an agenda.

3 Set up the committees and subcommittees you will need such as publicity and finance, and select a chair for each based on experience and interest. Develop and agree on the plan of action, committee goals, timeline and budget. Appoint a secretary to take minutes and e-mail them to the group the next day, along with everyone's contact information.

4 Create a mission statement for your group that will keep members positive and focused on the end result. See 374 Sharpen the Focus of an Organization.

5 Reiterate at the end of your first meeting what the action items are, who is responsible for each one and in what time frame. Pick a date for the next meeting.

Staying in touch

1 Communicate effectively using e-mail. This now-standard tool is a great way to update a group or solicit opinions. Keep in mind that people read their e-mail at different intervals, so don't expect an instant reply from everyone.

2 Contact your phone company. Ask about services that are accessed through an Internet connection, providing business-like features for a low monthly cost. Conference calls for up to 10 people and storing calls online are just two of the ways a group can stay in sync.

3 Create a Web site that reinforces your mission, provides updates and a schedule (see 372 Publicize an Event). Manage larger scale or more complex projects using a Web-based project management software, with timetables, task lists, project calendars and other handy planning tools. Some, such as Ace Project (aceproject.com), have a basic version available for free.

Tips

Select a first meeting date that the majority of members can attend. If you wait until everyone can be there, it probably won't happen.

Ask volunteers to be realistic about how much time and energy each can expend. This will help set practical and achievable goals.

Who Knew?

Recruit on a larger scale by launching a group through sites like MeetUp.com, or join a social networking group like Friendster.com. These allow you to connect with others interested in your topic, and either team up or share helpful information.

Warnings

Don't set up a Web site as a communication tool if you don't have someone to update it on a regular basis.

Beware of implementing a project management system that is more complicated than you need. It will only frustrate members and could derail the project.

Doing good work every day—that's the goal of every organization. Now and then it's vital that organizations take a break from the day-to-day frenzy to sit down together and make sure that those good works are getting done efficiently and effectively. Honing the organization's mission, vision and values is a time-tested technique.

Steps

Setting up a retreat

1 Identify your stakeholders. Go beyond the obvious people, such as the board of directors, management and so on. Include those on the front line who deliver the goods and services, and the people who receive them.

2 Schedule a meeting or retreat. It should be at least a half day long—a full day is preferable. Since a primary goal is to break free of the current mindset, get away to a neutral location.

3 Find a neutral facilitator. Remember, the goal is to bypass entrenched systems while brainstorming. You can also hire a professional meeting facilitator.

4 Open the meeting by talking about and celebrating the positive things your organization has accomplished.

5 State the purpose of the retreat and set the ground rules:

- Every idea gets written down.

- Everyone participates. No matter who they are, where they are in the organization's hierarchy and how they express themselves, everyone has something to say and offer.

- No saying no or putting ideas down while brainstorming. Everything gets recorded.

- Emotion is permissible in this intense, value-driven work—even useful. Anger is allowed as long as it's not personal.

Defining the mission

1 Start tossing out ideas about what the mission of the organization is in the first brainstorming session. Keep in mind that the mission is why people serve—and that the organizational mission is often driven by the personal missions of its members. Make sure everyone gets a chance to speak and all ideas get recorded.

2 Look for organizational strengths and similarities as the ideas flow. Also identify weaknesses and areas that need help.

3 Find out what everyone's view of the mission is. For example, one member of a preschool board of directors may feel the school's mission is early literacy, while another may encourage play-based learning. A fundamental disagreement could cause

Tips

Frontline employees, volunteers and core constituents often have very different ideas and values than management has. For example, a community-based television station may strongly value locally produced programming, but viewers can't do without a nationally produced travel show.

It's important to take a break after each working session. It's hard work, and participants need to relax and gather their thoughts before the next one.

The facilitator typically acts as timekeeper and secretary jotting down every idea on large flip charts or a white board.

See 372 Publicize an Event, 217 Form a Board of Directors and 220 Plan a Company Retreat.

Who Knew?

Senior Corps (seniorcorps .org) couples the experience, skills and talents of older citizens with organizations who need their help. Contact this group to see if it has facilitators willing to volunteer in your organization.

people to leave the organization, but this is a small price to pay to keep it on track.

Clarifying the vision

1 Begin the next brainstorming session by asking participants to talk about possible outcomes—otherwise known as the "vision." Encourage pie-in-the-sky thinking: What do participants *really* want the organization to accomplish?

2 Pay attention to the discord that may come up when people are expressing their own visions or dreams. Those differences are indicators of the different values people hold.

3 Reiterate the importance of everyone participating regardless of their position. Intense discussions should be managed by the facilitator who can help individuals fully articulate their views.

Expounding on values

1 Conduct an exercise where participants are asked to write down the five things that are most important to them—whether they are personal, professional, family, physical or artistic in nature. Each statement should begin with the words "I value" to help clarify the difference between the things you want to accomplish (vision) and what you value (see 16 Set Goals). These do not need to be shared.

2 Go back to the initial drafts of the mission statement. Are there any that are a particularly good fit with the vision and values participants have expressed?

3 End session one of the retreat. Give copies of the notes to all participants. Schedule the next phase in a month or so.

Wrapping it up

1 Introduce phase two of the retreat with the goal of crafting a mission statement that is in alignment with the organization's vision and values. You are trying to draft a common story of why you exist to share with the world: This will be your mission statement.

2 Discuss possible scenarios. At this point, participants will decide if the work the organization does is in alignment with their personal values. If there is a disconnect, individuals may decide to leave the organization. Or, the organization's vision may need changing. Or, the group can look for a way to incorporate their values into the vision.

3 Use the mission statement to develop a strategic plan including marketing and publicity, organizational priorities, and recruitment—of staff, volunteers and board members.

When you're working to identify values, the words that come up are along the lines of honesty, integrity, accountability, cooperation, camaraderie, or helping someone or something bigger than yourself.

Where discussing the mission is an intellectual exercise, and articulating vision is an emotional one, articulating your values gets to the very essence of your beliefs.

Your vision, for example, might be to help people develop the skills to build a house. Driving that vision might be a wide range of values that includes self-improvement, self-reliance, responsibility and giving back to the community.

Bear in mind that the donors who support a nonprofit organization give money in alignment with their values.

Mark Twain once said, "I have never let my schooling interfere with my education." There's no question that building a partnership between the community and the school strengthens both. The bottom line is, of course, whether your child's school stimulates and nurtures his or her emotional, intellectual and social development to its highest potential.

Steps

1 Cultivate positive relationships with each of your child's teachers, administrative staff, directors, principals and even the superintendent. Do this by joining the PTA if it's a public school or the board of directors if it's a nonprofit or private school. You'll be privy to what is going on in the school district and get a sense of how the school stacks up against other schools.

2 Keep in touch with teachers on a regular basis to see how your child is doing and to address any concerns. Don't wait for the school to call you when there is a problem; be on top of things before there is an issue. Keep an open mind to anything the teacher might say—even if you've never seen your child behaving in a particular way at home.

3 Volunteer your time, whether that means becoming a PTA member, a playground monitor or a homework hotline counselor. It doesn't matter what you do as long as you stay involved.

4 Help your child with homework. If the lessons are too easy or too difficult, let the teacher or guidance counselor know.

5 Encourage high expectations. Share your goals with your child's teacher and guidance counselor so they'll help your child work to his or her full potential. Get involved with the PTA and the board of education, and ask about the school district's expectations for the whole student body.

6 Investigate the standards of your child's school. Does a hefty percentage of the graduating class attend four-year colleges? Does the school offer enrichment and honors classes? If you feel the standards aren't high enough, encourage the teachers, principal and superintendent, as well as other parents, to fight to raise the standards.

7 Make the school accountable for its discipline. In this litigious society, school districts are careful about punishing students for bad behavior. Bullying is a prime example. Too often schools won't properly address a bullying situation, and the victims become subject to irreversible taunting humiliation. If there isn't a coherent bullying policy at your child's school, volunteer to assist in creating one. You may need to take this up to the board of education for a system-wide policy.

Tips

If you sense your child might have any kind of learning disability, ask the school to run the appropriate tests.

Being bored with school can be a sign that your child is gifted. Have your child tested. If he or she is gifted, get together with the teacher to develop supplemental work that will be sufficiently challenging. See 270 Homeschool Your Child.

Make sure you understand the curriculum requirements for your high-school student and the best time that he or she should take advanced courses. See 150 Get Into a Top College or University.

Research board of education candidates by attending pre-election debates, reading the literature they hand out and reading about them in the local papers. And certainly vote at school board elections. These folks have the power to hire and fire teachers, make decisions about curriculum and dictate the school budget—so you should elect them carefully. See 392 Run for Local Office.

Who Knew?

The Harwood Institute (theharwoodinstitute.org) is a national organization dedicated to connecting communities and schools.

Ahh, prom night. This adolescent rite of passage is ripe with memories: Mom fighting back tears of joy, Dad dispensing sage advice, a stretch limo packed with your friends. Follow these steps and your prom will be a night to remember.

Steps

1 Select a student chairperson and form an organizing committee with the teacher or administrator in charge of class or school activities. Discuss budget, decorations, menu, safety and entertainment. Brainstorm fund-raising and theme ideas. See 381 Plan a Fund-Raising Event and 373 Plan an Organizational Meeting.

2 Create a budget and choose a theme. If you have room in your budget, you can purchase a prom kit from various catalogs, but they can be pricey and require assembly. Build your own or check out options at a party rental company.

3 Find a venue and book it, sometimes as far as a year in advance. Bring a checklist with you to determine the following: How is the venue's sound capability? Can it handle a large band? Is there adequate parking? Are food, decorations and security included? Be sure to get a specific price quote. Some sites will include security, but in most cases you must provide your own.

4 Have committee members listen to at least three bands or DJs before hiring one. The band should play several styles of music. If you decide to go with a DJ, ask what the fee includes. Make sure the DJ has an up-to-date music library. Ask for and call references. Get everything in writing, including time, date, location and the names of the DJ or band musicians. Confirm that the band or DJ has liability insurance. See 335 Hire a Band.

5 Hire a caterer and photographer as soon as you set the prom date. Read 330 Hire a Photographer and 331 Hire a Caterer.

6 Brainstorm decorating and invitation ideas. Surf the Web for ideas and consult with art teachers. Make mood-creating scenery and lighting a priority.

7 Order invitations, tickets and any extras such as programs about three months before the prom. To cut costs, make your own invitations (for online sources, type "invitation kits" into a search engine) and tickets. Mail invitations and start selling tickets six weeks in advance.

8 Publicize the prom by hanging posters around the school about three months in advance. See 372 Publicize an Event.

Tips

Lay the groundwork for your prom as early as sophomore year if the class size is particularly large.

Plan to have postprom parties that begin immediately following the prom. Volunteer parents, the PTA or the junior class can organize these parties.

See 226 Set Up a Budget.

Who Knew?

Once you select the DJ or band, check their space needs for equipment and find out if they have any special power requirements. Provide a list of songs your class wants played at the event, including the prom theme song.

Calling all drama queens—and kings! Community theater is perfect for serious actors as well as those who think they have what it takes to be a star. It's also a terrific outlet for directors, set designers, costume designers and musicians. So enter stage left, and break a leg!

Tips

Contact a high-school or college theater department. Ask students to offer their expertise in directing, stage direction, lighting design or set design. In exchange, see if the students can receive credit or offer them a role in the new troupe.

For more ideas, check out CommunityTheater.org.

Steps

1 Hold an informal meeting to stir up excitement. Publicize the meeting in a library, grocery store and newspaper. Brainstorm ideas and gauge the community's level of interest. See 373 Plan an Organizational Meeting.

2 Visit other community theaters in the region and see as many productions as possible. Ask if you can attend one of their organizational meetings; meet the directors and pick their brains for ideas and advice.

3 Determine whether you want to produce adult theater or include a youth theater group or senior group. In any case, you should be able to provide many opportunities on and offstage for community members of all ages.

4 Discuss how you will select the productions. Will you consider original plays? Will you produce musicals or only dramas? Or perform strictly Shakespeare?

5 Scout around for possible stages: a community center, a church hall, a school auditorium or even a vacant building.

6 Figure out how your theater group will be funded. Through ticket sales? Grants? Concession sales? See 381 Plan a Fund-Raising Event.

7 Consider whether to offer dinner or dessert with performances. Talk to a caterer to ask if they'd be interested in working with your theater. See 331 Hire a Caterer.

8 Create your organizational structure. Will you have a board of directors? If not, form a committee backed by subcommittees. Talk to a lawyer about creating a nonprofit organization and about insurance issues. See 217 Form a Board of Directors.

9 Decide if you will have any paid staff, such as a skilled lighting designer or other production person.

10 Select which plays or musicals you will perform your first year. Don't be overambitious. See what kind of productions—and how many—other successful groups produced when they were starting out. Check out www.eserver.org/drama to get started.

11 Choose a director, an assistant director and a stage manager. The board should be in charge of this task. If you don't have one, form a committee to do so.

12 Get out your calendar and pick performance dates. Avoid holiday weekends, when many folks travel out of town.

13 Hold auditions at least six months in advance. Place casting calls in the regional newspapers and on cable TV community bulletin boards. List the name of the play or musical and give specific information about the characters, including age and physical characteristics.

14 Publicize the performances at least a month in advance. See 372 Publicize an Event.

See 372 Publicize an Event.

Who Knew?

Consider offering bulk discounted ticket sales to schools and senior centers to help fill seats.

378 Plan a Concert in the Park

Keep your neighborhood in complete harmony by organizing a concert or a series of performances in a park. Summer, of course, is the perfect time for people to gather on a lazy Sunday afternoon or beneath a blanket of stars to hear local virtuosi strut their stuff.

Steps

1 Determine if your concert will be a free event or a fund-raiser to support a charity or community organization (see 381 Plan a Fund-Raising Event).

2 Discuss your idea with town's park and recreation officials who issue permits and get the paperwork you need. Ask what they'll do to make sure the park looks its best and is litter-free on the big day. Use the concert as an opportunity to raise awareness of any plans to improve the park. You may be eligible for a grant to bring art into the community.

3 Choose a genre: Broadway hits, jazz, big band or rock 'n' roll.

4 Set the performance date—and a rain date. Keep your fingers crossed for good weather but always have a plan B, such as relocating to a school or other building.

5 Canvas businesses to underwrite the event. They get advertising while you get funding.

6 Find your headliner. Work your contacts (see 201 Make a Networking Plan) and tune in to a band or musician who will play for a nominal fee, or ask a choir to perform.

7 Find out what equipment the band needs. Appoint someone who knows what they're doing and speaks the language to set up the technical equipment including lighting, power and the stage.

8 Publicize the event as far in advance as possible. Hang banners and posters, and place notices in papers, coffee shops, community centers and schools. Read 372 Publicize an Event.

Tips

Approach a well-known musician who lives nearby to see if he or she would be interested in playing.

Include a fund-raising component such as a small-scale carnival in conjunction with the concert.

Enlist a school band to warm up the crowd.

Arrange for local artists to set up booths.

Warning

Find out about local noise ordinances well before the concert date.

An international concert tour can broaden, inspire and unify any musical group, from humble church choirs to renowned symphony orchestras. Traveling as a group can make a fabulous trip affordable to many people, and give you all a chance to share your music with the world.

Steps

1 Start planning at least a year in advance. You'll save money and have a better choice of destinations and venues. Poll your members about their interests before you start planning.

2 Form a tour committee of four to six people to choose a general destination and create a rough itinerary (see 418 Prepare an Itinerary and 373 Plan an Organizational Meeting). Consider how long you want to travel, how often you want to perform, what type of venues you want to perform in, how often you want to change lodgings and preferred mode of travel. (Most tours travel by bus, but trains or short-hop airlines are other options.) The tour committee's primary task is to choose the venues and confirm there's an audience at each stop to hear your group perform.

3 Submit your rough itinerary to at least two tour companies that specialize in musical tours. Ask each for a proposal that includes estimated costs and payment schedules, recommendations for lodging and concert venues, and an on-site guide who will travel with your group and be responsible for logistics. (Remember that nothing can be finalized until payments start coming in.) You may need to provide an estimated number of people, a demo recording and a photo of the group with your request for a proposal. Get references when you're checking out tour companies—and call them!

4 Use the proposals you receive as a basis for negotiations with the tour companies. Give the organizing committee the opportunity to preview the entire proposed contract; there may be hidden costs that aren't discovered until after a thorough read. When you're satisfied with an itinerary, the tour company and their references, sign a contract. Stay flexible—and keep negotiating—to improve your itinerary. The bottom line is that the tour company—not just the itinerary—will make or break the trip.

5 Understand how the tour company will promote your concerts. After all, why travel around the world if nobody knows you're performing?

6 Build in enough free time so that members of your group can relax after performances. Plan no group activities on actual performance days to give members time to prepare without feeling rushed. Optional day trips on off-days are a good way to add rest and recreation. See 459 Plan the Perfect Day Abroad.

Tips

Small towns often provide friendly, appreciative audiences and interesting concert venues. Perhaps they won't be as glamorous as La Scala in Milan or the Concertgebouw in Amsterdam, but they can be more fun.

Choose a repertoire that's appropriate to your group and its venues. Some churches won't allow performance of secular literature, for example.

See 417 Prepare a Vacation Countdown Checklist and 419 Pack for a Trip.

Who Knew?

Consider renting large instruments or other equipment locally. It can be less costly and troublesome than carting along your own. Be sure your contract specifies the quality of instruments you need and what the insurance policy covers.

Make ample allowances for cultural differences when traveling abroad. Prepare for unforeseen adventures when dealing with language, facilities, food, methods of transportation and certainly local customs and expectations. See 431 Travel Abroad and 436 Plan a Trip to a Different Culture.

380 Organize a Film Festival

Lights, camera, action! Have you ever wanted to be in the movies or go behind the scenes to see how a film is actually put together? Share your passion for movies by planning a film festival for your community.

Steps

1 Give yourself at least a year to put the festival together. Given that you will need to secure a venue (possibly several), contact a wide range of film makers and arrange for viewings, one year is a realistic target for a small film festival.

2 Assemble a planning committee (see 373 Plan an Organizational Meeting). Narrow the focus of your event. Will you showcase a particular genre? Is the festival a fund-raiser, for profit or for fun?

3 Create a budget. Continually monitor costs to ensure that your budget remains in line with expenses. See 2 Set Priorities.

4 Secure a venue depending on anticipated attendance. Will this be a large event that will take place in a movie theater or a smaller event that will take place in several cozier venues?

5 Solicit sponsors. Donations can take the form of corporate gifts, small business donations and in-kind donations. Gifts-in-kind are a great way to acquire food, beverages, printing, supplies and more in exchange for publicity. See 372 Publicize an Event.

6 Consider the timeline of the event and which days and/or nights supporting events may occur. How long will the festival run? Will you have a gala event for major donors, a meet-and-greet with directors and stars, or an awards ceremony?

7 Decide how many films you plan to show and if you are going to have a call for entry. If so, be sure to request two copies of each film in case one gets damaged during shipping.

8 Invite directors, writers and producers to introduce their films. Showcase their involvement in the program guide to draw eager devotees. Plan a welcome reception for your VIPs.

9 Set the programming for the festival. Once you receive the films, create a method to judge them. Ask committee members to watch a few of the films and provide their feedback. Multiple judges will provide a more diverse score.

10 Secure volunteers, including an audio/visual crew, for the festival to keep things running smoothly during film showings and parties. Designate a leader to coordinate and manage all volunteers.

11 Feature movie descriptions, director and writer profiles, sponsor and in-kind donor listings, logos and ads, and special event information in the festival guide. List the committee and all volunteers.

12 Assign walkie-talkie headsets to all project leads so they can stay in communication. Keep check on all special guests and be sure they are certain of their movie introduction schedule.

Tips

See 226 Set Up a Budget and 381 Plan a Fund-Raising Event.

To find out more about calling for entries, contact festival coordinators from other film festivals. They should be able to provide you with insight and resources, and perhaps even sample letters.

Honoring an established actor or a director can be a great draw, adding glitz and glamour to the festival.

Who Knew?

Producing the event is where the bulk of the money goes: buying, renting or previewing films, shipping fees, office supplies, postage, festival gifts, and graphic design and printing costs for invitations, posters and brochures.

Make sure all VIPs have hotel rooms, welcome packages and speaking schedules.

Warnings

Don't panic if something is not going as planned. Take a deep breath, collect your thoughts and make a quick yet thoughtful plan of action. Remember that generally, most people will not recognize the difference.

Write thank-you notes to all sponsors, in-kind donors, large ticket purchasers, VIPs, committee members and volunteers after the event.

381 | Plan a Fund-Raising Event

Fund-raisers are truly a win-win situation. People like to get involved in activities that help others—and worthy individuals or causes benefit from those efforts. There are tons of reasons to raise money, and there are just as many types of fund-raisers. Raising money requires careful organizing. But if you have a clear plan, the money will flow.

KEY ELEMENTS	WHAT TO DO
Define the Cause	• Clarify your goals (see 16 Set Goals) and determine who will get the money your raise. If you want to raise funds for breast cancer, for example, narrow your cause to raising money for breast cancer research in a specific region of the country, or for families of terminally ill breast cancer victims. • Hook up with a national or local organization. It will help you create more awareness for your cause, and it can also give you established guidelines for time-tested fund-raising ideas.
Decide on the Type of Fund-Raiser	• Letter campaigns are cheap and easy to orchestrate. Write a letter requesting donations and send it to your family, friends and anyone you've ever met. Get qualified help from writers and marketing types (especially if you can afford to buy a mailing list). • Plan a low-key event such as a pancake breakfast (see 382 Organize a Pancake Breakfast), a car wash or a bake sale. • Hold a large-scale event such as an auction, a casino night or a run/walk (see 385 Organize a Charity Walk or Run), which will demand considerable planning, time and effort—and sometimes money.
Get Help	• Put out a call for volunteers. Ask not only for a volunteer's time, but also for any talents he or she may have, as well as important connections, donations or gifts in-kind. • Delegate carefully. Create committees and subcommittees. (See 373 Plan an Organizational Meeting.) Hold periodic meetings to monitor the progress of your preparations. Make sure volunteers are clear about their responsibilities. Ask them for a list of contacts to tap for contributions or to add to the invite list. See 201 Make a Networking Plan.
Secure a Speaker or Choose an Honoree	• Choose an honoree who has a relationship with your organization or cause, and will add an element of glamour or urgency for the cause. Consider a high-profile businessperson or celebrity.
Set the Date	• Choose a date far enough in advance to give you ample time to prepare. Create a timeline and event checklist. See 324 Create the Ultimate Wedding Checklist for an example. • Be aware of conflicting local and/or national events, as well as holidays. Or coordinate your event with a significant date or time of year. For example, raise money for melanoma research during Skin Cancer Awareness Month (May) or hold a tennis tournament at the same time as Wimbledon (July). See 371 Run a Sports Tournament.

KEY ELEMENTS	WHAT TO DO
Set a Budget	• Draw up a budget that will keep operating costs at a minimum so you can make a profit. Estimate attendance, cost of decorations, refreshments, printing, mailing expenses and so on. Set the couvert (the cost of expenses per person) and then the ticket prices. Read 226 Set Up a Budget.
Get Seed Money	• Ask businesses—mom-and-pop stores as well as big corporations—to underwrite certain aspects of the event, such as the venue rental, advertisements, programs and invitations, and music. Request in-kind donations of food and drink in exchange for a listing in the ad or program. • Provide each donor with a letter expressing the nature of the gift, cash value and tax-deductible information.
Choose a Venue	• Look for a suitable venue. Network with the Lions Club, American Legion, the town hall, galleries, schools and churches. Check out restaurants and catering halls, too. Book the venue as far in advance as possible. Be prepared to put down a deposit. Ask for a nonprofit discount. • Confirm your reservation with the venue as the event nears. • See 330 Hire a Photographer and 331 Hire a Caterer.
Legalities	• Know your financial liability. Some charity fund-raisers are subject to taxes. Tax requirements vary greatly depending on the amount of money that gets raised, the venue, and the charity that the funds will benefit. Play it safe and check with your accountant or the IRS. • Clarify if donations are tax-deductible. If the organization has 501(c)(3) status, the answer is yes. See 403 Set Up a Nongovernmental Organization. • Contact local law enforcement and ask about any procedures you may need to follow if you're holding the event in a public space. • Determine the need for security and liability insurance.
Create Invitations	• List everyone on your committee—invitation recipients will be looking for people they know. The honoree's name should be prominent. • Include tax deduction information, a description of the organization, sponsors and donors. • Save money by soliciting pro bono work from a talented designer and using only two colors to lower printing costs. • Invite reporters and photographers to your event for publicity.
Print a Program	• This booklet offers another opportunity to sell ads and thank sponsors and donors, and can be printed shortly before the event.
Follow Up After the Event	• Immediately add new contacts to the organization's mailing list. See 11 Organize Your Contacts. • Start mailing thank-you letters. Do not forget your volunteers. • Calculate your net and gross income. • Do a postmortem with your committee and make notes for next year.

382 | Organize a Pancake Breakfast

In this carbohydrate-obsessed world, planning a pancake breakfast can be as sticky as syrup. Never fear, they're one of the easiest and most popular fund-raisers to pull off. Start flipping those hot cakes!

Steps

1 See 373 Plan an Organizational Meeting and 381 Plan a Fund-Raising Event. Form committees to oversee the budget, menu planning, setup, supplies, cooking, publicity and cleanup.

2 Find a venue such as a school, church or synagogue, or fire house with an existing kitchen. Otherwise you'll have to rent cooking equipment, tables and chairs, and get a food permit.

3 Factor in rental fees, supplies, equipment and food, and set prices accordingly. Set tiered ticket prices: Kids under 2 eat free; youngsters aged 3 to 18 and seniors get a discount, and adults pay full price. Remember, you'll need to make a profit in order to raise money.

4 Encourage businesses to kick in. Perhaps a grocery store can contribute the pancake mix, bacon, syrup and milk. Other businesses can underwrite the cost of table and chair rentals, for example, in exchange for an ad in the event program. State your event's objective when requesting a donation.

5 Hold a meeting the day before the big gig to confirm that the venue is ready to go. Arrange to pick up the ingredients. Review with committee members tasks such as setting and clearing tables, garbage patrol, and cooking and serving food.

Tips

Give all volunteers and corporate contributors a mention in a flyer or an ad—and a big thank-you (in writing) when the event is over.

Raffle off or have a silent auction of donated items to raise more money. Or sell ads on placemats.

Keep the kids occupied with face-painting or balloon animals.

Music is key. For a quiet Sunday breakfast, hire a harpist—or raise the roof with a gospel choir.

Read 372 Publicize an Event.

383 | Plan a Toy Drive

Communities participating in relief efforts draw closer during difficult times. You'll be surprised and humbled at the amount of donations you'll receive once you get the word out.

Steps

1 Create a committee (see 373 Plan an Organizational Meeting). Goods need to be sorted by age, size, gender or use, and you must be able to distribute them to the people in need.

2 Partner with police or firefighters whose well-known programs such as Toys for Tots (toysfortots.org) enjoy hefty media exposure and public awareness.

3 Round up volunteers to help collect, load, organize and deliver the goods.

4 Designate a single drop-off point or scatter several around the city. Make sure they are well marked and supervised.

Tips

Ask a car rental agency or moving company to donate a van or other large vehicle.

Remember that people need food, clothing and toys year-round, not just during the holidays.

See 12 Get Rid of What You Don't Want.

5 Contact hospitals, Boys and Girls' Clubs, shelters, the Salvation Army and other local organizations to find out if they're interested in receiving donations, and for guidelines in doing so.

6 Determine what types of toys (gender- or-age-appropriate) and condition (gently used or brand new) are acceptable. Clarify whether toys should be wrapped before donating.

Who Knew?

The most difficult part of your drive will be storing the donated items.

384 | Hold a Barn Raising

Barn raising was once a celebrated tradition in rural America where neighbors helped neighbors to support the entire community. These days, neighbors still gather to build something, although it's usually not a barn. Working together, helping people in need and celebrating afterwards at an outdoor feast? Hey, it's all in a day's work.

Steps

1 Decide what structure you want to build and for whom. Maybe a family in town got flooded out and needs a new garage. Or you know a sick child who would love a tree fort. Or the kids are in need of a place to play (see 387 Build a Community Play Structure).

2 Discuss the scope of the project at your initial meeting (see 373 Plan an Organizational Meeting). Determine who will purchase or supply necessary materials, tools and equipment.

3 Set up teams to cover all aspects of preparation, construction, electrical, plumbing, painting, landscaping, cleanup, and food and drink. Assign a skilled captain to head up each team, direct all work and make sure it's built to code.

4 Get the word out: Put up flyers and let the newspapers know what you're doing. See 372 Publicize an Event.

5 Find volunteers. Historically, all able-bodied community members participated in a barn raising. These days, there's plenty of work for everyone who wants to help.

6 Contact Rebuilding Together (rebuildingtogether.org), formerly called Christmas in April. This national organization combines hordes of enthusiastic volunteers with skilled professionals to fix, rebuild, paint and otherwise spiff up dilapidated homes in communities around the country. See 386 Build Low-Income Housing.

7 Rally the troops on the big day and get to work.

8 Celebrate your accomplishment with a party afterward. Find a band to entertain your tired crew, and fire up the barbecue (see 321 Plan an Outdoor Party).

Tips

Older teens can certainly pitch in on the construction, while younger kids can pass out lemonade and water.

Choose a date when warm weather is most likely.

Save jobs like digging, cleaning and painting for volunteers who may lack experience—but not enthusiasm.

Pass out brightly colored T-shirts or caps to the whole crew as a thank-you. You might give captains a different color for easy identification.

Warning

Find out from your city hall if you need a permit and what codes you need to abide by.

385 | Organize a Charity Walk or Run

A charity walk or run raises money for a good cause by capitalizing on people's desire to help as well as get in shape. And there are any number of good causes that need cash infusions—from cystic fibrosis, AIDS or breast cancer research to school districts that face music and sports cutbacks without additional revenues. Whatever the cause, read 381 Plan a Fund-Raising Event, then get on your mark, get set and go!

Steps

1 Sit down with key people to get things going. See 373 Plan an Organizational Meeting.

2 Identify the charity you want to support. For greater exposure, plan your event during a designated charity's day or month. Set a date—rain or shine. Choose a starting time, and determine the length of the race and the route.

3 Decide how many participants your team (and the course) can successfully handle. An event with several thousand runners or walkers is a whole different beast than one with several hundred. The more participants, the more spectators come to watch.

4 Set a registration fee. For a short race like a 5K, charging runners and walkers a fee is preferable to having participants line up sponsors who pay by the mile.

5 Hold your initial planning meeting. Establish procedures and discuss policies for registration, media relations and publicity, volunteers, safety, traffic management, first aid and other services such as massage and foot care, food, rest rooms, accommodations, cleanup and entertainment.

6 Approach potential sponsors to help finance, publicize or even organize the event. Contact an athletic or sporting-goods store, a running club, a podiatrist, and local sports hero. Solicit corporate donations for water, energy bars, other snacks and sports drinks to be handed out along the route and at the end of the race. Sponsors will always want to promote their product with giveaways such as T-shirts, caps and water bottles.

7 Contact law enforcement agencies about local ordinances, road closures, traffic barricades, crowd control and security issues.

8 Get the word out to as many volunteers, runners and walkers as possible. See 372 Publicize an Event and contact a local TV station to see if it will get involved; maybe a news anchor is an avid runner.

9 Organize training sessions prior to the event for participants to get in shape. How many and how far in advance they should begin are determined by the length and intensity of the event. Assume some participants are total couch potatoes and schedule training sessions and plan instructional materials accordingly.

Tips

At the start of the race, position volunteers with pace signs reading "sub 7-minute mile," "8-minute mile," "9-minute mile" and so on. Runners stand behind the sign that best describes their pace. This way you ensure that the rabbits don't trample the slower runners.

Depending on the number of participants, you may want wheelchair participants, walkers or anyone running slower than a 12-minute mile to start early.

Have a shorter race only for kids prior to the main event.

Encourage residents to come out and cheer on the runners and walkers. Set up areas where people can watch safely.

Who Knew?

Delegate as much as possible on race day to your staff. As race director, you should not be in charge of any one particular task but act as the trouble shooter making sure the overall event is running as planned.

Warnings

Set a cutoff time at the last checkpoint and have the sag wagon pick up those folks who need a ride.

Marathons and two- and three-day walks require at least six months of training. A 5- or 10K requires more casual preparation—or none at all.

Always have more supplies, food, water and volunteers than you think you'll need.

386 Build Low-Income Housing

Announce that you're going to build or fix a home for a deserving family and you might have more volunteers than you know what to do with. With hefty donations of money, materials and labor, together you and your community will hit a home run by building and rehabilitating homes. These projects are a winner for everyone.

Steps

1 Research the demographics of your community and get information on the demand and availability of low-income housing. Evaluate whether or not a building program would work in your neighborhood (these days, there's hardly a community that wouldn't benefit from some form of affordable housing for the poor). Solicit opinions from friends and neighbors.

2 Contact one of the established organizations:

- Habitat for Humanity International (or HFHI; habitat.org) builds homes for the poor, from the foundation on up. Apply to become an official affiliate. If approved, follow the advice of HFHI. They've got the process organized down to every nut and bolt. Families are selected according to their need, their ability to repay a no-profit, no-interest mortgage and their willingness to work with the organization. The homeowners must make a down payment and the monthly mortgage payments, and help build the home. The homeowners' mortgage payments are then used to build more homes.

- Rebuilding Together (rebuildingtogether.org) preserves and revitalizes houses and communities by helping low-income homeowners (or nonprofit organizations) by making repairs, painting, updating electricity or plumbing, weatherizing, and building disabled-access ramps. Rebuilding Together requires that recipient families be low-income, elderly, disabled or with children, and unable to do the work themselves. This national group is also meticulously organized, and project volunteers can trust they'll be in professional hands throughout the process.

3 Encourage licensed carpenters, contractors, painters, plumbers and electricians to get involved in the project. It's good for corporate community relations, and the more skilled hands the better.

4 Get ready for high-spirited hard work, tremendous productivity, new friendships made and a great party at the end of it all.

Tips

Some recruits have no carpentry, construction or painting skills whatsoever. Assure them there are other ways they can get involved: identifying and choosing qualified families, supplying refreshments, helping with publicity, entertaining the volunteers on building day—and there's always cleaning up.

See 384 Hold a Barn Raising and 404 Build a School in a Third World Country for more ways to help out.

Get the media interested. This is the kind of good news and community-building story that media outlets love—and more important, so do their audiences. Keep the regional media, including radio and TV stations, abreast of the developments. See 372 Publicize an Event.

Who Knew?

Look for other organizations dedicated to this cause on the Web.

387 Build a Community Play Structure

Nothing makes a group of kids happier than swinging on swings, jumping off towers and sliding down slides. The bad news is that often playground equipment is no longer safe or, worse, there is none: Less than half of America's children have a playground within walking distance. The good news is that parents, neighbors and corporate partners are teaming up to build safe and creative playgrounds.

Steps

1 Identify what the playground problem is—antiquated swings, rusty slide, not enough equipment. Next, decide what the community wants to do about it. Replace the old stuff or build an entirely new structure?

2 Spread the word. The best spots to interact with parents are schools, recreation centers, soccer and baseball fields, after-school programs and the YMCA. Hang up posters in pediatrician offices. Contact elected officials to gain their support.

3 Hold a meeting (see 373 Plan an Organizational Meeting). Form committees to coordinate fund-raising, design, scheduling and construction.

4 Come up with creative ideas to make money—you'll need lots of it. Sell personalized tiles to pave a walkway or bricks to build a wall. Contact organizations or companies that may be willing to lend construction expertise, write grants to raise funds or underwrite the entire effort. See 381 Plan a Fund-Raising Event.

5 Schedule a series of meetings to increase the number of volunteers. Publicize these meetings creatively: "Calling all swingers."

6 Identify a pool of architects familiar with playground design. Find ones who will donate their time to design the structure.

7 Set up a meeting with the kids who will use the playground and ask them what they'd like included. The architect should incorporate their ideas into the final design.

8 Submit the design to the city or town for approval. Expect safety issues, zoning issues and conformity issues to be scrutinized.

9 Solicit donations from businesses and corporate sponsors. Ask for monetary contributions toward the building of the playground or for the donation of building materials.

10 Develop a construction schedule. Decide what weekend is best to build the playground and then contact contractors and other handy people to pitch in.

11 Publicize the date that the playground will be constructed and ask everyone in the community (including nonbuilders) to get in the swing of things. Anyone can help by doing last-minute hardware store runs; keeping track of screws, bolts and nuts; and, most important, lending moral support.

Tips

Contact Girl Scout and Boy Scout troops. Ask them to coordinate a refreshment stand on playground building day. Perhaps they can earn a badge for their service.

Dedicate the playground to a respected person in the community.

See 372 Publicize an Event and 384 Hold a Barn Raising.

388 | Throw a Block Party

In today's busy world, neighbors are often greeted with a quick wave at best. Have a block party where everyone can relax, have fun and get to know each other—and soon you'll be having coffee together, swapping kids or whoopin' it up with a pitcher of margaritas.

Steps

1 Put a flyer in neighbors' mailboxes inviting them to meet to discuss a block party. At the meeting, discuss possible dates and who will do what. See 373 Plan an Organizational Meeting.

2 Distribute sign-up sheets for tables, chairs, glasses, plates, napkins, utensils, barbecue grills, side dishes and other party essentials. Have plenty of trash cans and bins for recycling bottles and cans. Rent a portable toilet if necessary.

3 Plan the food and drinks. Call it international night and have each family make a dish that is unique to its heritage. Or have everyone bring their own food to grill. This is a surprisingly effective way to get strangers to mingle easily—they feel less awkward with something to do. Have everyone prepare his or her favorite cocktails and munchies for a happy hour. Don't forget nonalcoholic punches for those who don't drink alcohol and for kids.

4 Dress up the block with colorful decorations. Buy lots of balloons and have everyone tie them to trees and fences on their property. You might consider a block theme color and decorate accordingly. Ask each family to make a family banner to display on its front lawn. Hang piñatas for the kids. Tiki torches and lots of twinkling lights are festive when the sun sets.

5 Organize entertainment. Bring in pony rides or a mobile petting zoo or rent an inflatable jumping structure for the kids. Ask the neighborhood fire station to send an engine by if they're available. Plan party games for kids and adults alike, such as a water balloon toss and an egg race.

6 Rock the street with music everyone will enjoy. Hook up a CD player outside or splurge on live music (see 335 Hire a Band).

7 Contact town officials to see about getting the road barricaded if it's a large enough group. You'll need to supply a map of the area where you'll be holding the event, including cross streets for barricades.

8 Send invitations to everyone on the block. Get the kids involved and have them stuff the invites in everyone's mailbox (check first to see if this is legal in your area).

Tips

See 342 Throw a Party and 316 Throw a Dinner Party for more ideas.

If you want to block the street off, you may need describe the event and get a petition signed by surrounding businesses and residents in the proposed area. There may also be a permit fee. Contact your police department or town officials for official requirements.

Ask about scheduling garbage pickup for the day after the party.

Warning

Remember to set a rain date.

389 Set Up a Neighborhood Watch

The idea behind a neighborhood watch is to educate private citizens on how to recognize and report suspicious activities while promoting better community relations. Neighborhood watch members serve as extra eyes and ears for the police and channel information between neighbors and law enforcement officials in their efforts to thwart crime.

Steps

1 Ask your police department how to set up a program. Schedule an initial meeting on your block. See 373 Plan an Organizational Meeting.

2 Establish the boundaries of the watch area at your first meeting. It must be an area that can be effectively watched and maintained. Discuss what, how and when to report activities to the police, and effective ways to use 911. The department liaison can recommend security measures for homes—such as locks, lights and alarms—and identify crime trends in your community.

3 Elect a rotating chairperson to oversee the program, and block captains to disseminate information and enlist volunteers.

4 Hold regular meetings with law enforcement personnel to educate neighbors on local crime patterns, effective crime prevention and crime reporting. Have your law enforcement representative present as a guide for the first few meetings and then return occasionally to address residents' questions and concerns.

5 Create a Web site and newsletter to post events and incidents. See 165 Produce a Newsletter.

6 Put together and distribute a list of all residents with their home and e-mail addresses, phone numbers and list of skills (which are also useful for emergencies—see 390 Create an Evacuation Plan). Update the list as families move in or out of the neighborhood.

7 Post neighborhood watch signs. Check with the police about regulations governing their posting and where to acquire them.

8 Contact the police department about developing a community-policing program. These partnerships are a collaborative effort between police, elected officials and residents, where the input of the entire community is utilized to reduce the incidence of crime and improve community relations.

Tip

Contact the National Crime Prevention Council (ncpc.org) for more information on neighborhood watches.

Who Knew?

Neighborhood watch programs require an annual meeting with representatives from the police department to maintain the commitment to the program, to keep communication channels open within the neighborhood, and to have a vehicle in place to address concerns as they arise.

National Night Out (nationaltownwatch.org) is held on one summer night each year. Police officers and firefighters appear at neighborhood ice-cream socials, block parties and parades nationwide.

390 | Create an Evacuation Plan

In an emergency, every second counts and a coherent evacuation plan minimizes confusion, chaos and fear. Cities located in areas where hurricanes, earthquakes, floods and wildfires are likely have contingency plans in place to cope with these serious incidents. Urban areas are also developing scenarios in the event of a terrorist attack, with coordinated efforts between police, emergency personnel, transit and local authorities. Make sure your community has a solid plan in place.

Steps

General readiness

1 Read 464 Formulate a Family Emergency Plan and get your own family prepared.

2 Browse the Federal Emergency Management Agency's Web site (fema.gov). FEMA details how to prepare for virtually every type of natural disaster and specific actions to take in the wake of one, such as how to treat contaminated water. Ready.gov has information about the appropriate response to specific hazards, including biological, chemical, radioactive and nuclear threats.

3 Get disaster-preparedness training with the American Red Cross (redcross.org) on such topics as basic first aid and what to do if a medical response is delayed. Pilot programs are underway to give teachers basic first aid training as well as train health care workers on proper decontamination procedures in case of a biological warfare (such as anthrax or saran) attack.

In your neighborhood

1 Keep your list of residents current with phone numbers, e-mail addresses and skills that would be useful in an emergency (see 389 Set Up a Neighborhood Watch).

2 Create a neighborhood emergency plan. Discuss the following:

- How to protect food and water sources.

- What to do if the electricity is out.

- What the local emergency signal sounds like, and which radio and TV stations to tune to for emergency information.

- Situations (such as chemical, biological and radiological) when residents will be required to stay in their homes.

- Optimal evacuation routes and shelter locations.

- A check-in procedure, so neighbors know quickly who has or has not been accounted for.

- Emergency kits geared toward particular disasters (see 466 Assemble Emergency Kits).

3 Make sure you have a good map and are familiar with evacuation routes. Plan a backup route in case roads are blocked off.

Tips

Update the evacuation plan periodically, especially when circumstances warrant it, such as major road construction projects that would directly affect evacuation routes.

Make sure your child's school has a sound evacuation plan in place. See 375 Improve Your Child's School.

Read 223 Prepare Your Business for the Unthinkable.

Who Knew?

FEMA offers a guide to citizen preparedness in the event of earthquakes, heat waves, fires, floods, hurricanes, mudslides, thunderstorms, tornadoes, tsunamis, volcanoes, winter storms and severe cold. See 105 Prepare Your Home for Nature's Worst and 465 Prepare for an Act of God.

PrepareNow.org and the American Red Cross have a wealth of additional information.

Warnings

If advised to evacuate, do so immediately. Be aware that pets are not allowed in shelters.

When evacuating, stay on main roads that are likely to be covered by firefighters and other emergency personnel.

391 | Hold a Voter-Registration Drive

As the 2000 presidential election proved, every vote counts. Becoming a registered voter is the first step. Make sure the people of your community have a voice in the next election.

Steps

1 Ask your state board of elections or county clerk about becoming a deputy registrar. Contact the Federal Election Commission (fec.gov) for regulations, news and instructions, and to download national voter registration forms.

2 Conduct an electronic voter-registration drive. You'll need to have several computers at the table so voters can access the Web. Again, the FEC site provides state-by-state guidelines and can answer any questions.

3 Get institutions involved in your registration drive. Register school students, church members or municipal workers. Or, canvas door to door.

4 Remember that your voter-registration drive must be nonpartisan—you cannot endorse a party or candidate while registering voters. In fact, the Federal Election Commission requires that a sign be posted or a written notice be available to registrants that states "Our voter registration services are available without regard to voters' political preference."

5 Ask the FEC or the League of Women Voters (lwv.org) how to properly store the completed voter-registration forms.

6 Finish the job by making sure all registration forms are returned to the election office or mailed, as required.

Who Knew?

The voting process is undergoing tremendous change. In 2002, Congress passed the Help America Vote Act (HAVA) to help states improve registering and voting procedures. In many states you can register online.

Warning

A person who commits or attempts to commit any fraud in connection with voting, votes a fraudulent ballot, or votes more than once in an election can be convicted of a felony of the third degree and fined up $5,000 and/or go to jail for up to 5 years.

392 | Run for Local Office

Turned down again by the zoning board? Outraged that your town has approved a cell tower? Many people—even political neophytes—declare their candidacy so that they can effect change directly. A campaign is time-consuming and expensive—financially and personally. So before you make the leap, carefully weigh all of your commitments.

Steps

1 Research elected positions that will be vacant at the next election such as trustee, councilperson or mayor, and determine which one you are best suited for—and have a chance to win. It helps to know whom you'll be running against.

2 Do your homework. Research your city's history, demographics, current events and the actions of your predecessors. You'll want to be prepared for formal and informal debates.

Tips

Get endorsements from influential political figures and other local heavyweights as early as possible.

Be proactive with the media. Give them your bio and platform early on. Call when there's a story that you can contribute a quote to.

3 Attend government and school board meetings, read the paper and talk to locals before establishing your campaign platform. Find out what issues and concerns really matter to a wide range of residents.

4 Understand that you'll be living in the limelight and be clear on the ramifications of that reality. Consult all family members when making your decision. Their lives will be radically altered along with yours.

5 Practice speaking before large, challenging and even potentially hostile groups. Re-evaluate your wardrobe and grooming habits. Hire a voice coach if necessary, and a PR consultant if you will be speaking in front of the cameras. Cultivate an image of professional competence.

6 Develop a thick skin. At the same time be open to constructive criticism. More than one candidate has discovered that hubris isn't the best characteristic to bring to a campaign.

7 Make sure you and your spouse have an impeccable record—personally, professionally, financially and legally. Have a professional handler vet you before members of the opposition do. And they will.

8 Introduce yourself to your possible constituency. You'll have to sell a lot of people on your ability to effect change. How will you stand out? What do you have that another candidate doesn't?

9 Ask people to volunteer their time on your behalf during the campaign stage. Divide the town into precincts and appoint a captain for each. Choose block captains to coordinate door-to-door canvassing to ask folks to vote for you. Commit to personally walking critical precincts. Read 373 Plan an Organizational Meeting.

10 Submit a petition with enough signatures, if required to get your name on the ballot. Some jurisdictions simply request that you file a form with the city clerk.

11 Read 372 Publicize an Event. Develop collateral materials to mail or hand out while canvassing neighborhoods. Create an effective Web presence (such as MoveOn.org) and use it to discuss the issues and present your platform, particularly to your younger constituents.

12 Campaign door to door, at public transportation stations, in front of the post office or other locations with lots of foot traffic.

13 Hold a fund-raising event to raise both money and awareness of your campaign. See 381 Plan a Fund-Raising Event.

14 Create lawn and window signs for supporters to display.

15 Rally your volunteers to call voters the night before and the day of the election to remind them to get out and vote.

Who Knew?

Get the address list of voters from your county board of elections (about $20).

Hire a writer to help you craft your bio and position statement; there's nothing worse than a candidate, especially a school board candidate, whose handouts contain grammatical errors.

Surround yourself with brilliant, well-educated advisers who have sterling characters and background. Make sure none of them has any connections to nefarious business practices. After you ask them, do a Better Business Bureau (bbb.org) search to confirm.

Warnings

Take care not to run as a one-issue candidate, or you'll risk being bored or overwhelmed by the number and complexity of issues you'll face once in office.

Don't ever take the efforts of your volunteers for granted.

393 | Organize a Petition

Collecting autographs becomes a political statement when they're attached to a petition. As one of the most powerful grassroots movements, petitions can bring together thousands of individuals who are devoted to a change or cause.

Steps

1 Identify the best person or group of people to receive your petition. Just who that is will depend on what you are petitioning to accomplish. For example, if it's to halt a business practice, send your petition to the firm's CEO or legal team.

2 Write a petition with a clearly defined message. See 374 Sharpen the Focus of an Organization.

3 Make copies of the petition and give them to as many supporters as possible to get signatures. Get clipboards and head for the grocery store. Make sure your signers include an address and/or a phone number. If you're trying to fight a local problem, the addresses will probably have to be in that jurisdiction. Depending on the scope of the problem and the petition, you may need to gather a required number of signatures. to find out, contact a lawyer, or a national organization petitioning a similar cause.

4 Get the word out in conjunction with petitioning. Your group can do that through the Internet, the media, posters, phone calls and word of mouth. See 372 Publicize an Event.

5 Deliver the completed forms and signatures to the appropriate person or organization.

Who Knew?

Check sites such as ThePetitionSite.com for petitions ranging from protecting the environment to disability access.

Find other people to join you—you don't have to do it alone.

394 | Organize a Recall

Anyone can change their mind, even a voting body. Grumbling aside, if you feel a politician's conduct has gone beyond acceptable boundaries, organize a recall.

Steps

1 Find out who's accountable. If an elected official at the city, county or state level has broken a law or simply displayed, in your mind, extreme incompetence, you can try to get the official recalled. Coordinate your efforts with fellow disgruntled citizens.

2 Contact your state or local officials to find out what rules govern the recall process. File a registration form with the city, county or state, depending on whom you want to recall.

3 Get enough signatures within the specified time period. Have the signatures validated, usually by the board of elections.

4 Work with officials to schedule a recall election.

Who Knew?

Elected state officials are accountable to the public in a handful of states; many more locally elected officials are similarly accountable. (Recalls do not apply to federal elections.)

Warning

Beware: It's a lot of work, and the replacement may not be any better.

395 | Get an Initiative on the Ballot

State laws vary, but it can take hundreds of thousands of signatures to get your initiative on the ballot. This requires lots of time and money. Still up for the job? Take a deep breath, dust off that folding table and start collecting signatures.

Steps

1 Understand that a ballot initiative does not effect change. But it tells legislators where voters stand on certain issues and how many people support certain action. Keep in mind that you'll ulti-mately need a certain number of votes to be effective, so voter turnout needs to be high. You might even purposely delay your initiative until a presidential election year, since voter turnout in off years tends to be low.

2 Hire a lawyer to help you draft a formal petition.

3 Collect the required number of signatures and make sure they are valid.

4 Spread the word about the initiative (see 393 Organize a Petition).

5 Get out the vote. Depending on the rules of your jurisdiction, you'll need a certain percentage of voters to vote in favor of the initiative in order for it to pass.

Who Knew?

At the local level, a nonbinding referendum serves the same purpose as a ballot initiative. A binding referendum, on the other hand, does change the laws.

396 | Organize a Protest or March

From Martin Luther King to Gandhi, nonviolent demonstrators have proved a powerful form of influence. To protest successfully, research local and state laws, sign on high-profile citizens and entice the press.

Steps

1 Determine if you want to shout your message loud and clear with an in-your-face protest, or stage an equally effective silent vigil.

2 Educate the public about the issue and cultivate public opinion. Write letters to newspaper editors and stage town hall-style meetings. Publicize the meetings in the papers (see 372 Publicize an Event).

3 Pick a popular and highly visible location, such as the town square, a centrally located park or a busy shopping mall parking lot. But be certain that the rally spot also relates to what you are protesting. For example, if your fight is to clean up the ocean, stage your protest or march at the beach.

4 Choose effective, high-profile speakers such as a city councilor or local celebrity. You and other protesters should also prepare speeches to rally the troops.

Tips

Check with local law enforcement about permit requirements, setting up roadblocks and safety regulations.

Discuss how you'll handle disruptive behavior and destruction during the protest. Share the informa-tion from the police with the leaders of the protest or march prior to the event.

Designate crowd leaders to be responsible for keeping the protesters in line.

397 Fight City Hall

Mad as heck and not going to take it anymore? This is politics at its most basic—and many times most effective—level. Creating change where you live is not easy but well worth the fight.

Steps

1 Build your case. Start by defining the crux of the problem, whether it's a controversial community issue or a recent decision made by elected officials. Sketch out what you'd do to correct it. Conduct exhaustive research. Talk to affected citizens and gather witnesses. Do as much of the legwork as possible.

2 Find out when open meetings are held and go on the record. Ask other articulate coalition members to attend the meeting with you and to speak up. Also, if possible, schedule an appointment with the appropriate government officials for yourself and several others from your side.

3 Form alliances with influential officials inside and outside of your town. For example, if you're fighting a town issue, contact the county supervisor and try to win his or her support. You may hear back from an intern, but it is a stepping-stone. Next, ask to set up a meeting with the government official.

4 If you can beat 'em, join 'em. Read 392 Run for Local Office.

Tips

Forge a coalition with other impassioned community members.

Visit your city government's Web site and e-mail your concerns or comments to the appropriate person.

398 Organize a Boycott

Nothing speaks louder than lost revenue, so an effective boycott can get a CEO's or board director's attention quickly. Vote with your dollars by refusing to buy products from companies that conduct business in ways you find unethical.

Steps

1 Identify whom or what you want to boycott. The beauty of a boycott is that you can have a major effect on a seemingly impenetrable multinational corporation by calling attention to how it conducts business. Keep the message simple yet emotionally appealing.

2 Research to death the product or group that you are interested in boycotting. Consider boycotting both the consumer and the seller. PETA, in its boycott of fur coats, intimidates the seller, the maker of fur coats, and the people who buy and wear them.

3 Warn the company early on of your plans to boycott. Sometimes just the threat of a boycott does the job.

4 Spread the word via word of mouth, e-mail and a Web site dedicated to the cause. Get a petition going (see 393 Organize a Petition).

Tip

Keep up the momentum. Sometimes a boycott takes years before it effects change. Don't give up.

Who Knew?

Consult a lawyer about how to boycott effectively without risking a slander or libel lawsuit.

America's corporate history is peppered with David and Goliath stories where an almighty corporation is taken on by a lone whistleblower determined to expose unlawful actions or dangerous products. Whether it's battling Big Tobacco, identifying cancer clusters in your community or getting a malfunctioning car seat taken off the market, if other people share your complaint, a class action lawsuit may offer the appropriate legal remedy.

Steps

1 Understand the legal terms: A class action is a procedure used to efficiently handle a lawsuit in which a large number of people have been injured by a common act, or set of actions, or product. A suit is not considered a class action until there is a court order making it such.

2 Research the scope of the problem. How you do this will depend greatly on the issue. The Web is a tremendous resource: Visit chat rooms and online support groups to find information that relates directly or tangentially to your lawsuit.

3 Hire an attorney who specializes in the type of lawsuit you are pursuing. For instance, if you are suing a current or former employer for discrimination or back wages, hire an employment or labor lawyer. There are also attorneys who specialize in securities, product liability and defective manufacturing. Many lawyers who take on class action suits work on a contingency basis, which might be more than 30 percent of the final settlement.

4 Determine with your lawyer whether your lawsuit has broad appeal. It all depends on the problem. Again, use the Web to help identify potential plaintiffs. Dig up information from government agencies or congressional representatives. Place an ad in a newspaper after a class action is certified by a court.

5 File your case, then a motion for class certification. In order to qualify you must prove that you have a sufficient number of plaintiffs involved, all of whom were subject to similar misconduct, and you must show that each person is making the same allegations. Your attorney must also prove that common questions predominate in the suit rather than individualized issues. He or she will handle this.

6 Send notices to potential members of the class suit. You as the plaintiff (and your lawyer) are responsible for this. The defendants must provide their names and addresses. Your legal team must also publish a notice in nationwide papers such as *The Wall Street Journal* and *The New York Times*. Some potential class lawsuit members may opt to sue on their own or not at all.

7 Prepare your case and get ready to go to court.

Who Knew?

You can be the lead plaintiff acting on behalf of the other members in the class action. You simply need to have enough coplaintiffs to justify the suit as a class action; and while that can be millions of people in some cases, it can be as few as 20 in others.

A class action suit can prove to be more efficient for the judicial system and reap larger settlements, so don't be surprised if lawyers push for a class action suit rather than individual litigation.

Talk to journalists at legal newspapers and magazines to get an objective perspective on the inner workings of class action suits. They may be able to help you research your case or suggest an appropriate attorney.

Warnings

Select your lawyer carefully. Some lawyers love class actions because of the exposure it brings them, not to mention the money. Word of mouth may be the best way to find a credible lawyer. You might also contact a lawyer referral service such as LegalMatch.net. Interview several potential attorneys before hiring one.

Many years can pass before a final settlement in a class action suit is made.

400 | Manage Growth in Your Community

It's not just America's waistlines that have expanded—city limits have too. The post–World War II boom in automobile sales, new superhighways and attractive loan programs resulted in homes and businesses moving farther away from city centers. Ain't progress grand? While change may be inevitable, there are beneficial ways to direct growth.

Steps

Do your homework

1 Recognize that managing growth is a highly politicized process where there is often no single right answer. The question isn't necessarily "What's the right thing to do?" but rather "How do we get key people on all sides of the issue in the same room, talking and working together?" When there is a plan in place for people to become involved, there's a much higher likelihood that the eventual resolution will serve the interests of the entire community.

2 Research your community's existing development and growth plan. The planning board is a good place to gather information, but you may have to go to the state level to get the big picture.

3 Contact local government officials to see what is being done to deal with urban sprawl. If your town has a redevelopment agency or an environmental protection department, these will be key operations in addition to the planning department. Research existing laws carefully, especially fees and taxes on new developments. Many cities have successfully used their fee and tax structure to encourage development in certain areas while discouraging it in others.

Get involved

1 Know the important players in the real estate and development market in your area. Speak informally of your concerns about fast-paced development in your community to residents and business owners. Don't be surprised if you're met with serious opposition: Many proponents of aggressive growth think it's a sign of a thriving economy.

2 Look at slow-growth development plans of other towns in your region or state. Study them and gather more information to incorporate into your plan. Join or form an alliance with existing organizations dedicated to eliminating urban sprawl or exploring similar problems.

3 Cultivate relationships with city officials and lobby them to revise ill-conceived legislation. When you interact with people from local and state government and business, consider them your partners rather than your adversaries. As an insider, you're far more effective when dealing with local government than an outsider can be.

Tips

Become a familiar face at town meetings. Run or volunteer for a position on the planning or zoning board.

Contact a college professor, high-school teacher, architect or city planner from a neighboring area who has a keen interest in the subject, and pick his or her brain. Ask if he or she would volunteer to educate your community about growth management options.

Read 395 Get an Initiative on the Ballot to give your plan some teeth.

Who Knew?

A *greenline* is an arbitrary line dividing rural areas from urban uses. A *greenbelt* is a band of open land that surrounds cities and towns. While a greenline might look good on paper, it can be a limiting, heavy-handed and rigid approach with the unintended effect of turning some areas into slums.

Advocates of smart growth value revitalizing existing cities and older neighborhoods—so that people can work, shop and go to school without traveling great distances—as well as preserving open space (see 401 Preserve Open Space).

4 Mobilize concerned citizens in your community to form a group (see 373 Plan an Organizational Meeting). Canvas other residents to see where they stand on the issue of urban sprawl. Publicize your efforts in the paper and at open city-hall meetings (see 372 Publicize an Event and 397 Fight City Hall). Ask fellow concerned citizens to help research and draft a plan for managed growth. Find other plans online to use as a template.

5 Vote smart. Research candidates running for local, state and national office to see where they stand on urban sprawl issues. Or run for office yourself (see 392 Run for Local Office).

6 Demand accountability from top state, county and city officials. Review zoning laws and public works proposals on the local and state level to see if they align with planning goals. Find out if your town has a Community Development Plan already in place.

Draft a plan

1 Isolate heavy industrial activity into defined zones. Incorporate long-term strategies to protect water, air and soil quality.

2 Consider thoughtful integration of commercial uses into residential areas. Elements to look at are population densities, making public transportation available, cultivating neighborhood shopping districts rather than introducing big-box retailers, and effective use of open space and a greenbelt within predominantly urban areas.

3 Provide a realistic assessment of how your plan will ensure adequate revenue for ongoing city needs such as road, sewer, police and fire expenses. Be familiar with the current city budget and address what impact your plan will have on it. Informed people will frequently look at this portion of any plan first.

4 Include the following in any managed growth plan:

- Projected population growth figures.
- Water and sewer plans.
- Any necessary environmental reports.
- Pedestrian-friendly designs for streets and public places.
- High-density housing in transportation corridors as a part of the urban plan.
- Greenbelts and parklands.
- Strategies to maintain the community's integrity, including preservation of cultural and historic landmarks and buildings (see 402 Save Historic Properties and Landmarks).
- Models of other communities that have been successful in controlling development.
- Economic development.

5 Remember, it's your right as a citizen to influence change.

Smart Growth America (smartgrowthamerica.com), Smart Growth (smartgrowth.org) and the Sierra Club (sierraclub.org) are all proactive in the fight to curb urban sprawl.

Request that your city government hold an open forum for residents to brainstorm ideas and concerns about development and growth. Share strategies with other organizations, gain access to information on "smart construction," learn about innovative financing, evaluate competing development options and initiate money-saving investments that provide economic and environmental benefits.

401 | Preserve Open Space

Communities across the country, facing a wide range of environmental challenges, are engaged in a fight to preserve open space, farmlands and wildlands. Open space provides a vital habitat for plants and animals, curbs pollution and protects the integrity of the natural landscape. Preserving the unspoiled beauty of open space is one of the toughest battles a community can wage, especially when powerful developers cast their eye on "empty" land.

Steps

1 Be aware of the broad range of issues surrounding open space. An open-space proponent seeks to limit urban sprawl by directing public and private investment into existing communities (rather than spreading them farther into open land), advocating intelligent regional transportation decisions, creating new plans for urban parks, developing multifamily housing units and revitalizing central cities.

2 Take action. Get involved in your community's planning process (see 400 Manage Growth in Your Community).

3 Join forces with groups working to protect open space and the greenbelt in your area. Become a member of existing environmental powerhouses, such as the National Audubon Society (audubon.org), the National Resources Defense Council (nrdc.org) and the Sierra Club (sierraclub.org)

4 Hold a public meeting to identify land that is in imminent risk of development. Launch a Web site to communicate your concerns and rally support. See 373 Plan an Organizational Meeting and 372 Publicize an Event.

5 Research programs that your community can put into place. For example, purchase of development rights (PDR) and transfer of development rights (TDR) programs are both cost-effective methods for preserving high-quality agricultural lands. Established by local zoning ordinances, TDRs allow landowners to transfer the right to develop one parcel of land to a different parcel of land. So, for example, an environmentally sensitive area would remain untouched while an underutilized urban zone is marked for development. With PDRs, landowners, such as farmers, are compensated for the fair market value of the development potential of the land instead of donating it. A cash payment is made in exchange for the land owner signing a deed restriction.

6 Canvas door to door to inform people about local projects that impact open space, such as development of new housing, strip malls, big-box retailers and so on.

7 Contact elected officials in your legislative district. Type "elected officials [your city]" into a search engine to find contact information.

Tips

Consider hiring a lawyer to force government compliance, or get involved in an existing lawsuit. Review your community's general plan. Many general plans have a stated goal of preserving open space. If you know of a project that violates this goal, you may have the basis for a lawsuit. See 399 Organize a Class Action Lawsuit.

See 208 Prepare a Speech and practice your message so that you're comfortable presenting it to different audiences. Hold a series of workshops to educate volunteers on issues surrounding the open-space debate so they, too, can clearly communicate the desired message.

Who Knew?

Open space—while highly political—is a nonpartisan issue, and efforts to recruit support should cross party lines.

Some communities have funds to purchase open space greenbelts.

402 | Save Historic Properties and Landmarks

In an era of ever-tightening fiscal belts, America's historic and cultural relics are in danger of disappearing due to decay and encroaching development. That turn-of-the-century home, the trading post that marked a pioneer's passage or the magnificent architectural treasure in a city's heart all tell stories of the area's heritage. The personal dedication of private donors and watchdogs is key to preserving these priceless treasures.

Steps

1 Contact your state historical society, preservation group or library to find out what preservation projects are under way and how you can help.

2 Research the history of your community. Seek out residents whose families have lived in the town for generations and ask about the history of your town and its early inhabitants. Visit museums that house community archives or inquire at city hall.

3 Determine if there is anything historic at risk of being razed or developed: significant properties, prominent landmarks such as monuments, historic routes and even venerable trees.

4 Dig into the details at SaveAmericasTreasures.org. Contact town officials or state preservation groups to see if there is a landmarks committee or other preservation group you can join. If there isn't, assess what guidelines your town has for historic preservation.

5 Rally neighbors and friends to join you in saving a site or an artifact. See 373 Plan an Organizational Meeting.

6 Start your own historical society if your town doesn't have one, or join forces with one in a neighboring town.

7 Remember that marketing is key: Write a piece featuring facts, figures and old photos to hand out (see 165 Produce a Newsletter). Contact the local newspaper and television station (see 372 Publicize an Event).

8 Raise money. Your group may need to fund-raise aggressively (see 381 Plan a Fund-Raising Event) to save properties in danger of being destroyed. Or hold an auction at which the public can bid on a building to salvage it—or purchase it outright.

9 Encourage the schools and teachers in your community to take an interest in historic landmarks. Help set up field trips to nearby sites and assist in furnishing appropriate teaching materials to ignite students' interest. See 276 Plan a Field Trip.

10 Contact Preserve America (preserveamerica.gov), a government organization that rewards communities by giving them a special designation for preserving historic resources.

Tips

Apply for grants and loans to help in your preservation efforts. Contact preservation agencies and organizations, as well as government officials, for more information.

Take advantage of Historic Preservation Month each May with an event to raise awareness of your project.

Who Knew?

Physical structures such as monuments, homes and other buildings aren't the only relics that are at risk. Historic books, documents and musical and spoken-word recordings also need preservation.

Historic preservation designation limits construction and renovation to keep areas and buildings in historic condition. Check with your city as to what you can and can't do to a property.

403 Set Up a Nongovernmental Organization

Greenpeace and the Red Cross are powerful examples of nongovernmental organizations. NGOs help millions of people around the globe, doing things that for whatever reason (lack of money, infrastructure or interest) governments don't do, typically in the areas of the environment, education, health care and human rights. NGOs can operate locally (working to block construction of a cell tower) or internationally (promoting economic development, education, health care). If you have an issue you feel passionate about, start your own NGO.

Steps

1 Clarify your goals and target a country or region to work in. Write a strong, specific mission statement, such as providing schooling for Nepalese girls who otherwise might be sold into prostitution. See 374 Sharpen the Focus of an Organization.

2 Research your issue exhaustively. Find out what other NGOs have done, and if their mission has any crossover with your core issues. Forming an alliance with other NGOs or grassroots organizations can greatly boost your power and influence.

3 Develop the bylaws, the set of rules under which the organization will operate. These include the board of directors' makeup and nomination process, financial management, project implementation, and how to amend the bylaws.

4 Establish a board of directors to help develop and implement policy (see 217 Form a Board of Directors).

5 Design and implement your programs. Track results and refine policies until they align with stated goals. If you aren't ready to make a go of it alone, try out what you want to do under the wing of an NGO whose core mission fits closely with yours. You'll benefit significantly from its expertise and in-country contacts without going through the huge headache of getting 501(c)(3) status. You'll enjoy fiscal sponsorship from the NGO and be able to raise money in its name. The NGO benefits because you expand its effectiveness with minimal administrative costs.

6 Register your NGO with the country's public authorities as well as with the target community to ensure acceptability, and build trust, and program and project effectiveness.

7 Apply for tax-exempt status in the country where your NGO does its work. If you plan to raise money from U.S. donors, it's crucial that you have 501(c)(3) status as well. The process may take several years and it's not assured that you'll receive the status.

8 Start raising cash for your cause. Target individuals as well as foundations and philanthropists (see 381 Plan a Fund-Raising Event). You'll need a plan in place for securing donations for short-term and long-term programs. Ask for in-kind donations as well, such as computers, desks and other office equipment.

Tips

Research what other groups are doing and discuss strategies at the NGO Café (www.gdrc.org/ngo/ncafe-ks.html).

Check with the local government registry or a similar agency to see if the proposed name of your organization is already in use.

Become a visible figure. Talk to elected officials and policy makers regularly. Fill them in on national and global events affecting your issue. Force them to debate the subject.

See www.irs.gov/eo for tax-exemption information for U.S. charitable organizations.

Apply for a nonprofit bulk-mail permit to receive additional discounts. Contact a local post office and request the necessary information.

See 404 Build a School in a Third World Country.

Who Knew?

An NGO can consist of just one or two people, or many. It is always self-governing and has voluntary and/or paid positions.

Aim high to receive consultative status with the United Nations' Economic and Social Council. The 1,500 NGOs with this status may send observers to public meetings of the council and its subsidiary bodies, and may submit written statements relevant to the council's work.

404 | Build a School in a Third World Country

As the old parable says: "Give a man a fish and he will eat for a day. Teach him to fish and he will eat for a lifetime." There are many ways to help build schools in remote areas of the world that desperately need them. Some people, ignited by personal passion, start their own foundations. Others join efforts that are under way, hammer in hand. But most people who care deeply about promoting education in the Third World are happy to help successful organizations in their efforts.

Steps

1 Research a country that interests you or that you feel particularly passionate about helping. Sir Edmund Hillary, through his Himalayan Trust (www.himalayantrust.co.uk), has been a tireless supporter of the Sherpa people of Nepal ever since his famous 1953 climb of Mount Everest. Greg Mortenson also made Third World education a personal mission. Acutely ill after climbing Pakistan's K2 in 1993, he stopped in a remote mountain village to recover. The people opened their hearts and homes to him, despite their overwhelming poverty, and nursed him back to health. Profoundly grateful, Mortenson returned to the United States, sold his belongings, took the cash back to the village and built a school. A decade later, his Central Asia Institute (ikat.org) has built 40 schools in Afghanistan and Pakistan, many for girls attending school for the first time.

2 Research your chosen country. Typically, children in remote areas have neither the choice nor the opportunity to go to school. The money they earn is often critical to their family's survival. In other places, only well-off families are able to send their kids (almost always boys) to boarding school. Children leave their families for years—and once they've tasted city life, many don't return. This has profound implications on family life and cultural preservation.

3 Investigate methods. Successful nongovernmental organizations (NGOs) build partnerships with the people they work with. They listen carefully, meet local needs, develop in-country partners who administer to the projects, and always respect the local culture and customs. Some NGOs focus on building schools for girls and start a powerful new cycle in their village when the students return as teachers or nurses, challenging long-held cultural assumptions that girls aren't worth educating. Other groups build schools in remote villages, allowing children to learn at home.

4 Link up with a well-established NGO active in your area of interest. See 403 Set Up a Nongovernmental Organization.

5 Become an active member. Spread the word about the good work the organization is doing, serve on the board and donate money. If you're heavy on talent and passion but don't have deep pockets, offer to help write or design the newsletter (see 165 Produce a Newsletter), maintain the Web site, stuff envelopes, answer phones and even write thank-you notes.

Who Knew?

Virtually every continent has programs in place helping to promote education and health care and preserve cultural heritage.

Young people find these causes very appealing. Some kids collect pennies or donate their birthday, bar mitzvah or babysitting money to help these groups. See PenniesForPeace.org.

Many terrific organizations would welcome your membership dollars: the American Himalayan Foundation (himalayan-foundation.org) and Habitat for Humanity International (habitat.org/intl) are only a few of the players. See 386 Build Low-Income Housing.

Free the Children (freethe children.com) has built more than 375 schools globally, educating more than 300,000 students daily.

ProPeru (properu.org) offers a three-week program in which you pay $1,900 to build schools and stay with a host family in Peru. Then again, consider how far that same $1,900 would go in a country where $200 pays the annual salary of one teacher.

Warning

Some organizations operating in politically or socially turbulent regions do not permit volunteers to work in-country for safety reasons. See 439 Plan a Trip to a Politically Unstable Region.

RGANIZE YOUR CONTACTS • GET RID OF WHAT YOU DON'T WANT • SAY NO WITHOUT FEELING GUILTY • BALANCE HOME AND WORK • L
BAIN • SCHEDULE TELEVISION WATCHING • DESIGN A HEALTHY LIFESTYLE • PLAN TO AVOID JUNK FOOD • CHOOSE A WEIGHT LOSS PL
EET AN ONLINE DATE • PLAN THE PERFECT DATE • MASTERMIND A BREAKUP • PLAN YOUR SOCIAL CALENDAR • MEET MR. OR MS. RIG
ORT YOUR SOCK DRAWER • RETURN RENTALS ON TIME • TAKE CONTROL OF YOUR JUNK DRAWER • ORGANIZE THE MEDICINE CABINET
AR CLEAN AND ORDERLY • DEAL WITH A PACK RAT • SELL STUFF ONLINE • ORGANIZE YOUR BOOKSHELVES • CATEGORIZE NEWSPAPEF
VE BETTER THROUGH LABELING • ORGANIZE JEWELRY • PLAN YOUR DREAM KITCHEN • CONQUER YOUR CLOSETS • ORGANIZE THE LI
RGANIZE SPRING CLEANING • KEEP THE FAMILY ROOM ORGANIZED • SET UP A BATHROOM SCHEDULE • ORGANIZE BATHROOMS • ORG
RGANIZE KIDS' ROOMS • ORGANIZE SPORTS EQUIPMENT • ORGANIZE KIDS' PLAY SPACES • SAFEGUARD YOUR HOME AGAINST ALLERG
OUSE • USE HOME DESIGN AND PLANNING SOFTWARE • ESTABLISH YOUR HOME'S SPACE PLAN • INCORPORATE UNIVERSAL DESIGN P
HE BASEMENT • ORGANIZE THE GARAGE • ORGANIZE A TOOLBOX • SET UP A WOODSHOP • ORGANIZE YOUR WINE COLLECTION • PLAN
TUDIO OR SMALL APARTMENT • MANAGE WARRANTY DOCUMENTS • MANAGE HOME-IMPROVEMENT PAPERWORK • MERGE TWO HOUS
RGANIC VEGETABLE GARDEN • PLANT A KITCHEN HERB GARDEN • PLAN A BUTTERFLY GARDEN • DESIGN A BIRD GARDEN • DESIGN A G
ORGANIZE GARDENING TOOLS • ADD A POTTING BENCH TO A YARD • SCHEDULE FRUIT TREE MAINTENANCE • LAY OUT A SPRINKLER S
ESIGN A GARDEN PATH • SET UP A COMPOST SYSTEM • WINTERIZE PLANTS • SCHEDULE YARD WORK • STORE ANYTHING • STORE BU
ND HOBBY MATERIALS • ORGANIZE ART SUPPLIES • ORGANIZE GIFT WRAP AND SEASONAL DECORATIONS • ORGANIZE KIDS' SCHOOLW
OUR WEDDING DRESS AND OTHER TEXTILES • STORE A FUR COAT • STORE BICYCLES AND GEAR • STORE SKI GEAR • ORGANIZE CAMF
HICH COLLEGE IS RIGHT FOR YOU • GET INTO A TOP COLLEGE OR UNIVERSITY • ACE THE COLLEGE ADMISSIONS TESTS • ORGANIZE Y
AW SCHOOL • PREPARE FOR THE BAR EXAM • GET A DEGREE WHILE YOU'RE WORKING • WORK AT HOME WITH KIDS • GO BACK TO WC
RGANIZE YOUR JOB SEARCH • PREPARE FOR A CAREER CHANGE • OPEN A RESTAURANT • BECOME A PHYSICIST • BECOME A CONCE
EALITY-SHOW CONCEPT • BECOME A TALK-SHOW HOST • BECOME A PHOTOJOURNALIST • BECOME A MOVIE DIRECTOR • BECOME A F
LING SYSTEM • ORGANIZE YOUR BRIEFCASE • ORGANIZE YOUR DESK • ORGANIZE YOUR WORKDAY • GET A HANDLE ON E-MAIL • ORG
ALARY REVIEW • CLIMB THE CORPORATE LADDER EFFECTIVELY • ADD A WORKSPACE TO ANY ROOM • ORGANIZE A HOME OFFICE • OF
RAVEL • WRITE A BUSINESS PLAN • SET UP A NEW BUSINESS • CREATE A MARKETING PLAN • AMASS A REAL-ESTATE EMPIRE • POLISH
MPLOYEE • FIRE AN EMPLOYEE • PASS ON A FAMILY BUSINESS • STAY ON TOP OF YOUR SALES GAME • RESTRUCTURE A COMPANY TC
EFEND AGAINST A HOSTILE TAKEOVER • ORGANIZE YOUR OFFICE FOR A MOVE • PREPARE YOUR BUSINESS FOR THE UNTHINKABLE • F
REPARE YOUR TAXES • ORGANIZE A LOAN APPLICATION • ORGANIZE IMPORTANT DOCUMENTS • SAVE FOR PRIVATE SCHOOLING • ORG
LUB • TRACK YOUR INVESTMENTS • SURVIVE BANKRUPTCY • PLAN FOR RETIREMENT • PREPARE A PRENUPTIAL AGREEMENT • CREAT
IONEY • PLAN YOUR FAMILY • BUDGET FOR A NEW BABY • ORCHESTRATE THE PERFECT CONCEPTION • PLAN FOR ARTIFICIAL INSEMIN
EAVE • ORDER BABY ANNOUNCEMENTS • ORGANIZE AN INTERNATIONAL ADOPTION • FOSTER A CHILD • ORGANIZE YOUR LIFE AS A NE
OORDINATE A FAMILY CALENDAR • PLAN FAMILY MEETINGS • ORGANIZE HOME SYSTEMS FOR ADD • PREPARE FOR A NEW CAT OR DO
ACK-TO-SCHOOL • WIN THE HOMEWORK WARS • PLAN A FIELD TRIP • PLAN YOUR CHILD'S ACTIVITIES • PLAN YOUR CHILDREN'S SUM
NLINE • ORGANIZE A GENEALOGICAL SEARCH • PREPARE FOR YOUR CHILD'S DEPARTURE FOR COLLEGE • ORGANIZE YOUR EMPTY N
LDERLY PARENTS' CARE • PREPARE FOR THE DEATH OF A SPOUSE • HELP YOUR ELDERLY PARENTS MOVE • ORGANIZE A HOME MEDIC
TORE TRIPS • SET UP ONLINE GROCERY SHOPPING • ORGANIZE RECIPES AND COOKBOOKS • PLAN THEME MENUS • CREATE EFFECT
EFRIGERATOR AND FREEZER • ORGANIZE CUTLERY AND KITCHEN TOOLS • ORGANIZE CUPBOARDS AND DRAWERS • ORGANIZE THE F
UNCHES FOR KIDS • PLAN PARTY FOODS AHEAD • THROW A DINNER PARTY • FINISH DINNER ON TIME • PULL OFF A LAST-MINUTE PAF
LTIMATE WEDDING CHECKLIST • BUDGET FOR A WEDDING • FIND THE PERFECT WEDDING RING • PLAN AN ELOPEMENT • SET UP A BA
IONOR • EXECUTE BEST MAN DUTIES • HIRE A BAND • HIRE A BARTENDER • PLAN A SHOWER • ORGANIZE THE REHEARSAL DINNER •
UCCESSFUL SLUMBER PARTY • PLAN A BAR OR BAT MITZVAH • PLAN A QUINCEAÑERA • PLAN A RETIREMENT PARTY • PLAN A FUNER
IANUKKAH PARTY • ORGANIZE A HOLIDAY CRAFT PARTY • PLAN TO SPEND CHRISTMAS SOLO • PLAN THE PERFECT HOLIDAY GIFT EXC
HE HOLIDAYS • STICK TO YOUR NEW YEAR'S RESOLUTIONS • PLAN THE PERFECT NEW YEAR'S EVE • PLAN A SEDER • PLAN A SPECIA
OOD TREE • ORGANIZE A BICYCLE SCAVENGER HUNT • RUN A SPORTS TOURNAMENT • PUBLICIZE AN EVENT • PLAN AN ORGANIZATIO
LAN A CONCERT IN THE PARK • ORGANIZE AN INTERNATIONAL CONCERT TOUR • ORGANIZE A FILM FESTIVAL • PLAN A FUND-RAISING
BUILD A COMMUNITY PLAY STRUCTURE • THROW A BLOCK PARTY • SET UP A NEIGHBORHOOD WATCH • CREATE AN EVACUATION PL
RGANIZE A PROTEST OR MARCH • FIGHT CITY HALL • ORGANIZE A BOYCOTT • ORGANIZE A CLASS ACTION LAWSUIT • MANAGE GRO
CHOOL IN A THIRD WORLD COUNTRY • PLAN A TRIP • PLAN A TRIP WITH CHILDREN • TRAVEL WITH TEENS • BOOK AIRLINE TICKETS •
IOTORCYCLE TRIP • PLAN A TRAIN TRIP IN THE UNITED STATES • RIDE THE RAILS ABROAD • PREPARE A VACATION COUNTDOWN CHE
UGGAGE • LOAD A BACKPACK PROPERLY • PLAN AN ELDERHOSTEL TRIP • ORGANIZE AN RV VACATION • PLAN A TRIP WITH AGING PA
VIDELY DIFFERENT PEOPLE • PLAN SPRING BREAK • PLAN AN OVERNIGHT GETAWAY WITH YOUR SPOUSE • PLAN A VACATION SEPARA
OLITICALLY UNSTABLE REGION • GET TRAVEL INSURANCE • GET IMMUNIZATIONS FOR TRAVELING • BOOK AN ADVENTURE VACATION
LAN A FISHING TRIP TO ALASKA • PACK FOR A CAMPING TRIP • LEAD A BACKPACK TRIP • HIKE A FAMOUS TRAIL • PLAN A TOUR OF T
NGLISH CANAL TRIP • PLAN A CROSS-COUNTRY AIRPLANE VOYAGE • PLAN THE PERFECT DAY ABROAD • PLAN A VISIT TO THE LOUVF
LAN • PREPARE FOR AN ACT OF GOD • ASSEMBLE EMERGENCY KITS • PREPARE FOR SURGERY • PLAN YOUR RECOVERY • SURVIVE
EING LOST • CONDUCT A SEARCH AND RESCUE OPERATION • PLAN AN INVASION • SURVIVE A POLITICAL COUP • PLAN FOR A TERRO

• SET GOALS • STREAMLINE YOUR MORNING ROUTINE • ORGANIZE A CHORE SCHEDULE FOR KIDS • ORGANIZE YOUR CHORES • NEW
YOUR WORKOUT SCHEDULE • SCHEDULE DOCTOR VISITS • PREPARE FOR COLD AND FLU SEASON • GET A DRASTIC MAKEOVER • ARRA
P • FIND YOUR KEYS • TIDY UP IN MINUTES • CONQUER CLUTTER • ACTUALLY SEE THE BOTTOM OF YOUR PURSE • ORGANIZE YOUR S
CAR MAINTENANCE • ORGANIZE PET SUPPLIES • MANAGE GARBAGE AND RECYCLABLES • PREPARE GRAB 'N' GO ACTIVITY BAGS • KE
NE CLIPPINGS • ORGANIZE YOUR PHOTOS • ARRANGE PHOTOS AND PICTURES • ARRANGE AN ART COLLECTION • END COLLECTION G
ORGANIZE YOUR LAUNDRY CENTER • CREATE A SEWING CENTER • GET READY FOR THE HOUSECLEANER • ORGANIZE CLEANING SUP
WAYS AND MUDROOMS • ORGANIZE A DORM ROOM • ORGANIZE YOUR SCHOOL LOCKER • MAKE YOUR HOME SAFE FOR SMALL CHILD
RE FOR SKYROCKETING ENERGY COSTS • USE FENG SHUI TO ORGANIZE YOUR HOME • DESIGN A NEW HOME WITH FENG SHUI • DESIG
LAN A REMODEL • PLAN A MULTIMEDIA CENTER • TURN A BASEMENT INTO A MEDIA ROOM OR PLAYROOM • ORGANIZE THE ATTIC • OR
UL ESTATE SALE • PLAN A YARD OR GARAGE SALE • PREPARE YOUR HOME FOR SALE • PLAN A MOVE • DOWNSIZE YOUR HOUSE • ORG
ORATE FOR THE SEASONS • PREPARE A VACATION HOME FOR THE OFF-SEASON • PREPARE YOUR HOME FOR NATURE'S WORST • PRE
ARDEN • PLANT A CUT-FLOWER GARDEN • DESIGN A SHADE GARDEN • DESIGN A DRY GARDEN • PLAN FOR A LONG-SEASON CONTAINE
AND PLANT A LAWN • DESIGN A NEW LANDSCAPE • PLAN AN OUTDOOR KITCHEN • DESIGN A DECK OR PATIO • DESIGN A WATER FEAT
S • STORAGE SOLUTIONS FOR ANY ROOM • THE CAPACITY OF A SMALL ROOM • ORGANIZE
WORK • ORGANIZE MOVIES, MUSIC AND O RLOOMS • STORE OUT-OF-SEASON CLOTHES •
T • STORE PAINT AND OTHER HAZARDOUS STORE A BOAT FOR THE WINTER • STORE A CA
APPLICATIONS • PLAN YOUR COURSE OF CH PAPER • GET INTO GRAD SCHOOL • GET INTO
NG ABSENCE • SET UP AN INTERNSHIP • N THE PEACE CORPS • PRODUCE A NEWSLETTER
BECOME A COWBOY • BECOME A BRAIN S ATHOLIC NUN • ORGANIZE AN EXHIBITION • DEVE
ME A STUNT PERSON • BECOME A TOUR G • CONQUER YOUR PAPER PILES • CREATE A FL
TER FILES • SCHEDULE APPOINTMENTS EF NCE CALL • PREPARE FOR A MEETING • PREPARE
E NETWORK • CHOOSE THE BEST PHONE TEM • MAKE A NETWORKING PLAN • PLAN YOUR
TATION SKILLS • PREPARE A SPEECH • PR AN AN IPO • DELEGATE RESPONSIBILITIES • HIRE
OFITS • FORM A BOARD OF DIRECTORS • AN A COMPANY PICNIC • PLAN A COMPANY RETR
AILING BUSINESS • DISMANTLE A BUSINE • DESIGN A SAVINGS PLAN • SIMPLIFY BILL PAYI
ANCIAL-AID PACKAGE • PLAN FOR COLLE E A HEALTH INSURANCE PLAN • START AN INVES
T • MAKE A WILL • EXECUTE A POWER OF S' ESTATE • PLAN YOUR ESTATE • TEACH YOUR K
E FOR AN IN VITRO FERTILIZATION • PREP ATERNITY WARDROBE • SET UP MATERNITY OR P
EPARE FOR CHILDBIRTH • STOCK A DIAPE LEND FAMILIES • CREATE A HOUSEHOLD ORGAN
L YOUR CHILD • SET UP A CARPOOL • S HE BEST ELEMENTARY SCHOOL • ORGANIZE KIDS
R SUMMER CAMP • CHOOSE A SUMMER S R FAMILY COMPUTER USE • PLAN TO KEEP YOUR
BOOMERANG KIDS • PLAN AN AMICABLE EMENTS • ORGANIZE MEDICAL RECORDS • PLAN
ARRANGE HOSPICE CARE • MAKE YOUR ECORDS • PLAN A WEEK OF MENUS • ORGANIZE
STS • COOK AHEAD • DETERMINE THE SH M WAREHOUSE STORES • EFFICIENTLY USE THE

**Travel &
Adventure**

NTLY USE SPACE UNDER THE SINK • STOW UR COUNTER SPACE • COOK FOR ONE • PLAN H
NNER PARTY FOR YOUR BOSS • PLAN DI PARTY • IMPRESS A DATE • PLAN A WEDDING • C
NT PLANNER • HIRE A PHOTOGRAPHER • ACHELORETTE PARTY • PREPARE TO BE THE MAI
YMOON • PLAN A BAPTISM • PLAN A BRIS • THROW A PARTY • PREPARE FOR HOUSE GUESTS • PLAN A CHILD'S BIRTHDAY PARTY • P
D CUSTOM • PLAN AHEAD FOR A LOW-STRESS HOLIDAY • STAY WITHIN A BUDGET THIS CHRISTMAS • PREPARE A HOLIDAY FEAST • TH
ZE GIFT-GIVING IN ADVANCE • STICK TO YOUR DIET DURING THE HOLIDAYS • PLAN A HOLIDAY OPEN HOUSE • REORGANIZE YOUR LIFE
ORGANIZE A HIGH-SCHOOL CLASS REUNION • PLAN A FAMILY REUNION • START A KNITTING CIRCLE • ORGANIZE A BOOK CLUB • SET
HARPEN THE FOCUS OF AN ORGANIZATION • IMPROVE YOUR CHILD'S SCHOOL • PLAN A PROM • ORGANIZE A COMMUNITY THEATER
ZE A PANCAKE BREAKFAST • PLAN A TOY DRIVE • HOLD A BARN RAISING • ORGANIZE A CHARITY WALK OR RUN • BUILD LOW-INCOME
R-REGISTRATION DRIVE • RUN FOR LOCAL OFFICE • ORGANIZE A PETITION • ORGANIZE A RECALL • GET AN INITIATIVE ON THE BALLO
MUNITY • PRESERVE OPEN SPACE • SAVE HISTORIC PROPERTIES AND LANDMARKS • SET UP A NONGOVERNMENTAL ORGANIZATION
E UNITED STATES • RENT A CAR ABROAD • MAKE HOTEL RESERVATIONS • ARRANGE EXECUTIVE ACCOMMODATIONS • PLAN A CRUISE
AN ITINERARY • PACK FOR A TRIP • PACK FOR A BUSINESS TRIP • PACK FOR A WEEK IN ONE CARRY-ON • PACK A DAY BAG • PREVEN
E A SAILING TEAM • PLAN A SAILBOAT CRUISE • PLAN A BICYCLE TRIP WITH A TOUR COMPANY • TRAVEL ABROAD • PLAN A VACATION
OUSE • PLAN A TRIP TO A DIFFERENT CULTURE • FORAGE ABROAD • MAIL PACKAGES BACK TO THE UNITED STATES • PLAN A TRIP TO
ROAD • PLAN A CLIMB OF MOUNT KILIMANJARO • PACK FOR A SAFARI • ORGANIZE A HUNTING TRIP • PACK FOR A FISHING OR HUNT
S • ORGANIZE A BACKCOUNTRY SKI TRIP • ORGANIZE A CAR RALLY • PLAN A WHALE-WATCHING TRIP • PACK FOR A VOYAGE AT SEA
NEY HARBOUR BRIDGE • PLAN A TRIP TO NEW ORLEANS FOR MARDI GRAS • PLAN A DAY AT DISNEYLAND • FORMULATE A FAMILY EM
YOU'RE ALONE • SURVIVE IF YOUR CAR BREAKS DOWN • DEAL WITH AMNESIA • FIGHT AN EBOLA OUTBREAK • FIGHT A FOREST FIRE
CUE A HOSTAGE • OUTSMART PIRATES • DELIVER A BABY • MAKE AN EMERGENCY LANDING • MAKE A JAIL BREAK • BECOME A MOVI

Planning a trip that's great fun and a great deal isn't as easy as the guidebooks and travel services Web sites would have you believe. After all, not everyone gets the best prices, packages and destinations, right? It pays to know how to wade through the glut of guidebooks and online opportunities to put together the best vacation—for you.

Steps

1 Choose a guidebook or Web site that shares your travel philosophy, style and budget to help you plan your getaway. LonelyPlanet.com, Frommers.com, Let's Go Travel Guides (letsgo.com) and Rick Steves' Europe (ricksteves.com) are all good places to look. Start by looking up your home city or another place you know well, and compare the kind of restaurants, hotels and hot spots it suggests with those you frequent.

2 Think out of the box—and into the ship, the train, even the bus. A cruise is a great way to cover a lot of ground and get the flavor of an area if you're visiting it for the first time (see 413 Plan a Cruise). If you want to see the countryside, a train can get you there at a leisurely pace in a seat with a view (see 415 Plan a Train Trip in the United States). And if you're going to a busy city where driving is a nightmare (think Rome, Lisbon, New York City), sign up for a single-day overview tour (see 459 Plan the Perfect Day Abroad).

3 Research your destination online to determine the best way to get there. If you're flying to Los Angeles, for example, and then want to visit Las Vegas, it helps to know in advance that it can be cheaper and easier to rent a car than to fly.

4 Look up area events, celebrations and holidays that occur during your stay. Download maps from city, state and national chambers of commerce (chamber-of-commerce.com or 2chambers.com). If you're planning to spend a quiet vacation in Oaxaca, Mexico, for example, you'll be glad to know that November 2 is *el Día de los Muertos* (Day of the Dead), the biggest celebration of the year. Beer fans heading to Germany might want to shoot for an end of September visit to Munich to join millions of fellow revelers at Oktoberfest. And if you *don't* want to attend the event, find out lodging availability as well as how to avoid traffic and crowds.

5 Book your lodging (see 411 Make Hotel Reservations).

6 Check the U.S. Department of State travel site for the latest warnings (travel.state.gov/travel_warnings.html) and travel advisories as well as passport requirements (state.gov/travel). Review 439 Plan a Trip to a Politically Unstable Region.

7 Find out if you need any shots prior to travel to certain countries, and be aware of any health warnings that may adversely affect your ability to travel to the destination. See 441 Get Immunizations for Traveling.

Tip

Surf online or look through guidebooks to compare prices and package deals. Be prepared to snap up a great deal fast—prices could change while you're checking out other sites.

Who Knew?

Book an international trip online for greater convenience, unless you're working with a U.S.-based tour operator or cruise line. You'll get a printable confirmation of your payment and reservation, and also a confirmed rate in both local currency and U.S. dollars ahead of time. You'll spare yourself the confusion of an expensive conversation, possibly in the middle of the night.

If you're planning a long road trip, rent a bargain-priced or roomier car instead of putting the wear and tear on your own.

Warning

Confirm that the site you are on is the one you think you're on. Many fraudulent sites nab victims by using common misspellings. Also confirm that the booking page is secure—usually the symbol of a padlock appears before you enter your payment information. Don't take chances with your vacation money.

406 | Plan a Trip With Children

Traveling together is one of the most rewarding experiences a family can have. Road-tripping, catching the Big One at the lake and hearing Mom scream on the roller coaster all make it worthwhile. Memories are there for the making—get those bags packed!

Steps

1 Choose a kid-friendly destination. Any cruise or resort will likely trump a big-city visit if you've got a child under the age of 5. Most cruise ships and some hotels offer camplike programs.

2 Consider the perils of jet lag on long-distance vacations. If you don't know how your child reacts to significant time changes, factor this into your choice of destination. He or she (and you) may be up all night and sleepy all day for the first half of the trip. Instead of wasting the vacation, take a shorter jaunt closer to home.

3 Establish the rules of the road before you even leave the house.

4 Create a boredom survival kit for each child: Action figures, dolls, and plastic or stuffed animals for younger kids; books, drawing supplies and handheld video games for older ones. For a long road trip, borrow books on tape from the library or invest in a portable DVD player (starting at less than $200). Or set kids up with their own CD players and headphones.

5 Take advantage of younger children's sleep patterns. Hit the road early so kids stay asleep for the first few hours. Plan for an easy breakfast break. Or drive late at night if you're not exhausted.

Tips

Be prepared for mobile mop-ups with bottled water, napkins, plastic bags for wet clothing or trash, and wet wipes to wipe down surfaces and people.

Pack the car the night before to avoid a frantic morning.

Klutz.com offers a wealth of travel kits for all ages.

Warnings

Expect the best, but prepare for the worst. Pack a first aid kit, motion-sickness medication, barf bags and a change of clothes for each child.

If you have a different surname than your child, carry a photocopy of the child's birth certificate at all times as evidence of guardianship.

407 | Travel With Teens

Time flies. Soon your high-schoolers will be leaving the nest, and you'll have to work harder to stay connected with their lives. Foster strong bonds now by planning a trip they'll enjoy and remember.

Steps

1 Don't be a trip dictator or the vacation could turn into a disaster. Respect your teen's input and feelings. Involve him or her in the planning stages by downloading maps (Mapquest.com), researching attractions, and creating the game plan (see 418 Prepare an Itinerary).

2 Consider vacationing at a resort or on a cruise that has activities for different age levels, such as Club Med's Teen Clubs (clubmed.com), so your teen can hang out with peers and get a rest from siblings.

3 Allot spending money for each teen, and let them make decisions on which extras to buy. See 248 Teach Your Kids About Money.

Tips

Teens often need more sleep and more calories than adults, so plan accordingly.

Give licensed teens practice driving and reading maps part of the way.

Warning

Allow your teen his or her independence and privacy, but not at the risk of safety. New cities and situations may require new rules.

408 Book Airline Tickets

Booking airline tickets has become an art form. One day too late, or choose the wrong layover, and you're paying hundreds more than you need to. It takes a lot of sleuthing and a bit of finesse to get the seat you want, the price you need and the dates you prefer. Here's how to get from point A to point B—on your own terms.

Steps

1 Start your search at least 21 days ahead of time to take advantage of advance-booking fares. Travel midweek and stay over a Saturday night whenever possible. Stay on your toes: The cheap seats always sell out first.

2 Look for flights on your frequent-flier carrier first and compare its cheapest rate to those on sites such as Priceline.com, Expedia.com and Travelocity.com. Also check out consolidators such as AirTravelCenter.com and auction sites. Many airline Web sites offer lower Internet-only fares.

3 Consider flying through a secondary airport. Orange County and Burbank are alternatives to LAX, and Newark International can substitute for the busier and oft-delayed JFK or LaGuardia airports. You may have to drive further, but if flights are impossible to get or impossibly expensive, you might be surprised by the ease of use and friendlier prices of smaller airports.

4 Request your seat preference (aisle or window) when buying your ticket. You could find yourself with a middle seat if you wait until check-in. SeatGuru.com has detailed maps of the best and worst seats on specific planes, so you can avoid seats that don't recline and keep an eye out for those with extra leg room.

5 Request any special assistance or equipment (such as a wheelchair) for disabled travelers prior to arriving at the airport.

6 Keep the length of the flight, the layovers, the amount of gear you're carrying and the time of day in mind when deciding whether to buy a seat (often discounted) for an infant. Domestic carriers permit you to hold children under 2 years of age on your lap, while international flights require a ticket and a seat for every passenger.

7 Place special meal orders at no extra charge, if they are offered on your flight. For example, United offers diabetic, low fat and low cholesterol, low-calorie, high-fiber, low-protein, low-sodium, kosher and vegan meals. There are also meals for children. These special meals are often tastier than the regular fare.

8 Find out whether tickets are refundable, transferable or changeable (and at what cost) before you buy. Get e-tickets when possible. Having paper tickets mailed usually involves an extra fee, and they're like cash: If you lose them, they're gone.

Tips

Join a frequent-flier program if you haven't yet. Even if you fly on a bunch of different airlines, the miles will eventually add up.

Print boarding passes online usually a day before your flight.

Sign up for e-mail newsletters from airlines to read about cheap fares.

Who Knew?

If you opt to fly with an infant on your lap, bring your car seat on board anyway, head directly to the very back (and most undesirable) row and install the seat next to the window as required by the Federal Aviation Administration (FAA). If the flight is not full, you will be allowed to keep your child in the car seat, which is far more comfortable (and safer) for both of you.

If your favorite airline doesn't go to your destination, ask if it has reciprocity with another airline. For example, United's partner for much of Western Europe is Lufthansa, so miles booked through United on Lufthansa earn you United frequent-flier miles. Northwest has a similar deal with Continental and KLM.

409 | Rent a Car in the United States

The freedom of having a car while you're away from home is liberating—no expensive taxis to take, no bus or train schedules to decipher. Keep your options open when negotiating for the best deal.

Steps

1 Make reservations as soon as your plans are firm. The earlier you book your car, the better your selection of class and price.

2 Shop online. Almost all car rental companies offer Internet-only rates. AAA, AARP or other group memberships may entitle you to an additional discount. Check out name-your-own-price sites such as Priceline.com.

3 Look for a package deal when you book your flight or hotel. These frequently include car rentals at deep discounts.

4 Consider a weekly rate if you are keeping the car for more than five days. Generally the sixth and seventh day end up being free in a weekly rental. Check the rental agency's policy on early returns before changing your itinerary.

5 Determine if you have sufficient insurance coverage to forgo the agency policy. Your credit card or homeowner's insurance may not cover SUVs or luxury cars. If your policy covers you no matter what car you're driving, decline extra coverage. Don't have car insurance? You'll be required to buy it from the rental agency.

6 Gas up on the cheapest no-name fuel you can find before returning the car to avoid being gouged at the company's pump. Or, if you're driving a long way, prepay for the tank and return it empty.

Tips

Don't give up until you're driving away: When you get to the counter, ask if there are any upgrade specials.

Get a discount on the rate and avoid paying common airport surcharges by picking up the car in town rather than at the airport.

Bring both upgrade and discount coupons. If the agency can't honor the upgrade (based on availability), it may still give you the discount.

Some states require car seats for kids up to 6 years old or 60 pounds (in New Jersey, up to 8 or 80 pounds).

If you have a poor driving record, you could be denied a car at pickup. Agencies run driver's license checks.

410 | Rent a Car Abroad

Drive on the other side of the road, pay exorbitant prices for petrol and suffer with no air conditioning and a manual transmission—the train is sounding better already. Still insist on renting a car abroad? Read on.

Steps

1 Make arrangements through a travel agent. By booking and even prepaying in U.S. dollars, you avoid unexpected rate changes and currency fluctuations. Avis and Hertz operate in many countries. Europcar (europcar.co.uk) rents in 118 countries.

2 Nail down your itinerary. Your choice of rental company may depend on whether you intend to hopscotch around countries. A 50 percent surcharge for just crossing a border is not unheard of.

3 Know the extent of your insurance coverage and provide proof. By declining coverage, you may be waiving the agency's recovery service from liable third parties.

Tips

Get an International Driver's Licenses (IDL) from AAA. Valid for one year, the IDL requires a passport-size photo, a nominal fee and a valid driver's license. An International Driving Permit (IDP), written in 10 languages, is officially recognized translation of your driver's license.

Most likely you'll pay extra for air conditioning and automatic transmission.

411 | Make Hotel Reservations

The steepest price a hotel charges is its *rack rate*—the standard price for a room with no discounts. How do you get well below that inflated figure? With package deals, off-season rates and savvy bargaining.

Steps

1 Comparison-shop online. Many hotels offer discounts for online transactions. Sites such as Orbitz.com, HotelDiscounts.com, Hotels.com and Expedia.com have arrangements with thousands of hotels. Name your own price on Priceline.com if your trip dates are set in stone—it offers no refunds.

2 Call the hotel directly during its office hours on a workday. That's when you're most likely to find an agent who knows the best deals and packages—and actually has the clout to give them to you.

3 Ask whether there are special rates or if a membership (AAA, frequent flier) entitles you to a further discount. Sometimes discounts are available for military or government employees, or even for just using a certain credit card. Those are the kind of deals agents won't normally tell you about.

4 Beware of hidden costs. Taxes, surcharges, resort and other incidental fees tacked onto your bill are common and rarely mentioned until you check out. Ask if there are any extra charges on the agreed room rate before you book your reservation: If they are tacked on without your prior approval, refuse to pay.

Tips

Be nice. You're more likely to get what you want—be it a better rate, a suite upgrade or breakfast—if you make a friendly connection.

If the hotel is full, ask for nearby alternatives. Also consider frequent stay programs (i.e., Marriott Rewards) to earn free nights.

If you're traveling with family, ask if a suite is cheaper than adjoining rooms.

Find out the exact date a hotel's off-season rates start.

If your confirmation doesn't specify "late arrival," some hotels will give away rooms after a short grace period, even if they have a deposit. Be sure to ask.

412 | Organize Executive Accommodations

Road warriors know the ins and outs of booking hotels. Many upscale hotels woo lucrative business travelers with premium mattresses, free Internet access and other perks. Take a few tips from their book.

Steps

1 Choose a hotel that's in close proximity to your meeting or client. Ask your client if they have a company discount with the hotel.

2 Use the promise of a long stay (or if you will return often over a period of time), as leverage to ask for extras:

• Negotiate for free breakfast and use of the gym or pool.

• Choose your room and request the same one every time.

• Ask if you can keep a small bag with the bellhop so you won't have to tote items back and forth.

3 Look for hotels with in-room amenities: voice mail availability, two-line speaker phone, fax/printer/copier, ergonomic chair, 24-hour room service, coffeemaker and ironing board.

Tips

Drop off shirts at the cleaners when you leave and pick up when you return.

Many hotels now offer wireless Internet connections in the lobby, but there may still be a charge for in-room connecting.

Join car companies frequent rental programs and take advantage of one-click booking and streamlined pickup, such as at Budget Fastbreak or Hertz Gold.

413 | Plan a Cruise

Few vacations require more decisions prior to leaving home—and fewer to make once you get there. That's because most cruises are all-inclusive affairs—with airfare, stateroom, meals and nightly entertainment all included in the seagoing package. So once you've said bon voyage to your friends, your biggest worry will be whether to have the pool attendant bring you a mai tai, an iced tea or a pillow.

Steps

1 Decide on a destination. Do you want to climb glaciers and kayak in Alaska, dive in the Caribbean or taste wines in France? Or maybe you want to sail across the Atlantic or through the Panama Canal.

2 Select a cruise line that appeals to your budget and lifestyle. These range from the five-star elegance of Crystal Cruises' trio of ships to the raucous booze cruises aboard the Carnival Cruise Line's fleet of Fun Ships. Consider theme cruises where you can meet people with similar lifestyles such as singles, gays and lesbians, or senior groups.

3 Decide how long you'd like to cruise. Some lines offer three-day sailings; others start at seven days and can extend a month or more for around-the-world adventures.

4 Consider essential amenities when making your decision. Do you want to ice skate, rock climb, gamble or relax in a spa? Features vary by ship, though virtually all have a gym, pool, entertainment and dining options ranging from black tie to poolside barbeques.

5 Select a stateroom. Options range from butler-staffed suites to inside staterooms without portholes, and they're priced accordingly. Frequent cruisers regularly get upgrades.

6 Select your ship. Cruise lines are churning out new ships all the time. Do you want to celebrate a new ship's inaugural sailing season, or relax on an older ship whose crew has worked out the inevitable service kinks?

7 Book early. Many cruise lines offer substantial discounts when you book several months or more in advance—and there are always off-peak specials. Check cruise company Web sites for hot Internet-only deals.

8 Make reservations for shore excursions in advance of your ship's departure. Although you can make reservations when you get onboard, many of the popular trips fill up quickly.

Tips

Find a certified travel agent who specializes in cruises. In addition to getting you special deals, they'll also take care of the final details—how you'll get to and from the airport, and requests for dining seating (early or late).

Set a shipboard budget. The price doesn't usually include alcoholic beverages and soda, shore excursions or tips, which average about $10 per day per person.

Check out sites such as CruiseCritic.com for the inside scoop and great bargains.

Who Knew?

Cruise ships have stepped up their efforts to enforce cleanliness and reduce onboard illnesses. Crystal, Holland America and others require hand sterilizing as part of the reboarding regimen at each port stop.

Learn while you're at sea. Many cruises now offer classes in topics from French lessons to Web design to napkin folding.

Going solo? Most big cruise ships have a few single cabins. Check SingleCruises.net for single-cabin and single-occupancy promotions.

414 | Plan a Motorcycle Trip

There's nothing better than being on the open road, the wind in your hair, the scenery rushing by. A little planning goes a long way, whether you're riding a Harley or a Honda.

Steps

1 Learn basic motorcycle repair. You should know how to check the oil and the tire pressure, and adjust the chain. If you don't already have one, buy a repair manual for your bike, available from the dealer or online from TheMotorBookstore.com.

2 Get an adequate tool kit. The kit that comes with most bikes is not high quality. Start with a small socket-wrench set, an adjustable wrench, a spark-plug wrench, a suspension adjustment wrench, a tire gauge, screwdrivers and an Allen wrench set.

3 Know your bike. Find out your gas tank range and how to safely attach luggage. Remember that a heavily loaded bike handles differently than it does without a load. Take test drives to find out how many miles or hours you can ride before you get tired or lose concentration.

4 Get out the maps and start planning. Look for scenic roads with light traffic. Freeways are monotonous—your bike wants to prowl on the back roads. Buy a campground and/or motel directory so you can make reservations while on the road.

5 Set a realistic schedule. For many people, riding more than 300 miles (483 km) per day is too much in terms of both comfort and safety. Make allowances for spontaneous discoveries, unexpected events or foul weather.

6 Discuss the planned route with your travel partner(s). Make sure everyone's goals are included in the itinerary. If you're traveling with other bikes, plan on starting each day with a route briefing: Lay out rest spots, lunch spots and meeting spots. See 418 Prepare an Itinerary.

7 Create your own maps. Use road map software and print a map of your route. Tape this map to the gas tank or clip it to the windshield for quick reference.

8 Outfit yourself with a helmet-to-helmet communication system that allows you to talk with your passenger, a much more effective and less frustrating system than yelling back and forth. This can be wired to your bike or powered by batteries.

9 Be realistic about expected temperatures and dress accordingly. Hypothermia is a real danger on a motorcycle and can affect your judgment and response time on the road. Widder Enterprises (widder.com) has been making electrically heated motorcycle clothing for many years. For hot weather, a hydration pack is a great asset. Shop for one at REI.com and other sites.

Tips

Don't wait until you have the perfect bike; go now! Any bike is capable of taking you on a tour. Motorcycle magazines would have you believe that only the latest, fastest, most complex bikes are worth having. Don't fall for this.

Pack light. Buy food and drinks along the way rather than loading down the bike. Keep clothing and gear to a minimum.

Who Knew?

Consider a more adventurous trip once you gain some experience. Motorcycle rentals are common in Europe, and the Alps feature some of the most spectacular riding in the world.

Go to the manufacturer's Web site for your brand of bike. Print out a list of every dealership address and phone number on your route. If you have a problem on the road, you'll know which dealer to call for help.

Warning

Motorcycle fatalities are on the increase. No matter what your age or experience level, be sure you have proper skills and training. Sign up for a Motorcycle Safety Foundation rider training class at msf-usa.org.

415 | Plan a Train Trip in the United States

Trains offer a magnificent and nostalgic way to get from one place to another. Evoking the glamour of an age gone by, riding the rails lets travelers delight in the trip itself, not just arriving at the destination.

Steps

1 Purchase destination tickets as far in advance as possible for the best prices and the best reserved seats (when available).

2 Check domestic fares at Amtrak.com. Ask about excursion fares, which, if available, can save you nearly half the round-trip fare. Also inquire about special rates for seniors, youths and families.

3 Catch the train from its point of origin (even if another stop is closer). It's often the only way to snag seats for the long haul, especially if you have a group traveling together.

4 Get sleeper reservations for an overnight trip with four or fewer people; the comfort is worth the cost if you can afford it. Otherwise, choose either a six-sleeper or general seating to save you a lot of money (although you may also lose a bit of sleep).

Tips

Check out Amtrak's vacation packages, which combine train travel with hotels and sightseeing tours.

Figure on a three-night journey to travel across the United States—and that's with two train changes and layovers.

Pack a robe; showers are usually down the hall. Keep track of your valuables.

If you're boarding the train late, head to the first car— it usually fills up last.

416 | Ride the Rails Abroad

Trains are the ideal mode of travel in many parts of the world. More comfortable, affordable and convenient than planes for some journeys, train travel is worth exploring. Beautiful scenery, sparkling conversation and the elegant dining car all add to the romance and pleasure.

Steps

1 Look into a world of trains. RailEurope.com offers a variety of European destinations and connections. Check country Web sites for more options: Russia (waytorussia.net), China (china-train-ticket.com), Australia (australianexplorer.com) and Southeast Asia (seat61.com). Take a spectacular journey through South Africa on The Pride of Africa (rovos.co.za)—dubbed the most luxurious train in the world. Or steep yourself in history with a trip on the legendary Orient-Express (orient-express.com).

2 Buy a train pass if you'd like to roam one country or many for a few days or longer. Europe's famous Eurail pass (eurail.com), for example, provides access to 17 countries on a 100,000-mile (161,000 km) network of tracks. With the cost-effective Eurail Selectpass, you can travel to any three bordering countries.

3 Mix train travel with driving. The Eurail Selectpass Drive includes travel by train and car throughout five countries. Rail 'n' Drive passes are for specific areas, such as France, Germany, the United Kingdom, Italy, Scandinavia and Spain, and include VAT (value-added tax) and unlimited mileage.

Who Knew?

Reserve sleeping cars in advance for an extra charge, unless you don't mind sleeping in your seat. If you're traveling overnight and want to meet the morning refreshed, it's worth the investment. Some cars even come with a private bath.

Warning

Eurail passes do not include a sleeper car or high-speed rail (TGV). Additional reservations and payments are required in most cases.

417 | Prepare a Vacation Countdown Checklist

You're finally taking that dream vacation. You've purchased the airline tickets, reserved the hotel room—it's really going to happen. Make sure you leave with everything—and with everything taken care of. You don't want to wake up in your hotel wondering whether you left the oven turned on at home. After you research your destination, use this checklist as you countdown to departure.

COUNTDOWN	WHAT TO DO
T-Minus Three Months or More	• Book your lodging. See 411 Make Hotel Reservations. • Make your flight reservation. See 408 Book Airline Tickets. • Plan your itinerary. See 418 Prepare an Itinerary. • Confirm that your passport is current if you're traveling abroad. If you need to renew it, normal processing time is estimated at six weeks. Apply for visas. Children need a notarized birth certificate for international travel if they don't have a passport yet. See 163 Work Abroad. • Check the Center for Disease Control's Traveler's Health site (www.cdc.gov/travel) to see if inoculations are required for travel. See 441 Get Immunizations for Traveling. • Start getting in shape if you're planning an adventure vacation.
T-Minus Two Months	• Arrange for pet boarding and/or a house sitter. If you are traveling in prime travel season, you may have to make arrangements even earlier.
T-Minus One Month	• Make sure your pet is current with its shots if you are boarding it or taking it with you. Ask your vet for specifics. • If you are divorced or traveling as a solo parent, get a notarized letter from your children's other parent authorizing you to take them out of the country—otherwise airlines may not let you board. • Buy any new clothes, shoes or accessories you'll need. Break in new shoes and make sure walking or climbing gear is comfortable. • Confirm that your health insurance is adequate and current. • Look into travel insurance. There are many low-cost policies available to cover you for the unexpected.
T-Minus Two Weeks	• Tune up the car if this is a road trip. • Hire someone to mow the lawn and water the plants. • Ask a neighbor to check on things, pick up leaflets and collect unexpected deliveries if you haven't hired a house sitter. Give him or her a key, your alarm code and emergency contact numbers. • Set up pet care: provide detailed written instructions for the care and feeding of your animals including the number of the vet and the maximum you'll spend on hospital costs for each animal in case of an emergency. • Get prescriptions refilled.

TIME FRAME	WHAT TO DO
T-Minus One Week	• Arrange travel to the airport (bus, limo, friend) if you aren't driving. • Update luggage tags. • Request a vacation stop of the mail and newspaper. • Alert the alarm company, if you have one, of your pending absence. • Make a list of everything you must take—from clothes to diapers to contact lens cases—and begin assembling things in a staging area or spare room. Replenish your toiletries kit as needed. See 3 Write an Effective To-Do List. • Pick up a good book (or two) for the plane. • Write a letter of instruction for your house sitter. Do a walk-through to make sure he or she knows where the remote is and how to use it, where household supplies are, emergency numbers, alarm code and so on. • Start packing.
T-Minus Two Days	• Get cash or travelers' checks.
T-Minus One Day	• Pay any bills that will come while you're gone. See 229 Simplify Bill Paying. • Pare down your wallet to the bare minimum of cards. • Finish packing. Check the weather at your destination and add any climate-specific garments. • Pack kids' carry-on backpacks with their help. Always put in a few surprise snacks and new toys, and keep a backup supply in your own bag. Also include a change of clothes for the kids. See 406 Plan a Trip with Children. • Set the autoreply message on your e-mail and update your voice message at work. Be sure to take the call-in number and password for your home answering machine so you can access it if necessary. • Purge the fridge of any perishables. • Take out the trash. Tidy up the house. • Water the plants. • Order a shuttle to the airport.
Blastoff!	• Turn the thermostat down to 55 degrees F (13 C) in winter. • Place lights on automatic timers. Close curtains and blinds. Take a final walk through the house. • Double-check that you have tickets, passports, money, driver's license, credit cards, frequent-flier cards, confirmation numbers, airline tickets and medications. • Call the airport to make sure your flight is on time. • If you're not taking your car, leave it in the driveway so it looks like someone's home. • Don't forget the most important thing of all—have a great trip!

418 | Prepare an Itinerary

Spontaneous travel is rarely as fun as it sounds. You arrive late and the hotel is booked. You've planned a museum visit on Wednesday but it's closed. Don't get tripped up: Put a little forethought into your itinerary and get set for smooth sailing.

Steps

1 Identify the number of days you'll have on the ground. Include air travel days so everyone's flight arrivals and departures can be included, and travelers know where to go on the first day.

2 Include the names, addresses, phone and fax numbers of hotels or private homes as well as the time difference (plus 8 hours from Mountain Standard time).

3 Research connecting options in advance. Pay particular attention to potential delays related to airport check-in, travel to and from airports or train stations, car rental, distances between attractions, time differences, unfamiliar roads, and even local traffic conditions at various times during the day.

4 Resist the impulse to overplan. Some destinations don't conform to schedules (ask anyone who's taken a train in India), and you want to stay flexible and be open to spontaneous opportunities. They will arise unexpectedly—a local will take you under his or her wing, or a fellow traveler will suggest a scenic detour.

5 Give a copy to someone at home who is not traveling with you (but is most definitely waiting for that postcard).

Tips

Contact tourism boards at your destination for brochures, coupons or referrals. Keep all pertinent trip information in one file.

Compile a list of flexible tasks to fill spare time while you wait for connections, particularly in Third World countries. Bring a book or magazine as well as bottled water. See 436 Plan a Trip to a Different Culture.

Who Knew?

Plan for jet lag. Nothing can throw a trip faster than nodding off at the big event to which you purchased expensive tickets far in advance.

419 | Pack for a Trip

Packing is not an innate skill. Through trial (more bags than hands) and error (coming home with a suitcase full of never-used items), you'll grow into a good—or at least better—packer.

Steps

1 Use the professional traveler's rule of thumb when choosing luggage: a 22-inch carry-on or backpack for one- to three-day trips; a 24-inch bag for three to seven days; a 26- or 27-inch bag for seven to 14 days; and a 29- or 30-inch case for longer than two weeks. Of course, this will depend on the weather, as wool sweaters take up more room than swim suits and shorts.

2 Devise a color-coordinated wardrobe with pieces that mix and match. Choose two or three color schemes to allow each item in your suitcase to do double duty. Dress in layers so you can adapt to changing temperature. Bring enough underwear for each day of your trip unless you'll be doing laundry.

Tips

Unless you are going to be hauling porcelain figurines, soft-sided luggage is the way to go. It's much lighter than hard-sided luggage and absorbs shock better. Get wheels on large duffels. Ross has great deals on luggage.

Shop sites such as TravelSmith.com for wrinkle-free and easy-to-wash clothing and accessories.

3 Zip zippers and button buttons. Cushion garments inside and out with plastic coverings from the dry-cleaners or fold them in tissue paper as the retail stores do to minimize wrinkling.

4 Roll or fold clothes to fit the suitcase. Start by folding the garment into a large rectangle, and then tightly roll from the bottom up. Fold less wrinkle-prone clothes (pajamas, jeans) and place on the bottom.

5 Create two sections for garments in the order in which you plan to wear the items. Fill corners and edges with shoes (bagged and stuffed with underwear and socks). Top off with delicate items.

6 Pack travel-size toiletries and first aid supplies, including sunscreen, pain relievers and bandages, in zipper-lock plastic bags for easy identification. Place these in zippered or netted areas inside the luggage top or in an outside compartment or pocket.

7 Stash important papers and documents, including passports, tickets and credit cards, in a single closable file or envelope. Bring a money belt to keep your cash and travelers' checks safe while you and your hands are occupied. Photocopy passports (black-and-white copies only—color copies are illegal) and other ID and write down emergency numbers in case of loss or theft, and carry separately from real ones.

Call the hotel prior to leaving home to inquire about items that come with the room (a blow dryer, an iron). Otherwise, pack travel-sized items. If you're heading to Europe or Australia, get the right plug adapter.

Pack a carry-on bag with fragile, expensive or irreplaceable items, including prescription medications and the actual written documents; contact info; and eyeglasses, contact lens solution and case.

Who Knew?

Handy extras include a compact umbrella, digital camera, sewing kit, and collapsible bag to fill with treasures collected along the way.

420 | Pack for a Business Trip

On the road again! If Willie Nelson is singing your personal theme song, you've probably already got your business travel packing down to a science. If not, glean nuggets from these tried-and-true tips.

Steps

1 Keep your standard business travel checklist near the front door, and never forget that cell phone charger again. See 3 Write an Effective To-Do List.

2 Pack a single carry-on or garment bag and a briefcase. Don't waste time waiting for checked luggage. See 421 Pack for a Week in One Carry-On.

3 Buy a wheeled suitcase with a easy-to-access pocket for your laptop for quick trips through security.

4 Bring work to do on the plane. Check SeatGuru.com to see if your seat has a power port. If not, pack an extra battery.

Tips

If you're taking your cell phone, computer or digital camera, bring the charger (and an adapter if you're going abroad). Your U.S. cell phone won't work in many countries, which have different phone systems. Buy an international phone card.

Read 412 Arrange Executive Accommodations.

421 | Pack for a Week in One Carry-On

You know the benefits of traveling light—there's less to pack, less to lose, less to lug. Yet boiling down an entire week's wardrobe to fit into a single carry-on requires giving each item serious thought before it actually makes the cut. What you bring will of course be determined by the purpose of your trip, but this will get the ball rolling.

Steps

1 Select two pairs of pants (or skirts) and three shirts or tops (short- and/or long-sleeved according to your destination's weather and the formality of trip), yielding six possible combinations. Stick to basic colors and jazz up with accessories. Add a bathing suit, shorts and a week's worth of underwear and socks. Bring workout gear if you plan to hit the gym.

2 Pack two pairs of shoes that work with all outfits. Wear one on the plane or train along with your jacket.

3 Choose travel-size toiletries or put favorite gels or lotions in small lightweight containers with labels.

4 Use a shoulder bag or backpack to carry daily essentials. See 422 Pack a Day Bag.

Tips

Instead of lugging computer accessories, look for the locations of Internet cafes at your destination before you leave home.

Ship souvenirs home.

Whenever possible, choose synthetic, no-iron, quick-drying garments that you can wash out in a sink with shampoo. See sites such as Orvis.com and TravelSmith.com for some great options.

Check out 420 Pack for a Business Trip.

422 | Pack a Day Bag

You'll be out of the hotel all day, so you've got to take everything you'll need for the next 12 hours of sightseeing. What goes in your day bag? All the essentials—but not enough to weigh you down.

Steps

1 Choose a lightweight, comfortable bag or backpack with several pockets. Put the same items in the same pockets every time so you can grab your camera fast enough to get those great shots.

2 Carry your driver's license, passport, money, credit cards and travelers' checks in a zipper-lock plastic bag, and place in a closable inside compartment. Is your book a must-have? What about pen, notepad, camera, memory cards and cell phone?

3 Check the weather and add a hat, sweater, windbreaker, gloves, scarf or umbrella as necessary. Keep in mind that although fleece is bulky, it's light and will keep you warm even if you get caught in a sudden downpour.

4 Put one-day's medications in a small pillbox. Add lip protection, sunglasses, travel-size bottles of saline solution (if you wear contacts), sunscreen and a tissue pack. Zip it all up in one plastic bag and stash in an outside pocket for easy access.

Tips

Buy bottled water and munchies. They're too heavy to carry all day comfortably.

Have bills and change handy and organized by denomination.

Who Knew?

If your bag lacks pockets, group like items in zipper-lock plastic bags to organize them as well as keep them clean and dry.

Check out the super-light windbreakers that fold into their own tiny pocket at REI.com and other stores.

423 | Prevent Lost Luggage

Check your luggage at the counter and you're at the mercy of the airlines. Although their (permanent) luggage loss rate is only .005 percent, you'll want to ensure that your bags don't visit Paris without you.

Steps

1 Attach permanent leather or plastic tags with your name and phone number to each suitcase and keep them current. Remove old flight destination tags before leaving home.

2 Put your contact info on everything, including glasses cases, cameras and cell phones. If you leave anything on the plane, it's essential that it be identifiable so it can be returned to you.

3 Put a copy of your itinerary in your suitcase. If your bags are found while you're away, they might get home before you do.

4 Make sure the airport tag on your bag matches your final destination. Confirm that luggage tags and the number of checked pieces matches. Keep your tags in a very secure place—they're your receipt and proof in the event of loss.

5 Find a baggage agent immediately if your luggage does not arrive in the claim area. Ask if your bags arrived on an earlier flight. If they are not in the holding area, fill out the forms. Get a phone number to call in case you need to follow up and give them yours. Most airlines will provide basic amenities—toothbrush, toothpaste and razor—while you're waiting for your bag.

Tips

Tag your carry-on bag in case you have to check it at the last minute.

Buy luggage tags with windows and insert your business card. Write the address and phone of your destination on the other side.

Tie a sturdy, brightly colored ribbon around your bag or its handle so no one else takes it by mistake.

Ensure that clasps and zippers are secure.

Warning

If you grab an earlier flight, your bags may not arrive with you.

424 | Load a Backpack Properly

There are as many ways to pack a backpack as there are people who carry them. Many organizational systems tend to break down during heavy use, but a few simple techniques can help.

Steps

1 Pack heavy items as close to your back as possible, not stuffed at the bottom. Put clothes and light items toward the outside.

2 Strap self-contained items like a tent or a sleeping bag to the outside of the pack, but avoid making the pack so wide that you can't swing your arms comfortably. Long straps with buckles are more secure than bungee cords for holding gear in place.

3 Put a garbage bag in your pack if you're preparing for inclement weather, and then load your clothes in the bag. Rain leaks into even the best packs at the seams and zippers.

4 Devote (only) one outside pocket to snacks, water and trash.

5 Put maps, books, a flashlight, sunblock and batteries in the top pocket so you can access them without breaking stride.

Tip

Don't strap items to the outside of your pack if you're checking it on a plane. Even if the airline allows it, your gear might get ripped loose.

Warnings

Avoid overstuffing the pack. Heavy loads can strain and pop zippers and seams.

Be security conscious. It's easy to get into the outside pockets of a pack, even while you're wearing it.

425 | Organize an Elderhostel Trip

You're retired and the kids are gone. You've got plenty of time and enough money, and you can't wait to see the world and meet other like-minded people. Elderhostels offers structured learning and travel programs for people over age 55. The nonprofit organization presents 10,000 programs in 90 countries to roughly 200,000 participants each year. All you have to do is pick the one that suits your fancy.

WHAT TO DO	OPTIONS AND CONSIDERATIONS
Nuts and Bolts	• Visit Elderhostel.org or call toll-free (877) 426-8056 for a free catalog. • Elderhostel programs encompass a broad range of interests and abilities: • Seniors can choose from active programs (bicycling through the Netherlands) to service programs (wildlife research or building affordable housing) to intergenerational programs (fly-fishing with the grandkids). There's even an astronaut-training program. • Elderhostel arranges everything and the fee includes all costs, except for travel to Elderhostels within the United States. • Experts direct the tours and programs at discounted rates. • Accommodations range from ship cabins, country inns and conference centers to retreats, hotels and safari tents. Charges are based on double occupancy. Most rooms have private baths. • Programs can usually accommodate common dietary restrictions (kosher, low-salt and so forth). • You must be at least 55 to attend (except for charter groups or intergenerational programs).
Choose a Destination	• United States and Canada: Travel expenses are not included in the cost, and you must make your own arrangements. • Pick a program that's as close to home as your neighborhood university, or as far away as Thailand or Australia. If you're planning a tour (unless you have unlimited time and resources), confine your tour to one geographic area so you won't waste time and money traveling from place to place. • Sign up for an international trip and a travel coordinator will contact you with flight choices, domestic connections and a range of tour options after your program ends. • International pricing usually includes travel. You will receive a packet of information telling you what you will need for the trip (inoculations, passport and so on).

WHAT TO DO	OPTIONS AND CONSIDERATIONS
Choose a Program to Suit Your Style	• Organize your tour by theme. History buffs can tour Civil War battlefields in Virginia or study history and legends in the Carpathian Mountains. Outdoor enthusiasts can camp in Baja and study gray whales.
	• Create your own program: Groups of 20 to 30 can charter a special seminar for members of any age on any topic. Your extended family could take a tour of Ireland and trace its roots. Or your book club could explore the countryside of the Brontë sisters. Charter programs have all the benefits of regular Elderhostel programs.
	• Since not every participant is at the same level of fitness, each program lists an activity level from 1 (you must be able to do three hours of activity per day) to 4 (you must be able to do six hours of activity per day).
	• Program descriptions in mountainous areas lists the altitude. Generally, you need to be in good health and able to sustain at least three hours of activity per day for a trip in these regions.
Program Lengths	• Elderhostel programs cover a broad range: a two-hour forum at a local college, a two-night tour of Washington, D.C., three nights at the marine science center on California's Catalina Island, a 26-night train trek through China—and all durations in between.
	• Check out Snapshot and Weekender programs for adventures that run only three to five days.
Fees	• Program costs (excluding travel) in the United States and Canada average about $115 per day. Fees for overseas programs usually cover transportation from the United States. All expenses (including gratuities and insurance) are included.
	• Some scholarships are available for domestic programs. Ask.
	• Minimize travel costs by attending programs within driving distance of home.
Registration	• Register online or by phone; a deposit is required. You will receive a packet of materials about the program, including things to read and do to prepare as well as packing lists and travel details. See 405 Plan a Trip and 419 Pack for a Trip.
WARNING	International facilities are not always disabled accessible. Be sure to ask well in advance.

426 | Organize an RV Vacation

People wanting to hit the road in any season for any length of time may find an RV just the ticket. You've got the travel bug, the resources and the inclination: become the master of your universe, with a kitchen and fridge on board, and no longer be a slave to bathroom breaks and fast-food meals. Before you gas up, however, do a few things to ensure that your vacation vision becomes your rolling reality.

Steps

1 Pore over some maps, browse online, and dream out loud with your traveling companion about the places you've always wanted to see. Let a route and game plan start to ferment.

2 Plan an itinerary that covers about 150 miles per day. Stay off freeways and take local roads. Contact RV clubs for help with your itinerary and visit GoRVing.com for tips on where to go on your trip, how to find a campground, how to get ready and fun things to do while you're on the road.

3 Consider what kind of RV you need. Ranging from trailers to state-of-the-art, 40-foot motor homes, there are big differences in price, comfort, mileage and navigability.

4 Rent an RV for a couple of short trips near home first. This not only allows you to practice driving and using it, but also helps you decide whether this model (and RVing all together) is right for your longer trip.

5 Take notes when you're shown how to operate all the equipment (start the generator, use the disposal hookup and so on), and practice. Remember that RVs don't stop on a dime like the mini-van does. Go for a test drive with an RV rental agent, and practice backing up and parking until you feel competent.

6 Discuss the rules of the road—such as who drives, for how long, how often you take breaks, and when you can choose to extend a stay—before you're actually on it.

7 Childproof the RV if you have small kids. Protect the carpet with rugs and the furniture with throws. See 406 Plan a Trip with Children.

8 Don't overload the living compartment—take only what you need. Get a set of both ignition and door keys for each driver.

9 Learn the lingo before you hit the road. Yes, the RV world has its own language—where phrases like *black water* (don't think too long about this dumping task) are as common as *boondocking* (camping in your RV without water or electrical hookups). Since you'll likely be on the road a while, you may as well know how to speak the language—just in case.

10 Leave a copy of your itinerary with friends. Arrange to check in every few days.

Tips

Know how much clearance your RV needs for bridges and overhangs.

Consider caravaning with friends. Everything—including RV travel—is more fun with a buddy or three. No takers? Join an RV tour group until you get comfortable with the equipment.

Who Knew?

Pack a complete set of extra fuses. Don't forget latex gloves for emptying black water.

Make reservations at one of the 16,000 campgrounds in the United States (check KOA.com as well as the U.S. National Forest Campground Guide at forestcamping.com) and try to arrive before nightfall. It can be difficult to hook up in the dark.

Warnings

If you have a trailer RV, no one can be in the trailer while you're towing it.

Pilot lights must be extinguished during fueling.

Your parents always wanted to take you abroad. Now you're both in a position to take yourselves on that dream vacation together at last. The unspoken reality is that this may be the last trip your parents will take, and wrenching emotions can and will be making the journey with you. Most important—be *extremely* flexible.

Steps

1 Choose a mutually agreeable—and manageable—destination. While you may dream about hiking the Swiss Alps, a sea-level favorite like the Caribbean islands might be a better choice for people with physical limitations. Find a lovely place close to home so just getting there isn't overwhelming.

2 Consider any medical restrictions or dietary needs when choosing a region or destination. Get copies of all prescriptions, refill them and keep all drugs in their original containers.

3 Reserve direct flights. Take out travel insurance if you're booking a trip with nonrefundable tickets. See 408 Book Airline Tickets.

4 Reserve any special equipment your parents might need at your destination, such as a wheelchair or oxygen tank. Better yet, call the airlines and hotel in advance and tell them about your situation. Ask: How can I make the trip special for my folks? Upgrades by airlines and hotels are not unheard of.

5 Help them get ready for the trip. Stop their mail and find someone to care for their yard and pets. Shop for what they need.

6 Find out what room arrangements they prefer: Single parents might like sleeping in your room: couples might prefer an adjoining room. Ask for disabled-accessible bathrooms.

7 Persuade any parent with limited independence to let you reserve a wheelchair for them at the airport, even if they don't need one at home. Explain that the airport will be crowded, you'll be juggling bags, and an agent with a wheelchair will zip your party to the head of the security line.

8 Plan an itinerary with your parents help but understand that they may not be able to keep up—no matter how much they want to. Schedule down days after long travel days. Be willing to change plans at the drop of a hat if your parents get fatigued or overwhelmed.

9 Plan leisurely days with very little walking and lots of rest stops. Find ways to avoid standing in lines, such as purchasing museum tickets for reserved entries or show tickets during off times.

10 Take a backpack on every outing, containing medicines, tissues, sweaters, umbrella, purse and wallet—anything they might need during the day. See 422 Pack a Day Bag.

11 Invest in cabs, and find out where the next public bathroom is.

Tips

See 293 Organize a Home Medication Regime.

Bring a night-light to help your parents get around easily in the hotel room.

When booking rooms, packages or tours, ask about senior and AARP discounts.

Check whether your health insurance plan covers travel abroad. See 440 Get Travel Insurance.

Who Knew?

Keep in mind that although the hotel you booked said it was within walking distance of downtown—it may not be walking distance for someone with limited mobility. Ask for specifics.

Warning

Elderly people are often very comfortable in their daily routine and *want* to travel the way they used to but simply can't. You're dealing with someone who may be in denial. Be prepared for consequences.

428 Organize a Sailing Team

Always wanted to enter your sailboat in a race? There are two vital elements to starting a racing career. First, read the latest edition of *Understanding the Racing Rules of Sailing*, by Dave Perry. Second, enter only casual races until you gain experience. Usually you need to have a membership at a yacht club recognized by the race committee.

Steps

1 Contact yacht clubs. Most clubs organize weeknight races designed more for fun than for cutthroat competition. Gather information from the organizers. Be sure you know the course, race time, location and starting signals.

2 Understand your crew needs. In windy conditions, you want to be as close as possible to the maximum allowable crew weight to help balance the boat. A 30-foot (9.1 meter) boat may sail with five to eight crew. Larger boats may have as many as 15 crew members. Most yacht clubs have a bulletin board or Web site listing crew members looking for a race boat. Keep an eye out for idle crew who often hang around the docks before a race.

3 Put one crew member in charge of equipment. This person is responsible for checking the boat and vital gear before and after each race to see if anything is missing or needs repair. Make sure he or she conducts a thorough check of safety gear, rigging, instruments, radio, engine and bilge pump.

4 Assign responsibilities to crew members. On most boats, the primary positions are driver (helmsman), tactician, bowman and mainsail trimmer. Few boats have enough skilled people to fully divide up these duties; the tactician might also be the mainsail trimmer, for example.

5 Convene a team meeting and discuss team goals (see 373 Plan an Organizational Meeting). Sensible captains and crews approach casual races with an attentive but lighthearted attitude. Do your best, and try to stay cool if you run into sail-handling problems or tactical errors.

6 Practice as much as possible in a wide range of sailing conditions, no matter how skilled the crew. Poor communication or clumsy steering can result in dangerous situations for everyone.

7 Discuss and agree on crew hierarchy, a common source of conflict. Few boats have an established chain of command, but all have a tacit hierarchy based on experience, personality and ownership of the boat. These relationships affect performance and safety. Allow for input from all crew members, and be sure the person at the helm can make decisions under pressure.

8 Have the team work on physical fitness. A stronger crew will sail faster. Encourage a daily regimen of sit-ups, push-ups, pull-ups and frequent stretching. See 25 Design Your Workout Schedule.

Tips

Most casual races follow a triangular or oblong course marked by temporary buoys and last only an hour or two.

As a novice racer, don't expect to attract the top people for each position. You'll have to make do with whoever is available.

Keep in mind that a novice sailor who always shows up and practices hard will soon be more valuable than a seasoned veteran who is rarely available.

Be clear about shared expenses and chores. Most owners provide lunch for their crew. Most crew help clean and prep the boat.

Who Knew?

Many boats are afflicted with high-strung captains who like to yell a lot, but no boat has ever sailed faster from yelling.

Boost team morale with hats, shirts or anything fun. Keep the mood positive by being relaxed and supportive.

Warnings

Keep your boat in safe condition. Be sure the rig and hull are sound. Personal floating devices and firefighting equipment should all be aboard and in good shape.

Avoid overloading any one person—few people can competently handle more than two duties.

Do you dream of chucking it all and setting off in a sailboat? For most people, it remains a dream. Enough folks manage it, however, to prove that it can be done, even with children along. The key is to have sufficient experience and knowledge to make it safe and fun.

Steps

1 Get a boat. Even a small one will let you practice sailing and boat-maintenance skills.

2 Make sure you and your family know what to expect from life aboard a boat. No matter how large your vessel, storage, space and fresh water are limited, and refrigeration is limited or nonexistent. Take a test cruise by chartering a boat for a week or two.

3 Take short overnight trips on the boat and gradually increase your exposure to the open ocean. Evaluate your skills and equipment, then prioritize what needs improving. Ask cruising veterans for advice. Most coastal marinas have a few captains with considerable ocean experience who are happy to share their knowledge.

4 Practice boat repair. The boatyard can handle repairs at home, but out at sea, you're the boatyard. Wise skippers know basic repairs for standing rigging, running rigging, the engine, through-hull fittings, Fiberglas, electrical and plumbing systems, and so on.

5 Become competent using ocean safety gear until you become expert—very high frequency (VHF) radio, radar, weather reports, charts, global positioning systems (GPS), life rafts, storm sails, sea anchors, Watermakers (reverse-osmosis desalination system, found at Watermakers.com) and harnesses. Then decide which of these items is essential—a topic of considerable debate among experienced boat owners.

6 Evaluate your boat. Is it large enough and suitable for extended ocean cruising? Will your new gear plus food, water, fuel and spare parts fit comfortably and safely? Most people are happiest with a cruising boat of 37 feet (11.3 meters) or more, but many sailors cruise in smaller boats. Construction quality and seaworthiness should take precedence over size.

7 Pore over charts. The Caribbean is a logical choice for sailors on the Atlantic; Mexico appeals to Pacific sailors. Both have balmy weather, warm water and plentiful harbors.

8 Set a realistic budget based on your preferred lifestyle. If you always anchor in remote spots and avoid flashy towns, you can cruise very cheaply. If you'd rather dock in marinas, occasionally sleep in hotels and eat in restaurants, budget several hundred dollars per day. See 226 Set Up a Budget.

9 Keep your boat in good shape and shop around for insurance. The Boat Owners Association of the United States (boatus.com) offers marine insurance to members.

Tips

There is no perfect boat, despite what some people will tell you. As long as it meets adequate construction and seaworthiness standards, get the boat that appeals to you.

Never buy a boat without hiring a qualified marine surveyor to provide a thorough examination and report. The cost is low compared with the risk.

Read magazines such as *Latitude 38* and literature geared toward cruising sailors. *This Old Boat* by Don Casey is a comprehensive guide to fixing everything on a sailboat.

Who Knew?

Longer boats are usually faster and more comfortable, while smaller boats are easier to handle and can be considerably cheaper to buy and maintain.

You might want to join an organized cruising group such as the Baja Ha-Ha from California to Mexico (departs in October) or the Atlantic Rally for Cruisers (departs from the Canary Islands for the Caribbean in November).

Warnings

It's no one's job to rescue fools from themselves. Make sure you have the necessary skills before you go.

See 480 Outsmart Pirates.

430 | Plan a Bicycle Trip with a Tour Company

Traveling by bicycle combines many of the best elements of transportation. Far faster than hiking, bikes allow you to cover much more ground than you ever could on foot. At the same time, you're moving slowly enough to see and experience things you would never notice in a car. For your first extended trip, sign on with a bicycle tour company to maximize your enjoyment and relaxation.

Steps

1 Take a look at some of the touring companies (see chart) and get an idea of what appeals to you. Are you looking for a cushy cruise with creature comforts (read: hotel, shower) at the end of the day or more of a roughing it kind of experience? Or do you want to really break away and take an international tour?

2 Research possible routes, the general weather and terrain. In mountainous areas, the overall amount of climbing you have to do is more important in terms of exertion than the mileage. Pick an area and a route that interest you and that aren't so challenging that you won't enjoy yourself.

3 Find a company that offers tours in your region of choice.

4 Ask for a list of recommended equipment from the tour company and pay close attention to it. Good-quality riding clothes, rainwear, a helmet, cycle shoes and sunglasses will enhance your enjoyment. On the other hand, pack light. There's no reason to saddle the group with a bunch of stuff you probably won't use.

5 Decide if your current bike is ready for a long trip. A bike shop will be happy to render an opinion. Or rent one of the tour company's bikes. You want proper fit, durability and comfort.

6 Tinker with your bike to make sure it's properly set up. Small adjustments of several millimeters to your seat or handlebars can make a big difference in fit and comfort. Seats can be raised, lowered, tilted or slid fore and aft, as can handlebars. If you're going to use a company bike, know your general bike size and have the pros adjust it for you.

7 Ask if you need to bring your own panniers (saddlebags for carrying gear), if they are provided, or if the van will carry everything.

8 Make sure you're physically prepared. Don't show up without having gotten some serious saddle time under your belt or your enjoyment will be compromised. Ask the company for training guidelines. See 25 Design Your Workout Schedule.

Tips

Most often, the tour price does not include airfare.

Know the tipping customs of any places you plan to visit. You will be responsible for tipping service personnel. Also, it's common to tip your tour staff at the end of an enjoyable trip.

See 489 Win the Tour de France and 142 Store Bicycles and Gear.

Who Knew?

Experienced tour operators typically provide a support van (sag wagon) that carries tools, spare tires, luggage and exhausted riders.

Warnings

Pay attention to the proficiency and difficulty ratings for various tours. This is a good time to remember that you may not still be the animal you surely once were.

Ask the tour operator about road safety and traffic before booking a trip to a foreign country.

Check the daily itinerary for the word transfer, a euphemism for the requisite van, bus or train ride to your next destination. Make sure these transfers are few and brief.

COMPANY	TOURS, SCHEDULES	TRIP LENGTH, COST
VBT (vbt.com)	• VBT (formerly known as Vermont Bicycle Tours) operates primarily in New England and the eastern United States, and less extensively throughout the western United States, Europe, Canada and New Zealand. • Tours run from late spring until early fall. Trips to Hawaii and New Zealand operate in November and December only.	• Trips average a week in length; add-on days possible. Accommodations, local transportation and 70 percent of the meals are included. • Europe: $1,800 to $2,100; North America: $1,100 to $1,500; Hawaii: $1,800; New Zealand: $2,200
Orchid Isle Bicycling (orchidislebicycling.com)	• Operates in the Hawaiian Islands. Features circumnavigation of the Big Island and a tour of the Kona Coast. • Tours operate year-round.	• Trips average a week in length. Accommodations, breakfast, local transportation included. • $1,700 to $2,200
Breaking Away Bicycle Tours (breakingaway.com)	• Specializes in tours of famous cycling routes across France and Italy. While not designed as a race, the focus is experiencing the history and excitement of European cycling competition. Note: no trips are rated for beginners. • May, June and July only.	• Trips average a week in length. Includes high-quality accommodations, breakfast and some dinners, and local transportation. • $2,600 to $2,800 Tour de France trip: $3,900
Canadian Trails Adventure Tours (canadiantrails.com)	• Operates mountain bike tours in the Calgary, Alberta and Whistler, British Columbia areas; road tours throughout Canada. Mountain bike tours more rugged. • July and August.	• Trips average a week in length. Include tents, cooking gear and meals, sleeping pads and local transportation. • $1,100 to $1,200
Backroads Bicycle Tours (backroads.com)	• Offers trips over much of the world, primarily North America, Europe, Central America and Asia. Backroads offers so many choices of destinations and dates that its Web site provides a destination selector page. This is the best way to begin planning your trip. • Year-round. • All levels of cycling ability.	• Length of trip varies by destination and preference. Most packages include high-quality hotel accommodations; a few are camping trips. All include local transportation and most meals. • Europe: $2,900 to $4,000; Asia and Pacific: $2,500 to $4,500; Latin America: $2,500 to $3,600; North America: $1,300 to $3,000

Traveling in foreign countries requires you to make smart decisions on the fly, to stay unruffled in the face of things you don't understand, to find comfort in a situation where every possible thing is foreign in every possible way—and to enjoy it all. Follow this basic road map.

Steps

Before you leave

1 Make reservations at least two to three months in advance during high tourist season. Be aware of hurricane season (late summer and early fall) in the Caribbean. Prices are much friendlier at this time, but expect the unexpected as the trade-off. See 465 Prepare for an Act of God.

2 Look into adding extra medical insurance to your policy if traveling to remote or primitive areas. You might want to tack on evacuation insurance (yes, there is such a thing), which covers the expense of bringing you—or your remains—home in case of a serious injury or illness. Review 440 Get Travel Insurance.

3 Renew your passport if it's not current. Apply for any necessary visas. Go to travel.state.gov/passport_services.html for more specifics.

4 Get required vaccinations two months in advance. Refill prescription drugs and keep them in their original containers. Bring proof of immunizations. (See 441 Get Immunizations for Traveling).

5 Research cash options. Find out if you can use your ATM card, credit card and travelers' checks at your destination. Don't exceed your credit limit on your cards—Americans have been arrested for this. Also know that toll-free numbers do not work from abroad.

6 Don't assume everyone speaks English. Prepare in whatever way you can, whether it's taking a class in the country's language or buying a phrasebook.

7 Clean out your wallet of unnecessary credit cards, Social Security card, library card and other items that could put you at risk for identity theft.

8 Create and carry a personal first aid kit with over-the-counter medications such as ibuprofen; cold, antidiarrhea and antacid medicines, antibiotic ointment plus sunscreen, insect repellent and prescription medications.

9 Make two additional copies of your passport's identification page, your airline tickets, your driver's license, and any credit

Tips

Dress and behave so as to not draw attention. In many countries, your American back-slapping, enthusiastic, cut-to-the-chase mannerisms may be offensive to locals. Learn to be patient, to be quiet, to wait, and not to force things to happen. See 436 Plan a Trip to a Different Culture.

Pay off your credit card balance before you go.

Visit travel.state.gov for up-to the minute specific entry requirements, inoculations or safety information.

Who Knew?

Countries that require sponsors for a visa may also require exit permits.

cards you are bringing. Leave one set with family or friends at home; pack the other separate from your valuables. Do the same with a list of the serial numbers of your travelers checks and cross off the numbers as you cash them.

10 File a travel plan with your family as well as with the local embassy if you are going to a remote or politically unstable area. See 439 Plan a Trip to a Politically Unstable Region.

While you're there

1 Check into your hotel and get to know the concierge. He or she will help you find the local treasures and arrange transportation as well as keep an eye out for you.

2 Have your hotel write its name on a card in the lingua franca for cab drivers.

3 Learn the local words for "help," "police," "food" and "bathroom." You never know when these might come in handy.

4 Wear sunscreen with a SPF above 30, even higher for kids. Wear a T-shirt over your bathing suit.

5 Eat only hot, cooked foods, and avoid ice and tap water, including foods that might have been washed in tap water, such as vegetables and fruits (see 437 Forage Abroad). In hot, dry climates, pack at least 1 gallon of water per day per person.

6 Ask before taking photos of people you don't know or of public or government places. Officials may confiscate your film and/or camera if they think the photos raise a security issue.

7 Research local customs first, particularly when traveling to Islamic countries. Do not bring cigarettes, alcohol, pornography or non-Islamic religious materials into the country. See 436 Plan a Trip to a Different Culture.

8 Take precautions. Tourists are easy targets for pickpockets and other nefarious types. Hide money, identification cards and credit cards in money belts or in a pouch around your neck. If you intend to sleep on a bus or train, use your backpack as a pillow. Don't read maps or guidebooks while standing on street corners.

Warnings

Reckless behavior and drug use in another country can do more than ruin your vacation—it can land you in a foreign jail (or worse).

Use official taxi stands. Cruising cabs could be a front for robbers.

In Africa, do not wade or swim in fresh water because of the risk of schistosomiasis (aka bilharzia or snail fever), a parasitic disease that leads to chronic ill health.

Some Arab countries will not permit entry if you have been to Israel previously.

Minimize the risk of kidnapping or terrorist attacks in unstable countries by scheduling direct flights and avoiding high-risk airports.

432 Plan a Vacation for Wildly Different People

Theoretically, you should be able to do what you want on a vacation. But unless you travel alone, vacations always involve compromise. And if you're traveling with people who have dramatically different interests, even more compromise is necessary. Work together to decide the how, when and where of your trip—and a good time will be had by all.

Steps

1 Check out destinations that offer a variety of options and activities within a short walking or driving distance. For example, if one traveler likes the nightlife and another likes to unwind on remote bike trails, choose a location with proximity to both.

2 Set sail on a cruise, especially if you are traveling with people of different ages and physical abilities. Most ships have children's programs, card and game rooms that appeal to less mobile and/or older travelers, stage shows for the whole gang, and all types of food at all hours of the day. See 413 Plan a Cruise.

3 Look into a packaged vacation such as those offered by Club Med (clubmed.com). These are perfect for large, multigenerational family gatherings because everyone gets to do exactly as they please. Hole up with a book on the beach or play tennis dawn to dusk. Dive, sail, swim, golf or do nothing at all. Everything—booze, towels, entertainment and food—is included.

4 Try to schedule at least one time or meal each day during which you can all gather and catch up. Maybe you've done something the rest of the group might be interested in after all.

Tips

If room sharing is part of the plan, pair early birds or party animals together.

Stay flexible and be willing to change plans occasionally.

Who Knew?

Check out Club Med's Kids Clubs. Your kids (infants to teens) will receive excellent care and have a ball—and you can have a *real* vacation. Put them in all day long or for just a few hours, as you wish.

Warning

Purchase trip insurance in the event of last-minute cancellations. Read 440 Get Travel Insurance.

433 Plan Spring Break

One week in March or April is a highlight of many a hard-working college student's year: the annual rite of spring break. Start planning now—leave it to the last minute and you might miss the good deals.

Steps

1 Get on the horn to your friends. Figure out who's going and how many people you can cram into one hotel room.

2 Decide where to go and how much you have to spend to get there. Most warm weather destinations—Mexico, Jamaica, the Bahamas—require flight reservations, but you can take a road trip to Florida and Texas. Or head to the mountains for a ski trip.

3 Research packages, but watch out for scams and hidden costs, such as booking and resort fees and peak week charges.

4 Budget about $350, in addition to hotel and airfare, for food and activities for the week.

Tips

Travel to Mexico, Jamaica or Bahamas requires a valid passport or a certified birth certificate copy and a valid government-issued photo ID. See 431 Travel Abroad.

Save on expensive hotel food with a prepurchased meal plan, or opt for an all-inclusive resort.

For an alternative spring break, work on a local or international project.

434 | Plan an Overnight Getaway With Your Spouse

What with the job, the kids, the TV and the dog, romance gets lost in life's daily details. A getaway can work wonders for a lethargic love life or a stressed-out spouse. The secret? Plan ahead for spontaneity.

Steps

1 Select a date and hire a sitter. Provide your cell phone number, but with the admonition to call only in case of a dire emergency.

2 Reserve a room at a nearby resort, inn or hotel. After all, the two of you don't want to waste your getaway time in the car. Select a small inn with peaceful surroundings where the service is more personal (that alone could set the mood) and distractions are limited.

3 Ask for a quiet room away from the elevator and busy street.

4 Book dinner reservations at a romantic restaurant. If the hotel's restaurant is good, eat there so you'll just have to stroll back to your room afterward.

5 Make absolutely no plans for the next day. Tell the front desk you'll be checking out late. Then let yourselves sleep in and enjoy breakfast in bed.

6 Set the date for your next escape before you return to reality.

Tips

Do not under any circumstances call the kids. Assume they are alive unless told otherwise. In fact, try not to even talk about them.

Leave relationship hot buttons for another time. To survive life's bumps, you need to pave your marital road with pleasant memories.

Warning

You thought you'd just see how the game's going for a minute? Check what's on the news? No, no, no, no.

435 | Plan a Vacation Separate From Your Spouse

Separate vacations? Isn't that a prelude to divorce? Actually, many therapists say it's an indicator of a long and happy marriage. When you see each other every day, you may fail to see each other at all. Separate vacations help you become your own person again—the one your spouse fell in love with.

Steps

1 Talk to your spouse. A separate vacation is fine, but unless you're aiming for a divorce, it should be a joint decision. If your spouse is adamantly opposed to a night-clubbing weekend with your mostly single friends, don't push it. You both need to be on safe ground to make this getaway an enjoyable one.

2 Travel with a friend. Rediscover what it's like to be one of the girls or guys instead of someone's husband or wife.

3 Take this opportunity to go somewhere your spouse would never go. Revisit long-held dreams and take a walk on the wild side. Read 442 Book an Adventure Vacation.

4 Indulge yourself. Eat and drink what you want when you want.

Tips

If childcare is a problem, consider taking turns: One parent takes care of the kids while the other parent vacations; then you switch.

Call each other. It doesn't have to be every day, but keep the connection alive. You'll both be happier for it.

Warning

Don't do anything to jeopardize your spouse's faith in you.

Travel & Adventure

The world wouldn't be so confusing if everyone would act more like we do, right? Maybe not. The whole point of travel is to experience difference—cultures, regions, landscapes, traditions. As always, the key to having a good time is your attitude. Read 439 Plan a Trip to a Politically Unstable Region, expect a little trouble and confusion and, when things don't seem to be working out, sip a cool drink in the shade for a few minutes until your smile returns.

ISSUE	ACTION
Language	• Take a language course. While learning a new language isn't easy, it will allow you to experience the culture deeply and personally. Consider enrolling in a language-immersion program based your destination. For example, if you want to explore Indonesia, choose one of the many language programs located in the city of Yogyakarta.
Religion	• Learn which religions have the greatest influence over local culture. Keep in mind that this is likely to vary by region even within a country. Awareness of dominant religions will yield insights into culture and history as well as customs. At a minimum, know what constitutes acceptable behavior with regard to areas of worship. You don't want to unwittingly defame the holiest shrine in the land.
	• Men and women are segregated in most Muslim mosques, and non-Muslims may not be allowed in. Many Hindu temples require visitors to wear special robes or sashes. Buddhists require covered knees, shoulders and feet.
Behavior, Dress	• This subject is guaranteed to start a lively debate. Some people feel it's their right to be themselves with regard to public behavior and dress. If you ignore the local customs and laws, you risk offending people and possibly getting arrested. To take an extreme example, in some countries women aren't allowed to drive. You may not feel this is right, but must still understand that when you enter a country, you agree to abide by its laws.
	• Know what is considered proper dress and behavior for any place you plan to visit. Religious sites frequently have different dress standards. Islamic countries usually expect women to remain mostly or even completely covered. Resort areas, with numerous international visitors, may have more lax standards than the rest of the country. But don't expect shorts and T-shirts to be acceptable everywhere. When in doubt, be discreet.
Frustration	• Traveling in a foreign country usually involves some frustration. Many countries take a different approach to time and punctuality than most Americans and Western Europeans are used to. Cultural sites, post offices and restaurants may not always be open, even though their signs say they are. Businesses may close for a national holiday without consulting you first.
	• Keep your schedule light, allowing for setbacks. If things don't work out, be flexible and move on. In many cultures, public displays of anger are absolutely unacceptable. If you arrive in Bali to find that your hotel reservation doesn't exist, yelling at the desk clerk will not only fail to get you results, but will make you appear as an insane person to be steered toward the emergency exit. Take 5 seconds and take a deep breath, then choose to be amused and inquire politely about your options.

437 | Forage Abroad

"When in Rome, do as the Romans do" was said by someone who never suffered from Montezuma's revenge. While the chance of getting sick is a real threat in many areas of the world, with a little common sense, you'll be enjoying every country's delicious and exotic fare.

Steps

1 Boil it, cook it, peel it—or forget it. Commit these simple rules to memory. Eat freshly cooked food and fruit that you peel yourself. Beware of street vendor food, which may have been sitting too long. Say no to raw foods and unpasteurized dairy products.

2 Drink bottled water (that includes brushing your teeth). Avoid tap water, fountain drinks and ice cubes. Beware of salads and thin-skinned fruits, which may have been washed in water. If you're uneasy about the food, choose rice, bread and baked goods, nuts, coffee, tea, sodas and canned foods, which are generally safe.

3 Stay calm if you're offered a nasty local delicacy—chicken feet soup, fried cricket, rancid yak-milk cheese—or risk offending your host. See 436 Plan a Trip to a Different Culture.

4 Take advantage of continental breakfasts offered at hostels and pensions. Many will even give you a bit extra to take with you.

Tips

Most large cities have hotels serving international guests. If you really need a break from the local cuisine, these hotels are likely to have familiar menu options.

Whether water is fit for consumption may differ depending on whether you're in the city or the countryside.

Talk to a doctor about bringing an antidiarrhea medication or antibiotic for severe cases.

Parents, look for signs of dehydration in children. Bring along Pedialyte or other products designed to prevent dehydration.

438 | Mail Packages Back to the United States

Decipher your host country's confusing set of shipping regulations, then factor in U.S. duty, taxes and customs fees. If you can't cram that sucker into your luggage, follow these steps and hope for the best.

Steps

1 Wrap your purchase as carefully as possible to avoid breakage. Write the mailing address on it (include U.S.A.), its contents, the fair retail value and whether the package is for personal use or a gift (which determines the exemption limit).

2 Ship the package via the nearest postal exchange. You'll pay a steep premium if you ship through Federal Express (gofedex.com) and UPS (ups.com). Insure valuable items.

3 Be prepared to pay a duty fee for your package when you return home. The U.S. Postal Service (USPS.gov) sends all foreign mail shipments to the U.S. Customs Service for examination.

4 Keep your receipts. You might need them to solve potential problems with customs. If you feel you've been charged too much duty on a package mailed from abroad, file a protest with the U.S. Customs Service.

Who Knew?

American embassies and consulates cannot forward, accept or hold mail for U.S. citizens abroad.

Some European countries waive the value added tax on items that you ship home.

Shipping wildlife souvenirs can be illegal, and antiques may be considered national treasures. At best you could be detained and fined; at worst, arrested.

Beware: No matter what a foreign postal employee or store owner may tell you, you cannot prepay duty fees.

Whether you have to travel to a politically unstable part of the world for work or you choose to trek through hostile environments for thrills, the key to coming home safely is acknowledging potentially dangerous situations and knowing how to avoid them. Careful planning isn't just smart—it may save your life.

Steps

1 Purchase newly updated guidebooks and get busy on the Internet familiarizing yourself with the local laws and customs. Even something as seemingly benign as taking a Buddha statue out of Thailand—a very politically stable country—could get you in big trouble. Other good resources include travel agents, Web sites and online travel community boards, and the embassies, consulates or tourist bureaus of the countries you plan to visit.

2 Check the current travel warnings issued by the U.S. State Department at travel.state.gov. Warnings advise Americans when and where they should not travel due to hostility or danger and are issued any time a perceived threat targets U.S. citizens as a group. Listen to them. Read the Consular Information Sheet specific to your destination (also at travel.state.gov), which provides details on the location of American embassies and consulates, unusual immigration practices, health conditions, political disturbances, unusual currency and entry regulations and crime, penalties and security information. Watch for public announcements on the same site about terrorist threats or other significant risks to the security of Americans abroad.

3 Apply for all necessary visas and make sure that your passport is valid for at least six months from the day you enter the country. Not having valid travel documents gives local authorities an easy—and valid—reason to detain and fine you.

4 Stay in larger hotels, which tend to have more elaborate security arrangements. Experts recommend booking rooms from the second to seventh floors: high enough to deter easy entry from outside, but low enough for fire equipment to reach.

5 Book nonstop flights whenever possible, since takeoffs and landings are the most dangerous times of a flight. See 408 Book Airline Tickets.

6 Purchase travel insurance and check that the coverage is appropriate. If your own policy doesn't cover you, purchase a short-term health and emergency assistance policy for travelers, that covers emergency medical evacuation.

7 Register at the nearest in-country U.S. embassy or consulate. This will make it easier if you urgently need to be located or evacuated. It will also facilitate the issuance of a new passport should yours be lost or stolen.

Tips

Travelers may obtain up-to-date information on security conditions by calling (888) 407-4747 or (317) 472-2328 (outside the United States and Canada).

Leave copies of all your important documents with someone at home, along with your itinerary, your flight numbers and, particularly, your return date. Tuck an extra set in your luggage.

Access consular information sheets, travel warnings and public announcements by calling the Office of Overseas Citizens Services at (202) 647-5225. Or get them from any of the 13 regional passport agencies; from U.S. embassies and consulates abroad; or by sending a self-addressed stamped envelope, indicating the desired country, to the Office of Overseas Citizens Services, Bureau of Consular Affairs, Room 4811, U.S. Department of State, Washington, D.C. 20520-4818.

Warnings

When you are in a foreign country, you are subject to its laws and are under its jurisdiction, not the protection of the U.S. Constitution.

Do not use short cuts, alleys or poorly lit streets. Try not to travel alone at night. Avoid public demonstrations.

440 | Get Travel Insurance

Travel insurance combines trip-cancellation insurance with 24-hour emergency assistance. It makes sense if you've planned an expensive vacation, but the trick is knowing which policy to buy, if any.

Steps

1 Decide which type of insurance is best suited for your destination (terrorism, emergency medical evacuation). Costs vary widely, depending on age, health, and the cost and length of your trip.

2 Determine whether the following is included in your policy: international medical insurance, emergency medical evacuation (including helicopter transport), accidental death and dismemberment, repatriation of remains and family travel benefits.

3 Have your travel agent buy an insurance plan for you or shop commission-free online. You'll find a wide selection of reputable insurance companies on the Web, including TravelGuard.com and AccessAmerica.com, that can get you a policy in 24 hours.

Tips

Check your existing insurance policies and credit card coverage before you buy travel insurance. You may already be covered.

Find out if your travel insurance provider offers 24-hour hotline service.

Warning

Many foreign doctors and hospitals require cash payments in advance.

441 | Get Immunizations for Traveling

Get only the shots you need before you travel abroad. Visit www.cdc.gov/travel to confirm immunization requirements in your destination country and get updates on outbreaks.

DESTINATION	NECESSARY IMMUNIZATION
Africa	Hepatitis A, hepatitis B, rabies, meningococcal, yellow fever, typhoid, tetanus and measles boosters and one-time polio vaccine.
Mexico, Central and South America	Hepatitis A, hepatitis B, rabies, typhoid, yellow fever (if traveling outside urban areas), tetanus and measles boosters (as needed).
Asia	Hepatitis A, hepatitis B, Japanese encephalitis (if you plan to visit rural areas for four weeks or more or during a known outbreak), rabies, typhoid, tetanus and measles boosters (as needed).
Australia and the South Pacific	Hepatitis A, typhoid (neither required for Australia and New Zealand), rabies, tetanus and measles boosters (as needed).
Indian Subcontinent	Hepatitis A, hepatitis B, Japanese encephalitis (if you plan to visit rural areas for four weeks or more or during a known outbreak), rabies, typhoid, tetanus and measles boosters (as needed) and one-time polio vaccine.
Middle East	Hepatitis A, hepatitis B, meningococcal, yellow fever, rabies, typhoid, tetanus and measles boosters (as needed) and one-time polio vaccine.
Eastern Europe	Hepatitis A, hepatitis B, rabies, typhoid, tetanus and measles boosters (as needed) and one-time polio vaccine.

If you'd rather be rock climbing than rumba-ing, camping than cabana-ing or sailing than sunning, choose a vacation that pushes you more than coddles you. But since an adventure is, by definition, not entirely predictable, it's good to have all of your bases covered.

Steps

1 Decide on your level of adventure and choose a destination. Trips range from Italian bicycle tours (see 430 Plan a Bicycle Trip With a Tour Company) to an Everest expedition. Be realistic about your budget, tolerance for adversity (see step 8), stamina and abilities. If you get in over your head, the trip may become expensive, scary or dangerous.

2 Research the climate. For example, avoid the monsoon season in tropical regions when travel becomes unpredictable.

3 Choose a primary activity such as kayaking, rafting, bicycling, mountain climbing, skiing, sailing, scuba diving or camping. An activity you're familiar with is good, but it's also fun to push yourself and try something new.

4 Consult a travel agent or do your own research. Search the Internet using key phrases such as "climb Denali," "ocean kayaking," "adventure travel for women" and so on.

5 Keep it fun. If your vacation involves a new or physically challenging activity, don't overestimate your ability. Talk to prospective traveling companions about what you hope to accomplish and what your abilities are. For example, if you're trekking in Nepal, make sure the group agrees on the schedule, level of difficulty, desired or necessary amenities and the pace of travel.

6 Create a budget, including extra for unexpected events. Base your budget in part on how much gear you must buy or can rent from the guide company. The hassle and expense of transporting gear on an airplane can make the rental option attractive. Ask yourself whether you expect to use the equipment for future adventures (and how much enjoyment you get out of owning cool gear). See 226 Set Up a Budget.

7 Choose how secluded you want to be. Do you want to be out of touch with the world—no phones, e-mail, radio or TV? Seclusion might mean serenity, but it also means fewer amenities and difficult evacuation in case of trouble.

8 Decide on the level of hardship or deprivation you can sustain. Is there fresh water for washing? What are the bathrooms like? What kind of food will you eat? How are meals prepared and by whom? How brave are the bugs and rodents? While many yearn for a simple life, there are very good reasons for the continued popularity of indoor plumbing, screen doors and pizza delivery.

Tips

Don't try to impress your adventure guide with how much you know. Most groups seem to have one customer who wants to act like a guide. Don't be this person.

There are numerous guide businesses that cater to the current desire for "extreme" sports adventures. Make sure any company you choose is reputable and thoroughly trains all their guides and staff.

See 439 Plan a Trip to a Politically Unstable Region and 444 Plan to Climb Mount Kilimanjaro.

Who Knew?

Look for travel options that fit your lifestyle and interests such as seniors, students or singles. Many adventure companies specialize in trips for specific groups. See 425 Organize an Elderhostel Trip.

Warning

Don't assume travel companies in other countries are subject to safety inspections and regulations. In some countries, there's nothing to stop an unqualified person from acting as a guide. As always, you're responsible for yourself. Use your own judgment about what's safe and what isn't.

443 | Travel the Silk Road

The Silk Road, a vast and ancient network of overland trade routes, spreads over Europe and Asia and passes through numerous present-day countries. Active trading along the route began sometime in the first millennium B.C.E., introduced the luxuries of the East to the Roman Empire and continued until the early Renaissance era. Travel this route today as part of a cultural and historical adventure.

Steps

1 Collect Silk Road literature. Numerous academic and popular works cover this subject, including art histories, anthropological studies, economic investigations and historical novels.

2 Study a map of the region, available online from the Silk Road Project (silkroadproject.org), and choose your route.

3 Read up on the countries that you plan to pass through. Knowledge about the currency, culture, ancient history, current situation and geography will all be helpful and interesting. Use a separate guidebook for each country—those from Lonely Planet Publications (lonelyplanet.com) offer well-rounded information.

4 Pick a method of travel. Determined adventurers might outfit a sturdy vehicle or even a motorcycle. More casual travelers may choose to break the trip into a series of train trips, stopping in the more interesting cities (see ChinaRailTravel.com). Luxurious charter trains also offer all-inclusive tours (try Voyages Jules Verne at vjv.co.uk). Any full-service travel agency can book such a trip; expect to pay several thousand dollars. See 416 Ride the Rails Abroad.

5 Focus on a single country if you want a less involved trip. Many countries are proud of their Silk Road history and promote it as a tourist experience. For example, the Tajikistan Web site (www.tajiktour.tajnet.com) provides contact information for the National Tourism Company as well as basic history and information about the country.

6 Prepare for mountain weather. Many areas of Turkmenistan, Afghanistan and Tajikistan are rugged mountains and subject to severe winter weather. Travel in the summer months if your route crosses any high mountain passes.

7 Use your guidebooks to gauge where you'll find amenities. Large cities are accustomed to travelers and provide a wide range of services. Smaller towns are likely to be less visited by travelers and may offer pleasingly low prices but fewer services.

8 Convert a small amount of currency for each country before you go. You won't need to carry a lot of cash if your ATM card is linked to a global network. Check with your bank.

Who Knew?

If you wanted to pass through the fewest possible countries, your journey would take you through Syria, Iraq, Turkmenistan, Iran, Afghanistan, Tajikistan and China.

The Chinese city of Xian is the old assembly point for huge caravans preparing to make the westward journey. Today the city is home to silk factories as well as famous archaeological sites.

Warning

Read 439 Plan a Trip to a Politically Unstable Region. Given the number of countries along the route and their recent political history, it's likely that a good part of your trip may border on the perilous.

444 | Plan to Climb Mount Kilimanjaro

From its first sightings by outsiders, Mount Kilimanjaro has had a romantic and mysterious appeal. Described by Ernest Hemingway as "wide as all the world, great, high, and unbelievably white in the sun," the famous glaciers that top the African continent's highest mountain (19,340 feet high; 5,895 m) attract many climbers every year. Yet despite its reputation as an "easy" peak to summit, roughly a dozen people die on Kilimanjaro every year.

Steps

1 Plan your trip to Tanzania sooner rather than later: Kilamanjaro's glaciers are melting fast. They've lost 82 percent of their mass since first being measured in 1912—and by all reports, will be gone entirely within 15 years. Find more information on National Geographic's Web site (news.nationalgeographic.com).

2 Decide whether you want to climb all the way to the top, part way up, or take a tour around the base. Most reasonably fit people who take the time to properly acclimatize, are adequately equipped, and carry sufficient food and water may be able to reach the summit. The trip shouldn't be taken lightly: Acute Mountain Sickness (AMS)—pulmonary and cerebral edema—along with hypothermia, kills climbers and porters alike. You may be happy ascending to 15,000 feet (4,572 m) or so, or just enjoy touring the dramatic scenery around Kilimanjaro's base.

3 Research guide companies, most of which operate a variety of tours. It is not possible to climb or tour the area without a guide service, so arrange this in advance. Many guide services can be found on the Internet. Seek out climbers who have been there, and ask lots of questions.

4 Start training at least three months ahead of time. Know how much weight you will be expected to carry on the climb. A good training day would be to complete a 3,000-foot (914 m) vertical ascent while carrying a pack of 25 to 45 pounds (11.3 to 20.4 kg). Try to do this once a week. The more weight and vertical gain the better. Climbing or walking at high elevations will also help. See 25 Design Your Workout Schedule.

5 Keep in mind that your level of fitness bears no relation to your susceptibility to mountain sickness. If you can run 5 miles in 45 minutes, you are probably fit enough to make the climb, but you still need to find out how your body handles the thin air of extreme altitude. Climb to 10,000 feet (3,048 m) at least once

Tips

The guides are there to provide expertise and assistance, but they're not babysitters. Be aware of your limitations and your surroundings, and rely on your own judgment. Then again, if altitude sickness makes a claim on your body, your judgment is one of the first things to go.

Kilimanjaro's rule of thumb: Don't climb fast.

Who Knew?

A pulse-oximeter is a medical device that accurately indicates how well you are adjusting to the altitude by measuring your oxygen saturation. A portable hyperbaric bag (or Gamov bag) is an artificial pressure chamber used in emergency situations to treat AMS if the patient cannot descend fast enough.

For a first-rate interactive presentation of Kilimanjaro's history, culture, geology, resources, fitness guidelines and tour recommendations, visit altrec.com/features /crownofafrica.

Check out the documentary *Kilimanjaro: To the Roof of Africa* (mos.org/kili) and read summit logs by other climbers at Peakware.com.

during your training. Ask your doctor what the symptoms of AMS are and what to do if it strikes you or a climbing companion.

6 Pay close attention to what is included in the guide service. Most offer porters, sleeping quarters, food, water and cooking arrangements on and near the mountain. Expect to pay $800 to $1,000 for the guide and porter service, with additional expenses for plush accommodations such as a fancy lodge at base camp. Find out if park fees are included in the package.

7 Select a route. Most guide companies offer a choice of routes up the mountain. The easiest, Marangu, is heavily traveled and less scenic than others. The more difficult Machame route is also very popular. A reputable guide service will help determine the best route for you based on your fitness and mountaineering experience.

8 Plan your overall schedule. If you're arriving in Africa after a long flight, rest up and go on a safari before heading for the mountain. Some companies will book a comprehensive trip for you, including round-trip airfare, and hotel and safari reservations. See 445 Pack for a Safari.

9 Research the weather. Climate zones on Kilimanjaro range from tropical to arctic. Kilimanjaro can be climbed any month of the year, but the least favorable weather is typically from March through May.

10 Get a detailed list of items you need to bring from the guide service and as well as items they will provide. Comprehensive lists are also found online at sites such as Peakware.com. If you're bringing your own equipment such as tent, sleeping bag or camp stove, make sure that you've taken it for a dry run at extreme altitude, and that all of your gear can handle potentially very rough weather. Mountaineering boots, synthetic thermal underwear, wind- and waterproof-outerwear, glacier sunglasses, a fleece hat and heavily insulated gloves are all essential.

11 Get several maps and study them before you go. The more you know beforehand, the more comfortable you'll be later.

12 Get all necessary vaccinations as directed. Make sure you have adequate health insurance, including medical evacuation, for your trip. See 431 Travel Abroad.

13 Be respectful of the guides and porters, and tip them at the end of the trip. When booking your trip, ask the guide service about tipping policies.

Warnings

People die every year from hypothermia caused by inadequate equipment and AMS. Many of those who die are local Chagga porters who are no more acclimatized than the tourists whose gear they carry on their heads.

The drinking tubes on hydration packs often freeze solid. Bring Nalgene bottles (nalgene-outdoor.com) to carry water as well or you won't have any to drink.

445 | Pack for a Safari

Assembling the gear for a safari could be as much fun as the trip itself. Think about it—every time a sales assistant says, "May I help you?" you can reply, "Why, yes, I'm in need of some safari accoutrements, my good man. Show me your finest items." If you've booked a trip with a tour company, ask for a recommended equipment list. Use the following steps as a general plan.

Steps

1 Research binoculars. You need a high-quality, comfortable pair. Go to a camera or sporting goods store where you can try them out. The viewing power of a given binocular is described using a two-number equation such as 7x35. The first number is the magnification and the second number is the size of the objective (front) lens. Bigger numbers allow for better images. Understand that as magnification increases, the field of view shrinks.

2 Decide on your camera preferences. A large camera with a telephoto lens will get great shots, but is also heavy, delicate and complicated to use. A small camera is easy to carry but may not show animals and scenery well.

3 Purchase mosquito netting (to put around your bed) and bug repellent from a camping supplier.

4 Select versatile clothing, such as lightweight nylon pants, that will keep bugs away and dry quickly. Consider long pants that you can convert to shorts by zipping off the legs.

5 Research your destination's climate. It may be hot during the day but cool at night.

6 Assemble your electronic gear, including cameras, watches, radios and cellular phones, and note all the types of batteries they use. Purchase plenty of spares before you go.

Tips

Guidebooks are an essential item, but also look for history, fiction and travel stories related to your destination. All of these will give you ideas about what to expect and what to look for.

Bring sunblock and a wide-brimmed hat.

Warning

Plan on being responsible for your own safety. If you're from the United States, you're probably used to well-marked dangers. This may not be true in other parts of the world. If your guide says, "Be careful walking around at night," you should probably listen.

446 | Organize a Hunting Trip

There are two kinds of guys in the world—those who go on hunting trips and those who wish they were allowed to go on hunting trips. Truth is, the actual hunting is not the best part—camping out with dangerous weapons is.

Steps

1 Investigate game options. For most areas of the United States, this might mean big game (deer, boar, bear or elk), rabbits or groundhogs, duck or pheasant. Decide what you and your fellow hunters are interested in pursuing.

Tips

Hone your skills. Practice at a shooting range for several weeks before you depart. You'll feel more confident and relaxed.

2 Find out when the hunting season is for the quarry of your choice. Many states have different seasons for different types of weapons. Contact your state's department of fish and game (www.offices.fws.gov/statelinks.html) to find out about all of the applicable regulations.

3 Consider your weapon choices. Some people enjoy hunting with a bow and arrow, while others prefer rifles, shotguns or handguns. Your choice will depend not only on your personal preference but also on your level of experience and skill, intended game, the terrain and local regulations. Be sure your weapon is appropriate and legal. If in doubt, consult a hunting equipment supplier or your state's department of fish and game.

4 Consult with the group about where they'd like to go. In general, more remote spots will have better game and fewer people, but getting there will require more effort and could consume a good deal of your hunting time.

5 Decide if you want to camp or stay in a hotel or lodge, or some of each. Camping allows for more mobility, location changes and solitude but requires more gear and effort. A lodge provides hot meals, warm beds and possibly maps, advice and guides.

6 Put one member of the group in charge of food supplies if you decide to camp. Include snacks and foods that require no preparation. Be sure to have access to or pack in sufficient water. Put another member in charge of getting maps and camping permits if necessary. See 447 Pack for a Fishing or Hunting Trip.

7 Make sure all hunters understand they are responsible for their own personal gear, including clothes, sleeping bag, ammunition, eating utensils, map and compass. Be sure each member of the group has the proper hunting license.

8 Discuss camping arrangements. Confirm that there is tent or camper space for each person. Divvy up responsibility for communal gear such as tents, camp stoves and cook pots.

9 Bring equipment for transporting and preserving game. Large coolers and dry ice are a good idea.

10 Review weapon safety, particularly if there are new members in the group. Everyone should know and observe strict rules about when weapons can be loaded, how they will be transported and where they will be stored in camp.

The happiest hunters are those who enjoy the whole process of getting outdoors. Don't focus exclusively on bagging game or you're bound to be disappointed eventually.

Who Knew?

Consult with a taxidermist before you go. If you bag an impressive animal, it might be worthwhile to have it preserved.

Warnings

Never shoot anything you can't see clearly. Accidents happen every year when hunters mistake a partner for game.

All weapons should be off limits when cocktail hour arrives.

Nothing makes you look more like a rookie than forgetting an important piece of gear on a big trip—and many people are reluctant to loan a prized fishing lure or piece of hunting gear for fear it will get lost or damaged. Start preparing well beforehand to avoid embarrassment. The following list is a starting point for any trip, but you'll want to include gear suited to your exact destination.

Steps

1 Know your itinerary and destination. Leave a detailed description of your itinerary, including a return time, with a responsible person. If you are alone, leave a note in your car explaining who you are, where you're going and when you expect to return.

2 Verify if you'll be hiking or driving to your final destination. If you need a backpack, make sure it is comfortable, large enough for all your gear, and has a large, padded waist belt that transfers some of the load to your hips.

3 Divide your gear into batches that you can store in small nylon bags, available at camping supply stores for a few dollars. Put fishing implements in one bag, cooking equipment in another and so on.

4 Invest in a hard case for your fishing rod or rifle. Available from hunting and fishing supply stores, they cost $200 to $400 for rifle cases and $100 to $200 for fishing rod cases.

5 Assess the maintenance needs of your fishing or hunting equipment. Have a small set of tools for working on your gear, including pliers, screwdriver, oil and cleaning supplies.

6 Check out handheld GPS (global positioning system) receivers at a camping store. Prices start at about $125. These devices are a great way to avoid getting lost, and you can use one to record secret fishing locations. Practice using it before you go. Remember that you still need a map and compass (and knowledge of how to use them).

7 Get good boots if you don't already have them. Purchase a pair at least a week beforehand and wear them for several hours to break them in. They should be water-resistant, have a thick, protective sole and toe, and have a high enough collar to keep dirt and water out. Got waders?

8 Pack extra socks. Medium-weight socks in a wool, synthetic or blend are extremely comfortable and suitable for almost any weather. Spend $10 or $15 per pair and your feet will love you.

9 Plan to dress in layers. Most trips will involve periods of activity followed by stretches of standing around, so you'll need to add

Tips

You don't need to make all your packing decisions at home. If you're unsure, bring extra items and leave them in the car when you get to the trailhead.

Put together a basic safety kit, including a whistle, map, compass, water purification tablets, and matches or lighter. These items will also come in handy if you get lost.

Buy or assemble a first aid kit with small bandages, tape, antiseptic, ibuprofen and any medications you regularly take.

Warning

Make sure your hunting partners understand gun safety. Don't hesitate to ask the group's members about their skills and habits.

and remove insulation. A base layer of long underwear (synthetic fabrics insulate and resist moisture better than cotton), followed by a pants and a sweater or fleece jacket, and topped off with a wind- and waterproof outer layer, is ideal.

448 Plan a Fishing Trip to Alaska

If hauling fish around on a string is your idea of a good time, Alaska is heaven. With salmon clogging the rivers and halibut carpeting the ocean floor, the 49th state has more great fishing than it does flannel-shirted, bearded guys looking for girlfriends.

Steps

1 Decide on what type of fishing you're after. Your choices are many, including fly-fishing, spin casting and various kinds of ocean fishing. Be sure the fish you're after are in season. For more information check with the Sport Fish Division of the Alaska Department of Fish and Game (sf.adfg.state.ak.us).

2 Explore what different areas have to offer. The coast contains more and larger cities offering charter boats for ocean and inlet fishing. Remote inland areas have numerous lakes and rivers with outstanding fly-fishing.

3 Choose a destination. Alaska is vast, with over 570,000 square miles (1,476,293 square km). (You can't cover it all.) Most Alaskans arrange travel on small airplanes. Some areas are accessible only by train.

4 Contact a guide service. There are hundreds available, offering a range of services including air and ground transportation, use of a boat, lodging and access to quality fishing spots. When making choices, weigh your budget against the level of service you want. Consult friends or travel agents for recommendations or do your own research online.

5 Expect rain and moderate temperatures on the coast during the summer. Appropriate clothing, including a wool shirt and durable rainwear, is essential. Inland areas can be warm in the summer and shockingly cold at any other time. Expect vicious mosquitoes and black flies. See 447 Pack for a Fishing or Hunting Trip.

6 Ask your guide about transporting fish home. If you don't have a guide, call the airlines for suggestions. Ask about vacuum-packing, freezing and shipping services.

7 Know your limits. Two halibut per person, any size, daily catch limit. Salmon varies depending on month. Halibut dresses out to 50 percent boneless meat at $6-per-pound market value.

Tips

Bring along a friend to take lots of pictures of you and your record catch.

Pack your gear in a soft bag, which is easier to stow on airplanes and boats.

Warning

Bears! Big, fast bears. Absolutely make sure you know what you're doing before venturing into bear country.

The wilderness can be unforgiving, even with the proper gear. The last thing you want is to reach a remote destination and find that you forgot something essential. Develop a plan to guarantee that you're well equipped.

Steps

1 Establish a staging area. Use a corner of your garage or living room and pile gear there prior to packing. If you have the space, begin moving gear to the staging area several days ahead of time. This prevents overloading your brain at the last minute.

2 Take a good look at your gear pile when you think it's complete. Spend a minute reviewing your checklist (see chart) and check everything on it.

3 Pack your clothing. You want to layer your clothing to meet changing temperatures and conditions. Pack spare clothing in case you get wet. Avoid cotton unless your trip is in a very warm climate—cotton dries slowly and offers no insulation when wet. Synthetic long underwear and jackets are best. Include a warm wool or fleece hat.

4 Test your gear before you go. Know how to operate your camp stove, and bring the proper fuel.

5 Purchase several small and medium nylon bags (stuff sacks) to divide your gear. Cooking gear can go in one bag, first aid items in another bag, and so on.

6 Plan your water supply. If water is scarce, consider having a large water bladder in your pack, such as those made by Camelback. In addition to offering a high capacity, water bladders have a hose that allows you to drink while you're on the move. Water purification tablets are indispensable.

7 Buy a good sleeping pad or two. Many people like to stack a full-length sleeping pad on top of a shorter one. The extra warmth and comfort makes the weight and bulk worthwhile. Camping stores have several brands of pads, from $20 to $100.

8 Plan your meals ahead, so you'll be guaranteed to have enough food. For short camping stints, your grocery list might include milk, butter, cheese and crackers, bread, buns, vegetables, fruit, dried and/or fresh, meat (burgers, hot dogs, shish kabobs), canned foods (chili and soup), condiments and spices, trail mix, energy bars, cookies, s'mores fixings, soda, juice, tea, cocoa, cider, coffee and alcoholic beverages.

9 Use the chart (right) as a general guideline. All of the items on the list are useful, but some are luxuries rather than absolute necessities (for instance, a handheld GPS is fun and helpful, but a map and compass work fine, too). Your specific destination may require additional gear or far less, if weight is an issue.

Tips

Read 424 Load a Backpack Properly.

Have some spare clothing, but resist the urge to bring everything in your closet. Most people don't use all the clothing they bring and regret having to carry it.

Remember to freeze ice packs the night before you leave.

Get a map of your destination. The best backpacking maps are the 7.5-minute series from the United States Geological Survey. These are available from backpacking stores or online at map-mart.com. The highly motivated should buy mapping software like National Geographic's Topo program, available for the United States by state and region.

Purchase a headlamp instead of a flashlight for hands-free convenience (available at REI.com for $20 to $40).

Warning

When you're hiking, stop frequently to look around. Note landmarks and you'll be less likely to get lost. Discuss with the group what to do if someone gets lost. See 474 Survive Being Lost and 475 Conduct a Search-and-Rescue Operation.

ISSUE	BASIC CAMPING CHECKLIST		
Necessities	☐ Day pack	☐ Batteries and bulbs	☐ Pocketknife
	☐ Sunglasses	☐ Battery charger	☐ Rope
	☐ Cloth or duct tape	☐ Camera	☐ Bungee cords, nylon string
	☐ Flashlight or headlamp	☐ Cellular phone, extra battery	☐ Signal whistle
	☐ Waterproof matches, lighter	☐ Weather radio	☐ Mallet or hammer
	☐ Lantern and stand	☐ GPS device	☐ Tarp
	☐ Candles	☐ Compass	☐ Tent, rain fly, poles and stakes
	☐ Water purification tablets	☐ Hiking guidebooks	
	☐ Water supply, canteen or water pack	☐ Maps: roads, park, forest	☐ Sleeping bags
		☐ Cash, driver's license	☐ Scissors
Extras and Entertainment	☐ Tent heater	☐ Whisk broom (for sweeping out tent)	☐ Books
	☐ Sleeping mat, air mattress		☐ Folding card table, chairs
	☐ Inflator or air pump	☐ Hammock	☐ Radio
	☐ Pillow	☐ Board games, deck of cards	☐ Sporting gear
Cooking	☐ Block or bags of ice, ice packs, ice chest	☐ Dish soap and sponge	☐ Zipper lock plastic bags (many)
	☐ Stove, propane or other fuel	☐ Can and bottle opener, corkscrew	☐ Dish towels
	☐ Paper or metal plates, bowls and cups	☐ Spatula	☐ Paper towels (two rolls)
		☐ Knives	☐ Coffeepot
	☐ Plastic or metal utensils	☐ BBQ grill, tongs	☐ Plastic food containers
	☐ Pots and pans (metal)	☐ Storage container with lid	☐ Tablecloth
	☐ Plastic trash bags (several)	☐ Aluminum foil (a roll)	
Fire	☐ Firewood	☐ Kindling, starter sticks	☐ Fire extinguisher
	☐ Campfire permit	☐ Newspaper	☐ Bellows pump
	☐ Shovel	☐ Metal fire ring	☐ Gloves to pick up hot things
	☐ Bucket	☐ Axe or wood saw	
Toiletries	☐ Sunblock	☐ Toothbrush and toothpaste	☐ Towel, washcloth
	☐ Insect repellent	☐ Soap	☐ Shaving kit
	☐ First aid kit	☐ Toilet paper (several rolls in plastic bags)	☐ Nail clippers
	☐ Medications		☐ Glasses, contacts, solution
	☐ Wet wipes	☐ Lip balm	
	☐ Personal items	☐ Tissues	

450 | Lead a Backpack Trip

Your friends must have a lot of faith in you if they choose you to lead them into the wilderness. Squash the drill sergeant fantasy, and take into consideration the needs and wants of the entire group.

Steps

1 Poll the group: Do they want to fish, hike or just read and relax? Groups that want to cover lots of miles might take a long loop trail. Less ambitious groups can set up a single base camp at a beautiful mountain lake and take day hikes.

2 Research potential destinations keeping the abilities of your group in mind. Beginners carrying a moderately heavy pack for 5 miles will have plenty of hiking—and altitude will definitely have an effect as well. Most outdoor stores have a variety of maps and guidebooks for popular areas.

3 Be aware that in the mountains, elevation change (climbing) is more relevant than distance in terms of the effort required. Using a topographical map, add up the distance you will have to climb on your route. For example, if your route traverses three 500-foot tall hills, total climbing for the day is 1,500 feet. Most novices would consider 2,000 feet of elevation change a full day.

4 Review water availability along your route: The more water along the route, the less people have to carry. Campsites must have water access. Purchase a bottle of water purification tablets at a sporting goods store or online at one such as REI.com.

5 Select a destination with the group's input. Use their feedback to make adjustments to your trip plan, making it either more or less ambitious. Let members review your choice with copies of the map and guidebook in hand. The more information they have, the happier they will be.

6 Be sure you have enough tent space for everyone and a way to keep gear out of the rain. If the group is inexperienced, throw an equipment party—one week before the trip, have everyone bring their gear to your house. Practice setting up the tents, packing packs and lighting camp stoves.

7 Review necessary gear. Each person should bring and carry a sleeping bag and pad, eating utensils, headlamp, matches, GPS, whistle, duct tape, knife, compass, map, toilet paper and water. Communal equipment, including tents, stove and pots, food and first-aid gear should be distributed among the group.

8 Leave clear instructions with a responsible person about your route, trip plan and expected return time. Instruct this person to notify authorities promptly if you don't return by a specified time.

9 Check weather reports. If conditions aren't good, postpone the trip unless your group is hardy, seasoned, prepared and game.

Tips

Plan on averaging about 2 miles per hour across hilly terrain, less if the trail is steep or difficult.

Always include destinations (mountaintop, waterfall, lake) in your route and as much scenery as possible. Dense forest is beautiful, but most people want the visual relief of an open vista at some point.

Plan for at least 5 liters of drinking water per day per person, more in hot or humid weather or during strenuous climbs.

Review 449 Pack for a Camping Trip.

Warnings

In the wilderness, expect to be a long way from medical care. Get as much first aid training as possible.

See 474 Survive Being Lost and 475 Conduct a Search and Rescue Operation.

451 | Hike a Famous Trail

The ultimate goal for some hard-core hikers is to walk across the United States on one of the three major trails: the Appalachian Trail, the Continental Divide Trail and the Pacific Crest Trail. Any one of them will provide you with the challenge of a lifetime; all require intense thinking and advance planning. Most people drastically underestimate the commitment that's required.

Steps

1 Read *A Walk in the Woods: Rediscovering America on the Appalachian Trail,* by Bill Bryson. In addition to being entertaining and well written, the story paints a sobering picture of what a 2,000-mile (3,219 km) stroll is like. Hint: He didn't make it. And he was getting paid.

2 Decide if you want to attempt an entire trail in one trip or do short sections over an extended period of time. The Appalachian Trail is almost 2,200 miles (3,541 km) long. At an average speed of 15 miles (24 km) per day, it would take over five months of steady walking. The Pacific Crest Trail is more than 2,600 miles (4,184 km), and the Continental Divide Trail is about 3,100 miles (4,989 km). All traverse mountainous areas and include countless thousands of feet in elevation changes.

3 Read maps and guidebooks to give you an idea about distances between supply points and to scrutinize your route. Pay close attention to elevation changes, and prepare for any weather. Bring warm clothes and rain gear: It can be summer at sea level but winter a few thousand feet up.

4 Plan your daily progress based on elevation change, not strictly distance. Traversing mountains with a heavy pack is slow work. On a day that requires significant elevation gain and loss, your mileage total will be way down. For example, a section of trail that includes a total climb of 5,000 feet (1,524 m) but covers less than 10 miles (16 km) of distance is a full day for most hikers.

5 Set up a physical fitness plan and get in shape. You can wait until you're on the trail and do your training and hiking at the same time, but this guarantees that you'll be tired and miserable at the beginning. Practice carrying a pack and covering miles. Fitness is safety: A fit person thinks more clearly, acts faster and covers more ground in case of emergency.

6 Collect your gear well ahead of time. Be sure your boots are broken in and you have experience using your tent, stove and pack.

7 Collect any necessary permits and be aware of restrictions. These issues are handled on a state or local basis, so permits may be required in some areas but not others. For information on specific trails, check out these Web sites: for the Pacific Crest, Pcta.org; for the Appalachian, www.Appalachiantrail.org; and for the Continental Divide, CDTrail.org.

Tips

Don't get too hung up on daily mileage goals. A steady demeanor and positive attitude are more important than sticking to a rigid plan.

Recognize that you are on your own in the wilderness. While a rescue might be possible, you should plan on taking care of yourself. If you can't accept this reality, don't go. See 474 Survive Being Lost.

Warnings

If you haven't exercised for a while, talk to your doctor before embarking on a long hike.

Be prepared to deal with annoying and dangerous animals, including mosquitoes, bears and snakes. Bug spray is a good idea. A bear-proof container for food is essential in many areas.

452 Arrange a Tour of the National Parks

A surprising number of Americans look overseas when it comes time to travel, forgetting the wealth of domestic attractions. The National Park System contains hundreds of scenic gems that would be one-of-a-kind wonders in many other countries. It's extremely ambitious to try to visit all the National Parks in one continuous trip, but you can certainly plan a route that includes many famous spots.

Steps

1 Research which parks appeal to you and your family. Parks can be divided into two broad categories—scenic and historical. Go to the National Park Service Web site (nps.gov). On the "Info Zone" page, click on "park maps" and find the "National Park System Map and Guide" in the alphabetical list.

2 Chart your course: Focus on a specific region, such as the Southwest, and visit parks that showcase both ancient civilizations and geology at Grand Canyon, Zion, Canyon de Chelly and others. Plan your trip around a historic event such as the Civil War (civilwarweekend.com). Or, follow your passion for a specific landscape and its inhabitants by touring parks that feature dripping rain forests, frozen tundra or wind-carved deserts.

3 Buy seven-day park passes for $5 to $20 per vehicle. Or get a National Parks Pass at nps.gov or by calling (888) GO-PARKS. This admits you to all national parks for one calendar year for $50.

4 Time your trip and activities to coincide with optimal weather conditions for that area. Death Valley in August contains only dead people, people who wish they were dead and a few hardy lizards. Wintertime is ideal for back-country skiers and ice-climbers, and at some parks, it's an ideal season to view wildlife.

5 Keep in mind that all national parks are likely to be packed with visitors during the peak summer and early fall seasons. Avoid major attractions such as Old Faithful and Yosemite Falls during these times if you want a more solitary experience. On the other hand, most parks encompass miles of terrain, offering visitors peaceful seclusion even during peak times.

6 Decide on how much camping vs. hotel time you want. Camping is great, but after a few days in the wilderness, a little room service isn't so bad. Many of the historical sites on the East Coast offer only limited camping options but many hotel options.

7 Choose your lodging (also at nps.gov) and book reservations well in advance. Parks offer a range of options, which vary from rustic to plush, with dining options running the gamut as well. In-park lodging is convenient because you don't have to drive from your motel into the park—and deal with traffic and parking—each day. Campgrounds and hotels outside of parks usually don't fill up as fast as those inside.

Tips

State departments of tourism can also be very helpful in planning your tour.

Go to nps.gov to view a map of the United States showing all of the parks, plus major roads and state boundaries.

Surf each park's Web site for additional information about camping options, lectures, classes and special events, as well as programs tailored especially for kids.

This chart features just a few of the many park options nationwide.

Warning

Follow rangers' instructions *exactly* when in bear territory. Do not keep food, wrappers, gum—even sunscreen and toothpaste—in your car. Ever. Hang food in trees when camping in wilderness areas and use all precautions to reduce the chances of confrontation.

SITE	STATE	POINTS OF INTEREST	TIPS FOR TRAVELERS
Fort Vancouver National Historic Reserve Center	Washington	Headquarters of the Hudson Bay Company's fur trading empire in the 1800s.	Programs and exhibits illustrate the fur trade and the role of Fort Vancouver in the exploration, settlement and development of the Pacific Northwest.
Voyageurs National Park	Minnesota	Water park named after the canoe paddling French-Canadians who plied these waters on the U.S.–Canadian border in the 1800s. Features some of the world's oldest exposed, glacially carved rock formations.	All campsites and many trails are accessible only by boat. Open year-round, with snow-mobiling, ice fishing and cross-country skiing in the winter.
Assateague Island National Seashore	Maryland, Virginia	Bands of wild horses roam this barrier island at the Atlantic Ocean's edge. Intriguing adaptations by plants and animals.	Wildlife viewing, swimming, fishing, other water sports. Watch for mosquitoes in the summertime.
Antietam National Battlefield	Maryland	Site of the first Northern invasion by Confederate forces in the Civil War. Resulted in the bloodiest single day in American history with 23,000 soldiers wounded or killed.	Self-guided driving tour, 8.5 miles long with 11 stops. Audio guides available. A 26-minute movie recreating the battle begins on the hour.
Big Bend National Park	Texas	Largest protected area of Chihuahuan Desert topography and ecology in the U.S. Serves as part of the boundary between the U.S. and Mexico. Spectacular canyons along the Rio Grande; rich cultural and historical landscape.	Extreme climate fluctuations: dry, hot weather in late spring; early summer days often exceeds 100 degrees F (38 C); occasionally winter temperatures drop below freezing.
Canyon de Chelly National Monument	Arizona	Sheer red sandstone cliffs house the caves and ruins of Indian villages built between AD 350 and 1300.	Programs and exhibits explore the lives of the earliest basket makers to the Navajo residents.
Carlsbad Caverns National Park	New Mexico	Features more than 100 known caves and one of the world's largest underground chambers.	Walking tours offered year-round, many wheelchair accessible. Underground temperature is only 56 degrees F (13 C).

453 | Organize a Backcountry Ski Trip

After years of listening to your ravings about great snow and scenery, your friends have finally agreed to accompany you on a backcountry ski tour. They'll thank you for introducing them to the vast ski experiences beyond the chairlifts and crowds—but only if the trip is fun, comfortable and safe.

Steps

1 Know everyone's skiing ability. When you ski in a group, you must stay on terrain that the least capable skier can handle. Unless your group is fairly large and includes several experienced skiers, breaking into smaller groups along the way is probably not a wise option.

2 Pick a destination. An ideal trip includes beautiful scenery, a pleasant lunch spot and a variety of terrain. If good weather seems likely, open areas with lots of sun are great. If the weather is likely to be stormy, choose a route with some tree coverage.

3 Research your destination carefully. Many outdoor stores have computerized topographical map displays that let you print a map of exactly the spot you're interested in. Be sure you understand how to read topographical depictions of terrain. Check out guidebooks that cover popular areas and include maps as well as written descriptions of quality ski spots.

4 Question members of the group beforehand about their familiarity with the basics of backcountry skiing. In addition to their ski gear, everyone in the group will need climbing skins, food, water and proper clothing. It's a good idea for each person to carry a headlamp, whistle, map, compass, GPS device, knife, first aid kit, matches and duct tape. If you take along beginners, you will need to check their gear, spend time showing them how to use it, and adjust your schedule and expectations accordingly.

5 Understand the route's avalanche risk. Safe travel in avalanche areas requires each member of the group to have a shovel, an avalanche probe and an avalanche beacon. Using this equipment effectively cannot be learned on the spot; repeated practice is essential. Evaluating terrain and snow conditions for avalanche risk also requires training. Many universities and outdoor stores in avalanche-prone regions offer training in avalanche safety.

6 Leave clear notice with a responsible person about your destination and expected return time. Instruct this person to notify authorities if you don't return by a given time. Know when the sun sets, and plan a turnaround time accordingly.

7 Check weather reports before you go. If things don't look good, consider postponing the trip.

Tips

Experienced backcountry skiers do not like to reveal all of their beloved spots. Plan on exploring to find your own favorites.

See 474 Survive Being Lost, 449 Pack for a Camping Trip and 143 Store Ski Gear.

Who Knew?

Make sure there is legal parking at your intended trailhead. You don't want to be parked illegally when the snowplow arrives.

Warning

Skiing and other mountain activities involve risk and require a high level of personal responsibility. Anyone who isn't prepared to accept this responsibility should look for another sport.

Car rallies come in many forms, but most are designed to provide entertainment while testing participants' ability to follow directions. There are both large and small rallies ones held around the world, from Italy's infamous Mille Miglia to local rallies around the United States. Running your own event is not difficult: Start small, keep it simple, and soon you'll be an experienced rallymaster.

Steps

1 Create a plan: Give each competing team, consisting of a driver and a navigator, a set of written instructions to follow a pre-determined course. Teams then drive the course independently, departing at set intervals, and strive to follow the course *exactly*. Scattered throughout the route are checkpoints where teams pick up directions to the next stop or have their times charted. Being late—or early—incurs penalty points.

2 Set up a *TSD*, or time-speed-distance rally, if you want teams to stay on your prescribed course while they drive exactly at the given speed between checkpoints. The winner covers the course and matches speed requirements with the greatest precision and fewest time penalties.

3 Opt for a *gimmick* rally for a low-key, goofy event. At checkpoints teams are given directions designed to test their ability to solve riddles, decipher clues or find obscure items such as the most turkey-shaped signs in a certain area.

4 Get technical with an *economy* rally, where the team with the best gas mileage wins, or a *shortest-distance* rally, where teams travel to marked locations in the fewest miles. Often teams are required to answer questions "What color is the church where Elm meets the railroad tracks?" to prove they made it.

5 Plan the route using a highly detailed map. Avoid congested areas, and keep in mind that highways are typically free zones with no checkpoints. Pick a relaxing spot for the finish, such as a city park or local restaurant, so teams can exchange war stories and vie for bragging rights while you tally the points.

6 Drive the route yourself to mark significant landmarks and check-points. Bring a partner to take detailed notes that will later aid you when writing riddles and cryptic instructions.

7 Write route directions. When you reference significant landmarks, don't explicitly name them. For example, rather than "Turn left at the multiplex theater," try "Roger Ebert gives two thumbs up for 'Left turn to Adventure'!"

8 Go over the course the morning of the rally and post the check-point flags, along with the questions and instructions.

9 Check your stopwatch, recharge your cell phone and hang on to that checkered flag—the rallymaster is ready to roll.

Tips

All rallies have traps, or instructions designed to steer you off-course. But fear not—routes are fail-safe. Even if you fail to stay on course, the rallymaster makes sure you'll still find the checkpoint.

Many cars are equipped with global-positioning systems (GPSs). Decide if these are to be allowed and instruct people to turn them off if they are not.

Checkpoints need to be where drivers can stop easily and safely. They do not, however, need to be staffed provided there is a secure spot to post instructions and questions.

Set the cutoff deadlines. If teams can't make all the checkpoints by a prescribed time, they must proceed directly to the finish line.

Who Knew?

Thomas Bros. Maps (www.thomas.com) is a great source for comprehensive street maps.

Warning

As the rallymaster, you may be liable if anyone gets hurt. Consult your insurance company or lawyer.

455 Plan a Whale-Watching Trip

Few animals are more exciting to see for the first time than whales. Their massive size and usually gentle nature make them unforgettable for many.

Steps

1 Go where the whales are. Some of the best spots are Baja California, Mexico; Cape Cod, Massachusetts; the Northern California coast; Vancouver Island, British Columbia; the Lofoten Islands, Norway; South Africa; and Shikoku, Japan.

2 Check whale migration seasons. On the California coast, for example, gray whales migrate south during the late fall and winter and return north in the spring. Winter provides the best viewing due to the lack of fog. On the east coast, the best viewing is in summer and fall. Some areas are home to whales year-round. Surf online to find the species and location that floats your boat.

3 Research the type of whale you're likely to see. Many species have a distinctive spout pattern and a unique dorsal fin shape. Check to see if any are likely to be traveling with calves. Look for tours that include a whale expert as part of the crew.

4 Check out tour companies. You can get information from any major hotel or tourist agency in a whale-watching area. Expect to pay $30 to $75 per person, depending on amenities and length of trip. Find out where the tour will go and what conditions to expect. It may be sunny and calm in the bay or harbor, but it could be foggy, cold and rough out on the open ocean.

5 Ask about safety: Is the boat equipped with modern navigation and safety gear? Are life jackets available for every passenger? If you're concerned, contact the local Coast Guard station and ask about the company's safety record.

6 Ask about guarantee sightings. Companies can't promise you'll see a whale, but some may be willing to. It doesn't hurt to ask.

7 Bring a camera, binoculars, sunblock, warm clothes and a waterproof layer against rain or spray.

8 Consider whale-watching from land. There are several locations around the country where whales can be seen from prominent points above the ocean. In fact, 94 percent of the world's gray whales swim within a mile of San Francisco's Point Reyes. The cliffs of Hermanus in South Africa are also well known for whale sightings. Keep in mind that rough seas, fog and wind can severely restrict your ability to see whales at a distance.

Tips

Bring two types of photographic film: ASA100 for bright sun and ASA400 for overcast conditions.

Consult your doctor regarding the many types of anti-seasickness treatments. Pharmacies usually carry over-the-counter medications like Dramamine, which can cause drowsiness. Some medications must be taken the night before. Another option is wrist bands.

Warning

Remember that you may encounter the menace of Mother Nature as well as her majesty. One whale-watching group was caught in the middle of an epic battle between a pod of killer whales and gray whales with their calves. The orcas formed a unified front to attack the calves, drove them away from their distraught mothers, then ate them.

456 | Pack for a Voyage at Sea

If you forget to bring an important item on an ocean voyage, you may have little recourse, as the briny deep is remarkably free of convenience stores. Obviously, you should know the duration and destination of your trip and plan accordingly, but the following ideas apply to both long and short excursions.

Steps

1 Know the boat's luggage capacity. If you're going on a small boat, you may not be able to bring everything you want. Ask the captain ahead of time. Larger boats (more than about 60 feet) should be able to stow a reasonable amount of luggage.

2 Make sure you have sufficient supplies of any prescription medications.

3 Bring warm clothing, no matter what the weather is like onshore.

4 Review step 3. Seriously, this is a major problem. When it's 90 degrees F (32 C) at the dock, it can be very hard to imagine dangerously cold temperatures offshore, but that's frequently the case. Bring a sweater (wool or synthetic) and a windproof outer layer. Long pants, a raincoat and a warm hat are also essential.

5 Pack your camera in a water-resistant bag. Anticipate storing film and equipment in damp, saltwater conditions for an extended time. Nikon, Canon, Olympus, Tamrac and many others make camera bags and cases, costing anywhere from $30 to $500.

6 Purchase motion-sickness medication and sunblock. The most common motion-sickness brands are Dramamine and Bonine. Both brands contain the same active ingredient and both come in regular and less-drowsy formulas.

7 Pack several good books. Any long voyage will have plenty of reading time.

8 Bring a sturdy pair of polarized sunglasses, a sunglasses retainer, and a hat for the glare that you can fasten securely to your head. Attach keys to a float.

9 Go to plan B if preparing for the voyage starts to lose its charm. See 413 Plan a Cruise.

Tip

If you like gadgets, consider bringing a GPS (global positioning system) to track your voyage. You can purchase a suitable GPS for $200 to $400 at marine or outdoor supply stores.

Warning

Make sure the boat is safe. If you're unsure, interview the captain ahead of time and inquire about life preservers, communications equipment and crew qualifications.

457 | Plan an English Canal Trip

Looking for a scenic and relaxing way to travel through England? A canal trip might be just the ticket. During the 18th and 19th centuries, Great Britain undertook numerous canal-digging projects as a way to move farm and industrial goods from production centers to markets. Today, the waterways offer a tranquil vacation for friends or family.

Steps

1 Read up on the system's 2,000 miles of waterways. The canals are mostly narrow and usually traverse flat areas (some use locks to raise or lower boats past inclines). Most canal trips pass both towns and countryside.

2 Check out the unique boats. Because the canals are narrow, the boats are also. In fact, the ideal rental is called a *narrow boat,* which is about 7 feet (2 m) wide and up to 70 feet (21 m) in length. Look for a boat with a *cruiser stern,* as these provide the best outdoor lounge space. If you're a beginner, steer clear of boats longer than about 55 feet (17 m).

3 Decide whether you will rent a boat with a captain or without one, taking into account your boat-handling skills. On the calm water of a canal, most people do fine after a little practice. Hire a skipper if you would rather not be responsible for 50 feet (15 m) of steel hull with a mind of its own.

4 Visualize life on board. "Cozy and charming" are boatspeak for limited storage, cramped kitchens and minimal bathroom space. And although many boats are modern and well equipped, life aboard could never be called spacious.

5 Research boat rental agencies online or through a travel agent. Since almost every section of canal has an agency, it makes sense to choose your starting destination first. For example, if you will be based in Oxford, start there to search for agencies.

6 Expect to pay $2,000 to $2,200 during peak periods (late summer and holidays) for a boat that sleeps four to six people. You can find significant savings during slow times.

7 Take a break and stretch your legs. Most canals are bordered by well-maintained paths for walking and cycling. Ask the canal-boat rental agency if bicycles are available to rent nearby and if they are allowed to be stored on deck.

Tips

Take your time and enjoy the countryside. Canal boats travel sedately, not swiftly.

Be sure to get instructions for navigating the many locks on the British canal system. Your rental agent should be able to provide this information.

WaterwaysHolidays.com allows you to book your English canal trip online and isn't tied to any one boat operator. It also offers useful information on canal boating.

Who Knew?

Some operations own a fleet of boats. Others broker privately owned boats. Either type of agency may offer special deals, depending on how busy they are.

Warning

Canal travel is not especially dangerous, but a large boat is capable of serious destruction if things go wrong. Ask for a thorough explanation of liability and insurance before leaving the dock, and make sure your boat has one lifejacket for each person.

Ever dream of flying from sea to shining sea? Once pilots reach a certain level of proficiency, it's natural to start thinking about endless adventures in the wild blue yonder. Making a long-distance flight in a small airplane is really just a series of one-day flights. As long as you don't take short cuts with standard flight procedures, everything should go fine on your journey.

Steps

1 Review the requirements governing cross-country flights and be sure that you and your aircraft meet them. Prerequisites include training in navigation, emergency procedures and knowledge of airport-traffic procedures, among many other things. In addition to your basic flying certificate, you will almost certainly need to have an instrument rating (ability to fly in low-visibility conditions, using only the instruments) in order to fly cross-country safely.

2 Chart your intended course from airport to airport. It is essential that you have your flight plan worked out ahead of time and that you're familiar with each airport. Know the location of alternative landing spots. Use a GPS plotter to enter your course information for the entire trip before you leave home.

3 Set an optimal schedule, but understand that flexibility is key since delays are likely. Small airports may not always have staff available to help with maintenance, and large airports may have crowded flight schedules that can cause problems with takeoff and landing times.

4 Study basic meteorology. Pilots need to be skilled at interpreting the weather patterns around them. Modern weather forecasting is very helpful, but there's no substitute for your own eyes. Call ahead to airports along the way and other planes in the area for up-to-date weather information.

5 Adjust your flight plan as the weather dictates. A reluctance to wait out bad weather is a major contributor to accidents. Don't be overconfident about your ability to handle bad weather. Listen to advice from more experienced people and know when to exercise caution. Sailors have a saying: "The captain with the most time gets the best weather." In other words, if things don't look good, wait an hour or a day until they improve.

6 Learn the technical and performance parameters of your plane. You should know your maximum flying range at various speeds and under different weather conditions, ceiling altitude, rate of climb, and required takeoff and landing distances.

7 Train yourself in basic airplane maintenance. Even if you never actually repair your own plane, this knowledge will help you handle problems as they arise. For example, knowing how the landing gear works could be very handy if it stops retracting.

Tips

Know the optimal season to travel. When is the jet stream most likely to be in a favorable position? When is the risk of hurricanes and tornadoes lowest?

See 491 Learn to Fly and 482 Make an Emergency Landing.

Who Knew?

Be sure you're comfortable flying over unfamiliar territory. New destinations mean that you'll be seeing landmarks and runways for the first time. You won't have any visual clues to guide you to a landing. If your navigation skills aren't honed, you can expect problems.

Warning

Assemble a survival pack. A search and rescue operation can be very fast and effective, but there's still a lot of empty country out there. Pack food, water, a first aid kit and spare clothes. In the event of a forced landing, stay with the aircraft; it's much easier to find than a wandering person. See 466 Assemble Emergency Kits and 474 Survive Being Lost.

459 | Plan the Perfect Day Abroad

Anybody can pay money to join a guided tour, but nothing beats the freedom and satisfaction of planning your own day abroad. Just say no to fixed schedules, bickering couples and tedious group dynamics, and hello to unfettered delight as you reap the rewards of a day designed expressly for you and yours.

Steps

1 Research, research, research. Long before you leave, scour your guidebooks and travel Web sites to find activities, dining destinations and places of exploration that interest you. Online travel community groups such as Frommers.com, Fodors.com and LonelyPlanet.com are excellent sources of "been there, done that" information on thousands of destinations. Check your newspaper's travel section for reader's suggestions; or read online newspapers in your destination country for insider tips.

2 Make a wish list that includes everything you'd like to see and do on your trip. Plot your ideas on a good map, and then break them down into day trips. Keep your group's stamina and style in mind (love to wander through local markets, hate the train, must be able to shop). See 427 Plan a Trip with Aging Parents.

3 Hire a driver for the entire day if the places you want to visit are more than walking distance apart, or you're traveling with people for whom getting around is difficult. In Bangkok, for example, hire your own private tuk-tuk (a sort of oversize three-wheeled golf cart); the driver often doubles as a guide.

4 Stop by the tourist office or ask the hotel concierge for additional maps, guides and advice. Ask about current or ongoing festivals and fairs, art exhibits, cultural performances and special events. They may also offer discounts and tips on getting around.

5 Always ask the locals for travel advice whenever an opportunity presents itself and discover hidden gems you might never have known about. Sometimes the best question to ask is "What's *your* favorite thing to do?"

Tips

See 422 Pack a Day Bag, 431 Travel Abroad, 418 Prepare an Itinerary and 405 Plan a Trip.

If your hotel doesn't offer concierge services, pop into one that does for a little advice on the sly.

Who Knew?

Check with professional organizations for tips on your destination. They can help you plan a day if your passion is architecture, local flora, antiquarian books and so on. See 432 Plan a Vacation for Wildly Different People.

Warnings

The biggest mistake travelers make is cramming too much into a single day. Allow yourself enough time to explore without rushing.

One small blister can ruin your entire vacation, so break in your walking shoes well in advance for a more enjoyable adventure.

460 | Plan a Visit to the Louvre

Putting the Louvre in Paris was poor planning. Is there not enough to see in Paris without the world's most fabulous museum, too? And the Louvre is huge and demanding, so have a solid game plan in place.

Steps

1 Plan your trip carefully. Forget August. Every French person and most of their German, Italian and British relatives are on vacation then and will be in line ahead of you.

Tips

Take an art history course before your trip to Paris.

There is no air-conditioning in the Louvre. Dress accordingly in the summer.

2 Take the Metro. It travels from downtown Paris to the Louvre. Consult your hotel concierge for times and stations.

3 Get advance tickets through TicketNet.com or TicketWeb.com and arrive early in the day for your best chance for a light crowd. Advance ticket holders bypass the long lines at the on-site ticket booths and go straight to the entrance.

4 Obtain a printed museum guide. A bookstore that sells travel literature should have one. Study the guide and identify the items you definitely want to see. Wandering about the museum might be relaxing and rewarding, but you will definitely miss something.

5 Rent an audio player for an low-key guided tour at your pace.

6 Review the major collections. You probably can't see them all, so focus on your favorites, including of course Da Vinci's Mona Lisa. In addition to famous European paintings, there are exhibits of Oriental art, Greek relics, and sculpture. Study as much history and background in advance for a truly memorable visit.

7 Check online (www.louvre.fr/louvrea.htm) to verify which exhibits are open. Different segments of the museum have different schedules, and timing the openings and closings is complicated.

8 Bring a lunch. Food is expensive and most spots will be crowded.

Be sure to express your opinion about the infamous I.M. Pei–designed glass pyramid in the courtyard.

Who Knew?

Practice using your camera indoors without a flash: Hold your camera very still when you take pictures (your shutter speeds will be slow to compensate for the low light). Film rated ASA400 is a good choice.

Buy postcards or reproductions at the Louvre, but save major book purchases for home. Museum stores in the United States carry the same or better material than is available at the Louvre store.

461 | Climb the Sydney Harbour Bridge

Add an unforgettable adventure to your trip to Sydney and scale the Harbour Bridge. Enjoy breathtaking views of one of the world's most beautiful harbors during the day–or the dazzling city lights by night.

Steps

1 Book your BridgeClimb online (bridgeclimb.com) well in advance. Trips fill up quickly, especially in the summer months.

2 Prepare to climb come rain, hail or shine—BridgeClimb operates in all weather. In bad weather, you will be provided with rain gear, gloves and headwear. Night climbers also get a headlamp. The climb—440 feet (134 m) above sea level—takes 3½ hours, including preparation time.

3 Complete a climb simulator to verify that you are comfortable using the ladder and your harness. Participants are attached to a static line on the bridge throughout the climb. The climb may not be suitable for people who are not able to climb a normal ladder or who become breathless walking short distances.

4 Learn about the history of the bridge and facts about the city as a professionally-trained BridgeClimb leader escorts you to the summit.

Tip

Relax in the sun on Bondi Beach following your climb or take a ferry ride for a closer look at the harbor. Visit Sydney.com.au or Visitnsw.com.au for more information on what to do during your stay.

Warning

Watch your alcohol consumption: Every participant is required to take a breath test. If your blood-alcohol limit registers over the legal driving limit of .05, you will not be allowed to climb.

462 Plan a Trip to New Orleans for Mardi Gras

The literal translation of Mardi Gras is *Fat Tuesday*, referring to the revelry that occurs prior to the Christian recognition of Lent, which is marked by acts of restraint. For many travelers, restraint is the last thing on their mind. New Orleans, a party town on the dullest days, goes famously nuts during Mardi Gras.

Steps

1 Schedule your visit around the holiday festivities. Mardi Gras is always the Tuesday before Ash Wednesday. However, nightly events begin two weeks before the actual day.

2 Arrange hotel reservations far in advance. Celebrations center around Bourbon Street in the charming French Quarter. This area may be too close to the action for people who actually want to sleep at night. The Riverwalk area also has many hotel options.

3 Prepare for lots of parades. The Krewes—large groups that organize them—attempt to outdo each other every year with wild costumes, music and much exuberance.

4 Experience the famous New Orleans music. Ask a Mardi Gras veteran what to see and how to get tickets, inquire about package tours that include music tickets, or call some clubs.

5 Arrange a meeting time and place in case you get separated from your travel companions on Bourbon Street.

Tips

Know what you're getting into. Mardi Gras is not a refined celebration set in the tranquil charm of the old South. It's more like a city-wide frat party, with all the drinking, carousing and debauchery that entails.

Check out mardigrasnew orleans.com for scheduling and Mardi Gras history.

Who Knew?

Don't drive to the French Quarter during Mardi Gras. Take public transportation.

Famous clubs include Tipitina's, House of Blues, Maple Leaf Club, Mermaid Lounge and Café Brazil.

463 Plan a Day at Disneyland

The key to enjoying the fun and excitement at Disneyland in Anaheim, California, is to keep the whole family happy and avoid the brutally long lines. Impossible, you say? Not at the Magic Kingdom. Try to schedule your visit midweek or during the winter months, plan ahead, use the FastPass—and dust off your sense of adventure (and humor!).

Steps

General tips

1 Browse around on Disneyland.com a few weeks before your trip. Take advantage of advance-purchase online ticket specials and have tickets held at will-call. If yours is a last-minute trip, arrive 30 minutes before the official opening time and get in line at the entrance gate. Print out a map, surf around and look at options, and start thinking about how you'd like to approach your visit.

2 Decide how long you'll stay. The park can be done in one day, but you'll miss a lot. If you have little kids or if it's crowded, plan a two-day trip (or even three with a Disneyland Hotel package). Avoid summer weekends and major holidays if at all possible.

Tips

Get a two- or three-day pass and see California Adventure (right next door), too.

Pick a meeting spot (like the drawbridge at Cinderella's castle) in case someone gets separated or lost. Having fully charged cellular phones is key when you're supposed to meet someone but are stuck in line.

Hit big rides during the lunch hour when people are eating. Eat at 11 or 2, or bring your own meal and skip the lines altogether.

3 Use a FastPass. Find kiosks at extremely popular rides such as Indiana Jones and Autopia. Slide in your park ticket, and the machine will print out a FastPass with a reservation time slot—11 a.m. to 1 p.m., for example. Come back to the ride anytime between 11 and 1 and blow right past the crowds by jumping into the FastPass line. Often you'll save an hour or more.

4 Sit down with your crew and your map to plan out the best route around the park. Your map also has scheduling details of all the productions, parades, and live entertainment.

5 Grab an early lunch at Frontierland's Blue Bayou, the only full-service restaurant in the park. Nearby (and less expensive) is the French Market Restaurant, a counter-service café. You'll find a wide variety in the $8 to $10 range, with kids' meals for about $5.

6 Give tired legs of all ages a rest by taking a ride on the Disneyland Railroad instead of walking. Or board the Mark Twain Riverboat or the Sailing Ship Columbia in Frontierland for a peaceful cruise. Tom Sawyer's Island is another great getaway.

Going with little kids

1 Set the ground rules: no whining, no fighting, and always keep a grown-up in sight. See 406 Plan a Trip with Children.

2 Pin a note to your child's back with "If I'm lost" written in bold letters. Inside the note, list your cellular number (but no name). If your group includes several children, dress them all in the same color shirt so you can spot them easily in the crowds.

3 Play it by ear with your littler kids. Head for Toon Town, where there's plenty to do even if the lines get too long (and go to Dumbo the Flying Elephant first to miss the crowds). Take a break while your 2- to 7-year-olds watch the Buzz Lightyear Adventure show at the Club Buzz Stage across from Autopia, or the Aladdin show (in Frontierland) next to the Jungle Cruise.

4 Snag a front-row sidewalk seat ahead of time for the Grand Parade at 7 p.m. on Main Street. It's fun for everyone, but an extraordinary treat for kids under 7 who see all their favorite characters—in the flesh.

Going with big kids (and really, really big kids)

1 Head straight to Indiana Jones, Space Mountain and the Matterhorn. If there are hardly any people in line, do any or all of these rides over and over again.

2 Indulge in sentimental favorites like Pirates of the Caribbean and the Haunted House. Pure kitsch—but it's a pirate's life for you.

3 Investigate grown up entertainment at the Courtyard Gallery on Main Street (with fabulous multimedia animation shows) or take yourself shopping: Disneyland has more buying opportunities per square foot than anyone can possibly imagine.

Punctuate long walks across the park with a show now and then so everyone can rest up a bit.

If you have small children (and a two- or three-day pass), consider a midday nap break at the hotel.

Divide and conquer when you have little and big kids.

Warnings

The temperature drops significantly after dark, even in summer, so bring a jacket or sweatshirt for everyone as well as an extra pair of sneakers for the kids. The water rides will soak their shoes, which won't dry by the evening.

Bring your own food if you don't want to drain your wallet completely. The vendors at Disneyland aren't cheap!

The Swiss Family Robinson Treehouse? Gone. They turned it into the cartoon-riddled Tarzan's Treehouse.

ORGANIZE YOUR CONTACTS • GET RID OF WHAT YOU DON'T WANT • SAY NO WITHOUT FEELING GUILTY • BALANCE HOME AND WORK •
GAIN • SCHEDULE TELEVISION WATCHING • DESIGN A HEALTHY LIFESTYLE • PLAN TO AVOID JUNK FOOD • CHOOSE A WEIGHT LOSS PL
MEET AN ONLINE DATE • PLAN THE PERFECT DATE • MASTERMIND A BREAKUP • PLAN YOUR SOCIAL CALENDAR • MEET MR. OR MS. RIG
SORT YOUR SOCK DRAWER • RETURN RENTALS ON TIME • TAKE CONTROL OF YOUR JUNK DRAWER • ORGANIZE THE MEDICINE CABINET
CAR CLEAN AND ORDERLY • DEAL WITH A PACK RAT • SELL STUFF ONLINE • ORGANIZE YOUR BOOKSHELVES • CATEGORIZE NEWSPAPEI
LIVE BETTER THROUGH LABELING • ORGANIZE JEWELRY • PLAN YOUR DREAM KITCHEN • CONQUER YOUR CLOSETS • ORGANIZE THE L
ORGANIZE SPRING CLEANING • KEEP THE FAMILY ROOM ORGANIZED • SET UP A BATHROOM SCHEDULE • ORGANIZE BATHROOMS • ORG
ORGANIZE KIDS' ROOMS • ORGANIZE SPORTS EQUIPMENT • ORGANIZE KIDS' PLAY SPACES • SAFEGUARD YOUR HOME AGAINST ALLERG
HOUSE • USE HOME DESIGN AND PLANNING SOFTWARE • ESTABLISH YOUR HOME'S SPACE PLAN • INCORPORATE UNIVERSAL DESIGN F
THE BASEMENT • ORGANIZE THE GARAGE • ORGANIZE A TOOLBOX • SET UP A WOODSHOP • ORGANIZE YOUR WINE COLLECTION • PLA
STUDIO OR SMALL APARTMENT • MANAGE WARRANTY DOCUMENTS • MANAGE HOME-IMPROVEMENT PAPERWORK • MERGE TWO HOUS
ORGANIC VEGETABLE GARDEN • PLANT A KITCHEN HERB GARDEN • PLAN A BUTTERFLY GARDEN • DESIGN A BIRD GARDEN • DESIGN A
ORGANIZE GARDENING TOOLS • ADD A POTTING BENCH TO A YARD • SCHEDULE FRUIT TREE MAINTENANCE • LAY OUT A SPRINKLER S
DESIGN A GARDEN PATH • SET UP A COMPOST SYSTEM • WINTERIZE PLANTS • SCHEDULE YARD WORK • STORE ANYTHING • STORE BU
AND HOBBY MATERIALS • ORGANIZE ART SUPPLIES • ORGANIZE GIFT WRAP AND SEASONAL DECORATIONS • ORGANIZE KIDS' SCHOOLV
YOUR WEDDING DRESS AND OTHER TEXTILES • STORE A FUR COAT • STORE BICYCLES AND GEAR • STORE SKI GEAR • ORGANIZE CAMI
WHICH COLLEGE IS RIGHT FOR YOU • GET INTO A TOP COLLEGE OR UNIVERSITY • ACE THE COLLEGE ADMISSIONS TESTS • ORGANIZE \
LAW SCHOOL • PREPARE FOR THE BAR EXAM • GET A DEGREE WHILE YOU'RE WORKING • WORK AT HOME WITH KIDS • GO BACK TO WO
ORGANIZE YOUR JOB SEARCH • PREPARE FOR A CAREER CHANGE • OPEN A RESTAURANT • BECOME A PHYSICIST • BECOME A CONCE
REALITY-SHOW CONCEPT • BECOME A TALK-SHOW HOST • BECOME A PHOTOJOURNALIST • BECOME A MOVIE DIRECTOR • BECOME A
FILING SYSTEM • ORGANIZE YOUR BRIEFCASE • ORGANIZE YOUR DESK • ORGANIZE YOUR WORKDAY • GET A HANDLE ON E-MAIL • ORG
SALARY REVIEW • CLIMB THE CORPORATE LADDER EFFECTIVELY • ADD A WORKSPACE TO ANY ROOM • ORGANIZE A HOME OFFICE • OF
TRAVEL • WRITE A BUSINESS PLAN • SET UP A NEW BUSINESS • CREATE A MARKETING PLAN • AMASS A REAL-ESTATE EMPIRE • POLISH
EMPLOYEE • FIRE AN EMPLOYEE • PASS ON A FAMILY BUSINESS • STAY ON TOP OF YOUR SALES GAME • RESTRUCTURE A COMPANY T
DEFEND AGAINST A HOSTILE TAKEOVER • ORGANIZE YOUR OFFICE FOR A MOVE • PREPARE YOUR BUSINESS FOR THE UNTHINKABLE •
PREPARE YOUR TAXES • ORGANIZE A LOAN APPLICATION • ORGANIZE IMPORTANT DOCUMENTS • SAVE FOR PRIVATE SCHOOLING • ORG
CLUB • TRACK YOUR INVESTMENTS • SURVIVE BANKRUPTCY • PLAN FOR RETIREMENT • PREPARE A PRENUPTIAL AGREEMENT • CREAT
MONEY • PLAN YOUR FAMILY • BUDGET FOR A NEW BABY • ORCHESTRATE THE PERFECT CONCEPTION • PLAN FOR ARTIFICIAL INSEMIN
LEAVE • ORDER BABY ANNOUNCEMENTS • ORGANIZE AN INTERNATIONAL ADOPTION • FOSTER A CHILD • ORGANIZE YOUR LIFE AS A NE
COORDINATE A FAMILY CALENDAR • PLAN FAMILY MEETINGS • ORGANIZE HOME SYSTEMS FOR ADD • PREPARE FOR A NEW CAT OR DO
BACK-TO-SCHOOL • WIN THE HOMEWORK WARS • PLAN A FIELD TRIP • PLAN YOUR CHILD'S ACTIVITIES • PLAN YOUR CHILDREN'S SUM
ONLINE • ORGANIZE A GENEALOGICAL SEARCH • PREPARE FOR YOUR CHILD'S DEPARTURE FOR COLLEGE • ORGANIZE YOUR EMPTY N
ELDERLY PARENTS' CARE • PREPARE FOR THE DEATH OF A SPOUSE • HELP YOUR ELDERLY PARENTS MOVE • ORGANIZE A HOME MEDIC
STORE TRIPS • SET UP ONLINE GROCERY SHOPPING • ORGANIZE RECIPES AND COOKBOOKS • PLAN THEME MENUS • CREATE EFFECT
REFRIGERATOR AND FREEZER • ORGANIZE CUTLERY AND KITCHEN TOOLS • ORGANIZE CUPBOARDS AND DRAWERS • ORGANIZE THE P
LUNCHES FOR KIDS • PLAN PARTY FOODS AHEAD • THROW A DINNER PARTY • FINISH DINNER ON TIME • PULL OFF A LAST-MINUTE PAF
ULTIMATE WEDDING CHECKLIST • BUDGET FOR A WEDDING • FIND THE PERFECT WEDDING RING • PLAN AN ELOPEMENT • SET UP A BA
HONOR • EXECUTE BEST MAN DUTIES • HIRE A BAND • HIRE A BARTENDER • PLAN A SHOWER • ORGANIZE THE REHEARSAL DINNER •
SUCCESSFUL SLUMBER PARTY • PLAN A BAR OR BAT MITZVAH • PLAN A QUINCEAÑERA • PLAN A RETIREMENT PARTY • PLAN A FUNER
HANUKKAH PARTY • ORGANIZE A HOLIDAY CRAFT PARTY • PLAN TO SPEND CHRISTMAS SOLO • PLAN THE PERFECT HOLIDAY GIFT EXC
THE HOLIDAYS • STICK TO YOUR NEW YEAR'S RESOLUTIONS • PLAN THE PERFECT NEW YEAR'S EVE • PLAN A SEDER • PLAN A SPECIA
FOOD TREE • ORGANIZE A BICYCLE SCAVENGER HUNT • RUN A SPORTS TOURNAMENT • PUBLICIZE AN EVENT • PLAN AN ORGANIZATIC
PLAN A CONCERT IN THE PARK • ORGANIZE AN INTERNATIONAL CONCERT TOUR • ORGANIZE A FILM FESTIVAL • PLAN A FUND-RAISING
BUILD A COMMUNITY PLAY STRUCTURE • THROW A BLOCK PARTY • SET UP A NEIGHBORHOOD WATCH • CREATE AN EVACUATION PL
ORGANIZE A PROTEST OR MARCH • FIGHT CITY HALL • ORGANIZE A BOYCOTT • ORGANIZE A CLASS ACTION LAWSUIT • MANAGE GRO
SCHOOL IN A THIRD WORLD COUNTRY • PLAN A TRIP • PLAN A TRIP WITH CHILDREN • TRAVEL WITH TEENS • BOOK AIRLINE TICKETS •
MOTORCYCLE TRIP • PLAN A TRAIN TRIP IN THE UNITED STATES • RIDE THE RAILS ABROAD • PREPARE A VACATION COUNTDOWN CHEC
LUGGAGE • LOAD A BACKPACK PROPERLY • PLAN AN ELDERHOSTEL TRIP • ORGANIZE AN RV VACATION • PLAN A TRIP WITH AGING PA
WIDELY DIFFERENT PEOPLE • PLAN SPRING BREAK • PLAN AN OVERNIGHT GETAWAY WITH YOUR SPOUSE • PLAN A VACATION SEPARAT
POLITICALLY UNSTABLE REGION • GET TRAVEL INSURANCE • GET IMMUNIZATIONS FOR TRAVELING • BOOK AN ADVENTURE VACATION
PLAN A FISHING TRIP TO ALASKA • PACK FOR A CAMPING TRIP • LEAD A BACKPACK TRIP • HIKE A FAMOUS TRAIL • PLAN A TOUR OF T
ENGLISH CANAL TRIP • PLAN A CROSS-COUNTRY AIRPLANE VOYAGE • PLAN THE PERFECT DAY ABROAD • PLAN A VISIT TO THE LOUVF
PLAN • PREPARE FOR AN ACT OF GOD • ASSEMBLE EMERGENCY KITS • PREPARE FOR SURGERY • PLAN YOUR RECOVERY • SURVIVE
BEING LOST • CONDUCT A SEARCH AND RESCUE OPERATION • PLAN AN INVASION • SURVIVE A POLITICAL COUP • PLAN FOR A TERRO
BECOME THE PRESIDENT OF THE UNITED STATES • WIN AN ACADEMY AWARD • BECOME AN OLYMPIAN • TRAIN FOR A MAJOR ATHLET

SS • SET GOALS • STREAMLINE YOUR MORNING ROUTINE • ORGANIZE A CHORE SCHEDULE FOR KIDS • ORGANIZE YOUR CHORES • NE
YOUR WORKOUT SCHEDULE • SCHEDULE DOCTOR VISITS • PREPARE FOR COLD AND FLU SEASON • GET A DRASTIC MAKEOVER • ARR
UP • FIND YOUR KEYS • TIDY UP IN MINUTES • CONQUER CLUTTER • ACTUALLY SEE THE BOTTOM OF YOUR PURSE • ORGANIZE YOUR :
E CAR MAINTENANCE • ORGANIZE PET SUPPLIES • MANAGE GARBAGE AND RECYCLABLES • PREPARE GRAB 'N' GO ACTIVITY BAGS • KE
INE CLIPPINGS • ORGANIZE YOUR PHOTOS • ARRANGE PHOTOS AND PICTURES • ARRANGE AN ART COLLECTION • END COLLECTION C
• ORGANIZE YOUR LAUNDRY CENTER • CREATE A SEWING CENTER • GET READY FOR THE HOUSECLEANER • ORGANIZE CLEANING SU
YWAYS AND MUDROOMS • ORGANIZE A DORM ROOM • ORGANIZE YOUR SCHOOL LOCKER • MAKE YOUR HOME SAFE FOR SMALL CHIL
ARE FOR SKYROCKETING ENERGY COSTS • USE FENG SHUI TO ORGANIZE YOUR HOME • DESIGN A NEW HOME WITH FENG SHUI • DESI
PLAN A REMODEL • PLAN A MULTIMEDIA CENTER • TURN A BASEMENT INTO A MEDIA ROOM OR PLAYROOM • ORGANIZE THE ATTIC • OF
FUL ESTATE SALE • PLAN A YARD OR GARAGE SALE • PREPARE YOUR HOME FOR SALE • PLAN A MOVE • DOWNSIZE YOUR HOUSE •
CORATE FOR THE SEASONS • PREPARE A VACATION HOME FOR THE OFF-SEASON • PREPARE YOUR HOME FOR NATURE'S WORST • PRE
GARDEN • PLANT A CUT-FLOWER GARDEN • DESIGN A SHADE GARDEN • DESIGN A DRY GARDEN • PLAN FOR A LONG-SEASON CONTAIN
N AND PLANT A LAWN • DESIGN A NEW LANDSCAPE • PLAN AN OUTDOOR KITCHEN • DESIGN A DECK OR PATIO • DESIGN A WATER FEA
ES • STORAGE SOLUTIONS FOR ANY ROOM   D THE CAPACITY OF A SMALL ROOM • ORGANIZ
TWORK • ORGANIZE MOVIES, MUSIC AND O   IRLOOMS • STORE OUT-OF-SEASON CLOTHES •
ENT • STORE PAINT AND OTHER HAZARDOUS   T • STORE A BOAT FOR THE WINTER • STORE A CA
E APPLICATIONS • PLAN YOUR COURSE OF   CH PAPER • GET INTO GRAD SCHOOL • GET INTO
LONG ABSENCE • SET UP AN INTERNSHIP •   N THE PEACE CORPS • PRODUCE A NEWSLETTE
BECOME A COWBOY • BECOME A BRAIN S   ATHOLIC NUN • ORGANIZE AN EXHIBITION • DEV
OME A STUNT PERSON • BECOME A TOUR G   G • CONQUER YOUR PAPER PILES • CREATE A FI
UTER FILES • SCHEDULE APPOINTMENTS EF   NCE CALL • PREPARE FOR A MEETING • PREPAR
ME NETWORK • CHOOSE THE BEST PHONE   TEM • MAKE A NETWORKING PLAN • PLAN YOUF
NTATION SKILLS • PREPARE A SPEECH • PR   AN AN IPO • DELEGATE RESPONSIBILITIES • HIRE
ROFITS • FORM A BOARD OF DIRECTORS •   A COMPANY PICNIC • PLAN A COMPANY RET
FAILING BUSINESS • DISMANTLE A BUSINE   • DESIGN A SAVINGS PLAN • SIMPLIFY BILL PAY
INANCIAL-AID PACKAGE • PLAN FOR COLLE   E A HEALTH INSURANCE PLAN • START AN INVE
ST • MAKE A WILL • EXECUTE A POWER OF   S' ESTATE • PLAN YOUR ESTATE • TEACH YOUR I
ARE FOR AN IN VITRO FERTILIZATION • PREP   ATERNITY WARDROBE • SET UP MATERNITY OR
REPARE FOR CHILDBIRTH • STOCK A DIAPE   LEND FAMILIES • CREATE A HOUSEHOLD ORGA
OOL YOUR CHILD • SET UP A CARPOOL • ST   HE BEST ELEMENTARY SCHOOL • ORGANIZE KID
OR SUMMER CAMP • CHOOSE A SUMMER S   R FAMILY COMPUTER USE • PLAN TO KEEP YOU
R BOOMERANG KIDS • PLAN AN AMICABLE   MENTS • ORGANIZE MEDICAL RECORDS • PLAN
• ARRANGE HOSPICE CARE • MAKE YOUR   RECORDS • PLAN A WEEK OF MENUS • ORGANIZ
ISTS • COOK AHEAD • DETERMINE THE SH   M WAREHOUSE STORES • EFFICIENTLY USE THE
ENTLY USE SPACE UNDER THE SINK • STOV   UR COUNTER SPACE • COOK FOR ONE • PLAN I
DINNER PARTY FOR YOUR BOSS • PLAN DI   PARTY • IMPRESS A DATE • PLAN A WEDDING •
ENT PLANNER • HIRE A PHOTOGRAPHER •   ACHELORETTE PARTY • PREPARE TO BE THE MA
NEYMOON • PLAN A BAPTISM • PLAN A BRI   THROW A PARTY • PREPARE FOR HOUSE GUESTS • PLAN A CHILD'S BIRTHDAY PARTY •
TO CUSTOM • PLAN AHEAD FOR A LOW-STRESS HOLIDAY • STAY WITHIN A BUDGET THIS CHRISTMAS • PREPARE A HOLIDAY FEAST • T
NIZE GIFT-GIVING IN ADVANCE • STICK TO YOUR DIET DURING THE HOLIDAYS • PLAN A HOLIDAY OPEN HOUSE • REORGANIZE YOUR LIF
• ORGANIZE A HIGH-SCHOOL CLASS REUNION • PLAN A FAMILY REUNION • START A KNITTING CIRCLE • ORGANIZE A BOOK CLUB • SE
SHARPEN THE FOCUS OF AN ORGANIZATION • IMPROVE YOUR CHILD'S SCHOOL • PLAN A PROM • ORGANIZE A COMMUNITY THEATER
NIZE A PANCAKE BREAKFAST • PLAN A TOY DRIVE • HOLD A BARN RAISING • ORGANIZE A CHARITY WALK OR RUN • BUILD LOW-INCOM
TER-REGISTRATION DRIVE • RUN FOR LOCAL OFFICE • ORGANIZE A PETITION • ORGANIZE A RECALL • GET AN INITIATIVE ON THE BALLO
OMMUNITY • PRESERVE OPEN SPACE • SAVE HISTORIC PROPERTIES AND LANDMARKS • SET UP A NONGOVERNMENTAL ORGANIZATION
THE UNITED STATES • RENT A CAR ABROAD • MAKE HOTEL RESERVATIONS • ARRANGE EXECUTIVE ACCOMMODATIONS • PLAN A CRUIS
E AN ITINERARY • PACK FOR A TRIP • PACK FOR A BUSINESS TRIP • PACK FOR A WEEK IN ONE CARRY-ON • PACK A DAY BAG • PREVEN
IZE A SAILING TEAM • PLAN A SAILBOAT CRUISE • PLAN A BICYCLE TRIP WITH A TOUR COMPANY • TRAVEL ABROAD • PLAN A VACATIO
POUSE • PLAN A TRIP TO A DIFFERENT CULTURE • FORAGE ABROAD • MAIL PACKAGES BACK TO THE UNITED STATES • PLAN A TRIP TC
LK ROAD • PLAN A CLIMB OF MOUNT KILIMANJARO • PACK FOR A SAFARI • ORGANIZE A HUNTING TRIP • PACK FOR A FISHING OR HUN
RKS • ORGANIZE A BACKCOUNTRY SKI TRIP • ORGANIZE A CAR RALLY • PLAN A WHALE-WATCHING TRIP • PACK FOR A VOYAGE AT SEA
YDNEY HARBOUR BRIDGE • PLAN A TRIP TO NEW ORLEANS FOR MARDI GRAS • PLAN A DAY AT DISNEYLAND • FORMULATE A FAMILY E
IF YOU'RE ALONE • SURVIVE IF YOUR CAR BREAKS DOWN • DEAL WITH AMNESIA • FIGHT AN EBOLA OUTBREAK • FIGHT A FOREST FIR
ESCUE A HOSTAGE • OUTSMART PIRATES • DELIVER A BABY • MAKE AN EMERGENCY LANDING • MAKE A JAIL BREAK • BECOME A MO

The Unexpected

464 Formulate a Family Emergency Plan

Having harm come to those you love is everyone's worst nightmare. But, like writing a will or getting life insurance, it's a relief to do something about it instead of worrying about it. These effective strategies will help you prepare for the most common types of emergencies.

Steps

General tips

1 Program clearly marked emergency numbers into your phone's speed dial.

2 Set up two places: one near your house in case of a sudden emergency such as fire or home invasion, and another outside the neighborhood, such as a school or friend's house, in case you can't get home. Also designate one family member to make decisions for the whole group during a crisis, including where to meet and what to do in case plans must change.

3 Designate an out-of-town relative or friend as your contact in the event that local phone service is interrupted. Family members should phone in as soon as possible if separated.

4 Create an emergency plan for children that details who will pick them up from school or daycare should parents be unable to, where that person will take them and what the plan is to meet up again. Be sure everyone involved has all the phone numbers.

5 Discuss, locate and prepare priority items such as photos and documents to save. Have your will, insurance paperwork and all legal documents in good order (see 232 Organize Important Documents and 244 Make a Will).

6 Prepare a backpack for each family member with extra clothing, shoes, jackets, medications, diapers and wipes for babies, insurance and medical information. Include a laminated picture of the entire family with names and numbers. Keep them in a chest by the front door, in a hall closet or in the trunk of your car.

7 Keep an emergency kit, including first aid supplies, in each car. See 466 Assemble Emergency Kits.

Home invasion

1 Leave immediately if you come home to find you've been robbed. Call the police from another location and don't re-enter the house until police officers have cleared the scene.

2 Get everyone out (if you can do it safely) if you're at home during a robbery. Use fire escape ladders, if you have them, and meet at the designated nearby safe location.

3 Buy a dog or install a security system. Burglars look for easy targets; the idea is to make it harder to break into your house than someone else's.

Tips

Ask a firefighter, police officer or insurance agent to review your house and suggest risk-reduction strategies as well as appropriate actions to take in an emergency. See 390 Create an Evacuation Plan.

Contact the American Red Cross (redcross.org) or the Federal Emergency Management Agency (FEMA.gov) for more information. See 105 Prepare Your Home for Nature's Worst.

Find out about the disaster plans at your workplace and your child's school. Read 223 Prepare Your Business for the Unthinkable and 375 Improve Your Child's School.

Take a course in CPR. Get to know your neighbors' special skills (medical, construction, electrical) and whether any disabled or elderly people require help in the event of an emergency. See 389 Set Up a Neighborhood Watch.

Warning

Use weapons as a last resort. There are many complications: Where do you store the weapon so it's unavailable to kids or burglars? Can you unlock, load and aim a gun under pressure and in the dark? Would you kill someone over a VCR? Do you know the legal limits of self-defense? Is there a chance you could shoot your neighbors or family by mistake?

Although they make great disaster-movie plots, fires, tornadoes and hurricanes aren't so fun off the big screen. If you live in an area prone to these natural disasters, it pays to be prepared.

Steps

Wildfire

1 Set up an evacuation plan from both your house and your neighborhood. Stick to the main roads. Smaller roads may be ignored by rescue crews or blocked by flames or burning debris.

2 Establish a family meeting place or check-in spot well away from the burn zone. This will be a different place than where you would go during a house fire.

3 Build a defensible area by clearing brush and deadwood from around your house. Check your firebreak every year and remove new brush and flammable debris. See 473 Fight a Forest Fire.

Tornadoes

1 Understand the alerts: a *tornado watch* means tornadoes are possible. Remain alert for approaching storms. Watch the sky and stay tuned to radio or television to know when warnings are issued. A *warning* means a tornado has been sighted or indicated by weather radar. Take shelter immediately.

2 Outfit your basement or storm cellar with emergency supplies. See 466 Assemble Emergency Kits. If an underground shelter is not available, an interior room or hallway on the lowest floor may be your best bet. Practice going to your shelter with your family.

3 Know the locations of designated shelters in places where you and your family spend time, such as public buildings and malls.

Hurricanes

1 Understand the alerts. *Watch* means storm conditions are possible in the specified area, usually within 36 hours. *Warning* means storm conditions are expected in the specified area, usually within 24 hours. Short-term watches and warnings provide detailed information on related hurricane threats, such as flash floods and tornadoes.

2 Prepare to survive on your emergency supplies for at least three days, since water may become undrinkable and stores may be closed. After sterilizing the bathtub and other containers with a diluted bleach solution, fill them with water to ensure a safe supply in case you are unable to evacuate or are told to stay put.

3 Make plans to secure your property. Permanent storm shutters offer the best protection for windows. A second option is to board up windows with five-eighth–inch plywood, cut to fit and ready to install. Tape does not prevent windows from breaking.

Tip

Review 105 Prepare Your Home for Nature's Worst and 390 Create an Evacuation Plan.

Warnings

Check out equipment and protective gear at online sources such as HomeFire FightingSystems.com, but be realistic about your skills and lack of training. If you live in a heavily forested area, it's unlikely you'll be able to stop a large fire from reaching your house and it's foolish to try. Outside hoses are useful for wetting the roof, which may provide a degree of safety, but during an inferno, all water may be diverted to professional firefighters.

Cooperate with rescue personnel and follow evacuation orders. Do not endanger your life to save your pets.

After a natural disaster, look out for broken glass and downed power lines. Check for injuries. Do not attempt to move seriously injured persons unless they are in immediate danger of death or further injury. If you must move an unconscious person, first stabilize the neck and back, then call for help immediately.

It may be a long time before rescue personnel get to you. Look online at RedCross.org for preparedness training courses near you.

Don't wait for an emergency to start scrambling for vital supplies—get ready now. Most necessary equipment is inexpensive and readily available. You'll need kits in the event of an earthquake, power outage, snowstorm, flood or hurricane. For long car trips, you need a mobile kit. Keep everything in water- and airtight containers. Also read 464 Formulate a Family Emergency Plan.

MOBILE KIT

Basic

- Flashlights or headlamps
- Batteries
- High-calorie foods such as energy bars
- Fire-starting kit: matches, lighter, paper
- Toilet paper and sanitary products in a zipper-lock plastic bag
- Battery-powered radio
- Jumper cables and instructions
- Ice scraper
- Tire chains
- Instant hand warmers (chemical packs)
- Space blanket (www.hisystems.co.uk)

Expanded (above items plus the following)

- Backpacking stove and fuel
- Cook pot, can opener, utensils
- Cans of food
- Boots, hats, gloves, other warm clothing
- Sleeping bags
- Snow shovel

In the desert, water is your most important resource. Be sure you have enough to drink, as well as to refill your car's radiator. In very hot weather, a gallon per day per person may be needed. Carry a three-day supply.

In cold and mountainous regions (and at nighttime in a desert), warm clothing and sleeping bags are vital. At higher elevations, snowstorms are possible any day of the year.

HOME KIT

Since this kit can be larger than the mobile kit, it contains far more bulky contents and even things that aren't strictly emergency items, such as books and toys. The contents are limited only by the amount of space you're able to devote to storage.

- One blanket or sleeping bag per person, sleeping pads, ground cloths and pillows
- Canned food and opener
- Portable stove and fuel (or propane barbecue setup)
- Fire-starting kit: matches, lighter, paper, candles
- Flashlights
- Battery-powered radio
- Books, writing pad and pencils
- Extra pair of glasses
- Three-day supply of water, one gallon per person
- Diapers and other child-related supplies
- Batteries for radio and flashlight
- Extra set of car keys

FIRST AID KIT

Create kits for both your home and car.

- Surgical tape, bandages, sterile gauze, antiseptic, antibacterial ointment, rubber gloves, ace bandage, finger splints, safety pins, scissors, chemical ice packs
- Ibuprofen, necessary prescription drugs, thermometer, decongestant, antihistamine cream for bug bites and poison oak or ivy.

TIPS Parents need to be careful not to scare their kids, but should also avoid turning drills into a game. Be serious, direct and simple when instructing your children.

Search online for "emergency resources" to find resources in your community.

Check out Ready.gov for a complete list of what to include in your first aid kit.

Given the stress of surgery, you may neglect to plan for it properly. There's a lot you can do to make sure your operation and recovery go as smoothly as possible. Much of this information can be applied to preparations for chemotherapy treatments as well.

Steps

Preoperative measures

1 Learn as much as possible about your surgical procedure. Have your doctor explain exactly what the surgical process is and why surgery is necessary. Get a second opinion if you haven't already. Some people get queasy discussing surgery, but many find that they relax as they gain information. If your doctor is not willing to take the time to discuss the procedure with you, find another one. There's a wealth of information online that will help you ask the right questions.

2 Be sure you understand all the risks and benefits of your surgery, as well as potential risks if you choose not to have the procedure done.

3 Discuss timing issues with your doctor: Do you need surgery in the immediate future or can you safely wait a few weeks? How difficult is it to get a surgery date? Assess your work and family schedule, and determine what is the most favorable period given your other commitments.

4 Bring someone with you to presurgical appointments to take notes. If this is impossible, bring a portable tape recorder. You'll hear a lot of information in a very short time, and it can be hard to digest and remember all the medical terms.

5 Ask for preoperative and postdischarge checklists and other materials in writing at this time. Get postoperative prescriptions filled ahead of surgery so you won't have to wait at the pharmacy or send someone out. (And you won't risk having the medication be unavailable.) Taking care of meds now will also give you time to work out any insurance copay issues. Buy dressings, ointments or gauze, and rent special equipment (hospital bed, wheelchair) ahead of time too.

6 Call your health insurance company. Be sure that your operation is covered and preauthorized, and that you're following all the procedures required by the insurance company. You don't want a surprise bill to come in the mail.

7 Collect information about expected recovery time from your doctor, and from friends who have had similar procedures. Visualize life during your recuperation. Will you be able to get around your house and office by yourself or will you need to line up help? Will

Continued on next page

Tips

As the old saying goes, minor surgery is surgery that happens to somebody else. Expect any surgery to be a big deal, even a procedure that sounds trivial, such as getting wisdom teeth pulled. Give yourself a day or two to rest and heal after even a seemingly small procedure.

If your surgery is in any way related to your inactive lifestyle, consider it a wake-up call.

Make sure both your physician *and* the hospital are participants in your network if you have a PPO.

Read 28 Get a Drastic Makeover and 172 Become a Brain Surgeon.

Who Knew?

Hospitals have discovered that the risk of infection related to surgery drops significantly when a few simple procedures are followed. Hair around a surgical site is clipped, not shaved, to prevent micro breaks in the skin. For major invasive surgeries, antibiotics should be started by injection 60 minutes prior to surgery and ended 24 hours after to maximize their effectiveness.

you be able to drive? Be sure to factor in the effect of medications that may make driving unsafe and possibly illegal.

8 Hire help if necessary. Ask your insurance provider if your treatments or conditions qualify you to have in-home care covered. Set up help with child care and housework as well.

9 Be realistic about how much energy and enthusiasm you will have following surgery. You may not be in the mood for dinner dates, a new work assignment or even movies for a while. Set up and enforce visiting hours (or ask your spouse or friend to act as enforcer) so you can get needed rest.

10 Make arrangements for a ride to and from the hospital, since any surgery requiring anesthesia will render you unable to drive yourself home. Line up a few helpers to be available during your first few days after surgery. You may also need help running errands, picking up prescriptions and driving to follow-up appointments.

11 Choose one trusted person to help you make medical decisions. Listening to a committee of family and friends is likely to be stressful and confusing.

12 Know your rehabilitation and physical therapy plan ahead of time. Commit to following it. Slacking off on your rehab is the surest way to have a botched recovery.

13 Have your financial affairs, your will and all legal documents in good order in case the worst happens. Ask your doctor or a patient advocate at the hospital if you need to complete a durable power of attorney for health-care decisions. See 244 Make a Will and 245 Execute a Power of Attorney.

General precautions

1 Identify yourself by name to your surgeon. This helps ensure that no mistakes are made about your identity and why you're there.

2 Mark your surgery site with an indelible pen. Many hospitals follow this procedure and will ask you to do this as you enter surgery. For example, if the operation is to occur on your left knee, mark a large **X** on that knee, or follow the surgeon's instructions.

3 Inform the surgical staff completely about medications you are already taking, including nonprescription drugs, herbal supplements, vitamins and the dosages. Also inform them of any allergies. See 289 Organize Medical Records.

4 Have someone stay at the hospital during your surgery. He or she can phone your family and friends as needed, collect information for you and watch your belongings.

5 Do not let the hospital send you home if you don't feel ready. Ask for help from the patient advocate if you feel pressured.

The purpose of getting a second opinion is not so much to get a different opinion as it is to increase your knowledge. The more information you can gather (and understand) the better you'll be able to make informed decisions.

Warnings

There are no risk-free procedures. Modern hospital techniques are very safe, but everything entails a risk. The more you know, the better decisions you can make about your treatment.

Make sure health professionals wash their hands and put on a fresh pair of gloves every time they walk into your room. Cross-infection is all too easy in a hospital setting.

Receiving the incorrect dosage or type of medication is one of the most common mistakes at hospitals. Ask for a list of all your medications and dosages, as well as who prescribed them: your doctor or a resident.

If you're diabetic, you already know being sick can wildly throw off your blood sugar levels. Receiving medication intravenously, as well as an irregular meal schedule, can contribute to this. Work with the nursing team to keep your levels steady.

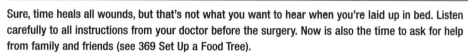

Sure, time heals all wounds, but that's not what you want to hear when you're laid up in bed. Listen carefully to all instructions from your doctor before the surgery. Now is also the time to ask for help from family and friends (see 369 Set Up a Food Tree).

MINOR SURGERY	
Pain Medication	Depending on the procedure, you may not need any medication beyond the initial anesthetic. If you think you might need something, have a prescription written and filled before you leave the surgery site. You don't want to wake up in the middle of the night with no pain relief available.
Sleeping Arrangements	You're likely to have a few uncomfortable nights. Try to convince your spouse that you need the bed all to yourself. If you're having leg surgery, you will probably want to spend a lot of time with your leg propped up on pillows— keep one tucked at the foot of the bed to hold covers off your foot or leg.
Around the House	Getting around the house may be difficult. Your spouse may be able to wait on you for a few days. But if it's going to be more than that, get help lined up in order not to burn out your major caretaker. Have refreshments stored by your bed or the couch in a cooler.
MAJOR SURGERY	
Pain Medication	You will be on pain medication for some time after surgery. Do not expect to drive. Side effects may include drowsiness and constipation.
Blood Supply	Consult with your doctor about storing some of your own blood (autologous blood transfusion) or blood from a person designated by you (directed donor transfusion) in advance of an elective or planned surgery. You will need to check with the hospital to make sure it's set up to store blood. Allow six weeks before your surgery to process and store the blood. You may need to find a blood match in your family to build up a supply for doctors to keep on hand.
The Surgical Nurse	A family's best friend in the operating room is the surgical nurse, who cares for the patient from pre-op to recovery. He or she usually acts as the conduit of information between the operating room and the waiting family. Be especially kind to and grateful for this person.
Sleeping Arrangements	Moving around the house may be difficult during recovery. If you expect to be in bed for extended periods, look into renting a hospital-type bed that tilts into various positions. These beds make it easier to rest, read, eat and watch television and can help relieve pain and stress in different parts of your body. Other necessary medical equipment may include a wheelchair, a bedpan, a bed pad, crutches, a trapeze to pull yourself up with, and adult diapers.
Around the House	Temporarily reorganize your house so that you don't need to go up or down stairs. If you're in a wheelchair or on crutches, carrying drinks and meals around the house is very hard if not impossible. Store refreshments by your bed or the couch in a cooler.

Many heart attacks are survivable, especially if you've taken the time to prepare yourself. Anyone who thinks they're at risk for a heart attack should get a complete medical evaluation as soon as possible. The information below is far from everything you need to know, but it's enough to point you in the right direction.

Steps

Be prepared

1 Listen only to advice from medical professionals. A widely circulated e-mail recently advocated a procedure called cough CPR as a way to treat a heart attack. The American Heart Association does not recommend that the public use this method in a situation where there is no medical supervision.

2 Limit your risk. Listen to your doctor and make changes in your lifestyle to lower your chances of a heart attack. Stop smoking, get regular exercise, improve your diet and reduce stress.

3 Buy a device such as the LifeAlert unit (lifealert.net), which automatically links you to rescue or hospital personnel when you press a button.

What to do

1 Recognize heart attack symptoms. Shortness of breath, pain or pressure in the chest, and pain in the neck or radiating down the arms are all associated with an attack.

2 Pull over if you suffer an attack while driving. You may only have seconds before you lose consciousness. Don't try to drive to the hospital no matter how close you are.

3 Call 911 and describe what symptoms you're feeling and where you are located.

4 Take an aspirin (325 mg) at the first sign of an attack. Aspirin makes blood platelets less likely to stick to each other, assisting blood flow and reducing clots. Chew it up if no drink is readily available—the time and oxygen you waste in waiting to get a sip of something isn't worth it when you're acutely symptomatic.

5 Take a beta-blocking drug immediately upon feeling an attack. This is a prescription-only drug; if you have a heart condition, you probably already have this medication.

6 Administer oxygen to yourself. You are likely to have bottled oxygen available only if you have a diagnosed heart condition.

7 Thump yourself on the chest as hard as possible. This is very effective when administered by someone else but can be hard to do to yourself.

Tips

For more information, contact the American Heart Association (american heart.org).

If you have a defibrillator, educate your family or neighbor on how to use it. Most have explicit voice and text prompts to guide users through the process. Many businesses also stock defibrillators and CPR kits.

Warnings

This advice is not a substitute for proper medical care. Consult your physician if you have concerns or questions.

Don't be confused by indigestion. If an antacid doesn't work in a few minutes, call 911 immediately. You could be having a heart attack—the doctors won't mind if it turns out to be "just gas."

470 | Survive If Your Car Breaks Down

Modern cars are generally very reliable. They don't break down and leave you stranded too often. But this reliability also means that if your wheels do conk out, you might be caught unprepared. To avoid being stranded, take these precautions before attempting a drive across an empty desert or a lonely mountain pass.

Steps

1 Pack a car emergency kit (see 466 Assemble Emergency Kits).

2 Teach yourself basic car repair. Know how to connect the battery, check the oil and radiator fluid, and change a tire. These are simple procedures that might get you out of a jam or, better still, prevent the jam from happening.

3 Stay with the car if you're in a remote area and don't know exactly where help is located. Rescuers are more likely to find the car than you alone, especially in bad weather. See 474 Survive Being Lost.

4 Conserve water at all costs if stuck in a desert area. Stay in the shade during the day. Get under the car if there's no shade. In extreme conditions, such as those found in Death Valley, hiking even 10 miles without water can be fatal. Drinking urine will not rehydrate you. And do not drink the water in your car's radiator, which is mixed with toxic ethylene glycol.

5 Be sure the exhaust is not entering the car if you've got the motor running for heat. Clear snow or dirt away from the tailpipe. If the car sounds louder than normal, you may have a leak in the exhaust system, increasing the risk of toxic carbon monoxide entering the passenger compartment.

6 Make yourself as visible as possible to rescuers. Open the hood of your car to indicate that you're having trouble. If it's snowing, periodically sweep the snow off your car. If an airplane passes, wave both arms over your head.

7 Keep your wits about you if you need to go find help, or if someone stops to help you. Your safety is at risk in any event, and it's hard to judge someone's character in the dark, if you're already rattled or if you desperately need help. Try to find a family or at least a group of people who can help you; stay away from single men. Be honest about your predicament—many people are wary of scam artists, so be understanding if they're skeptical at first.

8 Stay cool. This rule applies whether you're stuck in the mountains or in the scariest neighborhood of Bogotá. In the wilderness, you need to conserve energy and maintain a hopeful outlook. In the city, you need to look composed and confident. Nothing attracts bullies and miscreants more than an easy target.

Tips

Being able to call for help may be the single overriding reason to have a cellular phone with you.

Join an automobile club like AAA or sign up for roadside assistance program through your cellular phone service.

Increase your chances of being found by carrying a Personal Locator Beacon (PLB). When activated, a PLB broadcasts an emergency signal and your location. PLBs are available at outdoor supply stores for $500 and up and must be registered with the National Oceanic and Atmospheric Administration (noaa.gov) upon purchase.

I am Napoleon, Emperor of France! What? I'm not? I'm just a regular guy with a severe case of amnesia? Well, *zut alors,* I must postpone the invasion of Russia until I recover my memory. Amnesia, a loss of memory, is not purely Hollywood fiction. It commonly occurs after a concussion or other trauma to the brain.

Steps

1 Consult the doctor who treated you when you were initially injured. The circumstances that led to the onset of amnesia may provide clues about who you are and what you were doing. Find out where the incident occurred and who was with you.

2 Determine which type of amnesia you have:

- *Anterograde* amnesia is a selective memory deficit, resulting from brain injury in which the person is severely impaired in learning new information. Memories for events that occurred before the injury may be spared, but those that occurred since the injury could be lost. So you might remember much of your childhood and the years before the injury, but may remember little or nothing since. Short-term memory is generally spared, which means that you may be able to carry on a conversation; but as soon as you are distracted, the memory of the conversation fades.

- *Retrograde* amnesia means your brain can't access memories that happened before the traumatic event. The length of the period rendered inaccessible can range from minutes to years. Some amnesiacs remember autobiographical information but not public events, though more often it's the other way around.

3 Be patient. While most people recover their memory almost completely, recovery may take many months. It's common to never recall the exact events leading to the accident, but wholesale permanent loss is unlikely.

4 Hope for a memory trigger. As it did for Proust, the simple task of eating a madeleine (or another common event) may bring your old memories back in a rush, sometimes resulting in a full recovery.

5 Read 9 Organize Your Thoughts and 10 Set Up a Reminder System.

Tips

The Rutgers University Memory Disorders Project offers excellent information at memorylossonline.com.

Read *The Bourne Identity* by Robert Ludlum.

Who Knew?

Amnesiacs commonly retain or easily relearn old skills.

Memory loss can also be caused by a stroke or aneurysm, epilepsy, encephalitis, hypoxia, carbon monoxide poisoning, near-drowning or near-suffocation, and the earliest stages of Alzheimer's disease.

Warning

Be careful about whom you associate with. People can easily take advantage of you right now. For example, where's your savings account? Make sure the strange person claiming to be your investment manager isn't slanting your portfolio a little too heavily into horse races and limo rides (for him).

Medical professionals know that disease outbreaks, like earthquakes, are not a question of *if* but *when*—so it only makes sense to plan ahead. One minute you could be enjoying an exotic vacation, and the next, you could be acting as point person in the battle against a devastating epidemic of viral hemorrhagic fever.

Steps

1 Study Ebola basics before traveling to a region prone to outbreaks. First identified in humans about 25 years ago, the virus was named after the Ebola River in the Democratic Republic of the Congo, near where it first appeared. It is believed to be carried by animals in the region—transmission to humans is most likely through contact with a diseased animal. Outbreaks have occurred in several countries in central Africa.

2 Familiarize yourself with Ebola symptoms. In its early stage, symptoms include fever, aches and weakness, making a specific diagnosis difficult. An accurate diagnosis is usually not possible until the disease progresses to include skin rashes, bleeding from all orifices, and kidney and liver failure. Death is usually brought on by the failure of vital organs such as the lungs or the heart.

3 Mobilize international medical resources to handle the outbreak. Notify the International Red Cross (icrc.org) and the Centers for Disease Control and Prevention (cdc.gov). Distribute rubber gloves and surgical masks to anyone who might come into contact with an infected person.

4 Quarantine any person suspected of infection. Prevent exposure to any body fluids from an infected person. There is presently no cure or vaccine for Ebola, so preventing further infection is the only effective tool for managing an outbreak.

5 Maintain sanitary conditions. Ensure the proper disposal of sewage and medical waste. Disinfect reusable supplies and equipment, including gloves, thermometers, sheets, boots and clothing, with a bleach-and-water solution.

6 Make sure bodies are interred or cremated as soon as possible. Do not allow funeral rituals that bring mourners into contact with Ebola victims.

7 Maintain the victim's hydration and blood pressure. Treatment options are limited, but secondary conditions such as fever may respond to common medications such as ibuprofen.

8 Encourage your patients to maintain hope. Ebola is not always fatal. In past outbreaks, the mortality rate has fluctuated between 30 percent and 80 percent for all confirmed cases. Recent vaccine tests on monkeys are showing promise, and a deeper understanding of the virus is likely in the near future.

Tips

The World Health Organization (www.who.int), a component of the United Nations, is active around the world working to understand and control diseases like Ebola. Consider donating time or money to these efforts.

Warnings

Health-care workers are at risk while treating Ebola patients. Observe strict anti-infection protocols.

Do not eat meat from monkeys and other primates in potentially Ebola-affected areas. Eating infected animals is a likely transmission route for the virus.

473 | Fight a Forest Fire

Battling wildfires has got to be one of the toughest jobs in the world. Imagine being dropped from an airplane into the midst of a conflagration of biblical proportions, armed primarily with a shovel. It sounds more like a punishment than a career, but there are many people who are highly committed to it. You'll never approach their skill level, but you can try.

Steps

1 Take a course in forest fire control or fire science from an accredited university forestry program. You'll find that there's as much science involved as there is bravery and brawn. Meteorology, geography, engineering and management skills are all integral to forest fire control.

2 Study the weather. Wind shifts will play a big part in fire-fighting strategy; an unfavorable shift may defeat all your efforts. See 390 Create an Evacuation Plan.

3 Establish a defensive line. Without a large professional crew and airborne tankers, your only chance is to dig a firebreak. Look for a favorable spot, such as a road or a ridgetop.

4 Eliminate all flammable material along your firebreak. The wider you can make the line, the better. Remove deadwood and bushes and scatter them on the burning side of the line.

5 Soak the area along and behind the firebreak with water. If there are buildings in the area, soak them as well. Remove any vehicles.

6 Be wary of the fire jumping past your location and cutting you off. Watch for airborne embers. Also watch out for igniting treetops, which suggest a fast-moving crown fire.

Tips

Use earthmoving equipment to dig a defensive line.

Keep an evacuation route available. If this route looks threatened, get out.

Keep a charged cellular phone handy.

Warning

Highly trained professionals using the best possible gear regularly encounter fires they can't control. Don't kid yourself that you're better than them. Evacuate early.

474 | Survive Being Lost

Despite modern communications and equipment, more people than ever are getting lost in the wilderness. Cellular and satellite phones and global positioning systems (GPSs) make the world seem smaller, but the reality is, there's still a lot of emptiness out there and you can't always rely on technology for a rescue. It helps to have the best gear possible, but you also need to make smart choices.

Steps

General strategies

1 Stay put as soon as you realize you're lost. Rescue crews will find you faster if you stay in one spot. If you have no idea where you are or how to get back to where you started, further movement is just wasted energy.

Tips

Avoid the most common cause of delayed rescue: forgetting to tell anyone where you're going. Always leave a detailed description of your trip route and schedule with a responsible person. Direct that person to call the authorities if you don't return by a specific time or date.

2 Make yourself visible. Move to a clear area and do whatever you can to make a signal. Flags or markers can be made from food wrappers, clothing or anything that is colorful. If you're in the snow, stomp out a large **X.** In the desert, form an **X** with rocks.

3 Stay dry. Avoid crossing streams unless absolutely necessary. If you get warm, take off excess clothing before you become sweaty. Build a fire and dry wet clothes if possible. Getting wet can quickly lead to hypothermia, the inability of your body to warm itself. Don't wear cotton clothes in cold weather. Cotton retains water, providing little or no insulation when wet.

4 Stay hydrated. It's harder for your body to maintain the proper temperature if you're low on fluids. This is also very important if you're injured and have lost some blood: You need liquids in order to maintain normal blood pressure.

5 Make a shelter. Where it's hot, find shade. Where it's cold, create warmth. Tree branches, snow, sheets of plastic or cloth—almost anything can be fashioned into a basic shelter.

6 Treat any injuries. Dislocations, such as to a shoulder, should be replaced at the earliest opportunity. This will be extremely painful but will reduce overall trauma. Severe bleeding to an arm or a leg can be reduced with a tourniquet, a tight wrap of cloth around the limb above the wound. Study basic first aid before embarking on any potentially hazardous adventures.

7 Carry extra food. Energy bars and candy bars are easy to stash in pockets and provide many needed calories.

In the mountains

1 Prepare ahead of time by wearing and packing the proper clothing. Dress in several layers, starting with polypropylene underwear, then a fleece sweater and a waterproof outer jacket that extends below your waist. Use similar layers on your lower body, and make sure your pants cover your boot tops snugly to keep out snow. Boots should be tall and have a waterproof outer shell and plenty of insulation. A warm hat and gloves are also essential.

2 Understand avalanche risks before heading into the snow. Most avalanche accidents occur during or soon after a large snowfall. Forecasts are available for popular U.S. recreation sites, either through the National Weather Service (nws.noaa.gov) or the National Forest Service (www.fs.fed.us). Or call an outdoor recreation store for advice.

3 Descend as low as possible without making yourself invisible under trees or by descending into a remote spot. High elevations are colder and windier and have less oxygen. You'll work harder to stay warm.

Carry fire-starting equipment such as a cigarette lighter and toilet paper. In wet weather, your best bet for finding dry wood is to look for small dead branches at the base of evergreen trees.

See 466 Assemble Emergency Kits and 470 Survive If Your Car Breaks Down.

Who Knew?

You need to consume more calories in a cold climate than you do in a warm one.

Continued on next page

4 Dig into the snow at the base of a small incline to make a cave for shelter in snowy areas. If you anticipate an avalanche and can't leave the danger area, dig a snow trench. Shovel out a ditch and cover the top with tree branches and more snow. Line the floor of the shelter with more branches.

5 Remove any fresh snow from your signals so they remain visible.

6 Consider climbing to a high vantage point if rescue doesn't appear imminent and the weather is clear. You might see a familiar landmark. Be cautious about how far you hike out; it's easy to convince yourself that help is just over the next ridge.

7 Use snow for water. Stay hydrated or you'll have increasing difficulty keeping warm. If you have a water bottle, fill it with snow and hold it inside your jacket until it melts.

In the desert

1 Stay in the shade. You absolutely will not survive in the sun. Walking more than a few miles without a steady water supply is unrealistic. Stay with your car if you have one. Try to move only at night, if you must.

2 Dig at the base of cliffs in search of water. Avoid doing strenuous work in direct sunlight; find shade or wait for nightfall.

3 Resist the urge to drink your urine even if you feel desperate. You won't get any usable water from it because your body will just have to filter and excrete it all again.

4 Carry several clear plastic bags. Seal the bags around plants (except those with thorns) in bright sunlight. Water transpired by the plants condenses in the bags and can be collected.

At sea

1 Conserve as much energy as possible; avoid trying to row (or swim) to land unless you know exactly where it is.

2 Wait to trade a damaged or foundering boat for a life raft until you absolutely have to. There are countless stories of abandoned boats later being found intact while the raft is never seen again.

3 Supply yourself with as much freshwater as possible. Keep a tarp on hand to catch any rain.

4 Never drink seawater. Some people claim small amounts are OK (an appealing notion to someone in distress). Unfortunately, it's not true. In the absence of freshwater, seawater will destroy your liver and kill you.

5 Create shade and stay in it if it's hot or sunny.

6 Conserve water and energy by remaining inactive. Some life raft survivors claim they made it only by entering a trancelike state for days at a time.

Warnings

Distinguish between desert survival myths and truths. Many people believe you can squeeze drinkable water out of cactuses. That may be true of some cactuses, but others are toxic. If you're headed into the desert, pick up a guidebook that describes the various types. Also review poisonous reptiles and insects in case you think you might be dining al fresco à la Survivor.

Don't enter into any adventure with the expectation that you will find help in case of trouble, since there's no guarantee of rescue. Be responsible for yourself and plan as though rescue will not be possible.

Conduct a Search and Rescue Operation

You're camping in a remote spot with a group of friends. One member of the group decides to go on a short solo hike. But when the sun sets and he still hasn't returned, the group becomes concerned. What steps should you take to locate your missing friend, assuming you can't summon outside help immediately?

Steps

1 Assemble the rest of the group to discuss the situation and collect information. What was the intended destination of the missing person? How physically fit is he? What equipment was he carrying? A fit person with proper boots and clothing is likely to travel farther than someone who's out of shape and ill equipped.

2 Assign duties to the team based on skills and available equipment. If you have three walkie-talkies, for example, try to send out two searchers while keeping one walkie-talkie and team member at base camp. One person needs to stay at base camp, regardless of available equipment, in case the lost party returns.

3 Study an area map and review likely travel routes, such as trails, streams and ridgetops. The missing party's personal interests will offer clues. Rock climbers may head for cliffs; bird watchers may seek out wetlands or overlooks.

4 Equip each search team with a walkie-talkie, a topographic map and a global positioning system (GPS) unit. This gear allows for a constant flow of information between searchers and base camp.

5 Restrict the search teams to small, well-defined areas if walkie-talkies and GPSs are not available. Assign each team to an area; each should cross that area while calling for the victim and looking for tracks, then return to base. Repeat as needed.

6 Evaluate how much time and effort is needed to get outside help. If nobody locates the missing friend in several hours, it is probably a good idea to shift your efforts to contacting search-and-rescue authorities. A 911 dispatcher can initiate search operations. Provide the GPS fix of your base camp, if you have it.

7 Make preparations for evacuating an injured person. Check your map for possible helicopter landing sites (solid, level ground with no trees). Notify pilots of power lines, tall poles or anything else that is hard to spot from above.

8 Observe standard first aid techniques when evacuating an injured person. If a neck or back injury is suspected, move the victim only as a last resort if medical help cannot be brought to the site. Make sure an unconscious person is breathing and has clear airways and a stable heart rate. If the breathing and heart rate are not stable, perform CPR. Keep the victim warm and off the ground if possible. Warm up a hypothermic person immediately with extra clothing, hot drinks, a fire and close contact with another person.

Tips

The first rule of search and rescue is, don't make things worse. Don't send searchers into dangerous areas or allow them to race off and get lost themselves.

Educate your group ahead of time about the dangers of getting lost. Encourage people to note their surroundings at all times and to carry proper gear, including food and water. If anyone does get lost, they should stay where they are rather than wander continuously.

See 474 Survive Being Lost.

Warnings

Do not rub frostbitten extremities with snow.

Maps, compasses and GPS devices require practice. Become familiar with these tools and practice on several test runs before you set out on a wilderness adventure.

Very few high-quality countries are on the market these days. If you want one, you'll have to get it the old-fashioned way: Invade. Now, before you go running off half-cocked, keep in mind that, like marriage, many invasions receive the benefit of only vague, romantic thinking beforehand. Prepare properly and you could live a long, satisfying life as an illicit head of state.

Steps

1 Identify a potential target. Geographical proximity to your country of residence is handy, but many out-of-the-way spots provide good opportunities, especially if they don't attract much attention in the press. If you're totally at a loss, aim for the Caribbean.

2 Look for a country with a despicable dictator engaging in numerous human rights violations. You'll get instant support from any oppressed citizens in the country, and the rest of the world will likely adopt an "it couldn't get worse" attitude.

3 Manipulate the press if necessary (total silence is great but unlikely). Feed strongly negative reports about your target country to the world press in order to claim savior status later.

4 Evaluate your forces. Most military strategists prefer a three-to-one advantage in troops and armor for invasion forces operating against fixed defenses.

5 Employ code names whenever possible, such as "Operation Rolling Thunder." (Sorry, this one has already been used.) These can make even the most criminal plan sound compelling.

6 Strike as deeply and as early as possible to reduce the chances of the opposing army calling up reinforcements and stalling the invasion. Do anything possible to prevent a stalemate and a war of attrition, as such situations rarely favor invaders.

7 Achieve air superiority. This alone might ensure success. It makes movement by any opposing forces difficult to impossible.

8 Capture infrastructure. Immediate invasion goals should include communications structures, fuel supplies, rail lines, seaports and airports. You want to deny your opponent access to these facilities, ideally without destroying them. A completely razed country is hardly a bargain once your face is on the currency.

9 Allow your opponents an escape route. Military forces are more likely to retreat if a plausible route is open. If they're completely cut off, determined resistance can be expected.

10 Plan huge rallies to celebrate your victory. Toppling statues of the former dictator makes for great TV spots.

11 Find capable people to rebuild the country, undo civil rights abuses of the former boss, establish security and set the economy on a steady course.

Tips

Don't assume that the opposing army lacks loyalty to its despicable dictator. Tyrants tend to lavish favors on their generals in order to guarantee loyalty.

There will always be a few busybodies who will condemn you for the invasion. Do a good job with the economy and they'll be ignored quickly.

Read extensively. Become familiar with Napoleon's conquests and the works of Sun Tzu, Niccolò Machiavelli and military author John Keegan.

Who Knew?

Try not to let your weaker opponent occupy a geographically confined space, such as a mountain pass. Any battlefield that restricts mobility reduces the advantage held by the larger force.

Warning

This is dangerous work. You and scores of other people might be killed.

You're traveling in an exotic country that suddenly veers into anarchy due to a political coup. Many scary scenarios flood your mind, such as, "Will we all be killed?" and "Do they really eat rats in prison?" Anxiety is unavoidable, but there are practical steps you can take to ensure your safety.

Steps

1 Understand the political situation of any countries you travel or reside in. Nothing leaves you more unprotected than being uninformed. You need to know details of the political climate, key personalities and the mood of the people on the street. Review 439 Plan a Trip to a Politically Unstable Region.

2 Learn the language. Don't travel in a dangerous or unstable country without at least rudimentary language skills.

3 Avoid crowds and rallies. Crowds present many problems and only one attraction—excitement, which is not worth getting killed over. They are also the source of mob violence and brutal military and police repression. As a foreigner, you're an attractive target. If you're stuck in a crowd, don't be seen taking pictures.

4 Keep a low profile and trust no one. Stay inside as much as possible. If you're in a hotel, secure allies among the staff by being discreet and polite, and tipping lavishly. A house may be better than a hotel since it's impossible to know the political loyalties of all hotel staff. On the other hand, a hotel may be spared attacks and international scrutiny if foreigners are present.

5 Get out as soon as possible. The airport is likely to close to prevent enemies of the new ruler from escaping, but foreigners are usually allowed to leave.

6 Hire a local driver who is either newly married or has young children waiting for him at home. Avoid limousines. You want a common, nondescript car. Travel to the airport early in the morning, when the streets are most likely to be empty. Expect roadblocks and be prepared with some cash or jewelry to use as bribes.

7 Keep noncash resources on hand. In dire scenarios, paper money may quickly become worthless. People tend to shift focus to currency with intrinsic value (such as gold, gemstones and stereos) when they see the central bank in flames.

8 If your nationality is a potential problem, pretend to be from a different country. Canada is a popular choice for many American travelers—sew that maple leaf on your backpack!

9 Be flexible and able to respond fluidly to a changing situation. Balance the desire to leave quickly with the need to avoid unnecessary risks. If things are likely to calm down in a few days, consider laying low. If it's only getting worse, get out.

Tips

Few coups occur without some kind of warning. If a country's economy is rapidly breaking down, dramatic leadership changes are likely. Look for these signs, be prepared and make smart decisions.

Get to your embassy if mob activity appears imminent.

Warnings

Women should avoid traveling alone or without a male companion in certain countries.

If you carry a weapon, you'd better know how to use it.

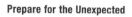

Sound extreme? Consider the full range of possible terrorist activities from both foreign and domestic sources, and it's reasonable to conclude that no location or person is completely safe in this post-9/11 era. The question, then, is what actions are effective and reasonable given your lifestyle and preferences.

Steps

1 Understand that terrorism is about creating terror. Fear is the real enemy. Do whatever it takes to make your family comfortable, but reinforce the point that the risk to any individual is very low. In statistical terms, traffic accidents are far more common than acts of terror, and few of us are scared about the prospect of being hit on the road.

2 Discuss terrorist activity with your family. If they have any fears, such as fear of flying outside the country, it's best to discuss them in the open and understand how they might play out.

3 Review possible action plans with your family, including where everyone may be at any given time and how to get all family members together again. Focus on actions each family member can take to reduce feelings of helplessness and fear. Review 464 Formulate a Family Emergency Plan.

4 Don't underestimate the benefit of activities that might seem ineffective to you but provide peace of mind to your family. For example, someone in your family may derive strength through church functions, discussion groups or even researching the root causes of terrorism. Encourage them to pursue such activities.

5 Review biohazard equipment and decide if buying it makes sense for you. While many experts feel there is little that any one person can do to ensure protection from a chemical or biological attack, it might be illuminating to inspect the gear. Just be sure you're not scaring your family; there's a fine line between being reassuringly prepared and creating panic and drama.

6 Research gas masks and protective suits. There are several online suppliers, including CivilianGasMasks.com and ApprovedGasMasks.com. These items may cost several hundred dollars each. Be sure the masks have proper filters and spares. An obvious problem to resolve is how to make this equipment available at all times. Unless you plan to carry it everywhere, there will be times when it's out of reach.

7 Stock up on emergency food, equipment and supplies (see 466 Assemble Emergency Kits).

Tips

Don't frighten children by including them in intense conversations; stick to describing "what to do" scenarios. Grown-ups can barely process this information, so limit what your kids hear to age-appropriate information and make them feel as safe as you can.

Stash an extra wired phone in your home and office. If the power goes out and your cordless unit dies, or cellular reception is impossible to get, an old-fashioned phone may save the day.

Who Knew?

Consider moving to an area with a lower risk of a terrorist attack. Cities with international stature have the highest risk of attack. Sharon Springs, Kansas, for example, has almost zero risk.

Warning

A gas mask won't protect you from all dangerous chemicals. Be sure you know which chemicals your filter is designed to protect against. Know the expiration date on its storage and how long it will last during use. View old army-surplus gas masks with extreme skepticism since many are outdated and useless.

Hostage situations are very unstable. In many cases, the perpetrators never wanted to take a hostage but felt forced to during an escape attempt, or decided their kidnap victim would help them make a political point. For both sides, hostage situations are hard to control. Anything can happen at any time.

Steps

1 Clear the surrounding area. Rescue personnel, spectators and reporters need to be kept well back. The more noise and activity, the higher the stress level for everyone and the less controlled the environment.

2 Identify a negotiator and prevent anyone except that person from communicating with or gaining access to the perpetrators.

3 Attempt to establish communication with the perpetrators. They undoubtedly have demands and are anxious to talk. At a minimum they should recognize that communication is the only way out. If a political group planned the hostage taking, expect exorbitant demands and a request for maximum media coverage.

4 Ascertain exactly how many perpetrators there are. This may be easy to do if they are making demands for transportation, as you can reasonably ask what capacity vehicle they need. If shooting starts, you need to know how many targets to track.

5 Establish the number of hostages taken. Determine if there is a way to evacuate all of them quickly.

6 Get a list of demands. Concede to some of them if possible in exchange for the release of some hostages.

7 Utilize high-tech tools to track the perpetrators' movements. Infrared sensors and listening devices can yield clues about perpetrators' numbers and plans. These devices need to be deployed in positions of close proximity, depending on the layout and architecture of the location and the technical limitations of the equipment.

8 Position sharpshooters in as many locations as possible. If there's only one perp and you get a good shot, take it.

9 Proceed slowly and recognize that the perpetrators don't hold all the cards. A perpetrator's threat of violence is therefore somewhat muted by his need to keep the negotiation moving.

10 Plan any intervention to occur at a transition point. If hostages and perpetrators are being driven to the airport, the move from car to airplane may offer an opportunity. The perpetrators have the least control at this time and are on terrain chosen by you.

11 Station additional sharpshooters and personnel at the intervention site. Assign targets to your team members and instruct them to shoot at your signal.

Tips

Seek assistance from people respected by the perpetrators. Parents, religious figures or political leaders may be helpful. These people can be put in touch with the perpetrators once you're assured of their support.

Check the phone book or the Internet for private firms that offer training in hostage rescue, as well as for security or bodyguard training.

Warnings

Agreeing to a terrorist's demands may be tempting, but it is, perhaps literally, a dead end. You are almost guaranteed to be targeted by additional groups.

Use extreme caution when placing tracking equipment, to avoid infuriating the perpetrators. A good time for your personnel to move is when the perpetrators are engaged in conversation with the official negotiator.

Arr, matey! 'Tis a dangerous life, the sea—full of giant beasts, raging storms and wayward ships bobbing around like steel icebergs. And that's not to mention the pirates. Sounds like an 18th-century fable, but the truth is, pirate attacks are a problem even today in some parts of the world. Small cargo ships and cruising sailboats are most at risk.

Steps

1 Research your route and find out if pirates have been spotted in the area. The Malay Peninsula, Somalia, parts of the South China Sea, and the Caribbean coast of South America are all active pirate spots. The International Maritime Bureau's Piracy Reporting Centre (www.iccwbo.org/ccs/menu_imb_piracy.asp) and sailing magazines frequently publish warnings as well.

2 Be aware of pirate tactics. They tend to follow a pattern, hitting the same routes or anchorages at certain times (moonless nights, for example). Adjust your route and schedule to minimize risk.

3 Form a fleet when traveling through dangerous waters. Single boats are far more likely to be attacked than groups. Maintain a speed that is comfortable for all boats in the flotilla, as well as a safe separation between boats. Post a watch at all times and come up with a fleet plan should any of the boats be attacked.

4 Maintain radio contact with the group. Or, if you're traveling alone, contact family or friends on shore at regular intervals. Rather than broadcast your exact position, establish an arbitrary reference point ahead of time and give your position in relation to it. Do not broadcast the coordinates of the reference point.

5 Keep in mind that most piracy incidents do not turn violent. The criminals take a few things and leave. But once pirates are aboard, armed resistance usually means a shootout. On the other hand, a visible show of arms before the pirates get close may convince them to choose an easier target.

6 Plant something in the safe so you can make a show of opening it and handing your valuables over. Conceal most other valuables in the many unlikely hiding places a boat offers. If pirates come aboard, they'll expect to leave with something, but that doesn't mean they have to find everything.

7 Make your boat less visible at night. Keep cabin lights off or concealed. In extremely dangerous locations, consider keeping your running lights off. The problem, of course, is that you're now invisible to other boats, including members of your own group. A collision might be more dangerous than a pirate incident.

8 Ram the pirates' boat. Most pirates use small powerboats and come alongside a sailboat or the stern ladder on a cargo ship. These small boats are no match for a sturdy cruising sailboat.

Tips

When in port, don't dress and act lavishly. Pirates live on land like the rest of us. They're likely to be in port and be keeping their eyes open for targets.

Purchase night-vision goggles. These are handy navigation tools anytime, but can also help you spot pirates before they spot you.

See 429 Plan a Sailboat Cruise.

Who Knew?

The International Chamber of Commerce (iccwbo.org) maintains a log of commercial piracy incidents. This might be helpful for identifying dangerous areas.

Warning

Guns are tempting to keep and use but introduce problems. When arriving at a new port or country, you will be asked about weapons. Your choice is to lie and possibly land in jail (which might make piracy seem like a holiday in comparison) or admit to having the guns (which may get them confiscated). See additional warnings in 464 Formulate a Family Emergency Plan.

481 | Deliver a Baby

The contractions are coming faster and the baby's not waiting. Whether you're the father, a friend or just an innocent bystander, you need to know that there's more to do than boil water and get towels. But remember, women have been having babies for millennia without much help, so don't try to do too much.

Steps

1 Call 911. Rally passersby to help (if you're really lucky, one will be a midwife or a doctor). Even if help is far away and you'll be on your own during the birth, you will want someone to walk you through it.

2 Do not freak out. Childbirth is designed to be noisy, messy and scary as a deterrent to the less committed. Your role is to be comforting and reassuring no matter how awful you feel.

3 Ask the woman if there are any problems you should be aware of in order to tell emergency personnel. Is she having twins? If the baby is oriented with its head up (a breech delivery), renew your efforts to get help quickly. In the meantime, wash your hands.

4 Talk to the woman. Tell her to breathe. If she feels like pushing, encourage her to pant instead. Wait until the contractions are strong and the baby is emerging (crowning). Have her push when contractions are strong and rest at other times.

5 Spread out a shower curtain, clean towels or newspaper. Help the woman sit at the edge of a bed or table with her hips hanging off and knees apart. If labor is too far along or it's too painful to climb on a bed or table, place a stack of newspapers or towels under her hips to raise them high enough to help deliver the baby's shoulders.

6 Cup the baby's head in your hands once it starts to come out and move it slightly downward as the woman pushes. If the umbilical cord is wrapped around the head or neck, gently work it free and clear the baby's mouth of any obstructions. Help the shoulders to ease out one at a time. Once both shoulders are clear, the baby should slip right out—so hang on!

7 Wipe the baby's face with a towel and check that the nose and mouth is clear. Suction the mouth if you have a syringe or bulb.

8 Wrap the baby in a clean towel or shirt and gently lay it on the mother's abdomen or at her breast (depending on how long the cord is). Nobody slaps newborns anymore.

9 Do not try to pull the placenta out. If it comes out on its own, wrap it in a newspaper or towel and keep it above the level of the baby's head until help arrives. Do not cut the cord.

10 Keep the mother and baby comfortable, warm and dry, and do nothing else if help is on the way. If help is not coming, get them to a hospital as soon as possible.

Tips

Many people choose to have a baby at home. Do plenty of research before you commit to this so you know both the risks and benefits and the amount of work involved. See 261 Prepare for Childbirth.

If you're in a car, have the woman lie down with one foot on the floor and the other on the seat.

Who Knew?

Collect towels and blankets (or a shirt or jacket) to dry off the baby and keep everyone warm afterward.

A woman's water can break hours before birth actually occurs. However, if contractions are less than two minutes apart, get ready. Irregular contractions could mean she's in false labor, and she probably has time to wait for help.

Warning

Don't drop the baby.

"This is niner, twelve, niner to tower. The pilot's unconscious, and the copilot is dead. How do I land this plane?!" Hey, it could happen. Would you know what to do to land a commercial airliner? Just remember, it's only the lives of yourself, the passengers and crew and those people on the ground that are at risk.

Steps

1 Remain calm. Don't do anything for a few seconds to get your bearings. As long as the plane is in steady flight, everything is OK for the time being.

2 Put your hands on the control yoke (the stick), right in front of you. It's simple—pull back to ascend, push forward to descend. Ascending sounds safe, but if you do so too aggressively, the engine will stall, a technical flying term that means "die." Keep the stick centered.

3 Locate the attitude indicator (usually on the console in front of you), which shows an image of a plane relative to a straight line (an artificial horizon). Nudge the yoke until the plane is level.

4 Locate the airspeed indicator, also in front of you. You must maintain airspeed in order to remain flying. Place a hand on the throttles, the largest levers in the center console. If the airspeed is dropping, nudge the levels forward for more power. Increase power until speed is stable in level flight.

5 Put on the radio headset, which will already be tuned to an active frequency. If the frequency dial is obvious, switch to 121.5 megahertz, the emergency frequency. The transmit button is on the yoke. Don't worry about radio protocol; just state your situation.

6 Wait for a reply and then follow instructions. The air controller may ask you to switch radio frequencies.

7 Look at the compass in front of you. You will be given a course to follow, for example, "Turn left (using the yoke) until the compass reads 175 degrees." Expect several course changes to line you up with an airfield.

8 Deploy the landing gear. Get confirmation from the ground that it's in place.

9 Decrease airspeed to the minimum instructed by ground control.

10 Extend the flaps fully once you're lined up with the landing strip.

11 Use the yoke to maintain a level or slightly nose-up position, and allow the plane to settle onto the ground. Don't aim down into the ground. Hang on tight when you touch down.

12 Apply the brakes fully once all wheels are down. Wait until the plane comes to a full and complete stop.

13 Get a drink. Then read 409 Rent a Car in the United States.

Tips

There are numerous types of commercial airplanes. Your helpers on the ground will probably know what you're flying, but look around the cockpit for clues. If nothing else, get a safety card from one of the passenger seats and read it from there.

See 491 Learn to Fly.

Who Knew?

The Aircraft Owners and Pilots Association (aopa.org) offers its Pinchhitter Course to anyone who spends a lot of time in a plane. This is a course for nonpilots who would like to know how to handle an emergency. It's popular among spouses of pilots.

The hardest part of most tasks is the planning. But that's no problem for you, is it, Sergeant Hard Time? You've got an empty schedule, a few clever ideas and plenty of motivation.

Steps

Preparing

1 Be patient. Sure, it's hard. If you possessed virtues like patience and foresight, you might not be locked up in the first place.

2 Keep your mouth shut. More crimes get solved because of stupid criminals than because of smart cops. Don't give anyone a chance to mess up your plan.

3 Study prison routines. When is staffing the lightest? Who are the least vigilant and capable guards? Which guards can you bribe? Are there periods when the general atmosphere is optimally confused and noisy?

4 Extend your planning to beyond the confines of the prison itself. You not only need to get out of this building, you need to get into a safe building. Have a hideout and some trustworthy collaborators waiting for you on the outside. Make sure that your henchmen don't harbor any grudges against you and that there isn't a tempting reward for turning you in.

5 Review your choices regarding hideouts. Another thing about stupid criminals: They're predictable. Stupidity and predictability go together like rats and cheese. Don't go to your girlfriend's or your mother's house.

Taking action

1 Have an accomplice get a job with the U.S. Post Office.

2 Get a job in the prison mail room. Become a model worker.

3 Make sure your accomplice has a set of clothes for you and perhaps a plane ticket and passport.

4 Have your accomplice drive the mail delivery truck to the jail.

5 After the day's mail is unloaded, load yourself in its place and drive out.

6 If this fails, just make the most of your free meals and wait for massive budget cuts that force the release of hundreds of prisoners.

Tips

Wouldn't it be easier to stay out of jail in the first place?

Your jail probably has guidelines about using deadly force on escaping prisoners. You might find these details interesting.

See 405 Plan a Trip.

Who Knew?

Turns out there is such a thing as a permanent record. This will definitely go on your permanent record.

ORGANIZED • SET PRIORITIES • WRITE AN EFFECTIVE TO-DO LIST •
GANIZE YOUR CONTACTS • GET RID OF WHAT YOU DON'T WANT • SAY NO WITHOUT FEELING GUILTY • BALANCE HOME AND WORK • LI
RAIN • SCHEDULE TELEVISION WATCHING • DESIGN A HEALTHY LIFESTYLE • PLAN TO AVOID JUNK FOOD • CHOOSE A WEIGHT LOSS PLA
EET AN ONLINE DATE • PLAN THE PERFECT DATE • MASTERMIND A BREAKUP • PLAN YOUR SOCIAL CALENDAR • MEET MR. OR MS. RIGH
ORT YOUR SOCK DRAWER • RETURN RENTALS ON TIME • TAKE CONTROL OF YOUR JUNK DRAWER • ORGANIZE THE MEDICINE CABINET
AR CLEAN AND ORDERLY • DEAL WITH A PACK RAT • SELL STUFF ONLINE • ORGANIZE YOUR BOOKSHELVES • CATEGORIZE NEWSPAPER
VE BETTER THROUGH LABELING • ORGANIZE JEWELRY • PLAN YOUR DREAM KITCHEN • CONQUER YOUR CLOSETS • ORGANIZE THE LIN
RGANIZE SPRING CLEANING • KEEP THE FAMILY ROOM ORGANIZED • SET UP A BATHROOM SCHEDULE • ORGANIZE BATHROOMS • ORG
RGANIZE KIDS' ROOMS • ORGANIZE SPORTS EQUIPMENT • ORGANIZE KIDS' PLAY SPACES • SAFEGUARD YOUR HOME AGAINST ALLERG
OUSE • USE HOME DESIGN AND PLANNING SOFTWARE • ESTABLISH YOUR HOME'S SPACE PLAN • INCORPORATE UNIVERSAL DESIGN PR
HE BASEMENT • ORGANIZE THE GARAGE • ORGANIZE A TOOLBOX • SET UP A WOODSHOP • ORGANIZE YOUR WINE COLLECTION • PLAN
TUDIO OR SMALL APARTMENT • MANAGE WARRANTY DOCUMENTS • MANAGE HOME-IMPROVEMENT PAPERWORK • MERGE TWO HOUSE
RGANIC VEGETABLE GARDEN • PLANT A KITCHEN HERB GARDEN • PLAN A BUTTERFLY GARDEN • DESIGN A BIRD GARDEN • DESIGN A C
ORGANIZE GARDENING TOOLS • ADD A POTTING BENCH TO A YARD • SCHEDULE FRUIT TREE MAINTENANCE • LAY OUT A SPRINKLER SY
ESIGN A GARDEN PATH • SET UP A COMPOST SYSTEM • WINTERIZE PLANTS • SCHEDULE YARD WORK • STORE ANYTHING • STORE BUL
ND HOBBY MATERIALS • ORGANIZE ART SUPPLIES • ORGANIZE GIFT WRAP AND SEASONAL DECORATIONS • ORGANIZE KIDS' SCHOOLW
OUR WEDDING DRESS AND OTHER TEXTILES • STORE A FUR COAT • STORE BICYCLES AND GEAR • STORE SKI GEAR • ORGANIZE CAMP
HICH COLLEGE IS RIGHT FOR YOU • GET INTO A TOP COLLEGE OR UNIVERSITY • ACE THE COLLEGE ADMISSIONS TESTS • ORGANIZE YO
AW SCHOOL • PREPARE FOR THE BAR EXAM • GET A DEGREE WHILE YOU'RE WORKING • WORK AT HOME WITH KIDS • GO BACK TO WO
RGANIZE YOUR JOB SEARCH • PREPARE FOR A CAREER CHANGE • OPEN A RESTAURANT • BECOME A PHYSICIST • BECOME A CONCER
EALITY-SHOW CONCEPT • BECOME A TALK-SHOW HOST • BECOME A PHOTOJOURNALIST • BECOME A MOVIE DIRECTOR • BECOME A M
LING SYSTEM • ORGANIZE YOUR BRIEFCASE • ORGANIZE YOUR DESK • ORGANIZE YOUR WORKDAY • GET A HANDLE ON E-MAIL • ORG
ALARY REVIEW • CLIMB THE CORPORATE LADDER EFFECTIVELY • ADD A WORKSPACE TO ANY ROOM • ORGANIZE A HOME OFFICE • OR
RAVEL • WRITE A BUSINESS PLAN • SET UP A NEW BUSINESS • CREATE A MARKETING PLAN • AMASS A REAL-ESTATE EMPIRE • POLISH
MPLOYEE • FIRE AN EMPLOYEE • PASS ON A FAMILY BUSINESS • STAY ON TOP OF YOUR SALES GAME • RESTRUCTURE A COMPANY TO
EFEND AGAINST A HOSTILE TAKEOVER • ORGANIZE YOUR OFFICE FOR A MOVE • PREPARE YOUR BUSINESS FOR THE UNTHINKABLE • R
REPARE YOUR TAXES • ORGANIZE A LOAN APPLICATION • ORGANIZE IMPORTANT DOCUMENTS • SAVE FOR PRIVATE SCHOOLING • ORG
LUB • TRACK YOUR INVESTMENTS • SURVIVE BANKRUPTCY • PLAN FOR RETIREMENT • PREPARE A PRENUPTIAL AGREEMENT • CREATE
ONEY • PLAN YOUR FAMILY • BUDGET FOR A NEW BABY • ORCHESTRATE THE PERFECT CONCEPTION • PLAN FOR ARTIFICIAL INSEMINA
EAVE • ORDER BABY ANNOUNCEMENTS • ORGANIZE AN INTERNATIONAL ADOPTION • FOSTER A CHILD • ORGANIZE YOUR LIFE AS A NEW
OORDINATE A FAMILY CALENDAR • PLAN FAMILY MEETINGS • ORGANIZE HOME SYSTEMS FOR ADD • PREPARE FOR A NEW CAT OR DOG
ACK-TO-SCHOOL • WIN THE HOMEWORK WARS • PLAN A FIELD TRIP • PLAN YOUR CHILD'S ACTIVITIES • PLAN YOUR CHILDREN'S SUM
NLINE • ORGANIZE A GENEALOGICAL SEARCH • PREPARE FOR YOUR CHILD'S DEPARTURE FOR COLLEGE • ORGANIZE YOUR EMPTY NE
LDERLY PARENTS' CARE • PREPARE FOR THE DEATH OF A SPOUSE • HELP YOUR ELDERLY PARENTS MOVE • ORGANIZE A HOME MEDICA
TORE TRIPS • SET UP ONLINE GROCERY SHOPPING • ORGANIZE RECIPES AND COOKBOOKS • PLAN THEME MENUS • CREATE EFFECTIV
EFRIGERATOR AND FREEZER • ORGANIZE CUTLERY AND KITCHEN TOOLS • ORGANIZE CUPBOARDS AND DRAWERS • ORGANIZE THE PA
UNCHES FOR KIDS • PLAN PARTY FOODS AHEAD • THROW A DINNER PARTY • FINISH DINNER ON TIME • PULL OFF A LAST-MINUTE PART
LTIMATE WEDDING CHECKLIST • BUDGET FOR A WEDDING • FIND THE PERFECT WEDDING RING • PLAN AN ELOPEMENT • SET UP A BAR
ONOR • EXECUTE BEST MAN DUTIES • HIRE A BAND • HIRE A BARTENDER • PLAN A SHOWER • ORGANIZE THE REHEARSAL DINNER • P
UCCESSFUL SLUMBER PARTY • PLAN A BAR OR BAT MITZVAH • PLAN A QUINCEAÑERA • PLAN A RETIREMENT PARTY • PLAN A FUNERA
ANUKKAH PARTY • ORGANIZE A HOLIDAY CRAFT PARTY • PLAN TO SPEND CHRISTMAS SOLO • PLAN THE PERFECT HOLIDAY GIFT EXCH
HE HOLIDAYS • STICK TO YOUR NEW YEAR'S RESOLUTIONS • PLAN THE PERFECT NEW YEAR'S EVE • PLAN A SEDER • PLAN A SPECIAL
OOD TREE • ORGANIZE A BICYCLE SCAVENGER HUNT • RUN A SPORTS TOURNAMENT • PUBLICIZE AN EVENT • PLAN AN ORGANIZATIO
LAN A CONCERT IN THE PARK • ORGANIZE AN INTERNATIONAL CONCERT TOUR • ORGANIZE A FILM FESTIVAL • PLAN A FUND-RAISING
BUILD A COMMUNITY PLAY STRUCTURE • THROW A BLOCK PARTY • SET UP A NEIGHBORHOOD WATCH • CREATE AN EVACUATION PLA
ORGANIZE A PROTEST OR MARCH • FIGHT CITY HALL • ORGANIZE A BOYCOTT • ORGANIZE A CLASS ACTION LAWSUIT • MANAGE GROW
CHOOL IN A THIRD WORLD COUNTRY • PLAN A TRIP • PLAN A TRIP WITH CHILDREN • TRAVEL WITH TEENS • BOOK AIRLINE TICKETS • P
MOTORCYCLE TRIP • PLAN A TRAIN TRIP IN THE UNITED STATES • RIDE THE RAILS ABROAD • PREPARE A VACATION COUNTDOWN CHEC
UGGAGE • LOAD A BACKPACK PROPERLY • PLAN AN ELDERHOSTEL TRIP • ORGANIZE AN RV VACATION • PLAN A TRIP WITH AGING PAR
IDELY DIFFERENT PEOPLE • PLAN SPRING BREAK • PLAN AN OVERNIGHT GETAWAY WITH YOUR SPOUSE • PLAN A VACATION SEPARATE
OLITICALLY UNSTABLE REGION • GET TRAVEL INSURANCE • GET IMMUNIZATIONS FOR TRAVELING • BOOK AN ADVENTURE VACATION •
LAN A FISHING TRIP TO ALASKA • PACK FOR A CAMPING TRIP • LEAD A BACKPACK TRIP • HIKE A FAMOUS TRAIL • PLAN A TOUR OF TH
NGLISH CANAL TRIP • PLAN A CROSS-COUNTRY AIRPLANE VOYAGE • PLAN THE PERFECT DAY ABROAD • PLAN A VISIT TO THE LOUVRE
LAN • PREPARE FOR AN ACT OF GOD • ASSEMBLE EMERGENCY KITS • PREPARE FOR SURGERY • PLAN YOUR RECOVERY • SURVIVE A
BEING LOST • CONDUCT A SEARCH AND RESCUE OPERATION • PLAN AN INVASION • SURVIVE A POLITICAL COUP • PLAN FOR A TERROR

ESS • SET GOALS • STREAMLINE YOUR MORNING ROUTINE • ORGANIZE A CHORE SCHEDULE FOR KIDS • ORGANIZE YOUR CHORES • N
YOUR WORKOUT SCHEDULE • SCHEDULE DOCTOR VISITS • PREPARE FOR COLD AND FLU SEASON • GET A DRASTIC MAKEOVER • AR
UP • FIND YOUR KEYS • TIDY UP IN MINUTES • CONQUER CLUTTER • ACTUALLY SEE THE BOTTOM OF YOUR PURSE • ORGANIZE YOUR
E CAR MAINTENANCE • ORGANIZE PET SUPPLIES • MANAGE GARBAGE AND RECYCLABLES • PREPARE GRAB 'N' GO ACTIVITY BAGS • K
ZINE CLIPPINGS • ORGANIZE YOUR PHOTOS • ARRANGE PHOTOS AND PICTURES • ARRANGE AN ART COLLECTION • END COLLECTION
T • ORGANIZE YOUR LAUNDRY CENTER • CREATE A SEWING CENTER • GET READY FOR THE HOUSECLEANER • ORGANIZE CLEANING SU
YWAYS AND MUDROOMS • ORGANIZE A DORM ROOM • ORGANIZE YOUR SCHOOL LOCKER • MAKE YOUR HOME SAFE FOR SMALL CHIL
ARE FOR SKYROCKETING ENERGY COSTS • USE FENG SHUI TO ORGANIZE YOUR HOME • DESIGN A NEW HOME WITH FENG SHUI • DES
PLAN A REMODEL • PLAN A MULTIMEDIA CENTER • TURN A BASEMENT INTO A MEDIA ROOM OR PLAYROOM • ORGANIZE THE ATTIC • C
SFUL ESTATE SALE • PLAN A YARD OR GARAGE SALE • PREPARE YOUR HOME FOR SALE • PLAN A MOVE • DOWNSIZE YOUR HOUSE • O
ECORATE FOR THE SEASONS • PREPARE A VACATION HOME FOR THE OFF-SEASON • PREPARE YOUR HOME FOR NATURE'S WORST • PR
GARDEN • PLANT A CUT-FLOWER GARDEN • DESIGN A SHADE GARDEN • DESIGN A DRY GARDEN • PLAN FOR A LONG-SEASON CONTAIN
AN AND PLANT A LAWN • DESIGN A NEW LANDSCAPE • PLAN AN OUTDOOR KITCHEN • DESIGN A DECK OR PATIO • DESIGN A WATER FEA
ES • STORAGE SOLUTIONS FOR ANY ROOM • [...] THE CAPACITY OF A SMALL ROOM • ORGANI
RTWORK • ORGANIZE MOVIES, MUSIC AND O[...] IRLOOMS • STORE OUT-OF-SEASON CLOTHES
ENT • STORE PAINT AND OTHER HAZARDOUS[...] STORE A BOAT FOR THE WINTER • STORE A C.
GE APPLICATIONS • PLAN YOUR COURSE OF[...] CH PAPER • GET INTO GRAD SCHOOL • GET INT
LONG ABSENCE • SET UP AN INTERNSHIP •[...] N THE PEACE CORPS • PRODUCE A NEWSLETTE
• BECOME A COWBOY • BECOME A BRAIN S[...] ATHOLIC NUN • ORGANIZE AN EXHIBITION • DE
OME A STUNT PERSON • BECOME A TOUR G[...] • CONQUER YOUR PAPER PILES • CREATE A F
UTER FILES • SCHEDULE APPOINTMENTS EF[...] NCE CALL • PREPARE FOR A MEETING • PREPAR
ME NETWORK • CHOOSE THE BEST PHONE [...] TEM • MAKE A NETWORKING PLAN • PLAN YOU
NTATION SKILLS • PREPARE A SPEECH • PR[...] AN AN IPO • DELEGATE RESPONSIBILITIES • HIR
ROFITS • FORM A BOARD OF DIRECTORS • [...] AN A COMPANY PICNIC • PLAN A COMPANY RET
A FAILING BUSINESS • DISMANTLE A BUSINE[...] • DESIGN A SAVINGS PLAN • SIMPLIFY BILL PAY
FINANCIAL-AID PACKAGE • PLAN FOR COLLE[...] E A HEALTH INSURANCE PLAN • START AN INVE
UST • MAKE A WILL • EXECUTE A POWER OF[...] S' ESTATE • PLAN YOUR ESTATE • TEACH YOUR
ARE FOR AN IN VITRO FERTILIZATION • PREP[...] ATERNITY WARDROBE • SET UP MATERNITY OR
PREPARE FOR CHILDBIRTH • STOCK A DIAPE[...] BLEND FAMILIES • CREATE A HOUSEHOLD ORGA
OOL YOUR CHILD • SET UP A CARPOOL • S[...] HE BEST ELEMENTARY SCHOOL • ORGANIZE KID
OR SUMMER CAMP • CHOOSE A SUMMER S[...] R FAMILY COMPUTER USE • PLAN TO KEEP YOU
R BOOMERANG KIDS • PLAN AN AMICABLE [...] EMENTS • ORGANIZE MEDICAL RECORDS • PLAN
E • ARRANGE HOSPICE CARE • MAKE YOUR [...] ECORDS • PLAN A WEEK OF MENUS • ORGANIZ
LISTS • COOK AHEAD • DETERMINE THE SH[...] M WAREHOUSE STORES • EFFICIENTLY USE THE
ENTLY USE SPACE UNDER THE SINK • STOV[...] UR COUNTER SPACE • COOK FOR ONE • PLAN I
DINNER PARTY FOR YOUR BOSS • PLAN DI[...] PARTY • IMPRESS A DATE • PLAN A WEDDING •
ENT PLANNER • HIRE A PHOTOGRAPHER • [...] ACHELORETTE PARTY • PREPARE TO BE THE MA
NEYMOON • PLAN A BAPTISM • PLAN A BRI[...] KNOW A PARTY • PREPARE FOR HOUSE GUESTS • PLAN A CHILD'S BIRTHDAY PARTY •

In Your Dreams

TO CUSTOM • PLAN AHEAD FOR A LOW-STRESS HOLIDAY • STAY WITHIN A BUDGET THIS CHRISTMAS • PREPARE A HOLIDAY FEAST • T
NIZE GIFT-GIVING IN ADVANCE • STICK TO YOUR DIET DURING THE HOLIDAYS • PLAN A HOLIDAY OPEN HOUSE • REORGANIZE YOUR LIF
• ORGANIZE A HIGH-SCHOOL CLASS REUNION • PLAN A FAMILY REUNION • START A KNITTING CIRCLE • ORGANIZE A BOOK CLUB • SE
• SHARPEN THE FOCUS OF AN ORGANIZATION • IMPROVE YOUR CHILD'S SCHOOL • PLAN A PROM • ORGANIZE A COMMUNITY THEATER
NIZE A PANCAKE BREAKFAST • PLAN A TOY DRIVE • HOLD A BARN RAISING • ORGANIZE A CHARITY WALK OR RUN • BUILD LOW-INCOM
TER-REGISTRATION DRIVE • RUN FOR LOCAL OFFICE • ORGANIZE A PETITION • ORGANIZE A RECALL • GET AN INITIATIVE ON THE BALL
OMMUNITY • PRESERVE OPEN SPACE • SAVE HISTORIC PROPERTIES AND LANDMARKS • SET UP A NONGOVERNMENTAL ORGANIZATION
THE UNITED STATES • RENT A CAR ABROAD • MAKE HOTEL RESERVATIONS • ARRANGE EXECUTIVE ACCOMMODATIONS • PLAN A CRUIS
RE AN ITINERARY • PACK FOR A TRIP • PACK FOR A BUSINESS TRIP • PACK FOR A WEEK IN ONE CARRY-ON • PACK A DAY BAG • PREVEN
IZE A SAILING TEAM • PLAN A SAILBOAT CRUISE • PLAN A BICYCLE TRIP WITH A TOUR COMPANY • TRAVEL ABROAD • PLAN A VACATIO
SPOUSE • PLAN A TRIP TO A DIFFERENT CULTURE • FORAGE ABROAD • MAIL PACKAGES BACK TO THE UNITED STATES • PLAN A TRIP TO
LK ROAD • PLAN A CLIMB OF MOUNT KILIMANJARO • PACK FOR A SAFARI • ORGANIZE A HUNTING TRIP • PACK FOR A FISHING OR HUN
RKS • ORGANIZE A BACKCOUNTRY SKI TRIP • ORGANIZE A CAR RALLY • PLAN A WHALE-WATCHING TRIP • PACK FOR A VOYAGE AT SEA
SYDNEY HARBOUR BRIDGE • PLAN A TRIP TO NEW ORLEANS FOR MARDI GRAS • PLAN A DAY AT DISNEYLAND • FORMULATE A FAMILY
IF YOU'RE ALONE • SURVIVE IF YOUR CAR BREAKS DOWN • DEAL WITH AMNESIA • FIGHT AN EBOLA OUTBREAK • FIGHT A FOREST FIR
ESCUE A HOSTAGE • OUTSMART PIRATES • DELIVER A BABY • MAKE AN EMERGENCY LANDING • MAKE A JAIL BREAK • BECOME A MO

Although there are many movie roles in the world that need filling, a scant few are starring roles for that irresistibly charming, fabulously talented actor around whom directors craft top movies. To get your star on the Walk of Fame, you need plenty of luck and talent. Don't invest in those Revo sunglasses yet—years of hard work lie ahead.

Steps

1 Start early. Try out for parts in school plays, community theater, anything that gives you stage time.

2 Take acting lessons from an accredited local theater company or university, or a professional actor's studio.

3 Attend one of the country's top notch drama and performing arts programs including those at New York University (nyu.edu), the Julliard School (julliard.edu), Yale (yale.edu), Carnegie Mellon (cmu.edu/cfa/drama), Northwestern University (northwestern.edu), North Carolina's School of the Arts (ncarts.edu), and the California Institute of the Arts (calarts.edu).

4 Audition for school films, indies and low-budget films. Go to Auditions.net to explore your options. Expect constant rejection: Perseverance and resilience are your greatest allies.

5 Join the Screen Actors Guild (SAG.org), the labor union from which major movies hire their acting talent. You can't become a SAG member until you land a role, and you can't be cast in a film until you become a SAG member, a catch-22 that many film careers have foundered on. In order to break the stalemate, you need to "know" somebody who will help you get a speaking role of just one word. Or, take advantage of SAG's recently introduced points system (sag.org). Work as an extra and attend sanctioned events to build up enough points to qualify for membership. Or, take your chances and audition at a cattle call—casting directors are always looking for new talent.

6 Move to New York or Los Angeles and get an agent. He or she gets information about auditions for roles, either directly from casting directors and producers or from "the breakdowns," a daily faxed list of roles being cast that is only available to agents, managers and union members. It's brutally tough to get an agent if you're not a SAG member, and you might have to make due with a manager until you get a break.

7 Look good. This isn't necessary for every role, but the better you look, the more buzz you'll get. In fact, if you look good enough, you can skip all the other steps. See 28 Get a Drastic Makeover.

8 Choose your films carefully. It may be impossible to predict a hit—in fact Hollywood is littered with stories of actors tuning down a role that turned out to be a sensation—but pick roles (and directors) that will further the development of your craft.

Tips

The New York Film Academy (nyfa.com) offers a summer acting camp for high school students.

See 486 Win an Academy Award and 377 Organize a Community Theater Troupe.

Work on your singing ability to open up new roles and expand your vocal skills.

Who Knew?

If you had to make a choice between being really gifted and really driven, choose drive. Hard work will get you farther than talent any day (but having talent helps!).

SAG membership can be expensive, with initiation fees of almost $1,200 and annual dues based your earnings.

Assemble a portfolio with professional head shots and descriptions of your roles and training. See 180 Become a Model for more tips. Make sure your headshot reflects the image you want to portray and the roles you're looking for.

Warning

Don't be a prima donna. If you're difficult to work with, you won't get call-backs.

American kids grow up hearing that anyone can become president, but so far fewer than 50 people have done it (and they've all been white men). You need drive, charisma, money and backing—not to mention experience, diplomacy, connections, cunning and a commanding knowledge of foreign and domestic issues.

Steps

1 Be at least 35 years old and a citizen born in the United States, Guam, Puerto Rico or the U.S. Virgin Islands (or to American parents abroad). You also need to have been a U.S. resident for at least 14 years.

2 Hold a law degree. Out of 43 presidents, 25 have been lawyers. It also helps to have government service on your résumé— 17 governors, 15 senators and 19 members of the House of Representatives have become president.

3 Start raising money—lots of it. You've got a long way to go. The Bush-Cheney ticket, for example, spent $186 million campaigning in 2000. See 381 Plan a Fund-Raising Event.

4 Gather a bright, devoted and tireless campaign staff, including strategists, spokespeople and speechwriters.

5 Campaign like crazy before and during your party's primaries and caucuses. They begin in January of each election year.

6 Name your running mate. When you look at potential candidates for vice president, take into consideration the voting block he or she is supported by and can help deliver (the South, the labor vote, women, senior citizens, military veterans). If your experience is weak in certain areas, your running mate can strengthen it with his our her own background. Bottom line: Pick someone who would be a good president should you die or otherwise leave office. See 349 Plan a Funeral According to Custom.

7 Win the majority of delegates who will vote at your party's national convention. If you don't have more than half in your camp going into the convention, work on the unpledged delegates. These include high-ranking party members, governors and congressional representatives.

8 Celebrate your convention victory, and campaign like crazy all over the country until elections in November.

9 Win a majority of the electoral college, which isn't the same thing as the popular vote. There are 538 electoral votes, and you need 270 of them to become president.

10 Practice reciting the oath for the inaugural ceremony on January 20: "I do solemnly swear (or affirm) that I will faithfully execute the office of president of the United States, and will to the best of my ability preserve, protect and defend the Constitution of the United States."

Tips

See 392 Run for Local Office.

If the final vote is close and not in your favor, find a reason to demand a recount. You may not win the presidency, but it will get you a footnote in history.

If you don't have a government background, be a victorious general. It has worked wonders for many candidates, from Washington to Eisenhower.

Also see 476 Plan an Invasion and 484 Become a Movie Star.

Who Knew?

The president of the United States makes $400,000 a year.

Shave your facial hair. Only five presidents have had beards when they entered the White House.

Five vice presidents were later elected president.

Warning

If you engage in adulterous affairs, don't get caught.

All the hard work and skill in the world might not be enough to win an Oscar as the Academy of Motion Picture Arts and Sciences (oscars.org) is famously erratic in its choices. There are, however, ways to increase your chances of putting a charming gold statuette on your bookshelf.

Tip

Read 484 Become a Movie Star, darling.

Steps

1 Work hard to perfect your craft. Alternate between work on big-budget and small independent films. It's impossible to know where the next hit is coming from, so you have to cast your net widely.

2 Avoid becoming associated with a sole film genre or type of character. Broaden your repertoire and develop your skills in a variety of films.

3 Be in a movie or release your film after September. You want the film or your performance to be fresh in Academy voters' minds.

4 Get your studio to create a buzz around yourself or your film. This means sending the film to every voting Academy member, marching you around to talk shows and angling you for magazine covers. If you win, it will translate into millions at the box office.

5 Win an award from another prestigious organization. This list includes the Chicago Film Critics, the National Board of Review, the New York Film Critics, the Los Angeles Film Critics, and especially the Hollywood Foreign Press Association's Golden Globe Awards, which in recent years has been the best indicator of who will win an Oscar.

6 Understand how the Oscar nomination process works. In most of the award categories (see Tips), three to five people or films are nominated (the number varies by year and depends on the category). The Academy is divided into branches: acting, directing, editing, writing, sound and music. Each member belongs to only one branch. In late December, Academy members receive a ballot and nominate people or films only for their branch. Note: Now is the time to cozy up to the members in your branch.

7 Wait for a call from your manager. In late January, the top five nominees are announced in each category. Final ballots are mailed soon after to Academy members.

8 Ask your manager to borrow a selection of gowns or tuxedos from the hottest designers, and some baubles from Harry Winston.

9 Attend the awards ceremony at the end of February and listen for your name. The Oscar winner for each category is voted on by the whole membership, not just the branch as with the nomination procedure.

10 Get your speech ready (see 208 Prepare a Speech).

Who Knew?

These are all of the "Best" award categories: picture, director, actor, actress, supporting actor, supporting actress, original screenplay, adapted screenplay, foreign language film, original song, original score, animated short film, cinematography, editing, costume design, art/set direction, sound, sound effects editing, visual effects, makeup, documentary feature, live action short film and documentary short subject.

Of the Academy members, actors can only nominate actors, while music branch members may nominate people for song and score. For documentary, live action short, animated and foreign, a preselected panel picks the nominees.

To be the absolute best in the world—it's a dream that drives Olympic hopefuls around the world. Every kid swimming her first 100-meter freestyle or kicking his first shot into the goal imagines a gold medal hanging around his or her neck. If you have superb genetic qualifications, possess incredible mental and physical strength and can commit to years of grueling training and tough competition, you just might see your country's flag rising above the podium one day.

Steps

1 Pick a sport. You have two paths—go with a sport you know and like, or pick an obscure one. A familiar sport may seem like an obvious choice, but think carefully—popular sports have millions of dedicated participants, and competition is stiff. Less well-known options, such as short-track speed skating, luge, bobsledding and pentathlon, have fewer competitors.

2 Evaluate your physique and choose a sport that suits it. No matter how dedicated you are, unless you have the physical makeup for extreme endurance, you'll never be an Olympic marathoner. And if you're tall and over the age of 16, kiss gymnastics goodbye. Consult a sports physiologist to establish your specific attributes.

3 Spend years and years working at your sport. Develop all aspects of fitness, strength and endurance. Incorporate cross-training into your regime to prevent boredom and injury.

4 Believe in yourself. Have your mental game ready, be tough in every aspect, refuse to give up.

5 Attend a sports academy. These schools provide intensive training in the sport of your choice at the high-school level. The experience, exposure and coaching that you get will qualify you for a college that excels in your sport.

6 Work with excellent coaches to develop your skills. Hire a sports psychologist to help you set and reach goals. Hire a private coach if needed. See 10 Set Goals.

7 Make the national team in your sport and train year-round (there is no off-season for an Olympian). Be able to perform well under incredible pressure and fend off all other competitors until you make the Olympic team.

8 Change your citizenship. It may be much easier to qualify for a spot on the Pakistani sailing team than on the U.S. team. Some countries ask for proof of ancestry, such as a grandparent born in the country.

Tips

Just because you're past your 20s, doesn't mean you can't go for the gold. Some sports, such as archery, curling and sailing, include competitors of many ages.

Go to a university that consistently wins the NCAA championships in your sport. You may get a scholarship as a bonus.

Join the association or governing body for your sport. This will keep you informed of major competitions, including the Olympic trials.

Move to an area that is well known for your sport. If you're a ski racer, for example, live in a major ski town with an active racing scene. Colorado is a mecca for bike racers.

See 488 Train for a Major Athletic Event, 489 Win the Tour de France and 490 Run a Marathon.

Who Knew?

In the past, only amateur athletes could compete. This is no longer the case, as was evidenced by the NBA-staffed Dream Team of the 1992 Barcelona Olympics.

If you change nationality, International Olympic Committee rules prevent you from competing in international events for three years.

488 | Train for a Major Athletic Event

If you've broken free of the 10K masses and have your heart set on competing in a major race, you'll need to create a solid plan and be prepared—mentally and physically—for a lot of hard work. The key thing is to incorporate a full range of aerobic, strength and endurance training into your schedule.

Steps

1 Create a training schedule that covers all aspects of your preparation, including strength training, endurance work, and building explosive power (if needed) in your sport. Consult your coach to adjust your workload and the workout intensity throughout your schedule to maximize results.

2 Train in different locations and at different times of the day so you don't get bored with your routine. Do a five- to ten-minute warm-up and full body stretch before and after every workout session.

3 Schedule regular rest days. Deep recovery is as vital to maximizing performance as any other aspect of your training.

4 Work with a sports psychologist to maximize your mental training. Hire a coach to watch your workouts regularly, suggest improved training methods and correct your technique.

5 Lessen the intensity of your training as the event approaches by gradually reducing your training load. This ensures that your fitness and recovery levels both peak on the day of the event. See 490 Run a Marathon.

6 Eat a well-balanced diet throughout your training. It should include plenty of complex carbohydrates to fuel your intense physical output. Drink at least 6 to 8 pints of water a day to prevent dehydration. Consume alcohol in moderation since it's dehydrating and interferes with your sleep cycle.

7 Rest as much as possible in the days leading up to the event. Focus on getting solid sleep at night, and continue tapering your workouts.

8 Eat your pre-event meal as close to the event as possible, but far enough in advance so that your stomach is empty when you start. For most people that's about three hours before the event. This is not the time to try new foods—and stay away from fish or spicy foods.

9 Arrive 30 minutes to an hour before the start of the event to collect your entry number, use the bathroom, stretch, prepare your equipment and mentally focus on the challenge ahead.

Tips

There's a tendency to focus on one particular aspect of the training process. A balanced program—including physical and mental training, motivation, technique and organization—will help raise your performance level.

Join a "team in training" group at your health club or local YMCA to get helpful advice and inspiration. This is also a much less expensive option than hiring a professional trainer.

Who Knew?

Stick to your plan: This is important. As the event comes ever closer, you may start to panic and begin to question your ability or preparation. Calm down. If you've done the long-term training, you should have no problems.

Warnings

Consult your physician before beginning any intense training program.

Obey your body rather than a book or a training program. If you feel exhausted, rest for a day or two.

The key to winning this century-old French bicycle race is to be Lance Armstrong. If you're not, then you'll need years of training, incredible power and stamina, several bikes, a coach, a sponsored team and at least eight months of course preparation. Don't forget a killer work ethic, superhuman willpower and superb strategy: The Tour de France is a test of human spirit as much as physical prowess.

Steps

1 Start pedaling: the Tour de France covers approximately 2,000 miles and 20 individual stages, with a different course every year. The lead changes hands several times during the three-week race, with time bonuses and penalties influencing overall time. When that last lap on the Champs-Elysées is completed, the rider with the lowest combined time (general classification) takes home the trophy—and the *maillot jaune* (yellow jersey).

2 Complete a single stage in the shortest time and you'll wear the coveted *maillot jaune*. The red-and-white polka-dot jersey goes to the King of the Mountains—the overall best climber. The most consistent finisher of all the stages (often a strong sprinter) wins the green jersey for most points, while the white jersey is awarded to the top finisher under the age of 25.

3 Begin your Tour de France training in November in order to get optimum results come July. For example, if you're shooting for the 2007 race, start your training program in November of '06.

4 Develop the ability to accelerate quickly to high speeds. Work on speed and endurance at least once a week. Set specific distances and track your times. Alternate all-out rides at top speed with slower rides in order to recover fully during training.

5 Develop explosive power and focus on your climbing stamina. While the rabbits might take some of the flatter stages, when the race moves into the brutal mountain passes, you'll be able to make your move. Ride all the mountain stages—which include jaunts through the Pyrenees and the Alps—relentlessly in the months leading up to the race. Study the course particularly as it approaches the finish line for each stage in order to take full advantage of strategy and tactics during the race itself.

6 Race the Individual Time Trials, where riders start at set intervals and cannot give or receive a draft. Then it's on to the Team Time Trials, where team members strive for the lowest cumulative time.

7 Work for your team's star rider in any way you can. *Domestiques* ride in front of him to reduce wind resistance or chase down breakaways to ensure that rivals don't escape and gain valuable minutes. Gain enough Tour experience and split off to form your own team and become the star.

8 Win the most difficult battle: the mental challenge. You must train your mind to keep pushing while your body is begging to stop.

Tips

You can benefit from the coaching principles that Lance Armstrong uses by contacting coach Chris Carmichael's staff at TrainRight.com.

Be prepared to swerve to avoid high-speed crashes and to race through extreme weather conditions.

Who Knew?

Race organizers invite about 20 teams, each with nine cyclists.

It's critical to eat and drink regularly on the bike because your body can store only 1,600 to 1,800 calories of carbohydrate energy in your muscles and liver. Consume 6,000 to 7,000 calories per race day, more on particularly long and hard days. Lance tries to get 70 percent of his daily calories from carbohydrates, 15 percent from fat, and 15 percent from protein.

Total prize money is about 16 million francs (approximately U.S. $2.1 million).

Warnings

Beware of the broom wagon, a van that follows the race and picks up the riders who have fallen so far back that they're unable to finish within the time limit for the stage.

Be sure to follow all the rules precisely to avoid being disqualified from the tour.

490 Run a Marathon

One sure way to cure that midlife crisis is to run a marathon. It's 26.2 miles (42.1 kilometers) of pain and suffering, but crossing that finish line for the first time will be one of the greatest accomplishments of your life. First, though, you have to be prepared, and to do that you need to set up your training schedule carefully.

Steps

1 Have six months to a year of solid running under your belt. Expect to spend at least 26 weeks in training, one week for every mile you'll complete in the race. Of course, this will vary depending on what shape you're in when you start, your current running base and the length of the runs that you are currently doing. For example, if you are already running 5 miles a day and you occasionally go out and run a half marathon, you would start your long runs at the half-marathon distance and increase from there.

2 Do some serious research before you begin. If you know people who have run marathons, talk to them and get their advice.

3 Investigate running clubs and organizations in your area. Many offer classes as well as provide the safety of group runs. Locate coaches and trainers at the Road Runners Club of America (rrca.org). There are also groups like the Leukemia & Lymphoma Society's Team in Training (teamintraining.org) and the Arthritis Foundation's Joints in Motion (arthritis.org), which will coach you in exchange for your getting donations for their charity.

4 Invest in a good pair of running shoes. This is critical. Shop for shoes at the end of the day when your feet have swelled slightly. Visit a couple of stores that specialize in running and speak with a qualified salesperson. You should be able to test-drive them in a jog around the block. Retire shoes after 300 to 400 miles since the cushioning breaks down, inviting injuries.

5 Dress in moisture-wicking layers appropriate to your climate. Wear a hat, sunscreen and sunglasses.

6 Purchase a performance-quality wristwatch with a stopwatch function to track your splits at each mile. This will help you regulate your pace.

7 Develop a training program that you can stick with. The general idea is to slowly increase your distance, and then your speed, over a 26-week period. Each week will build off the previous one and include five running days (one long run and four shorter runs) and two rest days. Remember, while you can skip an occasional shorter run, the long ones are essential to your training.

8 Stretch your muscles smoothly, without bouncing, before and after every run to keep them prepared and resilient. Give your hamstrings, quadriceps, calves, groin and hip flexors plenty of attention, slowly stretching each for at least 30 seconds.

Tips

Hire an experienced coach if your budget allows. He or she will help keep you motivated and make sure you're training properly.

Slather Bodyglide or Vaseline on those parts of your body that chafe (armpits, inside of thighs, under bra straps, inside of the knees). There is nothing worse than painfully chafing skin on a long run.

Keep a training diary to help you stay focused and identify how any injuries occurred.

Getting plenty of rest is a vital component of your training.

Who Knew?

Shop for shoes in a running store. The staffers are usually highly experienced runners. Bring an old pair along. An examination of the worn areas reveals quite a bit about the type of shoe you need.

Incorporate cross-training into your routing: walking, swimming, cycling and so on to increase endurance and strength and avoid boredom.

You don't have to run the entire 26.2 miles. Many marathoners walk a portion of the race to rest and rehydrate.

9 Eat meals that are high in carbohydrates and low in fat.

10 Stay hydrated and drink plenty of water, even on days when you're not running. During your training period you'll need to consume at least 6 to 8 pints (3 to 4 liters) of water a day. Carry a water bottle with you on the run or wear a hydration pack. Many seasoned runners eat small packets of easy-to-digest carbohydrate gel every 35 to 40 minutes during long runs.

11 Register a few weeks or months in advance if you're shooting for one of the major marathons, such as the races in Chicago and Los Angeles. The New York Marathon, for example, uses a lottery system to choose participants for the race, so not everyone who applies even gets to run. To enter the Boston Marathon you have to have qualifying times based upon your age on the date of the race you wish to run. (See bostonmarathon.org for more information.)

12 Start your taper three weeks before the marathon. Don't burn yourself out before the race begins.

13 Rest one to three days if you feel like you are getting an injury. You will be back on the road much sooner if you don't aggravate the problem. If your symptoms pass, resume gentle running; if they do not, see a medical professional.

14 Rest and eat properly the week before your race. If you stick to your plan, you don't need to load up on carbs the night before— and stay away from unknown restaurants, fish and spicy foods. Don't try anything for the first time on marathon day either: Test everything (gels, hydration packs, shoes and inserts, clothes— even your hat, but especially shoes) well before the race. Stock up on energy bars, gels and sports drinks for the big day.

15 Keep your pace even, or start out slow during the race and increase the pace during the second half or last third of the marathon. The surest way to crash and burn is to run too fast at the beginning. This is very hard when people are passing you. You can run faster if you are in good shape, but you need to resist. Run at your own pace and run it consistently. You will feel much better for a longer time in the race, and you can always speed up near the end if you have extra energy.

16 Stay on your feet right after the race and walk around in order to avoid some serious soreness. You'll heal much quicker if you stretch every day over the next week and get some easy running in. For example, run 1 mile at a 15-minute pace the day after the marathon. The next day, run 2 miles at a 13-minute pace. Then rest a day, but stretch. The fourth day, run 3 or 4 miles at an 11-minute pace, then take a day off. By the following weekend, you might run up to 6 miles, but slower. Listen to your body.

Warnings

Consult your physician before beginning any serious training programs.

Stay clear of alcohol and caffeinated beverages (coffee, tea, cola). They're diuretics and will quickly dehydrate you.

To avoid injury, never increase your distance from one week to the next by more than 10 percent.

Never train in worn-out shoes. If you feel pain in the knee, shin or foot, it may be time for a new pair.

491 | Learn to Fly

Flying is one of the great universal dreams. Who hasn't imagined the thrill of peaceful, effortless flight? The good news is that learning to fly is more accessible than you think. Instructors, flight schools and airports are readily available in much of the world. Your initial goal is to qualify for a private pilot's certificate (license) for single-engine planes.

Steps

1 Create a budget. Costs include fees for classroom instruction, flight instruction and airplane usage. Figure on about $6,000 to learn how to solo within a year of beginning. You will need to pay for about 30 hours of instructor time and 50 hours of airplane time. Your costs are likely to go up, due to the need for increased instruction time, if you take an extended break during your training.

2 Train in the type of airplane that you will eventually be flying on your own. Otherwise, you'll need to immediately get checked out in another plane once the licensing process is complete. For example, if you want to take friends on a weekend flight, make sure you do some training in a four-seater, not just a two-seater.

3 Evaluate your time commitments. You will need to devote time to both classroom instruction and flying time. If your schedule is already busy, wait until you can clear up more free time. An intensive period of instruction is far more effective than scheduling lessons with long breaks in between. Try to fly at least once per week.

4 Research flight schools. The phone book is a good starting point, but also talk to friends and colleagues who fly. Visit several schools and look around. Ask questions until you have a clear picture of the instruction process, costs and type of airplane that will be available to you.

5 Verify that the instruction schedule fits your needs. Ask about the availability of planes during the times that are convenient for you.

6 Interview flying instructors. Look for someone whose safety record is impeccable and with whom you feel comfortable. You'll be spending considerable time with this person. Ask each potential instructor how many students he or she has successfully guided through the entire license process and ask to contact former students.

7 Ask about insurance. Make sure you're adequately covered. Insurance is similar to automobile policies in terms of the risks that need to be covered. You want protection against property damage, airplane damage, liability, and medical coverage for yourself and anyone you might injure.

Tips

Take a few test flights with a qualified pilot. Make sure you enjoy being in a small plane before you invest a lot of time and money in lessons.

Get a flight instruction book and study on your own time. Your instructor can recommend suitable texts.

See 236 Buy Life Insurance.

Who Knew?

It's important that training planes have up-to-date avionics (airplane electronics) including communication equipment, GPS and flight instruments. It makes no sense to train on outdated equipment.

Plan on renting an airplane at first. If you're loaded, you might be tempted to buy one, but as you learn to fly, you'll also learn more about planes. Wait until you're knowledgeable and skilled so that the aircraft you eventually buy will satisfy you for years to come.

Who hasn't fantasized about blasting off into space? Many people have been (and continue to be) willing to risk their lives to make this dream happen. Read on to see if you've got the right stuff.

Steps

1 Be or become a U.S. citizen.

2 Excel in academics. Advanced math and science education is absolutely essential. Plan on getting at least a postgraduate degree in one of these fields. Consult with your academic adviser for information about the best course of study. The National Aeronautics and Space Administration (NASA) provides universities with information about recommended subjects.

3 Review the necessary skills. In the old days, the space program wanted pilots. The major challenge then was simply getting the craft into space and back to Earth. Now the goal is scientific research and exploration. Today's most sought-after candidates have the skills to advance the understanding of the universe, and are usually physicists, aerospace engineers and astronomers.

4 Work in a research environment after graduate school. NASA is looking for people with successful work experience, but also wants individuals who develop and pursue their own research projects. (Being a computer programmer will not get you a seat in the rocket—this is all done from the ground nowadays.)

5 Review the application procedure. (Go to NASA.gov for information.) Expect the process to take up to two years. Submit an application at any time, but understand that the review process is lengthy and NASA only makes job offers every other year.

6 Interview with the Astronaut Selection Board (ASB). The ASB interviews each candidate and assigns him or her a rating based on experience and potential, motivation, ability to function as a member of a team, communication skills and adaptability. Some applicants do not possess the required interpersonal skills and are rejected solely on that basis.

7 Decide which role you would like to play as member of the crew. *Pilot astronauts* serve as both space commanders and pilots. *Mission specialist astronauts* work with the commander and the pilot and have overall responsibility for coordinating operations in the following areas: systems, crew activity planning, consumables usage, and experiment and payload operations. *Payload specialists* are people other than NASA astronauts (including foreign nationals) who have specialized onboard duties; they may be added to shuttle crews if projects with unique requirements need more than the minimum crew of five to run.

8 Build your own spaceship, if all else fails. Check out the Ansari X Prize (xprize.org).

Tip

Astronauts must possess the following abilities and characteristics:

- Make choices and perform under pressure.
- Work well in teams.
- Work well in zero gravity and in cramped conditions.
- Have strong communication skills.
- Work with a complex body of knowledge.
- Be able to concentrate for long periods of time.
- Use good judgment in a crisis.
- Be able to work in dangerous conditions.
- Have good attention to detail.
- Be able to use advanced mathematical and statistical formulas and concepts.
- Know how to operate complicated lab equipment.
- Have excellent physical stamina.

Who Knew?

NASA has 130 to 140 active members of the Astronaut Corps. About half are federal civil servants. The remaining are armed services members detailed to NASA.

Look into Space Camp programs for both children and adults at spacecamp.com.

493 Live Off the Land

Ever gotten the urge to quit the rat race and live in the wilderness? In fact, it's very difficult for a solitary person to live comfortably off the land. Most people who do so are members of highly cooperative societies who balance the uncertainty of their existence with an intricate network of mutual support. You have no safety net if you're flying solo.

Steps

1 Clarify your objectives. Is your goal to experience a short-term wilderness retreat, live in harmony with nature for the long haul or just survive a reality-show stint in the South China Sea? What level of technology and tools will you employ: GPS device or compass and sextant? Zippo or flint and steel?

2 Enroll in a wilderness preparedness course, such as those offered by Outward Bound (outwardbound.com) or the National Outdoor Leadership School (www.nols.edu). You will learn vital skills such as navigating with a map and compass, shelter construction and first aid.

3 Choose an environment with significant opportunities for food, water and shelter. Solo adventures are really only feasible in warm or temperate climates. Abundant water is essential to survival. If you don't have a reliable source of clean water, become expert at purifying water in large quantities.

4 Become expert at starting a fire without matches. Your best bet is probably the bow-drill technique. For detailed instructions on this, go to www.wmuma.com/tracker/skills/fire/bowdrill/.

5 Learn how to make a basic shelter. Review 474 Survive Being Lost for instruction. Choose a camping spot with easy and reliable water access. Without a mechanical system of delivery and storage, obtaining water may be your biggest daily task.

6 Know how to use, repair and sharpen basic tools. Living off the land requires that you get very close to that land. Axes, knives, shovels, hoes and fishing gear will be essential to your survival.

7 Study the flora and fauna of your intended destination. Be able to identify edible plants and practice locating, harvesting and preparing them long before you set out.

8 Learn to see and feel changes in the weather and to take appropriate action.

9 Practice whatever hunting method you choose until you are an expert. Hunting is difficult and unpredictable; fishing is more reliable and requires less physical effort.

10 Learn how to process skins in order to make clothing. Practice harvesting reeds and grasses in order to make baskets and rope.

11 Keep an apartment in Manhattan for those times when you need to get away from it all.

Tips

Read *Into the Wild* by Jon Krakauer. In addition to serving as a warning for anyone who's thinking of disappearing into the wilderness, it also touches on the issues involved in removing oneself from modern technology.

Books that teach outdoor survival skills are popular, and any major bookstore will have several titles. All survival strategies, however, require that you practice until you're proficient.

Explore the medicinal properties of native vegetation.

See 106 Prepare an Organic Vegetable Garden. You'll need to plant a high-yield food garden.

Warnings

Be familiar with the animals in your environment. Some you may want to eat, and others may want to eat you—or your food. Animals tend to attack only when unable to run away.

Pay particular attention to identifying poisonous plants, insects and snakes.

Retain some means to make contact with society in case of an emergency.

Practice and be able to administer first aid to yourself. See 466 Assemble Emergency Kits.

Those who study food and distribution issues understand that hunger is not related to a shortfall in food production, but in the ability to pay for it. What can be done to ensure that all people around the globe can enjoy a suitable diet?

Steps

1 Share existing food, production technology, and water and land resources with developing countries. Pressure your political leaders to pursue policies that promote global cooperation.

2 Promote economic development of developing nations to allow its residents to earn more money and afford more food.

3 Support equal rights for all people. Promoting access to health care, education and jobs for women and minorities encourages economic development for the country as a whole. Birth rates are reduced with even basic education, further reducing the strain on the food supply. See 404 Build a School in a Third World Country.

4 Lobby the U.S. government to remove agriculture subsidies. Designed to help U.S. farmers with globally traded crops like wheat and corn, subsidies depress global prices, holding down the incomes of farmers in developing countries or even driving them out of business. Poor countries can make a strong argument that the developed world is intentionally preventing the creation of a level playing field.

5 Support increased funding of global-assistance programs. The United States uses only a tiny fraction of its money (less than one-half of one percent of the gross domestic product) for overseas food assistance. The nation could easily double or triple this figure without suffering economic harm.

6 Understand the impact that meat consumption has on the world food supply. Meat production is a biologically inefficient process; the amount of meat produced is infinitely smaller than the amount of feed grain the animals consume. Eating meat elevates consumption of scarce resources and increases pressure on the world food supply. The majority of meat is consumed by developed nations.

7 Contribute to private global assistance programs such as CARE (care.org) and the International Red Cross (icrc.org). Many churches and civic organizations also conduct hunger relief programs.

Tips

See 383 Plan a Toy Drive and 403 Set Up a Non-governmental Organization.

Check out many of the Web sites targeting world hunger, including the Hunger Project (thp.org) and the World Hunger Education Service (worldhunger.org).

Heifer International (heifer.org) aims to promote long-term financial prosperity. Livestock are given to subsistence farmers to develop a consistent source of income and food for their families and communities.

Warning

Famine and warfare frequently go hand in hand. If you're involved in hunger relief efforts, keep a lookout for armed conflicts around the globe. Focus your efforts on these spots.

495 | Become a Rhodes Scholar

This is so hard to do that most people don't even know what a Rhodes scholarship is. In 1903, British tycoon Cecil Rhodes established a scholarship at Oxford University to be awarded in an international competition. The recipients have been some of the world's brightest, most motivated students, and many, including former U.S. Senator Bill Bradley and former President Bill Clinton, have gone on to prominence.

Steps

1 Be between 18 and 24 years old, blisteringly smart and possessing excellent study habits. Complete your undergraduate degree by the time your Rhodes tenure would begin. The scholarship is theoretically available to students in all fields, but to continue your education at Oxford you must be in a course of study that the university offers (double check at www.ox.ac.uk).

2 Apply to the Rhodes Scholarship Trust (rhodesscholar.org). Your primary contact will be the Rhodes representative at your university, and this is your best source for application materials. Check with your academic adviser for the name of this person. Meet with him or her as early in your academic career as possible so that you can discuss the selection process.

3 Review the application. Keep in mind that recommendations from professors are more important than compelling answers to application questions. The selection committee is interested in assessing the impact you've made on your university and the people around you.

4 Develop effective and mutually beneficial relationships with your professors. You will need complete support from your department, your adviser and any professors you ask for recommendations. Scholarship winners are selected for leadership ability and character as much as for grades.

Tip

Have a backup plan ready. There's no way to predict the selection odds even for the brightest students.

Warning

Stifle any ironic comments about Cecil Rhodes during the application process. Though Rhodes himself was involved in both diamond mining and politics in South Africa, occupations not normally associated with the values promoted by the scholarship, the Rhodes Scholarship Trust emphasizes integrity and service to humankind.

496 | Write the Great American Novel

While you're free to write about anything you wish, your goal is to produce a work so universally in touch with the essential American character and experience that it becomes an integral component of every bookshelf. The hard part, of course, is that you have to write well.

Steps

1 Read classic and modern American literature voraciously. If you aspire to write the next Great American Novel, it's essential to become familiar with those that already exist. Develop a sense of the many recurring themes in American literature, such as defiance of the natural world or the individual versus society.

Tips

Many writers draw from personal experiences to provide settings and characters for their stories.

Research the National Writers Union's (nwu.org) many services.

2 Start writing. Create a permanent writing space in your house and set aside a block of time each day to work. Treat your writing time as seriously as you would a job.

3 Take a creative- or novel-writing class. You'll learn how to sketch out various aspects of a story, including characters, themes, conflicts, dialogue, pacing and structure. Get comfortable with critiques and glean feedback from instructors and colleagues.

4 Plot the entire story, but work on developing only the beginning. Though you should have a clear direction that the entire novel will follow, leave room for changes.

5 Polish and edit the beginning before proceeding. You can show this high-quality section to agents or publishers. The exercise forces you to define and develop your characters.

6 Have a qualified editor read your work. Ask for honest feedback. Develop a thick skin, listen carefully, and be thankful for the help, even if the comments are negative. Revise accordingly.

7 Purchase a directory of literary agents. Send your sample section to agents who are interested in your type of writing. If one offers to represent you, expect to pay the agent a percentage of any deal he or she negotiates with a publisher.

8 Start calling yourself a writer, if anyone asks.

Contrary to what you may have thought in high school, Herman Melville's *Moby Dick* is a phenomenal bit of writing, as is anything by William Faulkner. If you don't agree that these writers are geniuses, you're not ready to write the Great American Novel. Consider studying Proust and aiming to write the Pretty Good French Novel.

Join a critique group in your area or apply for a prestigious program such as the Iowa Writers' Workshop at the University of Iowa (www.uiowa.edu/~iww).

A commercial-length novel is about 85,000-plus words.

Warning

Don't quit your day job.

---

497 | Cure the Common Cold

Colds are caused by viruses, which are notoriously difficult to treat. Despite massive efforts to find a cure, the best treatment is to avoid infection in the first place.

Tips

There's a Nobel Prize waiting for the first person who finds a true cure.

See 27 Prepare for Cold and Flu Season.

Some experts think there's no chance of defeating these viruses, primarily because they have too many variations. And even if an effective treatment is found, it may lose its effectiveness over time as new virus variants appear. This is not the sort of attitude that eradicated smallpox and other deadly diseases.

Steps

1 Become an infectious-disease expert. Study the most common cold viruses, including rhinovirus, parvovirus and parainfluenza virus. Understanding exactly how these nasty creatures behave is the key to stopping them.

2 Secure a massive research grant and refine the latest medications. Oseltamivir phosphate and Amantadine are two drugs that show promise in fighting cold and flu viruses. Currently, their side effects are significant and their benefits limited, but research may improve these drugs.

3 Focus on the most common infection route of cold viruses— through the nasal cells. The nose is designed to receive chemical compounds from outside the body, and the nasal cells are full of receptor sites to which a virus can adhere. Blocking these receptor sites, without interfering with other body functions, may be the key to preventing infection.

Can anything you do really matter to the Earth? On a universal scale, no. The Earth will keep on spinning, evolving and sustaining life no matter what humans choose to do. There's much to do, however, to reduce the pressure on our Big Blue Marble's limited resources.

Steps

1 Consume less. Everything people do, including eating (especially meat), watering lawns, heating homes and driving cars, consumes resources. Everything people buy requires resources to produce and ship. Be conscious of all the small decisions you make in your everyday life that increase the total human impact on the planet. See 15 Live With Less, 493 Live Off the Land and 494 End World Hunger.

2 Choose to have fewer (or no) children. The pressure on Earth's resources by its ever-increasing human population is one of the most dire issues that the planet faces.

3 Learn what types of fish are in danger of being overfished and don't buy them at the store or order them in restaurants. The United Nations site offers background information (go to www.un.org and search for "overfishing"). For specific recommendations on which fish are caught and farmed in ways that support a healthy environment, check out Seafood Watch at the Monterey Bay Aquarium's site (mbayaq.org).

4 Consider driving a smaller or hybrid car. Of course, buying a new car equals more consumption, so approach this issue with some caution. But if you're already looking for a new car, get one that's energy efficient.

5 Support international agreements to limit the output of greenhouse gases. Reduce your own energy use as much as possible. See 78 Prepare for Skyrocketing Energy Costs.

6 Downsize your life. See 1 Get Organized, 12 Get Rid of What You Don't Want and 15 Live With Less.

7 Buy organic food. Pesticides take a toll on the environment and frequently spawn pesticide-resistant pests. Buying organic food directly from the growers supports small farms and promotes biodiversity. See 106 Prepare an Organic Vegetable Garden.

8 Lend your energy to protecting the drinking water supply on both micro and macro levels. Access to and availability of clean drinking water is a growing global crisis. Cut back on personal water use with water-wise gardens (see 113 Design a Dry Garden) and promote development of sound water policies in your town or region (see 400 Manage Growth in Your Community). Or join forces with scientists working to perfect the difficult and expensive process of desalinization (waterdesalination.com).

Tips

Read *50 Simple Things You Can Do to Save the Earth* by the Earthworks Group.

You can recycle many things, not just newspapers and bottles. Rather than throwing away old lumber, bicycles, furniture and clothes, give them to someone who will put them to use.

Read the vast array of books by authors dedicated to educating readers on global resources. Rachel Carson's famous *Silent Spring* is frequently credited with starting the environmental protection movement in the United States. Marc Reisner's *Cadillac Desert* describes the story of water use (and abuse) in the American West. It's a chilling description of how business and government manipulate the environment to serve economic development.

Who Knew?

Water-related disease is the number one cause of death and responsible for 80 percent of illness worldwide. Investigate online sources such as the Worldwatch Institute (worldwatch.org) or NationalGeographic.com for information on the global water crisis.

Thorsten Veblen, a 20th-century American economist, coined the term *conspicuous consumption,* the intentional buying of unnecessary goods to satisfy vanity and show status.

The fountain of youth might be a myth, but with the almost daily advances in medicine and health care, breaking the century mark is an attainable goal for many people. By the year 2050, America will be home to an estimated 1 million centenarians. In fact, you may already be well on your way.

Steps

1 Live an active life, both mentally and physically. You don't have to be an exercise nut, but keep moving. Walking, golfing, swimming—anything at all is good. Implement a stretching program to maintain your flexibility and lift weights to build muscle and prevent osteoporosis.

2 Stay married. Numerous studies indicate that married people live longer than single people. There's the old joke that it just *seems* longer for married people, but in reality it seems to help.

3 Maintain your ideal weight. Being overweight will definitely limit your chances of becoming a centenarian and is likely to make the journey a slow and painful one.

4 Drink moderately and don't smoke at all.

5 Have good genes. Extreme long life seems to run in families and may be based on common genetic and environmental factors. If you have a centenarian sibling, your chances of living past the century mark increase greatly. (Of course, you're probably pretty old already yourself.)

6 Eliminate unnecessary stress as it shortens your life. Finding satisfying, meaningful work is likely to contribute to a long life, and certainly does to having a life you enjoy. If you're retired, do something that gives purpose and value to your life. See 14 Balance Home and Work and 16 Set Goals.

7 Develop close and respectful relationships with your friends and loved ones. This may actually be harder than living for 100 years, but it's a big help if you can manage it.

8 Live simply (see 15 Live With Less). Huck Finn probably lived to 100 because he understood that today is what counts, fine clothes are itchy, and money is a burden.

Tips

Stay away from boring or depressing people. Even 100 years is too short a time to waste. There's fun stuff to do. Get going!

Calculate your life expectancy at LivingTo100.com.

Who Knew?

Activities that challenge your brain and require social interaction, such as bridge, chess, music, educational courses or micromanaging your children's lives, are also essential.

Warning

Avoid dwelling on negative or upsetting events. These thoughts can trigger physical responses, such as adrenaline output, that take a toll on the body over many years. A positive attitude can both lengthen your life and make it more pleasurable (see 501 Be Happy).

500 Die Rich

Presumably, dying rich also means you were able to live rich, which is the main point of having wealth. In order to get to the finish line with a hefty net worth, apply sound money management basics throughout your life: Work hard, don't buy stuff you don't need, save money, and invest wisely. The first step? Come up with a solid plan—in writing.

Steps

1 Write down your financial goals. Think about your "sky's the limit" dreams in all areas of your life and start devising out a plan to get there. See 16 Set Goals.

2 Become an inveterate saver (see 228 Design a Savings Plan). Sock away at least half of every pay raise and other windfalls like bonuses or tax returns. Make systematic investing your long-term goal once you've put away a six-month emergency fund.

3 Put your money to work. Even if you think you don't have much to invest with, open an account with a mutual fund company that includes no-load funds and low expense ratios. With a diverse portfolio, you can reasonably expect to earn 8 to 10 percent annually on your investments over the long haul.

4 Know the difference between wants and needs, and make conscious spending decisions: Would you rather have the latest cool gizmo or put your money someplace where it can do something for you? Spend significantly less than you bring home and save the rest. See 15 Live With Less.

5 Be aware of what you're charging on your credit cards. If you're carrying a balance every month, read step 3 again. Think of how much further the money you pay in interest charges could go if it was going directly into an interest-bearing account or an IRA. See 227 Get Out of Debt and 241 Plan for Retirement.

6 Start your own business. The majority of millionaires make their fortunes the hard way, not by inheriting it. Self-employment entails significant risk as well as rewards. Work hours and company policies are yours to decide; revenue is yours to control. Risk-takers and innovators stand to gain the rewards of running a successful business.

7 Hire a pro. A good financial planner can help you balance your portfolio with smart investments. Don't abdicate responsibility for your money, but do create a solid working relationship with your planner. If you can't afford to have one manage your money, many financial planners will review your portfolio and make recommendations for a onetime fee.

8 Concentrate on spiritual wealth instead of financial gain. If the point of being rich is so that you can be happy, why not just skip ahead to 501 Be Happy?

Tips

Set aside some money for a good biographer.

See 244 Make a Will, 247 Plan Your Estate and 239 Track Your Investments.

Who Knew?

Americans tend to save less and carry more household debt than people in many other industrialized nations.

Count on yourself, not on Social Security. When it comes to future Social Security payments, many economists have this to say to a young person entering the workforce: "Ha ha ha!" As the population ages, too many old people will be receiving payments while too few young workers will be paying taxes to support the system. See 241 Plan for Retirement.

501 | Be Happy

It would be nice if the U.S. Constitution guaranteed happiness, but it just allows you to run around pursuing happiness without giving directions on how to find it. Ultimately, of course, happiness is an inside job. Jump in with both feet and map out your own route to nirvana.

Steps

1 Dream big. Go out on a limb and pursue a life that interests you, not one others expect you to live. Read 16 Set Goals and go live the life you were born to.

2 Make a conscious decision to be happy. This is paradoxically the simplest and the most difficult aspect of the whole venture. As most cheery people will tell you, though, at some point they simply decided to be happy.

3 Have fun. (Seriously.) Get out there and do things that tickle your funny bone.

4 Live within your means so that you're not stressed out about money. See 15 Live With Less.

5 Take care of yourself—but focus on helping others. Living a meaningful life nurtures long-term happiness. See 499 Live to Be 100 Years Old.

6 Find activities that ignite your passion—from orchids to inventions, discover what fires you up. Find a hobby, such as knitting, cooking, gardening or woodworking, to serve as a creative outlet. See 367 Start a Knitting Circle and 92 Set Up a Woodshop.

7 Meet new people and experience places, near and far. Spend time in the wild soaking up the peace and tranquility found only in nature.

8 Slow down, turn off the phone and stop rushing. Be open to new experiences. Take time to notice what you have rather than what you don't. It's natural to feel discouraged at times—practice shifting your focus to what's positive.

9 Eat chocolate. Work out. Both will give you an endorphin rush (one just takes less effort). Getting regular exercise and staying fit will have you feeling great, staying healthy and looking marvelous. See 25 Design Your Workout Schedule.

10 Find satisfaction in simple things: Spend time with children and see the world through their eyes. Smell tiny babies, watch an ant trail with a toddler. Pick wild blackberries. Laugh. Eat ice cream. Turn up the music and dance!

Who Knew?

Mark Twain put the secret of happiness in a nutshell: "Twenty years from now you will be more disappointed by the things that you didn't do than by the ones you did do. So throw off the bowlines. Sail away from the safe harbor. Catch the trade winds in your sails. Explore. Dream. Discover."

Take responsibility for your actions. Many criminals and substance abusers share the common trait of blaming their circumstances on other people. You're in charge of you, so act like it.

Warnings

Get medical help when unhappiness has a psychological basis. Signs of depression include chronic fatigue, apathy and suicidal thoughts. If any of these symptoms apply to you, consult a doctor.

Stop complaining. It doesn't make you look smart and discerning; it makes you look like a complainer. It also causes you, your friends and colleagues to focus on the negative aspects of any situation.

INDEX

CONTRIBUTORS

Tara Aronson, aka Mrs. Clean Jeans (mrscleanjeans .com), is the mother of three and author of *Mrs. Clean Jeans' Housekeeping with Kids.* Her "Coming Clean" column appears twice monthly in the *San Francisco Chronicle's* Home & Garden section.

Ellen Conroy has, over the past 13-plus years, been a Web site content writer, a comedy writer for an entertainment production company, an interactive murder mystery scriptwriter, a copywriter and currently a freelance writer. She has also been an actress, singer, artist, craftswoman and interior decorator. Today she runs her own professional organizing company, In An Orderly Fashion.

Barbara Dunlap is editor and publisher of *Coming of Age,* an Oregon lifestyle magazine for Baby Boomers and their parents. She has been the assistant editor of the *San Francisco Chronicle* Home Section and the content manager for an award-winning human relations Web site. She received her master's degree in journalism from the University of Missouri at Columbia and was a Knight Fellow at the University of North Carolina at Chapel Hill.

Casey Ellis is a freelance writer in the San Francisco Bay Area specializing in articles on interior design, art and food. She is the co-author of *The Organized Home: Design Solutions for Clutter-Free Living,* although her closets still exemplify her credo of "Do as I say, not as I do."

Louise Kurzeka began helping business and individual clients clear clutter and improve productivity in 1992. Co-founder of Everything's Together, Kurzeka is a nationally recognized organization expert who appears regularly on HGTV's "TIPical Mary Ellen" and radio. She also offers seminars to clients such as 3M and Best Buy.

Mike MacCaskey Mike MacCaskey is an avid gardener of many years so has learned by experience a great deal about how to plan and organize a garden. Is his own garden the best organized one in the world? He respectfully declines to say.

Brian O'Connell is a Bucks County, Pennsylvania writer. The author of 10 books and two Book of the Month Club titles, O'Connell can be reached at brian.oco@verizon.net.

Matthew Richard Poole is a freelance travel writer who has authored more than two dozen guides to California, Hawaii and abroad. Before becoming a full-time writer and photographer, he worked as an English tutor in Prague, ski instructor in the Swiss Alps and scuba instructor in Maui and Thailand. Highly allergic to office buildings, he spends most of his time on the road doing research and avoiding commitments.

Fred Sandsmark is a freelance writer in the San Francisco Bay Area, covering technology and home-related subjects. Working on this book inspired him to organize his garage, a task that should be completed sometime next week.

Marcia Whyte Smart, a San Francisco-based freelance food writer, has written for *Cooking Light, Sunset, Robb Report, Parenting* and *BabyTalk* magazines. A graduate of Tante Marie's Cooking School professional program, she has a chronic sweet tooth and thinks everything tastes better with bacon.

Derek Wilson has acquired and organized more outdoor gear than any normal person should and if you don't believe him you're welcome to visit his garage and critique his arrangement of bicycles, skis and climbing gear. He lives in the Lake Tahoe area of California and divides his time between economic consulting and writing projects which include *Burritos: Hot on the Trail of the Little Burro,* and contributions to *How to Fix (Just About) Everything* and *How to Buy & Sell (Just About) Everything.*

Laurie Bain Wilson is a bestselling author and former travel editor at a national consumer magazine. She has also written articles for the *New York Times,* the *New York Daily News,* and travel and parenting magazines. She lives outside of New York City with her 13-year-old son.

Weldon Owen wishes to thank the following people for their generous support in the production of this book: Kelli Adams, Scott Adams, Jayne Benton PA-C, Tom Benton, Angelica Biggs, Elizabeth Block, Carol Breuner, Chris Breuner, Clay Breuner, Dave Breuner, Don Breuner, Kristen Best Breuner, Lisa Breuner, MD, Peyton Breuner, Riley Breuner, Gretchen Brooks, Keesha Bullock, Dan Caldwell, Karlene Caldwell, Steve Clark, Irene Cole RN, MS, CDE, Bob Crockett, Sinclair Crockett, Greg Crouch, Marty de Jonghe, Toni Fauver, Andi Fargeix, Claire Fargeix, Rebecca Forée, Ken Greenblatt, Meghan Hildebrand, Sioux Jennett, Devon Johnson, Andrea Martin, Dave Martin; Hon. Robert L. Martin, Deirdre McLoughlin, MSPT, Charlotte McKnight, Liz Miles, Virginia Miller, Eileen Moncoeur, Mary Anne Moore, Susan Neubauer, Lynn Ocone, Ed O'Dea, Ron Pratt, Louise Pratt RN, Alma Prins, Odette Pollar, Gayna Radtke, Mike Radtke, Dave Rees, Heather Rogers, Shelly Rogers, Sue Seide, Randy Shostak, Jason Solle, Chris Stevens, Jean Sturgeon, Dana Tillson, Kathy Toon, Lucy Weaver, Heidi Breuner Wilson, Peg Winkelman, Noah Winkelman, Blaze Woodlief and Anselm Yew.